Global Origins of the Modern Self, from Montaigne to Suzuki

Global Origins of the Modern Self, from Montaigne to Suzuki

AVRAM ALPERT

Cover: Clarissa Tossin, *Unmapping the World*, 2011 (detail). Ink on tracing paper, 33 in. × 46 in. Photograph by Hai Zhang.

Published by State University of New York Press, Albany

© 2019 State University of New York

All rights reserved

No part of this book may be used or reproduced in any manner whatsoever without written permission. No part of this book may be stored in a retrieval system or transmitted in any form or by any means including electronic, electrostatic, magnetic tape, mechanical, photocopying, recording, or otherwise without the prior permission in writing of the publisher.

For information, contact State University of New York Press, Albany, NY
www.sunypress.edu

Library of Congress Cataloging-in-Publication Data

Names: Alpert, Avram, 1984– author.
Title: Global origins of the modern self, from Montaigne to Suzuki / Avram
  Alpert.
Description: Albany : State University of New York, [2019] | Includes
  bibliographical references and index.
Identifiers: LCCN 2018021838 | ISBN 9781438473857 (hardcover : alk. paper) |
  ISBN 9781438473840 (pbk. : alk. paper) | ISBN 9781438473864 (ebook)
Subjects: LCSH: Self (Philosophy)—History.
Classification: LCC BD438.5 .A47 2019 | DDC 126.09—dc23
LC record available at https://lccn.loc.gov/2018021838

10 9 8 7 6 5 4 3 2 1

Thought in reality spaces itself out into the world.

—Édouard Glissant, *Poetics of Relation*

In this enchanted mood, thy spirit ebbs away to whence it came; becomes diffused through time and space . . . forming at last a part of every shore the round globe over.

There is no life in thee, now, except that rocking life imparted by a gentle rolling ship . . . But while this sleep, this dream is on ye, move your foot or hand an inch; slip your hold at all; and your identity comes back in horror. Over Descartian vortices you hover. And perhaps, at midday, in the fairest weather, with one half-throttled shriek you drop through that transparent air into the summer sea, no more to rise for ever. Heed it well, ye Pantheists!

—Herman Melville, *Moby Dick*

Contents

Preface	ix
Acknowledgments	xiii
Introduction	1
1 Montaigne and the Other History of Modernity	28
2 Foundations of Universalist Global Thought: Rousseau and Kant	61
3 Aesthetic Visions of the Global Self: Schiller and Senghor	97
4 Dialectics and Its Discontents: Hegel, Marx, Fanon	135
5 Radical Pluralism I: Emerson	189
6 Radical Pluralism II: Du Bois	221
7 Emptying the Global Self: Suzuki	249
Coda: Being-Toward-Bequeathment	291
Notes	295
Works Cited	385
Index	415

Preface

This book began as an analysis of the work of D. T. Suzuki and the impact he had on global culture. Suzuki, though rarely studied today, was "the man who brought Zen to the West." Through his English-language writings and lectures, which were quickly translated into French, German, Spanish, and other languages, he would influence a bewildering range of figures, including Simone Weil, Andy Warhol, Richard Wright, bell hooks, John Cage, Jorge Luis Borges, Octavio Paz, Severo Sarduy, Agnes Martin, Ad Reinhardt, Allen Kaprow, Allen Ginsberg, Erich Fromm, Karen Horney, Martin Heidegger, Carl Jung, Karl Jaspers, William Empson, Northrop Frye, Roland Barthes, Michel Foucault, and Gilles Deleuze. But throughout the 1980s and 1990s, and even in his day, Suzuki was criticized for "Westernizing" Zen. Buddhist studies scholars felt almost like Suzuki had put them in a prison of "Zen" simplicity, where everything was about freedom from anxiety, emptiness, the loss of ego, spontaneity, and other themes commonly associated with Zen today. Those who actually went to Japan or China or Southeast Asia quickly found, however, that Zen was as complex, corrupt, historical, and anxiety-filled as any other form of life. Suzuki had lied, they claimed, and the torrents of critique began to rain down.

My first thought was simply to reread Suzuki himself, understanding that although he had reinvented Zen, his reinvention was still meaningful and deserved consideration (as much as any other modernization of religion, such as those by Martin Buber or Paul Tillich). Moreover, certainly there was something to say about figures like Cage, Foucault, and Paz and how they should be understood in light of this critical reception of Suzuki. But I quickly realized that the excessive (if correct) critiques of Buddhist studies scholars were not, in fact, the problem. Because the more I read of Suzuki's work, the more I realized he was in dialogue with figures like Kant, Schiller, Hegel, and Emerson, and that if I was to understand Suzuki, I would have to understand these thinkers as well.

And this presented a new challenge. For just as Suzuki was read as a "Westernizer," *so were they*. Of course that seems obvious—they were Western. And yet their works are filled with references to peoples and philosophical systems the world over. Montaigne, Rousseau, Kant, and Emerson read as much about non-European cultures as Suzuki did about European cultures. Why is he viewed as a "Westernizer," while they are viewed as global thinkers? What if we were to change the frame in which we read both Suzuki and the Euro-American tradition, and consider their works from the point of view of how they engaged the globe? Might that also affect how we read figures like Du Bois and Fanon—no longer as outside critics of the European tradition, but rather as entangled in the same struggle for global thought? These are the questions that animate this study.

My claim is that the question of the globe—that is, the question of what kinds of selves and institutions we should form to confront our global connectedness—is as central to modernity as the discourses of rationality, autonomy, or aesthetics. In fact, as I show in the chapters that follow, the question of the globe helps to *constitute* these other discourses. *That* this happened is undeniable—it's right there in the texts. Its meaning, however, is disputable. The argument of this book is not that we should discard Europe because of its impoverished understanding of others, nor should we brush European thinkers' mistakes aside as if they were mere historical blunders. (Early pluralist figures like Montaigne and Herder haunt our ability to historicize away the racism of the canon.) Rather, we should take the problem of the globe seriously and understand how the attempt to think it was dealt with by different thinkers at different times and different places.

To rethink Suzuki's work, then, I had to go back through many writers before him. As I worked back to Kant, I realized he was incomprehensible without Rousseau, and Rousseau in turn without Montaigne, and this whole history without critics such as Fanon, Du Bois, and bell hooks—all of whom, significantly, worked in the form of the essay. From Montaigne to Emerson to Suzuki to hooks, I am tracing a style—essaying the globe—that is neither philosophy nor literature, but rather a tentative thinking through of ideas about how to inhabit this planet that remains reflective about how those ideas are made in time, place, and language. This book is the story of how different writers at different times and places attempted this tenuous and difficult practice. In it, I argue for some of their solutions and against others. To do this, I develop an ethical vocabulary around unbearability, identity, globality, and the need for a more radical pluralism. Suzuki is no longer the focus of the book, but his vision of a subject who undoes her ego so that she may experience the totality of global being will, I hope, find its place in a history of global thought.

Acknowledgments

This book first developed during my undergraduate education more than a decade ago. Since that time I have accrued debts both intellectual and personal, which are far more extensive than this brief acknowledgment can fairly accomplish. As an undergraduate, Étienne Balibar, Rosalyn Deutsche, Bruce Robbins, and David Scott provided me with my first lessons in philosophical, literary, and cultural criticism. I frequently returned to their words and works throughout my writing. I owe special thanks to Bruce for keeping up a dialogue with me about this work over many years.

At McGill University, where I was for a year by the generosity of the Sauvé Foundation, Cora Dean, Ken Dean, and Tom LaMarre showed remarkable generosity as they disabused me of my ahistorical approach to Buddhism and introduced to me the world of critical Buddhist studies.

The Independent Study Program at the Whitney Museum, run by Ron Clark, provided me with an ongoing intellectual home outside the university. The friendships and working relationships forged during and after my time there—too many to name—have been perhaps the single most important aspect of both my professional and personal life for the past decade.

During my time in Philadelphia, Gabriel Rockhill and Alexi Kukuljevic invited me to join their recently founded "Machete Group," which provided opportunities for public encounters with my work that were invaluable. Our conversations over the years also fundamentally shaped many of my concerns here, and Gabriel has remained one of my most constant intellectual interlocutors.

In my graduate years at Penn, the Program in Comparative Literature provided an ideal intellectual home. The Benjamin Franklin and Penfield fellowships gave me time to think and read and enabled me to visit the D. T. Suzuki archives in Japan. I thank especially Nancy Bentley, Charles Bernstein, Warren Breckman, JoAnne Dubil, Amy Kaplan, Kevin Platt, and

Jean-Michel Rabaté. Branka Arsić and Don Pease also gave me much needed advice from afar. Jean-Michel was an ideal advisor—supportive, incisive, engaging—and has remained a close and exacting reader of my works.

My friends and colleagues in and around Philadelphia, who joined me in any number of both academic and extracurricular activities, kept me both sane and excited for this work. I owe special thanks to Tal Corem, Nadia Ellis, Mashinka Firunts, Kristen Gjesdal, Lewis Gordon, Jane Gordon, Cetin Gurer, Nick Keys, Grace Lavery, Astrid Lorange, Danny Marcus, Laura McMahon, Jessica Rosenberg, Danny Snelson, Daniela Tanner, Yannik Thiem, and Leif Weatherby. Laura Levitt also went out of her way to offer advice and help guide this book toward publication. My "performative" work as the collective Research Service with Danny and Mashinka has been a constant source of joy and inspiration, as has their friendship.

This book would not have taken the form it did without the support of an Andrew W. Mellon Postdoctoral Fellowship at the Center for Cultural Analysis, Rutgers University. I thank Henry Turner and Colin Jager for their excitement about my work and for bringing me to Rutgers. Many thanks are also due to Billy Galperin for his tireless support and engagement as director of the Center, and for our many fascinating impromptu conversations as office neighbors. David Kurnick and Rebecca Walkowitz, as directors of the Center seminar on "Totality," also provided invaluable feedback and conversations as I wrote. My thanks also to Jeff Lawrence, who read and commented on several portions of this manuscript.

As always, my para-institutional engagements remain central to my thinking and expression. It was a great privilege to organize the "Dictionary of the Possible" discussions with Sreshta Rit Premnath at the New School for the past two years. Many of the ideas in this book were tested there. Special thanks to our regular participants: Eric Anglès, Lindsay Benedict, Brian Block, Danilo Correale, Shadi Harouni, Margarita Sanchez, Edward Schexnayder, Adam Spanos, Keith Tilford, and Mimi Winick. Adam and Eric also kindly and critically commented on portions of the manuscript.

Over the years I have had the great fortune to present aspects of this work to engaged and provocative audiences at the ACLA, C19, and Caribbean Philosophical Association conferences and at Berkeley, Columbia, Humboldt, the Jan van Eyck Academie, Johns Hopkins, Princeton, Rutgers, UCLA, the University of Florida, the University of Pennsylvania, and the University of Toronto. I owe a debt to all who came, listened, and engaged.

This book would not have taken the shape it did had it not been for the support of Christopher Ahn at SUNY Press, who secured for me two wonderfully helpful anonymous readers' reports. Chelsea Miller, Diane Ganeles, Kate Seburyamo, and the rest of the staff also helped greatly with all the details of publication. The final writing of the book in response to those reports took place at Princeton, where a grant from the humanities research fund allowed me to hire Anna Leader, whose work and diligence as a research assistant was unparalleled, and Michael Hu, who carefully edited the final manuscript. As the project neared completion, an outpouring of scholarly generosity from experts on the figures I write about here improved the manuscript immeasurably. I cannot offer enough thanks to Jeremy Adelman, Bachir Diagne, Richard Jaffe, Michael Monahan, Inés Valdez, and Johannes Voelz. Eric Cheyfitz and Lawrence Buell were also kind enough to offer some brief reflections. The errors that remain are of course my own.

A book that attempts to span as much time and space as this one is only possible because of a larger community of scholars I have never met—many of whom can be found throughout the footnotes—who have done penetrating work in their respective archives. I imagine that some specialists will find my claims too broad or at times unconvincing, and it would be a great honor if they took the time to correct me. But I hope that they will also consider my provocation that the place of the globe and the span of the centuries change how we read canonical works.

My family first introduced me to the rigors and demands of intellectual life and showed me the many ways of thought and action that could contribute to this world. They have been my most tireless advocates, kindest supporters, and, when necessary, my gentlest critics. Without them, none of this would have been possible. Special thanks are due to my mother, Rebecca Alpert, who showed me how to do this work and who, in spite of the endless reading of her own intellectual labors, somehow found time to read, comment on, and edit the entire manuscript.

And finally, to my partner, Anthea Behm, who makes the past bearable, the present a joy, and the future a blessing.

An earlier version of the section on Foucault in the introduction first appeared in "Sounding Conscience: *Walden*'s Global Bottoms," *J19: The Journal of 19th Century Americanists* 4, no. 1 (2016): 41–63. An earlier version of the section on Rousseau first appeared in " 'Melancholy Wildness': The Failure of Cross-Cultural Engagement in Rousseau's *Discourse on the Origin of Inequality* and Brown's *Edgar Huntly*," *Early American Literature* 49, no. 1 (2014): 121–47. An earlier version of the section on Hegel appeared in *Intersubjectivity Volume 2*, ed. Katherine Rochester and Lou Cantor (Berlin: Sternberg Press, 2018).

Introduction

This discovery of a boundless country seems worthy of consideration. I don't know if I can guarantee that some other such discovery will not be made in the future, so many personages greater than ourselves having been mistaken about this one. I am afraid we have eyes bigger than our stomachs, and more curiosity than capacity. We embrace everything, but clasp only wind.

—Michel de Montaigne, "Of Cannibals" (1578)

This right, to present oneself for society, belongs to all human beings by virtue of the right of possession in common of the earth's surface, on which, as a sphere, they cannot disperse infinitely but must finally put up with being near one another.

—Immanuel Kant, "Toward Perpetual Peace" (1795)

The civility of no race can be perfect whilst another race is degraded. It is a doctrine alike of the oldest, and of the newest philosophy, that man is one, and that you cannot injure any member, without a sympathetic injury to all the members.

—Ralph Waldo Emerson, "Address on
Emancipation in the West Indies" (1844)

The modern world must . . . remember that in this age, when the ends of the world are being brought so near together, the millions of black men in Africa, America and the islands of the sea, not to speak of the brown and yellow myriads elsewhere, are bound to have great influence upon the world in the future . . . If . . . the black world is to be exploited and ravished and degraded, the results must be deplorable, if not fatal, not simply to them but to the high ideals of justice, freedom, and culture.

—W. E. B. Du Bois, "To the Nations of the World" (1900)

Human dignity enters with knowledge, the whole world changes for the enlightened man and he becomes more effective. When one is enlightened, he does not stand out from the rest of the world, but embraces it . . . The very moment of enlightenment experience takes in the whole world and is totality.

—D. T. Suzuki, Lecture at Columbia University (1952)

The Negro-African . . . does not observe that he thinks; he feels that he feels, he feels his *existence*, he feels himself. Because he feels himself, he feels the Other; and because he feels the Other, he goes towards the Other, through the rhythm of the Other to know-him-in-being-born-with-him [*con-naître*] and the world.

—Léopold Senghor, "The Negro-African Aesthetic" (1956)

Our existential condition is a global one.[1] To reflect on the self is to reflect on the world. To be alive today is to be connected to processes across the globe that remain always beyond one's control. As the sampling of quotes above shows, this relation of self and world has a long history in modern thought from around the world. Whether from France or Brazil, Germany or Japan, Senegal or the United States, those who have asked what it means to be human have placed at the center of their reflections how humans relate to each other across time and space. The resulting questions are not easy to answer: What does it mean to have a self if that self is so diffused to all the corners of the globe? How do the histories of power and domination unevenly shape the histories of global self-making? What kinds of concepts would we need in order to be aware of these differences while simultaneously appreciative of our extensive connections? The following pages demonstrate again and again that these types of questions are inseparable from modern self-making.

And yet the claim that the modern self is a global one might sound strange to some readers. We are accustomed to thinking of who we are in modernity as either intensely personal—as in the Cartesian self, founded precisely by turning away from the world—or deeply cultural—as in the anthropological understanding epitomized in Marx's expression "social being determines consciousness." The questions this volume poses in response are: What if the Cartesian moment of turning in is not the founding moment of modernity, but the evasion of its global demands? And what if our "social being" is mediated not just by our nation or culture, but also by our global connections? The questions are raised not so much against these other formulations, but rather as part of an attempt to tell other parts of the story of who we (fragmented, uneven, but global nevertheless) are. There of course would be many histories of such global selves, many positions within this global frame that are denied access to it, many denials of the very idea of having a "self" in the first place. But my claim here is that such questions are part of the general problem that confronts us in the modern world: How are we to relate who we are to individuals across a finite planet, whose existence and meaning are connected to ours, whether viscerally or not?

I have learned how to tell this history in part through my reading of two canonical histories of the self that take as their geographic orientation the history of Europe and the invented tradition that links Europe to the Greek and Roman past: Michel Foucault's lectures, *The Hermeneutics of the Subject* (1981–82); and Charles Taylor's *Sources of the Self* (1989). In the pages to follow, I engage more closely with Foucault than with Taylor and disagree with both of them. But from each I have taken the central idea that to tell a history of the self is to tell a cultural, philosophical, and political history; that is to say, that to speak of who we are is to speak, as much as possible, of the totality of our condition. Moreover, I have learned to think of our ideas of who we are as having histories constituted in part by our cultural and philosophical inheritance. What I have denied are simply the ideas that our most important modern inheritance has to do with Greek and Roman sources and that the most significant context of modern Europe had to do with changes in the scientific worldview.[2] Rather, following globalist and postcolonial[3] scholarship, I have tried to show how the making of the modern self was profoundly framed by global encounters both violent and peaceful, and that taking this into view can change how we understood who we are, what constitutes our condition, and what liberatory practices may entail. This story, then, is not about our relation to the philosophical past or how the mathematization of nature changed our role in the world. Rather, I speak of how the modern self was made by uneven, violent, overlapping, hopeless, hopeful, loving, confusing, dominating, liberating, skeptical, mystical, universalizing, pluralizing, and revolutionary crossings of people and places across space and time.

Readers more aligned with these varieties of global and postcolonial theory might find this claim rather banal. Have we not known since at least the opening pages of Edward Said's *Orientalism* (1978) that Europe made itself "by setting itself off against the Orient [and other Others] as a sort of surrogate and even underground self"?[4] Indeed, at the heart of postcolonial theory has been the claim—again in Said's vocabulary, borrowed from Raymond Williams—that the modern world and those in it were "*constituted*" by colonial encounters.[5] To be sure, there is a vast amount of literature on how modern ideas of selfhood were constituted globally, and I am indebted to it here.[6] But, for reasons that become increasingly apparent in the pages to follow, I think there remain significant gaps in our understanding of this global constitution. There simply does not exist, for example, a narrative that highlights the historical linkages that would bind together the six seemingly disparate thinkers quoted in my epigraphs, as I do here. The extent and specificity of how ideas about global life constituted the history of Euro-American thought still require further exploration, and so do the complex ways in which thinkers from Asia, Africa, the Caribbean, and elsewhere were part of this same global conversation. In calling the object of this study the "modern self," I follow recent critics like Gary Wilder and Shu-mei Shih, who register this fact of a shared—if violently different—history of the modern world.[7]

This book thus speaks to both the traditional and the postcolonial versions of intellectual history. It also works to show both of these traditions why they should engage seriously with Buddhist thinkers. To do so, I have demonstrated how some of the canonical Euro-American thinkers of the modern self—such as Jean-Jacques Rousseau, G. W. F. Hegel, and Ralph Waldo Emerson—formed their major ideas in the crucible of international relations. In *re*constituting this global history, I thus continue to pry open the canon and show how the question of global self-making is at the heart of even the most Eurocentric thinking. Europe, then, is not the founder of modernity, but is itself a reactive formation created in the face of global pressures.[8] This in turn allows me to show how figures like W. E. B. Du Bois, Frantz Fanon, and D. T. Suzuki are not outsiders to the Western tradition clamoring to make their voices heard, but rather part of a single, shared, wildly uneven, and violent history of global self-making.

This basic reframing leads me to critically engage with a number of the leading thinkers in both critical and postcolonial theory across the breadth of this book. Too often, I find, even those who think about global concerns still place a deglobalized European philosophical history at the center of their theorizing. This happens either by locating the problems of the world solely in "Western metaphysics" or by "using" critical theorists to analyze global conditions without considering the global histories that inform their theories in the first place. By suggesting that the philosophical history of modernity is a global one, I hope to push contemporary theorists to remap their critical analyses of the present. If the problem is not just Western metaphysics but more specifically particular ways of configuring global relations, then the proposed solutions will need to respond to these ideas about global life.

Essaying the Globe

Thinkers coming from such radically different times and places will of course produce different ideas about the global self, and that's the whole point: the history of the modern self is a pluralist history of attempts to make who we are adequate to the task of being global. I sometimes refer to taking up this task as "essaying the globe," in part because the writers I consider all worked in the essay form. They likely did so because the essay, as an attempt or trial that works through the many parts of an object, is a form ideally suited to trying to understand one's place in the extensions of the global. The challenge of these essayists was to understand the whole world from their limited position on it, and to do so not merely at the level of intellectual understanding, but also by transforming themselves into subjects at once humble and critical, at once local and far-flung, at once firmly directed and open to the wild contingencies of life. I follow an interconnected series of essayists who took up that challenge with greater and lesser success from Renaissance Europe to modern Japan and Senegal. I consider skeptics, rationalists, universalists, pluralists, revolutionaries, and mystics as they responded to each other (either with praise or critique) across five continents and four centuries. These thinkers were appalled by specialization and had no interest in limiting themselves to one country or century or genre or discipline. I follow their provocations to think so broadly in this book.[9]

To understand their relationship to the world, the whole world, and nothing less was their task. This was not hubris on their part (although some of their propositions are hubristic). Rather, they believed, as Cornelius Castoriadis put it, that theory should be "the always uncertain attempt to realize the project of elucidating the world."[10] For Castoriadis, elucidation does not mean explanation; it means that we are constituted by forces outside ourselves (heteronomy), which we must work through in order to make them clear (lucid) and our own (autonomy). Essaying the globe is the difficult practice of gathering up the fragments of the world that make us who we are and developing concepts and ways of life that can come to terms with this connectedness. The task of these writers was to make the unbearable mass of the world's impression on their souls something that they could come to shoulder. This essaying required them to turn fragments of others into some real understanding. They restlessly pursued as much knowledge about as many peoples and ideas and things as they could.

Still, the essay—in spite of the excessive praise it sometimes receives—is no perfect form, and it may be put to as many different ends as any other form.[11] In the chapters to follow, I look at five modes of global essay writing: skeptical (in which the essay leaves us in a state of doubt with regard to all given cultures), teleological (in which the essay tries to move us toward a singular, global vision), alternating (in which the essay enjoins us to move back and forth between different visions of the world without attempting to synthesize them into a single whole), revolutionary (in which the essay attempts to intervene in and transform a given reality—ideally through pluralistic alliances) and emptying (in which the essay seeks, through silences, nonsensical asides, anecdotes, repetitions, and other means, to undo the ego of the reader and provoke an enlightenment experience). A single essay can, of course, embody components of each, but most essays studied here tend toward one specific mode. Sometimes the essaying attempts led these writers to achieve understanding; sometimes they did not. That uneven progress is the history of essaying the globe.

While the book thus aims to present a rival account to the "Ancient Greece to modern Europe" framings of Taylor and Foucault, it does not share their ambition to tell a complete history of the present. To the contrary, my claim here is that such denials of one's own partiality are part of why we continue to have such skewed visions of the modern self. I do not think it is possible to exhaustively tell a history of the "sources of the self" precisely because those sources are so vast and global and mean different things for different subjects—and often, of course, for the same subject at different times in her life. Rather than attempting to synthesize some general movements like Taylor's disengaged reason versus Romanticism or Foucault's rise of biopower and loss of the practices of the self, I aim to show how different solutions were broached in response to the problem of what I call "unbearable identities." These are the various ways in which global being overwhelmed the subject and made life for her intolerable. I do not pretend that the problem of "unbearability" is the *ur*-problem of the modern self or that my list of solutions (skepticism, universalism, pluralism, revolution, aesthetics, mysticism) is exhaustive. I merely suggest it as one plausible narrative vocabulary for understanding how global connections have constituted and continue to constitute who we are. More specifically still, I suggest it as a way of understanding the strange and surprising history that will connect essay writers from Montaigne to Kant to Emerson to Du Bois to Senghor to Suzuki.

Unbearable Identities

Identities are understood here as how personhood is conceived and crafted in relation to the world. I am not particularly concerned—as Taylor is, for example—with whether the very idea of a deep, internal self is a unique invention of modernity. However one conceives of personhood—and we come across a great many differing conceptions here—what concerns me is how this diverse set of thinkers has conceived of what it means to be any kind of individual since the sixteenth century, when, as Sanjay Subrahmanyam tells us, the long-standing human fascination with cultural difference "crystallized around the idea of a world that had been 'encompassed.' "[12] By this he means the realization that there were not just different people "out there," but that we were all bound to eventually run into each other on this finite, "encompassed" sphere. My question is: How did our thinking about identity respond to this condition?

The answer I am suggesting here is that, quite simply, it became unbearable, and in several different ways. Of course the primary sense of this unbearability was the exacerbation of the all too human will to dominate others. The focus of this study is in how this will interacted with other transformations of self-understanding. The first, such as we find in Montaigne, is when we realize that our inherited knowledges cannot bear the weight of these new connections. The kinds of identities one might once have sculpted—a Greco-Roman man of letters, for instance—do not have the resources to make sense of being alive in this new configuration. The Cartesian response to refind certainty in the self, which is supposed to be the founding of modern subjectivity, is thus in fact only its evasion. This did not mean, however, that engaging the global necessarily overcame the problem. Another path, such as we find in Kant, is a universalism that seeks to make sense of the situation by attempting to bear on its shoulders—or in its mind—a basic set of truths to govern the whole world. This, too, proves unbearable, and in two senses: first, because it is simply too much for any one thinker or cultural system to bear the world's diversity, and, second, because in attempting to do so, one tends to impose unbearable demands on others to live up to one's ideals. This thus produces another kind of unbearable identity, such as we find negotiated in Du Bois: the unbearable burdens of having a degraded and often violently oppressed position within someone else's universal scheme. (This will in turn produce potential forms of self-essentializing, which I consider with Senghor, although I believe he ultimately avoids this self-imposed version of unbearability.)

Overcoming these primary forms of unbearable identities will produce other possible modes of subjectivity, including, on the conceptual side, a traditional pluralist way of both respecting and maintaining difference, and, on the more active side, the revolutionary subjectivity of attempting to overthrow the conditions of unbearable imposition. Indeed, without social transformations, practices of the global self fall back into mere changes in subjectivity that are equally incapable of bearing the needs of the modern world. Thus, while social change is not the immediate focus of this book, it is a crucial context that I discuss throughout. Traditional pluralism and revolution also each have their own constraints in turn: pluralism runs the risk of encasing others in static—if no longer denigrated—identities. And revolution, when it does not proceed through pluralistic alliances forged in deep organizing, may impose its rightful transformations in an unbearable manner.[13]

The final form of unbearability that is my focus here is that of mysticism. In this model, such as we find in Suzuki, unbearability is overcome through the negation of the very idea of a subject that is separate from the world. Only such separation, Suzuki suggests, lets one feel the world as other than oneself and thus as a possible burden to oneself. While this model may have great efficacy, it runs into a limit—one that Suzuki admits—when it has to deal with the difficult questions of everyday political choices in the face of human suffering. The mystical release simply cannot bear the burden of these demands.

In cataloguing these modes of unbearable identities throughout the book, I do not suggest that they are entirely flawed. There is within Montaigne's skepticism, Kant's universalism, Suzuki's mysticism, and so forth values that can be named and upheld as methods within themselves for overcoming the unbearability of global relations. And indeed, this kind of radically pluralist response, one that insists on the plurality of all ideas, peoples, individuals, and natures and thus can engage with different ways of being at different moments without dissolving into infinite particulars, is what I suggest as the most fortuitous method of overcoming the unbearable identities found in this history.

Radical Pluralism

I later trace the roots of radical pluralism to the writings of Ralph Waldo Emerson and W. E. B. Du Bois. The idea of radical pluralism is that plurality is not just between things, but within them as well. We all know that cultures have drastic differences within themselves and that individuals are hardly ever consistent. Nevertheless, cultural theory tends to minimize these internal differences in the name of "ideal type" analyses that can summarize a cultural moment. Our era as one globally saturated with neoliberal rationality is a good example. And indeed, critical theory requires our ability to demarcate cultural trends so as to be able to support or fight against them. Otherwise we are lost in the empty and muddled multiplicity of the present moment. We need to reconcile the demands of critique with the reality of internal and external difference.

There are of course a great many writers who have theorized individuals and cultures in these terms, and I have learned from each of them.[14] However, I have often found that we lack the language to articulate both the reality of constituted entities (be they individuals or cultures or ideas) and the fact of their internal multiplicity. This leads to an ensuing failure of our critical vocabulary to be able to denounce those aspects of any entity that create unbearable conditions for others without denouncing the totality of that entity. To properly articulate this dual relation is the hope of a radical pluralism. It is "radical" in the etymological sense of the term—it goes all the way down to the roots (radicals) of things. There is no essential substrate to be found, only the ceaseless multiplicity of life. But it also insists that real entities, themselves plural, emerge from these infinitely plural roots, and these entities must in turn be ethically and politically negotiated. Thus it is also radical in the sense that it does not accept any given strata of a plurality simply because it exists. It demands that all strata of a society be accountable to the tasks of liberation in a globally connected world.[15] In the ethical language of this book, that means that radical pluralism contributes to the overcoming of unbearable identities, and that it effectively does so is my argument in the chapters to follow.

The existence of concrete realities does not reduce those entities to singular traits. Radical pluralism posits that each resulting, worldly entity—

individual, society, nature—is made of infinite constituent parts. These constituent parts form concrete, conventional designations such as table, self, world. No such entities have an essence. (Readers of philosophical Buddhism will recognize the distinction between conventional and ultimate reality here, and I return in the chapter on Suzuki to the role of this philosophy in the generation of radical pluralism.) A table may be used as much for writing as for eating; a person may vacillate between fits of generosity and miserliness; the world may teeter between hope and apocalypse. Radical pluralists do not simply throw up their hands at this relativity, however. They analyze the ways in which entities congeal around specific nodes. Within each constitution there is a variety of strands, threads, voices. Each takes priority at different times—Emerson calls these "master-tones."[16] But there are also minor keys and unheard sounds. The trick, as we will see more deeply in Emerson, is to learn to move between these different sides both internally and externally and, furthermore, to see the world as this alternating complex with which our plural selves engage. It is this capacity of alternation that at once ensures and endangers progress, and the task of radical pluralists is to lend their weight to the elements of the world that overcome unbearability without, in the process, neglecting to encourage the freedom to be plural.

Traditional pluralism assumes that there are multiple ways of being in the world, and it sometimes suggests that "modernity" is the site of the mixing of these ways of being. Traditional pluralism tells us to be aware of the other ways of living, but the internal plurality of those other ways is not emphasized. It can thus become unbearable because, especially when coupled with dominating powers, it can force people into a prescribed role as much as universalism can. This was the case, for example, with South Africa's terrifying Bantu Education Act (1953), which furthered apartheid by enforcing prescribed "tribal" rules for educating nonwhite South Africans.[17] There are already many good theories of pluralism that have moved past traditional pluralism. In addition to classic works by William James, W. E. B. Du Bois, and Hannah Arendt (and I would add Léopold Senghor to this list for reasons that may not yet be apparent to all readers), we might also include recent theorists like Richard Bernstein, William Connolly, Janet Jakobsen, María Lugones, Mariana Ortega, and James Tully.[18] My point is not so much to disagree with these authors as to build on and extend their insights into the histories of global-self-making.[19]

The consistently pluralist approach I present here can be schematized in nine claims. First, that all cultures are within themselves plural, dynamic, and not definable by a single essence.[20] Second, that every individual is plural within themselves because we are all made up a series of competing or complementary dispositions and desires. By combining these first two claims, we arrive at the third: that within a given culture, any individual has the capacity to move, or, as Emerson put it, "alternate," between the different ways of being within a culture. (That freedom requires an openness to alternation is a theme that is especially evident in the sections on Du Bois, Fanon, and hooks.) Fourth, that the plural forms of life that come into being within one culture do not exhaust the totality of the ways of being. This is what requires us to engage with a plurality beyond the plurality into which we are born. Given that cultures have always mixed, it is rarely the case that there is an idea to be found in one archive that is completely absent in another, but there are certainly modes of life that have been deepened in one site or another. (We will see a version of this argument in Senghor's aesthetics in chapter 3.) Therefore, fifth, that any individual who is open to it can alternate to another way of being outside of their own cultural space (where avoiding the risk of projection and appropriation requires great vigilance). Just as cultures and individuals grow, interact, and mutate, so do concepts, and thus, sixth, that concepts are themselves plural. Seventh, and related to this, that pluralism itself is plural. As we will see with Emerson and Du Bois, for example, different subjects in different times and places will develop different emphases in their articulations of pluralism. (They also sometimes need to ignore their plurality for political or personal reasons; I call these "strategic partialisms.") Eighth, that all of these cultural mutations do not take place on a single substratum, Nature, but rather within the context of what Eduardo Viveiros de Castro calls "multi-naturalism," or the idea that the world itself is plural.[21] Finally, ninth, the concept of radical pluralism has appeared in different forms in different times and places. This does not make it eternal or a transcendental form of human life. It is a way of understanding the world and our place in it, and as those things both change, radical pluralism may itself disappear. I offer it here as a universal in the sense that radical pluralism intends all universal claims: as strategic partializations of ontology. This way of thinking about diversity calls on us to constantly negotiate the multiplicities that we are with the multiplicities that the world is. It is a difficult and never fully resolvable task, but it is the intellectual challenge posed by the plurality inherent in our lives.

If we apply this model to the idea of "the West," for example, what we see is that "the West" is a real entity with historical power that has emerged through global constitutions. At the same time, we can appreciate that its reality effects are plural and that they are received differently in different times and places and even differently by different subjects within the same time and place.[22] Furthermore, we can appreciate the multiplicity of what has come to be within the West and the fact that different ideas were generated there, ideas that are worth finding and rearticulating.[23] The result, as I discuss in the context of Foucault below, is that our aim becomes less about "overcoming Western metaphysics" and more about overcoming certain versions of global life that were produced in the West (although certainly not only there—terrible ideas come from all corners of the globe).[24]

To sum up: the claim here is that all entities are plural and global, constituted by the multiplicity of the world. Radical pluralism enables global subjects to overcome unbearable identities, for its practitioners are no longer trying to bear the burden of the world in a single vision, nor are they forcing others to have singular places within our schemes. Rather, they learn that they are always already sharing the burden of global being, and the task becomes learning how to share this better. The tragedy of life is that this sharing is not particularly easy either. But it is, at least, bearable.

Reconstitution

These epistemological and ethical claims about the plurality of existence are coincident with a historical methodology that I, following Said, call "reconstitution." The aim of reconstitution is to show how constituted entities—like "the modern self"—were formed through a multiplicity of processes and interactions. Unlike a standard comparative method in which the givenness of two constituted entities is taken for granted and then each is analyzed (as in Erich Auerbach's wonderful exposition of the differences in time consciousness between Greek and Hebraic forms of representation), the reconstitutive method begins by first showing how interactions across boundaries *produced* these entities in the first place.[25] It thus affirms that differences are real, but also that their reality is dependent on multiple factors. Unlike a dialectical method, which might seek the shared ground of these differences via a third category that unites them, or a deconstructive method, which might rest content with exposing the fact of mutual constitution, reconstitution thus aligns with a radically pluralist view of the world that holds reality and transformation together in a single vision.

Reconstitution shares a fair amount with what theorists like Jane Gordon, Michael Monahan, and Neil Roberts call "creolization" and what Shu-mei

Shih calls "relational comparison."²⁶ I have used the term "reconstitution" for two primary reasons. First, because it leads more logically to a sense of maintaining difference than these other categories because of its link to what is "constituted." Second, because I view this work as part of a tradition that uses Said's thinking about mutual constitution to understand how concepts seemingly formed in only one place in fact have their origins in global interactions. A long tradition of scholarship has attempted to show precisely this constitutive role, including Martin Bernal's *Black Athena* (1987), Paul Gilroy's *The Black Atlantic* (1993), Gayatri Spviak's *A Critique of Postcolonial Reason* (1999), Susan Buck-Morss's "Hegel and Haiti" (2000/2009), Peter van der Veer's *Imperial Encounters* (2001), Sankar Muthu's *Enlightenment against Empire* (2003), Antony Anghie's *Imperialism, Sovereignty, and the Making of International Law* (2004), Kevin Anderson's *Marx at the Margins* (2010), Lisa Lowe's *The Intimacy of Four Continents* (2015), and Gary Wilder's *Freedom Time* (2015).²⁷ But in spite of this extensive work, David Scott noted in 2010 that such claims still remain outside the mainstream accounts of European intellectual history: "It is not typically imagined that knowledges and institutions in these worlds [outside Europe] . . . might have had a role in the shaping of Europe and the discourses that *constitute* its cultural and philosophic identity."²⁸ Part of my work here, then, is simply continuing to do the constitutive work that these other scholars have called for. But I also want to keep advancing the conversation through critical engagements with these critics. I thus hope to expand this field in several ways: by giving a broader narrative of this history of European thought in works stretching from Montaigne to Foucault; by taking up, revising, and disagreeing with some of the specific claims about these authors by previous global postcolonial critics; and by showing the connections between this constitutive history of European thought and its ramifications for how we understand American Transcendentalism, Africana thought, and modern Zen.

One example of these claims can be seen in the alternative history of dialectics that I trace across this book. Dialectical thought, of course, has been a critical resource for thinkers of the global since Hegel and Marx. The dialectical insight that history progresses through struggles generated by complex relations between self and other certainly speaks to how we might understand the modern history of global interactions. Recent critics including Buck-Morss, Timothy Brennan, and George Ciccariello-Maher have offered renewed visions of the power of dialectics for advancing radical critiques of philosophical traditions and our present conditions.²⁹ But while all of these works push dialectics beyond their Hegelian origins, and while Buck-Morss and Brennan argue that Hegel frequently had colonialism on his mind, none of them argues that dialectics *itself*, as a way of understanding the world, was constituted in global interactions. For them the dialectic might have been *applied* to these interactions, but it was not itself formed in them.[30]

But of course dialectics as a way of thinking does have origins. Most scholars would argue that those origins are in the science of the times (polarity and magnetism), or the history of Greek or Medieval philosophy. What I argue (in chapters 2–4) is that the very idea of the modern dialectic itself was (in part) constituted by geographic thinking. I trace a history of dialectics from Jean-Baptiste Du Tertre's colonial ethnography into Rousseau's *Discourse on the Origin of Inequality* and then on to Schiller and Hegel. I show the specific ways in which dialectics developed through ideas about primitive life and how, simply by looking for it, we can see clearly the global origins of modern dialectical thought. Having established this history, I argue that key moments in the history of dialectics do not include just their Marxist revisions, but also the various refutations and reformulations of dialectical thought that we find in thinkers as diverse as Senghor, Fanon, and Suzuki.[31]

Rather than "deconstruct" dialectics, then, I reconstitute its history. And I am thus less interested in the ongoing debate in postcolonial studies between deconstruction and dialectics and more concerned to show how both of these philosophies were *themselves* formed in the modern history of global interactions.[32] Nevertheless, throughout this book, I engage this debate as it occurs around some of the authors considered here and argue for why a radical pluralism that is aware of this constitutive history offers a powerful alternative route out of some of the impasses of contemporary criticism.

The other broad argument being advanced through the example of dialectics is that the history of thought is in part a history of geographic claims about how cultures can and should relate to each other, and that by ignoring this history we ignore the work of the theories themselves. As Linda Martín Alcoff puts it in a discussion of modern philosophy's relation to colonialism: "If . . . the meaning of philosophy is simply the history of philosophy . . . then European philosophy does not understand what philosophy is because it does not understand its own history of philosophy."[33] The aim of constitutive criticism is, following Alcoff, to make a stronger case for why the appearance of other cultures *matters* for the history of thought.[34] In the past few decades, several other methods have been used to understand the place of global cultures within the history of Western thought. Said, for example, focused on the *representation* of others and how those representations went hand in hand with the political regime of colonialism.[35] Spivak, meanwhile, investigated the *rhetoric* of others, showing how admittedly marginal moments in texts create the conditions of possibility for their arguments.[36] Others asked what *resources* a thinker provides in spite of their hostile representations, as in, for example, recent works by Judith Butler on Levinas, or Brennan on Hegel, or Amy Allen on Adorno and Foucault.[37] All of these methods have a certain power and logic that I do not intend to dispute. My concern with them is that they allow us to continue to write and read as if these moments are discardable: "If our focus is not politics, why engage with representations?" "If this is just marginal rhetoric, then it does not touch the philosophy itself." "If the resources are there, why does it matter what people actually said?" I believe that focusing more and more on questions of constitution can help rebut the logic of such questions. That is to say, we need to "rummage" back through intellectual history to reconstitute texts whose claims about others have been discarded.[38] In so doing, we can begin to reconstitute the canon itself, showing how these are not just matters of external representation, marginal rhetoric, or latent resources, but concerns at the heart of the texts themselves. Combined with a radically pluralist approach to criticism, this can also allow us to be up-front about what is problematic in theorists whose work in other domains we might appreciate.

Such a reconstitution does not work to determine once and for all the meaning of a concept or movement, but rather creates a narrative whose reconstruction shows the ongoing effects of these prior moments in our present. We constitute ourselves by reconstituting the forms that already inhabit our thinking. And in this reconstituting we also open ourselves up to new forms simply by following other possible implications that we might not, or even could not, have otherwise considered. Thus, for example, reconstituting the globality of Zen led me to need to reconstitute the globality of the European thought that preceded it. In turn, I have reconstituted a history that does not stretch from Rousseau to German and French critical theory, but rather from Rousseau to postcolonial critique and modern Zen.

Practices of the Global Self

This act of reconstitution thus forms a challenge to the history of critical theory. Critical theorists have often taken as their target some problem in "Western thought" whose overturning they view as central to new forms of political liberation. This takes many forms, such as the framing of the world by technology and the "forgetting of being" in Heidegger (which I discuss in more detail in chapter 1), phallogocentrism and "the metaphysics of presence" in Derrida, biopower in Foucault, disembodied viewpoints in Haraway, the state of exception in Agamben, or neoliberalism for Wendy Brown. Across all the different diagnoses of how to name the failures of modern life, these thinkers all take as their central object of critique something whose origin begins in European thought. It is of course the case that all theories only diagnose an aspect of the problem, and most critical theorists would admit this. Still, there are moments, especially in the excessive concluding words of some of Agamben's books, when it seems that theorists might just believe that overcoming a problem in the philosophies of Europe could bring about the revolution tomorrow.[39]

But if the claims I make here, building on these traditions of reconstitution, have any value, then there must be something askew in this mode of critique. For, as van der Veer puts it, "[a] Eurocentric philosophical history . . . however brilliantly presented, ignores the importance of the global dimension of the issues it discusses."[40] It is of course the case that in discussing global dimensions, one will equally miss some more specific and local issues, and I return to this problem below. My point here is not that the "truth" of our concerns lies in the global. Rather, it is that this work of reconstitution allows us to see problems otherwise obscured when the focus remains on supposedly internal European dynamics.

Throughout this book, my main example of what this change of focus could look like is with reference to the late work of Michel Foucault, whose research into what he called the "technologies" or "practices" of the self has been influential for my thinking about the global self. For Foucault, such practices mean that the truth is not available to us as we are, but that we must change who we are to be adequate to the tasks of truthful living. To be sure, becoming global requires transformations of the self; it requires us to become new kinds of subjects who can relate to global processes. Thus it requires us to develop practices (such as new forms of writing, new ways of thinking, and new practices of meditation) to enact those changes. Foucault, however, never once mentions such global transformations. Instead, he follows a standard Eurocentric trajectory, arguing that the rich practices of the self developed by Hellenic and Roman authors have been lost in modernity. I break with Foucault by arguing that what we witness in modernity is not so much a disappearance as a transformation: ancient techniques give way to modern practices of the global self. In other words, self-transformation in the modern era is about making oneself the kind of subject who can overcome the unbearability of identity produced by global connections.

Foucault developed these ideas in his late work, especially in the lecture course "The Hermeneutics of the Subject." In these lectures, he worked to understand what he called a transformation in the "history of truth."[41] He argued that philosophy seeks to know not what is true and false, but rather "the conditions and limits of the subject's access to truth." What Foucault found in his excavation was that there was a long tradition of "spirituality," understood as "the search, practice, and experience through which the subject carries out the necessary transformations on himself in order to have access to the truth."[42] He argued that the modern era of this history—which he heuristically dubbed the "Cartesian moment"—began when spirituality split off from philosophy, and it was assumed that the subject, as she is, is capable of the truth without any work of transformation. We have enshrined "know thyself" above all and have forgotten how to care for ourselves.[43]

Foucault wanted to excavate and reassert the importance of these lost "practices of the self," but he found in the modern era a series of binds that limited such a reinvention: "I do not think we have anything to be proud of in our current efforts to reconstitute an ethic of the self . . . I think we may have to suspect that we find it impossible today to constitute an ethic of the self, even though it may be an urgent, fundamental and politically indispensable task."[44] This was, and remains, an urgent need for a number of reasons according to Foucault's analysis of the functioning of power since the eighteenth century. In brief, Foucault was concerned that our analyses of political power had limited themselves to the question of the "juridico-discursive," or the top-down legal institutions of a society.[45] He believed that these mattered, but also wanted us to turn our attention to the ways in which "power mechanisms . . . took charge of men's existence, men as living bodies." There we would see "new methods of power whose operation is not ensured by right but by technique."[46] Because power operates at the level of our existence, we must also confront it there by developing different techniques or practices of the self. This meant combating ossified notions of truth as they manifested in madness, criminality, or sexuality in Foucault's early and middle works. In these late lectures, he began to focus on a more general theorization of the lost "relationship of self to self" through spiritual techniques.[47]

We can see here the correspondence between Foucault's analysis and his proposed solutions. Because he, like Agamben and Brown after him, focuses on transformations in Western social, legal, and economic formations, he develops his solutions on these grounds. Indeed, Foucault is explicit about this: his concern is with a problem produced by "the set of phenomena and historical processes we call our 'culture.'"[48] In spite of the scare quotes and the genuine sense that a "culture" is a complex and heterogenous assemblage of forces,[49] Foucault, whose analyses on so many other topics were dedicated to taking apart the presumptions he inherited, nevertheless believed strongly in this idea of "our culture." Indeed, Foucault's most famous analyses in many ways spring from an insight, recorded in the very first sentence of *The Order of Things* (1966), about the constrictions imposed on thought by Western methods of classification: "This book first arose out of a passage in Borges, out of the laughter that shattered, as I read the passage, all the familiar landmarks of my thought—*our* thought, the thought bears the stamp of our age and our geography."[50] It is only by isolating "*our* thought" as only one possible mode of thought that Foucault can name and describe it and thus find the leverage through which to pry it open.

Foucault's enormous success in illuminating the systems of thought that undergird ideas of madness, of language, of sexuality, and of punishment, among others, shows that this is far from a futile task. Indeed, because "the West" *is* a constituted entity whose formation *is* in part through local and immediate concerns, such local analyses can of course produce tremendous results. But, as critics since at least Ann Stoler have pointed out in response to Foucault's histories of the self, taking into consideration "a wider imperial context resituates the work of racial thinking in the making of European bourgeois identity."[51] Indeed, as historians of philosophy like Robert Bernasconi and Peter Park have shown, racist thinking was the primary reason why thinkers from outside Europe have been excluded from the canon of "philosophy," and why someone like Foucault, constituted by global connections he did not fully grasp, would come to presume "the West" as "his culture."[52] Building on these scholars' research, my argument here is that focusing the question of the practices of the self on their Greco-Roman roots ignores the very precise ways in which these practices were constituted globally. And if *part* of the modern self is a global self, then at least *part* of the solution to its problems must be sought in new forms of global relations.

What is ironic here is that Foucault himself seems to have known this. In his lectures on *The Birth of Biopolitics* (1978–79), for example, he was explicit that the eighteenth century saw the rise of "a new type of global calculation in European governmental practice . . . a new form of global rationality . . . a new calculation on the scale of the world."[53] If part of the techniques of power were globally constituted for the past several centuries, then it makes sense to say that Foucault should have devised practices of the self that were formed in this same, ongoing global constitution. And, in a sense, he in fact did. The Borges passage mentioned above, after all, references a "Chinese encyclopedia." Throughout *The History of Sexuality* (1984), Foucault contrasts the "Western" approach to sexuality with those of other cultures. And, especially in the mid- to late 1970s, he began explicit and ongoing engagements with Zen Buddhism and what he called the "political spirituality" of the Iranian revolution.[54]

However, when Foucault looked beyond the West, he did so not as a point of contact, but rather as a space of rupture. When he speaks of "political spirituality" in the context of Iran, he speaks of "this thing whose possibility *we* have forgotten since the Renaissance."[55] And when he considers the possibility of comparative philosophy in dialogue with a Zen monk, it is only in its possible future birth: "if philosophy of the future exists, it must be born outside of Europe or equally in consequence of meetings and impacts between Europe and non-Europe."[56] Foucault's theorizing the loss of practice in the West while at the same time practicing global engagement is the fundamental irony of his study. Whereas he theorized that the West lost its spiritual practice and therefore had to locate spirituality elsewhere, I argue that *what happened to spirituality in the modern era was that it became precisely this global task. Modern subjectivity is not devoid of spirituality; it practices spirituality (for better and for worse) through attempts to make itself adequate to the globe.* The problem is not, or is not just, "our culture"; it is also how we relate to the world. Contemporary theory in general needs to understand this broader history in order to make more cogent interventions.

Several of Foucault's excellent readers have similarly followed his partition between the question of globalism and the act of self-transformation.[57] Thus Judith Butler, in *Precarious Life* (2004), argues that we are in a moment "in which an inevitable interdependency becomes acknowledged as the basis for global community."[58] She continues, "I confess to not knowing how to theorize that interdependency," but then gives a very interesting theorization:

> I would suggest, however, that both our political and ethical responsibilities are rooted in the recognition that radical forms of self-sufficiency and unbridled sovereignty are, by definition, disrupted by the larger global processes of which they are a part, that no final control can be secured, and that final control is not, cannot be, an ultimate value.[59]

There would be reasons to question some of the terms of this statement, but that is not my present concern. Rather, what interests me is that this text appeared shortly before Butler's extended engagement with Foucault's late work in *Giving an Account of Oneself* (2005).[60] But although Butler had just the previous year called for a development of global subjectivity, this concern disappears from her account of self-transformation, and she accepts (or at least does not pause to question) Foucault's basic notion of "the West" as a tradition of thought that shapes certain people's subjectivity.[61] The question of how one's subjective life is constituted globally thus does not, at this point in her work, get raised. This partition marks the history of critical theory in the present, even in thinkers as committed to global questions as Butler.

Some of the purpose of this book is to connect these two lines of thought through a long history of the methods used to theorize global interdependency and what that means for subjectivity. Foucault thinks that we can read a history of thinkers from Montaigne to Heidegger along the lines of attempted "practices of the self" that continually founder.[62] We need to be able to have a new spirituality, but we are unable to define one. For Foucault, this is because of the regimes of disciplinarity and control and the discourse of science, and because we simply have not yet done what Foucault is attempting: to set out the explicit terms of the discourse.[63] Another problem, I am suggesting, is that we have not yet fully set these concerns within the actually existing geographic frame of modernity, that is, our fraught global condition. It is not that we do not have practices of the self in the modern era; it is that those practices are aimed at developing diverse modes of global subjectivity. To analyze the successes and failures of those practices, we must, at the very least, acknowledge their existence. Hence I have rewritten Foucault's historical stretch from Montaigne to Heidegger to that from Montaigne to Suzuki, globalizing each figure along the way.

A Partial History: The Narrative of this Book

A word on the choice of figures represented in this book. It might seem that the task I embark on—to trace the attempts at global subjectivity in a series of essay writers from Montaigne to Suzuki and his followers—is an impossibly ambitious project. To my mind, however, it remains unbearably parochial. Although this book is informed by the complex pasts of the peoples whom Europeans once called "without history," the pre–twentieth century writers studied here are largely European born. Little mention is made of the global subjectivities being enacted *simultaneously* in the Americas, South Asia, sub-Saharan Africa, the Levant, the Pacific, or the Maghreb, or elsewhere. I do not in the least mean to imply that no such indigenous accounts exist—even some sixteenth-century European writers were aware of and engaged with them.[64] I discuss the importance of such engagements in the section on Montaigne but then focus mostly on how the willful misunderstanding of the lives of these peoples shaped the philosophical history that follows him. My aim in doing so, again, is to continue the work of reconstituting the fraught global origins of what is still taken to be a self-contained European history of philosophy.

There are other limits here. The liberal tradition, so important in shaping the colonial world, has also been relegated to marginalia.[65] There remains, further, a complete absence of noncanonical theorists and enacters of "planetary consciousness," such as those painstakingly detailed in Linebaugh and Rediker's *Many-Headed Hydra*.[66] And, while references are given to original language works for the major figures considered, the debates engaged here are grounded in the bibliography of primarily Anglophone scholarship.[67] Nor do I address the question of the World Wide Web, or the digital more generally, which is perhaps the most significant way in which global selves are being sculpted (if not essayed) minute by minute today. And the question of climate change, perhaps *the* global issue of the day, is not discussed until the coda.

There is, further still, a general absence of female writers in the primary figures studied (with the exception of bell hooks), although I raise questions about the role of women in a number of the authors considered here. In this context, it is also important to mark a debt in the methodology of reconstitutive reading that I owe feminist studies as much as to the postcolonial theory mentioned above. The general concern is well expressed in an essay by Hazel Carby. Carby questions the idea that the problems with patriarchal ideas "speak for themselves." If that were the case, Carby argues, then such ideas "are merely superficial, easily recognized, and quickly accounted for, enabling real intellectual work to continue elsewhere." The result is a space in which male intellectuals maintain "a politically correct posture of making an obligatory, though finally empty, gesture toward [feminist critique]."[68] Although my main focus is not on gender or sexuality, Carby's criticism of the idea that the "real intellectual work" is "elsewhere" has guided my reflection on understanding how global cultures formed modern selves. Thus feminists like Carby taught me to read for othering—for how the act of othering *mattered*, for how we could not insulate the philosophical insights from this act's constitutive force—and it is this sensibility that I bring to the philosophical texts that have mattered for so much contemporary theory, feminist and otherwise. I have no doubt that *other* histories of the global origins of the modern self can be told, have been told, and should be told.

As I wrote in the preface, the selection choices were animated by my aim to reconstruct the global intellectual history that resulted in Suzuki's own writing. As such, the development of a fully fledged understanding of practices of the global self beyond a certain number of canonical, mostly male figures remains beyond the scope of this book. It is instead primarily concerned with how a series of male writers—a number of them racialized as white—attempted to come to terms with global identity, and largely through their encounters with peoples and traditions outside white identity. One-half of the book, then, is a study of a kind of white, masculinist practices of the global self. But it is not blindly so, and thus the other half of the narrative is concerned with how this construction of the self was one among others. Equally, all of this is undertaken in the context of radical pluralism, which again is the insistence on layers of plurality all the way down. This means, first, that none of the positions offered here is represented as *the* truth. Second, it is not presumed that simply because the identities of the thinkers considered are white and male that the totality of their positions can be circumscribed by their identities—any more than Fanon's or Du Bois's thoughts are circumscribed by theirs.[69] My hope is that this canonical focus does not detract from the work so much as continue to open mainstream critical theory to other writings.[70] By opening up the canon to these same concerns of self-making in a global world, I hope this book might further other investigations by showing how deeply practical, global concerns were to even the supposedly most abstract thought.

I make these qualifications along the lines of what the novelist Wilson Harris has called "confessions of partiality."[71] In admitting to our own limitations, Harris argues, we refuse the instinct to universalize our own ideas, and, at the same time, we unravel claims to sovereign universality that others might make. The claim that I am making about practices of the global self is true for a *part* of modern subjectivity, but it is, on the whole, only a part. The idea of a *partial history* is based on the fundamental multiplicity of any historical epoch. It is partial both because it is a part and because it is *not* impartial—it represents the concerns of just one author when faced with the history of attempts to essay the globe. As Emerson admonishes, "You have not got rid of your parts by denying them, but are the more partial."⁷²

The chapters of this partial history are as follows.

In chapter 1, I suggest that the realization that we live on a single, interdependent, rapidly connecting planet led early writers like Montaigne to realize that private wisdom could no longer bear the weight of modern responsibility. The book begins with a reading of his "Of Cannibals," as an essayistic practice of the self in which Montaigne attempts to transform who he is so that he can understand his relation to the Tupi people he meets in 1562 in Rouen, France. I look especially at how Montaigne uses the method of skepticism to break down his prejudices and then eclecticism to build an early pluralist mode of thought. I conclude my reading of Montaigne by responding to the criticism of him levied by Sankar Muthu in his important work on enlightenment and colonialism. Then, in a comparison with ideas of subjectivity found in Shakespeare's *Hamlet* and Descartes's cogito, I polemically suggest that Montaigne's essay, more than these other writings, ought to be understood as the foundation of modern thinking. Hamlet and Descartes are representatives of the attempt to hold onto singular identity in the face of globality. As a result, they produce a line of identity thinking connected to the anxiety of trying to bear the truth of the whole world in a single subject that I follow into the work of Martin Heidegger. Despite his famous attempt to overcome the Cartesian self, Heidegger remains wedded to its evasive, monocultural practices. I am especially concerned here to question the common use of Heidegger as a theorist of modernity given his unrepentant Eurocentrism.

Following this argument, I work to reposition a line of post-Montaigne global thought stretching from Rousseau to Marx. Montaigne left a pervasive impact on Jean-Jacques Rousseau, whose earliest essays register the same desire to transform his thinking in order to comprehend global cultures. A large part of this book is dedicated to unpacking the wide-ranging yet underappreciated influence of Rousseau's ideas about the global self on writers around the world. Rousseau broke with Montaigne's open approach and began to plot a specific evolution for human subjectivity. While still a pluralist, Rousseau came to believe that there is a singular true path for Europeans. That path is staked along the route of evolutionary history, and Rousseau's key intervention is to use conjectural histories (speculative histories about human origins based on colonial ethnography) to understand how to construct a global self. Willfully misreading missionary accounts from the Americas, Rousseau suggests that "savage" life is happy but without reflection or justice. Civilized life, meanwhile, is unhappy and alienated, but contains the seeds of perfection. Rousseau's solution is to combine the best of both conditions through the dialectical sublation of the savage and the bourgeois into the cultured state of "instinctual reason." (This is a term I use throughout the book. By "instinctual reason" I do not mean an essential human instinct for reason. Rather, I refer to the achievement of making reason a kind of instinct.)

The remaining chapters detail how extensive the influence of Rousseau's narrative was on seemingly unrelated concepts, including Kant's enlightenment, Schiller's aesthetic, Hegel's dialectic, and Marx's communism. It will also be central to those who opposed or repurposed his vision of the modern self, including Emerson, who suggested we alternate between reason and instinct rather than combine them; Fanon, who refused the reduction to instinct; and Suzuki, who kept Rousseau's aim of instinctual reason but critiqued his methods. I conclude this chapter with the significant response to Rousseau by Immanuel Kant. Kant's use of conjectural history informed his theories of progress, cosmopolitanism, and enlightenment, as he argued that both individuals and nations needed to combine instinct and rationality in their constitutions. In so doing, Kant connected practices of the global self to global practices for the self, which is to say that he prescribed a general way of being for the entire world. In concluding the chapter, I discuss how this global history of Kant should shift his place in contemporary theory. These brief remarks are part of my overall attempt to show how telling a more global history transforms how we theorize the present.

In the next two chapters, I then discuss how Rousseau's implicit concept of sublation is a fundamental idea that underpins German idealism in the work of Schiller and Hegel. At the same time, I begin to bring other voices into the conversation, showing how the globalizing visions of these thinkers were contested by Senghor (paired with Schiller) and Marx and Fanon (paired with Hegel). Schiller argues that aesthetic experience can create the kind of instinctually rational subject imagined by Rousseau. His argument for the role of aesthetics in the making of the subject is in fact inseparable from the conjectural history he tells, in which the goal of the aesthetic life is to combine the best aspects of primitive instinct with the best aspects of rationality through the use of beauty and play. Senghor provides a powerful, if implicit, response to Schiller by arguing that Idealist aesthetics fundamentally misunderstood the importance of intuition as a meaningful way of being in itself. Rather than seeking to sublate intuition and reason into a single mode, Senghor instead embraced a plurality of ways of engaging the world—each of which, he argued, had developed more profoundly in different geographic spaces. In rewriting the racialized philosophies of modernity, he sought to remap the geography of aesthetic theory. Building on trenchant analyses of Senghor's work by Souleymane Bachir Diagne and Gary Wilder, I argue that Senghor's work is part of the "radical pluralist" tradition and that his insights on aesthetics as a mode of global thinking remain an untapped resource for the practices of global selves.

Hegel, meanwhile, brings Rousseau's individual pedagogy onto a grand historical scale, showing how contradictions in each moment of development lead to new stages in world history. The trouble with both Schiller and Hegel, as with Kant, is that they prescribe this teleological movement for the entire globe. While recent theorists such as Timothy Brennan, Susan Buck-Morss, and Andrew Cole have argued for the liberating potential of Hegel's "Master Slave Dialectic," I show how his work is another form of conjectural history that risks creating unbearable identities for the colonized. Rereading Hegel in light of contemporary research, I suggest that a reconstitution of dialectics allows us to see how his ideas are premised, in part, on racist beliefs. We cannot simply "negate" those parts, but we can constitute new, more pluralized forms of dialectics that develop in their absence. This, I argue in the rest of the chapter, is what we can see at work in Karl Marx and Frantz Fanon. In responding to Hegel, Marx, though he largely began his career as a traditional Idealist, eventually came to understand that his youthful universalism would mean the horrific destruction of whole ways of life and that communism must in fact proceed through multiple forms of social organization. He also made the fundamental claim that practices of the self cannot be thought of as separate from the economic systems in which they are formed. I conclude the chapter on dialectics by showing how Frantz Fanon offers a counterhistory of being to what we find in Heidegger and others, one that understands the profound need of global research and denies the claim that there is an ontology of being to be found outside historical and geographic interactions. It is on these grounds that he will partialize the applicability of the dialectic. Fanon's essaying also pushes back against the unbearable identities created by Rousseau and others by showing how the encasement of people by "epidermalization" destroyed their identity and reduced them to their skin.

Marx's reformist ideas were coincident with the development of "radical pluralism" in the essays of Emerson and, later, Du Bois, which I analyze in chapters 5 and 6. Radical pluralism, again, is the idea that the plurality of existence goes all the way down. All cultures are pluralities; all individuals are pluralities; all natures are pluralities. The task for radical pluralists is thus not solely to respect difference, but also to learn how to engage with different elements from different traditions. What interests Emerson is the capacity of "alternation," or the ability to move between the different modes of life that each collective plurality makes possible. Reconceiving conjectural history, Emerson posits multiple dispositions rather than singular instinct at the origins of humanity. This is what opens his thought to a radical pluralism. He thus seeks a mode of essay writing that brings out the many layers available and coexistent in the present. His essays seek to make subjects who can both discern and move through these layers. I argue that Du Bois was one of Emerson's most perceptive readers and that his idea of "double consciousness" grows out of Emerson's use of the same phrase. However, Du Bois was also critical of Emerson because Du Bois understood that alternations require different practices for those who have been forced to "alter nations" through slavery and exile. His complex essay form thus seeks to enable global identity formation while simultaneously working to overcome the debilitating identities of modern racism. Freedom here becomes the subject's capacity to alternate without compulsion. Radical pluralism, Du Bois proved, is itself plural and requires different practices for different life situations. Such pluralism, I ultimately argue, manages to overcome the unbearable identity by learning to share the burden of global subjectivity—never abandoning the task, but never claiming a final solution either.

It is in this broad context that I situate the global mysticism of D. T. Suzuki. Suzuki departed from both synthesis and pluralism in his version of essaying the globe. According to him, the only path to global enlightenment was through the undoing of all our inherited concepts. This required a "pure experience" of the world, unmediated by language. Whereas all the other thinkers sought a resolution *after* contact, Suzuki argued that our ability to bear the world would only be possible if we got in touch with a moment *before* the division of subject and object even began. Suzuki's essays used anecdote, repetition, nonsensical asides, and other tactics to try to jolt readers out of their conceptual world and into the world itself. The chapter explores Suzuki's relationship to idealism and transcendentalism and investigates the fraught relationship between this nonconceptual experience and the historical contexts of Japanese imperialism and neoliberal capitalism. In these contexts, Suzuki's Zen also becomes an unbearable identity because such difficult times call for an active and discriminating intellect. Suzuki believed, nevertheless, that even a momentary experience of egolessness could produce global subjects more concerned with equality and justice than with individual gain. By shifting the framework of our understanding, we can stop reading Suzuki as a mere Westernizer of Zen and recognize him as an important theorist of global subjectivity worthy of further study.

I conclude the chapter by showing the importance of Suzuki's reworking of Zen for John Cage and bell hooks. In Cage I find a performative exploration of Suzuki's ideals as he seeks "world-enlightenment" through his music and writings. Cage also used Suzuki's notions of silence to develop a way of working through his sexuality outside what he found to be the unbearable frames of psychoanalysis and the disclosure of identity. The analysis of hooks similarly follows how Zen helped in her development of what she calls an "identity in resistance" because Zen foregrounds the fact that politics is about overcoming suffering that is both psychic and social. Like Cage, hooks shows how subjects within different social groups can use practices of the global self for purposes beyond their original intention. She is an important critical voice warning against a nonconceptual practice that could blindly write over the realities of sexism, racism, and classism.

Finally, in a brief coda, I argue that our practices today should be guided toward "being-toward-bequeathment." Rather than the individual angst of "being-toward-death," in other words, we should develop ways of being on this planet that guide our subjectivity toward the creation of sustainable futures. This "being-toward-bequeathment" must be matched by the next generation's capacity to "bear" the "responsibility of inheritance," as Stanley Cavell puts it.[73] This reciprocal structure is perhaps the best way to preserve the very globe on which we, collectively, can develop ourselves.

The resulting narrative functions both diachronically and synchronically. It works across time to show the historical and thematic connections that unite these diverse thinkers into a single tradition of engagement and debate. In turn, it shows how our reading of each figure changes when seen from the angle of this unfolding narrative. While each section thus should be meaningful on its own, the book makes most sense as a complete narrative. Most chapters also have an engagement with contemporary theorists or critics at the end to show how the reading within this narrative might help resituate some of the themes and concerns of contemporary criticism and theory. While the general trajectory of the narrative is chronological, I have moved thinkers around to draw out the connections between them through immediate comparisons. I also wanted to avoid the impression of a teleological narrative toward resolution: there are insights to be gleaned across these writers.

The task I have set myself is to evaluate these forms in my own essayistic engagements. I have used the notion of unbearable identity to understand the normative limit against which all attempts to essay the globe in this partial history will be judged. That is to say, I consider the extent to which authors manage to produce a vision of global subjectivity that does not result in the production of a new unbearable identity for themselves or others. The argument, again, is that radical pluralism best satisfies this demand. But because radical pluralism itself depends on the constant production of new ways of being in the world, this is not a teleological story leading to its invention. Indeed, this book that started with trying to understand Suzuki and his influence now ends with a chapter on his thought. Although I ultimately critique Suzuki, this does not exclude the validity of his claims any more than Kant's production of the unbearable identity of primitive life destroys the value of his universalism. A radically pluralist analysis seeks to find as much value in a form of thought as it can while always remaining vigilant against master tones that drown out others. It restlessly seeks out new forms of life that may add to the richness of existence. Such an essay of essays is the project of this book.

1

Montaigne and the Other History of Modernity

In his essay on education, Michel de Montaigne provides a critique of what radical pedagogue Paolo Freire would later call the "'banking' concept of education."[1] Montaigne, like Freire, is concerned that we are taught to memorize deposits of facts rather than to become conscious and active subjects. "Our tutors," Montaigne writes, "never stop bawling into our ears, as though they were pouring water into a funnel." Against this he would have the trial and error method of experiential education that we now associate with Freire and others: "I should like the tutor to correct this practice, and right from the start . . . to begin putting it [the student's mind] through its paces, making it taste things, choose them, and discern them by itself; sometimes clearing the way for him, sometimes letting him clear his own way."[2] This critique of education is central to Montaigne's way of thinking and writing in general. His essay—his attempt, or test, or trial—is not so much about getting the "right" answer as it is about becoming the kind of subject who can engage with and make judgments about the world around her.

His three books of *Essays* are thus scattered with a combination of knowledge and practices of the self.[3] He does not merely state facts about the world, nor does he simply show how facts can change his way of thinking. He realizes an even deeper truth: that he cannot even recognize a fact unless he continually transforms his very being. This transformation becomes his abiding goal: "To compose our character is our duty, not to compose books, and to win, not battles and provinces, but order and tranquility in our conduct. Our great and glorious masterpiece is to live appropriately."[4] Although Montaigne frequently disparages books and learning, his real point is that we should not merely have passive knowledge accumulated in our head, but should only read or write to the extent that those activities help us to live better. (This is equally a warning for today's scholars: "This fellow, all dirty, with running nose and eyes, whom you see coming out of his study after midnight, do you think he is seeking among his books how to make himself a better, happier, and wiser man? No such news. He is going to teach posterity the meter of Plautus' verses and the true spelling of a Latin word, or die in the attempt.")[5]

Throughout his *Essays*, Montaigne is concerned with the particular kind of learning that is also my concern here: how to develop global subjectivity. And he is concerned that just as scholars and pedagogues narrowly focus on minutiae, so travelers miss the real meaning of their travel. They bring back measurements, accounts of riches, and gossip, but really they should "bring back knowledge of the characters and ways of those nations, and to rub and polish [*frotter and limer*] our brains by contact with those of others."[6] "Of Cannibals," perhaps Montaigne's most famous essay, is concerned with this task of confronting his knowledge with the knowledge of others. It is his record of meeting three Tupi people in France in 1562 and his struggle to reconcile his classical learning with his discovery of these people and their continent. Only through a complex set of practices of the self will he be able to accomplish this task of engagement.[7]

Montaigne's Global Self

As we see in the quotes above, Montaigne dedicated his life to the task of tranquility. He wanted to compose and arrange his moods and thoughts such that, by constant self-reflection and awareness, he could maintain his resolution in the face of difficulties both large and small. "Greatness of soul is not so much pressing upward and forward as knowing how to set oneself in order and circumscribe [*circonscrire*] oneself."[8] The essay is precisely this form of circum*scription*: Montaigne is writing around his life, encircling it, strengthening it. And yet he is very much aware that there is no all-encompassing circle. In the words of his disciple Emerson: "Around every circle can be drawn another one."[9] This is precisely what Montaigne believes has shocked his age. Around the geographic circle they thought they lived in, another one—the globe itself—has been drawn. It makes him wonder if this globe is in fact the whole and if other entire worlds will yet be found.[10] And also like Emerson, he believes that the loss of a circle is something to celebrate, not mourn, if we manage to recognize it as an opportunity to transform our imperfect ways of life.[11]

How does one become circumscribed within this new circle? How does one circumscribe others within one's own circle? Moreover, how does one circumscribe others without dominating them? These are the questions that drive Montaigne's reflections. In answering them, he provides us with an early blueprint of how one might essay a global self. Central to Montaigne's writing are two practices: eclecticism and skepticism. I mean eclectic here in a very specific sense, one that is close to what we find in Diderot:

> The eclectic is a philosopher who, trampling underfoot prejudice, tradition, antiquity, general agreement, authority . . . dares to think for himself, returns to the clearest general principles, examines them, discusses them, admits nothing that is not based on the testimony of his experience and his reason.[12]

Diderot here could practically be describing the structure of Montaigne's essay, except that Montaigne is not trampling anything. On the basis of his reason and experience, Montaigne interrogates assumptions and prejudices, but his eclectic method extends even to these. His task is, again, "to rub and polish" knowledges by each other, not discarding anything that might be useful. In "Of Cannibals," he tests and compares what wisdom he has inherited against the world in which he has found himself.

And Montaigne knows that he cannot simply circumscribe this new world within his present existence: he must go through a transformation of his thought to do so. This is the role of his skepticism, described well by Emerson:

> I neither affirm nor deny. I stand here to try the case. I am here to consider . . . to consider how it is . . . This, then, is the right ground of the skeptic,—this of consideration, of self-containing [circumscription]; not at all of unbelief . . . He is the considerer, the prudent, taking in sail, counting stock, husbanding his means . . . The philosophy we want is one of fluxions and mobility. We want some coat woven of elastic steel.[13]

To be an eclectic one must also be a skeptic. That is to say, to choose what is best, one must continually consider the possibilities of the world, their meanings, their consequences, their contingencies. This does not mean relativism. It does not mean that everything is in doubt. It means only that all sides will be judged with respect to each other and with respect for each other. And this becomes a "coat" because these are ideas and practices that must be tried on. They cannot be judged abstractly and from a distance, but only through engagement.

This, in turn, should make us doubt one standard reading of Montaigne's essay: that the space of the New World is only a fantastic projection that allows him to critique his own society.[14] Such a presumption goes against Montaigne's creed that "it is a common vice, not of the vulgar only but of almost all men, to fix their aim and limit by the ways to which they were born."[15] Montaigne is not simply imagining another world by which to compare his own; he is testing it to see if it offers other ways of life, or means of emending his own faults. As a skeptic who considers all, he is also not shy of criticizing: "This long attention that I devote to studying myself [*me considerer*] trains me also to judge passably of others, and there are few things of which I speak more felicitously and excusably."[16] Montaigne is not projecting, or at least he hopes he is not. Rather, he is criticizing customs by bringing them into contact with each other. Indeed, one of the customs he is criticizing is projection itself. This, in fact, is where the essay begins.

The opening paragraph of the essay describes the reactions of Greek and Roman kings who, when they thought they were fighting barbarians who lacked order or logic, were suddenly overrun by well-ordered opponents. This bit of ancient wisdom serves as a propaedeutic for the work of the essay: "Thus we should beware of clinging to vulgar opinions, and judge things by reason's way [*voye*], not by popular say [*voix*]."[17] The homonym here (at least in contemporary pronunciation) of *la voye* (way or path) and *la voix* (voice) is not merely clever. It also shows the unwanted but necessary proximity of the two. Reason's way is not something that one can just jump into and access; it is mixed up with, indeed informed by, the voices of society that inhabit us.[18] There is no "reason," after all, that can simply be separated out *from* the world, because the whole point of reason is to enable our ever improving engagement *in* the world. The place of the world in us must be "elucidated" in Castoriadis's sense. The problem is not that our reason is mixed up with our language, but that it is mixed up with a language we have not made our own.[19] The key is to transform the "popular say" (what is "vulgar") so that it aligns with this better engagement. As we will see, the transformation of language itself remains central throughout the essay.

If our reason is polluted with opinions about others, then we must learn to transform our subjectivity in order to be able to think globally. Montaigne teaches us to begin with not only skepticism, but a skepticism that is born of the experience of others:

> This discovery of a boundless country seems worthy of consideration. I don't know if I can guarantee that some other such discovery will not be made in the future, so many personages greater than ourselves having been mistaken about this one. I am afraid we have eyes bigger than our stomachs, and more curiosity than capacity. We embrace everything, but clasp only wind.[20]

It is not simply that the discovery calls into question what Europeans think about other peoples. It calls into question the entire tradition of knowledge in which Montaigne has been trained. Plato claimed to know the truth of the invisible world, but he did not even know the shape of the visible one. He claimed to be able to build a perfect republic, but he did not know that one that surpassed his vision was already existent on this planet.[21] If Europeans are to judge the peoples of these new lands, they should first remember that they are not only ignorant, but also ignorant of their ignorance. Because of this double ignorance, they attempt to bear more than they possibly can and thus to *claim* (both philosophically and geographically) more than is their right.

This is part of Montaigne's analysis of the unbearable identity. On the one hand, the identity bequeathed to him—that of a man of Greco-Roman knowledge—is simply not able to bear the weight of the world in which he finds himself. And so he must develop new practices. At the same time, he is remarkably aware that the solution to his problem is not to rush in and presume that he understands these new spaces or these new peoples. This would be unbearable in the second and third senses of this concept: that it would be more than he has the capacity to hold and that, in his attempt to hold more than was his share, he would destroy others. "So many cities razed, so many nations exterminated, so many millions of people put to the sword, and the richest and most beautiful part of the world turned upside down, for the traffic in pearls and pepper!"[22]

This is one of the several meanings embedded in Montaigne's evocative phrase "We embrace everything, but clasp only wind." The Europeans clasped the wind that brought them to the New World and quickly preceded to reduce everything there to wind and ashes. The irony for Montaigne is that this is the opposite of actually "clasping the wind," which is to say, learning its lessons: "We are all wind [*nous sommes par tout vent*]. And even the wind, more wisely than we, loves to make a noise and move about, and is content with its own functions, without wishing for stability and solidity, qualities that do not belong to us."[23] We are *all* wind in that we are alive by our breath, and *we* are all wind in that all humans are composed of the same elements. Thus while we, like the wind, by the aid of the wind, may travel the whole earth, we must, like the wind, by the aid of our understanding of the wind, remain content with our functions, and not try to establish ourselves masters over what, and whom, we are not.

Montaigne proceeds by way of what appears to be a digression into accounts of lost islands mentioned in the works of Plato and Aristotle. The most obvious context is again to test the knowledge of antiquity against the knowledge of the present. But it is also important that Montaigne carefully selects the details of these accounts. The account from Plato is about the kings of the rumored island of Atlantis and how they attempted to "subjugate" a number of nations until they lost to the Athenians. When he speaks of Aristotle, Montaigne mentions an island of great fertility and wealth to which many escaped until the "lords of Carthage . . . expressly forbade anyone to go there any more."[24] With these stories, he marks the two poles of European exploration: on the one hand, the desire for global dominance; on the other, the desire for alternative modes of life outside governmental or economic exploitation. That the first story ends with "the Flood" perhaps suggests that it is in part the sin of empire that caused the Flood.[25] And that the lords of Carthage came to forbid the alternative life practiced in antiquity perhaps signals the destruction of alternative lifeworlds that European conquest was unleashing.[26] Thus, although Montaigne rules out the possibility that the New World was known in antiquity, he subtly hints that antiquity provides lessons for the lost hopes and actual horrors of discovery.[27]

This twin potential of subjugation and the creation of free autonomous spaces is directly linked to one of the more complex features of Montaigne's essay: whom he claims as his informant about "cannibals" (actually, the Tupi of Brazil). Although it appears that Montaigne closely read the travel accounts of some of his contemporaries, especially Jean de Léry, he tells us that his best informant was a servant of his who had spent a decade or so in Brazil.[28] What he praises about his servant is this man's simplicity: he is "so simple that he has not the stuff to build up false inventions and give them plausibility; and [he is] wedded to no theory."[29] If he were cleverer, Montaigne suggests, he could not but add his own thoughts to things and not present them as they are: "to give credence to their judgment and attract you to it, they [clever people] are prone to add something to their matter, to stretch it out and amplify it."[30] Now because there is in fact no evidence of this servant ever having actually existed,[31] one wonders if what

Montaigne, the too-clever man, has added here to give credence to his account is nothing other than this servant himself.

For Stephen Greenblatt, this cross-identification that Montaigne performs between his servant and the Tupi is part of his general attempt to overcome possession—of labor, of land, and of self. Greenblatt deals elegantly with the complexity of privilege that allows Montaigne to attempt this overcoming:

> To be sure, this circulation is paradoxically intertwined in Montaigne with a powerful sense of what it means to possess the estate and the title of Montaigne. But that possession, constitutive of his name and essential to his identity, is none the less shot through with intimations of loss . . . [He is] one who has abjured the desire to possess the souls of others and, for that matter, to possess himself.[32]

The attempt to overcome one's self by way of identification with others of course always runs the risk of both appropriation and essentialization. That is to say, it risks reducing others to a single, identifiable trait (simplicity) and then taking from them the one thing power has reduced them to when it proves useful to you (something like literary gentrification). I think we can safely say that Montaigne is guilty of this, though he does take steps against it: he attempts to see the world differently than his habits and his class have disposed him to. This is not a question of positively valuing what had been once negatively valued (the folksiness of the plain folk, say), but rather of leveling the distinction between folks and seeing that we are all the admixture of our natures and nurtures and that those natures and nurtures are never themselves pure and essentializable so much as constantly varying within themselves the ranges of human reason. "Human reason is a tincture infused in about equal strength in all our opinions and ways, whatever their form: infinite in substance, infinite in diversity."[33]

We are being apprised here of another fact that will prove central to the closing sections of the essay, namely, that transforming himself in relation to the New World will also force Montaigne to transform his relation to his own immediate surroundings. For he has realized that his difference from "[his] manual laborers" is no vaster than his difference from "Scythians and Indians."[34] "I often say it is pure stupidity that makes us run after foreign and scholarly examples . . . [W]e have not the wit to pick out and put to use what happens before our eyes."[35] Here is another element of his eclecticism—to consult ancient philosophers, but also to consult the ordinary: "from the most ordinary, commonplace, familiar things, if we could put them in their proper light, can be formed the greatest miracles of nature and the most wondrous examples, especially on the subject of human actions."[36] Long before "the ordinary" became a subject of Romantic fascination, or a critical site of the critique of labor, Montaigne understood that within the most quotidian moments of our lives roared the toil and wonder of the whole globe. For him to understand himself, or a Tupi man, or a man who worked for him, required equal strengths of attention and grace. That the practices of the global self are intimately related to the question of class, and that, conversely, the question of class requires a new relation to our global self, will remain crucial into the work of D. T. Suzuki.

Montaigne never gives us easy answers; the interpretations always slip away. He is duplicitous here, telling us he hasn't consulted the cosmographers when we know he has. He is not simple or plain; he is cleverer than he has told us he wants to be. But perhaps this is precisely where his honesty lies. He is not trying to pretend to be able to do more than he can. He is telling us that in spite of his efforts he cannot but project, that he has failed to register fully, that he cannot become transparent, and that he cannot, in a sense, tell the truth. He is trying, still. And he should remind us that we are no better. We, too, have prejudices about others, both local and distant. We, too, are formed differently by our lives, all of which offer advantages and disadvantages. Our task is to learn to sort through these, live within limits, and transform what we can. He lies to remind us that he cannot but lie—clever people, after all, "cannot help altering history a little."[37] And he exposes his prejudice because he is trying to write through it; because he is trying to recircumscribe himself in a new, more just, more global circle, and he knows that he is not there yet.

One of the reasons for his limitation is the ambiguity of language itself. Turning back to the subject at hand—the accounts of the New World—Montaigne offers a preliminary conclusion that "there is nothing barbarous and savage in that nation . . . except that each man calls barbarism whatever is not his own practice."[38] Barbarian itself once simply meant "foreign, non-Hellenic," and it referred to those who did not speak Greek.[39] The idea that the barbarian, the outsider, the non-speaker, was also rough, vicious, or crude was a meaning that slowly accrued on the word.[40] This etymology of the arrogance of barbarism had been used in 1559 by Joachim du Bellay in his *Defense and Enrichment of the French Language*. Du Bellay noted a similar reversal to what we find in Montaigne: "As Anarchasis said, the Scythians were barbarians among the Athenians, but so were the Athenians among the Scythians."[41] For du Bellay, the "vulgar" French that both he and Montaigne use should not be thought of as barbarous in the pejorative sense. It is simply not Greek, and perhaps for that the better. Montaigne implicitly draws on the fact that his own language was once considered barbarous to underscore the relativity of the appellation.

About language more generally, Stanley Cavell has argued that "our words are our calls or claims upon the objects and contexts of our world."[42] Montaigne's point is precisely that calling some peoples barbarian makes a claim on our right to possess their world. To question the word barbarian is to question this claim. There can be no practice of the global self that does not interrogate the language that we use to speak of others or ourselves. This will not always mean that the language we need is available. Our languages alternate too quickly between the poles of singularization and collectivization to be able to speak meaningfully about the plurality of existence. Knowing this, and knowing that he cannot jump out of language, Montaigne will ask us to consider it: what it does, how it shapes our thought, how we repeat it without making it our own. Cavell continues: "This mode of controlling ambiguity shows that our mind is chanced, but not forced, by language. The point is to get us to assess our orientation or position toward what we say."[43] And, equally, whom we say it about.

Montaigne returns to his conjecture about why we are chanced by language: "it seems we have no other test of truth and reason than the example and pattern of the opinions and customs of the country we live in."[44] This is *not* a lament about our knowledge. This is not about escaping customs in order to find some universal truth outside custom. This is a statement of fact about our knowledge. There simply does not exist a way [*une voye*] of thinking that is outside the language [*la voix*] of our countries.[45] But there does exist the possibility that by confronting that language with other languages, we may begin to develop a more complex understanding of the world.

And then again, we may not. There is nothing intrinsically just about the attempt to essay the globe. One might quickly fall prey to prejudice, or domination, or presumption. Montaigne follows the above sentence about custom: "*There* is always the perfect religion, the perfect government, the perfect and accomplished manner in all things." Grammatically, "there" should refer to "the country we live in" that precedes it. And, indeed, the sentence reads like an ironically stated critique of chauvinism. But it might also be seen to spring forward, with "there" referring not to one's own country, but rather to one's imagination about the perfection of another. Thus he continues: "Those people are wild, just as we call wild the fruits that Nature has produced by herself and in her normal course."[46] And because Montaigne then proceeds to an encomium to nature, it would seem that perfection *is* "*there*"—in that other world that has just been encountered in his century.

This is one way at least to understand an ambivalence in the essay. In the following paragraph, Montaigne gives his famous account, cited by Gonzalo in Shakespeare's *The Tempest*, of a land without any of the trappings of civilization, yet still exceeding the "idealized . . . golden age" of Greek philosophers and poets.[47] Montaigne would seem here to present the new world as one of natural perfection and harmony, without human artifice or reflection. And yet, a few pages later, he criticizes this very conception: "And lest it be thought that all this is done through a simple and servile bondage to usage and through the pressure of the authority of their ancient customs, without reasoning or judgment . . . I must cite some examples of their capacity."[48] This "capacity" is demonstrated not only by their own poetry, valor, and practices of love, but also by the critique of French society that Montaigne hears three Tupi men give in 1562. We will return to this. The question for now is, why does Montaigne begin by insisting on the naturalness of people, only later to revoke and critique that very description?

One plausible answer is that the essay itself charts the progress of his learning—from reading accounts, to listening to witnesses who had been there, to finally meeting and discoursing with men from Brazil. This movement also appears less linearly within the essay, perhaps because it represents a dance between his constituted self—who makes claims—and his constituting self—who is trying to feel the claim of another on him. But the key point, I believe, is that we can see the famous passage of primitive idealization as a performance of the very kind of thing that a clever as opposed to an honest witness would say. Indeed, the citations to Propertius, Lycurgus, Plato, Seneca, and Virgil that wind through the brief encomium to nature would seem to demonstrate that this is Montaigne's imagination, and not his servant, who is speaking. Moreover, we know that the list of attributes—"no sort of traffic, no knowledge of letters, no science of numbers, no name for a magistrate or for political superiority . . ."—is not in fact Montaigne's. As Margaret Hogden has noted when arguing that someone other than Montaigne might have influenced Shakespeare's Gonzalo: "[This kind of description] was on the tip of every pen whenever the peoples of the New World were under discussion; or when the qualities of early, or far-off, or barbarous, or uncivil, or primitive man were subjects of debate."[49] The formula was so much in circulation that Hogden, a chronicler of sixteenth-century anthropology, avoids suggesting a definitive, original source.

This perhaps explains why Montaigne separates out this passage from the factual description of the ways of life of the Tupi people that follows. In nonromanticized terms, he describes their climate, architecture, daily routines, food, activities, hobbies, crafts, religious beliefs, ethical codes, and then, finally, within the context of warfare, anthropophagy. He does nearly as well as anyone could at his time to understand this practice.[50] The work of contextual understanding is certainly part of essaying the globe. Montaigne uses what evidence he can, and the way that he shifts positions throughout "On Cannibals" perhaps shows less his inconsistency and more his willingness to admit that he might be wrong. At the same time, he is perfectly willing to take a position. Like Emerson's "coat of elastic steel," he is both flexible and willing to make assertions. But because he knows that his knowledge is imperfect and that he himself is imperfect, he will not make judgments that are not also self-reflective: "I am not sorry that we notice the barbarous horror of such acts, but I am heartily sorry that, judging their faults rightly, we should be so blind to our own."[51] In a time and a place such as I live in, the bellicose United States of the early twenty-first century, this kind of judgmental humility is a practice of the global self that many of our political leaders and private citizens should strive harder to embody. Indeed, even looking back in time, we might note that Montaigne's representations remain inadequate and flawed, while also recognizing that our own culture, and our own representations, will always struggle with difference.

One more practice for handling this is to turn it to an advantage: we, like Montaigne, might leverage difference for the purposes of critique. At the essay's close, Montaigne reveals that he met three Tupi men in Rouen, France, in 1562. He dialogued with them, albeit through an interpreter whose competence he severely doubts. Language here, as ever, is the means by which customs speak for themselves and compare themselves with other ways of life. And it also marks another moment of Montaigne's insistence on humility against the presumption of comprehension about how others live when we don't even understand what they say. But of what Montaigne does manage to grasp, he tells us that there were three things, "of which I have forgotten the third, and I am very sorry for it."[52] George Hoffmann speculates that the third thing may have been the Tupi's critique of Christian practices, which he takes as the fundamental subtext of the essay.[53] But it seems equally plausible that Montaigne really has forgotten and simply wants to mark for us the contingency of knowledge—a knowledge that he, so to speak, hungers after, because he knows that imbibing it will help to "rub and polish" his thought.

That he wishes to remember the third thus serves to underscore the importance of the two things he does recall: first, that the Tupi cannot understand why so many men serve a child-king; and, second, how the impoverished of France, "emaciated with hunger and poverty," can "endure such an injustice," and why they "did not take the others by the throat, or set fire to their houses."[54] The movement of the essay's close is abrupt. Montaigne mentions these drastic acts, seeming almost to praise them, and turns away from the point to discuss briefly some practices of war. The essay then ends with the ironic remark "All this is not too bad—but what's the use? They don't wear breeches."[55] It's as if Montaigne suddenly throws up his hands, realizing the worthlessness of his contemporaries, and decrying that even the most important practices—the abolition of hierarchy, the overcoming of injustice, the dispossession of possession that Greenblatt commends—are unachievable by countrymen who won't even take them seriously because of a difference as absurd as clothing.

But perhaps by mentioning that he has forgotten the third point, he has something else in mind linked to his essaying practice. I began this section with a discussion of his essay on education because I believe these two essays to be deeply linked. After all, if Montaigne's contemporaries cannot solve the problems of injustice, perhaps a new generation will be able to. This is his final lesson about essaying the globe: that it must gesture toward the future as much as it relies on the past. Here is the significant passage from the education essay that glosses his method:

> There are in Plutarch . . . a thousand [insights] that he has only just touched on; he merely points out with his finger where we are to go, if we like, and sometimes is content to make only a stab at the heart of the subject. Just as that remark of his, that the inhabitants of Asia served one single man because they could not pronounce one single syllable, which is "No," may have given the matter and the impulsion to La Boétie for his *Voluntary Servitude*. Just to see him pick out that trivial action in a man's life, or a word which seems unimportant: that is a treatise in itself.[56]

Here are all the practices of "Of Cannibals" lovingly condensed: consult the ancients, consult cultural difference, read beyond what is given, compare one's image of one's self against how one actually lives, pay attention to language and the ordinary, and bring all this to bear on the political limits of one's own life and time. Neither Plutarch nor La Boétie nor Montaigne can rip apart the world and resuture it with justice. But they can gesture us toward the kinds of practices that, with due diligence of application, might enable us to be the kinds of subjects who can be just both at home and abroad. And here is a final reason for Montaigne to mark that he has forgotten one of the three things he learned—to prod us to go out and find it. For "if learning is to us any good, we must not merely lodge it within us, we must espouse it."[57]

Montaigne's Anti-Imperialism

A very different reading of Montaigne has recently been offered by Sankar Muthu in his book *Enlightenment against Empire*. Muthu's widely praised account was significant for several reasons. First, it helped transform the canon of European political thought by insisting that non-European peoples and the question of imperialism were central (and not merely marginal) interests of European Enlightenment thinkers. He also helped move us away from too constraining a view of *the* Enlightenment as a monolithic enterprise and focused on understudied writers like Diderot and Herder. A central claim of his study, however, is one that goes directly against what I have argued here. For Muthu, a thinker like Montaigne is part of the "noble savage tradition." This tradition is said to view the peoples of the New World as not fully human, because it considers them "natural" and not what Muthu calls "cultural agents." The former may be noble, but they are so because of contingent nature and not any genius of their own invention. The latter are "beings who, by their nature, diversely exercise their reason, memory and imagination, and who are necessarily embedded within and yet are also able to transform social practices and institutions."[58] By rendering the Tupi "naturally good" rather than as cultural agents, Muthu finds that Montaigne writes them out of humanity itself.[59] Montaigne, in spite of his protestations against imperialism, cannot properly generate an anti-imperial *theory*, because *only* the notion of humans as cultural agents can do that.

There are several things that can be said in response to this. First of all, it is, as we have seen, a weak reading of Montaigne. It ignores the complexity of his positions and the ways in which the essay embodies his auto-critique and development. For example, consider Muthu's reading of the moment when Montaigne inveighs against his reader's assumption that the Tupi lack "reasoning or judgment": Montaigne cites only the songs of war and love "to prove that Amerindians are not simply creatures of custom (note that he does not, of course, aim to challenge the view that they are largely creatures of *nature*)."[60] This very idea that there exists a pure nature outside custom is of course one of the targets of the *Essays* as a whole. If we have not seen enough evidence already, we can also note that Montaigne even argues that this is true of animals: "Moreover, what sort of faculty of ours do we not recognize in the actions of the animals? Is there a society regulated with more order, diversified into more charges and functions, and more consistently maintained, than that of the honeybees?"[61] If he says this of bees, it's hard to see how it wouldn't apply to the Tupi! Furthermore, Montaigne does not just cite the songs, he also cites the Tupi's critique of French society. He is saying that these are a people not only as barbarous as we, but as capable of cross-cultural critique as we. They have philosophies of love and justice, and their philosophies challenge ours. This is erased from Muthu's summary. In an ironic moment, then, it is Muthu who silences the Tupi voice, not Montaigne.

My point is not, however, that Montaigne in fact fits within Muthu's category of anti-imperial thought as the idea of cultural agency. Quite to the contrary, Montaigne troubles this very conclusion that anti-imperialism relies *solely* on this notion. For Montaigne, after all, there is no such strict separation of agency and instinct, as Muthu claims. They mix into each other. But even in those instances where we rely more on nature than on reflection, what, exactly, is wrong with the spontaneous production of virtue? Should we always have to rationally reproduce it? And in the attempt to do so, is there not a real possibility that we will find ourselves too alienated from reality to be able to implement the desired changes? As Jean-Jacques Rousseau will come to suggest, there is a very plausible argument to be made that reflection is in fact injurious to virtue. By alienating us from our actions, "rationality" produces the possibility of distance, distraction, estrangement, and indifference. As Rousseau writes: "Reason is what turns man in upon himself. Reason is what separates him from all that troubles him and afflicts him. Philosophy is what isolates him and what moves him to say in secret, at the sight of a suffering man, 'Perish if you will; I am safe and sound.'"[62] In his writings on Montaigne and Rousseau, Muthu never submits reason itself to the kind of analyses that they both did.

Moreover, the idea that only the theory of cultural agency can fight imperialism is itself a kind of "ontological imperialism," or the idea that only one's own theory of human nature is the only correct one. Never broached in Muthu's account is what it is exactly that the Tupi themselves may have believed. In insisting that Montaigne was only ever concerned with his own society, Muthu is in fact admitting that this is *his* only concern. As anthropologist Eduardo Viveiros de Castro puts it, "[B]y thinking that under the mask of the other it is always just 'us' contemplating ourselves, we end up contenting ourselves with a mere shortcut to the goal and an interest only in what 'interests us'—ourselves."[63] Recent anthropological and archival work by Viveiros de Castro has challenged Muthu's proposed universal idea in at least two ways. First, it has suggested that the idea of a specifically human notion of cultural agency is entirely foreign to the Tupi worldview, wherein the relationships between humans are no more important than the relationships between humans, animals, plants, and the earth.[64] This is explicitly disavowed in the tradition Muthu advocates, as when he approvingly cites Herder's idea that "[n]either the pongo nor the gibbon is your brother: the American and the Negro are. These . . . therefore you should not oppress . . . for they are humans, like you; with the ape, you cannot enter into fraternity."[65] But what does it mean to enter into fraternity with Amerindians or others who believe themselves to be in fraternity with nonhuman and even nonsentient beings? What would it mean to not merely accept the fact of this difference, but to learn to essay it—to try it on—as part of a practice of the global self? How many of us are truly capable of thinking not just "inter-species being," but the humanity of all "species"?

Second, Viveiros de Castro has called into question the ethnocentric idea that primitivism is the province of Europeans alone: "The Europeans offered to the Tupi an opportunity for self-transfiguration, a sign of the reunion of that which had been rent asunder at the origin of culture . . . Thus it was perhaps the Amerindians, not the Europeans, who saw the 'vision of paradise' in the American (mis)(sed) encounter."[66] I take "(mis)(sed) encounter" to mean both a "mis-encounter"—the ways of life in the Americas were not properly understood—and a "missed encounter"—the opportunity for exchange was lost. Montaigne's cross-cultural critique shows the possibility of an encounter in which peoples try their best to understand each other and, in so doing, truly shift their very notions of what it means to be human. I believe that Muthu unwittingly continues the (mis)(sed) encounter by relying solely on the notion of cultural agency as the grounding of universal politics. My point is not that this is a uniquely European idea or that it is entirely a bad one. But it is simply not the only one available to us. We might conceive of human subjectivity as spread across a number of different potential relations to nature, as Philippe Descola has shown, or we might insist on "other modalities of agency," as Saba Mahmood has done. Or we might think of the human not as singular agent but as intersubjective node, as Hakugen Ichikawa has suggested, or we might follow Gandhi in insisting that the uniqueness of humanity is not agency but rather our ability to overcome violence.[67] The real question lies in the interstices of these conceptions, that is, in trying to see how such different visions of humanness can meaningfully speak to each other. As I come to argue, global relations are less about a single mode of understanding and more about learning how to negotiate what is shared and what differs across cultures. In this negotiation, sometimes we will rely on instinct, sometimes on reflection, and sometimes on any of our many other human capacities.

Finally, critiques like Muthu's do not give us any ability to parse the ways in which peoples invent their own past golden ages replete with critiques of modern rationality. Writers working on vastly different regions, such as James C. Scott in rural Malaysia, Partha Chatterjee in urban Bengal, and Frantz Fanon in revolutionary Algeria and colonial France, have all shown how this mode of nostalgia functions as a critique of actually existing exploitation.[68] We see this also today with "*buen vivir*" movements in Latin America, where there is a strong focus on renewing "indigenous ecology" and ways of life and reintegrating them into contemporary practices. Again the point here is not that these movements call for an anachronistic return, but rather that they oppose a single, dominant model of capitalist or even socialist rationality as the supreme value.[69] It is also the case, as Scott has argued based on his fieldwork on Zomia (in the steppes of central Asia), that what is often called "primitive" is often a "secondary" phenomenon. Scott's point is that people live what appear to be primitive lives not because they are evolutionarily "stuck" but rather because they have, in their own times and ways, rejected the pressures to state formation and its attendant oppressions and inequalities (although they may keep and create still other problems in the process).[70]

Pluralism, or at the least the kind of radical pluralism that I am advocating in this book, cannot simply mean respect of others' customs. It must insist that the plurality of humanity goes all the way down and that the challenge of a pluralistic politics includes ontological and cosmological diversity. As I argue more extensively when looking at the work of Immanuel Kant, this is precisely what is foreclosed by the tradition that Muthu advocates. Montaigne partakes of another tradition, one that, through complex practices of the global self, seeks to become the kind of person who can inhabit multiple ways of thought with a "fallibilistic" sense.[71] There are no ahistorical values here, and there is no reason to praise ourselves or others for abstraction. After all, only a culture of war needs a theory of peace. Only a culture of economic stratification needs a theory of economic justice. Only a culture of slavery needs a theory of liberation.

This is not to say, of course, that Montaigne manages to accomplish a completely just essay of the globe. For example, the place of women in "Of Cannibals," as throughout his *Essays*, relegates them to the status of male fantasy and desire: "Being more concerned for their husbands' honor than for anything else, they [Tupi women] strive and scheme to [find their husbands] as many companions as they can, since that is a sign of their husbands' valor."[72] For Montaigne, this functions as a critique of the jealousy of French women rather than as a point at which "to rub and polish" the different possibilities for gender relations against each other. Many of the authors who attempt to "essay the globe" fail precisely on this front: they construct ideas and practices that, while not necessarily gendered in themselves, they often mark as being "for men only." This is a problematic traced throughout this book.

Montaigne, limited though he may remain, opens our discussion because of the fundamental role he played in establishing the relationship between the essay form and the construction of global subjectivity. Erich Auerbach wrote of Montaigne and his *Essays*:

> His book manifests the excitement which sprang from the sudden and tremendous enrichment of the world picture and from the presentiment of the yet untapped possibilities the world contained. And—still more significant—among all his contemporaries he had the clearest conception of the problem of man's self-orientation; that is, the task of making oneself at home in existence without fixed points of support. In him for the first time, man's life—the random personal life as a whole—becomes problematic in the modern sense.[73]

This task of self-orientation in a suddenly expanding world is precisely what I track through the rest of this book. But the tremendous excitement of it was of course not wonderful for all. Some, like Montaigne, were the recipients of a world that shook their parochialism and forced them on the thrilling path of self-transformation. Others found themselves encased and enslaved in identities that they are still fighting to overcome. Others still never took up this challenge at all. It is to this last group that I now turn.

The Evasive Mood: Descartes, *Hamlet*, and Heidegger

It is perhaps counterintuitive for Auerbach to locate Montaigne as the first modern thinker because of his worldliness. Is not the modern, after all, the rise of the private, bourgeois subject, of individualism, of nationalism? To be sure, these transformations are part of the story of modernity. We see in texts like Shakespeare's *Hamlet* (1603) and Descartes's *Discourse on Method* (1637) the distinct turn that Charles Taylor has called "inwardness"—"the sense of ourselves as beings with inner depths, and the connected notion that we are 'selves.'"[74] Taylor has argued that this is a form of thinking about humans that not only marks modernity, but is a unique modern invention that arose in a given time and place and may expire sometime in the future.[75] *Hamlet* and the *Discourse* are in some senses the two poles of this notion of the self. In the latter, we find the idea that the inward turn guarantees not only personal identity, but also the very possibility of truth. In the former, the inward turn is expressed as a prison house that vitiates our capacity to think clearly or act perspicaciously. But while the *Discourse* presents inwardness as a success story and *Hamlet* frames it as an abject failure, both mark the modern subject as a being whose truth is in her own mind.

As we have seen, this "Cartesian moment" is also where Michel Foucault located the loss of practices of the self in modernity. The subject became capable of thinking the truth within herself and therefore did not have to transform who she was to become a truthful subject. For Taylor, the difference between Descartes and Montaigne is between two visions of this inward turn: Montaigne's "forms of self-exploration" and Descartes's "forms of self-control."[76] In either case, the question of the global is not factored into these accounts.

Some years ago, Cornel West spoke of the power of American pragmatism as what he called its "evasion of philosophy." The pragmatists, following Emerson, avoided the Cartesian turn, with its quest for certainty and secure foundations of knowledge.[77] Emerson instead turned philosophy into a form of social criticism, focusing on "power, provocation, and personality."[78] While appreciative of how this makes sense of one possible narrative of modernity, I want to suggest in this section that Cartesianism *itself* was the evasion. Descartes is not the founding point of modernity that must be gotten around to ground new ways of thinking. Rather, his thought itself is an evasion of the need to become a global subject that marks modern thought. Descartes, like Hamlet, exists in the evasive mood—a kind of thinking marked by the burdens of the inward turn that includes skepticism, paranoia, melancholy, and alienation.[79] At the same time, of course, evasion is an important mood. It can enable us to break with the doxa of the present; it can create a space for the imagination to grow; it can be a way of critiquing imperial engagements.[80] It only becomes unbearable when it presumes that the truth of being is to be found *only* in private subjective transformations.

This evasion of the world and retreat into the self is precisely what we find in Descartes's *Discourse on Method*. Descartes tells the reader that he offers his "essay" "merely as a story," which is to say, he simply wants to show us what it would be like to take on the transformations of self that he himself has gone through.[81] Part of Descartes's practice is to at once insist on his humility and to suggest that his methods form the only path to truth. Thus when he relates that he continued on his path because others saw his genius (not he himself), he says that it was probably only because they saw how he openly confessed his ignorance.[82] His is the ironic humility of Benjamin Franklin: "Humility: Imitate Socrates and Jesus."[83] So we can somewhat brush aside his self-effacing remarks and see that what he offers here is more than a mere story; it is a discourse that claims nothing less than the method for arriving at the truth of the world.

The Discourse follows a somewhat consistent pattern of disappointment. Descartes goes through a course of study that he believes will lead him to the truth until he realizes that, in fact, he remains caught in the multiplicity of opinions to be found across cultures and therefore sets out for another foundation. The possibility that this quest for a foundation is itself at fault, as Montaigne claimed, is precisely what Descartes feels he must refute. He decides that there are two ways to set about discovering the solid foundation for knowledge: either by studying "the great book of the world" or by studying himself.[84] He begins with the former but is chagrined to quickly find "as much diversity [in the world] as I had previously found among the opinions of the philosophers."[85] Thus the somewhat ironic lesson that Descartes learns from travel is that one need not travel, because what traveling apprises one of is merely the fact that most humans only hold opinions derived from customs. One does not go traveling in order to learn from others; rather, one goes traveling in order to learn that one can only learn from oneself.

And so Descartes shuts himself up in a room in Germany and begins to converse with himself. One of his first thoughts, he tells us, was that the greatest works are made not by many hands, but by a single expert craftsman. The reason for this is that a building will be more securely built if it is made well from scratch than if it is constantly worked and reworked. Descartes then makes a leap of logic, averring that because this is true for buildings, it must be true for civilizations as well. As such: "Peoples who, having once been half savages and having been civilized only little by little . . . could not be as well ordered as those who, from the very beginning of their coming together, have followed the fundamental precepts of some prudent legislator."[86] But how is one to arrive at such a state if one is not already there? Descartes suggests that this simply cannot be done but at the individual level: only with regard to one's private thoughts may one tear down the foundations and begin to build again. This, then, is what he resolves to do: to clear out everything within his thinking that is not his own so that he can arrive at the most basic truths of the world.

The important point to see in Descartes's story, I believe, is that he only comes to this conclusion *because* of his experience in the world. It is not because of Descartes's inward resources that he realizes he must turn inward. It is, rather, because the external world proves too vast, diverse, and incoherent. Descartes notes this explicitly:

> I considered how one and the same man with the very same mind, were he brought up from infancy among the French or the Germans, would become different from what he would be had he always lived among the Chinese or the Cannibals[87] . . . Thus it is more custom and example that persuades us than any certain knowledge . . . Hence I could not choose anyone whose opinions seemed to me should be preferred over those of the others, and I found myself, as it were, constrained to try to guide myself on my own.[88]

It is then, at least in part, *because of this situation of cultural relativity* that Descartes goes on to develop a four-step method for thinking by himself and without the aid of others.[89] For Montaigne, thought is mixed up with the world and can only improve by elucidating the traces of the world in ourselves. For Descartes, thought is mixed up with the world and can only improve by negating the world in ourselves.

The trouble, however, is that no such pure negation is possible. As Descartes quickly notes, before tearing down his whole house, he had better have another place to live in the meantime. And so he resolves to follow a few basic maxims:

The first was to obey the laws and the customs of my country . . . [because] although there may perhaps be people among the Persians or the Chinese just as judicious as there are among ourselves, it seemed to me that the most useful thing was to rule myself in accordance with those with whom I had to live.[90]

Here is the heart of Descartes's evasion: he wants to avoid the world and go into himself, but he nevertheless finds that the world is already there within him—without it, he would have no language, no concept of truth or God, no idea what a home is. The question, then, is not whether or not he engages the world, but how he does so. He claims he will simply follow the rules of his immediate surroundings. In so doing, he is in fact rejecting the world around him—the very people he cites, the very products of the world that flow into his experience. He refuses the task of elucidating these references.

Was it mere coincidence that Montaigne had Tupi near him, and Descartes did not? This does not seem to be the crux of the matter, because Montaigne and Descartes both clearly have been reading about the world regardless of who they physically meet. While Montaigne chooses to engage this broader world, Descartes evades it. This move of refusing to engage the world under the guise of seeking truth is part of the origin of the Cartesian self. This is not the self who founds modernity, then; it is the self who avoids the global task of modernity.

Such evasion is not necessarily a bad thing. Descartes notes, for example, that self-reliance results in a kind of critique of empire: if we are content with what we have, "we will have no more regrets about lacking those [goods] that seem owed to us as our birthright when we are deprived of them through no fault of our own, than we have in not possessing the kingdoms of China or Mexico."[91] But it also results in the depths of doubt to which he is plunged as he tries to bear the burden of the whole truth of the world in his soul. Moreover, he offers us no resources for how to engage with others. Rather than enabling us to comprehend our interconnectedness, Descartes encourages us to shun it. He leaves us without a constructive option beyond empire or isolation.

Foucault is explicit in his lectures that the "Cartesian moment" does not refer to anything specific in Descartes's work so much as a general transformation away from care of the self to absolute knowledge of the world. Foucault acknowledges that Descartes goes through transformations in order to arrive at the truth, but marks the key difference: classical practices of the self aimed at making the subject adequate to the changing demands of an uncertain world; Descartes's practices aimed at making the subject's knowledge adequate (equal) to the truth of the world.⁹²

In his earlier writings on the history of madness, Foucault saw the split between Montaigne and Descartes originating in the disappearance of the possibility of taking madness seriously as a mode of thought. "A new dividing line has appeared, rendering that experience so familiar to the Renaissance—unreasonable Reason, or reasoned Unreason—impossible. Between Montaigne and Descartes an event has taken place, which concerns the advent of the ratio."⁹³ Another way to understand the difference between Montaigne and Descartes is here in this turn away from the globe. Descartes attempts to banish the globe and find that truth can be founded in the individual soul, whereas Montaigne seeks to essay a new global self. Foucault's early analysis continued: "But the advent of a ratio in the Western world meant far more than the appearance of a 'rationalism.' More secretly, but in equal measure, it also meant the movement whereby Unreason was driven underground, to disappear, indeed, but also take root."⁹⁴ Unlike madness, globalism was not driven underground, at least not at the time. But in our retrospective imaginations, the globe disappeared from modern thought, and the abstracted Cartesian subject came to take pride of place.

Such a disappearance has been contested by several Latin American philosophers concerned with the colonial origins of philosophy. Enrique Dussel, Nelson Maldonado-Torres, and Linda Martín Alcoff, among others, have kept the centrality of Cartesian reason while adding a new angle of critique. They argue that Descartes provides the philosophical language for the colonial encounters that precede him. Dussel, who first articulated the critique, claims that the Cartesian subject who announces *ego cogito* has a "protohistory" in the *ego conquiro*, or "I conquer" of the conquistadors. Dussel repeats this claim frequently, though without always clearly specifying what he means. At one level, the claim seems to imply a relationship between the specifics of Descartes's philosophy (on his reading, a universalizing rationality predicated on a mind-body dualism) and the philosophy of colonialism.⁹⁵ At another, more historical level, the claim—one we will see in slightly different form in Rousseau's critique of Locke's colonialism—is that the conquistadors pronounced their ownership of the world by refusing to acknowledge the meaningful existence of those already living on the land. The "I conquer this land in the name of Spain" thus treats the inhabitants of the Americas as Descartes treats all the world outside his head: as immaterial.⁹⁶ Maldonado-Torres furthers this argument by recalling that this proclamation in Descartes is preceded by his passage through skepticism. Maldonado-Torres suggests that this philosophical skepticism is itself informed by a colonial skepticism about the humanity of others.[97] Calling the humanity of others into question is what subtends Cartesian doubt.

For Dussel and Maldonado-Torres, then, Descartes is not the evasion of modernity, but the central philosophical expression of its colonial force. In a later essay, however, Dussel suggests a slightly different possibility. Responding indirectly to Foucault and Taylor, he suggests that the important comparison is not between Descartes and Montaigne, but rather between Descartes and Bartalomé de las Casas (a Franciscan missionary who argued for the humanity of Amerindians) as well as Felipe Guamán Poma de Ayala (a Quecha critic of the horrors of the Spanish conquest). De las Casas is, according to Dussel, the writer of the "first modern philosophy."[98] "Modern" here, as Alcoff explains, has two meanings: "(1) as a normative or evaluative term, which distinguishes between better and worse modes of thinking, and (2) as a descriptive term denoting the historical period post-Conquest."[99] If Descartes is modern only in the latter sense, de las Casas and Guamán Poma de Ayala are modern in both senses. Descartes is no longer the paradigmatic modern thinker, but only because a normative distinction has been introduced.

While I believe there is tremendous value in this rethinking of modern philosophy and the need to change the canon, my framework for understanding modernity is slightly different. This framework derives from Subrahmanyam's insight into the switch from universal to global history when the world became "encompassed."[100] In other words, it begins from the idea that to be modern is to make the attempt—for better or for worse—to relate oneself to the finite and interdependent globe. In effect, this idea of modernity collapses Dussel's distinction (as explicated by Alcoff), suggesting that "being modern" means developing the normative grounds for understanding our post-(European) conquest global relations. Descartes begins his journey in this space, trying to understand his relation to the world. However, when he turns in, when he decides that he cannot know the world and can only know himself, he explicitly evades this modern task.

I am appreciative of how Alcoff, Dussel, and Maldonado-Torres link the history of modern philosophy to the problem of colonialism. And I profoundly agree with Alcoff's conclusion, cited above, that "If . . . the meaning of philosophy is simply the history of philosophy . . . then European philosophy does not understand what philosophy is because it does not understand its own history of philosophy."[101] That is an economic phrasing of the claims I am trying to articulate. This agreement, however, does not, of course, preclude us from engaging in ongoing debates about what a revised history of philosophy would be; indeed, this revision will require as robust a history of debated scholarship as we find in the mainstream position today. I am suggesting a different way of reading the history of philosophy's relation to colonialism in part because I am suggesting a different method of reading.

Dussel and Maldonado-Torres find analogical relations between Cartesian philosophy (the abstract ego and the doubts about others) and the practices of colonialism (the ego that denies others and questions their humanity).[102] My interest is in reading what the philosophy says, *explicitly*, about intercultural relations. What Descartes writes is, in a sense, anticolonial: he does not conquer, but rather refuses to engage with others, and he is even explicit that Europeans should *not* want to "possess . . . the kingdoms of China and Mexico." These ways of reading are certainly not incompatible, as Dussel's later essay suggests. It is entirely possible that, in spite of what Descartes says, the forces around his thought lead his conclusions elsewhere.[103] So while I am not opposed to symptomatic readings such as these, I do think that if we are to convince a wider range of scholars to take seriously the impact that colonial relations have on modern thought, it is worth pointing to what is simply there in the text. That, at least, is what I am trying to do here.

In this context, I am ultimately unconvinced by the idea that merely stating "cogito ergo sum" is the logical end of colonialism. In Descartes's writings, it seems, rather, to function as his attempt to avoid others entirely. In so doing, he undoubtedly fails to use his voice to criticize atrocities, as de las Casas and Guamán Poma de Ayala did, and, in an encompassed world, such a failure is no minor thing. Nevertheless, the writings on other cultures in Descartes's texts suggest that the "I think" is in fact in (weak) opposition to the "I conquer," not an expression of it. And overcoming the "I think" thus provides no determinate path to improved global relations. This is the key point, for as we will see with the examples of Hegel's belief in the self-world relation and Heidegger's attempt to overcome the subject-object dualism, the abstract rejection of Cartesian philosophy may just as well lead to colonialist and racist claims.

There is nothing inherent in most abstract philosophies about what constitutes thinking that will lead us to better or worse global relations. One may perfectly well believe steadfastly in the mind-body dualism and still believe that it is unethical to impose that thought on others, or even that the logical conclusion of such a dualism is a political program that guarantees both liberal rights (for the mind) and economic rights (for the body). What matters here is what we think and what we do in connected spaces; how we connect and transform our ways of being to the specific contents and contexts we engage. This is this question that I believe lies at the heart of what it means to be modern—for better and for worse.

We can continue to see the frequently unnoticed importance of the globe in a literary example often considered paradigmatic of modernity: Shakespeare's *Hamlet*. Hamlet is famously bound within his own consciousness and unable to act in the world. But there are hints in the play that, again, the question of consciousness for Hamlet cannot be separated from his geographic relations. Read in this light, Hamlet might emerge as part of a line of figures who failed not because of their excessive thinking, but because of their evasion of globality. This is, for example, the context of Hamlet's famous line "There is nothing either good or bad but thinking makes it so":

> *Ham.* Denmark's a prison.
> *Ros.* Then is the world one.
> *Ham.* A goodly one in which there are many confines, wards, and dungeons, Denmark being one o'th' worst.
> *Ros.* We think not so, my lord.
> *Ham.* Why, then 'tis none to you; for there is nothing either good or bad but thinking makes it so.[104]

Hamlet is trapped in Denmark, trapped in the allegiances and worries of his times, even as his scholarly mind seeks to expand beyond them. Rather than performing an act of extension and moving on to a new space, he embraces the prisons of nationalism and subjectivity. His problem is not that he is not a good enough thinker within his culture, but that his culture is now overwhelmed by the demands of global engagement. (This is signaled in the play by his temporary escape to England and Fortinbras's imminent threats.)

That Hamlet chooses the prison of Denmark, and that Denmark represents the prison of his mind and the insanity bound to afflict one who cannot live in this new, global world, is signaled by a pun in his conversation with the gravedigger. Hamlet, whose identity is not known in this scene, asks the gravedigger "upon what ground" the mad prince is said to have lost his wits, asking, most directly, what the cause of his madness is. The reply encapsulates the play's geographic logic perfectly: "Why, here in Denmark."[105] The ground—the reason—of Hamlet's losing his mind is his decision to return to the ground of Denmark. He is tied up in its grounds—its logic of inheritance and vengeance over dispossession. Thus this scene segues on to Hamlet's passionate outburst over the grave of Ophelia: "This is I, Hamlet the Dane."[106] In claiming his throne, he claims his fate to die avenging it.

This is indeed what occurs in the play: Hamlet stays within the bounds of Denmark, and in the play's famously excessive ending, all those around him die as a result. Perhaps Hamlet at last learns this lesson in the moment of his death. As he lies dying, his friend Horatio decides to take his own life. Horatio states: "I am more an antique Roman than a Dane."[107] He seeks, like Hamlet early in the play, to evade his present duties by falling back on ancient ideals. (This is, recall, a mode of evasion that Montaigne explicitly critiqued.) And, like Hamlet, he presumes that the only other option available is the prison and madness of living in Denmark. But if Hamlet has learned anything, it is that a new kind of artistry is required to live in this world. He does not know what it is, but he can ask it of Horatio: "And in this harsh world draw thy breath in pain / To tell my story."[108] It is no coincidence, then, that Horatio gathers to tell this story to the international audience that has gathered—"You from the Polack wars and you from England."[109]

In perhaps the most famous (and briefest) of all modern readings of *Hamlet*, Freud located his struggles within the tragedy of *Oedipus Rex*. *Hamlet*, in other words, is a family drama. But my sense is that the family drama in *Hamlet* is not necessary. Indeed, the lesson of the later *Oedipus at Colonus* is precisely that we should stop repeating these family dramas and learn how to learn from others. Hence the play begins with Oedipus commanding Antigone: "Set me there securely, that we may find out where we are; we have come to be learners as foreigners from citizens, to do as we are told."[110] The drama of *Antigone*, then, will be that Antigone refuses this global modality and insists—rightly or not—on returning home to deal with her brothers' feud. This is the same troubled return that will undo Hamlet. Why, then, have so many read *Hamlet* within the family drama and not explored its questions about national identity in a global world?[111]

These concerns would augment rather than displace the fascinations with Hamlet's psyche. They would show us that a kind of insanity is the mode of being that accompanies modern isolation. Hamlet famously ponders, "To be or not to be, that is the question," but Oswald de Andrade ingeniously replies in the *Cannibal Manifesto* (1928), "Tupi or not Tupi, that is the question."[112] To understand the *question of being* in the modern age is to ask that question less about one's own life and more about one's capacity for solidarity and exchange. Tupi or not Tupi: Are you isolated in your worries or are you trying to engage? That is to say, how much have you worked on your practices of the global self? The evasive mood, the mood of doubt, melancholy, and disarray, is one that has refused to answer the question.

Of course, not all modern thinkers have believed that understanding the "question of being" in the modern era requires us to engage with global histories and practices. Indeed, the thinker who most famously asserted the question of being in twentieth-century philosophy—Martin Heidegger—was explicit that such historical and ethnographic engagements only obscured our search for truth. Early in his *Being and Time* (1927), he raises the question of the value of anthropology for a philosophy of what the human is. Without wading too deeply into his philosophy, we can say that he is grappling with a question that might be posed to his thought: "You are trying to understand what is the fundamental ontology, the most basic meaning of being, for humans. Can this not be found in accounts of primitive peoples?" Heidegger's response is no for two reasons.[113] First, in a quasi-progressive gesture, he maintains that so-called primitive peoples are like all peoples who can lead both authentic and inauthentic lives. Second (following Rousseau, as we will see), he claims that ethnologists bring with them a conception of the human, and contact alone is not sufficient to shake off the prejudice of one's own culture. Knowing more about other cultures does not yield insight; rather, "this plethora of information seduces us into failing to see the real problem."[114]

To see the real problem, Heidegger maintains, we do not need ethnology but, rather, a very specific kind of philosophy. Later in the book, he stresses that all of "primitivism," whether in the Christian variety of a Fall story or in the accounts of travelers, misses the fundamental point about who humans are and have always been. It does not understand the difference between what Heidegger calls "*Verfallenheit*" (falling prey or falling into) and the "*Fall*." It is not that there is some primordial condition we have fallen from, but rather that in our way of being-in-the-world, we "fall into," or "fall prey to," everyday social existence. We are always immersed in our given world, whether Tupi or not Tupi. This is not a Fall, then, because it is how we are, and it is from within this "always already" condition of fallenness that we can achieve some individuation and authenticity.[115]

The question for Heidegger is: If anthropological research does not reveal some true primordial condition, but only variable human conditions with their own abilities for authenticity, then what is the good of understanding other cultures? The answer is, in its simplest terms, none. In his own language:

> The opinion may now arise that understanding the most foreign cultures and "synthesizing" them with our own may lead to the thorough and first genuine enlightenment of Da-sein about itself. Versatile curiosity and restlessly knowing it all masquerade as a universal understanding of Da-sein. But fundamentally it remains undetermined and unasked *what* is then really to be understood; nor has it been understood that understanding itself is a potentiality for being which must become *free* solely in one's *ownmost* Da-sein.[116]

Heidegger thus raises two challenges: one, that knowledge of other cultures is a distraction, and, two, that it is a distraction because understanding what human beings are and can be can *only* be found via an experience of the self within a delimited culture. Perhaps not surprisingly, and in spite of his attempts to overcome Cartesian thinking, Heidegger remains very Cartesian about this. What he describes is an experience of angst, or anxiety, in which we realize that we have no explicit purpose as living beings. But in that very moment in which we glimpse the nullity of our existence in our inevitable death, we realize that, nevertheless, we continue to invent projects for our future. Our individuation occurs at that moment of breakdown, when we stop simply projecting ourselves and grasp the fact that we are beings who make projects.[117] There is much more to say about this movement through anxiety, but a precise understanding of Heidegger's philosophy is not presently our concern so much as to respond to his claim that knowing who we are requires less an understanding of other cultures and more a grasping of ourselves qua humans through whatever cultural condition we find ourselves in.

It does not seem to me possible to present a complete engagement here, especially because this question of the historical formation of being spans Heidegger's formidable (and increasingly obscure) body of writing. Quite frankly, it is entirely possible that under all the manifestations of human being there is a fundamental split between different ways of approaching our lives and a kind of grasping of who we are that enables authentic existence. But it does seem to me possible to question this presumption based on Heidegger's own insistence on history. For central to the argument of *Being and Time* is that Heidegger is offering a "history of ontology." Unlike Descartes, he does not believe that the question of being can be posed anterior to a philosophical tradition. "Within the scope of this treatise [*Being and Time*], which has as its goal a fundamental elaboration of the question of being, the destructuring [*Destruktion*] can be carried out only with regard to the fundamentally decisive stages of this history."[118] For Heidegger, these stages are the movement from pre-Socratic philosophy, to the categories of Aristotle, through Scholasticism, and into Descartes and Kant. But the challenge posed by global theory is to suggest that such a history of philosophy *cannot understand itself*. All that traditional philosophy can produce is the evasion of global engagement that Heidegger continues to practice. He wants to overcome the Cartesian subject, and his concept of Dasein as a being-in-the-world (rather than a foundational thinking subject) certainly achieves this at some profound level. He does thus destruct the subject of evasion, but that evasive subject is only one of multiple ways of operating in the world. To assume that because one has overcome a philosophical heritage one has therefore transformed the very history of being everywhere is profoundly absurd for two reasons. The first has to do with the globality of the West: Heidegger does not see that the Cartesian subject is itself an evasion of another way of being "within his tradition," one that begins with Montaigne and passes through Rousseau on its way to Kant, and that, therefore, to "destructure" the history of being in the West would require an engagement with the globality of the Western subject, not just its Cartesian interiority. The second has to do with the diversity of global modes of being: his project ought not lay claim to universal insights if it refuses to engage with other possible ontologies and epistemologies. In the first instance, Heidegger fails at his own methodology. In the second, he fails by the methodologies of diverse thinkers the world over.

Heidegger might very well have responded that the task of philosophy is precisely to transcend local limitations through the aperture that a historical condition offers,[119] but, again, much of what I want to argue in this book is that *even the conditions* on which we could do so require a broader comprehension of the global geography of modern thought than Heidegger can manage. Or again: *if it is through our condition that we claim some universal insight, then we had better have a very good grasp on what our condition is.* Heidegger himself admits this specificity while misreading its geography when he states:

> It is my conviction that any reversal of the modern technological world can only occur from out of the same location in which it originated. It cannot take place through the adoption of Zen Buddhism or other Eastern experiences of the world. In order to achieve a shift in thinking, one needs the European tradition as well as a new appropriation of it. Thinking will only be transformed through thought that has the same origin and determination.[120]

I return to this engagement with Zen Buddhism in the final chapter. For now, what is at stake in addressing the question of global cultures for our thought today is to better understand (with Heidegger) what the historical conditions of thought are, while also working to understand (against Heidegger) that it is not so easy to separate out a "European" and an "Eastern" tradition, or a Northern and a Southern tradition, or any other such division, and that, rather, our task is to understand how all these global conditions are constitutive of each other. In other words, even if we accept Heidegger's demand to grasp the fundamental ontology, or to overcome the modern-technological tradition and repose the question of being, this can only be done on the grounds of understanding the extensive geographic constitution of that condition.

In his refusal to do so, Heidegger also exhibits one of the dangers of the evasive mood. For while for Descartes it meant avoiding the attempt to transform the world, for Heidegger, disastrously, it meant attempting to purge one's culture of anything believed to be outside. This is yet another form of unbearable identity: to insist so greatly on one's singular importance as to refuse to share the planet with anyone else.[121] There is another history of modern thought, running counter to the evasive mood, that seeks to understand one's place in a world always larger than one's immediate surroundings. This, too, will have negative potentials, because it may result in imperialism as much as in critical, pluralist engagement. The point is not that going out into the world is necessarily better. The point is that whether one travels or stays home, the task is to overcome unbearable identities in all their forms.

These dueling histories leave one with a choice: either to follow Montaigne and believe that engagement with the "Cannibals" is a necessary part of the constitution of the modern self, or to follow Descartes and, *because of* the Cannibals, decide to go into one's self. In missing this option at the heart of modernity, we have obscured two primary elements in the history of modern thought. First, the primacy of the global. The general belief is that *as a reaction* to Cartesian interiority, to what Taylor calls "disengaged reason," to what Schiller and Weber called the "disenchantment of the world," later thinkers would turn out toward primitive life as a site of renewal.[122] But if we follow modernity through this other route I am sketching, then the situation reverses itself: Cartesian modernity *itself* is an evasion of the globe. Primitivism is tertiary. The second (related) element that has been obscured in our understanding of modernity is the fact that modern thought in Europe and the United States was never solely a project of cultural interiority. Indeed, as we will see over the course of this book, it is practically impossible to find a Euro-American thinker who did not in some way comment on world cultures—even if, as Descartes did, in order to avoid them. To make sense of the history of modern thought, we need to attend to the archive of the varieties of practices of the global self. There is perhaps no thinker who more obviously speaks to this vital tradition than Jean-Jacques Rousseau. In him we will see both its promises and perils enacted on a grand scale. If Descartes, Hamlet, and Heidegger are overwrought by evasion, Rousseau will be undone by his attempt to claim more of the world than he rightly can.

2

Foundations of Universalist Global Thought
Rousseau and Kant

Rousseau: Global Thought against Inequality

Jean-Jacques Rousseau's *Discourse on the Origin and Foundations of Inequality among Men*, also known as his *Second Discourse* (1755), is, like Montaigne's "Of Cannibals," deceptively simple. In true essayistic style, Rousseau's argument unfolds as a continual attempt to understand a reality that always exceeds the capacities of prose. The essay's ambition is fantastic: to peel away all the layers of society and try to understand what the human animal was originally like. It is a fantasy that stretches back to the earliest myths of all peoples, and one that evolutionary biology and astrophysics continue to investigate today. The difficulty of this task does not escape Rousseau, and he emphasizes it from the outset: "*What experiments [expériences] would be necessary to achieve knowledge of natural man? And what are the means of carrying out these experiments in the midst of society?*"[1]

Arguably the central methodological claim of the *Second Discourse* is that there are no such experiments that can be undertaken if we remain within the confines of our "own" society. Indeed, what keeps Rousseau's contemporaries from knowing human nature is the fact that they keep projecting their current ways of life backward: "They spoke about savage man, and it was civil man they depicted."[2] Sociological analysis will only allow us to see what is, and then we can try to derive what was from what continues to exist. But Rousseau argues forcefully that what is need not be. His maxim: never mistake fact for truth. The state of society is just one possible configuration of human life, and, by Rousseau's standards, it is perhaps the worst one. Society is unequal, unfree, and unjust.

For Hobbes and others, inequality and injustice had been the natural condition of human life. And because humans were naturally unequal and unruly, it took the strong hand of a singular sovereign to crush their brutal ways and make an ordered world. For Rousseau, the result of this logic is clear:

> [It] gave new fetters to the weak and new forces to the rich, irretrievably destroyed natural liberty, established forever the law of property and of inequality, changed adroit usurpation into an irrevocable right, and for the profit of a few ambitious men henceforth subjugated the entire human race to labor, servitude and misery.[3]

The question of the origins of humanity, then, is no mere hypothetical question. It is an incredibly powerful idea that underwrites all of our social formations.[4] The question is: how can we get outside mere sociological analysis and truly grasp the nature of human life, with its latent potential for alternative social formations? Rousseau's answer is to provide a *conjectural history* of human life.[5] He sets aside "all the scientific books which teach us only to see men as they have made themselves" and equally "all the facts, for they have no bearing on the question."[6] What concerns him then is not the *fact* of what is, but the *truth* of what might be. To the end of uncovering this truth, he will offer "conjectures, drawn solely from the nature of man and the beings that surround him, concerning what the human race could have become."[7]

But this does not necessarily answer our question about methodology. How is it that Rousseau, immersed in society, will manage to formulate such conjectures? Will not the prejudices of his time seep even into his imagination? Undoubtedly. But this is precisely the point from which his methodology begins. We must understand that human truth is historical because human beings themselves are historical. It is our very historicity, that is, our being subject to historical change, that both enables us to rise to our greatest heights and to sink to our greatest lows. This is what Rousseau calls our "*perfectibility*," for to be perfectible is also, as it were, to be imperfectible. There is no *necessary* teleology to human history for Rousseau. We are as likely to succeed as to fail. It is this very perfectibility, inherent to the human condition, which eventually drew us out of the state of nature.[8] Our latent capacity for perfectibility, combined with a series of historical accidents, made us seek to perfect our social world as well.[9] There is no guarantee that this move was a gain for humanity, but there is a constant challenge to ensure that it be so. If the human being is both perfectible and imperfectible, then it makes sense to consider various forms of life in order to analyze what is most perfect for humans.

This practice of comparison is the key to Rousseau's method. He will not merely conjecture in abstraction.[10] He will use the data of colonial ethnographers and missionaries to construct his conjectures. And, like Montaigne, he will demonstrate that the inequality of Europe looks foolish when viewed from the potentials of equality manifested elsewhere in the world. The starting point of Rousseau's practice of the global self, then, is that he will use comparative and conjectural methods to deduce how it is best for human beings to comport themselves. This will require that he develop modes for transforming both societies and individuals, as testified to by his treatises on government and pedagogy. We will come to these in turn.

Rousseau also uses an implicit comparison to distinguish his methodology from that of others. In what is generally taken to be an allusion to Descartes's physics,[11] Rousseau writes that his conjectures are "better suited to shedding light on the nature of things than on pointing out their true origin, like those our physicists make everyday with regard to the formation of the world."[12] In his *Discourse on Method*, Descartes describes a hypothetical experiment from his book *The World*, which was only published posthumously because of his fears after the trial of Galileo. In the account in the *Discourse*, he imagined how God could have created the world beginning from chaos and then "let nature act in accordance with the laws he had established."[13] Descartes goes on to consider what this would mean for the growth of the human being. But because, as we have seen, he is not interested in cultural comparisons, he focuses his method on anatomy, specifically the movement of the blood through the body. He then builds up an entire picture of the human mind and body from this basic principle of life, including impressions, the senses, and dreams.[14] But there is one thing Descartes leaves outside the purview of his conjectural history: "the rational soul." This, he tells us, "can in no way be derived from the potentiality of matter . . . but rather . . . it must be expressly created [by God]."[15]

Because Rousseau's concern is perfectibility, and because for him that implies happiness and equality, there is nothing special to him about the rational soul. Indeed, his great fear is that the rational soul is incapable of achieving happiness and equality, and many of his energies—his sentimental novels, pedagogical treatises, and political tracts—will be dedicated to the attempt to achieve these ends given the ambivalent value of the rise of rational reflection. He does not, as such, attempt to tell a story about the ascent of human beings into rational creatures. Rather, he tells a comparative history about the different ways of life in which human beings might find happiness and achieve equality. He does *not* believe that such perfection is the original condition of mankind. But he *does* believe that there was a moment when we achieved it: "a middle position between the indolence of our primitive state and the petulant activity of our egocentrism, must have been the happiest and most durable epoch."[16] And what is his evidence? "The example of savages, almost all of whom have been found in this state."[17] Rousseau's point, and he is explicit about this here and elsewhere, is not that we could, or even should, attempt to return to this state. Rather, it is twofold: first, that rationality (*pace* Muthu)[18] is not the sign of human civilization, and we should only judge human communities on the basis of their actualization of justice and tranquility; second, that Europeans will need to develop new modes of relating both to themselves and to others if they are to become just and happy subjects on this shared globe. We do not have to succumb to primitivist fantasy to appreciate Rousseau's basic insight: a more just and equal world is possible.[19]

In evading the Cartesian inward turn, Rousseau explicitly returns to Montaigne. Rousseau agrees with Montaigne that "practices of the self" are fundamental to life and to education. And Rousseau does not believe in writing essays as a value in themselves, or beyond the ways in which they make it possible for subjects to transform themselves. The link between education and global practices of the self from Montaigne will be echoed—quite explicitly—in Rousseau's work. We can see this by looking at two unnamed citations to Montaigne that end Rousseau's first two discourses. In the first, *The Discourse on the Arts and Sciences* (1750), Rousseau repeats an argument from Montaigne's essays on education that the first principle of education should be active and not reflective virtue. For example, the Romans did well when they "had been content to practice virtue; all was lost when they began to study it."[20] This distinction carries through to the essay's close, where Rousseau speaks of "that glorious distinction observed long ago between two great peoples: that the one knew how to speak well, the other how to act well [*que l'un savoit bien dire, et l'autre, bien faire*]."[21] The two great peoples are those of Athens and Sparta, and the line very clearly echoes this from Montaigne: "At Athens they learned to speak well, here [Sparta] to do well [*à Athenes on aprenoit à bien dire, et icy, à bien faire*]."[22]

This allusion at the end of the *First Discourse* is echoed by one at the end of the *Second*. Rousseau concludes the latter by writing, "It is obviously contrary to the law of nature, however it may be defined, for a child to command an old man, for an imbecile to lead a wise man, and for a handful of people to gorge themselves on superfluities while the starving multitude lacks necessities."[23] Two of these are, of course, the critiques made by the Tupi during their visit to Rouen. Rousseau, perhaps following Montaigne's spur to complete the triad of critiques, adds that an imbecile should not lead the wise. Indeed, it is possible to read the *Second Discourse* largely as a completion of Montaigne's "Of Cannibals" in much the same way that Montaigne had said La Boétie's *Involuntary Servitude* was the completion of a suggestion in Plutarch. Rousseau takes Montaigne's basic idea that the confrontation of knowledges between Amerindians and Europeans should result in a critique of poor leadership and inequality, and he develops an extensive philosophical, historical, and anthropological argument for why this is the case.

The method by which he does this is not through witness testimony, but rather conjectural history. This is a key innovation in the history of essaying the global self. And Rousseau is insistent that one cannot make such an essay simply by imagining what other peoples are like. In what reads like a plea for a patron, and marks the passage that Claude Lévi-Strauss will come to call the founding moment of the human sciences,[24] Rousseau laments, "The entire earth is covered with nations of which we know only the names [and, in truth, not even that], and we dabble in judging the human race!" He calls for someone to fund the greatest minds of his time to venture forth to learn about these other peoples, and return to write their stories, so that "we ourselves would see a new world sally forth from their pen, and we could thus learn to know our own."[25] It would be crucial that those who go forth to learn do not bring their presuppositions with them. Otherwise it would remain the case that "individuals may well come and go . . . [but] philosophy travels nowhere."[26]

And, unfortunately, Rousseau himself is not traveling. He does not have his desired patron, and so he must imagine these modalities of global comprehension that he is calling for. To this end, his first task will be to never assume to understand the practices of other peoples based on his own. It is frequently said that Rousseau romanticizes those whom he called "savages." This is largely true, and it forms a debilitation in his thought to which we will return. But it is important to remember that his remarks in this essay generally fall under the category of the critique of inequality. And so right after he speaks of the "example of savages" in a perfect middle condition, he proceeds to leverage this idea to deplore inequality:

> As long as men were content [in this way of life] . . . they lived as free, healthy, good and happy as they could in accordance with their nature . . . But as soon as one man needed the help of another, as soon as one man realized that it was useful for a single individual to have provisions for two, equality disappeared, property came into existence, labor became necessary. Vast forests were transformed into smiling fields which had to be watered with men's sweat, and in which slavery and misery were soon to germinate and grow with the crops.[27]

What Rousseau is in effect doing is providing a genealogy by which the gap between the Tupi and Montaigne's France makes sense. He is trying, in his conjectural history, to understand how it is that we went from basic, if inconvenient, equality to a life full of conveniences but bereft of an egalitarian praxis.

Moreover, he is insisting that it is only by shaking off one's assumptions about the superiority of one's own form of life that one is truly able to get at the heart of this critique. Just as we need "means" to understand the original condition of humans, so we need them to appreciate human difference: "But what are the means [*le moyen*] by which we are to imagine the sort of pleasure a savage takes in spending his life alone amidst the woods?"[28] These are the practices of the global self that Rousseau seeks to build in his essaying. To answer this question takes us to the heart of Rousseau's revolutionary philosophy, for it requires unveiling the lack of freedom at the heart of supposedly liberal Europe. Indeed, Rousseau makes the connection between European confusion about others and about themselves explicit: "Politicians produce the same sophisms about the love of liberty that philosophers have made about the state of nature. By the things they see they render judgments about very different things they have not seen."[29] Just as the state of nature is inferred backward from the state of society, so is the desire for liberty denied backward from the actuality of submission to authority. If one is to understand the desire for liberty that is at the heart of human life, one has to understand equally well the natural liberty into which we were all born. The fact that Amerindians are fighting back against the encroachments of European colonialists underscores this insight for Rousseau: "When I see multitudes of completely naked savages scorn European voluptuousness and brave hunger, fire, sword and death, simply to preserve their independence, I sense that it is inappropriate for slaves to reason about liberty."[30]

One of the things that Europeans seem particularly incapable of understanding is liberty with regard to the land. The second part of the *Second Discourse* begins with these famous lines: "The first person who, having enclosed a plot of land, took it into his head to say *this is mine* and found people simple enough to believe him, was the true founder of civil society. What crimes, wars, murders, what miseries and horrors would the human race have been spared" if someone had stopped him.[31] It is infrequently noted that this famous idea of Rousseau's is linked to his critique of colonization. Civil society having been stupidly founded in Europe (in Rousseau's account), it proceeds to claim that it can liberate others by imposing the same idea on them. This act creates some of the "miseries and horrors" to which Rousseau refers. After all, it was John Locke, to whom Rousseau is responding throughout the essay, who had famously asserted that the lack of private cultivation of land in the New World is precisely what allows for European usurpation. Rousseau rebuts: this is a category mistake; it is an application of an idea of civil society to a different form of social life.[32]

This is illustrated by a clever and brief parable in *Emile* (1762). Locke, in his *Second Treatise on Civil Government* (1689), argues that Europeans have a right to land claims in America where that land has not been obviously cultivated. The Amerindians have rights to what they hunt or reap from nature, but because they do not sow, they cannot properly own the land.[33] In *Emile*, Rousseau appears to adopt Locke's basic principle that mixing one's labor with the land gives one a right to it: "the idea of property naturally goes back to the right of the first occupant by labor."[34] But he complicates this idea in a subtle parable in which Emile *thinks* that he is the first one to plant beans in a field, whereas it turns out that, *unseen to him*, the gardener has already laid melons there. They negotiate a settlement wherein the gardener keeps the majority of the land and Emile is allowed a small plot, but from which he must give the farmer half his crops. Though Rousseau accepts Locke's definition, he opens it up to the critique that what labor is may not be obvious to the invading power. Hence he frames the parable by comparing the legitimacy of Emile's possession of the land with Spain's in the New World: "And surely this possession is more sacred and more respectable [even though it *still* turns out to be false] than that taken of South America when Núñez Balboa in the name of the King of Spain planted his standard on the shore of the south sea."[35]

This point is repeated almost verbatim from *On the Social Contract* (1762), where Rousseau doubts, in direct political terms, that Núñez Balboa could legitimately claim lands and dispossess people without understanding the land or how it had been cultivated. He adds a satirical line that if this were the case, "[a]ll the Catholic King had to do was to take possession of the universe all at once from his private room."[36] As Greenblatt argued about Montaigne, so we might say here about Rousseau: he is trying to dispossess himself and Europe of the things that it has wrongly taken as possessions. Those possessions include not only land claims, but also claims about the nature of humanity: its inner savagery, its instinct for servitude, and what would constitute its true liberty. With his argument for indigenous land rights, Rousseau is broaching a claim that Europe must dispossess the land as a precondition of freedom. For freedom implies not only liberty from subjection, but also liberty from possession. Possession may be a part of human life, but no one can be free who is possessed by her possessions.

Rousseau's solution to this problem is not to get rid of possessions. Rather, it is to shift the possession from the individual to the communal: "each particular individual's right to his very own store is always subordinate to the community's right to all."[37] We work not for private gain that might accidentally trickle down to the community; we work for the community such that all will gain privately. This alone guarantees for Rousseau the possibility that society might be perfectible even after the loss of our middle state:

> Instead of destroying natural equality, the fundamental compact, on the contrary, substitutes a moral and legitimate equality to whatever physical inequality nature may have been able to impose upon men, and that, however, unequal in force or intelligence they may be, men all become equal by convention and by right.[38]

This seeming preference for the social contract is sometimes seen as a contradiction in Rousseau's thought between the *Second Discourse* and the *Social Contract*. But Rousseau is not suddenly disavowing other forms of life; he is merely trying to understand how his own immediate form of life can learn from the critique of inequality that his global essaying has taught him. To break from his cultural norms so as to approach an understanding of Amerindians is to essay the human condition. This does not mean that the Amerindians are "truer" humans for Rousseau any more than it means that Europeans are more "rational" in a positive sense. It only means that one cannot possibly understand humanity unless one understands the different ways in which humanity might organize itself.

Rousseau is not affirming here that all peoples must join in some singular, global mode of governance, as we will shortly see Kant do. He falls, rather, into a traditional pluralism. He affirms that "aside from the maxims common to all [such as equality], each people has within itself some cause that organizes them in a particular way and renders its legislation proper for it alone."[39] This cause in Rousseau is solely geographic, and it has to do with how the land where a collectivity resides is best able to provide sustenance. Rousseau does not see that the circuits of international trade are dissolving this logic and that soon all peoples will be ruled by an absurd and overwhelming economic necessity. Rousseau writes, for example, "Does the sea wash against nothing on your coasts but virtually inaccessible rocks? Remain barbarous and fish-eating. You will live in greater tranquility, better perhaps and certainly happily."[40] One might think here of Hubert Sauper's 2004 documentary *Darwin's Nightmare*, about the devastation wreaked on Lake Victoria by the introduction of the Nile perch. The fish is cultivated in the lake solely for European consumption and denied to the local fisherman but for rotting scraps. Sauper eventually unveils this to the viewer, as well as the fact that not even a minuscule amount of money is entering the local economy. These fish are being shipped to Europe in exchange for armaments. However, we do not in fact have to wait until the present to find such terrifying modes of exchange. The conditions Rousseau imagines are not the actual conditions of the people he writes about. As Nelson Maldonado-Torres concludes his appreciative but critical reading of Rousseau: "Rousseau searches for 'savage' man, but does not consider that the 'savages' have turned, for the most part, into the 'colonized.'"[41] At this level, Rousseau continues Descartes's evasion.

The Antillean Origins of the Dialectic

We can see this failure of Rousseau's vision in one particularly famous anecdote in the *Second Discourse* that Rousseau took from Jean-Baptiste Du Tertre. (There will be more to say about this anecdote, whose impact on contemporary thought will go all the way to Suzuki.) In 1667, Du Tertre, a French missionary in Guadeloupe, published his *General History of the Antilles*. It chronicles both the original inhabitants of the islands and the French interactions with them. In a chapter on exchange, Du Tertre takes a tone that is both mocking and sensitive to the Island Carib peoples he is writing about. (The "Island Caribs," I should note, call themselves Kalinago, and this has been known by Europeans since 1665. I refer to "Caribs" here, a generic term in Arawak likely denoting strength and bravery, because this is how it is done in the texts being discussed and also because the appellation remains standard in the scholarship. This is in part because Carib is a more general term developed during the colonial era and the mere replacement of Carib with Kalinago creates a false equivalence.[42]) On the one hand, Du Tertre is appreciative of the basic differences in the mind-set about trade between the Caribs and the French: "The Caribs wish the French would have the attitude that Caribs have among themselves. That is to say that the French should give generously everything which is asked of them."[43] On the other hand, he thinks that the Caribs' attitude is essentially inferior: "In a word, all their commerce and trade is a childish game, and often when they come among us they cost more to feed than the profits that one has made out of the goods bought from them."[44]

Du Tertre tells one brief anecdote in his account of exchange about a hoodwinked man and his lost bed. It might appear a trifling tale of colonial woe at first glance, but, as I show in the chapters to follow, it is a central moment not just in the development of the dialectic, but in a worldly history of modern, global subjectivity. Here is Du Tertre's version of the story, offset as it is by the remarks on the differences in the concept of trade:

> As our French are shrewder than the Caribs, they easily deceive them. The traders never bargain for a hammock [*lit de coton*] in the evening since these good people will then have it present in their minds that they have an approaching need for it, and they would not give up their beds at any price. But in the morning they give them up cheaply without a thought that when night comes they will need them as much as before. At the end of the day they always return in order to exchange their purchase, simply saying that they cannot sleep on the ground. When they see that the traders do not intend to return them, the Caribs almost weep in vexation.[45]

We have here in miniature form what Rousseau, the critic of private property, should have seen as the greatest threat to happiness and tranquility: the imposition of private property onto the entire planet, a practice that E. P. Thompson called "imperialist essays in translation."[46]

But this is not what Rousseau sees when he retells the anecdote in his *Discourse*. Rousseau's version of the story, which is not offset by any remarks about the specific relations or different ways of thinking to be found among the French and Caribs, is as follows:

His soul, agitated by nothing, is given over to the single feeling of his own present existence, without any idea of the future, however, near it may be, and his project, as limited as his views, hardly extend to the end of the day. Such is, even today, the extent of the Carib's foresight. In the morning he sells his bed of cotton and in the evening he returns in tears to buy it back, for want of having foreseen that he would need it that night.[47]

Whereas in Du Tertre it is at least clear that the unfortunate Carib *assumes* the French will trade back in the evening, in Rousseau this difference in economy is erased, and the Carib is posited as a being who cannot *make assumptions* at all. Rousseau may just be a bad reader, but something more than this is at stake. He is taking the actual history of human contact, erasing the actual events and histories, and positing a specific evolutionary scheme of the human comprehension of time. Philosophy is attempting to constitute itself via the erasure of material history.

The trouble here is the split between Rousseau the fierce critic of imperialism and Rousseau the existential philosopher. Rousseau the critic sees global populations rising up against European usurpation of lands and destruction of forms of life. Rousseau the philosopher sees evidence for a primordial condition of humanity that has a unique relationship with time. At this moment, with this anecdote, Rousseau offers a fundamentally different practice of the global self. Rather than leveraging difference as a point of critique for inequality, he transforms inequality into existential practice. This is no longer about the difference between a culture of perpetual exchange and one of finite relations of property. Rather, it is about the relationship between human beings and time. Rousseau's practice of the global self here initiates a problematic split between politics and happiness. The Carib supposedly loses happiness because of a new imposition of *temporality*. What a just practice of the global self will truly require is to see the intimate link between existential temporality and global politics. Rousseau erases the former as he pursues the latter. In attempting to overcome his own unbearable identity of alienation, he imposes a double unbearable identity on the Caribs: first, that they are purely instinctual; second that their identity will become a cure for Rousseau's malaise.

Other critics have made this point. In a reading of Rousseau through the lens of decolonial studies, for example, Maldonado-Torres concludes that though Rousseau importantly registers "the need of encountering the other as part of the knowledge of the self, his method falls short of acknowledging and accounting for the full humanity of the other that he investigates."[48] Maldonado-Torres thus criticizes the representation of others in the history of philosophy and argues that this failed representation cannot be merely set aside, for it impinges on the very point of Rousseau's philosophy: to understand the purpose and meaning of human life in modernity. Maldonado-Torres's position is, among other things, an advance beyond the tendency in mainstream philosophy to simply discuss Rousseau's writing about savages as if he were not writing about real people at all. For an example, taken almost at random given how generalized the practice is, one could look at Robert Pippin's suggestion that Rousseau initiates a fundamental problem in modern philosophy by asking the question of whether or not the "savage" individual is actually free, or if freedom is only available in social relations.[49] Pippin writes as if Rousseau's "savages" were not real people, part of real societies and with real concerns that exceeded the philosopher's vision.[50] He writes, in other words, as if centuries of anticolonial critique and agitation had never occurred.

Charles Taylor, whose ongoing work after *Sources of the Self* to expand beyond Eurocentrism is commendable, similarly marks the fundamental importance of Rousseau without registering that part of what makes him so important was that he engaged—even if poorly—in global thinking. While Taylor at least notes the reality of those whom Rousseau writes about (an imagination "nourished partly by tales of 'uncivilized' people abroad"), he ignores the importance of the actuality of those people.[51] His reading is essentially the same as Pippin's: what appears as Rousseau's engagement abroad is only actually his critique of a "calculating other-dependence . . . [and] the force of opinion and ambitions it engendered" at home.[52] Taylor concludes: "Rousseau is at the origin point of a great deal of contemporary culture, of the philosophies of self-exploration, as well as of the creeds which make self-determining freedom the key to virtue. He is the starting point of a transformation in modern culture towards a deeper inwardness and a radical autonomy."[53] Certainly Rousseau reflected at length on himself. But to leave the summary of his impact here overlooks how Rousseau was also central in the transformation of the modern self toward an understanding that *inwardness itself* was shaped by global circuits of influence. It is not so much that I disagree with Taylor on this point; it is that he only paints part of the picture and thus, in turn, gives us confused visions of our global selves—their history, their destinations, and their futures.

One option here, which Maldonado-Torres and others have pursued, is to engage the philosophical productions of the diverse human populations that Rousseau covers over. Part of my argument in this book is that reconstitutive work on currently canonical figures can aid such important engagements by continuing to show why the hegemonic philosophical position of writers like Pippin and Taylor needs to be responsive to these claims, lest they risk misunderstanding their own claimed sites of expertise. That is, we need to see how the problematic assumptions in Rousseau are part of his *general philosophy* and are *embedded in* and *constitutive of* his concepts. There is no history of modern philosophy, in short, without the European fantasies of the colonial encounter. Taking this encounter head-on means not only criticizing representations; it also means showing how those representations cannot be separated from his philosophical positions or the philosophical history to follow.

One way to address this issue is to take up Pippin's question about the dialectic of freedom between individual and society. Indeed, we can see that this seemingly minor anecdote about the Carib's relation to French traders is not only a pivotal moment in Rousseau's thought, but also a surprising foundation for the entire modern concept of the dialectic. Modern dialectical thinking is usually traced to Hegel. The idea at its most basic is that something is what it is only through a relationship with what appears to contradict it. The self, for example, might classically be thought of as a unique and separate entity. The opposite of the self is therefore the other. But for Hegel, the self is interdependent with others and could only be what it was through both an internal and external relationship with otherness. This interdependence is rarely harmonious: self and other often exist in an antagonistic relationship. For Hegel this is a good thing, because it is from this inner opposition that static forms break down and newness is introduced into the world. That newness both preserves and cancels some elements of the previous entity, hopefully reconciling at least some of their contradiction in a new, third element, which itself will be subject to change and transformation. This process is called *Aufhebung*, which is usually translated as "sublation." The word in German has the unique characteristic of meaning canceling, preserving, and lifting up. The process proceeds by "determinate negation," which means negating a specific part of something to bring something new out of it without destroying the entity itself.

One can see why this might be of use to global theory: it shows a dynamic process of relations between self and other that can result in new ways of being. And, indeed, several recent works argue that Hegel's dialectic is fundamental to modern critical theory in our global age: Susan Buck-Morss's *Hegel, Haiti, and Universal History* (2009); Timothy Brennan's *Borrowed Light* (2014); Andrew Cole's *The Birth of Theory* (2014); and George

Ciccariello-Maher's *Decolonizing Dialectics* (2017). Each offers an expansion of the history of the dialectic beyond mere philosophy: into the Haitian Revolution for Buck-Morss; into anti-colonial theory for Brennan; into the critique of the remnants of feudalism for Cole; into revolutionary politics, especially in Latin America, for Ciccariello-Maher.[54] Differences between these authors aside, their approaches all complement each other in giving Hegel's dialectic pride of place in the birth of a worldly critical theory.

Moreover, while they change the geographic and temporal focus of Hegel's *data*, they do not question the European origins of his *concepts*: none asks whether the international contexts of his times may have influenced the concept of the dialectic itself. Perhaps they cannot suggest this, for to do so would deny the very universal applicability of the dialectic that they seek to defend. Thus, for example, Buck-Morss writes, "The actual and successful revolution of Caribbean slaves against their masters is the moment when the dialectical logic of recognition becomes visible as the thematics of world history, the story of the universal recognition of freedom."[55] The "Master Slave Dialectic" may thus be about real slaves and real revolts, but the conceptual thinking behind it remains abstract and philosophical. But what if we question this assumption? What if we flip the tables and replace the question "How does the dialectic explain global history?" with "How does global history explain the dialectic?" One place to start to answer this question, surprisingly enough, is in this history of French colonialism in Guadeloupe.

What's important for the history of the dialectic is how the anecdote fits into Rousseau's larger project. He both envies and deprecates the Caribbean men he writes about. He, too, wants a soul "agitated by nothing" that is simply carried away by the present. As he will later write, all happiness requires us to have "no need to remember the past or reach into the future, where time is nothing to [us], where the present runs on indefinitely but this duration goes unnoticed . . . As long as this state lasts [supposedly the state of the Carib], we can call ourselves happy."[56] And yet, based on his own misreading of Du Tertre's story, he accuses this man of lacking foresight. And Rousseau will later claim that the ability to "substitute justice for instinct," that is, to break with the present in order to see the consequences of our actions, is the basis of moral life.[57] Thus our happiness—in the instinctual "state of nature"—and our morality—in the reflective "state of society"—are fundamentally at odds.

Rousseau's question becomes: How can we combine reflexive temporality with presentness, and abstract justice with its instinctual application? This question is what leads us to the birth of modern, global dialectics. Here is Rousseau's proposal: First, one must preserve all the happy presentness of instinct. At the same time, one must negate all that is unruly and unhelpful in it. In so doing, one achieves a rational distance on the world. But this distance itself proves unstable. As Rousseau writes, "[the Carib's] entire soul is elevated to such a height that, if the abuse of this new condition did not often lower his status to beneath the level he left, he ought constantly to bless the happy moment that pulled him away from . . . [the state of nature] forever."[58] Thus a second process here begins: what is good in rational abstraction must be preserved, but its own capacity for abuse and alienation must be negated. Then, in the all-important final step, these two processes must be combined, and an instinctually rational subject, in the present but not blinded to time, rational but not devoid of instinct, should emerge. Rousseau gives this a formula when he says that Emile should become "a savage made to inhabit cities."[59] We will see this formula evolve into Kant's claim about art returning to nature and Schiller's claim that primitives are who we were and who we should become again. As we go, then, we will see how dialectical ideas about cultural relations are both formed by them and later applied to them. This culminates in a reading of Hegel's "Master Slave Dialectic" along these lines.

To see the general direction of this movement, consider a "textbook" definition of Hegel's dialectical method from Michael Forster:

> Beginning from a category A, Hegel seeks to show that upon conceptual analysis, category A proves to contain a contrary category, B, and conversely that category B proves to contain category A, thus showing both categories to be self-contradictory. He then seeks to show that this negative result has a positive outcome, a new category, C . . . This new category unites—as Hegel puts it—the preceding categories A and B . . . But it unites them in such a way that they are not only preserved but also abolished (to use Hegel's term of art for this paradoxical-sounding process, they are *aufgehoben*).[60]

The French and the Caribs, representing reason and instinct, may appear irreconcilable at first. But what we should see—when Emile becomes a savage made to inhabit cities—is that they are united in the concept of the human who can embody both sides of this false divide. As I discuss in chapter 4, there are a great many complexities to Hegel's dialectics not to be found in Rousseau. But there is clearly a thematic overlap here, and thus I argue over the next few chapters that one of the origins of this kind of thinking in modernity is *very explicitly* to be found in Rousseau's appropriation of Du Tertre.

Indeed, I am certainly not the first to suggest that Rousseau's way of thinking contains the germ of dialectics—Ernst Cassirer and Jean Starobinski have suggested as much.[61] Rousseau had a tremendous and well-known impact on his German readers, including Hegel, as I discuss further in the chapters that follow.[62] But no one, to my knowledge, has noted that Rousseau's incipient dialectic finds an origin (though not the only one) in this anecdote from a colonial encounter, and that this origin carries into the work of Hegel and others. It is as if Rousseau's hammock has been exchanged for the history of the concept itself.

By situating concepts within global histories like these, and, more generally, by showing the explicit ways in which global cultures are invoked in canonical texts, I am arguing that concepts are neither abstract philosophical instruments nor neutral descriptors of history, but rather are constituted by histories and geographies that find some part of their origins in global commerce (economic and otherwise). My claim is not that a concept like the dialectic is fully determined by this colonial origin, but that the dialectic is useful today insofar as we tarry with its colonial history. Global thought cannot understand its own history if it discards these moments of constitution by simultaneous appropriation and neglect. *Pace* Cole, then, "the birth of theory" is not in Hegel's dialectic (or at least not there alone), but in global dialectics produced in the encounter between cultures. This is one of the reasons that anthropology has a singular place in the classics of critical theory (such as Adorno and Horkheimer's *Dialectic of Enlightenment*, Derrida's *Of Grammatology*, and Deleuze and Guatarri's *Capitalism and Schizophrenia*). Theory is born in the violence of global encounters, and, like Rousseau, it registers this impact without always being aware of its implications. This is also one of the reasons that works that question the colonial origins of the dialectic, like Fanon's *Black Skin, White Masks* and Senghor's essays in *Liberté*, are as central to the history of critical theory as any others. Indeed, theory could not have been born without African and Antillean cultures, and it cannot proceed without a proper reckoning with the histories and futures of these global sites.

Let us return to Rousseau's overall position, then. There was for him perhaps no more fundamental problem for human happiness than that of our relationship to time. We have seen this already when he describes how the Carib's soul is "agitated by nothing" because it has no foresight. Later, in *Emile*, he will exclaim, "Foresight! Foresight, which takes us ceaselessly beyond ourselves and often places us where we shall never arrive . . . O man, draw your existence up within yourself, and you will no longer be miserable."[63] Happiness is presentness. Anxiety is nothing more than the gap between where we are and another temporality—past trauma, future challenge—that impinges itself on us. If we can only live in the present, like the Carib, we shall have no reason for anxiety. No reason, that is, except the appearance of the French traders who make it impossible for us to enjoy these reveries. Thus where the politics of exchange has disappeared, the politics of time has returned.

Rousseau does not, however, pursue this politics. In the *Reveries* (1782), he quickly admits that such intensities of presentness are only fleetingly available to us and of only limited good to those who remain engaged with the duties of social life.[64] And in *Emile*, his task is not to come up with a global situation in which we collectively engage with each other about the potentials of temporality, but instead to develop a temporality specific to his own time and place, even if dependent on the supposed temporalities of others. His practice of the global self, then, is not for all global selves, but for his own self in relation to the globe as he sees it. Because "savage" presentness is happiness, but social life requires foresight, Emile will need to find a way to combine them both:

> I have not raised my Emile to desire or to wait but to enjoy; and when he extends his desires beyond the present, his ardor is not so impetuous that he is bothered by the slowness of time. He will enjoy not only the pleasure of desiring but that of going to the object he desires, and his passions are so moderate that he is always more where he is than where he will be.[65]

These are practices of the self in relation to time.

However, unlike the practices Foucault traced in the Hellenic world, they are specifically about a relationship between the self and the plurality of ways of life on this globe. As I argued in my introduction, Rousseau and others do not abandon ancient practices of the self when they fashion their own. Rather, they update them by globalizing them. Just as the Hellenic philosopher would invent practices of the self to moderate their relationship to time, so Rousseau invents practices of the global self that create a relationship to time based on his global vision. Indeed, the relationship between Rousseau's vision here and his readings in Greek and Latin sources is explicit. His rewriting of the Du Tertre anecdote, for example, closely parallels one of Seneca's *Letters to Lucilius*. Seneca has told his pupil that fear and hope are linked. This is so, he says, because

> Both are mainly due to projecting our thoughts far ahead of us instead of adapting ourselves to the present. Thus it is that foresight, the greatest blessing humanity has been given, is transformed into a curse. *Wild animals* run from the dangers they actually see, and once they have escaped they worry no more. We however are tormented alike by what is past and what is to come. A number of our blessings do us harm, for memory brings back the agony of fear while foresight brings it on prematurely. No one confines his unhappiness to the present.[66]

Seneca, like Rousseau, is concerned with how to use the future and the past to adapt ourselves to the present. But whereas Seneca makes recourse to an analogy with wild animals, Rousseau speaks of the Caribs. The key thing to see here is that modern thinking, even when it borrows from ancient writers, is continually led to think about those same problems in terms of cultural geography.

This is also apparent in the very methodology of conjectural history. Rousseau's central focus on foresight as something that is not in fact proper to the human is also found in another mode of conjectural history: myths. Here, specifically, the Greek myth of Prometheus and Epimetheus. The version of this story related in Plato's *Protagoras* nearly parallels Rousseau's *Second Discourse* as a whole:

> When the destined time arrived to bring [animals and humans] forth into the light, the gods shaped and compounded them within the earth from earth and fire, and charged Prometheus and Epimetheus, Forethought and Afterthought, with the task of distributing to the animals . . . their natures and powers. Epimetheus took it upon himself to do this . . . But he squandered his stock of powers, and when it was time for men to be brought forth, he had nothing to give. Man was left naked and unarmed. It was Prometheus who saved the situation, stealing from the gods their own prerogatives, fire and the arts,

and giving them to men so that they might survive . . . Other animals were much stronger, so that men were forced to band together for protection and to live in cities. But they quarreled and wronged each other because they did not have the art of politics, with the result that they were dispersed again and in danger of extinction. Zeus, to prevent their destruction, sent Hermes to bring them . . . right and reverence or shame, so that there would be proper order in their cities and associations bound by friendship.[67]

Notice that human beings are not only originally an animal, but originally an animal without any characteristics proper to themselves. This is essentially how Rousseau defines the human animal: "whereas each species has only its own instincts, man, who may perhaps have none that belongs to him, appropriates all of them to himself."[68] The essence of the human, as in the myth, is that they have no essence other than the capacity to acquire other ways of being. The human is properly equated with the nudity and presentness of Epimetheus, not the futurity and fire of the Gods brought to them by Prometheus. To not have foresight, to simply live as an animal among other animals, was the original condition of human beings. Staying in that condition, they might have gone on to live happy and equal lives. But the bringing of fire and the arts to human beings deracinated their hold in the earth, and brought them into cities where, like Emile, they must learn the art of politics—the social contract.[69] Again, Rousseau's story differs from Plato's in that it makes sense of human life within the context of global geography.[70] Social science replaces the myth of gods with the myth of sociobiological origins.

The importance of this translation for the history of thought to follow cannot be underestimated both because of this transformation from myth to social science and because of the *specific content* of Rousseau's new myth. There are many ways to understand humanity and where we come from. That Rousseau chose to emplot our history in an evolutionary trajectory from instinct to rationality to their sublation not only changed who he was, but also whom he claimed others should be. Rousseau does not explicitly state that everyone the world over *must* pass through this process. But he does, at the very least, seem to believe that every European *should*, and that everyone else eventually, by default of conquest, will. At the end of history, we will all be savages made to inhabit cities.

Nevertheless, it is worth recalling the value of Rousseau's primary practice of the global self: conjectural history. What Rousseau proposes here is fundamental: we should never presume that our own modes of life or perceptions of others are anything more than evanescent facts. The point is to see past these appearances to the structure of human potential that he calls perfectibility. There is nothing in the notion of perfectibility that implies a singular, universal end. Indeed, Rousseau is clear that there are at least two moments of perfection in human history: one that has been lost and one that may come into being in the future. Conjectural history as a practice of the global self offers us the possibility of constructing narratives about human lives that overcome the very stereotypes and presumptions that Rousseau himself fell into. It allows us to suggest that there are many ways for human life to perfect itself. Moreover, it reminds us that every story we tell about human origins and destinies is a political story with ramifications for how we view others. At the heart of Rousseau's history is a bifurcation. On the one hand, he tells a story that disrupts the belief in the necessity of inequality both inter- and intraculturally. On the other, he tells a story about a rising, perfect soul who will dawn only in the West.

Other conjectural histories would open up other possibilities for our global selves. Rousseau's method has been used in texts as diverse as Mary Wollstonecraft's *Vindication of the Rights of Women*, Friedrich Nietzsche's *On the Genealogy of Morals*, Thorstein Veblen's *Theory of the Leisure Class*, and Sigmund Freud's *Civilization and Its Discontents*. And more complex conjectural histories, ones that refused to posit an essence of human origins, helped initiate new forms of radical critique. Here Jacques Derrida's *Of Grammatology* is perhaps best known, but we will come across earlier versions of this in the works of Ralph Waldo Emerson and W. E. B. Du Bois. First, however, it is important to follow Rousseau's history into German idealism. Not only we will see how notions of primitive life underwrite many of idealism's seemingly most abstract concepts, but we will also continue on our path to the surprising foundations of modern Zen.

Kant after Rousseau

Immanuel Kant has had a tremendous global influence for a man who never left his hometown of Königsberg.[71] Kant initiated a "Copernican revolution" in theoretical philosophy by placing the structures of consciousness at the center of the question of knowledge. Epistemology after Kant is no longer about the world itself, but about how the human can manage to comprehend that world at all. He was also foundational in the development of moral philosophy, and his "categorical imperative" remains one of the best-known, and most debated, concepts in moral thought. As if that were not enough, Kant has also been extremely influential in global political philosophy: his idea for a world federation of states informs the modern United Nations and our ideas of cosmopolitical life more generally.[72] But Kant did not just shape the modern world; he was also shaped by it. He was a recipient of global ideas, and he was especially influenced by Rousseau's conjectural history. In this section I look at how Kant systematizes Rousseau's thinking into a global program of transformation.

The key point is this: for Kant, there can be no practice of the self that is not related to the entire transformation of the globe. As he put it, "As a single individual, the human being cannot yet thus make himself perfect, until the whole of society will be perfect."[73] This is a tremendous idea. In fact, it is too tremendous: because history does not align with this possibility, the best Kant says we can do in this life is accept providence, hope for a future cosmopolitical order of instinctual reason by both states and peoples, and act as if this future can be brought about through our activities. This is also a tremendously unbearable idea. It is unbearable in both senses of the term: it tries to encapsulate more of the world than it can possibly accomplish, and, in so doing, it places others within an unbearable schema that forces conformity and denies the very freedom it promises.

My aim in this section is less to criticize Kant than to elucidate the residues of the globe on his thinking and of his global thinking on our own. In the era in which Kant wrote, no doubt, the thought of universalism was a wild achievement. It broke through the barriers of caste and clan and prejudice and made possible a belief in humanity's emergence into a more peaceful and enlightened age. But we can now see, as Du Bois, Fanon, and others argue, that universalism needs to be partialized. While we do share a tremendous amount as a species, we need to realize that part of what we share is a diversity that singular systems do not encompass.

Furthermore, later thinkers also needed to respond to the ways in which Kant helped further the discourse of race. While I focus here more on his remarks about cultural difference, it is important to note that Kant helped lay the groundwork for the biological ideas of race to which later thinkers respond.[74] An account of the history of the concept of race and its relation to concepts of culture and biology would be a contentious undertaking beyond the scope of this study. Thus when I speak later in the book of the "racial" history of philosophy to which Du Bois, Senghor, and Fanon respond, I mean only to invoke the general ways in which writers like Kant thought about forms of cultural racism.[75] The later writers will of course also be responding to the pseudoscientific notions of race that form in the nineteenth century, but I do not trace the development of that discourse here.

Kant is not the first in this history to suggest that there can be no effective transformation of the self without a transformation of the world. Rousseau had said as much. But Rousseau, as Lévi-Strauss noted, had followed a basic rule: "the society we belong to is the only society we are in a position to transform without any risk of destroying it."[76] Kant, as we will see, believed in this rule in abstract morality. But he also believed, as Hegel, Schiller, and Marx will believe after him, and as many believe today, that the only path to true human progress is through the dialectical destruction of cultures outside Europe (and "backward" cultures within). For Kant, although there is no *right* to change any other culture, there is a historical teleology of human progress that means that those cultures *ought* to change in order to join the European conception of states. In other words, Europe is never morally justified in colonialism, but it is historically so. We will see that the process by which the globe—and all its citizens—perfect themselves is what defines Kant's idea of "enlightenment." To arrive at it, he will pass through a conjectural history of the human species very similar to Rousseau's, but with this additional teleology at the end. In positing enlightenment as this total transformation of the globe, Kant invents a practice of the self that is about making who we are adequate to the globe at the same time that it tries to make the globe adequate to ourselves.

It was largely in response to Rousseau that Kant framed his ideas on the global self. Indeed, Kant once admitted that before reading Rousseau, he only concerned himself with theoretical questions, and, more than this, he looked down on those who did not philosophize:

> There was a time when I thought that this [pursuit of knowledge] alone could constitute the honor of mankind, and I despised the common man who knows nothing. Rousseau set me right. This blind prejudice vanished; I learned to respect human nature, and I should consider myself far more useless than the ordinary working man if I did not believe that this view could give worth to all the others to establish the rights of man.[77]

By Kant's own account, then, Rousseau affected an entire revolution in his thought. Upon reading him, Kant realized that his task as a philosopher was not only to set knowledge on firmer grounds, but also to help establish the dignity of all humanity. Noble though this task may be, there are questions to be raised in how Kant set about his pursuit.

Although Kant makes that remark about Rousseau already in 1764, we can see a prejudice about the common man run throughout his work. In the 1785 *Groundwork of the Metaphysics of Morals*, for example, he speaks of "the more common run of people, who are closer to the guidance of mere natural instinct and do not allow their reason much influence on their behavior."[78] Kant's point throughout his later writings is that "common people" *can* and *ought* to use their reason. (He loses his prejudice that they do not *have* reason, but he maintains his prejudice that they do not use it.) A lot of the mistakes Kant will make in his thinking follow Rousseau in this sense. As we saw above, Rousseau believed that rationality was a general human potential only actualized of late. The difference was that Rousseau questioned rationality and insisted on the values of different ways of life and thought, whereas Kant questions Rousseau's questioning itself. For example, in this passage in the *Groundwork*, Kant is responding to Rousseau's "*misology*, that is, hatred of reason."[79] He believes that Rousseau has correctly diagnosed the pains and failures of rationality thus far, but claims Rousseau has not seen that these failures are merely symptomatic of our current low state in the development of humankind. Rousseau "envies" the common man whom Kant used to despise, and this envy teaches Kant the value of all humanity.[80] But Kant finds that value not because of humanity's diversity and its various potentials, but only because he believes that he can essay a trajectory by which all humanity will progress on a path from dumb instinct, to alienated reason, and then to a perfected instinctual reason in a world federation of enlightened states. In short, humans will "suffer injury from progressing culture and injure culture in turn, until perfect art again becomes nature, which is the ultimate goal and the moral vocation of the human species."[81]

This last quote comes from Kant's conjectural history in his 1786 essay "Conjectural Beginning of Human History." It is one of his more interesting texts, in part because it satirizes the attempt made by his former student turned enemy, Johann Gottfried Herder, to use the story of Genesis as a document for reading human history.[82] At one point in the essay, Kant mentions the mythical moment when a human being made "the first attempt at a free choice." He therein discovered the "faculty of choosing for himself a way of living and not being bound to a single one, as other animals are."[83] But this distinction of the species, and this sudden discovery of rationality as a freedom to choose the path of one's life, was a Pyrrhic victory:

> Yet upon the momentary delight that this marked superiority might have awakened in him, anxiety and fright must have followed right away, concerning how he, who still did not know the hidden properties and remote effects of anything, should deal with this newly discovered faculty. He stood, as it were, on the brink of an abyss; for instead of the single objects of his desire to which instinct had up to now directed him, there opened an infinity of them, and he did not know how to relate to the choice between them; and from this estate of freedom, once he had tasted it, it was nevertheless wholly impossible for him to turn back again to that of servitude (under the dominion of instinct).[84]

What this Adamic man "tastes," then—his "original sin"—is his faculty of rational choice and, with it, his freedom from instinct. (That this man suddenly overwhelmed by choices resembles Rousseau's Carib and his blanket is no coincidence—indeed, Kant mentions the anecdote in his anthropology lectures from the 1784–85 academic year, a fact to which I return.[85]) But this freedom has produced a terrifying anxiety. Suddenly we have an infinity of choices, and we have no idea which of them may be correct. The kind of anxiety I have traced into Hamlet, Descartes, and Heidegger, one might say, is born in this moment.

Kant sees very well that this anxiety is meaningful and real. The colonial travelogues have brought to him accounts, which he appears to uncritically believe, about peoples "still" living under the domain of pure instinct. Moreover, he sees that in the world around him, humanity remains trapped between this rational capacity and its instinctual yearnings. Kant then makes an amazing intellectual move and claims that individuals simply must suffer in this gap. There is not yet in history the possibility for a moral law to prevail in ourselves, in our states, and in between states on the international stage. He credits Rousseau with perceiving this problematic and offers a perceptive reading of the link between the first two discourses and later works like *Emile* and *On the Social Contract*. In the first works, Rousseau "shows quite correctly the unavoidable conflict of culture with the nature of the human species as a *physical* species." And in the later works, "he seeks . . . to solve the problem of how culture must proceed in order properly to develop the predispositions of humanity as a *moral* species to their vocation, so that the latter no longer conflict with humanity as a natural species."[86]

But Kant has now snuck in an idea that is not, in fact, in Rousseau when he writes "how culture must proceed." This was not Rousseau's point at all. Rousseau simply attempted to resolve the conflict, not set history on a teleological path. It is in Kant's essaying that this happens. And it requires for him not only this transformation in the human soul, but also the development of "a perfect civil constitution (the uttermost goal of culture)."[87] As Emmanuel Eze argued in his foundational essay on Kant, Rousseau, and race: "Kant . . . elevated and reinterpreted Rousseau's supposedly hypothetical, or ideal, assumptions as to the origin and development of *European civilization* into a general statement on *humanity as such*."[88] If we turn to his "Idea for a Universal History with a Cosmopolitan Aim" (1784), as well as to some of his later political texts, we can see that the structure of the individual argument maps onto Kant's claim about the nation: nations, like individuals, must move from instinct to reason to instinctual reason, and this must happen across the species—all nations—as well.

In his "Universal History" essay, Kant aims to unpack the logic of the human world analogically to how Kepler and Newton unlocked the secrets of the natural world.[89] His purpose, he states at the end of the essay, is to help further the "aim of nature" by providing humans with a "guiding thread" to follow.[90] This is what marks Kant's essay form and makes it distinct from Montaigne and Rousseau: this is no longer about eclecticism, or a conjectural essay that can disrupt the present. This is a *teleological essay*, and its task is to bring together the diversity of human lives, tame the disruptions of the present, and tie them up into a neat claim about the destiny of humankind. It echoes Adorno's claim that in the essay, "thought's utopian vision of hitting the bullseye is united with the consciousness of its own fallibility and provisional character."[91] But if for Adorno that fallibility is ever present, and thus the essay is a site of tension between error and perfection, Kant's teleological essay aims to pull the error in the direction of an eventual perfection. The problem with teleology in this sense is not that it is bad in itself. There is nothing inherently wrong about trying to show the possible order out of the chaotic logic of human life. The problem here is that Kant forces all of human life into his teleological pattern. Like Prospero, he shapes the globe, taming it, bringing all of its strange powers under his rational domain.

The essay begins by arguing that the "predispositions of a creature" are destined to eventually flourish.[92] For human beings, as we have seen, this flourishing will occur not in the individual, but in the species. But because individuals begin their history, according to Kant, simply immersed in nature, there must be some mechanism to break them from their instinctual routines. Kant proposes here that our innate "unsociable sociability," that is, our yearning both to be with others and to harm each other when close (what Schopenhauer will later speak of as our porcupine problem) is the mechanism that draws us out of nature.[93] In a remarkable passage, he says that this inner antagonism is a blessing because without it, "all [human] talents would, in an arcadian pastoral life of perfect concord, contentment and mutual love, remain eternally hidden in their germs . . . [Human beings] would not fill the void in creation in regard to their end as rational nature."[94] The passage is surprising. Kant says that "perfect concord, contentment and mutual love" are our original condition, but it would have been terrible for us to live in this condition. "Thanks be to nature," he continues, "for the incompatibility, for the spiteful competitive vanity, for the insatiable desire to possess or even to dominate!"[95] One wants Kant to be tongue-in-cheek in these lines, but it is clear from the context that he is not. By his logic, pastoral happiness denies the true vocation of the human to develop reason in accord with freedom. We should be as we were in our original condition, but we must only get there via a diremption from and later return to this condition.

In his *Religion within the Boundaries of Mere Reason* (1793), Kant enters into a brief dialogue with Hobbes and Rousseau. This engagement can help us better understand the rest of his argument in the "Universal History" essay. Kant's argument in the later text is, in effect, a combination of those of his two predecessors. He appreciates Rousseau's desire for contentment and peace, but he has himself read widely in travel accounts, and he sees that Hobbes had some truth:

> If we wish to draw our examples from that state in which many a philosopher especially hoped to meet the natural goodliness of human nature, namely from the so-called *state of nature*, let one but compare with this hypothesis the scenes of unprovoked cruelty in the ritual murders of Tofoa, New Zealand, and the Navigator Islands, and the never-ending cruelty (which Captain Hearne reports) in the wide wastes of northwestern America.[96]

This duality of war and peace found in the travelogues was part of our inherent "unsocial sociability."[97] The key point for Kant in the *Religion* is that we need to break from these competing instincts and make a free choice for peace. To this end, he redescribes the "state of nature" by making a one-word emendation to Hobbes's Latin: "*status hominum naturalis est bellum omnium in omnes* [the natural state of men *is* a war of all against all], has no other fault apart from this: it should say, *est status belli* [is a state of war]."⁹⁸ What he means by this is that Hobbes is wrong to assume that humans are *naturally* at war: they are not *naturally* any determinate *thing*; they are only destined/determined [*bestimmt*] to the attempt to perfect their reason.⁹⁹ The natural condition is a state of war not because it *is* war, but because there is nothing to *prevent* war from occurring. There is, for example, nothing to prevent the Caribs from being colonized by the French, nor the Tupi by the Portuguese.

What Kant thus argues in "Universal History," and it is an argument that will carry through into his last published texts, is that we need a "perfectly *just civil constitution*," which is to say, one that allows for our freedom but can coercively compel us to respect the freedom of others as well.¹⁰⁰ This leads Kant to make one of his most controversial statements (which was immediately criticized by Herder); namely, that humans are animals who "need a *master*."¹⁰¹ Otherwise, by Kant's logic, we will always attempt to use our freedom to limit the freedom of others or allow our inclinations to overwhelm our sense of right. As Emerson will later put it, "We permit all things to ourselves, and that which we call sin in others is experiment for us."¹⁰² But Kant's history enters into a paradox here: because the master must be a human who can regulate our affairs, what is to stop him or her from doing the same? There seems to be nothing, and thus we appear to have made no progress. We remain in a condition of war.

But it is here that Kant comes up with his famous solution. The inadequacies of the individual lead to the state, and the inadequacies of the state lead to the federation. States, like individuals, must "go beyond a lawless condition of savages and enter into a federation of nations."¹⁰³ Thus, "states must be compelled to the decision (as difficult as it is for them) to which the savage human being was just as reluctantly compelled, namely, of giving up his brute freedom and seeking tranquility and security in a lawful constitution."¹⁰⁴ And just as the perfect art of the human will eventually return to nature, so will the alienated nation eventually act with peace and "preserve itself like an *automaton*."¹⁰⁵ Kant warns his readers that this last step—toward the federation of nations—will be among the hardest. Thus "*Rousseau* was not so wrong" when he spoke of Caribbean life as better than European life, but that is only the case until this final moment, when states combine together and forge a means of keeping the peace, ending war, and ensuring the continual economic and spiritual growth of their peoples.¹⁰⁶

I would be remiss not to pause and note the fallacy of Kant's arguments here. Unlike Rousseau or Montaigne, who understood that meaningful political institutions existed outside Europe, Kant, like Hobbes and Locke, explicitly denies this. He believes that only the written constitution of a republic counts as proper governance. This prejudice continues to haunt our political imagination. There is an implicit assumption that either there is the state or there is lawless anarchy. Pierre Clastres's lesson—that there is also *society*—has not been fully understood outside anarchist circles. Clastres argues that there are ways in which power can be held without the threat of coercion: "[The chief] must appease quarrels and settle disputes—not by employing a force he does not possess and which would not be acknowledged in any case, but by relying solely on the strength of his prestige, his fairness, and his verbal ability."[107] Clastres's point is not solely anarchist; it is also pluralist. It is a claim that there are other ways to hold power than through the monopoly of violence. Given the injustice that steadily marks so-called civilized law, one wonders if the state's centralization of power can in fact achieve its stated aim of ending arbitrary violence.

Some critics have suggested that Kant, in spite of what appears to be clear evidence in these texts, did not in fact believe that all peoples of the earth *must* join such a global federation. Thus Sankar Muthu argues, for instance, that "although the duty to join a civil society is mandatory, from a moral viewpoint, Kant always makes a curious exception to it in his descriptions of it."[108] He cites as evidence a passage from *The Metaphysics of Morals* (1797): "*when you cannot avoid living side by side with all others*, you ought to leave the state of nature and proceed with them into a rightful condition."[109] The emphasis here is Muthu's. He takes it that Kant believes that some people can avoid living side by side with others, and he cites as evidence a remark in the "Conjectural History" about how Bedouin society is still to this day nomadic.[110] But for a thinker as systematic as Kant, this simply does not hold. His point throughout these works is that human beings must have a federation of states; otherwise the logic of the whole argument falls apart. For if there is not a supervening power over states, we are sent back to the states themselves, which are necessarily ruled by flawed humans. If Muthu is right that some can live outside Kant's system, then Kant has no system at all, and then all Muthu has proven is that Kant failed in his attempt. But Kant, I believe, is consistent. He has a complete, teleological practice of the global self, which requires the transformation of the entire globe. And he says this unequivocally himself in *Toward Perpetual Peace* (1795): "This right, to present oneself for society, belongs to all human beings by virtue of the right of possession in common of the earth's surface, on which, as a sphere, *they cannot* disperse infinitely but must finally put up with being near one another."[111] Thus what Muthu reads in the *Metaphysics of Morals* as Kant's "curious exception" is in fact entirely the opposite: he is saying that although one may not *force* others to join (because such force is against freedom), they nevertheless eventually *must* because they have no choice but to live side by side on this finite sphere.[112]

Muthu deserves immense credit for turning our attention to the fact of Kant's thoroughgoing anti-imperialism. Kant was among the first to argue against imperialism as a civilizing mission in *The Metaphysics of Morals*, and in the *Religion*, he makes an argument that remains important to this day when he inveighs against the idea that a people must be prepared for freedom before they can be free as incoherent with the very idea of freedom, which can only develop on its own and cannot be imposed.[113] But the fact of Kant's moral position against colonialism simply does not mean that he did not also believe it historically necessary as part of his practice of the global self. If we do not see this fact, we will fail to learn one of Kant's most important lessons, one that he teaches us negatively: namely, that it is unbearable for a practice of the global self to try to make the world adequate to one's ideal conception of it.

Pauline Kleingold has attempted to nuance Muthu's position and suggest that Kant only became an anti-colonialist sometime in the 1790s.[114] But while it appears true, as she points out, that anti-colonialism becomes explicit for the first time only in his later works, it never erased his overarching belief that all peoples and all states would eventually follow Europe's lead. We can see this by returning to the anecdote about the Caribbean man and his blanket. Kant's reading departs from Rousseau's entire hermeneutic methodology. While for Rousseau it was absolutely essential that philosophy travel and learn other ways of life that could change how one viewed the world, for Kant (as for Heidegger later), travel was only a distraction. "The knowledge which the new travels have disseminated about the manifoldnesses in the human species so far have contributed more to exciting the understanding to investigation on this point than to satisfying it." He continues with his singular methodological claim: "one finds in experience what one needs only if one knows in advance what to look for."[115] Kant's point is that Rousseau was too easily seduced by the seeming ease of life in the Caribbean and so failed to think through this anecdote as part of the concept of humanity as such. If Rousseau's reading denied the economic realities of the situation, Kant's reading obliterates them and replaces the "manifoldedness" of life with a strict, linear teleology.

When Kant retells the anecdote in the final book version of his anthropology lectures, *Anthropology from a Pragmatic Point of View* (1798/1800), he does so, not surprisingly, in a section on foresight.[116] Kant begins the section by saying that foresight is the faculty that "interests us more than any other, because it is the condition of all possible practice and of the ends to which the human being relates the use of his powers."[117] Because the Caribbean man is said not to have these powers, he is supposedly happier. Nevertheless, Kant is unerringly specific in his critique: the Carib fails to live up to the dignity and purpose of the human vocation and wastes away in his happy, pastoral life. Lest there is any doubt about the fact that the Caribs must leave their condition and join Kant's federation, the closing pages of the *Anthropology* simply repeat what Kant had been saying since the mid-1780s:

> The character of the species, as it is known from the experience of all ages and by all peoples, is this: that, taken collectively . . . it is a multitude of persons, existing successively and side by side, who cannot *do without* being together peacefully and yet cannot *avoid* constantly being objectionable to one another. Consequently, they feel destined by nature to [develop], through mutual compulsion under laws that come from themselves, into a *cosmopolitan society* (*cosmopolitismus*) . . . [This] is only a regulative principle: to pursue this diligently as the destiny of the human race . . . [This will happen not] by the free agreement of *individuals*, but only by a progressive organization of citizens of the earth into and toward the species as a system that is cosmopolitically united.[118]

With that final clause, Kant's *Anthropology* ends. Individuals, to become the people they ought to be, must became part of a universal, cosmopolitan system of republican states.[119] There is no other choice. In a final quip, then, we might say that Kant was a pluralist in the same way that Henry Ford believed in consumer choice: "Any customer can have a car painted any colour that he wants so long as it is black."[120]

Kant's Geographic Lesson for the Present

One phrase that Kant might have used to describe the combination of individual, social, and international advancement that he seeks is "cosmopolitical enlightenment." Kant makes this link between his notion of cosmopolitics and enlightenment explicit in "Universal History," when he connects enlightenment as the increased freedom of the individual to the more general form: "This enlightenment [of the individual] . . . must ascend bit by bit up to the thrones and have its influence even on their principles of government."[121] In the brief essay "What Is Enlightenment?" (1784), Kant is also explicit that the reason for enlightenment in the sense of the public use of one's reason is that it is only through this antagonistic engagement that the "original vocation" of the human as a progressive being can be realized.[122]

When Michel Foucault gave his famous reading of this short text in the 1980s, he argued that it lay at the crossroads of Kant's critical project for a transcendental knowledge and his historical project to understand human development.[123] Reading this text alongside Baudelaire's reflections on modernity, Foucault argued that if we were to see ourselves, our present, and what we needed to do in the midst of that present, we needed to understand ourselves as "beings who are historically determined, to a certain extent, by the Enlightenment."[124] This does not mean that we are constituted by rationality and universality alone, but rather by a more general task to understand how to make ourselves into "autonomous subjects."[125] This requires keeping the Kantian project of historical analysis of the self, but abandoning the Kantian project for universal structures of knowledge, and asking instead how it is that what appears as universal is in fact contingent. It turns, then, from transcendental critiques to practical ones, and asks how we can carry out the "undefined work of freedom."[126] This means turning away from all projects that, like Kant's, "claim to be radical or global [*globaux et radicaux*]."[127] Instead, they must focus on the kinds of specific conjunctures that Foucault himself highlighted throughout his writing: sexuality, madness, the relationship of self to self, and so forth.

What I want to suggest here, and what I have been suggesting throughout, is that the type of "historical ontology of ourselves" that Foucault calls for simply cannot be done as he attempts to do it—through reference to "the West" and its practices.[128] Foucault is right to deny the "global" as universal prescription, but he does not see what else "global" might mean. The problem with global practices is that, in Kant's hands, the globe becomes something that we must transform to be in our own singular vision. But if Foucault is right that we should undertake "historical analyses that are as precise as possible," and I think he is, then we must understand that history to have been globally constituted.[129] A historical ontology of ourselves should be informed by how diverse geographies have constituted who we are. Part of our task in the present is to continue to develop the kinds of practices of the self that relate us to the globe but do not constrain the globe in that process.

I discussed in the introduction some of the problems that resulted from Foucault's own misconception of the globality of the present. To see the prevalence of this kind of misconception, I want to briefly turn to the very interesting work of François Jullien. In his *Treatise on Efficacy*, Jullien argues that "we" in the West have inherited a Greek notion of efficacy as part of a means-end or theory-practice continuum. Based on the model of heroic action, we think of ideas as plans to be implemented. Jullien assumes, in effect, that all of us "Westerners" believe in a kind of rational means-ends model that, if any modern thinker were to embody, we might imagine that it would be Kant. But, as we have seen, Kant's ultimate schema of efficacy lies elsewhere. He locates true efficaciousness only in the future: once "perfect art returns to nature" and governments pursue peace like "automatons."

Opposing his made-up West to a made-up and monolithic China, Jullien writes: "But far away in China we discover a concept of efficacy that teaches one to learn how to allow an effect to come about: not to aim for it (directly) but to implicate it (as a consequence), in other words, not to seek it, but simply to welcome it—to allow it to result."[130] For Jullien, the concern is that we need a "way out of our rut" of abstract thinking, and China is that way.[131] While I am sympathetic to his claim that we need to engage other ways of thinking, and that learning how to let things be is a possible mode of action, I am skeptical about the precision of his sense of the rut and his rather acritical conception of cultural thought. One of the problems, for example, is that the assumption that "Western" thought is an inheritance directly from the Greeks misses the very cross-cultural and transatlantic ways in which we have seen the problem of decision making develop in Montaigne, Descartes, Rousseau, and Kant. Even if we are in a rut, in other words, it strikes me as a very different one than what Jullien imagines. Or, better put, we all are in multiple ruts the world over.

By assuming that our subjectivity is crafted solely as an inheritance from Greece, he cannot see, for example, the historical production of an idea about efficacy as the uniting of global culture in the name of instinctual reason. Indeed, it seems to me that Jullien himself writes from within a rut, one in which the presumed solution to the West's ills and the South's savagery is almost always the East, which, as I discuss with Suzuki, increasingly becomes the site of the proposed resolution of reason and instinct in the figures of Tao and Zen. (We will see how deftly Suzuki negotiates this context.)

It is here again that the work of geographic reconstitution can help us break with a frequent assumption of comparative method: that it compares two constituted entities. One cannot simply say that one belongs to a Western tradition that needs to rethink itself in terms of other traditions, or, at least, one cannot *begin* here. Methodologically, rather, one has to understand how it is that the West, and China, were *already* constituted by ideas about others as part of their global subject formations and how, in turn, one's own conceptions of things like "the outside" and "China" and "the West" continue to be part of this project.[132] We might then reasonably find what Jullien speaks of as "resources" of thought that are different in different cultural formations, but we would have a clearer conception of *how* those resources formed and *why* we desire them.[133]

The lesson from Kant, *pace* Foucault, is not to understand who "we" as Western subjects of the Enlightenment are, but rather to continue to understand the complexity of the Enlightenment as a global phenomenon, one that is *constituted* by global interactions and that continues to *constitute* them. It is neither, then, about searching for other geographic thoughts that can displace our own, nor about coalescing around a single thought that can displace others. Rather, the task of enlightenment is now, as it was before Kant, a question about how to constitute global relations in such a way as to bring about both peace and plurality. Kant's answer to this question will continue to have impacts that I follow into Schiller, Hegel, and Marx. But there are also other answers, and their logics come to preoccupy later chapters.

There is one other recent criticism of Kant that I would like to briefly engage before moving on. In *A Critique of Postcolonial Reason*, Gayatri Spivak engages with the marginal references to aboriginal peoples in Kant's *Critique of the Power of Judgment*. She writes:

> I will call my reading of Kant "mistaken." I believe there are just disciplinary grounds for irritation at my introduction of "the empirical and the anthropological" into a philosophical text that slowly leads us toward the rational study of morals as such. I rehearse it in the hope that such a reading might take into account that philosophy has been and continues to be travestied in the service of the narrativization of history. My exercise may be called a scrupulous travesty in the interest of producing a

counternarrative that will make visible the foreclosure of the subject whose lack of access to the position of narrator is the condition of possibility of the consolidation of Kant's position.[134]

Here Spivak begins by accepting the split between philosophy and anthropology, although she will slowly work to show how deconstruction can bridge the two "strategically."[135] This can be done because although philosophy claims an abstraction, it is still constantly *used* in the service of imperial narratives. Because philosophy becomes anthropological and empirical in spite of itself, we had better, Spivak suggests, intervene at these levels. And what this intervention necessarily shows is that the anthropological was there all along. However, the anthropological subject—the native informant—has been "foreclosed." If the native informants were allowed to narrate this story, they would be able to speak of their human complexity that cannot be easily assimilated into Kant's philosophical system, for what that system requires is, like Rousseau's, their unthinking simplicity. Just as settler colonialism forecloses indigenous land, so does colonial philosophy foreclose indigenous subjectivity: not just by denying it, but also by taking from it.[136]

Spivak tells us earlier that she takes the term "foreclosure" from Laplanche and Pontalis's *Language of Psychoanalysis*.[137] But she doesn't tell us why she does so until a footnote a few pages later, where she discusses feminist readings of Kant. She makes this distinction: the woman is disavowed; the native informant is foreclosed. "Was it in this rift," she asks, "that the seeds of the civilizing mission of today's universalist feminism were sown?"[138] The difference between disavowal and foreclosure hinges on the difference between denial and expulsion. To be denied is to be refused recognition; to be expelled is to be expropriated. The psychoanalytic language used here, in other words, is coextensive with a political argument: recognition or redistribution? The critique of a "universalist feminism" is the critique not just of the one without the other, but of the fact that these poles have become a normative assumption about the possibilities of justice. What other ways of thinking about justice—including what other ideas of gender—might have been heard were it not for this silencing?

On these points I would agree. But where I disagree is further down in the same footnote:

> I am not suggesting that Kant's expressed views on the matter of colonialism and race, to be found . . . in relatively peripheral

texts . . . should be ignored, although their assumptions are historically interpretable as well. I am suggesting that a revised politics of reading can give sufficient value to the deployment of rhetorical energy in the margins of texts acknowledged to be central.[139]

This seems to me to displace the counternarrative to the marginalia and to take what has become canonized as "central" texts for granted.[140] Equally, it deprivileges historical interpretation in the name of rhetorical reading. What I have sought to do in this book is to raise the stakes of the counternarrative back to the level of history as a whole. Through historical reading, we can make claims similar to Spivak's, and, building on her work, we can challenge the marginalized position of these claims as well. Then what we are doing is not trespassing on disciplinary grounds through rhetorical methods. Rather, we are simply pointing out to philosophy *what it has been doing all along*. In terms of rhetoric more traditionally conceived, this reconstitution strikes me as a more powerful move.

Further, this can lead us to a clearer understanding of the relation between Kant's historical and transcendental writings. As Foucault notes, they cross over each other in essays such as "What is Enlightenment?" where Kant works to understand his present with regard to the broader structures of the universe. It is not incidental that this happens in the form of the essay. As Adorno writes (and perhaps Foucault echoes):

> Hence the essay challenges the notion that what has been produced historically is not a fit object of theory. The distinction between a *prima philosophia*, a first philosophy, and a mere philosophy of culture that would presuppose the first philosophy and build upon it—the distinction used as a theoretical rationalization for the taboo on the essay—cannot be salvaged.[141]

A deeper investigation of the ways in which Kant's anthropology informs his aesthetic and philosophical theories will have to be left to thinkers better versed in his three *Critiques* than I am—work, I note, that has already begun.[142] But if the analysis I have laid out in this book is correct, then the presuppositions of that study will need to flip. In other words, they will not ask "How does Kant's work on global cultures fit within his critical system?" but rather "How is Kant's critical system a response to the problem posed by global cultures?" In other words, how might we understand Kant's research into the universal structures of the mind as, in part, an attempt to secure the foundations of knowledge in the face of the world's "manifoldedness"?

And in fact Kant himself suggests this in the first edition of the *Critique of Pure Reason* when he makes political analogies for the philosophical positions of dogmatism and skepticism based on his sense of history. Metaphysics, the former queen of the sciences, has now been exiled by science and mathematics. Kant wants to restore the rule of metaphysics not "by mere decrees," but rather as a new body of legislated "eternal and unchangeable laws" so that *we* can make "rightful claims" about reason and knowledge.[143] The problem with metaphysics thus far has been its failure to assert its right legitimately:

> In the beginning, under the administration of the dogmatists, her rule was despotic. Yet because her legislation still retained traces of ancient barbarism, this rule gradually degenerated through internal wars into complete anarchy; and the skeptics, a kind of nomads who abhor all permanent cultivation of the soil, shattered civil unity from time to time.[144]

Proper metaphysics, in other words, does not proceed ahistorically. It arrives at a certain moment in human history—a moment in which the skeptics (the "savages") are brought under the domain of its system. The story of metaphysics that Kant tells here, in 1781, is not so far from the versions of history that he will essay a few years later and that he had been teaching in his anthropology courses for nearly a decade. Whatever one makes of this fact, it seems safe to say at the very least that even Kant's most seemingly abstract thoughts had a relationship to the question of how to live on this shared globe.

3

Aesthetic Visions of the Global Self
Schiller and Senghor

In the previous chapter I began an argument that modern dialectical thinking has its roots in Rousseau's misreading of an anecdote about colonial trading practices in Guadeloupe. This chapter continues this argument by showing how Rousseau's ideas passed from Kant to Friedrich Schiller. Schiller adds to this story an argument for how aesthetics functions as a way of creating the new, global subject that Rousseau and Kant had envisioned. In brief, it is a variation on the same story we have seen: primitive instinct confronts alienated reason, and the two must be reconciled. Schiller's innovation is to suggest that aesthetics is the path toward this reconciliation. Schiller's aesthetics is a powerful method for understanding the movement of history. The trouble is when his thinking, like Kant's, presumes its capacity to explain the whole world and, in so doing, forces others into unbearable identities within its scheme. The section on Schiller thus closes with some philosophical critiques of the overextension of his work, especially those by Jacques Rancière and Gayatri Spivak.

While these are powerful critiques, I argue that they are limited inasmuch as they do not take up the anthropological origins of Schiller's thinking. Although he does not address Schiller directly, I suggest that Léopold Senghor ingeniously reimagined Schiller's global aesthetics from precisely this position. Building on recent studies of Négritude, I show how Senghor did not merely claim that the instinct Schiller wanted to incorporate was a good in itself. Rather, I show how he argued that it was *rational* in itself. Against Schiller's global aesthetics, then, Senghor posited a pluralist global aesthetics whose insights have not yet fully been appreciated. The bulk of this chapter is dedicated to unpacking the complexity of Senghor's vision.

Schiller: A Universal Aesthetics of the Global Self

Friedrich Schiller's *Letters on the Aesthetic Education of Man* (1795) mark a key moment in the history of the practices of the global self. Schiller not only systematizes the dialectical method that we have seen developing in Rousseau and Kant, but he also adds a new category—"aesthetic education"—into the realm of practices.[1] Some Schiller scholars have noted that Schiller's letters rely on what Frederick Beiser calls a "protracted and complex anthropological argument that art constitutes the crucial transitional stage between natural and civilized man," but none, to my knowledge, has really unpacked the significance of this fact for not only Schiller's work, but for contemporary aesthetic theory as well.[2] To understand Schiller's work, its place in the history of practices of the global self, and its continued relevance, we will have to more closely follow this anthropological argument across his essayistic letters. We will see that Schiller synthesizes Rousseau's conjectural method into his theory of aesthetics, just as Kant did for his theory of political enlightenment.

Schiller's *Letters on the Aesthetic Education of Man* emerge out of a long history of Franco-German attempts to make philosophy adequate to the tasks of global life. Rousseau and Kant, as we have seen, sought to understand how philosophy needed to change if it wanted to properly address the conditions of global contact created by European colonialism. They also sought to create subjectivities that incorporated their (often very problematic) beliefs about those they called primitive. The basic idea was that there were peoples still unalienated and immersed in nature in the Americas, whereas Europeans had lost their immediate contact with reality through arts and civilization. And yet, at the same time, it was deemed necessary to preserve the values of the arts of civilization and also to negate what was unruly about human nature. This sublation of nature was central to the formation of Schiller's aesthetic. We can see this process beginning in Rousseau when he writes, for example, that his student Emile should become "a savage made to inhabit cities."[3] We find it again when Kant says that everyone, globally, needs to struggle for progress "until perfect art again becomes nature, which is the ultimate goal and the moral vocation of the human species."[4] And it reappears when Schiller claims that art and education need to be combined into an aesthetic education in order to create these new, global subjectivities. He will eventually give this process a formula: "They are what we were; they are what we should become again."[5]

As Wilkinson and Willoughby, Schiller's English translators, note in their helpful and extensive introduction, the letters are meant to work on the reader more as an essay than as a treatise; that is, they are meant to replicate a kind of experience of insight, hesitation, and doubt, leading us not to a resolution, but to the yearning to become the kind of subjects described by their closing lines: "men make their way, with undismayed simplicity and tranquil innocence, through even the most involved and complex situations, free . . . of the compulsion to infringe the freedom of others in order to assert their own."[6] We should notice immediately that the rough outlines of Rousseau's desire inform this concluding goal of Schiller's: to maintain tranquil simplicity ("savages") in the heart of chaotic complexity ("cities"). This individual arises through an "aesthetic modulation of the psyche," which is not achieved and then held, but rather continually renewed in "the aesthetic life."[7] It is in many ways a beautiful dream for the kinds of subjects we might become, and we should not too quickly dismiss Schiller's vision, even if we will have to call into question the geographical basis that informs it and the universalizing pretentions that overwhelm it.

Part of Schiller's aim in the text is to understand freedom, as both a political right and a modality of the soul. His concern is that although political rights can guarantee a certain kind of freedom, they may do so by compulsion, as Kant argued. Schiller points to the obvious contradiction here of a freedom guaranteed by non-freedom. To resolve the contradiction requires of him no less than a history of the human species. For what he wants to understand is not only compulsion by the state, but also the compulsion by desirous nature that the state is meant to suppress. He wants humans who are determined neither by sense nor by formal laws, but who, through the making of themselves in the aesthetic life, become noncompelled subjects who still follow the necessity of the rational law. This is the meaning of freedom for Schiller.

Central to his construction of this idea of freedom is his presupposition that there exists a primordial human state in which we are subjected to sense-impressions and instinctual drives—what he will come to call the "sensuous drive."[8] This drive originates in the famous "state of nature," although Schiller, like Kant and Rousseau before him, is insistent that there are no peoples who really live in this state and that it is only a regulative idea by which to understand human progress.[9] And yet, as with his forebears, it is clear that he has been influenced by empirical and anthropological accounts and that he is telling an evolutionary, conjectural history. This is perhaps most obvious in letter XXVI when he argues, "If we inquire of history, however far back, we find that [the signs of 'the savage's entry upon humanity'] are the same in all races which have emerged from the slavery of the animal condition: delight in semblance, and a propensity to ornamentation and play."[10] Thus in Schiller's evolutionary narrative, what brings the human being out of the natural condition is beauty. This is different from Rousseau's account of perfectibility, or Kant's notion of unsocial sociability, or the recognition by an "other" that one finds in Hegel. But in all of these, we can see that central to the *episteme* of this philosophical era is the explanation, based on a combination of conjecture and colonial anthropology, of how we left the state of nature.

Once lifted out of this state, another impulse—incipient but hitherto undeveloped—comes to the fore. Schiller will call this the "formal drive."[11] It is from the formal drive that our universal morality develops. Beauty will perform its second role here: it will lead this abstract morality back to our sense-impressions. As Schiller puts it:

> In order to be adequate to this twofold task, melting beauty will therefore reveal herself under two different guises. First, as tranquil form, she will assuage the violence of life, and pave the way which leads from sensation to thought. Second, as living image, she will arm abstract form with sensuous power, lead concept back to intuition, and law back to feeling. The first of these services she renders to natural man, the second to civilized man.[12]

The central role of beauty in this treatise on beauty, then, is inextricably tied to a vision of primitive life as an unthinking condition that must be transformed and incorporated into "civilized man."

There can be no doubt that this double structure of beauty is at the heart of Schiller's text. This statement, after all, matches up almost line for line with the programmatic description he gives in letter III. It's worth looking at that earlier statement in full as well, not only because it underlines so clearly Schiller's program, but also because it hints at the central solution that he will develop; namely, sublation, the dialectical movement of preserving, canceling, and raising up into a third term. Schiller writes:

> It would, therefore, be a question of abstracting from man's physical character its arbitrariness, and from his moral character its freedom; of making the first conformable to laws, and the

second dependent upon sense-impressions; of removing the former somewhat further from matter, and bringing the latter somewhat closer to it; and all this with the aim of bringing into being a third character which, kin to both the others, might prepare the way for a transition from the rule of mere force to the rule of law, and which, without in any way impeding the development of moral character, might on the contrary serve as a pledge in the sensible world of a morality as yet unseen.[13]

Again, what is at stake here is the idea that human progress requires a dialectical relationship between "primitive" and "civilized" ways of being. The dialectical process described here is not abstract; it is deeply imbricated in the violence of colonial history. Schiller is explicit: the savage must be made civilized, just as the civilized must use their contact with the savage to return themselves to sense. In this process, both disappear, and a "third character" will prepare the way for a new world order.

To arrive at this "third character" will require of Schiller a third drive, whose task will precisely be this work of preserving what is good, canceling out what is bad, and finding a way to combine the two together. Where all others before him have failed is in the task of finding this third drive, which Schiller will call "the play drive."[14] Schiller notes immediately that this idea of "play" needs justification. He claims that it is "fully justified by linguistic usage, which is wont to designate as 'play' everything which is neither subjectively nor objectively contingent, and yet imposes no kind of constraint either from within or from without."[15] Play is not contingent, because it has a set of rules (forms), yet it is not constraining either, because it is definitionally not bound by those rules and requires the constant creations of its actors. It thus implies a free range of the senses, but within the context of rules. Play in Schiller, then, is not frivolity, nor is it a category of leisure secured only after the partitions of modernity. Rather, it is a transhistorical human drive that embodies the two other drives and, in so doing, paves the way for their reconciliation. It is then in the aesthetic, in the "contemplation of the beautiful" where "the psyche finds itself in a happy medium between the realm of law and the sphere of physical exigency," that the human being will become most fully human, in Schiller's terms.[16] (This is all laid out in letter XV, which has been the subject of extensive engagement by Jacques Rancière, to whose work I turn below.)

It is in this context that Schiller will finally speak of his dialectical method through sublation. He argues that the problem with previous studies of beauty is that they have not understood how to use the play drive and its embodiment in the free realm of aesthetic contemplation as the means of securing the reconciliation of form and sense, or reason and instinct. Like oil and water, they can only be combined if the properties that force their separation are removed: "Since, however, both conditions remain everlastingly opposed to each other, there is no other way of uniting them except by sublating them [*sie aufgehoben werden*]."[17] The ultimate aim of this act of sublation is that the previous conditions "completely disappear [*gänzlich verschwinden*]," and a new kind of subject, who keeps only the best of the two previous conditions, emerges.[18] This will be the instinctally rational subject, who has returned art to nature and goes on to perform a continual enactment of her aesthetic education. Schiller's vision, which forms the seemingly abstract basis of the modern theory of dialectics that is so crucial for Hegel, is unthinkable without this actual, geographic vision of humanity across the colonial divide.

Moreover, for Schiller, this is the *only* path by which this can happen: "In a word, there is no other way [*es gibt keinen andern Weg*] of making sensuous man rational except by first making him aesthetic."[19] The path of the movement from sense to form to aesthetic is the only dignified path for *all* humanity. He spells this out more clearly in *On the Naïve and Sentimental in Poetry* (1795). There he gives us what we might call his formula for an aesthetic education of the global self. Speaking of "our" relation to what is natural in flora and fauna, in children, country people, and primitives, Schiller writes: "They *are* what we *were*; they are what we *should become* again." This is the formula. He explains further: "We were natural like them and our culture should lead us back to nature along the path of reason and freedom . . . *In ourselves* we see a merit which they lack but which they can either never possess, like the unreasoning, or only if they travel on the same path *as us*, like children."[20] We must incorporate them into who we are, and they must follow along the same path we have. For Schiller, as for Kant, there simply is no other way.

Schiller demonstrates this unilateral movement toward European domination of both self and world with a story about Columbus. He writes:

> The most complex tasks must be solved by the genius with undemanding simplicity and ease; the story of Columbus and the egg applies to every decision of genius. In this way alone genius justifies itself as such, by triumphing over complex art by means of simplicity. It does not proceed according to known principles but according to sudden notions and feelings; but its

sudden notions are inspirations from a god . . . *its feelings are laws for all periods and for all races of people* [*seine Gefühle sind Gesetze für alle Zeiten und für alle Geschlechter der Menschen*].²¹

We see here again that genius is the capacity for instinctual reason. It breaks with the normal flow of nature, but only to reinsert itself all the more powerfully into nature. Moreover, we see the claim of genius' universality. The allusion to Columbus and the egg seals the conquering, synthetic genius as lawgiver to all peoples. The basic story is this: Columbus is at dinner, and someone says that his sailing to the Americas was no great feat because someone else would have done it eventually. Columbus responds by asking if anyone can make an egg stand on one side. Everyone fails until Columbus smashes one side of the egg and makes it stand up. The moral is clear: it is easy to do something after genius has shown you the simple law by which it can be done. And now that we live on a shared globe, we all must follow the same (aesthetic) laws.

What is important here is that Schiller is not simply saying that this is one way to understand human life or that the aesthetic is one path to developing a kind of instinctual reason. Rather, he is saying that *this is the only way* (*es gibt keinen andern Weg*) to overcome the unbearability of our split identities and become a free subject. For Rousseau, rationality was unbearable and instinct had limits. For Kant, instinct was unbearable and rationality had limits. For Schiller, both are unbearable identities. The *only* solution is the aesthetic education that "sublates" both drives—the civilized form of the rational and the primitive instinct of the sensual. The *only* way out of the unbearable identities of either our primitive or civilized condition is the uniting of the two in such a way that their best qualities are preserved and their worst attributes are shed. And the *only* way to do it is through aesthetic play. The fact that this argument, relying on absurd ideas about human history, is at the center of this founding text of aesthetic theory is remarkably absent from the major critical engagements with Schiller today.

∾

Schiller's *Letters* are a constant reference point in contemporary discussions of aesthetic theory. Authors' engagements with Schiller range from brief invocations (T. J. Demos and Sven Lütticken) to general overviews (Peter Bürger) to declamations of his revolution in the entire field of art and politics (Jacques Rancière) to quasi-rewritings of his opus (Gayatri Spivak).²² What is remarkable across these engagements (especially in those essays concerned with global art today—Demos, Lütticken, and Spivak) is the fact that they don't engage with the anthropological argument. According to Beiser, this argument is "crucial" to the *Letters*, but all the aesthetic theorists today seem to ignore it, or, like Bürger and Rancière, invoke it without taking its origin seriously, as if the colonial imprint of the claim does not matter.[23]

We can begin to see how this geographic history could affect contemporary discussions about aesthetics by turning briefly to Peter Bürger's *Theory of the Avant-Garde*. Bürger's classic text proposed that the historical avant-garde was informed by the meaningful but tragic attempt to reunite art and life, while the neo avant-gardes of the 1950s and 1960s marked the farcical return of the same desire. Schiller is used by Bürger as the foil to the avant-garde. He argues that Schiller's theory of the aesthetic removes art from life, and that this theory of the "autonomy of art" is "a category of bourgeois society" because it is about the sensuous pleasures of one particular leisure class.[24] If only that were the case! Schiller's claims are not at all confined to a particular class, but rather are prescriptions for the entire globe. Bürger mentions Schiller's "speculative history" but then immediately states that it is not his purpose to trace his thought in its entirety.[25] Be that as it may, such "speculative histories" are themselves central to modern artists and to the entire discourse of the avant-garde, which is so drenched in primitivism and exoticism,[26] as well as more dialogic engagements across geographic spaces,[27] that to ignore it is to ignore much of the art itself.

But this is not just a problem of content; it is a *theoretical* problem as well. What Bürger does is to set up a history of art's autonomization and then diagnose the attempts to rupture this process in the name of a radical critique of bourgeois society. But the problem of bourgeois art is simply not this autonomous movement, or at least not that alone. The deep concern, the concern that no doubt speaks more pertinently to the actual "global art world" of the present, is about globalization itself. To imagine aesthetics as a theoretical practice of an isolated European bourgeois leisure class is to ignore not only the actual and often brutal history, but also the actual theoretical claims as well. What is it, after all, that drives the supposed wedge between art and life that Bürger and Schiller want so desperately to heal? To be sure, it is a context of mechanization and the division of labor that Schiller was reading about in the work of the Scottish Enlightenment.[28] But the art and life problematic also emerged at the moment when art was felt sundered from life, as instinct from reason, as self from world, because these themes became culturally and geographically coded. *There*, in the Americas, art and life are one. *There* instinct reigns supreme. *Here*, in Europe, art and life are fragmented. *Here* our instincts are vitiated. (Or, in the reverse voice of Senghor that we are approaching: *Here* emotion is a logic of life and art. *There* rationality is a logic of life and art.) Once we understand that it is because the globe itself produced the vision of the division between art and life, then we can understand why it is only in the globe that Schiller—and so many artists and writers since the nineteenth century—have imagined the healing of this rupture through new global arts. In short, Bürger's Eurocentric focus simply cannot account for the very history he seeks to tell.

This other history of aesthetics may also lead us to rethink some of the more recent innovations in aesthetic theory. In his engagement with Schiller, Jacques Rancière has produced a very different story from the one offered by Bürger. For Rancière, Schiller's model is not what the avant-gardes rebel against. Rather, the avant-garde's condition of possibility is the very regime Schiller initiates—what Rancière calls "the aesthetic regime of art." According to Rancière, the key claim of Schiller's text lies in one single conjunction: that the idea of play is capable "of bearing the whole edifice of the art of the beautiful *and* of the still more difficult art of living."[29] Rancière argues that the key to modern aesthetics is here: not in the removal of art from life, but rather in the continual reversibility of the relationship of art to life, and the autonomy and heteronomy of each: "To the extent that the aesthetic formula ties art to non-art from the start, it sets that life up between two vanishing points: art becoming mere life, or art becoming mere art."[30]

Pace Bürger, then, Rancière is claiming that the attempt to unite art and life is entirely consistent with the general modern regime of art. Also against Bürger, his claim is not that this movement between art and life is good or bad for politics per se or that the achievement of their sublation would be a good thing. Rather, he wants to understand more generally how regimes of art and politics make possible different "distributions of the sensible," that is, different ways of regulating what can be spoken, seen, and enacted.[31] The underlying goal is an ongoing practice that enables the fundamental equality of subjects, although this cannot be institutionalized in a particular form of art or governance. As Gabriel Rockhill comments, "Equality [for Rancière] . . . is an activity rather than a state of being, an intermittent process of actualization rather than a goal to be attained once and for all."[32]

There is something persuasive about this as a nonutopian goal of political action, although it runs the risk of undercutting the importance of organization and institution building. My concern here, in any case, is with how to understand this claim in relation to the geographic histories I have been unpacking. And I would propose that the "aesthetic regime," the regime concerned with the relation of art and life, is really more a subsidiary of a larger framework: what we might call in revisionist fashion the "global regime of art." My point is not that the aesthetic regime is inoperative or inaccurate, but that it is itself a response to the broader question: How do we live in this suddenly (post-1492) encompassed, incomprehensibly diverse, unbearably unequal world? How do we make sense of it? And how do we make ourselves the kinds of subjects who can make sense of it? Schiller's aesthetic education is precisely about becoming that kind of subject. So, I would say, are large swaths of modern aesthetics. The art-life relation, within this global regime, *cannot be resolved* without the type of global imagination that we find in Schiller.

My point is this: the idea of a "Western" history of art, aesthetics, or political theory not only ignores the rest of the world, but it ignores the West itself and the endless series of global connections that made it both what it was and what it wanted to be. To understand history as global history is not to deny local realities, but it is to insist that those local realities are dependent on much broader connections. The global regime is not confined to a time and place—people have always traveled and conquered—but it has been accelerated since European colonization of the globe. To understand aesthetic experience and politics within that framework opens up different ways of conceiving of the distribution of the sensible as well. Rancière's concern is with the perpetual (if often foreclosed) potential for the enactment of equality. This should lead him to be as concerned with global inequalities as with class inequalities within Europe. We might wonder, however, if Rancière's focus on a single conjunction in Schiller's work between art and life runs the risk of erasing another one: that between the worker *and* those interpellated as primitive. I have suggested that the formula of global aesthetics proposed by Schiller is "*they* are what we should become again" rather than the tying of art to non-art that Rancière nominates. The "they" in Schiller's sentence is embodied "in the customs of country people *and* the primitive world" ("*in den Sitten des Landvolks* und *der Urwelt*)."[33] Schiller's crucial "and" is thus also the one that links the customs of those who are immersed in nature as against those who are civilized. A geographic history of aesthetics would focus on this plurality of geographic inequalities both at home and abroad. It would seem that our sensibilities are still not able to understand the globe as they ought to. It would work on a redistribution of vision to both geographic histories and geographic presents. And it would also focus on the fact of plurality more generally: that Schiller's formula was but one of many offered in the modern era, and certainly not the best.

One of the more general stakes here is the fundamental equality of intelligence that is at the heart of Rancière's work. For the past few centuries, peoples outside Europe have consistently been denied this equality. It is important to supplement Rancière's trenchant critique of class politics within Europe with this more global frame: to insist on the equality of intelligences we ought to take hold of this conjunction as much as we ought to insist that gender or sexuality, or physical or mental ability, do not impinge on such equality. Ecological movements will add nature itself to this list. In such ways of thinking, the definition of intelligence itself becomes central. Because the claim is not that everything and everyone has the same kind of intelligence. It is rather that intelligence itself is plural and that all living creatures manifest it in different ways.

In two fantastic works, Rancière has demonstrated the practical ways in which humans have manifested their equality of intelligence in surprising places: illiterate peasants who taught themselves to read and activist workers who had utopian dreams and wrote "high literature."[34] I think we can profitably pair Rancière's interventions with long-standing work on racial equality, such as Anténor Firmin's 1885 text *The Equality of the Human Races*,[35] or with much of the work of contemporary anthropologists, from Claude Lévi-Strauss to Saba Mahmood and Eduardo Viveiros de Castro, who have similarly insisted on intellectual equality; again, not in the sense that everything is the same, but in the sense that everything has its own power and logic.[36] Or, as I discuss in the next section, with the revolutionary movement of Négritude, whose theorization by Senghor is one of the most fundamental refutations of Schiller's global aesthetics.

Interestingly, it is not only Euro-focused theorists like Rancière who have missed this geographic history, but also critics more directly engaged in the history of postcolonial thought. In Akeel Bilgrami's recent work on Romanticism (which germinates in M. H. Abrams's reading of Schiller and others), for example, he suggests that we add Gandhi to a list of critics "within the West" who have criticized the pretentions of the scientific Enlightenment since the seventeenth century. For Bilgrami, this means seeing Gandhi as part of a tradition of "internal" critics of the mathematization and rationalization of the world that includes radicals like Winstanley, early ecologists like Thoreau, and arts and crafts workers like William Morris.[37] To be sure, there are connections here, but at no point does Bilgrami question the idea that Gandhi is a geographic outsider to this tradition, which seems to be able to span an ocean but not a landmass. The historical record, however, suggests a more global history: Winstanley, for example, had already critiqued slavery and colonialism conjunctively in 1649, writing that "the heathens shall rise up in judgement against you," demonstrating what Linebaugh and Rediker call his movement "toward a planetary consciousness of class."[38] Why not see Winstanley, Thoreau, Morris, and Gandhi as part of this shared groping toward planetary consciousness, rather than Gandhi as an external addition to a "Western" tradition?

This question recurs for me when reading through Gayatri Spivak's *An Aesthetic Education in the Era of Globalization* (2012), whose title of course rewrites Schiller's own. Whereas in her previous work, *A Critique of Postcolonial Reason* (1999), Spivak looked at the place of globality within the philosophical texts of Kant, Hegel, and Marx, in this newer book she does not discuss the role of geography in Schiller at all. Her work shows that one does not need to take into account this geographic history to make questions of global relations today central to one's thinking. But she does raise the question of how the historical record might change were critics to do so. Most centrally, I argue here, it would mean abandoning the project of transcendental philosophy in the name of a more contingent, historical, and geographic theory of the present.

Spivak's book is a dense and difficult journey in an explicitly essayistic style that calls for an "interactive reader" to engage with its many allusions, digressions, and extensions across some five hundred pages.[39] This reader is interactive for Spivak not only in the sense that they make the connections within her own book, but also that they are willing to track down her intertexts as well. In a metamoment, she reminds us that this kind of tracking and creating of intertextuality is simply one of the tasks of a "literary academic."[40] Given the range of Spivak's references across genres, regions, and languages, her book almost seems to lead its reader to global aesthetics through a kind of pedagogic shaming: shame that you do not read as widely, as closely, in as many languages. And, given that one of Spivak's key claims in this text is that a modern aesthetic education is an education to be an active citizen, shame that you are also not doing enough![41] And fair enough, although there of course remain limits to what each of us can do, and a real question of whether or not such relentless labor is at the service of freedom, if, as Spivak quotes Marx, the precondition of freedom is the "reduction of the working day."[42] Spivak would call this, now following Gregory Bateson, a "double bind," in the sense that we must work relentlessly because capital works relentlessly, even though our goal is to undo the relentless labor forced on us by capital.[43] No wonder she tells us from the start that hers is a book written on the side of doubt against hope.[44]

Spivak and Rancière share a sense that there is a "plot" in Schiller that still constrains us. And they share as well, I think, a concern with the real intelligence of those who are marginalized. But their work is also fundamentally opposed in significant ways. For Spivak, "globalization takes place only in capital and data. Everything else is damage control." She suggests the totalizing existence of a global capital that we subjects can only "productively undo" with our doubt, our imagination, our teaching and learning.[45] And as far as I can tell, she believes in something called philosophy, a transcendental activity that delineates the structural possibilities for human thought. If so, she is earnest in calling her previous book a *Critique* in the Kantian sense and in taking seriously the idea that the empirical is an infringement on philosophy. Like Derrida, she seems to believe that the transcendental conditions of thought are never finalized. However, that very lack of finality is not a refutation of philosophy, but an instance of what Derrida himself called the "ultra-transcendental."[46]

Rancière, on the other hand, has explicitly set himself against both of these ideas. He argues that we should never see a regime as totalizing and should understand politics itself as the belief that "every situation can be cracked open from the inside, reconfigured in a different regime of perception and signification."[47] Philosophy, meanwhile, is an "accidental activity."[48] It does not seek transcendental or ultra-transcendental structures, it is not a persistent and necessary gadfly, it is not part of our ontology as beings who question. Philosophy's task, like any other structure, is simply to arrange the sensible in such a way as to continually produce the activity of equality. Perhaps the combination of Spivak's global vision with Rancière's skepticism can help us begin to find a path out of Schiller's plot. (This is some of what we will find in Senghor.)

Because Rancière views neither philosophy nor art as necessary, he takes issue with Schiller's utopian belief in a perfected, universal humankind through a perfected practice of aesthetic philosophy. Because Spivak believes in philosophy and the totalizing force of globalization, she opposes Schiller for his philosophical mistakes and his emplotment of a singular, global destiny. "If Kant's system is always about to break down under its own critical weight, Schiller smoothly moves from polarity to polarity. Today's praise of the humanities must not make this niche-marketing mistake."[49] In Spivak's vision, Kant emerges as the critical, doubting hero to Schiller's smooth movements. This reading, I think, undercuts the subtlety of Schiller's argument as well as the teleological thrust of Kant's historical writings.[50] More to the point, it gives us a vision of globalization as being something outside philosophy and does not let us see clearly what Spivak herself seeks: "the fault lines of the doing."[51] If Spivak's self-stated goal is "the persistent and shifting pursuit of the global history of the present," it is worth asking why that global history is not foregrounded in her philosophical investigations.[52] Perhaps she simply did not find it germane to the topic here or felt she had already addressed it in previous work. But part of the reason may also be that Spivak, like Derrida, puts forward deconstruction as a way of thinking that is ultra-transcendental and thus, although formed historically, ultimately applies to all of history.

The deconstructive logic comes forward in Spivak's maxim: "the task of the aesthetic education we are proposing: at all cost to enter another's text."[53] The key word here, I believe, is "text." Spivak is not calling on us to enter the "culture" of others, or their "value system" or "way of being." She is saying that we must enter "another's text," which is to say not only the "texture" of their interwoven ways of existing, but also the fundamental role that language universally plays in the construction of worlds. This, I think, goes back to Spivak's early work translating Derrida, in which she registers both a critique and an appreciation. Throughout *Of Grammatology*, Derrida criticizes writers like Lévi-Strauss and Rousseau, who practice what he calls "an ethnocentrism thinking itself as antiethnocentrism, an ethnocentrism in the consciousness of a liberating progressivism."[54] The masked ethnocentrism that Derrida follows in the book is one in which writers "constitute . . . the other as a model of original and natural goodness," largely because they lack writing, and instead have the authenticity of speech.[55]

Derrida in response will famously claim, "*il n'y a pas de hors-texte*," that is, simply put, there is no such presence or idea or history or place or people or person who is not constituted, at least in part, by text.[56] Spivak will say that "Derrida's chief concern . . . might be . . . to problematize the proper," and her admiration for this critique of ethnocentrism is noted and ongoing.[57] But, because Derrida focuses solely on how this is a part of "Western metaphysics," she notes a certain irony here: "Yet, paradoxically, and almost by a reverse ethnocentrism, Derrida insists that logocentrism is a property of the West."[58] In other words: Derrida finds a hidden ethnocentrism in the anthropological attempts to critique one's own culture, while Spivak finds a hidden ethnocentrism in Derrida's claim that only

European anthropologists do this. If there is no "*hors-texte*," there is no immediate outside to logocentrism either. Spivak is emending the translation: although nothing arrives in the full presence of its being beyond text, there are, nevertheless, multiple texts. And it is fair to say that Schiller, like Kant and Rousseau, failed to recognize that the world outside Europe was not one of pure instinct and irrationality, but rather equally one of texts and intertexts, of crossings and engagements and disagreements that was as rational—if differently rational—and ethnocentric—if differently ethnocentric—than his own. And thus, and I take this to be indicative of the deconstructive response to dialectics in general, the whole movement, the whole process by which opposites should confront and reconcile, falls apart before it even gets started, because the opposition was only imagined in the first place.

This is an incredibly powerful strategy, though, as I remark in various places in this book, I worry that it can become too powerful. For example, in an essay later in the book, Spivak speaks of Martin Luther King's call to "understand their feelings [those of one's enemies] even if we do not condone their actions" as an example of this act of entering another's text. Spivak says that this is an example of what she has called for: "Here is a setting to work of what in the secular imagination is the literary impulse: to imagine the other who does not resemble the self." However, Spivak cannot follow King's transcendental narrative, because for her all narratives are narratives, and none is transcendental (that's the meaning of the ultra-transcendental). "For the secular imagination, that transcendental narrative is, I repeat, a narrative, singular and unverifiable." What King's call possibly enables, Spivak tells us, is for "the probable" (our imagination of why someone might act as they do) to overcome "that which has been possible" (that which we have been able to imagine until now). Thus King's transcendental vision is subsumed within the ultra-transcendental. For Spivak this means that the narrative arc toward justice—secured for King by God—has no verifiable anchoring in the world.[59]

While I would personally tend to agree with Spivak, and while I want to fully register the power of her critique and how it overcomes some of the failures of Schiller, I think there are reasons to wonder about the limits of deconstruction here. While there may be an infinite plurality of texts, it seems, in the end, they can *only* be texts. While I would not exactly deny that there is textuality everywhere, I would equally say that text itself is made up of the things it is not: of silence, of rhythm, of the cry (as Levinas had said in response to Derrida[60]), or other imaginations than we have yet imagined. In terms of ways of responding to Schiller's global aesthetics, an option other than deconstruction has been imagined in precisely this way in the work of Léopold Senghor.

Senghor: A Radically Pluralist Aesthetics of the Global Self

The past few years have witnessed a resurgence of interest in the work of Léopold Sédar Senghor. The philosopher, essayist, poet, and politician had long faded from popularity based on assumptions of his racial essentialism and mixed tenure as president. Today, the picture is more nuanced, as even critical scholars present an appreciation of the colonial context, the limits of what was possible in that era, and the contributions that Senghor managed to make regardless.[61] Recent publications by Souleymane Bachir Diagne (translated from the French)[62] and Gary Wilder have further enabled the discussion by offering new visions of Senghor's writings, arguing that he makes not just a limited intervention in his own time, but also a major contribution to *global thought* into the present.[63] Without taking sides per se in the ongoing debate, I move in the same direction as Diagne and Wilder because their arguments have convinced me that there are underappreciated merits in Senghor's work to "essay" Négritude.[64] In this section, I build on their work to argue that Senghor revised the notion of global aesthetics by at once showing the limits of Schiller's model and proposing a different aesthetico-political vision of global pluralism.[65]

In thinking Senghor within the global history I have outlined so far, I am engaging his work in a way aligned with Wilder's positioning of him, alongside Aimé Césaire, within the critical theory tradition.[66] Wilder writes: "The point is not to reduce their thinking to continental or hexagonal parameters nor speciously to evaluate or legitimate it by placing it alongside canonical works. It is, rather, to use their work and acts to rethink, or unthink, the supposedly European parameters of modern thought."[67] In his writing, Wilder shows illuminating links between the two authors and figures ranging from Kant and Mazzini to Benjamin and Derrida. My aim is to extend these comparisons by showing how these Négritude authors are part of the long-standing tradition of global thought that I have thus far traced in this book. More specifically, as I have shown how fundamental false views of the peoples of Africa and the Americas were to the *conceptual* development of modern thought, I argue in this section that Senghor's rewriting of African ways of knowing was absolutely central not only to developing "other" modes of critical, global thinking, but, moreover, to challenging the terms on which earlier global thought had occurred.

This shifts slightly from Wilder's concerns. In his book, for example, he uses Kant's cosmopolitanism as an example of a kind of non-national thinking that is a possible precedent for Senghor's federalism.[68] I would not deny this, but, as I argue in the previous chapter, I think it is equally important to recall that Kant's vision was formed based on problematic views about peoples outside Europe. His federation was not with "primitives"; it was against them. I thus find it more apposite to describe Senghor's implicit critique of Schiller's vision by refuting his ascription of pure instinct to peoples outside Europe. At this level of engagement, then, my work shares something with Donna Jones, who has written about the "complex, constitutive relation between vitalism and racialism" as she traces the relation between Senghor and the vitalist philosophy of Henri Bergson.[69] I do not, for reasons outlined in part below, entirely agree with Jones's conclusions about Senghor (or necessarily Bergson), but I do share her interest in the questions of how the racial discourses of the history of philosophy are at the heart of global thinking from writers around the world in "complex, constitutive" ways.

Let me be clear at the outset that I share with critics of Négritude some suspicion about how these ideas were articulated by Senghor and Césaire. But I do think it is worth taking seriously their claim about cultural and racial differences because we have to remember that they were responding to a history of *global modern self-making* that had denied the value of these differences. While for Emerson, as we will see for example, it was thus more important to criticize his culture, for Senghor and others it was necessary to build up theirs. Négritude was not just necessary as a revindication of black humanity, then. It was necessary as a rewriting of a philosophical canon that refused (and continues to refuse) to acknowledge that mixed forms of global thinking were not just excisable and regrettable remarks by great philosophers, but part of the constitution of the very ideas through which they understand the world and their place in it. This was, as I argue with Schiller above, true for the foundation of modern aesthetics. Overcoming this global tradition (not just "Western metaphysics") thus meant challenging the cultural assumptions of this philosophical history head-on.[70]

On my reading, aesthetics serves a dual purpose in Senghor. First, it intervenes in the discourse of philosophical aesthetics initiated by Schiller by reconceptualizing the idea of primitive instinct. Whereas Schiller had argued that primitivism needed to be incorporated into a new, global universal ("they are what we were; they are what we should become again"), Senghor suggested that this dialectical scheme was based on a misunderstanding of the "contributions [*apports*]" of non-European cultures. In his complex understanding of cultural dynamics, to which I return, Senghor posited that different cultures worked out different potentials for humanity as their dominant norms. Senghor agrees that post-Cartesian Europeans and Africans exist in the world differently, but he eliminates the hierarchy between these ways of being. What Schiller misread as pure instinct was, according to Senghor, simply a different kind of reason, which he alternatively calls "intuitive reason" (after Bergson), "touch-reason," and "embrace-reason."[71] I explore this frequently maligned and misunderstood idea below, but the main point is that Senghor, by valuing two different kinds of approaches to the world, insists not on their sublation but on their mutual cultivation. Rather than deconstructing aesthetics, as Spivak does, or neglecting its global formations, as Rancière and Bürger do, Senghor pluralizes it.

I thus read him, as I do other figures throughout this book, as responding to global conditions in an attempt to overcome unbearable identities. Senghor, to be sure, frequently veers into a language of an encased African identity. Such identities are unbearable in the dual way we have already seen: they force people and peoples into a singular mode of identification that will inevitably misrecognize their residual attributes, and they cannot in fact bear either the facts or needs of a complex world. *However*, as recent scholarship has insisted, this language in Senghor is more complicated than it first appears. His work in fact makes available a set of aesthetic practices and modes of being for the global self *through* his essayistic language of identity.[72] Once the pluralistic substratum of Senghor's thinking is understood, we can see that he sought to overcome unbearability through a unique version of what I have called radical pluralism.

Thus, although the aim of this section is to explore Senghor's aesthetics as a radically pluralist response to our global condition, there is also a meta-argument at stake. Throughout this book, I have questioned how contemporary theory tends to view writers through the polarity of deconstruction and dialectics (represented in this chapter by Spivak's writing on Schiller). In this framework, one either shows how the perpetual instability of mutually constitutive form-contents creates the nonteleological movement of our lives, or one argues that that instability is part of an evolving progress toward ever more universal norms. In this duality, pluralism, as a philosophy that can embrace both angles (showing how, for example, some things progress while others do not), is entirely neglected or treated as an insufficient deconstruction (as we can see with writing on Senghor), or a stalled dialectic (as we will see with Emerson). In speaking of radical pluralism—that is, again, a pluralism of all entities that maintains a radical politics through a critique of unbearable impositions—I have sought to show the importance and meaning of thinkers like Senghor who offer another vision. In his writings, as we will see, deconstruction and dialectics are both utilized as part of a broader, radically pluralist strategy of understanding the possibilities for the global self.[73]

This pluralization of aesthetics in turn causes a transformation of the political dimensions of aesthetic thinking in a global frame. Schiller's aesthetics moves from the sublation of the individual soul to the political lawgiver for all mankind. Senghor, meanwhile, moves from a pluralistic soul, connected to the universe and others in different ways, with different logics, to a belief in the ever unfolding possibilities for how to make human communities. After the Second World War, this took the concrete—if unrealized—possibility of a "decentralized, interdependent, plural, and transnational" egalitarian federation between France and its former colonies.[74] But the point for my analysis is less about the specific form that Senghor's ideas took and more about the fact that his revision of human life led him to imagine different possibilities for how humans could share the world together. As we have seen, the ideas of Rousseau, Kant, and Schiller led them to propose very specific universal forms of government. Senghor's understanding of the plurality that constituted existence led him to envision plural possibilities.

Senghor is of course most famous in literary and philosophical circles for his promulgation—along with Aimé Césaire, Suzanne Césaire, Léon Damas, Jean Nardal, and Paulette Nardal—of the concept and practice of Négritude. Senghor periodizes his own definition of the word. In 1962, for example, he wrote that it was originally (in the 1930s) designed clearly in opposition to Europe: "the communal warmth, the image-symbol, and the cosmic rhythm which instead of dividing and sterilizing [as in Europe], unified and made fertile."[75] Later, perhaps in response to Jean-Paul Sartre's claim that Négritude would eventually be surpassed in the universal dialectic of class (to which I return), he will give it the more economic definition of "the sum total of the values of the civilization of the African world."[76] (Such a definition, it often goes unnoticed, implies a multiplicity of values condensed into a unifying term.) He would also add, at various moments, a third possibility: that Négritude was the "concrete manner, for each black person and for each black people, to live life as Black."[77] Négritude was thus a specific expression, a general set of values, and a means of constant adaptation to a changing world from a group of people who had been historically formed as "black."

To say that Senghor's conception refers to "historical formation" is to deny a certain essentialist way of reading his work. I largely agree with Diagne that Senghor in fact exhibits a "strategic essentialism" and that "the discourse of hybridity is always at work, rendering fluid the identities on display."[78] I would say this in a slightly different vocabulary, however, one that I have used throughout this book. (Senghor notes the importance of "enriching our vocabulary, which is to say, our conceptual arsenal."[79]) Instead of strategic essentialism, I speak of strategic partialism, and instead of always fluid identities, I speak of radical pluralities that manifest in shifting parts. The point of this shift in vocabulary, as the reader will hopefully see with Senghor and later in greater depth with Emerson and Du Bois, is that it allows us to make sense of cultural norms in the midst of the flux of life (be that Senghorian rhythm or modern American neoliberalism) without collapsing into the language of essence. At the same time, it reminds us that whenever we speak of such an element, we are in no way speaking of an essence, but only making a claim about a part of an evolving plural formation, which we may seek (and struggle) to partialize otherwise.

Senghor did not quite have this vocabulary, but he wrote so frequently of history and change and cultural transformation that the critical insistence on his essentialism is at times surprising. Diagne, again, puts it succinctly: Senghor "is a philosopher of mixture [*métissage*] at least as much as of Négritude."[80] Or, even more, he is a philosopher of how Négritude is a strategic *partialization* of the *métissage* that created the continent of Africa. Thus, for example, he begins his 1947 essay on "Black Africa" with the following: "A mixture of pygmies in the Guinean and Equatorial forests, of Semitic-Hamites in the Sudanese plains, the black-African does not fail to present a remarkable unity under their great somatic and cultural diversity."[81] The first word in French here is *métissé*, mixed. Mixture is the foundation of what it means to be a black African. This mixing produces tremendous diversity, and this diversity produces various effects, some of which, Senghor argues—rightly or wrongly—form a specific way of inhabiting the world (a "sum total" of "values" and variable means of comportment in a raced and racist world). Before we explore more specifically how that particular mode of inhabitation manifests, it is worth exploring in more detail how Senghor understands cultural diversity. Although Senghor was not a builder of systems, I do think that a system of thought emerges through his writings, at least around these questions of cultural diversity. I would schematically describe it as follows.

First, there is what Leo Apostels calls a "pluralistic energetism" at the base of reality.[82] This energetism is described as a "network of diverse forces" that Senghor defines as "the expression of virtualities encased [*enfermées*] in God." These expressions result in things, to be sure, but "all things, in themselves, are nodes of more basic forces." They result *not* from the expression of an essence, but from the "dialogue" of these elements. This is a dialogue both internal to things as they form through multiplicities, and external to them as they form in relation to other cohered multiplicities.[83] A different vocabulary, as we will see, yields a similar distinction between conventional and ultimate reality in Suzuki's Buddhism.

This process that happens on the level of individual elements also happens at the level of cultures. Diagne points to a key passage in Senghor's essay "The Negro-African Aesthetic" (1956). In the conclusion of that essay, Senghor concedes that some may say that the values that he ascribes to African cultures can be found in many cultural spaces. He readily admits this. It makes sense within his understanding because "[e]ach people reunites, in its image [*en son visage*], the diverse traits of the human condition." But, Senghor continues, the specific "equilibrium" that resulted in the "despotism of rhythm" is unique to "Negro-African" culture.[84] Diagne comments astutely: "What constitutes originality . . . is not a specific feature that would belong solely and exclusively to one race but, rather, a certain 'equilibrium,' let us say a certain ratio,[85] between various features that can be found everywhere because together they make up the human condition." This results in a theory of what constitutes culture: "Different cultures, then, will be characterized by different ratios between the same features that they combine in separate ways."[86]

Senghor puts it equally economically a few years later using a simile that further clarifies the connection between individual and cultural ontology: "Like every man, each civilization possesses, along with its traits, all the values of the human condition. But, faithful to its climate, to its past, to its people, it has only cultivated a few."[87] This is radical pluralism: there are a great many attributes to the world, all of which we are connected to, but not all of which we tap into. Individuals and cultures are plural within themselves and in their relation to others. They in turn generate a predominate mode, but that predominate mode is always shifting, layered, and available to others. Senghor writes: "Nature has done well" by arranging it such that "each people, each race, each continent would cultivate, with a particular dilection, certain virtues of Man."[88] Senghor's remarks here are a revision of Kant's geographic history. For Kant, humans had scattered so as to gain dominion over more territory, but all that they cultivated there was new land, not their souls.[89] Senghor sees that he can rewrite this racialist history by arguing that different human groups developed different aspects of the human condition.

This vision of culture thus does not at all mean that cultures are complete and everlasting or that they lack differences within themselves. This internal difference, again, occurs both at the individual and cultural levels: "We realize that, even in Europe, humans are all different from each other, and that there is not *the Civilization*, but several civilizations, born of the crossing of many influences: history, language, race, geography . . ."[90] This *crossing* is fundamental. These civilizations come into being, like all things, through a dialogue both internal and external. In a 1976 lecture, Senghor schematizes this by offering two basic principles for understanding the history of humanity: first, "after the appearance of *homo sapiens*, two races or two peoples in contact have always mixed with each other"; second, "every great civilization is a [result of] cultural mixture."[91]

Senghor traces this latter idea of the fundamental fact of mixture to two experiences in his life. First, to his studies with Paul Rivet (ethnologist and founder of the *Musée de l'Homme*) in the 1930s, to whom he credits the idea that all great civilizations are the result of the crossing of peoples.[92] Second, when Senghor was a prisoner of war in Germany during the Second World War, this message came home with terrifying force. With some free time in the midst of the horror, Senghor read whatever he could. Reading through the classics, he noticed that the Greeks, "from Homer to Strabo," offered eulogies of the " 'Ethiopians,' which is to say, the Blacks." He realized that the " 'miracle' of Greek civilization was not that of the Indo-European spirit, but rather that of the biological mixing between Prehellenics and Hellenics; [it was] above all the miracle of cultural mixing." If Senghor had not fully absorbed Rivet's message at this point, the context of this new reading brought it home: "This discovery, remade in the face of Nazism, helped me transform my life, to reorient myself, little by little, towards the theory of cultural mixing as the ideal of civilization."[93] Even though this reorientation came relatively early in Senghor's life (he would live and work for nearly another six decades), the shift in his views may explain in part why he is so often viewed as an essentialist—even though he kept reformulating Négritude throughout his life, readers still hear the original 1930s formulation. (And even this, as we shall see, is more complicated than it appears.)

Senghor gave something of a formula for this reorientation in his speech "Everyone Must Be Mixed in Their Own Fashion" (1975). He tells his audience that he has "simply paraphrased" Goethe's line "Everyone must be Greek in their own fashion, but they must be Greek."[94] Later (1981) he will say that he has "translated [what] Goethe's spirit told him." This takes a more specific form: "Everyone must be a cultural mixture, living the symbiosis of five continents, of the sensibility and of the will, of discursive and intuitive reason."[95] Again, Senghor clearly does not call for sublation or deconstruction but for symbiosis: living side by side in beneficial interaction. The fact that Senghor calls this a "spiritual translation" or "simple rephrasing" is significant. He is not saying that whereas Goethe said we all need to be Greek, he is breaking with this Eurocentrism and positing the need for mixture. He is, I think, being more subversive still: he is saying that Eurocentrism is a lie, that "to be Greek" is already to be mixed. Long before Martin Bernal's *Black Athena* (1987), after all, French (Rivet), American (Frank M. Snowden, Du Bois), Senegalese (Cheikh Anta Diop), and other historians had noted that Hellenic Greece was a cultural hybrid, a mixture, just as Senegal was. Thus, another way of saying that one must be Greek in one's own way is to say that one must be mixed in one's own way.

But this question of mixture in Senghor and Goethe is not about a generalized hybridity. It also refers (as Senghor makes explicit in the 1981 "translation") to the fact of doubleness, to the need of combining multiple aspects in one's self. In fact, Senghor had noted this as early as 1949 in an homage to Goethe, who, he tells his audience, taught him to overcome his youthful and defiant Négritude and embrace the multiplicities of the earth. Goethe taught Senghor to seek "the perfect equilibrium"—the same word he uses to explain what defines a culture—"between two complementary values, the heart and the head, the instinct and the imagination, the real and the accomplished [*le fait*]."[96]

Senghor is not the only one in this history to engage with Goethe's ideas of doubleness. Goethe will later influence Emerson and Du Bois with the famous lines:

> You only know one driving force, / and may you never seek to know the other! / Two souls, alas! reside within my breast, / and each is eager for a separation: / in throes of coarse desire, one

grips / the earth with all its senses; / the other struggles from the dust / to rise to high ancestral spheres.⁹⁷

I discuss the idea of what will come to be called "double consciousness" at length when interpreting Emerson and Du Bois. They responded to Faust's lament by propounding another form of double consciousness, one that Senghor also sees: the possibility that cultural development would mean the possibility of *alternating* between these movements rather than having them tear the soul asunder or trying forcefully to reconcile them into a new whole (as Schiller had done). What Goethe teaches, once translated, is not just the fact of mixture, but the fact of mixing in a specific way, one that tarries with the dual tendencies to the earth and to the stars that result within all cohered entities.

What this will mean for Senghor is a particular way of understanding the relationship between race, culture, and ideals. Thus, "[t]he true culture is rooting [*enracinement*] and uprooting [*déracinement*]. Rooting down to the deepest depths of one's birth land . . . But also uprooting: opening to the rain and sun, to the contributions [*apports*] of foreign civilizations."⁹⁸ This desire for both rootedness and expansion is the movement against which Faust cries out. The possibility of a positive form of this back-and-forth movement is what Senghor is essaying toward. And he seems to find it in the idea of a nonessentialist race-thinking that is committed to cross-cultural and cross-racial engagements. This may be signaled by a pun in these lines between root (*racine*) and race (*race*). Thus Senghor is insistent here, as always: he is not giving up on his claims about Négritude. Rather, he is learning to see Négritude as one possible offering in a world that requires both particular values and universal connections.

To summarize where we are in explicating Senghor's philosophy: there is a universal, plural energy that manifests as objects, beings, and cultures that are formed through an internal dialogue that is itself part of an ongoing external dialogue. The resulting formed entities are coherent and semiclosed, which is to say that we can define their dominant and residual attributes even if we must acknowledge that they are always taking part in ongoing processes of mixture and transformation. Because "radical" is another word for roots, this is another way of naming radical pluralism: the process of simultaneously engaging in one's own plurality and opening up in a fallibilistic, engaged manner to the pluralities that constitute other individuals and cultures.

Just as this movement of alternation differs from dialectics, so it is something other than deconstruction. Consider in this context a "deconstructive" version of the same claim that "to be Greek is to be mixed," which we find in Simon Critchley's essay "Black Socrates?"[99] In an engaged reading and conversation with then recent work in postcolonial theory (Said, Gilroy, Bernal, and Bhabha), Critchley accepts the basic claim that history is the history of hybridity. This claim, he suggests, shares the basic contours of Derrida's philosophy, in which what is supposedly "outside" is shown time and again to constitute the given entity.[100] Critchley posits: "On a deconstructive account, then, any attempt to interpret tradition and culture in terms of a desire for unity, univocity and purity must be rigorously undermined in order to show how this desire is always already contaminated by that which it attempts to resist and exclude. If deconstruction has a sociology, then it is a sociology of impurity, of contamination."[101] This leads him to three basic concluding points: we all operate out of particular traditions; these traditions are never "pure" but rather always the result of relations; there is no "pure" outside that can save us.[102] He offers instead a vision of philosophy as the study of "a series of constructed, contingent, invented and possible non-narratable contrapuntal ensembles."[103] This all seems to me to largely align with Senghor, and its vocabulary may avoid the problems of his presumed essentialism. However, this loss of "essentialism" is achieved at a cost: the essay is missing a specific understanding of what, exactly, those "contrapuntal ensembles" are, or how they might interact. Instead, Critchley concludes his essay by asking if philosophy will find its "future flourishing" in the discourse of hybridity.[104] Hybridity in itself thus becomes the sole *value* of the essay, and Critchley himself quickly comes to doubt this value in a postscript. Imperialism and racial capitalism, after all, are as hybrid formations as anything else. Hybridity is a good value for resisting racist discourse, but not so good for resisting other forms of domination.[105] What is lacking, in Critchley's estimation, is a "*critical* or *utopian* moment."[106] Beyond this, I would say, what is lacking is a sense of the plural values that might emerge from such hybridity. Without an account of this (which is what pluralism should provide), it is easy to get stuck in an unsatisfactory paean to hybridity for hybridity's sake.

It is not my contention that deconstruction as such lacks such a moment, or a potential. Indeed, I think it is quite clear (as we have seen from Spivak and Critchley, and will see with Mbembe below) that the foremost practitioners of deconstruction are always aware of how the act of disassembling also results in the assembling of something new. The question is—as Critchley puts it—whether that something new is simply a way of being that has become self-conscious about deconstruction. If so, that is a value in itself, and an important one. But there are other values, other ways of seeing and being, that can be combined with this deconstructive understanding. In other words, even as it does the incredibly valuable work of pulling apart claims to mastery, deconstruction tends to reinscribe that very work as a discourse of mastery, about which it, in turn, may have doubts.[107] The false hope of the West must be deconstructed so that some new possibility may arise, but, at the same time, the appeal to some insurgent other who would redeem us must be deconstructed. So, in turn, must the sense of generalized hybridity that such a situation would inevitably lead to. Deconstruction is undoubtedly valuable in its honesty and precision, but perhaps limited in its relentlessness. Senghor (and radical pluralism more generally) offers us a way to think about traditions in terms that combine deconstructive awareness with further elements.

As mentioned above, we share with deconstruction the insistence that constituted entities have been made through what they appear to exclude. And the philosophical language of Derrida and his critics may help explain this position to those who are put off by Senghor's religious explanations. Hence, deconstruction may be a part of a radical pluralism. But rather than focusing just on the undoing of opposites, we learn to move between two truths: the deconstructive process of dissolution, and an empirical reality of entities—humans, paper, computers, cultures. This deconstructive process, just like radical pluralism, may itself someday disappear, or we may find a way of thinking beyond it, and this is why I resist the gesture of making it an "ultra-transcendental." As I said in the introduction, even if throughout this book I suggest alternations and radical pluralism as potential ways of thinking to universalize, I do so as a strategic partialization of ontology. We then accept this separation and learn from it in a movement of rooting and uprooting. (Emerson will call this the movement of "unhanding" and "alternation.") In this rooting and uprooting, we produce specific individuals and cultures that, while never erasing their fundamental plurality, still bring forth specific and definable values and ways of being.

These values are then to be exchanged globally in what Senghor, following Césaire, calls the "rendez-vous of giving and receiving."[108] This should not be understood as some banal form of exchange based on the general goodness of all cultures. Senghor was clear: "I do not believe in congenitally good or bad races or nations. They are all more or less rich in qualities and faults."[109] Senghor admits this about Négritude itself.[110] Indeed, the *limits* of any culture to exhaust the possibilities of being in fact bring about the need for pluralism in the first place. The point, it would seem, is less to create some final, perfected world than it is to use the available elements of the current world to create new civilizations from new mixtures.[111] Senghor frequently spoke of this as the "civilization of the universal." I take this to be a pun: both a civilization based on the universal contributions of equal groups of humans[112] and an act of "civilizing" the universal itself by stripping it of the kind of pretentions that we have seen in Schiller. Senghor invokes this pun when he says the "new civilization [will be] more civilized because total and social."[113]

"Total" does not, as I understand it, refer to some finality, but rather to a grouping of human virtues in a planetary way that has not yet been imagined. Senghor is fully aware that "a collective, planetary madness would not be any less a madness."[114] Indeed, as many critics of globalization have noted, going planetary can be much worse. What would come on the other side of this civilized universal is impossible to predict. All Senghor or others could say is that we must remain vigilant about how we are creating this new world. Furthermore, Senghor and Césaire are both explicit that this act of "giving and receiving" cannot be achieved by the presumptive enforcement of one culture's universality onto another—not only because it is ethically wrong, but also because it can only result in a degradation on both accounts. As Senghor put it, one can force assimilation, destroy what is good about another culture, and perhaps even remove its faults, but "I doubt that they can, in this way, give us [*nous donner*] their qualities." Rather, "one risks turning us into mere, pale French copies."[115] Senghor issued a similar warning in 1954 as part of his argument for an Afro-French federation against the expanding American empire. Otherwise, he warned, "[i]n a few years perhaps Africa will be ripe for American propaganda. It would be the triumph of American policy in Africa and in the overseas territories. It would indeed be the end of France and the triumph of capitalism and a racialism which would invariably lead us into war, to the destruction, that is, of the planet and the end of the hope of man."[116] The risk here is that the erasure of difference will not in fact lead to a civilized universal, but only to a new conquering power, and a new war.

What is sometimes read as antiquated racialism in Senghor and Césaire is in fact a trenchant critique of the imposition of culture as a false evocation of gift giving and a concomitant realization that universalism risks creating only a "pale" world, bound together by domination, and without any residual resources for resistance. The fact that actual, specific, and worthwhile gifts were possible for exchange between civilizations was in part why Césaire refused deconstructions of race in his own time:

> I believe that the civilization that has given Negro sculpture to the world of art; that the civilization that has given to the political and social world original communitarian institutions such as village democracy, or age-group fraternities, or familial property, that negation of capitalism, or so many institutions bearing the stamp of the spirit of solidarity; that this civilization that on another level has given to the moral world an original philosophy based on respect for life and integration within the cosmos; I refuse to believe that this civilization, insufficient though it may be, must be annihilated or denied as a precondition of the renaissance of black peoples . . . In our culture that is to be born, without a doubt, there will be old and new. Which new elements? Which old elements? Our ignorance begins only here. And in truth it is not for the individual to give the answer. The answer can only be given by the community. But at least we can confirm here and now that *it will be given* and not verbally but by facts and in action.[117]

This is what radical pluralism offers: an appreciation of the constructedness of values and an acknowledgement than none is eternal or necessary, but, nevertheless, a positing of the fact that values do exist and develop (in a person, in peoples, in civilizations, even across humanity), and that these value systems can *meaningfully* interact with each other.

This hope for meaningful exchange is why what matters is not only giving and receiving, but also the terms on which that exchange takes place. In "Culture and Colonization" (1956), Césaire critiqued the idea that colonization was a kind of cultural exchange. Citing the noted anthropologist Bronisław Malinowski, he spoke instead of the "selective gift" that was colonization. As Malinowski saw it, colonization happily gave orders, infrastructure (which helped it mine and retrieve wealth), and laws (which helped it maintain its hegemony), but it certainly never gave freely. True giving would mean equally sharing military might, sovereignty, material wealth, and positions of power.[118] It is against this "selective gift" that Césaire proposes the possibility of a future gifting from Africans to the world, which will differ not only from the contents of colonization, but also from its form of contact.

Philosophically, this also formed a large part of the troubled reaction to Sartre's claims in "Black Orpheus." Sartre, recall, had posited that Négritude would be overcome in the dialectic of history and be superseded by class consciousness. The problem with this argument for Senghor and Césaire (and also for Fanon, whom I discuss in the next chapter) was not that they did not agree that Négritude would be *part of* this broader struggle in the civilization of the universal, but that Sartre had forestalled the *other dialectics* at work in history. Thus Césaire, speaking not directly to Sartre but to the general colonial mentality that his claim expresses, will state again in "Culture and Colonization": "The great reproach that we justly level at Europe is that it broke the momentum of civilizations that had not yet reached their full promise, that it did not permit them to develop and to realize the full richness of the forms held within them."[119] Senghor, in a lecture given at Césaire's invitation, would also state that he was not rejecting the dialectics of development per se, but rather the imposition of a dialectic from the outside. "I believe, like Jean-Paul Sartre, that 'Négritude is dialectical'; I do not believe that it will 'cede its place to new values.' More precisely, I believe . . . Négritude will constitute, already constitutes . . . an ensemble of essential contributions [*d'apports essentiels*]."[120]

This is, again, a move beyond deconstruction and dialectics made by radical pluralists. The point is not simply the breakdown of imposing visions, nor is it the possible achievement of those visions after their violence is done. Rather, it is the overarching claim that there are many dialectics always producing new ways of being in the world and then always offering from themselves an exchange while still always denying the unbearable imposition of someone else's partiality. Radical pluralists do not deny the value of dialectics, as a way of making new mixtures, or of deconstruction, as a way of denying purity, supremacy, or universalizability. In fact, they embrace both within a vision of individuals, cultures, genders, races, sexualities, collectivities, and others in the ongoing process of making ways of being and radically critiquing impositions of being.

In 1956, in his letter announcing his decision to exit the Communist Party, Césaire spoke of the need for a "Copernican Revolution": "There is a veritable Copernican revolution to be imposed here, so ingrained in Europe (from the extreme right to the extreme left) is the habit of doing for us, arranging for us, thinking for us—in short, the habit of challenging our possession of this right to initiative of which I have just spoken, which is, at the end of the day, the right to personality."[121] If, in his "Copernican Revolution," Kant recentered philosophy around the subject, and then Freud decentered the recentered subject through the unconscious, Césaire is saying here: where is the cultural relation in all of this? What do these ideas about humanity have to do with how humans live with each other? And where

Kant and Freud both reduced peoples outside Europe to primitives trapped under the dominion of nature or community, Césaire is advocating another Copernican Revolution wherein we achieve not a generic intersubjectivity (already contained in Hegel and Freud), but rather a specific kind of intersubjectivity, one in which it is assumed that all subjects are valuable, plural, and capable of giving and receiving.[122]

The question of what exactly Négritude is offering is where we enter into the more controversial thoughts of Senghor. Senghor, as I noted above, suggested that Négritude offered, among other things, a very specific way of inhabiting the world. In a talk simply titled "Of Négritude" (1969), he offers this summary: "A rare gift [*don*] of emotion, an existential and unitary ontology, culminating, through a mystical surrealism, in an art [that is] engaged [*engagé*] and functional, collective and actual, [and] whose style is characterized by the analogical image and asymmetric parallelism."[123] What is happening here is much more complex than we normally give Senghor credit for. (When Fanon wrote that Senghor spoke of a simplistic "rhythm!" he may have missed a beat.) I have already explored the basis of the "existential and unitary" ontology. The rest of these terms now need to be unpacked to understand Senghor's aesthetics and how they relate to global thought and being.

At a general level, what Senghor suggests here is not that we need to deracialize aesthetics so much as to revalue the very geographies on which aesthetics racialized itself. So if Schiller claims that aesthetics marks the moment when the sensuousness of primitive humans is united with the rationality of civilized humans, Senghor will say, to the contrary, that aesthetics is a plural act and that there is a logic of sense just as much as there is a logic of intellect. Rather than uniting them, we are to learn to develop each of them to their utmost capacities. The development of the logic of sense is what Senghor calls in the title of one of his best-known essays, "what the black man contributes [*apporte*]" (1939).[124] Diagne locates in this essay the beginnings of his mature aesthetics, and it is here where Senghor writes the line to which Fanon, and many following him, have taken such exception: "Emotion is Negro, as reason is Hellenic."[125]

It is not hard to see what is problematic in this line: the idea that there is a singular "Negro" culture and that that culture is about emotion rather than reason. But some important qualifications need to be made. This statement does *not* mean that Senghor is giving a positive spin to the unthinking power of Schiller's "sensuous drive." He is explicit from the very beginning of the essay that he is speaking of a "civilization," that is, a complete worldview.[126] He is not claiming to valorize unthinking sense. Rather, he is setting out to deny the belief that sense is unthinking. He is interested in the "non-intellectual qualities of ideas."[127] As Diagne (to whom I owe much of my understanding of Senghor's aesthetics) has argued, Senghor means "emotion" in a strictly philosophical way, one that was given expression in the work of Henri Bergson.

In Bergson, Senghor found expressed this *other* quality of ideas that opened onto an *other* philosophy.[128] Diagne cites this all-important passage from *Creative Evolution*:

> Consciousness, in man, is pre-eminently intellect. It might have been, it ought, so it seems, to have been also intuition. Intuition and intellect represent two opposite directions of the work of consciousness: intuition goes in the very direction of life, intellect goes in the inverse direction, and thus finds itself naturally in accordance with the movement of matter. A complete and perfect humanity would be that in which these two forms of conscious activity should attain their full development.[129]

Bergson helped Senghor articulate a reevaluation of the entire discourse around so-called primitive life that existed since at least Rousseau. Bergson's work not only allowed for a reevaluation of African history, as the recoveries of ethnologists like Leo Frobenius had done, but also it enabled the dissolution of the category of primitive thought as such.[130] Now it could be shown, from within the Eurocentric archive itself, not only that the senses had an inherent intellectual quality, but also that in the modern world, that quality had unfortunately been overridden by the intellect.[131] Bergson showed that intuitive thinking—alongside (not replacing) analytic thinking—was necessary for humanity. Senghor realized that Bergson's insight changed the racial history of ontology and opened up a new set of practices for global aesthetics: the use of engaging art for the increase of intuition[132] and the need of art to engage other cultural forms to open up new practices of the global self.[133]

So what exactly does Senghor mean by emotion, this word that he puts at the beginning of his definition of Négritude again thirty years later? It means a particular way of engaging with the world. While analytic reason decomposes its object into traits and characteristics, this emotive reason "goes beyond the visible, straight to the under-reality [*sous-realité*] of the object, so that it can go beyond the sign and grasp the meaning."[134] This is not, then, just some generic immersion in reality, but an actual *achievement* of a way of being in the world. Where Schiller sees blind instinct, Senghor sees emotion as a capacity to be affected (*ému*). "Water affects him, not because it washes, but because it purifies; fire, because of its power of destruction, not because of its heat or color."[135] It is possible to call this a banal mysticism or a degradation of the scientific method.[136] But it is equally possible to say that there is something very wrong with a humanity that *only* sees the technical, property-laden definitions of things and cannot think in meaningful ways about the natural world and the human place in it. These are, as such, practices of the self specifically designed to enable our shared habitation of the planet.

The possibility of being emotive (affected) is thus the possibility of seeing the world through this "surrealistic mysticism." But this vision, Senghor continues, leads back into the making of an art that is "engaged and functional, collective and actual." The use of the Sartrean term *engagé* suggests that Senghor is thinking about the life fostered by this way of being and making as a kind of political act. If surreal vision seems divorced from Sartrean engagement, that is only because we have forgotten the impact of Surrealism, with its critique of colonialism and demands for total liberation, on Sartre. There is in fact an intimate connection between a liberated vision of the world and the hope for a liberated humanity. Like Schiller, Senghor thus envisions a relation between aesthetic transformation and politics. But again, unlike Schiller, he does not envision that politics as a decided format that will once and for all be given in a universal law. He sees it rather as a constant engagement with the changing forces of a plural reality.

As Wilder has explicated so well, this meant for Senghor a continually engaged vision of how best to use the immanent structures of a postimperial world to create a just future. This meant both the transformation of Africa *and* the transformation of France: "Senghor called neither for France to decolonize Africa nor for Africa to liberate itself, but for Africans to *decolonize* France. African socialism would play a vanguard role in a process whereby the imperial republic would be elevated into a plural democracy."[137] "African socialism" would redress not only the economic alienation of humans, but also our spiritual fractures. Senghor thus frequently cited both Marx's early humanist texts and his late writings on the global plurality that could bring about transformation. Senghor ended his own lecture on "Marxism and Humanism" (1948) with Marx's line, discussed below, that communism was not the ultimate goal of humanity, but a particular arrangement that made sense at the present time.[138] As Wilder has shown, this grappling with a conjuncture, this being *engagé* with both the facts of the present and their hidden, surrealistic potentials for emancipation, marked the ongoing development of Senghor's (at times deeply flawed) political positions.[139]

Senghor summed up this pluralist and transformative political vision when he argued in favor of a postimperial Federation as follows:

> Autonomy is not an end for us, but a means. In other words, we want less to rid ourselves of the tutelage of the metropole than of the tyranny of international capitalism. We think that an autonomy that simply brings us back to the feudal regime of castes would not solve the problem. We are not rebels, but revolutionaries. We want to construct a better world, better than the colonial world of yesterday, better as well than our world before the European conquest. We will build it taking inspiration from European socialism and the old African collectivism. We will thus reconcile modern technique and African humanism. For it is a question of building a new world where, in an organized society, men will be equal and fraternal, without distinctions of class, race, or religion.[140]

The model for Senghor here as elsewhere is for a new kind of global formation. All past civilizations have been the result of crossings in some more or less haphazard ways. Senghor believes—or at least hopes—that a future civilization of the universal will make new kinds of global mixtures, but now through what Du Bois will call a "conscientious" mode of interaction.

We can see how Senghor defined Négritude as existing through a complex understanding of emotion and a thoroughgoing pluralist ontology that leads, through a mystical surrealism of how to perceive the meaning of the world, to an engaged and functional art that is based on the collective and seeks to make itself actual. Senghor, in conclusion, characterizes the resulting "style" of this art as based in the "analogical image" and an "asymmetric parallelism." Briefly, he defines this type of image as one in which "the word suggests much more than it says." At the same time, the words chosen are meant to evoke what is at once "concrete and emotional."[141] The images of Négritude—often specific to their articulation in different languages—are thus ones that embody a certain duality that does not speak itself, but allows itself to unfold in the sense-making of the listener or viewer.[142] We have already seen the "asymmetric parallelism": it is the way of thinking and being that is at once with and against, rooted and uprooted, weak and strong, and so forth. It is the mode of living in the world as a radically plural being who draws sustenance from the virtual to intervene in the actual and, in turn, retreats from the actual to the virtual to draw new energy for imagination and action. The "analogical image" helps us to see this multiplicity of possibility and actuality within what appears to be a brute reality.

We can now understand Senghor's infamous analogy to mean that African culture has worked on intuitive living to the highest degree, just as Hellenic culture did for rationality.[143] His claim is not one of cultural superiority; it is of cultural equality. If Athens gave reason and Jerusalem law (as Levinas had it), Senghor is now saying that Africa gave emotion. None of these works fully without the other (as Levinas did not understand).[144] Of equal importance is that none of these merges completely into the other, as they did in Schiller. The point is for each of us now, in our global world, to learn to operate in these different modalities as the situation calls for. Senghor's insight ought to be combined with Fanon's claim that the skin is not a "repository of specific values."[145] We must be vigilant—perhaps more vigilant than Senghor himself was—to not imprison anyone in a particular mode of existence, simply because of how they look or where they are from.[146]

This of course also extends to other aspects of an individual, including gender. As T. Denean Sharpley-Whiting has shown, black women in France in the early twentieth century, especially Jane and Paulette Nardal, were central to the growth of Négritude, both as writers and as salon organizers. They also formed the crucial bridge that opened A. Césaire, Senghor, and Dumas to the Harlem Renaissance.[147] Senghor writes in "What the Black Man Contributes," "How many were devoured by the Minotaur, who would not have strayed with the help of Ariadne, Emotion-Femininity?"[148] The continual movement of unbearable identities is again apparent here. Senghor, in escaping the identity imposed on him, runs the risk of imposing that same identity on another. The black *man* contributes, but the contribution of the black woman appears here only as the guide to lead him to his contribution. A possible bridge here—a rethinking of "woman" as an intuitive being along with his rethinking of "Negro"—never occurs. Perhaps more importantly, the fact that this rethinking of gender might need to proceed along different lines than the rethinking of race is not present. Senghor seems to want to loop women into his reappraisal of intuition, but it's unclear how that claim intersects with the divided geography of the rest of his text. (Are women in Europe the same as in Africa, although men are not?) The development of practices of the global self requires us to constantly be aware of how particular histories require specific practices and how one can never overcome an unbearable identity by creating a new unbearable identity for others, because unbearability is intimately connected to global interdependence.

Other worries persist in our taking hold of the relevance of Senghor for the present. This was brought home in a spectacular fashion in 2007, when then French president Nicolas Sarkozy gave a speech in Dakar that Wilder calls "remarkable"; that is: "Remarkable in its display of ignorance and arrogance, this moralizing lecture chastised a primitive and stagnant Africa for choosing stubbornly to remain outside the stream of modern history."[149] During the speech, Sarkozy had recourse to selectively invoke Senghor, "transforming" him, as Wilder summarized, "into a Francophile apologist for empire."[150] While Wilder's essay on the speech and its use of Senghor sought a corrective, Achille Mbembe wrote a stark rebuttal of both Sarkozy and Senghor.

Although appreciative of the fact that Négritude was born in a particular time in place—one in which the "humanity of Blacks was contested"—Mbembe nevertheless argued that Senghor (at least in his line about Hellenic versus African) wrote in a continuity "with the most racist vocabulary of the era." Senghor today, in Mbembe's estimation, has been "largely refuted."[151] Mbembe has offered more nuanced positions on Senghor elsewhere.[152] Nevertheless, his concern, shared by the many critics of Négritude, is that its own vocabulary remains marked by a moment of racial solidarity that no longer speaks to the present, when what is at stake is less the "humanity of Blacks" than the humanity of all of us in a world "becoming Black" through the ongoing dominations of empire and capital.[153] Furthermore, what appears to concern Mbembe is that the vocabulary of Négritude is now too much available to those like Sarkozy. Even if he supports a mission like Wilder's to revive the thinking of Senghor and Césaire (he offers a very positive blurb on the back of the book), he may doubt that their specific naming of the problem speaks to our present condition.

In the conclusion to his 2010 book *Sortir de la grande nuit*,[154] Mbembe writes: "We must therefore move on to something other [à autre chose] [than Afrocentrism and Négritude] if we are to reanimate the life of the African spirit and, in so doing, the possibilities of an art, a philosophy, an aesthetic that can say something new and meaningful to the world at large."[155] His primary offering at this point was a suggested replacement in vocabulary: "Afropolitanism."[156] If Négritude (as it is perceived) is too bound up with the concept of race, then Afropolitanism is meant to offer ways of thinking that speak to the conditions of African and Africana lives, freed as much as possible of the baggage of histories of racial dominance and capable of recognizing the multiply raced existences of the African continent.[157]

In these early works, Mbembe speaks more of the potentials of this African thinking than giving it much specificity. In his next book, *Critique of Black Reason* (2013), he begins to offer some specific suggestions, especially in the chapter "The Clinic of the Subject." Mbembe continues to question the resources of Négritude, even as he writes at some length about the contributions of Césaire.[158] Mbembe is clear that Césaire's "concern for the Black Man does not lead to secession from the world but rather to the affirmation of its plurality."[159] This, he says, is something that Césaire shares with Senghor.[160] If we are to speak of the legacy of Négritude today, then, we need to be "post-Césairian." That is to say, we need to "embrace and retain the signifier 'Black' not with the goal of finding solace within it but rather as a way of clouding the term in order to gain distance from it."[161] The results of this process offer a possible new vision of "what the black man contributes."

Mbembe suggests that the "wellspring for such ascetic work will be found in the best of our Afro-American and South African political, religious, and cultural traditions." He speaks especially of art, noting that the purpose of art in these traditions "has never been to represent, illustrate, or narrate reality." Rather, they engage in a process of transforming the object in a "space where the optic and tactile functions, along with the world of the senses, were united in a single movement aimed at revealing the double of the world."[162] These are quotes, with their ideas of doubling, of the senses, of the importance of art in understanding the African way of "being-in-the-world," that could come straight from Senghor. Indeed, we might speak of what Mbembe offers here as a "paraphrasing" of Senghor in the same way that Senghor paraphrased Goethe. Mbembe's version—a version I sincerely appreciate—might be something like "each must relate to the world in their own way, but they must relate to the world." This is what Mbembe calls "[t]he question of the world—what it is, what the relationship is between its various parts, what the extent of its resources is and to whom they belong, how to live in it, what moves and threatens it, where it is going, what its borders and limits, and its possible end, are." Mbembe further argues that this situation is inseparable from the question of "the Black man" because it is bound up with the history of slavery.[163]

For Mbembe, as again with Senghor and Césaire, our relation to the world must be an ethical one. It would take me too far into Mbembe's extensive thinking to fully explore his thoughts here, but my sense is that what this ultimately amounts to is what he calls a "critique of life," which can roughly be glossed as the need to move past a politics of violence and death and into a "meditation on the conditions that make the struggle to live, to stay alive, to survive, in sum, to live a human life, the most important aesthetic—and therefore political—question."[164] This meditation would lead us to a vision of art as constant renewal and politics as the distribution of "equal shares."[165] Speaking in a language of religious rebirth, Mbembe argues that African art has always been about this question of life to be gained and relived, of a "future to come." And it is here where he marks a potential difference from Senghor: "There has therefore never been anything traditional in this art, if only because it has always been charged with exposing the extraordinary fragility of the social order. It is a form of art that has constantly reinvented myths and redirected tradition in order to undermine them through the very act that pretended to anchor and ratify them."[166] If Schiller's aesthetics led to a single universal order, and Senghor's to a constant reconfiguration, Mbembe's is more "deconstructive" in the sense that it plumbs the reminder that the world is not how it should be, and thus should be unmade and remade again.[167] Art, rather than a mode of knowledge, becomes a method of (re)creation: "artistic creation . . . aims to free the individual and their community from the world as it has been and as it is."[168] If Senghor founds a new pluralism in African art, Mbembe founds a new deconstruction and, in so doing, reminds us that all discourses are themselves plural and evolving. I imagine that this "Afropolitan" imagination will continue to generate new ways of thinking through these problems of global relation in the years to come. It will thus contribute as much to new pluralisms as to new deconstructions.

I would continue to agree with Wilder and Diagne by insisting on the fact that Senghor's aesthetic thinking was always itself a global thinking, a way of relating to the world—not only in the sense that it articulates itself in response to the global imaginings of other philosophers, but also in that it offers Négritude as a practice of the global self. As Diagne puts it: "Even when he insists on the specificity of the Negro African aesthetic, it is ultimately for the purpose of making it one of the possibilities everywhere, in all cultural spheres and in various ages, to human creativity."[169]

Senghor outlines how what he offers is a worldly and global practice in the essay on "The Negro-African Aesthetic" right before the lines cited above about how nature had "done well" to distribute different faculties to different peoples. He writes: "The Negro-African . . . does not observe that he thinks; he feels that he feels [il sent qu'il sent],[170] he feels his existence, he feels himself. Because he feels himself, he feels the Other [within himself]; and because he feels the Other, he goes towards the Other, through the rhythm of the Other to know-him-in-being-born-with-him [con-naître] and the world."[171] He continues by noting that this feeling for the "vital force" is throughout African life, but is best expressed in literature and art.[172] Aesthetics, in other words, was always for Senghor a way of getting to know others and the world. This is perhaps why this passage precedes the one about the diversity of human cultures and values: because it is through the aesthetic faculty that we can best learn of others. While Mbembe's vision of a gift of undoing is powerful, there is still, I think, something to be said for this specific way of knowing that Senghor's aesthetics offers.

Schiller developed his aesthetic based on analytic reason. He divided the world into rational and instinctual and then sought out an abstraction—sublation—to unite the two. Senghor developed his aesthetic based on this other kind of knowing, which he developed not only in his contacts with Senegalese (and other forms of) thinking, being, writing, and art making, but also through his sympathetic reading of Bergson (and others). African aesthetics thus represented for him a way of understanding that enables one to enter global space without destroying others or blindly folding them into one's schema. His understanding of an other reason is not just an epistemology, it is an offered modality for how to engage others in global space, how to be part of the "rendez-vous of giving and receiving."

4

Dialectics and Its Discontents
Hegel, Marx, Fanon

Hegel: The Colonial Dialectic of History

The cross-century and cross-continent debate between Schiller and Senghor about aesthetics also plays out in the realm of history in the writings of Hegel, Marx, and Fanon. In Hegel's work, the colonial logic of Rousseau's dialectic becomes increasingly explicit, and Marx and Fanon will each work in his own way to overcome the unbearable identities Hegel creates in the process. Hegel departs from Rousseau and Schiller and sides with Hobbes in declaring that the state of nature is a savage, war-ravaged state. And no less than any of these thinkers, Hegel develops his ideas by thinking through the "state of nature" and the means of exiting from it. I argue here that this history is at the heart of his famous "Master Slave Dialectic" (MSD).[1]

Hegel presents a particular difficulty here because, of all the texts I have addressed thus far, his provoke the most tendentious debates—not only about his position, but also about whether or not a description of his position is accurate. I engage some of these debates here, necessarily, but in part by evading them. It seems to me rather clear, for instance, that what Hegel means by sublation and dialectics is endlessly complicated, and I would tend to side with those who view his ideas as evolving and contextual. Although "dialectics" is a universal movement in Hegel, there is also always a relation between form and content. Thus the dialectical process will differ within and between entities.[2] What particularly interests me here is what happens to Hegel's dialectical thinking when he discusses non-European spaces. In these moments, all the vitality he usually describes vanishes, and these spaces are viewed as stuck, "dormant," and in need of contact with Europe.

All the thinkers I consider who follow Hegel—Emerson, Du Bois, Fanon, Césaire, Senghor, and (to a lesser extent) Suzuki—find meaningful resources in his philosophical positions. In general, his ideas about the relation of politics to thought, the process of history, and the way in which struggle can create progress will be valuable resources for thinkers to follow. At the same time, his Eurocentric vision of these processes will create problems. As we have seen with Senghor and Césaire, for example, and will see again in Fanon, they used one kind of dialectics to push back against Sartre's imposition of another dialectics. That is to say, Hegel's idea of "self-sublation," or a dialectic internal to Négritude, helped them to oppose another version of sublation, one in which Négritude would be dialectically negated as it was swept up in the universal revolutions of European thought. Unfortunately, this kind of Sartrean opposition between cultures originates in Hegel himself. More unfortunately still, Hegel argues that it is only through the violent encounter between cultures that what he calls the "dormancy" of spaces outside of Europe can be overcome.[3] I do not think there is a route to understanding Hegel's global thinking without tackling these problems head-on, and I argue here that we cannot get at what is valuable in Hegel without first working through the problematic elements of his thought. In this sense I follow not only more standard "philosophical" readers of Hegel, but also a number of contemporary critics.[4]

However, my aim in this section, as in the book as a whole, is to connect traditional and postcolonial interpretations because these connections are present in the writings themselves. While Hegel's remarks about other cultures have been vigorously documented and debated, there remains something to be said about how cultural ideas inform the concepts of his thinking. As I suggested briefly in the chapter on Rousseau, and continued to follow into Kant and Schiller, the very idea of dialectical thinking has one of its origins in Du Tertre's colonial ethnography. In Rousseau's Second Discourse, with which Hegel was intimately familiar, Du Tertre's anecdote of colonial trade became a philosophical anthropology of the difference between the French and Caribs. In this anthropology, recall, the goal becomes to negate what is unruly in the Caribs while preserving their instinctual ways of being and, at the same time, to negate what is alienated in the French while still preserving their capacity for foresight. The hoped-for result is what Rousseau calls a "savage made to inhabit cities," that is, someone who dialectically combines these traits in a perfected soul. I argued there, in effect, that at this moment Rousseau lays the groundwork for the modern form of the dialectic. I have followed thus far how this gets further interpreted and reworked in Kant's politics and Schiller's aesthetics. In this chapter, I show how it continues to play out in Hegel's thinking about the dialectics of history. To do so, I focus on how the global history we have seen so far forms the background for his famous MSD. I want to show that Hegel's dialectical thinking germinates in this historical matrix and then is applied to it in his writings on the state of nature. In other words, by failing to come to terms with the ways in which his own concepts had global origins, Hegel replayed the histories of erasure and domination in his philosophy. This is the risk we all face when—as Hegel himself might have taught us—we lack self-conscious reflection on our global histories.[5]

In his *Philosophy of Subjective Spirit* (1817–1830), Hegel makes the following remark about Europe's relation to the world:

> The European spirit opposes the world to itself, and while freeing itself from it, sublates this opposition by taking back into the simplicity of its own self the manifoldedness of this its other. This accounts for the dominance of the European's infinite thirst for knowledge, which is alien to other races [*Racen*]. The world interests the European, he wants to get to know it, to possess the other with which he is confronted, to bring into intuition the inner rationality of the particularities of the world, of the genus, the law, the universal, of thought. In what is practical, as in what is theoretical, the European spirit strives to bring forth unity between itself and the external world. It subdues the external world to its purposes with an energy which has ensured for it the mastery of the world [*die Herrschaft*[6] *der Welt*].[7]

One can learn a great deal about Hegel from this quote. It encapsulates his dialectical method and the process of external sublation, his views on the relation of culture to nature, and his unapologetic Eurocentrism. Hegel is saying, essentially, that most world cultures only concern themselves with their immediate surroundings. They have yet to break from the culturally specific into the universal. This is part of a longer story in Hegel, in which Spirit moves out from Nature (in which Spirit is always latent but not always actualized) in order to begin to realize itself.[8] Elsewhere he calls this "culture and its laborious emergence from the immediacy of substantial life."⁹ As culture emerges from its immediacy in nature (a story that should be familiar from Rousseau), it first only grasps its immediate surroundings. What makes Europe unique is that it moves from this primary rupture into an attempt to understand others. Europe thus invents anthropology, which is to say, a self-conscious reflection on culture, and, through this invention, earns its rightful mastery over the world.

The idea that Europe alone invented anthropology is not hard to find in contemporary critical theory. Cornelius Castoriadis repeats it, for example: "That the ethnologist, the historian, or the philosopher is in a position to reflect upon societies other than his own and, indeed, even upon his own society becomes a possibility and a reality only within this particular historical tradition—the Greco-Western tradition."[10] This is absurd, and not only because the historical record contradicts it.[11] Because Hegel and Castoriadis both must have known that trade existed between societies throughout history, they must force themselves into the absurd conclusion that no one, as she trafficked back and forth between cultural norms, stopped and wondered why it was that the people she traded with had different customs, habits, and languages than her own. For representatives of the culture claiming to have invented knowledge about the other, Hegel and Castoriadis seem rather terrible at gaining such knowledge![12]

Hegel does get something right: the modern subject is created in her attempts to know the world. What Hegel does not see (and the reason that Senghor's work is so important) is that there are meaningful ways of getting to know the world in the places he calls "without history." What matters more than simply engaging with other cultures is how one does so. The Hegelian subject, I argue in this section, is deeply troubled by certain presumptions about history—about the supremacy of Europe, the necessary movements between stages of culture, and the assumption that life is originally submerged in nature.

In this section I focus on the MSD, just one small part of Hegel's epic essay of the globe, the *Phenomenology of Spirit* (1807), and relate it to broader themes in his work. I also track the variations of the MSD as it appears in *The Philosophy of Subjective Spirit* (1817) and *The Philosophy of Right* (1820). The MSD has arguably been the most influential part of Hegel's *Phenomenology*.[13] Although this section can be (and has been) read as liberatory, I argue that reconstituting the global origins of the MSD shows a darker side to its logic, one that justifies slavery and, later, European colonial rule. I show how this part of the *Phenomenology* is less about real masters and slaves, as Susan Buck-Morss has argued, or real feudal lords and peasants, as Andrew Cole has argued, and more about the historical movement by which one leaves the so-called state of nature (in which one is slave to immediacy and instinct). Hegel, I argue, is making a conjectural history of human development, just as Rousseau, Kant, and Schiller did. Further, I argue that this conjectural history is not a general abstraction about an imagined state of nature, but an actual engagement with real peoples about whom Hegel was reading.[14] This history offers, unlike Rousseau's version, an affirmation of the necessity of the present (what Marx will later call Hegel's "uncritical positivism"). Although Hegel believes slavery and colonization ought to eventually be abolished, he also believes that they were necessary moments in which Spirit broke with the domain of nature. The MSD emplots human history as beginning in a blind savagery that only European civilization can now help the world overcome. While it is often taken as a call to overcome the unbearable identity of slavery, I argue that it produces too many other unbearable concepts in arriving at this point.

Such a reconsideration, I should note, does not mean that we should entirely condemn or ignore Hegel. It only means that we should understand his conceptual labor as constituted by layers of meaning, some of which we need to excavate and remove if the others are to have their proper power. Hegel is open to the future, but, like Schiller, he believes that there is only one path to that future: the march of Spirit after its diremption from "the state of nature." There is diversity in this future for Hegel, but that diversity is only meaningful *after* civil society has been instantiated and can recognize it. Hegel offers to the global self the concepts of struggle, recognition, and ongoing process. But he short-circuits his insights by insisting on the necessity of diremption, violence, and "the right of heroes," as well as the claim of the inherent unfreedom of non-European forms of life. My point here, as throughout this book, is to elucidate and reconstitute: Hegel's thought is informed by the globe, and his global thinking, in turn, informs critical theory today. One of the key claims of this section is that reconstituting Hegel requires us to set him within the context of the global thinking of his predecessors: Rousseau, Kant, and Schiller. It is in this context that the logic of his global thinking emerges.

Hegel understood very well the need for self-transformation in order to think globally. The "spirit of Europe" had to be continually enacted and perfected. To some degree, this explains the difficulty of reading a text like the *Phenomenology of Spirit*, in which Hegel is trying to create in the subject a transformative process of passing through stages of knowledge. This is why the *Phenomenology* begins with a critique of standard philosophical practices that haunt academic writing to this day: the thesis statement and the literature review. The former, Hegel asserts, is contrary to the very way "in which to expound philosophical truth" because philosophy unfolds as a process, not as an achieved statement.[15] The latter, meanwhile, gives the impression that one is rejecting previous claims, whereas, in fact, all these claims are part of the "progressive unfolding of truth."[16] To write philosophy for Hegel is to write through this evolving process, not to make declarations from the start about what one has already achieved, nor to discard as irrelevant the historical tradition in which one works. In Hegel's famous line "The True is the whole," thus, what is true contains also the false.[17] Philosophy is not a statement of abstract knowledge, but the entire mode of coming to know something. It must, therefore, show "the result together with the process through which it came about."[18] In this sense of showing the trial and process of thinking, we might think of the *Phenomenology* as an essay of nothing less than all of human history. The question for me is how Hegel essays the globe in that process.[19]

The *Phenomenology* begins with the history of consciousness. After discussing how the mind relates to external objects ("Consciousness"), Hegel transitions in the MSD to how the mind moves from that external, object-oriented focus to an internal, self-reflexive one ("Self-consciousness"). Hegel here makes the interesting claim that the move to self-consciousness in history (that is, the move from Nature to Spirit, not unrelated to what we have been calling instinct and reason) is created by a social relation. Famously: "Self-consciousness exists in and for itself when, and by the fact that, it so exists for another; that is, it exists only in being acknowledged."[20] Self-consciousness only exists, then, when it is recognized by another *human* self-consciousness. But when they first meet in the MSD, the two consciousnesses on display are barely human because they are still attached to their object-like natural existence, and they still presume this of the other: "they are for one another like ordinary objects."[21] What this means, in Hegel's language, is that they have "certainty [*Gewißheit*]" of themselves, but they do not yet experience the "truth [*Wahrheit*]" of their self-consciousness, because truth is not found in the certainty of the individual mind (as it had been for Descartes, for example), but only in the shared, historical, communal meeting of minds. This is another of Hegel's worthwhile and revolutionary ideas, although the same questions remain: How does Hegel define the historical community? Who is included in it and who is excluded from it? And how does one enter into it in the first place? It is especially this latter point that is of concern in the MSD.

In the MSD, Hegel suggests that although all human beings unequivocally possess the concept of truth (the capacity for mutual recognition), they do not all in fact achieve it. In mapping the process of reaching truth, Hegel argues that one path is through the violence of a life-and-death struggle.[22] It is not immediately clear why this is the case. The two characters in his myth of human origins are two unnamed "self-consciousnesses" who are "*self-sufficient* shapes absorbed within the *being* of *life*."[23] Their task is the "destruction of all immediate being."[24] In other words, these are two beings who are submerged in "natural existence" and must find a way to move from natural immersion to self-conscious reflection.[25] *Only* if "the entire contents of its natural consciousness" have been "jeopardized" can the willful individual move from self-seeking natural life into communal life.[26] It is this act of jeopardizing that will require violent struggle.

For self-consciousness to prove that it is not a mere object, and that it is more than its natural existence, it must repudiate all attachment to that existence. And it *must also insist* that no one else remain in a state of natural existence. This is what is required by the idea of recognition: if I am not free except by your recognition, and if no one is free who is chained to merely natural existence, then I must both stake my life and your life in the name of our mutual freedom. Hegel's language about this in the *Phenomenology* is daunting, but he lays it out relatively clearly in the *Philosophy of Subjective Spirit*[27]:

> Freedom therefore demands of the self-conscious subject that it should neither allow its own naturality to subsist, nor tolerate that of others, but that it should be indifferent to existence in that in its immediate and individual dealings it stakes its own life and that of others in order to achieve freedom . . . At this juncture man only displays [*nur dadurch*] his capacity for it in that he brings himself, as he brings others, into peril of death.[28]

"*Only* displays." This language of necessity also appears in the *Phenomenology*.[29] If these two naturally bound self-consciousnesses are to move beyond immediate existence, there is not, at this hypothetical moment in history, another path.

Hegel traces here how the figures of "Lord" and "Bondsman," or "Master" and "Slave," are created through this process and what happens in their relation. What he argues is that during the life-and-death struggle, one of the figures must remain attached to life (otherwise one would die and the movement of recognition could not continue). This is the one who becomes the slave; the other is the master. The master thus becomes an independent self-consciousness. In this role, he continues to break with natural existence because he no longer has to work on things. He is free to go deeper and deeper into his consciousness while he enjoys the fruits of the other's labor.[30] But this proves unsatisfactory, because by enslaving the other he has robbed himself of the possibility of mutual freedom that was supposed to be his goal for the struggle in the first place. We might again pause here and wonder why he enslaves the other, because Hegel had previously told us that he seeks the death of the other in the name of the other's freedom. It seems that, even if we accept this initial claim, we have no reason to follow it to this result. However, Hegel's master *cannot* remember this original desire for freedom and end the servitude, because in his schema the slave must fight for his freedom. This seemingly progressive call for rebellion here becomes a conservative claim for the necessity of slavery until revolution.

Perhaps this possibility for slavery to advance history is why Hegel also sees the slave as helping to overcome natural existence. Although the master seems to be the one who completely overcame natural life through his willingness to die, he did so only abstractly. He did not experience the fear of death, the fear of the fact that this life offers neither stability nor guarantee. It is this *experience* of fear that allows the slave to actually know "the simple, essential nature of self-consciousness," both implicitly through his experience and explicitly through the continued presence of the master.[31] Further still, Hegel adds, this fear of the other in turn drives the slave to work. Work in this context has two functions. First, because it is for another, it allows the slave to "rid . . . himself of his attachment to natural existence in every single detail."[32] He is no longer just struggling to survive for himself; he is learning to work for another. But if this first experience is alienating, the second element of work begins to restore him to himself: in working and shaping the external world, the slave moves past the absolute fear of death and instability and begins to realize that there is the possibility of permanence through the making of the communal world.[33] As Hegel writes in the "Preface" when criticizing the commonsense morals of Adam Smith and others, "it is the nature of humanity to press onward to agreement with others; human nature only really exists in an achieved community of minds." He continues, and here we see his critique of natural existence: "The anti-human, the merely animal, consists in staying within the sphere of feeling, and being able to communicate only at that level."[34]

The natural sphere must be destroyed for community to emerge, and here Hegel is advocating for slavery as the means of destroying that will.[35]

So much of what is called Continental philosophy is given articulation in these few, dense passages: Kierkegaard's concept of dread, Marx's vision of the power of capitalism, Heidegger's being-toward-death, and Arendt's concept of work, to name a few. There is no doubt a profound mind at work here. But one of the claims of this book is that profundity goes awry when it claims universal necessity for what is in fact only one possible experience. Claims about necessary, precise steps, for which many philosophers the world over are guilty, haunt Hegel's argument: "If consciousness fashions the thing without that initial absolute fear, it is only an empty self-centred attitude." "If it has not experienced absolute fear . . . the negative being has remained for it something external." "Since the entire contents of its natural consciousness have not been jeopardized . . . [it has] a freedom which is still enmeshed in servitude."[36] Why does Hegel make these precise claims? Although he believes that slavery is unethical, he wants to find the logic that allows humans to make meaning of these moments. The danger here is that this results in a justification of violence and slavery as moments in the unfolding of human life. And what justifies violence and slavery? The fact that they tear human beings out of their immersion in self-centered, "merely natural existence." A significant part of Hegel's philosophy is thus grounded on inaccurate anthropological assumptions of humanity's original immersion in nature and his deprecation of the intuition and instinct supposedly found there. Rousseau, Kant, and Schiller had all answered this question otherwise. Hegel makes a choice in his interpretation.

The possibility that aggression could be a means to exiting the "state of nature" was debated in the conjectural histories of those who followed in Rousseau's wake. Rousseau himself never posited the path to society as one of struggle; he simply mapped a slow progression of social and natural causes.[37] But Hobbes of course did, and both Kant and Schiller discussed whether aggression between subjects in the "state of nature" could be what propels society forward. Speaking of mutual aggression, Kant writes, "Thus happens the first steps from crudity toward culture, which really consists in the social worth of the human being."[38] (Kant also, like Hegel, posits that the same thing that drives individuals toward culture will have a similar function in the relations between states.[39]) Schiller, on the other hand, argued that aggression between peoples only drove them further into themselves. There is no causal mechanism here. What we need instead is a "kindly nature" that allows reflective consciousness to grow.[40]

Hegel sides here with Kant, but with an interesting innovation that, in a sense, gives more credit to those outside Europe than his predecessor did. Hegel posited the desire for freedom as the *cause* of aggression, not only its effect. Nevertheless, he believed non-Europeans to be stuck in this early developmental stage—fighting ceaselessly for freedom but never arriving at it.[41] His racism is apparent in the explanation for this state of affairs: non-Europeans are incapable of seeing others as others, and thus never progress in the dialectic. One way out of this original condition was to pass through the same process of establishing the unbearable identities of master and slave so as to enable the dialectical movement toward freedom through recognition. Michael Monahan has argued that a reading of the MSD in the context of Hegel's work as a whole suggests the possibility of "recognition beyond struggle."[42] I am convinced of this. Nevertheless—as I think Monahan would agree—it remains the case that we have to deal with the problematic justifications for slavery (and later colonialism) that this *specific* path recommends.[43]

This reading of the MSD puts pressure on works such as Susan Buck-Morss's *Hegel, Haiti, and Universal History* and Andrew Cole's *The Birth of Theory*.[44] For these critics, Hegel's story is a progressive unfolding of a powerful critique of slavery. For Cole, this is specific to Hegel's critique of Medieval feudalism.[45] For Buck-Morss, this is about how he incorporated the Haitian Revolution into his philosophy. Buck-Morss expressed shock that no other reader of Hegel had yet connected the MSD to the ongoing slave revolution in Haiti, about which, she meticulously argues, Hegel would certainly have been reading when he was writing the *Phenomenology*.[46] (Of course, whether he read about something and what he wrote about are not the same thing, but the themes of revolutions against slavery were clearly on his mind.) She suggests that his work performs a contextual revolution because of its engagement with Haiti: Hegel thought of "not slavery versus some mythical state of nature (as those from Hobbes to Rousseau had done earlier), but slaves versus masters, thus bringing into his text the present, historical realities that surrounded it like invisible ink."[47] But I have two concerns here. First, it presumes that Rousseau and others wrote about "some mythic state of nature," rather than the actual travel accounts they were reading, as I have argued. It thus erases the place of global history in the making of European thought, which is what Buck-Morss otherwise rightly claims her whole text is about! Second, it ignores the fact that this globally produced concept of the "state of nature" *is* central to Hegel himself. Hegel writes repeatedly about "the state of nature," and always extremely critically.⁴⁸ Indeed, what I have argued here is that this not-so-mythic state of nature is a stand-in for the non-European world, and that the need to overcome this state is precisely what Hegel is discussing in the MSD. The dialectic, first formed in a forgotten history of colonial exchange, is now being used to explain the very cultures being colonized.

If this claim about the MSD remains obscure in the dense and existential language of the *Phenomenology*, it comes out clearly in the *Philosophy of Subjective Spirit*. It would be a mistake to simply read the later text as if it defined the former because the task of each is different, and Hegel may very well have changed his mind in the interim. But, if the later text functions in a way as Hegel's own reading of his earlier work, and given that this is also a concern of his earlier ruminations on "natural slavery,"⁴⁹ then my reading of the MSD is consistent with his later remarks on the life-and-death struggle for recognition:

> In order to avoid eventual misunderstandings of the point of view just presented [the life and death struggle], it has also to be observed that the struggle for recognition in the extreme form in which it is here presented *can occur only in the state of nature*, in which men are simply singular beings. It remains alien to both civil society and the state, within which the recognition constituting the result of this struggle is already present.⁵⁰

If this is true, the struggle simply cannot (or at least not primarily) refer to Haiti or feudalism at this point.⁵¹ Rather, here this struggle is explicitly said to be the answer to the question Hegel has inherited from Rousseau, Kant, and Schiller: How do we transition from the state of nature to civil society, or from immersive instinct to rational reflection to communal integration? Hegel is explicit about this: "It is through the appearance of this struggle for recognition and submission to a master, that states have been initiated out of the social life of men." Further still: it "constitute[s] the *necessary* and *justified* moment by which self-consciousness makes the transition from the *condition* of being immersed in desire and singularity into that of its universality."⁵² The MSD is Hegel's use of conjectural history to justify the present.

If we are to actually read the MSD, if we are to take it seriously *as* philosophy, then we need to understand the role it played within the philosophical history of its time. Because we have erased the question of the global from the history of philosophy, it appears as if what Hegel says about other cultures is alien to his "central" philosophy. (In her writing against this tendency, I very much agree with and am indebted to Buck-Morss.) But what we can see here, at the very center of his most central work, at the most famous moment of his most famous text, is that he is continuing to work within the tradition of conjectural history inaugurated by Rousseau. And more than this, he is disagreeing with Rousseau for the purpose of denying validity to forms of life that exist beyond what he views as the necessary and proper form of society. Further still, as we will see in a moment, he will justify colonialism through the same story. When Hegel sets out to essay the globe, he does not, like Montaigne, seek to transform himself so that he may become the kind of subject who can understand the values of other ways of life. Rather, like Kant and Schiller, he seeks to transform himself *and the globe* in unison.

In the "Preface" to the *Phenomenology*, Hegel tells us that the "onset of the new spirit is the product of a widespread upheaval in various forms of culture."[53] He is referring, undoubtedly, to the revolutionary transformations in Europe at the time, as well as those in Haiti and elsewhere, as Buck-Morss points out. The trouble is that this "widespread upheaval" of course is also the ongoing destruction of lifeworlds across the globe. We need not make a facile claim to "cultural preservation" to be able to say that such upheaval is destructive not only of existing complex cultures, but also of possible contact between them. As Césaire writes, "the great historical tragedy of Africa has been not so much that it was too late in making contact with the rest of the world, *as the manner in which that contact was brought about.*"[54] As we have seen in Senghor and will see with Fanon, none of these authors therefore denies the power of Hegelian thinking. Rather, they negate those parts of Hegel's system—those unnecessary impositions—that bring about contact in the wrong manner. Hegel may have an abstract idea about this, but, at least with reference to colonial spaces, he has no *grounded* (in both senses of the word) theory of intercultural contact. Rather than advocating a mode of contact that brings pluralities into conversation, Hegel believes in singular, universal transformations that are absolute and binding for all. Thus, in the final paragraph of the *Phenomenology*, he writes that each Spirit "took over the empire of the world [*Reich der Welt*] from its predecessor."[55]

Hegel is often criticized for seeming to suggest that the current form of the world is the final shape of Spirit, but this is not what he says at all. As some readers rightly point out, all that has happened in the current shape of Spirit is that Spirit has come to know itself in the form of the state and in the expressive mode of philosophical prose.[56] But what I am suggesting is that while Hegel is indeed more complex than a total, final vision, this complexity disappears when he writes about the colonies, particularly the Americas and Africa. For them, he *does* have a total vision: they will succumb to this European mastery of the very idea of historical change. Even if through overcoming Europe they may eventually take over "the empire of the world," we are still left with the problem of a philosophy of history that promises a single law for the entire globe.

Buck-Morss offers a positive take on what a future Spirit might look like when she writes, "The definition of universal history that begins to emerge here is this: rather than giving multiple, distinct cultures equal due . . . human universality emerges in the historical event at the point of rupture."[57] Her concern is with the loss of shared values in the face of colonial or capitalist onslaught. But she poses an either/or question between universalism and pluralism, and so, like Hegel, she loses sight of a truly radical pluralism that can at once affirm humanity and difference. As I have suggested with Senghor, and argue in later chapters, this is not about universalism versus traditional pluralism, but rather a singular universal vision versus a radical pluralism that allows for shared visions at the same time that it does not disable the multiplicity of human experience. There is no reason why universal values need to emerge at the point of rupture, rather than, say, the communication of shared values in what Senghor punningly called the "civilization of the universal." We can instead imagine the complex meetings between lifeworlds that Hegel, had he moved past his colonial prejudices, could have himself imagined. And there is great risk when we rely only on rupture, only the violent movement of tearing out of the given, rather than finding the complexity of the given. My concern with Hegel's global vision—even in the progressive forms envisioned by Buck-Morss and others—is that it does not, in its global *constitution*, make room for finding the complexity of worldviews in colonial spaces, even if it has the *resources* for doing so.

If the reader is not yet convinced that the state of nature arguments that Hegel derived from his readings in global cultures create a dangerously colonial dialectical logic, we need only turn to the *Philosophy of Right*, where he unequivocally deploys the MSD in his defense of both slavery and colonialism. Hegel first deploys the MSD in his discussion of slavery. He begins by clarifying the relationship between the human being as a concept and "his *immediate* existence in himself."[58] The concept of a human being includes its immediate existence, but the immediate existence does not yet comprehend the concept. In other words, the "natural" human being made up of instincts and desires is not a human being as such until he has a concept of himself *as* a human being: "it is only through the *development* of his own body and spirit, *essentially* by means of *his self-consciousness comprehending itself as free*, that he takes possession of himself."[59] Now all humans, Hegel says, are part of Spirit, and so have the "capacity" to reflect on themselves, but they do not necessarily do so. This is the essential difference between Nature and Spirit that I noted above. The possibility of slavery for Hegel comes down to this fact: that spirit can rest in-itself with a capacity that remains only formal until it is objectified and made for-itself.

In remarks to this section (§57), Hegel explains this in more detail. All justifications of slavery "depend on regarding the human being as a *natural being* whose *existence* . . . is not in conformity with his concept." In other words, the justification of slavery rests on a false idea that any human being could simply be a natural being. This fails to see that the natural human *contains his concept*, but simply has not asserted it yet. But, Hegel continues, this does *not* mean that all slavery is wrong: "the claim that slavery is absolutely contrary to right is firmly tied to the *concept* of the human being as spirit . . . and is one-sided inasmuch as it regards the human being as *by nature* free."[60] Freedom, Hegel asserts, is the province of the for-itself only. Now to be as fair to Hegel as possible, there is a certain logic here. For one thing, he outright rebuts the idea of natural slavery. It is as incoherent to him as natural freedom. Furthermore, he helps us to clarify the social meaning of civil liberty in a way akin to Schiller. If I am free as I am and with whatever unruly desires I have, then social life can only be thought of as a restriction on my desires. If, however, my freedom *only* exists when it rationally inhabits a social structure built on self-conscious reflection, then there is no contradiction between what I want and what society is: the two become seamless.[61]

What we have found in this period, especially since Rousseau, is a distinction between two kinds of liberty: natural and civil. While Rousseau praised natural liberty and did not seek to impose European forms of civil liberty on all, he did ultimately believe that civil liberty promised a higher condition of existence. For Kant and Schiller, as we have seen, not only is natural liberty a precarious and dangerous state, but it is also one that must be globally overcome. For them, being chained to natural instinct *is* slavery. To overcome this servitude to nature, one must rise up to the level of reason. But then reason, in turn, can be its own enslavement. One must thus find the path back to natural liberty through a civil constitution: this is Kant's "vocation" of the human species and Schiller's "they are what we were; they are what we should become again."

The distinction between natural and civil liberty is also central to Hegel's thought, if only because he goes to some length to reject it. There is no natural liberty in Hegel:

> The notion . . . [that] man lived in *freedom* in a so-called state of nature . . . is mistaken. [In that condition], spirituality was immersed in nature, and hence [it is] a condition of savagery and unfreedom . . . freedom consists *solely* in the reflection of the spiritual into itself, its distinction from the natural, and its reflection upon the latter.[62]

There is only civil liberty. But because you cannot get something from nothing, there must be something in nature that allows for this civil condition to emerge. Hegel suggests that what is inherent to our nature is only the *concept* of our freedom. Because of this, he is at least ontologically opposed to slavery. However, as he makes exceedingly clear in *The Philosophy of Right*, he is not opposed to it *historically*:

> The Idea of freedom is truly present only as *the state* . . . If we hold firmly to the view that the human being in and for himself is free, we thereby condemn slavery. But if someone is a slave, his own will is responsible, just as the responsibility lies with the will of a people if that people is subjugated . . . Slavery occurs in the transitional phase between natural human existence and the truly ethical condition; it occurs in a world where a wrong is still right. Here, the wrong *is valid*, so that the position it occupies is a necessary one.[63]

Hegel's defenders have a lot to explain here. First of all, how it is that someone who is supposedly so aware of forces and conditions of modern life is utterly clueless about the actual operations of institutional power and enforcement? Then there is the absurd slippage between an individual will and the "will of a people," something that, even if it potentially exists, by Hegel's own logic should be a tremendous historical achievement, one that does not exist anywhere in the world. But most immediately, why does slavery exist "in the transitional phase," and why is that phase "necessary"?

Some Hegel scholars, like Brennan and Buck-Morss, have offered a defense of Hegel on the basis of the fact that he is openly advocating slave revolts. Indeed, the above passage from the *Philosophy of Right* is claiming that individuals and peoples have not only the right, but the absolute necessity to fight for their freedom. This is not meaningless. Hegel is openly advocating against empire, and, in this sense, he is far ahead of many in his day and in ours. But we should be careful before praising him absolutely. As I have suggested, and as Robert Bernasconi has also argued, there is good reason to believe that Hegel's revolutionary arguments carry with them a deeply problematic idea: that—barring some revolutionary spark that their "dormancy" seems to preclude—peoples outside Europe must pass through domination by Europe to achieve true freedom.[64]

This is true for Hegel at both individual and global levels. Like Kant in his "Conjectural History," Hegel will go on to argue that this relation between individuals as masters and slaves repeats itself in the relation between states (colonizer and colonized). In the section on "International Law," Hegel writes, "Without relations with other states, the state can no more be an actual individual than an individual can be an actual person without a relationship with other persons." Just as with the Master and Slave, this further moment requires *mutual recognition* in Hegel's very specific sense. Here's the rub: "In the case of a nomadic people, for example, or any people at a low level of culture, the question even arises of how far this people can be regarded as a state."[65] In the original MSD, freedom depended on taking the life of the other; likewise, in this version, European countries have what amounts to a "duty to freedom" to colonize. Hegel says it is *"the right of heroes"* to use violence and wrong to establish states.[66] Hegel introduces this right earlier in the text with regard to the concept of coercion. Coercion is justified, he says, when it is "directed against savagery and barbarism [*Wildheit und Rohheit*] . . . Either there is . . . the family or state . . . or there is nothing other than a state of nature . . . in which case the Idea sets up a *right of heroes* against it."[67] The right of heroes is thus the right of coercion against the supposed unfreedom of those who do not live within the structures that Hegel manages to recognize.

Unable to recognize meaningful forms of governance other than his own, Hegel says that the right of heroes "entitles civilized nations to regard and treat as barbarians" these others. "Consequently," he continues, "the wars and conflicts which arise in these circumstances . . . are struggles for recognition with reference to a specific content."[68] To be sure, as in the original MSD, Hegel is critical of colonialism, and he does believe that these colonized states should eventually rise up and overthrow their masters.[69] In this instance, Haiti may very well be on his mind—but even if it is, it is only so, as Bernasconi argues, because it brings Haiti into the fold of Eurocentric conceptions of the state.[70] From beginning to end, the MSD is a conjectural history that ends with European dominance of both souls and nations, even if this dominance is meant to yield to universality someday. The birth of Hegel's notions of struggle, freedom, and the state, just like dialectics itself (as I argued in the preceding chapters), is indissociable from how the defense of colonialism constituted his philosophical positions. Given all of this, it is perhaps not surprising that Hegel does not (so far as I know) repeat the anecdote about the Caribbean man and the French trader from Du Tertre, Rousseau, and Kant. All that he says of the Caribs is this: "The Caribs of earlier times are almost entirely extinct. These savages die out when brought into contact with brandy and guns."[71]

In spite of all these problems, Hegel has often been taken up as a useful resource for global thinking. In an essay in praise of "cultural translation," for example, Judith Butler has argued that "[Hegel] makes plain that the categories by which the world becomes available to us are continually remade by the encounter with the world that they facilitate . . . [He] makes it clear that universality is not a feature of a subjective cognitive capacity but linked to the problem of reciprocal recognition."[72] Hegel, she argues, thus undercuts arguments to cultural supremacy and forces us to see how our ideas actually play out when engaging others. While this is true, I worry that it, in Hegel's own phrase, carries in too many presuppositions "behind the back of consciousness."[73] For what we have seen is that "reciprocal recognition" in Hegel is not an abstract idea that can be applied for global thinking; rather, it has already arisen through global contacts. And in that space, what "reciprocal recognition" implies is an entire history of slavery and dominance that purports to result in equal subjects but in reality seems only to produce perpetual war. Such a conception of recognition simply carries too much baggage and undercuts the very kinds of translations that Butler is proposing. Before we can get at what might be of interest in Hegel for essaying a global self, I think, we first need to come to terms with the geography that already informs his work.

How do we unsettle that geography? We will shortly encounter one path in Fanon: to play out the history of the dialectic until its overextended reach leads to its own shattering. Another tactic is to go back behind the story and question its Eurocentric origins.[74] Then we would ask, what if human history does not have blind instinct at its origin? What does our story of the global self look like with a vision that does not assume that in breaking the natural impulse and stagnation of primitive life, European reason could unleash a synthetic justice on the world? One way to respond is to follow Butler's guidance and continue to push our "acts of knowledge" about different cultural formations. In the context of the MSD, then, we can re-ask the question, "What happened when two consciousnesses met in the world before Columbus?" and answer it differently than Hegel does. Because it was Hegel's readings in anthropology that drove his initial reflections, perhaps it makes sense to turn to contemporary anthropology for other answers.[75]

This task—as conjectural as those of Rousseau, Kant, Schiller, and Hegel—was recently taken up by Philippe Descola, a philosophically trained anthropologist. Descola begins by updating the anthropological data from both travelers' accounts and recent ethnographic research. He finds that "physicality" and "interiority" are not European achievements, but are generally distributed across human populations—they are "not Western constructs . . . for despite the known diversity of conceptions of the person, notions of physicality and interiority seem to be universally present, although with an infinite variety of modalities of connections and interactions between the two planes."[76] Descola proceeds to reconduct Hegel's thought experiment with the supposition in mind that even in the "state of nature," some sense of the duality of interiority and physicality exists. He then graphs the types of identifications this hypothetical subject would make "when confronted with an as yet unspecified *alter*, whether human or non-human."[77] This is the rewriting of the moment when the two consciousnesses meet. This "or non-human" is important because it radically shifts our scene. Hegel is revealed to have retroactively snuck an inappropriate supposition into his thought experiment: that humans only recognize other humans as having self-consciousness. In fact, the anthropological record suggests that recognition on these terms happens only in one of four (there may be more, but Descola claims four) existing human ontological schemes: naturalism. In naturalism alone is it presumed that animals with similar physical forms to humans are "devoid of interiority." The other three options are animism (similar interiority, different physicality); totemism (analogous interiority and physicality); and analogism (completely distinct interiority and physicality).[78]

Without exploring these fascinating categories in any greater detail, the point is simply to suggest that there is no basis for assuming a) that recognition begins with humans, b) that recognition is concerned with differentiation, c) that any of these options for response represents a "progressive development," or d) most importantly, that violence of necessity ensues at this moment.[79] Aggression, Descola suggests, is just one in a range of possible relations, including also friendship, exchange, and seduction. This option of shifting the geography of thought, then, keeps Hegel's scheme while rejecting Hegel's history. It allows us, from inside his text, to open up his concept of recognition and intersubjectivity to a much broader, nonhierarchical, and not necessarily violent world. By tapping into the originary moment at which Hegel's global history went awry, it opens up the concepts of that history to other, less-Eurocentric possibilities.

Another option plays more directly with Hegel on his own terms, although it overthrows the regime of recognition entirely. If some of what Hegel claims to do is to bring philosophic intelligence to raw data, then we might also ask how well he manages to interpret those data. The Brazilian anthropologist Eduardo Viveiros de Castro has reinterpreted the missionary accounts of the same peoples who had fascinated Montaigne: the Tupi. Viveiros de Castro accepts Hegel's basic claim that one primary formation of the peoples of the Americas was cannibalism. In Hegel, cannibalism means that one fails to recognize the other *as* other, but only sees him as a part of herself, and thus cannot establish self-consciousness. Viveiros de Castro says nothing could be further from the truth:

> That which we might call the alloplastic or allomorphic impulse of the Tupi cannot be farther from the pathos of alienation or the mirroring of the Master and the Slave. It is the necessary counterpart to a generalized cannibalism, which distinguishes itself radically from the other-annihilating frenzy proper to imperialisms, Western or other.[80] Efforts to interpret Tupian person-eating in the simplistic terms of an impulse to control the other . . . neglect this double face and this double movement: to incorporate the other is to take on the other's alterity . . . The Tupinambá idea of "becoming White and Christian" did not match up at all to what the missionaries wanted.[81]

As I discussed in the first chapter, Viveiros de Castro's general claim is that, at the beginning, the Tupi (though certainly not every tribe) were in fact very happy to see the Europeans because their group formation was based on continual exchange with others. Thus, "mutual recognition" for the Tupi, even on the grounds of Hegel's schema, is less interesting than how to *exchange* (both materially and symbolically) with others. This reading does not, like Descola, offer us a new path to keeping the insight that Butler wants. Rather, it shows that modes of thinking other than "reciprocal recognition" must contribute to our accounts of how to essay a global self—here, a wildly protean one.

My intention here has not been merely to criticize Hegel for these remarks, although I am happy to criticize present-day Hegelians who remain unwilling to discuss these topics in serious and engaging ways because they insist that his "true philosophy" is elsewhere. This is not at all to say that everyone always need discuss Hegel's geographic imagination; there is much more in his philosophy than this, and there is much more in the world than geography. My concern is simply that geographic imaginings not be displaced, especially when theorists today are looking for global thinking. After all, geography is at the basis of the structure of knowledge that informs Hegel's history, his politics, arguably his philosophy as a whole, because the history of philosophy, in his own terms, is a geographical history.[82] We have no cause to be embarrassed by Hegel's scheme, but should rather seek to understand the logic of this global geography—why does he tell it at all? Because, as I have been arguing, part of the *episteme* of modern thought is that it is consistently framed geographically. One cannot be a thinker—whether German or Tupi—after 1492 without commenting on intercultural relations. If the problem is posed in these terms, then a different set of questions about freedom and the actuality of culture opens up. This would be a possible rewriting of Hegel's geographic history: that what we are seeking is not a resolution to the question "How can freedom be incarnated in a global society?" but rather to the question "How can thought be a meaningful endeavor on the side of freedom across cultural/civilizational/colonial difference?" (Equally: What values other than freedom will we need in order to offset the negative sides that this, like any concept, necessarily carries with it?) It seems to me that writers since Montaigne *were themselves asking* this type of question. And it seems to me that Hegel's answer, while it has some merits in notions such as recognition, is limited by his refusal to see the meaningfulness of lifeworlds outside Europe. It was left up to one of Hegel's most penetrating readers—Karl Marx—to overcome the blindnesses of German idealism and restore the task of crafting a radically pluralist global self that had been covered over by Rousseau's hammock.

Marx: Political Economy, Revolution, and the Return of Pluralism

We do not have to wait until twenty-first-century anthropology to find critics of Hegel's vision of global humanity. As early as 1844, Karl Marx understood that a flaw in Hegel's philosophy produced a flaw in his vision of empirical reality. He saw, furthermore, that a direct line connected this problem from the *Phenomenology* to the late works:

> In the *Phenomenology* . . . despite its thoroughly negative and critical appearance and despite the fact that its criticism is genuine and often well ahead of its time, the uncritical positivism and equally uncritical idealism of Hegel's later works, the philosophical dissolution and restoration of the empirical world, is already to be found in latent form, in embryo, as a potentiality and a secret.[83]

This relationship of an "uncritical positivism" to an "uncritical idealism" is at the heart of Marx's critique of Hegel. The idealism is uncritical because it denies human reality in the name of a greater "Idea," which that reality is meant to incarnate. And yet, because it incarnates that Idea, already existing empirical reality, as we saw above, is often needlessly and uncritically affirmed as part of the logic of history.[84]

This insistence on the unity of all in the Idea was part of why Hegel viewed all things through the movement of mediation and dialectical transformation. Marx saw the link between this uncritical idealism and the fallacy of the always present dialectic. In his critique of Hegel's *Philosophy of Right* (1843–44), Marx thus distinguishes between three kinds of oppositions: those that are opposites but share a common essence (the example given is male and female sharing the essence of the human), those that appear to be opposite but only because of a false partialization (the example given is religion and philosophy, with religion being but the illusory expression of the truth of philosophy), and those that are "real extremes" (the example given is that of a pole to a "non-pole").[85] "Real extremes," Marx continues, "cannot be mediated precisely because they are real extremes. Nor do they require mediation, for their natures are wholly opposed."[86] In other words, it is a mistake to see the dialectic at work everywhere, making events appear as logical by history, even though they never should have been at all (such as slavery or colonialism, as we have seen in *The Philosophy of Right*). In a merciless criticism, Marx shows time and again that Hegel converts the real extremes that riddle German political life into mystical unities whose contradiction can be overcome.[87] Marx gives the example of right to rule by birth, which Hegel affirms. According to Marx, "what is striking and even *miraculous* is to conceive of an immediate identity, an immediate coincidence, between the *birth of an individual* and the individual conceived as *the individual embodiment of a particular social position or function.*"[88] This is a clear example of how a "real extreme" (the non-relation between simply being born and being worthy of holding office) is reconciled in a mystical identity by which "zoology is the secret of nobility."[89]

Nevertheless, a concern that haunts Marx's works (and certainly not his alone) is the extent to which he himself was able to break with his own uncritical idealism and uncritical positivism. As I detail more extensively below, Marx did not necessarily bring these critical insights about Hegel to bear in his thinking about global cultures in most of his early writing. He himself would sometimes employ the very dialectic that he rightly claimed was misapplied in Germany to discuss how to incorporate "savage life" in the communist future, or why the British presence in India was part of the dialectical unfolding of history. What Marx saw to be true about Germany or the North and South Poles, he did not yet see to be true in his global thinking.

Louis Althusser famously suggested that it was not until Marx's later development of a theory of history as the relation of productive forces that Marx could truly develop an economic "science" and break with this "ideological" position.[90] Althusser, an engaged reader of Lévi-Strauss, Maurice Godelier, and other anthropologists, was not unaware of the impact of anthropology for the possibility of such a break in Marx's thought. Indeed, he is explicit that breaking with the anthropological model of the human as a being with needs who exchanges, trucks and barters (as Smith had put it) to meet those needs was at the heart of a fallacious and retroactive universalization of human nature.[91] But Althusser is also explicit that the "detour via primitive societies will only have been necessary in order to see clearly in them what our own society hides from us: i.e., in order to see clearly in them that the economic is never clearly visible."[92] In other words, as is sometimes also claimed in readings of Montaigne and Rousseau, so-called primitive societies provide only for what we might call "comparative relief" in a double sense; that is, they relieve us of uncritical affirmation of our own societies by putting into perspective (relief) the historicity of our forms of life. This seems to accord with some of Marx's basic writings on anthropology, as when he states in *Capital* (1867), "The whole mystery of commodities, all the magic and necromancy that surrounds the products of labour on the basis of commodity production, vanishes therefore as soon as we come to other forms of production."[93]

My argument in this section, however, is that Marx came to find more than relief through his comparisons. As his works progress, they become increasingly concerned with institutional alliances and increasingly pluralistic. They do not just show us how to arrange productive forces *after* capitalism; they also show us how to arrange societies in ways *other than* capitalism. Marx thus became a revolutionary pluralist rather than a teleological essayist. He shared the Kantian insight that one must change the world in order to change the self, but—at least by the end of his life—he tried not to impose his vision on the globe.[94] When he did impose his vision, as in his infamous writings on British colonialism, his revolutionary essaying became unbearable for others. But communism, at its best, would be formed through pluralistic alliances that would change both self and world. Others have noticed this as well. Indeed, my arguments here largely follow the pioneering work of Kevin Anderson's *Marx at the Margins*, which reads Marx's development from the angle of his global reading and writing.[95]

To break with the elements of uncritical idealism and uncritical positivism in his own thinking, Marx had to break with the idea that anthropology in the form of conjectural history only showed us something about the human past that could be reincorporated in the human future. He had to see that cultural difference did not need to be sublated into a single global schema, but rather could be leveraged to form pluralistic human alliances against any form of degradation, regardless of whether the source of that degradation was capitalism, feudalism, or some other force that crushed human lives in the name of a false order and progress. And this anthropology is not just relief for Marx; it is also a site for the production of alternatives. In this section I track the movement in Marx's work away from his early proximity to Hegel's global thinking into this new pluralist space. In so doing, I suggest (as of course many others have before) that Althusser's schema does not hold. This is not, however, based on an argument about Marx's continued humanism so much as on how his engaged reading methods allowed him to dislodge certain Eurocentric premises that overwhelmed his otherwise always strong critique of universal dialectics.[96] Viewed from the angle of his readings in anthropology, Marx's progress was not so much an "epistemological break" as an extensive "practice of the global self" that allowed him to work through the prejudiced elements of his thinking.[97] In a sense, Marx's great advance was simply to connect his critique of logic to his critique of Eurocentrism.[98]

This would take some development on Marx's part. Indeed, one of the most impressive things about his intellectual trajectory was his willingness to discard his anthropological assumptions as he read more deeply and widely. After all, Marx *did* begin his intellectual labor with an uncritical idealism and an uncritical positivism. He believed, like many before him, that human life was an original unity that had been sundered from its natural position in the world. Also like those before him, he believed that the task of philosophy was to reunite our alienated world with that original immersion. In the *1844 Manuscripts*, he thus wrote:

> *Communism* is the *positive* supersession [*Aufhebung*] of *private property* as *human self-estrangement*, and hence the true *appropriation of the human* essence through and for man; it is complete restoration of man to himself as a *social*, i.e., human, being—*a restoration which has become conscious, and which takes place within the entire wealth of previous periods of development* [my emphasis]. This communism . . . is the *genuine* resolution of the conflict between man and nature and between man and man, the true resolution of the conflict between existence and essence, between objectification and self-affirmation, between freedom and necessity, between individual and species. It is the solution of the riddle of history and it knows itself to be the solution.[99]

Communism is presented here as the universal fulfillment of an ongoing process that stretches across humanity; its problematic is humanity's alienation from itself, from nature, and from the world around it. Marx, like Rousseau, believes alienation to have arisen historically. At this point, his anthropological conjectures are as generic as his predecessor's: "The savage in his cave . . . does not experience his environment as alien; he feels just as much at home as a *fish* in water." This is opposed to the poor man's "basement dwelling"—a dingy space only claimed through his "sweat and blood," it is a product of many layers of alienated existence.[100] The "savage" here does not so much provide relief as show the geographic historicity of alienation. Marx is not yet concerned that this formulation traps those called "savage" in unbearably parochial identities. His concept of alienation is thus negatively constituted through his anthropological claims: through his belief that there are savages out there who live unalienated lives, he diagnoses the alienation present in Europe, much as Rousseau did.[101]

Nevertheless, we can already see here that Marx is trying to understand how conjectural histories of the human race have gone astray. He is trying to overcome their misplaced theories that presume that theoretical revolutions, rather than practical, economically aware ones, can solve the problem of alienation. But he is still taking for granted that alienation is historically produced in the transition from savage immersion to civilized reflection. While he is more insistent than his predecessors that the means of overcoming this split requires an economic transformation, he retains at this point (and perhaps will to some extent always) a basic sense that once upon a time we were all happy, immersed beings and that communism can return us to this happiness at a higher level. Continuity through Marx's writings can be seen in the recurrence of this statement in a draft of his famous 1881 letter to Vera Zasulich (often cited by Senghor)[102]: the "crisis [of capitalism in Europe and the United States] will end through its own elimination, through the *return of modern societies to a higher form of an 'archaic' type of collective ownership and production.*"[103] But this is, so to speak, a repetition with a difference: what Marx means by this statement at the end of his career is somewhat different from what he means at the beginning.

The most important difference, as has been painstakingly traced by Anderson in his rich work *Marx at the Margins*, is that Marx moves away from the largely unilinear vision of history that we find in the *1844 Manuscripts*. As Anderson notes, that unilinear conception had led Marx early in his life to write more positively about the disruptive forces of global capitalism. This was most famously signaled in the *Communist Manifesto* (1848), where Marx and Engels wrote:

> All fixed, fast-frozen relations, with their train of ancient and venerable prejudices and opinions, are swept away, all new formed ones become antiquated before they can ossify. All that is solid melts into air, all that is holy is profaned, and man is at last compelled to face with sober senses, his real conditions of life, and his relations with his kind.[104]

It is the destructive force of capitalism (at least in their early understanding here) that wipes away the failures of premodern life: "The need of a constantly expanding market for its products chases the bourgeoisie over the whole surface of the globe . . . The bourgeoisie . . . draws all, even the most barbarian, nations into civilization."[105] They amended this slightly a few sentences later: capital "compels them to introduce *what it calls* civilization."[106] Although Marx and Engels clearly were not siding with the bourgeoisie, they were, as is well known, praising its capacity to negate previous despotisms and create the global networks that would allow for the communist revolution. There is indeed even some praise of capital's ability to get rid of "ancient and venerable prejudices and opinions," and this continues when they say that the bourgeoisie "rescued a considerable part of the population from the idiocy of rural life."[107] The point is not, of course, that this new bourgeois civilization is necessarily better; only that it is the condition of possibility for the revolution. Thus, this opening section of the *Manifesto* prepared the way for its concluding rally call: "The proletarians have nothing to lose but their chains. They have a world to win. WORKING MEN OF ALL COUNTRIES, UNITE!"[108] This act of reconnecting the global self to economic transformation is the fundamental early Marxist idea of a practice of the global self.

But while the goal is noble, its global thinking with regard to the past is problematic. Indeed, it led to some of the worst formulations of Marx's career, especially as evidenced by his controversial writings on India in 1853. There Marx claimed that the supposed village idylls of India were in fact "the solid foundation of Oriental despotism, that they restrained the human mind within the smallest possible compass, making it the unresisting tool of superstition, enslaving it beneath traditional rules, depriving it of all grandeur and historical energies."[109] Like Hegel, Marx posits that positive primitivism in fact masks over the problematic lack of freedom in non-European civilizational practices. And also like Hegel, he believes that to be free from that blind determination, a struggle for recognition must be brought about:

> England, it is true, in causing a social revolution in Hindoostan, was actuated only by the vilest interests, and was stupid in her manner of enforcing them. But that is not the question. The question is, can mankind fulfill its destiny without a fundamental revolution in the social state of Asia? If not, whatever may have been the crimes of England she was the unconscious tool of history in bringing about that revolution.[110]

What interests me about Marx's comments here is not their place in an old debate about whether or not he was an Orientalist.[111] The passage raises for me a different concern: that these are the kinds of statements one might be led to make when one envisions history as beginning in a problematic state that modernity might disrupt. We saw this, too, in Hegel's defenses of slavery and colonialism. Indeed, Marx should have known better—his own 1844 writings on Hegel criticize Hegel's application of dialectics to sites where it did not belong. This writing about India is a blatant act of an uncritical idealism leading to an uncritical positivism. To say this is not to deny the profound problems that existed in India or its caste system, against which Dalits continue to struggle. It is simply to recall Césaire's point that ethical exchange, not the force of colonialism, forms the solution to such issues. My sense is that Marx himself came to (or returned to) this conclusion, and there is ample evidence that his position on India became increasingly nuanced over time.[112] Indeed, this necessity of imposition will gradually be erased from Marx's thought as a whole, as evidenced by the fact that when Marx and Engels wrote a new preface to the Russian edition of the *Communist Manifesto* in 1882, they emphasized the continuity of Russian forms of landholding from the past into the future.[113] But this turn in their later work is unfortunately not always noticed, and we continue to think of Marx within the framework of his early Eurocentric position, even as works like Anderson's challenge this narrative.[114]

Marx offers us more than a reminder of the need to think in terms of multilateral global formations: he offers a vision of the practice of that as well. He continued reading and thinking and learning new languages (perhaps most importantly Russian) throughout his life.[115] And not only did he learn from this reading; he often saw past the anthropologist's own ethnographic blinders. Here one important practice that he reinforces is Rousseau's basic insight that the European depictions of people in the so-called state of nature were often fantastic projections of one's own prejudices. In his *Ethnological Notebooks* (1879–82), for example, he comments acidly on a passage from John Lubbock's *The Origin of Civilization and the Primitive Condition of Man*: "these civilized jackasses cannot get themselves free of their own conventionalities."[116] The path to developing a global self is not simply to read about the globe; it is to expand one's capacities of thought so that, however one may judge another culture, one at least understands its basic categories first. (This, recall, was the lesson of the watermelon patch that Rousseau taught Emile.)

A second key practice emerges in Marx's reading of Maxim Kovalevsky's *Communal Landownership: The Causes, Course, and Consequences of Its Decline*. Anderson singles out a passage copied down by Marx: "The government has nothing to do with the totality of the communal possessors of a given village . . . Yet *between these atoms certain connections continue to exist*, distantly reminiscent of the earlier communal village landowning groups."[117] The absolutely central point here, as Anderson notes, is that capitalism is not a total system. Within its dominance there remain what Raymond Williams would later call "residual" and "emergent" cultures.[118] (I return to the contemporary debate about the universalization of capital below.) Whereas earlier Marx theorized the total disappearance of all "fixed, fast-frozen relations," he now emphasizes the possible points of resistance that could emanate from such residual communal practices. He thus shows us the need to think not in terms of domination alone, but also in terms of the various strata of the present that can be linked up in a global practice. This methodology of focusing on the multiplicity of the present is something I have insisted on throughout.

This leads us to another of Marx's contributions: he thinks about these residual practices not as benefits in themselves, but as nodes to be connected up with other points of resistance. This is why, in the 1882 preface to the Russian edition of the *Communist Manifesto*, Marx and Engels do not merely tout the power of the commune. Rather, they insist, "If the Russian Revolution becomes the signal for a proletarian revolution in the West, so that both complement each other, the present Russian common ownership of land may serve as the starting-point for a communist development."[119] Marx never stopped insisting on the fact that any possible transformation within the nation would have to be related to other global struggles—workers of the world, unite! Indeed, he only strengthened this insistence by opening his thought to the possibility that such a universal struggle would only be achieved through a variety of different global situations that would also contain difference within themselves. This does not of course mean that Marx became a romantic primitivist or believed in the necessity of the commune any more than in the necessity of any other form. It is simply that he opens up to the possibility of the variety of forms that the future world might take.[120]

Perhaps in part because of his early critique of Hegel's universalism, these insights do not just come later in Marx's career, and we can find elements of them across his writings. In addition to the *1844 Manuscripts*, this is evident in his notebooks for the *Grundrisse* (1857), for example. Indeed, in the very first paragraph of the notebooks, Marx argues against the anthropological assumptions of political economy.[121] All of them, he notes, are based on visions of primitive life, but these "in no way express merely a reaction against over-sophistication and a return to a *misunderstood* natural life, as cultural historians imagine."[122] Rather, these visions provide an alibi for the isolated individual of modernity. By imagining back to an original, singular individual separated from community, these thinkers can imagine that *this* separateness is the natural condition of human life that governments and societies stamp out. Marx suggests, both following and critiquing Rousseau, that this is merely a projection back from one's own way of life.

Breaking with this conception orients him toward a vision of the good life based first and foremost on social praxis. These readings in global histories of economy and property gave Marx a historical basis for the claim that the task of the economy was not the creation of wealth or personal liberty, as was becoming axiomatic. Throughout the *Grundrisse* notebooks, Marx considers different concepts of property. He concludes: "The relation to the earth as property is always mediated through the occupation of the land and soil, peacefully *or* violently, by the tribe, the commune, in some *more or less* naturally arisen *or* already historically developed form."[123] Elsewhere he speaks of earlier community systems as either "more despotic *or* . . . more democratic."[124] The point of the constant use of the conjunction "or" is for Marx to show that he refuses any originary determination of how humans can and should relate to property. He believes that, within certain natural limits and historical conditions, humans can make and remake their history at the same time that they embrace its "natural" development. The task is to find the mode of property relation that, as he says, they sought to consecrate in ancient Rome: the mode that "creates the best citizens."[125] Anthropological and historical difference enabled his argument that property is not a good in itself; it is subordinate to its value for citizenship as a whole. Unlike the liberals, whose visions of the state of nature informed their argument that property and liberty were the sole guarantors of human flourishing, Marx was able to see otherwise. This does not mean he was right, but it does mean he helps overturn the unbearable assumptions of human nature found in much liberalism.

As an aside, I note that this question of anthropology haunts mid-twentieth-century liberal economics as well. As Friedrich Hayek wrote in *The Road to Serfdom* (1944), based on seemingly blind prejudice:

> From the primitive man, who was bound by an elaborate ritual in almost every one of his daily activities, who was limited by innumerable taboos, and who could scarcely conceive of doing things in a way different from his fellows, morals have more

and more tended to become merely limits circumscribing the sphere within which the individual could behave as he liked. The adoption of a common ethical code comprehensive enough to determine a unitary economic plan would mean complete reversal of this tendency.[126]

Hayek's history is simply wrong: all cultures, then as now, have dominant modes as well as residual and emergent properties, as Raymond Williams phrased it. The question is which mode do we wish to become dominant. We certainly do have a comprehensive value structure today: one based on profit and the growth of wealth.

This was precisely what Karl Polanyi understood in his anthropologically and historically rich counter to Hayek, *The Great Transformation* (also 1944). For Polanyi, the reverse of Hayek's argument was true: modern society is the first ever to be "shaped in one common matrix," that is, "the self-regulating market": "Nineteenth-century civilization alone . . . chose to base itself on a motive only rarely acknowledged as valid in the history of human societies, and certainly never before raised to the level of justification of action and behavior in everyday life, namely, gain."[127] Primitive societies, by contrast, were built on social systems of value, of which the economic was but one factor. The point again is not whether we "regress" or "progress," but how we use our understanding (and imagination) of history to critique or justify the present. This is perhaps why much of Marx's late work, like that of other anthropologically minded economists such as Polanyi and Thorstein Veblen, took aim at the false historical anthropology of the Robinsonades and other fantasies of human life.[128]

To return to Marx. He moves beyond liberalism's ethnocentric accounts and realizes that the ways in which humans describe different cultures produce profound transformations in their visions of the good life. And as we think back on Montaigne, Rousseau, Kant, Schiller, and Hegel, it is abundantly clear that the more negative their visions of extra-European cultures, the more pronounced their imperialism became.[129] As Marx refines his own vision, he begins to see that there may be paths to revolution *other* than through the destructive power of capitalism. Indeed, he begins to discover that thinking *with* other cultures not only disrupts his own culture—not only throws it into comparative relief—but also opens up other potential ways of thinking and being.

This revision by Marx also issued a challenge to the general primitivist basis of much early European global thought. In the chapter on Rousseau,

I argued that the dialectic as an ideological concept was invented by erasing economic difference. Rousseau took an anecdote from Du Tertre about differences in methods of exchange between the French and Caribs, erased its economic base, and transformed it into a parable about the human relationship to time. In so doing, he invented an injunction for global thought: to be able to negate unruly human nature while at the same preserving and uplifting its more noble qualities. This, I have argued, initiated a colonial dialectic about how European colonization would lead to global subjects who had dialectically combined reason and instinct. I have traced this into Kant's ideal of enlightenment, Schiller's aesthetics, and Hegel's historical vision. Marx eventually pierced through this ideological history, realizing that conjectural histories had often been created precisely to cover over an uncritical positivism with regard to economic realities. While he did not necessarily redeem the complexity of the Carib's way of life, he did at least see that the Carib's history had been rent to fit a troubling narrative of European dominance. Still following Rousseau's basic model of conjectural history, Marx turned it back against its creator. The task became to recover the economic foundations of the global self and to construct new social orders on those foundations.

Across his writings, Marx preserves some of the basic features of conjectural history. He never appears to abandon his youthful vision of a sublated community of equals. He keeps the basic trajectory from immersion to alienation to reconnection at a higher level; he simply gives the story an economic twist. He keeps throughout his writings a basic sense of historical development toward a society that he describes in *Capital* as "an association of free men, working with the means of production held in common, and expending their many different forms of labour-power in full self-awareness as one single social labour force."[130] What he loses is the sense that there is only one path to this way of life—a path through the blood and fire of capital. He makes this explicit in an 1877 letter to a Russian critic who fears that Marx had imposed his vision of capital on the world. Marx writes of this critic that he "transform[s] my historical sketch of the genesis of capitalism in western Europe into a historico-philosophical theory of the general course, fatally imposed upon all peoples, whatever the historical circumstances in which they find themselves placed."[131] Rather than such a general theory, Marx calls for a comparative analysis of different historical situations, such that this analysis might yield a way of thinking the path toward communal justice that would be linked across different spaces. In the end, then, it would seem that Marx pluralized the path but maintained a singular goal.

And yet a sentence from his *1844 Manuscripts* suggests that even this may not be the case: "*Communism* is the necessary form and the dynamic principle of the immediate future, but communism is not as such the goal of human development—the form of human society."[132] The current situation calls for communism, but humanity, as a progressive force contingently developing with historical changes, may yet find other forms in which to live.[133] In moments like these, we can see again that Marx's greatest insights did not come when he broke from his youth, but when he learned to think some of his youthful insights all the way through. Plural paths may yet lead to plural destinies, hopefully ones that move beyond the grinding labor and natural destruction that have marked all growth-based economies to this day.

A Brief Note on Chakrabarty on Marx (and Heidegger)

One of the most significant treatments of Marx from the question of global thought remains Dipesh Chakrabarty's *Provincializing Europe* (2000). Chakrabarty explores two modes of history writing that he famously calls "History 1" and "History 2."[134] The former is "the indispensable and universal narrative of capital," while the latter explores "diverse ways of being human, the infinite incommensurabilities through which we struggle."[135] To "provincialize Europe," then, is to show how its attempt to tell "History 1" is meaningful but partial in ways that it does not admit. It is to insist that "thought [is] related to place" and thus that all universal claims also come from and collide with local histories.[136] We need universal histories like Marx's story of capital, Chakrabarty explains, because they enable the commitment to securing life, equality, and liberty for all that is the most valuable contribution of political modernity. But we cannot allow this universal vision to wash over the meaningful diversity of human existence, which is as valuable to global humanity as biodiversity is to the environment. Moreover, we cannot lose the explanatory power of bearing both of these modes of history in mind. As Chakrabarty shows, the assumption of European universalization makes it impossible to understand the actual lives that colonialism created. "My aim," he writes in one of the book's later chapters, "is to make room for the proposition that Bengali modernity may have imagined life-worlds in ways that never aimed to replicate either the political or the domestic ideals of modern European thought."[137] The universalizing narrative both should not and cannot write over the diversity of human life. But, equally, the diversity of human life does not absolve us from the need to essay to understand what may be universal in our conditions. In the end, the aim is "to struggle to hold in a state of permanent tension a dialogue [between History 1 and History 2]."[138]

There is much of value in Chakrabarty's work, but I want to offer another mode of thinking that gets us past such "tensions" and "incommensurabilities." Part of the problem here is that these ideas by necessity deny internal pluralities, as I mentioned in the introduction. To put it schematically: the cost of provincializing Europe is the depluralization of both Europe and India. Chakrabarty himself admits as much: "I am aware that an entity called 'the European intellectual tradition' stretching back to the ancient Greeks is a fabrication of relatively recent European history . . . The point, however, is that . . . this is the genealogy of thought in which social scientists finds themselves inserted."[139] In other words, although "Europe" may be a historical construction, it was not presented to Chakrabarty and his colleagues across South Asia in that manner.[140] Without denying the importance of what Chakrabarty unearths through this strategic partialization of Europe—that is, the history of the denial of Europe's own sense of place and its resulting violent imposition on other places—it remains the case that, like all partializations, this move ignores other complexities.

A persistent concern of Chakrabarty's critics has thus been that his critique of Eurocentrism reverts to Eurocentric positions that suggest that universality is invented in Europe and that Indian traditions remain parochial and belated.[141] Sanjay Subrahmanyam has noted, for example, that Chakrabarty is forced to deny that "History 1" was being written in more places than Europe, even though there is a long tradition of universal history writing in South Asia that can easily be documented. Subrahmanyam further notes the ironic result that this "provincialization" of Europe plays into the hands of those like Hegel who believe in the "exceptionalism" of Europe as the only place to have discovered History in the universal sense.[142] In a more recent critique, Harry Harootunian makes the same basic claim: "It was the postcolonial impulse to exceptionalize culture exemplified in Dipesh Chakrabarty's discourse that paradoxically led to restoring the privilege of the West."[143] The harshest words come, not surprisingly, from Chakrabarty's most strident critic, Vivek Chibber: "What is objectionable about postcolonial theory is not that it insists on 'provincializing Europe,' but that, in the name of this project, it *relentlessly promotes Eurocentrism*—a portrayal of the West as the site of reason, rationality, secularism, democratic culture, and the like, and the East as an unchanging miasma of tradition, unreason, religiosity, and so on."[144] This heavy-handed critique is unwarranted. Indeed, it is near impossible to read Chakrabarty's chapters on colonial Bengal and see in them the "miasma of tradition, unreason, religiosity, and so on." Indeed, Chakrabarty's interest, especially in the second half of the book, has little to do with these things and much to do with how meaningful lifeworlds with highly developed concepts and practices of imagination, fraternity, and conviviality created ways of being in modernity that simply do not match onto the European habitus.[145]

Chibber and Harootunian are particularly concerned with how Chakrabarty, among others, misunderstands "universalization" in Marx. They both show (correctly on my reading) that even in Marx's most generalized writings, capital's tendency to expand in no way implies a homogeneity of what that expansion looks like or how local forces will respond to it.[146] Chibber and Harootunian thus criticize Chakrabarty's insistence that he differs from Marx when he points out local differences in how capitalism gets absorbed in Bengal. This, they say, merely affirms that Marx was right. On this point, I think, their critique is apt. However, this neglects the fact that Chakrabarty uses Marx as an *example* of universal thought. Chapter 6, thus, is mostly about how the category of "imagination" in Bengal differs from what we find in Benedict Anderson's *Imagined Communities*, and chapter 8 looks at how social contract theory there differs from Locke's ideas. There may very well be problems with Chakrabarty's arguments here, too, but to criticize his whole project one would first have to recognize that his interest is not simply in debating Marxism (although he certainly does do this), but also in questioning how general theoretical ideas are applied to local contexts in ways that do not register the actuality of those contexts. At this level, not only do I think that Chakrabarty is correct, but I also assume that Chibber's and Harootunian's commitments to understanding local transformations of capital in fact commit them to some element of Chakrabarty's framework in spite of themselves.

In a review of Chibber's critique, Bruce Robbins registered a potential resulting problem in Chakrabarty: "Any history from below naturally provokes the charge of essentializing and/or idealizing the worldview of the lowly, and the related objection that it rejects any perspective on the lowly from above."[147] This is the risk that Chakrabarty runs and for which he is duly criticized. Indeed, where I think these criticisms of Chakrabarty have real merit—at least in terms of my concerns here (which are, again, less about the question of capital and more about how people respond to whatever regime it is that makes the globe at once interdependent and unequal)—is in their sense that diversity inheres within the universal, and that, conversely, universality may appear from nearly any local position. This is the heart of what concerns Subrahmanyam.

Nevertheless, history from below need not "naturally" lead to charges of essentialization. This is precisely what the doctrine of radical pluralism is meant to address. Within the understanding of radical pluralism, we can certainly generalize about local practices, which make pluralism possible—but that generalization becomes an unbearable identity as soon as it claims to go all the way down (the refusal of such totalizing claims is what makes pluralism radical). The problem occurs once the generalization claims, for example, that there were no subalterns in colonial Bengal who had doubts about contemporary religious practices, who supported the capitalist class, who adopted liberal ideals of the family, whose imaginations neither matched onto *darsan* nor Hobbes, and whose fundamental worldview was more or less the same as that of a seamstress in New England or a merchant in Beijing. What is missing in Chakrabarty's account, on my reading (and I think this most accords with Subrahmanyam's critique), is the sense that plurality does not just mean a German or a Bengali way of viewing things, but also pluralities *within* both places. As this is simply a brute fact of reality, I cannot imagine that Chakrabarty would deny this point. He does not, however, craft his theories from this angle.

The History 1 and History 2 model is thus limited in that it ignores the internal pluralities of either conceptual formation. There are multiple ways of conceiving of both the universal and the local, and often these multiplicities meet. As Chakrabarty himself notes, right after discussing the absoluteness of European thought when it arrived in India: "South Asian(ist) social scientists would argue passionately with a Marx or a Weber without feeling any need to historicize them in their European intellectual contexts."[148] Two things are revealing here: these figures are not received singularly, but are intensely debated, and their original formation is in multiple contexts. One of those contexts—the one I have stressed throughout this book—was how to develop global thought. This impulse to understand global interdependence, including moments of disconnection, is what Marx and Chakrabarty share across the colonial divide. This reckoning with the question of being in the context of a violent, fractured, yet connected world is, I am insisting, absolutely central to the history of the modern self and its conceptual developments.

This is why it is important also to note that Chakrabarty famously juxtaposed Heidegger with Marx to make the case for this diversity.[149] Heidegger, he argued, understood the localization of being in a way that Marx's universal thought overrode. I have argued here that this is an inaccurate characterization of Marx, and, as I discussed in chapter 1, Heidegger was quite explicit that the understanding of being did not require an investigation of different lifeworlds. In fact, he thought that such investigation only masked our understanding of ontology. I cite again: "Versatile curiosity and restlessly knowing it all masquerade as a universal understanding of Da-sein."[150] In a sense, I would argue, Chakrabarty reversed the insights of Marx and Heidegger: Marx understood the plurality of human life, whereas Heidegger insisted on a universal ontology.[151]

This is not just a nitpicky matter of scholarship; it is a part of understanding the traditions through which we build our practices of the global self. Marx may have started without a sense of human diversity, but he continued to read and displace himself, even learning new languages, until his last years. Heidegger, meanwhile, maintained a parochial vision of Europe into his last interview. The fact that he did so touches his philosophy because it shows that his philosophy misunderstands how we live in the world (a point I address more extensively in discussing Fanon and Du Bois). What is important in Marx is the development of his thought and the fact that open and sensitive reading about cultural diversity is a fundamental practice for any person who wants to move past the unbearable identity of cultural chauvinism or cultural imposition. Following Marx, then, I want to suggest that rather than seeing two modes of history in incommensurable tension, we ought to see them as two different modes of expression with their own internal pluralities. There are, after all, multiple ways of describing what is universal, and every local space will have its own sets of differences and conflicts. The tensions that we find in the world are not just between universal and particular. They are also *within* universal and particular. This is because what is "universal" are the ever flowing, alternating patterns of pluralisms and partialisms. Articulating the problem in this way, I hope, enables us to understand global identity differently: as the ongoing (sometimes brutal, sometimes peaceful) meeting of dynamic multiplicities.

Fanon: The End of the Colonial Dialectic

Frantz Fanon's first book, *Black Skin, White Masks* (1952), begins its narration of the global self by situating this history in the unbearable identities produced by colonialism. He describes this with an epigraph from his teacher Aimé Césaire: "I am talking about millions of men whom they have knowingly instilled with fear and a complex of inferiority, whom they have infused with despair and trained to tremble, to kneel and behave like flunkeys."[152] Here Fanon is analyzing what Enrique Dussel and others have called the "the underside of modernity."[153] For Montaigne or Rousseau, the modern world called on them to reduce their nationalist and individualist ego and to open themselves up to the diversity of the planet. For Fanon, under the brute force of colonial rule, the individualist and nationalist ego was precisely what had been crushed and needed to be reconstructed. What was unbearable for him was not the ego as such, but rather the ideological ego, the ego of a "flunkey," that had been constructed for him. His published works—many of which fall within the essay tradition—labored to both describe and enact the transformations of self and world that he believed necessary in order to overcome the unbearability of colonial identity.

In this search for a practice of transformation, Fanon, like Marx, Césaire, and Senghor before him, showed a strong ambivalence about the powers of dialectics, which he demonstrated had both a liberatory and colonial form. At the same time, he remained skeptical of Négritude itself and was a primary expounder of the critique of racial identity. This is certainly part of why Fanon remains more central to critical theory today. There are many critical writings on the complexity of Fanon's relation to Négritude[154] and his relation to Hegel and dialectics.[155] I want to build on them here by interpreting Fanon within the contexts thus far developed in this book. That is to say, I show how he contributes practices to overcome unbearability through his idea of invention, to radical pluralism through his focus on futurity, and to our understanding of the global self by his demand for the deracialization (rather than Négritude's reracialization) of the history of thought.

Fanon's analysis focuses on unbearability through the triad of racialization, colonization, and violence. He states the obvious truths that it is unbearable to be reduced to one's skin, to have one's geographic home controlled by others, and to be subject to random violence; furthermore, he explores how unbearable it is to have to take up race, nation, and violence in order to overcome this primary unbearability. In other words, he explores not just the brutality of colonialism, but also that it leaves open only horrific channels for its overcoming. It is in this context that Fanon will make use of the dialectic as a moving force of history. But it is absolutely central that the dialectic in Fanon's work must first itself be deracialized and decolonized. Although his analysis is not explicitly predicated on reconstituting the history I have set out above in the work of Rousseau, it directly speaks to the colonial violence that underwrites many philosophical concepts. If Fanon uses the dialectic, it is not because of its transhistorical truth, but only because its decolonized form will allow him to overcome the specific modes of unbearability that appear in his life and prevent his becoming a free and creative subject in a just and equal world.

The making of such a world cannot be accomplished by simply asserting the abstract equality of humanity. That is easy enough, Fanon tells us, and that has been done. He is not interested in a "treatise [*un discours*] on the universal," because he knows very well that treatises often come backed by guns and that "the supremacy of white values" is maintained by violence and aggression.[156] Moreover, like Montaigne and Rousseau, he knows that to speak well does not necessarily mean to act well: "[the native knows] that no professor of ethics, no priest has ever come to be beaten in his place, nor to share their bread with him."[157] In brief: "today we know with what sufferings humanity has paid for every one of their [Europeans'] triumphs of the mind."[158]

But while he devalues the discourse on the universal as an abstraction that underwrites the violent imposition of values, he utilizes the essay as a form of writing that can break into incipient transformation. The original title of *Black Skin, White Masks* in fact was "an essay on the disalienation of the black man."[159] And it is crucial to understanding Fanon's famous chapter "Concerning Violence [*De la violence*]" that it is an essayistic attempt to understand the complexity of violence. As we will see, the writing of the essay is not quite for Fanon what it was for Montaigne—a complete activity of the self—but it remained part of a broader set of revolutionary practices. He is explicit that the writing and reading of the book ought to function at the level of transformation: "My book is, I hope, a mirror with a progressive infrastructure where the black man can find the path to disalienation."[160] To the extent that the work is an autobiography, it is safe to say that he is, in part, the person for whom he is mirroring that path. As in Montaigne, then, the act of writing in Fanon is also an act of developing a new path for the self. Unlike Montaigne, however, Fanon will come to the explicit realization that all the work he does on himself is insufficient if it is not aligned with the overcoming of injustice in the world.

Fanon's work operates at the level of both cultural assumptions and political realities. "What we are striving for is to liberate the black man from the arsenal of complexes that germinated in a colonial situation."[161] This will need to happen at two levels, at least. One is at the level of culture, fighting against being "imprison[ed] . . . at an uncivilized and primitive level."[162] It was of course in this sphere that Rousseau's and others' overcoming of their unbearable identity produced the unbearable identity for Fanon and others. The other level is that of politics, which will require overcoming the colonial situation itself. Fanon's most famous works will be dedicated to that task.

Many fascinating threads make up Fanon's first book.[163] I focus my analysis, following the discussions above, on how Fanon takes up of the question of being in a way that is clearly opposed to Heidegger's. For Heidegger, again, the task of philosophy was to understand the meaning of human life from a universal standpoint enabled by, but ultimately divorced from, one's own cultural configuration. He believed that in order to achieve this standpoint from within one's culture, one had to first perform a "destruction of the history of ontology" so as to clear out misconceptions and allow a new understanding to come forth. Fanon attempted to be part of this journey: "I came into this world solicitous to bring out the meaning of things, my soul full of the desire to be at the origin of the world."[164] But what he found was that he was immediately racialized and rendered an object for the white gaze: "Look! A Negro!"[165] Thus "the question" for him was not "to be or not to be"; he could not pose the question of being freely. Rather, it was "Black or White, that is the question."[166] Race imposes itself on being before the nonracialized question of being can even emerge. Thus, a general history of concepts of Being is not what is required to overcome alienation and unbearability; rather, it is the specific racial history of being that has short-circuited the very possibility of philosophy. In *Black Skin*, Fanon sets out to "destructure" the racial history of ontology. It is through such a destructuring, he implicitly suggests, that he can reapproach the question of being.

This analysis carries across the entirety of Fanon's book, from his reflections on the travails of language and love at the beginning to the rethinking of psychoanalysis and call for revolution at the end. He maintains throughout that we do not yet have the philosophical resources to deal with the problem of racialization (whether biological or cultural). Neither European philosophy, which has improperly posed the question, nor African philosophy, which is too focused on uncovering its past, provides the resources that Fanon seeks.[167] Indeed, this search extends across everything Fanon wrote: he is "Striving for a New Humanism" on the first page of *Black Skin*, and he continues to call for a "new man" in the closing words of *Wretched of the Earth*.[168] The conditions of possibility for this new human require both a new understanding of race and the end of colonial rule. To begin to analyze this first aspect, let us turn to the rightfully famous fifth chapter of *Black Skin*, "The Lived Experience of the Black Man."

The chapter begins with the quote cited above about Fanon's desire to engage the meaning of a world that imprisons him in his blackness before he can even ask the question. He shares with W. E. B. Du Bois the sense that the black body and soul exist in a dimension that is always present but not always apparent.[169] "Beneath the body schema," Fanon puts it with reference to Merleau-Ponty's phenomenology of embodiment, "I had created a historical-racial schema."[170] This splits Fanon's body as well as his consciousness. Whereas any person lives in the world in both first and third person—both as a subject and an object—Fanon finds that he lives "no longer in the third person but in triple."[171] He is subject, object, *and* an entire "historical-racial schema."[172] He is not just who he is, a body moving in time among other bodies, responsible for its actions. He is also "responsible . . . for my race and my ancestors."[173] Much of the aim of *Black Skin, White Masks* is to overcome this condition, so that by the end of the book Fanon will state, "I am not a slave to the Slavery that dehumanized my forebears."[174] *Black Skin, White Masks* brings the racial-historical schema to light in order to set the world on a new path. This does *not* mean that race will be eliminated in toto, but only that its congealment into figures—like that of the noble savage—will be slackened, and new potentials for solidarity and collectivity will emerge.

One of Fanon's methodological tools for attaining this movement is what he calls *assumption* [*assumer*], which is wrongly translated as "accept."[175] To get to the point where he is not the slave of past slavery, he has to pass through the fact that others view him this way. He has to "assume" their views, take them up, and then keep moving. The chapter on "The Lived Experience of the Black" is Fanon's recording of the dangers of this process. At various moments, he explodes (89, 117, 119), feels amputated (94, 119), and becomes "disjointed" (93). But this is the struggle of assumption he takes on so that the intersubjective, social change he demands can take place. The endgame is not perfection: "Genuine disalienation will have been achieved only when things, in the most materialist sense, have resumed their rightful place."[176] In the meantime, the only authentic position will be that of "refusal" of the given order and the way in which it prescribes "[current] reality as definitive."[177] "The Lived Experience of the Black Man" charts the movements of twentieth-century black writers along the path of this refusal.

Readers may get some sense of the narrative movement of the chapter, but we should also note that its style consciously reproduces the disorienting effects of racism. Some of the difficulty of understanding the chapter is that it at once charts a logical progression of modes of assumption at the same time that a cacophony of white voices intercedes to remind Fanon of his blackness. Each time he thinks he has developed a schema of disalienation, a new response insists on the insipidity of blackness in a world of white supremacy. By the end of the chapter, all of his solutions frustrated, Fanon will weep at the unbearability of the present situation.[178]

Fanon's first assumption is the legacy of slavery. He will take on this identity just as "President Lebrun [president of France from 1932–40] was the grandson of peasants who had been exploited."[179] But Fanon quickly realizes that whereas a white man might rise through the ranks and leave his past behind, even a successful black man always carries the burden of his racial history with him. "I knew for instance that if the [black] physician made one false move, it was over for him and for all those who came after him."[180] No matter how wise he was, no matter how "well he behaved," there was nothing that the black man could do that did not draw the suspicion and ire of whites. As Fanon reads into the problem, he discovers the reason given by the white world: "color prejudice." And if prejudice is simply a mistake of judgment, then it should be correctable by rational means.

So Fanon begins to assume rationality, only to find that the white world continues to inscribe the problem not only in the black body but also in the black past. "At the start of my history that others have fabricated for me, the pedestal of cannibalism was given pride of place so that I wouldn't forget."[181] The pronouncement of the white world is a kind of "affective ankylosis."[182] In other words, it is an emotional stiffening of the body that refuses rational reflection. This being the case, Fanon assumes another position: taking up blackness and resignifying its value.

This is what Fanon finds in Léopold Senghor's philosophy of Négritude. (Senghor's work is more complex than Fanon allows, as I have argued above.) Senghor grounds the new value of black identity in a capacity for "*Rhythm!*"[183] The idea, as Fanon sees it, is to switch from a degraded past to one that assumes the subjective position of a kind of noble savagery. He associates this idea with Senghor's work on African sculpture and especially the phrase "*Emotion is Negro as reason is Greek.*"[184] If rationality is where the white world operates, then irrationality is what the black man will claim as his main contribution. Not only this, but he will be better at it than the alienated white man, who has lost touch with the world. Irrational immediacy will be the province of the black man alone. There is a brief moment of exultation: "At last I had been recognized; I was no longer a nonentity."[185]

But it does not take much for this position to crumble. While Fanon devotes several pages to unpacking the claims of Négritude, it is all undone by just a few sentences from an anonymous white voice: "Your distinctive qualities have been exhausted by us. We have had our back-to-nature mystics such as you will never have. Take a closer look at our history and you'll understand how far this fusion has gone."[186] The brevity of the response perhaps underscores how insufficient Fanon found the claim of rhythm (even if he himself misunderstood some of Senghor's profundity) as the distinct contribution of black humanity. And indeed he seems to recognize the truth of the fact that no single race can lay claim to instinct as its sole possession. He weeps at this loss of identity and then sets out on his path again.

Now he joins Césaire and Senghor along a different path: the discovery of "black antiquity." This teaches him that he need not simply hold up the power of instinct in order to confront the image of cannibalism. Indeed, "[t]he white man was wrong, I was not a primitive or a subhuman; I belonged to a race that had already been working silver and gold 2,000 years ago."[187] And not only did Africa have civilization; it had an arguably superior one. Fanon quotes Césaire: "European civilization is but one among many—and not the most merciful."[188] But this, too, is undone, as the white voice returns. It's very nice, it says, that Africa had civilizations, but those civilizations are simply out of touch in "a society such as ours, industrialized to the extreme." In such a world, the black man does not even have rhythm for himself. He only has it the extent to which it becomes useful for white identity: "You are so authentic in your life, so playful . . . In a sense, you reconcile us with ourselves."[189] Now Fanon feels as if he has no way out: "[T]hey were countering my irrationality with rationality, my rationality with the 'true rationality.'"[190]

It is in this space that he feels he is betrayed by a white friend who should have offered him the different kind of recognition he needed; namely, Jean-Paul Sartre. In "Black Orpheus," Sartre's introduction to *An Anthology of the New Black and Malagasy Poetry*, he had argued that, in Fanon's words, "my reasoning was nothing but a phase in the dialectic."[191] Indeed, Sartre had claimed that Négritude was a kind of "antiracist racism" that essentialized black identity only to posit an antithesis to the claims of white supremacy. Thus, now in Sartre's words as cited by Fanon, Négritude merely "serves to pave the way for the synthesis or the realization of the human society without race."[192] This puts Fanon in a difficult position. On the one hand, a way out of the binds of race is exactly what he is looking for. On the other hand, he finds in Sartre's voice the same whiteness that has relentlessly pursued him in the chapter; the one who, no matter what he says, claims to know his position in the world better.

Fanon had established his disagreement with Sartre earlier in the book when he questioned whether Sartre's analysis of failed love was an ontological claim or one produced by racial and other inequities within a society.[193] Earlier in the "Lived Experience" chapter, he also questioned the relevance of Hegel's ontology for thinking about colonial situations.[194] Fanon has thus continually been doubting whether philosophical claims, even those that claim to be grounded in historical becoming, have adequately come to terms with their racialized conditions. Fanon *profoundly* disagrees with Sartre's analysis, even though he has tremendous respect for the potentials of his work in general. And precisely what is at stake here is the question of practices of the global self. Fanon says that in naming the path of black existence as a movement toward a postracial humanity, Sartre is completely oblivious to the process of transformation by which that might occur.[195] In writing these lines, Sartre has encased him once again in the unbearable identity of European projection, and now there is no longer any way for him to proceed.

To signal this, Fanon invokes a double entendre on the word "sens" (which means both "meaning" and "direction") that is lost in translation: "*Et voilà, ce n'est pas moi qui me crée un sens, mais c'est le sens qui était là, pré-existant, m'attendant* ["And there it was: it wasn't I who created meaning/direction (*sens*), but it was meaning/direction that was there, pre-existing, waiting for me"].[196] Any just practice of the global self must come from the meeting of subject and world and cannot be imposed from the world onto the subject. But this imposition is precisely what Sartre has done, and so Fanon not only loses meaning (the question of being), but he also loses his path and his direction (the question of method). There is simply no way for him to construct the process of his becoming if that process is imposed on him.

Lewis Gordon (from whose writings and lectures I have learned a great deal about Fanon) argues that each chapter of *Black Skin, White Masks* "represents options offered the ['white construction called the black'] . . . by modern Western thought." The epic "hero" of the narrative attempts to live each of these out, but constantly finds that what these options amount to is "living simply as a white."[197] Gordon further ties this to the passage about Sartre: "What Sartre didn't understand was that he was in effect counseling the death of blackness through eventual absorption into the light of whiteness."[198] I would revise this slightly—and I don't think Gordon would disagree[199]—to note that the "light of whiteness" is *already itself* the absorption of blackness, as in Ralph Ellison's famous image from *Invisible Man* in which the "purest white" paint is made by absorbing drops of blackness.[200] Equally, the dialectic, as I have argued throughout this book, is made by absorbing the history of the world into itself and then presenting itself as universal. It is a structure we might call "handing the world" (for reasons that become clear in the next chapter), in which cultures are grabbed by the hands of European thought, erased by a sleight of hand that calls that grabbing merely a reflection on the "state of nature," and then handed back to peoples outside Europe as if it were a new, unrelated offering. This handing not only denies the history of how this happened, but it also, as we have now seen in Césaire, Senghor, and Fanon, denies the internal pluralities and transformations of the cultures it has grabbed.[201]

This is why Fanon must undertake the destructuring of the racial history of ontology. For now it is not only your average, everyday racism that oppresses, but an entire philosophical history that had told him that it was the practice of freedom. This is perhaps why Sartre's betrayal wounds Fanon so deeply—it comes from the thinker who had understood freedom and its relation to human existence better than any other. And yet Sartre, too, is trapped by this history of cultural racism because, as I have tried to demonstrate above, the philosophical history of modernity is *partially* (of course not entirely) determined by this cultural and racial history, even at the most seemingly abstract and conceptual level.

And thus the dialectic, born in a sense in Du Tertre's writings in Guadeloupe in 1667, will shatter once again, as it had in the hands of Césaire and Senghor, when Fanon writes: "The dialectic that introduces necessity as a *point d'appui* for my freedom expels me from myself."[202] When dialectics imposes itself as an identity for all the world, it denies the very freedom it promises. It is not by coincidence that Fanon uses the military term "*point d'appui*" here, for he recognizes that this is a violent struggle. And so he is fighting back against this imposition, exposing the futility of an abstract dialectical movement when it confronts the reality of the situation.[203]

This does not of course mean, again, that Fanon rejected dialectics, only that he rejected it as an imposition. Thus, for example, in his speech "On National Culture," given in 1959 and published in *Wretched of the Earth* (1963), he returns to this moment. And, indeed, he does suggest that there is a dialectic at play, but it is not the one that Sartre had assumed. In the lived experience of the black man, the thesis is the mimicry of white culture. The antithesis contains a reworking of ancient myths for present times. And the synthesis is not Marxism,[204] as Sartre had declared, but the moment when, "[i]nstead of according the people's lethargy an honored place in his esteem, [the writer] turns himself into an awakener of the people; hence comes a fighting literature, a revolutionary literature, and a national literature."[205] Fanon does not abandon the dialectic, but he does refute the assumption that white and black are antitheses that will eventually result in a synthetic, unified humanity, perhaps replete with the instinctual reason of which Rousseau had dreamed. Against this, he locates an internal dialectic in the art of a colonized people, the Algerians specifically.

He had set up this general opposition between the external dialectic (Hegel, Sartre) and the internal dialectic (what they should have realized) in *Black Skin*: "My black consciousness does not claim to be a loss. It *is*. It merges with itself . . . For there is not *one* Negro—there are *many* black men."[206] The dialectical force that wants to simply posit Négritude as a single antithetical moment is itself shattered by the reality of internal difference.[207] (This is a claim that, as we have seen, was later made by Césaire and Senghor in their own responses to Sartre.) And this is not difference for difference's sake, but a call to understand difference as part of the demands of equality and justice. For there can be no "new humanism" that continues to keep the ossifying categories of the old humanism and its scientific racism.

This leads Fanon to the necessity of invention. He is not interested in returning to the practices of the self that were used a millennium ago, not in Greece or Mecca or Algiers. Thus he ends *Black Skin, White Masks* with the desire for "the reader to feel with us the open dimension of every consciousness."[208] Like Marx, from whose writings he takes his epigraph to the conclusion, Fanon believed that the "social revolution cannot draw its poetry from its past, but only from the future."[209] We get a concrete sense of this when we turn to Fanon's analysis of the veil in *A Dying Colonialism* (1959). Although these pages have drawn some concern from feminist critics,[210] they show Fanon's mind at work, trying to develop a historically situated account of how social differences lead to different practices of the self. He is as critical of the veil as he is aware of the historical situation under which the colonial regime used it to reinforce ideas of Western superiority.[211]

But mostly what interests him is how the choice to wear or not wear the veil relates to the political praxis of revolutionary transformation.[212] The veil for Fanon is a site at which Algerian women transformed themselves to be the kinds of subjects that the political situation called for. For a woman to suddenly shed her veil and attempt to appear in the city in new disguise—as a militant pretending to be a subservient subject—was "an authentic birth in a pure state, without preliminary instruction."[213] There was no past to draw on; there was only a current subjective state to construct:

> Each time she ventures into the European city, the Algerian woman must achieve a victory over herself, over her childish fears. She must consider the image of the occupier lodged somewhere in her mind and in her body, remodel it, initiate the essential work of eroding it, make it inessential, remove something of the shame that is attached to it, devalidate it.[214]

She must, in short, go through a series of practices of the self in order to enable herself to participate in the revolution.

To get a sense of how much this analysis fits within the very set of practices that Foucault says was lost in modernity, compare the above Fanon passage with a reading of Aurelius in Foucault's lectures. Foucault summarizes Aurelius's method of "the decomposition of things," breaking them down to their constituent parts to see their essential emptiness.[215] By breaking them down, "we will be able to free ourselves from the bombast . . . from the bewitchment with which they are in danger of capturing and captivating us."[216] This is precisely what the Algerian woman is doing—but she is doing it without reference to Aurelius. She is inventing the new way of being that the global imperialism of her time calls for. She is not fretting about the loss of old practices—she perhaps knows all too well that she *might* have been excluded from learning them—but simply inventing them in the course of pursuing her freedom. It is fitting, then, that the original Italian translation of the work added this subtitle: "How a people transforms itself in the course of its emancipation."[217]

But this transformation is not a process that can simply happen through subjective transformations. Just as writing helps form the global comprehension capacity of a private self, so social changes open up new potentials for anticolonial subjectivity. We have seen how for Montaigne there was the need to work through the popular "voice" (*la voix*) that intercedes on the path (*la voye*) of reason. In Fanon, we see how the claim to reason by the French impedes the possibility of a popular voice for the Algerian people. Before the creation of a radio station, *The Voice of Fighting Algeria*, Fanon tells us, the radio was "solely tuned in on the occupier." By creating a station, the radio became a "technique" against power. Thus the "Algerian experienced and concretely discovered the existence of voices other than the voice of the dominator which formerly had been immeasurably amplified because of his own silence."[218] With the analysis of voice and the radio, we see Fanon again insisting that practices of the global self be related to specific historical circumstances. To "essay" a self in the Algerian context required the attempt to construct a voice or, better put, the realization that one had a voice all along.

It is difficult to talk about Fanon's practices without discussing the one for which he is—in my opinion unjustifiably—most famous. That is, violence. I have reserved a discussion of his work on violence for the end of this section not only because *The Wretched of the Earth* was his last published book, but also because I want to contextualize his discussion of violence as but one moment in his essay of an anticolonial, global self. It is important to remember that Fanon's essay "De la violence" is called just that: "Of Violence." It is an essay exploring a phenomenon, and it announces itself as such already in its title. This is "of" something, just as Montaigne's essay is "Of Cannibals." It is not *for* violence. Fanon then would have titled it "Pour la violence." In many ways, what Fanon is interested in here has not transformed from his earliest writing in *Black Skin, White Masks*. He is concerned with unpacking the "lived experience" of violence. This will include setting it within broader international contexts and questioning its long-term legitimacy as a practice. But it is also a phenomenological account of what it *feels like* to act violently in a revolutionary context. Some of Fanon's most inflammatory lines, we will see, speak more to the affects of war than to ahistorical claims about the legitimacy of violence.

Fanon actually discusses revolutionary violence very little in the essay. He begins his analysis by setting it in the colonial context. Colonization itself, he notes, has created a perpetually violent situation: "Their first encounter was marked by violence and their existence together—that is to say the exploitation of the native by the settler—was carried on by dint of a great array of bayonets and cannons."[219] One might criticize the seeming simplicity of this understanding, the way it appears to evade recognizing the role of a native elite, for example, but one will quickly find that Fanon is all too aware of this fact. His point is of course not that Algerians never oppress Algerians, but that the determining context in which this occurs is the colonial one. An Algerian might become wealthy under the French, but he will still only ever rule the country at the behest of the French. And, ultimately, he will be enabled to do so by the French military might. Moreover, Fanon's general concern is not with the colonized elite, but with the colonized masses. He wants to understand how they are acting to transform themselves and their situation.

And in fact after analyzing the basic violence of the situation, he discusses things other than violence: the process of creating a national identity; an analysis of colonized intellectuals and the transformation of their ideas; the development of new language; a discussion of the practice of self-criticism; an analysis of the dreams of the colonized; an interrogation of the revival of "tribal feuds"; an anthropology of magic and dancing; an investigation of mainstream politics, including political parties and the discourses of compromise and nonviolence; a critique of capitalism and religion; and finally a brief discussion of colonization in an international frame. After introducing the theme of violence, in other words, Fanon then spends about twenty-five pages analyzing the material and psychic conditions in which that violence is occurring.[220] Only then does he say, "But let us return to that atmosphere of violence."

And what he turns to is not a paean to violence, but a continued analysis of the new forms of international violence that now ensnare a colonial people:

> Already we see that violence used in specific ways at the moment of the struggle for freedom does not magically disappear after the ceremony of trooping the national colors. It has all the less reason for disappearing since the construction of the nation continues within the framework of cutthroat competition between capitalism and socialism.[221]

To understand anticolonial violence is neither to let it off the hook for failing to achieve its aims of a new, peaceful nation nor to assume that such a peaceful nation can meaningfully come into being in a violent world. Thus, Fanon will later conclude, "What counts today, the question which is looming on the horizon, is the need for a redistribution of wealth. Humanity must reply to this question, or be shaken to pieces by it."[222] This shaking persists as the cracking foundation of contemporary life.

But to understand this violence *is* also to understand what it means for the subject, and what possible benefits it might have for them. Fanon writes, "At the level of individuals, violence removes a toxin [*désintoxique*].[223] It frees the native from this inferiority complex and from his despair and inaction; it makes him fearless and restores his self-respect."[224] Moreover, Fanon continues, it means for the subject that he or she has taken part in a specific action, that they have had a share in the political transformation, and that is something no demagogue or bureaucrat can take away from them. The sentiment is not so different from that expressed in Shakespeare: "We few, we happy few, we band of brothers / For he to-day that sheds his blood with me / Shall be my brother . . . And gentlemen in England now a-bed / Shall think themselves accursed they were not here."[225] The making of the bonds of the nation is felt to be the effect of carving through blood and battle. And, in the colonial context, it is part of a movement against the violence that has imprisoned subjects. It allows them to become subjects again, even if it makes them do it—in an unbearable catch-22—through the very violence they wish to escape.[226]

Fanon signals throughout that violence is not the end of the story with his insistence on understanding the larger colonial context. The end of the essay, right after this moment of seeming praise for violence, turns back out to look at the problem within "the international context."[227] Here Fanon reminds his readers—who are, in spite of Sartre's claim in the preface,[228] intended to be Europeans as well as Algerians and others—that global practices *must* be global. The anticolonial revolutions simply have no hope of sustaining their power if they end in violent overthrow. The key is to move from this overthrow into a new world: "This huge task which consists of reintroducing mankind into the world, the whole of mankind, will be carried out with the indispensable help of the European peoples . . . To achieve this the European peoples must first decide to wake up and shake themselves, use their brains, and stop playing the stupid game of the Sleeping Beauty."[229]

Fanon also insists elsewhere that violence *need not* have occurred in the anticolonial fight: "It is clear that other peoples have come to the same conclusion [self-consciousness as an independent nation] in different ways."[230] His point is simply that it did happen, that it happened because of a context of colonial violence, that it meant something for those who took up arms, and that other forms of exploitative violence will continue so long as we do not deal with the problems of economic violence that continue to profit some people at the expense of others. Anticolonial violence for Fanon was a *reaction*, and his steadfast belief, as we have seen, is that practices for future humanity must be inventions that spring from the demands of their historical and political context. Any meaningful practices of the global self, he insisted, must come from a new internationalism, not old reactions. Fanon is the end of the dialectic in this double sense: he brings to an end its racist history at the same time that he (dialectically) preserves the method in order to show its true purpose (end) in specific contexts. In the closing words of his last book: "For Europe, for ourselves, and for humanity, comrades, we must shed our old skin, we must invent new thinking, and try to set afoot a new man."[231]

∽

Fanon has long been criticized for his supposed naiveté here. Even early admirers found his romanticism foolish in the face of the neocolonial onslaught. I have suggested above why this reading of Fanon is itself naive, depending as it does on too quick an analysis of his thought. But several critiques of Fanon have emerged in the past decade or so that call for a response. There is, first, Pheng Cheah's concern with what he calls Fanon's "organicism," or a belief that the nation is the organic, expressive chronotope that can effectively incarnate freedom. In Cheah's reading, Fanon falls prey to a long-standing idealist discourse in which "the unacknowledged frame guiding contemporary . . . research . . . invariably associate[s] freedom with [organic] life."[232] But such a claim, I would argue, is dependent on its own incarnational logic—that is, it takes the idea of organicism and incarnates it in Fanon's writings. While it is certainly true, as Cheah ably demonstrates, that Fanon argued for a kind of organic, national culture, it is nevertheless completely contrary to Fanon's argument to say that his is a practice of incarnating the ideal. Quite to the contrary, as we have seen, Fanon is a thinker of historically emergent practices, and his main focus is on *invention in the future*.

The point for Fanon is not to come up with the ontological truth of the relation between real and ideal as it is for Cheah. Rather, it is to insist that this question, posed as an abstraction that relates to, but is philosophically different from, racialization or colonization, is to pose the wrong problem in the first place. In turn, my work thus far in this book has been to offer a different model than Cheah's for historicizing modern thought: one that seeks to understand it as a globally created and ongoing process of transforming self and world in conjunction with each other, rather than as a set of abstract propositions about truth that are divorced from geography and history.[233] The ontological question, we have seen Fanon argue, is not "*the*" question. "Black or White" is. In other words, the question of being in the modern era is about the ways in which we learn to cohabit a diverse world together, and what kinds of practices we can generate to act justly in such a space. There are reasons to criticize Fanon's *practice*, as there is with anyone's, but it is unfair to criticize his philosophy without acknowledging that it is philosophy itself that he has set out to critique.[234]

Reading Fanon in this way also puts pressure on the incisive critique of Fanonian thinking offered by David Scott. I highlight Fanon*ian* here, because Scott's concern is less Fanon per se and more his belief that the problems that animated Fanon's thought are no longer ours. In brief, Scott situates Fanon within an anticolonial moment that charted decolonization as the progress from alienated and degraded peoples to their proper realization as a liberated humanity through the conduit of national sovereignty. Scott calls this the "Fanonian narrative of liberation."[235] It is a narrative that, he has argued across his last three books, is both politically and philosophically untenable.[236] Philosophically, the ideas rely too much on a concept of a true human essence that can be liberated once and for all, and politically they imagine a kind of homogenous, national community that is violently exclusive.[237] Interestingly for my purposes, Scott turns to Foucault to think a new Fanon for the present. Focusing on "*ruud bwai* [rude boy] self-fashioning," he compares a classic Fanonian reading with one more grounded in Foucault's late work. Under the Fanonian reading, the antisocial violence of *ruud bwai* culture is taken to be an expression of their alienated position in neocolonial Jamaica. Scott suggests, however, that this reading presumes a possible liberal normative order that could effectively incorporate the whole nation.[238] Against such a homogenizing vision, he proposes a politics of plurality that allows for various modes of self-making and collectivity building.[239]

What this all means for Scott, at the level of theoretical reading practices, is that "we [still] need Fanon" because his insistence on decisive action, the refusal of the neocolonial state, the openness to the vernacular, and siding with the oppressed remain crucial practices. But we need to jettison the Fanon of authenticity and Romantic liberation and replace him with a more Foucauldian set of concerns about the exclusive violence of national communities, embodied modes of liberatory practice, and the possibility of plurality within shared space.[240]

This is all well and good, and Scott's insistence on pluralism is something that I echo throughout this book. But I am concerned with the ways in which he has positioned Fanon in relation to Foucault here. I am trying to argue in this book that these Foucauldian practices of the self cannot properly be thought of in Foucauldian terms, because those terms themselves were forged through an exclusive community of intellectual history—namely, the West. I have been arguing throughout that central to modern thought has been, and continues to be, a shared but unequal process of understanding how to cohabit this planet. If we are to think about how Foucault's ideas of practices of the self are to be useful in this space, we must first consider how those ideas themselves are part of this broader global history. It is within this history, I am suggesting, that aspects of Fanon's work can be understood. If we simply import Foucault's thinking, we run the risk of letting his racial history of ontology stand.

To conceive of practices of the global self, then, it seems to me that we need to read Foucault through Fanon, rather than the other way around. And then we might see, for example, how much Foucault's late work on the relationship between politics and care of the self—the very ideas that drive Scott's reading of *ruud bwai* culture—is indebted to Fanon. I don't know if Foucault ever read Fanon, and, if he did, one suspects that he would have had precisely the concerns that Scott raises: that Fanon's work was too indebted to Sartrean notions of an "authentic self." (How much that is an accurate representation of Sartre or Fanon and how much it has to do with Foucault's own anxiety of influence is a question for another time.) Direct influence aside, much of Foucault's late thinking about politics was forged in the crucible of his (mis)encounter with the Iranian Revolution,[241] and certainly some of the intellectual fire of that revolution was generated through Fanon's work—as by, for example, the translations of his work into Farsi by Ali Shariati that were incorporated into the thinking of Khomeini.[242]

The specificity of this example aside, the larger point is to consider one of the injunctions of the modern as the need to come up with means of self-transformation that enable one to think globally. In this sense, I agree with Scott that a key task for postcolonial criticism today is to move toward a "critical interrogation of the practices, modalities, and projects through which the varied forms of its [that is, European modernity's] insertion into the lives of the colonized were constructed and organized."[243] For Scott, following Foucault's work on biopolitics and governmentality, the "first distinctive feature of modern power that needs to be foregrounded" is a kind of economic rationality that uses administrative apparatuses to control the biological productivity of the colonized in order to make and extract capital.[244] I am trying to suggest that we can see *this move itself* as a response to the underlying question: How are we to cohabit the planet? The answer given by colonialism—that some minority should rule over the majority of the world's population, and that part of that rule would include the invention of a global teleological movement toward a singular thing called "reason" embodied by a specific form of government and economy—was only one mode of how global selves have been essayed since Montaigne. It has, to the unshakeable and nearly irreparable damage of us all, been the most powerful answer. But it is not the only one. And it is the contention of this book that understanding that response as but one among many may open up other kinds of pluralistic self- and communal-fashioning for our shared futures. The understanding that plurality belongs to our future, that our future is not determined, is one of Fanon's greatest legacies.[245] I have argued that Montaigne, Rousseau, Marx, Senghor, and Fanon, though each with his own limitations, provide foundational resources for thinking these other paths. I now turn to how Ralph Waldo Emerson and W. E. B. Du Bois broke with idealism's vision of the global self in the name of a new, radically pluralistic way of being.

5

Radical Pluralism I

Emerson

It may come as a surprise to some readers that Ralph Waldo Emerson is, in my estimation, one of the greatest writers in favor of the pluralist global self. In spite of recent scholarship arguing for Emerson's pluralism, as well as the ongoing reevaluation of the ethical, political, and philosophical merits of his work, many readers remain skeptical of Emerson, and often for good reason.[1] Some of the remarks that Emerson makes about global cultures are appalling. Others are remarkable in their critique of Eurocentrism and white supremacy and their straightforward call for a deep engagement with the values of civilizations across the world. Reading Emerson can give us cerebral whiplash. For example, in the very same book of essays, *The Conduct of Life* (1860), we find the two following quotes: "The rest or remains of it [the 'savage spirit'] in the civil and moral man, are worth all the cannibals in the Pacific." And "As Nature has put fruits apart in latitudes, a new fruit in every degree, so knowledge and fine moral quality she lodges in distant men."[2] Similarly, in his 1844 address on "Emancipation in the West Indies," he states, "Our planet, before the age of written history, had its races of savages . . . We do not wish a world of bugs or of birds; neither afterward of Scythians, Caraibs, or Feejees." And then he adds in the very next paragraph, "The civility of no race can be perfect whilst another race is degraded. It is a doctrine alike of the oldest, and of the newest philosophy, that, man is one, and that you cannot injure any member, without a sympathetic injury to all the members."[3]

There are ways of responding to these inconsistencies in Emerson beyond simply marking them as such. To take but two recent examples that are important to my reading here: one might, as Eduardo Cadava has done, suggest that some of the worst moments are when Emerson "ventriloquizes" the voices of other racists as part of his acts of refutation.[4] This provides an important logic for understanding some aspects of Emerson's essays, and I return to the idea in my reading of the essay "Fate." To see where and how Emerson does this, we need to read his essays carefully and never presume that the words on the page can be taken at face value.

Another method is proposed by Johannes Voelz, who argues that we should understand Emerson's vacillations as "dynamic responses to the given," which engage the shifting demands and conditions of a burgeoning modernity.[5] Rather than criticizing Emerson for not living up to ethical standards, Voelz suggests, we would do better to understand him as perpetually provoking his listeners and readers to "experience their own infinitude."[6] In the quotes above, this plays out when Emerson seems to call for an ideal—such as primitive strength—and then expresses the limits of such an ideal to fully capture the infinitude of existence. At the same time, he suggests that not all of the possible ideals of the world are available where his audience sits, and thus they must break with their chauvinism and look abroad. Voelz calls this Emerson's "fractured idealism."[7]

That Emerson did this in the racist language of his times—whether ventriloquized or not—cannot be brushed aside, any more than with any of the other figures studied here. My argument here is that what we see in Emerson (in addition to what Cadava and Voelz note) is a process of learning to be a global self. He begins this learning, as Marx did, with very stereotypical and problematic images of others. But he also, as Marx did, works to overcome these faulty visions and learns to see the pluralist values and dynamic differences of all cultures. One finds when reading Emerson that he never fully arrived at this vision, but the process through which he attempted to overcome his prejudices is still instructive. And it was through this process of unevenly unlearning his assumptions and relearning how to think globally that he produced the radical pluralism of his thought.

I thus want to build on the recent studies of Emerson to consider how he developed (without naming) radical pluralism as a response to the unbearability of global modernity. What this means is that there are specific values that emerge in Emerson's reading: the refusal of imposition, the demand for global learning, and the belief in alternation over synthesis. This is accompanied by an epistemology that stresses the fact that all entities embody the struggle over competing ideals. As a radical and critical pluralist, Emerson criticizes certain layers of the plurality that constitute a given culture, while praising others. It is generally true that Emerson speaks of the same entity in two incompatible ways. But this does not make him—as the critical literature so long believed—a failed dialectician.[8] What he is in fact doing is showing how the entity itself—be it an individual, a race, a culture, a nation, a world, or the very concept of truth—is made up of multiple components, some of which he embraces and some of which he belittles.[9]

In Emerson, it is plurality that both enables change and requires it, because within a plural formation there are bound to be layers of existence that are no longer—or never were—useful. A grave concern (one that will recur in Du Bois) appears when a single idea overwhelms an entire way of life and thus appears to disable change entirely. For example, in his anniversary address on West Indian Emancipation in 1844, he states: "There are many faculties in man, each of which takes its turn of activity, and that faculty which is paramount in any period, and exerts itself through the strongest nation, determines the civility of that age; and each age thinks its own the perfection of reason."[10] Careless readers of Emerson will focus on the words "strongest," "civility," and "perfection" to suggest an implied link here, as if for him might made right. However, what is crucial here is that each "*thinks*" itself to be the perfection of reason. Recent readers of Emerson are right to claim that there is no such perfection and that there is always another moment of transformation.[11] The risk thus is that some will try to hold off this change in their claim of perfection.

Emerson gives concrete practices for the global self who faces such claims. What becomes necessary is what he calls "alternations," that is, the process of reminding oneself and others of the plurality of existence and learning to move between the different possibilities for existence that are available. (Some processes, such as slavery, will be excluded from what should be available to alternation. The logic given here is the universal right for alternation, and this is precisely what slavery attempts to deny a subject, as it works, but never succeeds,[12] to reduce a human being to their brute capacity for labor and reproduction.) Thus, in the Emancipation Address, Emerson names the ideal that currently seems to bind the United States as a nation: it is "very cheap and intelligible . . . It is that of a trading nation; it is a shopkeeping civility."[13] The idea that guides a nation at the "perfection of reason" is to place economic advantage over humanity. "But," Emerson continues, with a heavy dose of irony,[14] "most unhappily, gentlemen, man is born with intellect, as well as with a love of sugar, with a sense of justice, as well as with a taste for strong drink."[15] There is a struggle over which ideas ought to guide the world, and a reminder that we will need to tarry with a human soul that alternates between intellect, pleasure, insouciance, and justice.

A key to Emerson's mature thinking on this topic can be found in the essay "Culture" (1860) when he writes:

> Culture is the suggestion from certain best thoughts, that a man has a range of affinities, through which he can modulate the violence of any master-tones that have a droning preponderance in his scale, and succor him against himself. Culture redresses his balance, puts him among his equals and superiors, revives the delicious sense of sympathy, and warns him of the dangers of solitude and repulsion.[16]

Plurality runs through this passage, but it is against a traditional pluralism. Culture should not be restricted to a single dominant idea, but rather to a compilation of "best thoughts." (This is perhaps close to what Senghor calls the "civilization of the universal"—even if he, because of his historical position, offered a version of radical pluralism more concerned with demonstrating the existing values of his culture.) This plurality in culture aims to restore the plurality within an individual, who must recall her "range of affinities" and overcome "master-tones," which I take to mean both the dominant tones of one's soul and the presumption of mastery over others' souls. (This is where Senghor's emphasis on "rhythm," as Fanon argues, poses a danger of unbearability: when its sounds overwhelm the plurality of African cultures.) A culture guided by emancipatory ideals will have what Emerson elsewhere calls a "sound relation," in which the various connective threads of a culture harmonize with each other.[17] (And this of course is what Senghor's emphasis on rhythm is meant to sound like.) In the opposite case, when slavery and economy rule: "If any mention was made of homicide, madness, adultery, and intolerable tortures, we would let the church-bells ring louder, the church-organ swell its peal and drown the hideous sound."[18] These are the "master-tones" that result when one idea too strongly holds a people or a person.

In this attempt to overcome these cultural conditions, Emerson is perfectly willing to criticize cultures other than his own, and he often does so in what is at best a flat-footed manner; at worst, it plays into the very cultures of dominance he sets out to critique. As with Kant and Hegel, Emerson's willingness to name the being of another culture led him into racist statements that cannot merely be excused by the discourse of his times. However, unlike them, he did *not* view other cultures as being guided only and always by a single instinct or idea. Rather, he understood that there existed, across humankind, what he called the "singular equality of all ages."[19] This "singular equality" did not mean that all cultures are the same, but that all must wrestle with one basic fact of human existence: polarity, or a continual pull in opposite directions that can never ultimately be reconciled.[20] As he put it: "Our geometry cannot span the huge *orbits* of the prevailing ideas, behold their return, and reconcile their opposition." We cannot, in short, complete the act of sublation. "We can only obey our own polarity."[21]

What this meant for Emerson was a fundamental break with the Idealism that preceded him. Because the singularity of human life manifests not as an incipient instinct that breaks into reason, but rather as an eternal push and pull between the values of any such dichotomy, Emerson does not aim for the desired sublation we have seen since Rousseau. The goal for Emerson's global subject is not to restore some lost instinctual way of being at a higher level. Rather, the goal is for this subject to learn to recognize its own internal plurality—formed by alternating oppositions—as a sign of the plurality of the other individuals, cultures, and conceptual formations in the world with which it must interact. It learns to "obey" this constant movement of life that never achieves resolution and, in so doing, learns to respect difference at the same time that it learns to critique false attempts at reconciliation and impositions of singularity. No claim is made that others live solely under the domain of instinct or reason or anything else. Everyone is plural, alternating, contributing to new ways of life, developing old ones, eradicating failures. No culture or individual is now burdened with one identity. And no culture or individual can claim to bear the whole world on its shoulders. Rather, we all work with and shape different ways of being, both within ourselves and with others. This is Emerson's screed against phrenologists wherever he finds them: those "[t]heoretic kidnappers and slave-drivers" who prescribe to others "the law of [their] being." He continues: "I had fancied that the value of life lay in its inscrutable possibilities; in the fact that I never know, in addressing myself to a new individual, what may befall me . . . Shall I preclude my future, by taking a high seat, and kindly adapting my conversations to the shape of heads?"[22]

According to Emerson, then, an individual finds within herself multiple dispositions (of course from both nature and nurture), some of which find immediate expression in her culture and some of which do not. Her aim is to develop means of expression for those elements of herself that do not find ready outlets. (Emerson calls these practices "aversion" and "contradiction.")[23] Sometimes this means alternating out of her culture—into visions of transcendence, into nature, and into other cultures. In Emerson's phrasing, there will sometimes be "required some foreign force, some diversion or alternative to prevent stagnation."[24] But in none of these spaces will she find singularity. There will always be a new plurality, and she will have to engage that new space as such. She breaks with Lévi-Strauss's law that one is only responsible for one's own culture, but not because she imposes her way of being on others.[25] Rather, she opposes only those practices that result in the unbearable identity—that is, in the constriction of plurality to singularity—whether that is by misogyny, slavery, classism, or culturalism. But she is careful never to presume that she is not like Emile in his watermelon patch and that she has understood the context in which she makes these claims.

This kind of pluralism may enable the overcoming of the unbearable identities that global interdependence has produced. In previous versions of the global self, unbearability surfaced in a number of forms. It was, first of all, the fact that private practices of the self could no longer bear the burden that the individual was being forced to confront by the fact of globality. In response, Rousseau and his German followers suggested a universal form of global being that could, in theory, unite the world under rational rule. This, however, produced two new unbearable identities: one for those universalists who attempted to shoulder more of the world's being than they possibly could, and one for all those outside Europe, who were now hailed as being stuck in a particular moment in the evolution toward universalism.

Traditional pluralism attempts to resolve the first impasse by suggesting that there are many ways of being in the world, and each culture has a right to set forth its own logic for how to be in an interconnected world. But this notion does not overcome the second problem, for it keeps all those within a cultural space bounded to a particular definition of how to be. Nor does it make room for the internal plurality of any given subject. Radical pluralism, on the other hand, resolves both of these issues by insisting that plurality goes down to the roots (the radicals) of existence. At the same time, by criticizing any way of being that refuses to recognize the plurality of others, it avoids the problem of relativism. Further still, because it recognizes that pluralities have real, existent layers (even if those layers are contingent and historical), it avoids the problem of never being able to generalize. By thus distributing the burden of global being and opening up the possibilities for subjectivity to the multiplicity of every soul, radical pluralism overcomes the unbearable identity.

Of course, this does not mean that it makes life easy: it simply removes *a* layer of unbearability from the challenges and tragedies of being. A truly radical pluralism, one that embodies the political meaning of the adjective radical, will also work to remove other layers of being that make life unbearable—those that, for example, disable our collective capacities to make available even the bare necessities of life for all citizens of the world. This is where pluralism and revolution are symbiotic.

William Connolly has suggested that this combination of pluralism and practices of the self can be traced to "The Nietzschean/Foucauldian conception of the self as a contingent formation modestly open to further strategies of craftmanship [that] authorizes the practice of self as 'work of art.'"[26] By discussing Emerson rather than Nietzsche and Foucault, I am not simply hoping to replicate Stanley Cavell's historical claim that Emerson stands behind much of what came back to US-based philosophy as European thinking.[27] Rather, I am following a genealogy of practices of the self that does not arrive at Foucault's partition of the geographies of the world; that is, that does not assume "our culture" to have lost practices that are available elsewhere. Emerson develops a very similar understanding to Connolly's about the necessity of pluralist practices of the self, but he does so from the angle of an actual and ongoing engagement with global ways of being. Foucault, as I previously discussed, also attempted this in his engagements with the Iranian Revolution and Zen Buddhism. When he did so, however, he believed that he was breaking out of the confines of a Western history, but what he in fact encountered were "foreign" practices that had been shaped in the same global matrix. We have seen this with Fanon and Iran, and we will see this with Suzuki and Zen in the next chapter. What I want to continue to suggest here is that Foucault, and Nietzsche before him and Connolly after him, were also themselves *already* constituted by these global interactions in ways that their theorizing does not recognize—but that Emerson did.

Connolly continues with the following overview of practices:

> [This self] works experimentally and cautiously upon itself and the relationships through which it is constituted. It patiently applies tactics to itself to modify itself, prying open thereby some creative distance between itself and the institutional disciplines of normalization . . . [It] draws open fragments of its contingent subjectivity to work patiently and cautiously upon

those elements in its code of identity, desire, and judgment that are ugly, vengeful, and otherwise less admirable than they might be. A self that works on itself to develop critical responsiveness to that which it is not, to cultivate critical responsiveness to those identities whose very mode of formation may tap into differences within it.[28]

As we work through the historical progress of Emerson's writings on other cultures, we can see him arrive at many of these same modalities of self-transformation in the spirit of pluralization. What makes his work important in the genealogy of pluralism is that he did so through the global, historical understanding necessary for the practices of the global self. The challenge of life in this mode of understanding is to learn to move between positions without losing oneself in the haphazard alternations to which skepticism leaves us open.

One result of this process is that Emerson, and the figures he champions, *will* occasionally put forward universal sentiments. While this might seem contradictory, we might also ask how we could have pluralism if we do not have people proclaiming truths. Does pluralism not rely on the availability of such claims—such as Senghor's? For Emerson, universalism (including dialectical universalism) is not to be discarded so much as *partialized*.[29] It is to be understood as a "mood" of pluralism, as one way of speaking and acting among others. We might put forward "justice" or "emancipation" or "satori" as universal ideals, or "dialectics" or "rhythm" as processes of history, while remaining respectful of the fact that what those universals mean will have plural interpretations, and that at times other values will contradict their aims. (I have no particular interest in the "emancipation" of capital from regulation, for example. And, following Marx, I have no interest in making dialectical those entities that are "real opposites.") The trouble, then, is less univeralism per se than that "our moods do not believe in each other."[30] The part of us that knows the truth of diversity is not always in touch with the part of us that simply wants to add her voice as a truth of the world. The trick is not to refute this mood entirely; it is to get one mood to believe in another mood—that of humility, that which refuses to think that there is something special about what *I* think. The rejection of such humility is how Emerson defines fanaticism: "The pretence that he has another call, a summons by name and personal election . . . is fanaticism, and betrays obtuseness to perceive that there is one mind in all the individuals, and no respect of persons therein."[31]

Another question might arise here: What is this "one mind," and does it imply that the truth is, in spite of surface diversity, in fact singular? For Emerson, however, this one is never one, but is always splitting and engendering new oppositions: "All the universe over, there is but one thing, this old Two-Face, creator-creature, mind-matter, right-wrong."[32] The one is always two, and two are always producing newness in their alternations and interactions, and as we develop new ways of relating to them. With each alternation of this alternating complex, something new is produced, and we individuals are the accumulations of all this production. As Emerson writes elsewhere: "I am an aggregate of infinitesimal parts . . . What is a man but a congress of nations?"[33] It is because of this universal multiplicity that Emerson can at once promote and deny private genius, depending on whether or not it also recognizes this universality. As Emerson puts it, "The orator distrusts at first the fitness of his frank confessions . . . until he finds that he is the complement of his hearers."[34]

To see that the one is many and the many is one, that we need to both partialize and pluralize—these are the tasks of Emerson's radical pluralism. The failure to see this clearly and the resulting belief in the exceptionalism of Europe is the problem of German Idealism. Emerson's essays guide us to be the kinds of subjects who can connect their moods and learn how to move through different states of being. He develops a series of concepts—alternation, unhanding, double consciousness—that allow the individual to learn to be who she is as a plural being in a plural world. After a look at Emerson's early writings on global cultures, this chapter follows the development of those concepts and how they helped him overcome his prejudices.

Like Marx and many of his other contemporaries, Emerson began his intellectual life in a Eurocentric haze. In a journal entry from 1824, he discusses "those distant lands where the barbarous rudiments of society are still seen, where still, no knowledge is transmitted, no knowledge desired, no metals wrought, no institutions framed, no future explored, no God known."[35] These are, roughly, the same features mentioned by Montaigne in "Of Cannibals" and echoed by Gonzalo in *The Tempest*. But Emerson has no vision of a more perfect organization here. Citing Columbus, Cook, and Humboldt, Emerson demurs: "Man had grown no wiser in the solitude of the Pacific[36] . . . The common brotherhood of the same race that keeps even beasts from devouring each other, was altogether forgotten in a nauseous outrage that humanity shudders to name."[37] Emerson chooses to praise the missionaries instead, who brought art and science and truth. He even agrees with the "[m]odern Political Economists that the moral character of a community is mended or relaxed with the greater or less security of property."[38]

This is a position he will outright deny in later writings.[39] It has long been understood in Emerson scholarship that the 1820s marked a profound transformation in his thought as he moved away from some of the conventional beliefs of his youth and began to adopt his more radical and unique stance. Sheldon Liebman's essay on this period notes that part of the change occurs around these questions of how Emerson views others: "Both the child and the savage—before, examples of uncivilized and therefore asocial or presocial beings—are now seen as epitomes of unfettered man, outside the boundaries of stale authority and beyond the reach of corrupting sects or parties."[40] Alan Hodder has similarly argued that these are the years when Emerson breaks with his Romantic Orientalism.[41] As Emerson moves away from views about the necessity of the given social order, those outside it come to be objects of praise rather than of derision. But generic praise is not the same as actual engagement. What we will eventually see in Emerson's work is more than exoticism: it is a slow growth of the idea of alternation across cultural modalities.

This was also true for Emerson's position on race. What was becoming pronounced in Kant's time (and in part because of Kant's own ideas) was the idea of a *determining* biological notion of race. While there are elements of such thinking in Emerson's writings on race and culture, Ian Finseth and Laura Dassow Walls, among others, have observed that Emerson's thinking about race grows through a slow, uneven evolution that does not shed all his prejudices until the late 1840s, if then.[42] As Finseth and Dassow Walls have both convincingly shown, this thinking for Emerson is bound up with his studies in natural history. As the natural world loses its fixity in the doctrines of what would come to be called evolution, so does the supposed naturalness of race. But, they further show, this transformation in Emerson's thinking is not only due to his growing aversion to racial discourse. As an increasingly vocal opponent of slavery from the 1840s on, Emerson also realized that the discourses of white supremacy and black racial inferiority were part of the ideological matrix that justified the terrifying institution.

Emerson's intellectual struggles with racial and cultural thinking can be seen in 1838, when he deploys the philosophical parable of choice from Du Tertre, Rousseau, and Kant:

The savage surrenders to his senses; he is subject to paroxysms of joy and fear; he is lewd, and a drunkard. The Esquimaux[43] in the exhilaration of the morning sun, when he is invigorated by sleep, will sell his bed . . . And there is an Esquimaux in every man which makes us believe in the permanence of this moment's state of our game more than our own experience will warrant.[44]

Emerson's use of this story appears even worse than his predecessors. Although the geographic space has changed, the formal structure of the anecdote is the same. And the absurdity of people in the freezing north thinking at any point in the day that they might not need a blanket shows that Emerson, in his too-quick assumptions, submits to these prejudices of native life.[45] Seduced by this false gaze, Emerson again shifts the meaning of the story. Du Tertre had used it to describe the incommensurability of French and Caribbean trading practices. Rousseau had used it to at once praise the happiness of the Carib and despair at his lack of foresight. Kant saw in it the key to move past Rousseau's obsession with the happiness of the primitive and understand the necessity of civilization. Emerson has the most extreme exacerbation. There is nothing positive here, not even happy instinct. There is only the delusion and "despotism" of the senses.[46]

However, even though Emerson has not yet fully arrived at his revision of racial thinking, it is important to remember the context of the citation: it is not the "Esquimaux" that he is critiquing per se so much as the general failure to play what he calls "the game" here and, in a later essay, specifies as the "game of thought."[47] In this game, "every fact is related on one side to sensation, and, on the other to morals. The game of thought is, on the appearance of one of these two sides, to find the other."[48] What the "Esquimaux" names here is the capacity in "every man" to get stuck on one side. If there is an "Esquimaux" in "every man," then there is also more to them than this.

In lectures the previous year (1837) on "The Philosophy of History," Emerson stated that it is "pedantry to insist much upon distinctions so evanescent and unphilosophical as those of mere time."[49] He suggests that we tend to look back and see cultures and peoples defined by something, but to foist this definition on them as an essence is to neglect the fact of historical change and potential internal differences. Emerson is slowly breaking with historicist theories of development at the same time that he is breaking with the assumption that cultures are bound to a single idea or framework. "Many of the broad lines we might mark as characterising our age, are only visible because it is now present, and were as prominent in every preceding age but perish without memory."[50] Emerson calls this the "singular equality" of all ages and holds that "[o]ut of all periods, out of all forms of life and thought pour rivers of light upon the hour and the man that now is."[51] One will find little like this in Kant or Hegel. It harks back, rather, to the roots of essaying the globe in Montaigne and the young Rousseau.

The imperfect progress of Emerson's thought can be seen two decades later in similar remarks about gender. In the essay "Power," he writes: "In every company, there is not only the active and passive sex, but, in both men and women, a deeper and more important *sex of mind*, namely, the inventive or creative class of both men and women, and the uninventive or accepting class."[52] It is worth asking yet again to what extent Emerson's thinking is meant to be available across the spectrum of human sexes and genders. The same duality that troubles his understanding of indigenous life in the Americas appears here. On the one hand, he suggests that there is a duality between active (male) and passive (female), just as there is between cerebral (Euro-American) and sensual (indigenous). On the other hand, he suggests that these distinctions are doubled within the very categories, so that women exhibit both activity and passivity, and indigenous peoples exhibit both rationality and sensuality. Unfortunately, the very things that Emerson might use to undermine his generalizations are what he uses to support them.[53]

It is difficult to come up with a single judgment of Emerson here. This impasse is part of what pluralist analysis necessarily entails. To be sure, a more progressive Emerson would not have located pure sensation in the "Esquimaux" or passivity in one gender. At the same time, there is still an important point here that we—both "Esquimaux" and New Englanders—may be bereaved by our senses as much as we may rely on them for precision of action. And we may be alienated by our intellect as much as we may use it to think past the tyranny of circumstance. Throughout his life, Emerson spoke unevenly on questions of race and culture, and his broad-minded claims against slavery and stereotypes often sat uneasily with his racist asides.[54] As I have argued about other figures throughout this book, these asides cannot be brushed aside and need to be understood as factors in Emerson's essaying of a global self. Although he never fully achieved a nonracist consciousness (who can truly say they have, while living in a racist culture?), he took steps toward a philosophy of *anti*racism.[55] At the heart of this was his basic pluralism, his basic sense that a human being is a "congress of nations," and that each nation is, in itself, a plural and dynamic entity. This is a move toward abolishing the very racism Emerson himself employs in constraining the "Esquimaux" to the tyranny of sense.

Alternations

There is even reason to think that Emerson's break with racism comes out of this kind of writing. In his misreading of indigenous cultures, Emerson is slowly pushing toward a practice of the global self that enables radical pluralism: the practice of alternation. Emerson outlines the concept of alternation in a number of places. For example:

> The daily history of the Intellect is this alternating of expansions and concentrations. The expansions are the invitations from heaven to try a larger sweep, a higher pitch than we have yet climbed, and to leave all our past for this enlarged scope. Present power, on the other hand, requires concentration on the moment and the thing to be done.[56]

We do not (or at least do not always) seek to unite the expansion and the contraction into some higher, third thought. Rather, we learn to move between these modes of life as, in an image Emerson frequently employed, riders in a circus learn to move between horses. "Our strength is transitional, alternating." "Here again, as so often, Nature delights to put us between extreme antagonisms, and our safety is in the skill with which we keep the diagonal line."[57] And as cited above: "Every fact is related on one side to sensation, and, on the other to morals. The game of thought is, on the appearance of one of these two sides, to find the other."[58] Through alternations into other parts of ourselves, into other plural cultures, and into natures, we begin to slough off our limits and our prejudices and create new capacities for engagement and action. It is alternation's universal plurality—the fact that it is available to all peoples at all times and places without constraining them to an essence or denying them their actual formations—that will make it a liberating concept, a rupture in the fabric of prejudice that had claimed some peoples to be submerged in instinct, waiting for the rupture of history.[59]

The Idealists aimed at sublation, that is, the uniting of divergent terms into a higher third concept, such as instinctual reason. It is often said that

Emerson sought and failed to achieve a dialectical synthesis, but he explicitly refuted the goal of even attempting the project.[60] Emerson certainly agrees with the dialectical hope that our instincts can become more rational and our rationality more embedded in our senses—"More wise desires, and simpler manners," as Wordsworth had it.[61] But Emerson seeks less to envelop contraries into a third category and more to develop each as a mode of life to alternate into. He doesn't get rid of dialectics; he just, like Marx, refuses to impose it as a universal operation. At some moments in our lives, we will need to rely on our instincts; at others, on our reasons. More than this, we will need to realize that our instincts and reasons are both themselves plural categories with their own internal contradictions. Emerson thus not only universalizes multiplicity, he, like Senghor after him, revalues different segments of those multiplicities. And like Senghor, he argues that the trick is to bring these different segments into contact through alternation.

A general example of this process can be found in the essay "Society and Solitude" (1857). There Emerson vacillates between the virtues and misgivings of both private and public life. What kind of synthesis could be achieved here? The dialectic is simply inapplicable: you are either alone or with others; there is not a third option. (You might, in your solitude, think of others or, in company, retreat to a mental solitude, but these are practices of alternation, not reconciliation.) Emerson recommends that, rather than seek some impossible synthesis, we learn to move back and forth between society and solitude. Solitude gives us time to think and explore our aversions. Community gives our explorations meaning and forces our aversions to find spaces for institutionalization so as to become real. If we cannot make them real, then we still have our solitude as a kind of private joy. And when society is overwhelmed by conformity to a horrific cause, it is from solitude that one draws the strength to rebel. (Here Hegel and Emerson agree to an extent.[62]) Through these endless processes, each side is improved: "The remedy is to reinforce each of these moods from the other."[63]

As Dassow Walls has shown, this thinking in Emerson goes back to the late 1820s when he first saw a demonstration of a magnet. Grasping that magnets function through a relation of polarity, Emerson began to see polarity as a driving force in the universe. Dassow Walls further situates Emerson's excitement with the general trend in post-Kantian thought: "Emerson's reading confirmed that polarity was the keystone that divided, connected, and stabilized the arc of the universe."[64] This was not just an abstraction about universal principles, however, but also a specific understanding of how the globe worked. This was brought home for Emerson in the writings of the Swiss immigrant Arnold Guyot. For Guyot, according to Dassow Walls, the forces of polarity mean that "the globe may be said to be *alive*" and bounded by "connection" and "mutual dependence."[65] I have argued that this connectivity of a mutually dependent globe through both natural and human forces was the condition of possibility for the production of global self-making in modernity. But we also see in Guyot the same ethnocentrism of his European contemporaries. He, too, suggests that the energy of human life in "the South" is inert and must be reenergized with contact from "the North."[66] This is polarity without pluralism.

Emerson offers us another vision of the globe in his essay "Nominalist and Realist" (1844). He begins: "I cannot often enough say, that a man is only a relative and representative nature."[67] He explains by this that we are all parts of the evolving and multiplying truth of the universe and can never fully embody it. This is not because we are weak or hypocritical or because we fail to "incarnate the ideal" but because what we are—nature, culture, and concept combined—is multiple. To deal with this, we ought not to insist on some single trait that defines us, but rather to embrace our diversity. As Emerson writes, "You have not got rid of your parts by denying them, but are the more partial."[68]

It might seem that in the essay, Emerson is suggesting why nominalists and realists both have a share of the truth. Nominalists can show that the vaunted quality of an individual or nation is contradicted by other facts, while realists can point to the existence of general qualities even though they may be belied by details. "England, strong, punctual, practical, well-spoken England, I should not find, if I should go to the island to seek it."[69] But if I am correct about Emerson's struggle to articulate a radical pluralism, then the essay "Nominalist and Realist" is in fact opposed to this way of viewing things. Realism and nominalism *share* a denial of radical pluralism, because the former relies on universals and the latter on particulars, with neither recognizing that an object is *both* general and particular and, even beyond this, partakes of multiple generals and particulars.[70]

Moreover, this is not simply an abstract problem for Emerson, but one (explicitly in the essay) of global contact. Emerson is explicit that the globe cannot become a unified circle that encompasses all of human nature in a single form: "You are one thing, but nature is *one thing and the other thing* . . . She will not remain *orbed in thought*, but rushes into persons . . . [T]here will be somebody else, and the world will be round."[71] Nature's ceaseless multiples bristle against attempts to grasp and fasten the world. Emerson makes this point explicitly also with regard to philosophical doctrines: "Each man, too, is a tyrant in tendency, because he would impose his idea on others . . . Jesus would absorb the race; but Tom Paine or the coarsest blasphemer helps humanity by resisting the exuberance of power."[72] Speaking then of utopian communities like Brook Farm, Emerson criticizes the call to "baptise them" and then asks the crucial question: "Why have only two or three ways of life, and not thousands?" He answers: "Every man is wanted, and no man is wanted much."[73] There should be as many ways of life as do not exclude the creation of other ways of life.

This is not merely Emerson's philosophical understanding of the world, but an understanding based in the fact of our shared global condition. The language of culture thus runs through this essay, even though critics tend to skip over it even as they cite it.[74] For Emerson, the philosophical questions of nominalism and realism must be thought through as part of our globality. He is reacting against attempts to capture the globe and "orb" thought, and thus equally against attempts to name cultures or individuals as bounded by a singular essence. He instead argues for a multiplicity that cuts across these domains. In the battle between nominalist and realist, the radical pluralist wins. She alone can articulate the nature of a world that is an always evolving sphere of relations that produces real entities with no substantial and permanent existence. This fact of production through shifting relations is also central to what Emerson has to say in the essay. "Really, all things and persons are related to us, but according to our nature, they act on us or not at once, but in succession, and we are made aware of their presence one at a time."[75] Emerson does not suggest that the "really" true fact of interdependence matters more than the actual fact of our shifting attentions. He does not lead us to think that there is, around the corner, some complete knowledge that will hold all of these strands of existence together. Nor does he lead us to get lost in the infinite particulars and neglect the totality of relations. He argues against both completion and dissolution.

He leads us instead to simply remember that as we grasp real and existent parts of being, we are inevitably ignoring the many others unfolding around us. If we tend to forget this, Emerson lets us see that we are not alone in so doing: "The end and the means, the gamester and the game,—life is made up of the intermixture and reaction of these two amicable powers, whose marriage appears beforehand monstrous, as each denies and tends to abolish the other."[76] Just as any relationship in which one party obliterates the reality of the other is monstrous, so is our epistemology when it forgets the plurality of existence. Our task, here as ever, is to keep alive the "game" of alternation, always learning to see the duality of the pulsing world that manifests as the plurality of our lived experience.

There will of course be times in that plurality when we have to live a singularity. As I noted above, for example, society and solitude are simply opposites. Deciding when to focus on one side of the equation or the other is the role of partialization: we are to learn how to, at once, respect the plurality of the world and know that one element of that plurality will manifest in the need of precise decisions. This is the process of alternation described above: the process of learning when to expand and when to contract. At times, we are too accustomed to the given—what he calls "the imposing actual"—and must learn to move into the possible and the plural before returning to the specific.[77] At other times, singularities are necessary, both to critique dominant modes of a culture and to construct our own positions.

Gayatri Spivak famously spoke of this latter mode as "strategic essentialism," or, more precisely, "a *strategic* use of positivist essentialism in a scrupulously visible political interest."[78] In other words, accepting an idea of an essence of a group (say, women) in spite of the problematic connotations of such an essence (say, the feminine ideal) for a political purpose (say, fighting against the very idea of a feminine ideal). Spivak herself eventually abandoned the phrase (if not the practice), fearing that it had become a "union ticket for essentialism" rather than a serious reckoning with the *strategy* and its political uses.[79] The difficulty here is I think a good example of both the power and limits of deconstruction in the shaping of a critical vocabulary.

My suggestion is that there is a way of getting at the same idea without recourse to essentialism, which is to call these kinds of tactics *strategic partialisms*. Given that everything is plural, and that a certain part of a plurality often becomes or can be made to become the dominant factor, there appears a way of talking about this dominant part without reverting to a false essentialism. For what essentialism itself is, is nothing other than partializing a plurality and then insisting that the part grasped contains the whole within it. To speak instead of strategic partialization admits that parts of an entity can be grasped, but insists that no part can ever claim to speak for the whole. Much of what we struggle over is how we partialize an entity: not what we understand its essence to be so much as what we want its hegemonic partialization to be or which parts we want to exist together and how. When partialization becomes essentialization, it comes to support the unbearable identity of a culture.

To avoid this unbearability, we must keep alternating. The point of these alternations for Emerson is not to come to a final, perfected order of society, but to always be allowing for new modes of life to emerge. "The way of life is wonderful: it is by abandonment."[80] It is abandonment that keeps us from becoming too fixated on a single thought or idea. Even good ideas, after all, become unbearable when lived to excess: "Truth is our element of life, yet if a man fasten his attention on a single aspect of truth, and apply himself to that alone for a long time, the truth becomes distorted and not itself."[81] Of course if this is true of good ideas, it is even more so for bad ones. Again in his "Emancipation Address," Emerson noted that the dominant idea that had shaped slavery was economy. All considerations of truth were pushed aside save for the single pursuit of profit. But the power of life is in its ability to keep generating pluralities. I cite again: "man is born with intellect, as well as with a love of sugar, and with a sense of justice, as well as a taste for strong drink."[82] It is through alternation that we move away from a master-tone and into a new range of affinities. To begin the process of alternation we must first move away from the "imposing actual." This is the process of unhanding.

Unhanding

One step along this path is to cease our ingrained habits of trying to grasp the world. This structure of Emerson's thought is what could be called—in response to Idealism's "handing the globe"—"unhanding the globe." Stanley Cavell has done brilliant analyses of the figure of "unhanding" in Emerson, and it is from his work that I begin my own formulation. Cavell focuses on a line from Emerson's essay "Experience" (1844): "I take this evanescence and lubricity of all objects, which lets them slip through our fingers then when we clutch hardest, to be the most unhandsome part of our condition."[83] Speaking at a more or less purely theoretical level, Cavell explains that what is "un*hand*some" here is not the objects themselves, but the fact that we clutch at them, "as grasping something, say *synthesizing*."[84] What would be "handsome," then, is, in Cavell's recognition of Emerson's pun, *attraction*—not that I clutch objects, but that I attract them to me, draw them in, receive them.

Cavell also focuses on a second line from "Experience" when Emerson speaks of "this new yet unapproachable America I have *found* in the West."[85] He reads this "found" as having two meanings. First, that America is unapproachable without others, that one cannot found a country alone because finding is reception and explicitly *not* claiming. Emerson cannot go ahead and found America and call it his fiefdom. He must draw this other America to him. Second, this finding replaces founding. In other words, if what Hegel had sought to do was to *found* a system with a solid foundation, what Emerson has done is to *find* himself in an unfounded place and to begin his thought from there. Cavell sums up this historical positioning:

> If the generation after Hegel has announced the completion of philosophy, American writers must be free to discover whether the edifice of Western philosophy is as such European or whether it has an American inflection. (Here is where Emerson's and Thoreau's attraction to Eastern philosophy is crucial . . . America's search for philosophy continues, by indirection, Columbus' great voyage of indirection, redefining the West by persisting to the East.)[86]

In context, Cavell is claiming that Emerson's idea of unhanding precedes similar thoughts in Wittgenstein, and will, through Nietzsche, influence Heidegger. He is suggesting that the history of Western philosophy cannot effectively be told without America. Furthermore, he pushes Hegel's idea that philosophy rises in the East and sets in the West by showing that for Emerson there is always a new dawn, a new day, and so there can be no "setting" of philosophy. Cavell is no doubt aware as well of the resonance of Emerson's ideas with the doctrine of nonattachment in the *Bhagavad Gita* and the critique of grasping in the *Tao Te Ching*. I am concerned here, in part, with why this does not lead him to posit the incoherence—or at least the partiality—of the framing of philosophy or literature as national disciplines.

It was largely because of Cavell's inspiring work that I, like many others, first dedicated myself to reading Emerson. But whereas his interest over the past four decades has been to turn to Emerson to sculpt a history of American philosophy, my aim is to see how Emerson, as an American, strove to become a global essayist. I do not see him, then, turning to the East to overcome the West and to make American thought; I see him turning in as many directions as he can to liberate his thought *from* his national confines to be part of *global* thought. "I appeal from your customs," as he says in "Self-Reliance" (1841).[87] And, from the "American Scholar" (1837): "Thinking is a partial act," both in the sense that it is part of action but not yet a full act in itself, and also in the sense that any one person's thinking is only a part of a larger open-ended process of thought.[88]

This partiality is part of an origin myth about hands that we find in that earlier essay: "It is one of those fables, which, out of an unknown antiquity, convey an unlooked-for wisdom, that the gods, in the beginning, divided Man into men, that he might be more helpful to himself; just as the hand was divided into fingers, the better to answer its end."[89] Again, alternations require both internal and external cultural difference. This difference is not meant to be a site of deprecation (the lazy Esquimaux), but a space to explore another way to be human. Nor is this difference to be celebrated just because it is different: it is to be engaged and, where necessary, critiqued. Or, as with Montaigne, used to critique one's own culture. It is in the alternation of handing and unhanding—of giving and receiving—that this process is enabled.

Another way to read "unhandsome," then, is as a command: unhand some. Let go a little. This is the *act* I must perform on myself: to accept my partiality, work it over, but not then claim it as *the* world, and offer it rather as part of *a* world. What this requires, says Emerson, is "health and a day":

> Give me health and a day, and I will make the pomp of emperors ridiculous. The dawn is my Assyria; the sun-set and moon-rise my Paphos, and unimaginable realms of faerie; broad noon shall be my England of the senses and the understanding; the night shall be my Germany of mystic philosophy and dreams.[90]

Notice here that there are four regions of life named—Assyria, Paphos, England and Germany—and Emerson's "I" makes the fifth. What is his contribution to the hand? To make "the pomp of emperors ridiculous." His task, in other words, is to keep the other fingers—in thought or in action—from claiming more than is their rightful share. The trick is to keep unhanding and alternating.

Double Consciousness

Emerson knows that this process of alternation can be problematic. It can, for example, leave us feeling a painful split between our sensual and spiritual life, as Goethe had noted. Emerson takes up this problematic and offers a solution to it with the idea of "double consciousness." The phrase first appears in the essay "The Transcendentalist" (1842),[91] where Emerson focuses on a specific kind of experience that seems to exist for all self-professed transcendentalists: that they have glimpsed, for "the space of an hour," a truth that shook the foundations of their belief and showed them another, more harmonious way of life beyond the paltriness of daily human affairs.[92] This other truth appears misaligned with the real world. The perfect harmony appears untetherable to the terrible diversity it in fact manifests. This split in modes of thought becomes a split in life: transcendentalists are at times elated and free, clear and purposeful, direct and untouched by doubt; at others, they are woefully distant from this head space, trapped in everyday concerns, perplexed as to where their clarity has gone. Double consciousness is thus not just two different states, but the experience of one state that makes the other feel tawdry and inept:

> The worst feature of this double consciousness is, that the two lives, of the understanding and of the soul, which we lead, show very little relation to each other, never meet and measure each other: one prevails now, all buzz and din; and the other prevails then, all infinitude and paradise; and, with the progress of life, the two discover no greater disposition to reconcile themselves.[93]

The very hope that they should reconcile themselves, however, is what makes the experience unbearable. If we conceive of our identities as polarities that must become synthesized, we will always seek to impose that synthesis on our wildly alternating natures. In so doing, we will not only feel the pain of disconnect, but we will also close off the possibilities for who we are and can be that exist in our alternations. We are plural, and our power and freedom come from our learning which parts of ourselves to rely on and at which times. This is one meaning of "self-reliance." The way to overcome the unbearable identity is to not force it into a singular manifestation. This is as true for ourselves as for the world.

Emerson found another way of understanding the double consciousness around the same time that he was critiquing the "Transcendentalist." In an 1842 journal entry, he spoke of a conversation with Sampson Reed, who appears to have suggested to Emerson that a certain perfection was possible "in the other world." Emerson records his response with language he will recycle in "Nominalist and Realist": " 'Other world?' I reply, 'there is no other world; here or nowhere is the whole fact; all the Universe over, there is but one thing,—this old double, Creator-creature, mind-matter, right-wrong.' "[94] The critique of "double consciousness" is similar to Feuerbach's famous critique of religion: that it projects into the other world what are in fact problems in this world. In this instance, the very idea of the other world is itself an effect of the "double consciousness." The fact that the world itself is multiple is projected into the idea of a world different from this one. The result is a double alienation: from this world, which we imagine imperfect, and from the other real world, which is the alternation (alternative) that this world could be.

The question for Emerson was if—once the "other world" was recognized as simply the double of this world—there would be some way of handling this doubling rather than self-alienation. Emerson, I think, found this strategy when he rewrote the idea of double consciousness some years later in the essay "Fate" (1854/1860). Here he will find for it a positive meaning:

> One key, one solution to the mysteries of human condition, one solution to the old knots of fate, freedom and foreknowledge, exists, the propounding, namely, of the double consciousness. A man must ride *alternately* on the horses of his private and his public nature, as the equestrians in the circus throw themselves nimbly from horse to horse, or plant one foot on the back of one, and the other foot on the back of the other. So when a man is the victim of his fate . . . he is to rally on his relation to the Universe, which his ruin benefits. Leaving the daemon who suffers, he is to take sides with the Deity who secures universal benefit by his pain.[95]

The key point for my reading is the movement of alternation, this double consciousness (a double whose two sides, we must remember, are plural in themselves), which provides a solution to handle personal and—to an extent—political troubles. While in "The Transcendentalist" double consciousness meant an uneasy balance between worldliness and transcendence, Emerson here develops a solution to that problem through the same device. Rather than a consciousness torn asunder between a better and a real world, we now have a consciousness that is capable of using the vision of another world as the means of recharging power in this world. Equally, she uses this world to keep herself from becoming too bound up with the beauty of utopic transcendence. The problem of free will is resolved not by Kant's claim that I cannot know whether I have free will but may act as if I do, but rather by Emerson's response that I know I can only have it sometimes. Sometimes I am bound to a cause—call that the public or the deity—greater than myself. Sometimes I can extract myself and act with abandon. Some of the time, perhaps most of the time in an ideal society, I am positioned between the two.[96]

Others might disagree that this is really a solution. The movement here appears as not too dissimilar from what we find in Hegel's *Phenomenology of*

Spirit in the problem of the "unhappy consciousness," which Hegel defines as "the consciousness of self as a dual-natured, merely contradictory being."[97] These two sides are the "simple Unchangeable" and the "protean Changeable," and the task for Hegel's subject is to realize that in fact, the subject (as Spirit) is already a "single undivided consciousness [of] a dual nature."[98] Hegel discusses the same problem even more explicitly in his lectures on aesthetics. Setting up his discussion of Schiller, he writes:

> For, on the one side, we see man a prisoner in common reality and earthly temporality . . . On the other side, he exalts himself to eternal ideas, to a realm of thought and freedom. Such a discrepancy in life and consciousness involves for modern culture and its understanding the demand that the contradiction should be resolved. Yet the understanding cannot release itself from the fixity of these antitheses. The solution, therefore, remains for consciousness a mere *ought*, and the present and reality only stir themselves in the unrest of a perpetual to and fro, which seeks a reconciliation without finding it . . . All that philosophy does is to furnish a reflective insight into the essence of the antithesis in as far as it shows that what constitutes truth is merely the resolution of this antithesis, and that not in the sense that the conflict and its aspects in any way *are not*, but in the sense that they *are, in reconciliation*.[99]

I quote this passage at such length for several reasons. First, because it shows clearly the shared ground of the problem. Hegel, like Emerson and others, is trying to understand the relationship between our earthly and spiritual sides. And he makes an important qualification that both Marx and Emerson will echo, although the latter perhaps not as strongly as one would like. This is that the hoped-for reconciliation can only be *explained* by philosophy: its achievement must occur in the world itself. But this is also the danger of Hegel's philosophy: that it will seek to impose that philosophical vision onto the world. Emerson, denying reconciliation, also denies imposition. His politics of the present will be generated *through* the contradiction, as we shall see.

For Hegel, the task is to reconcile the poles and bring them under the domain of the singular process of history. For Emerson, the task is to learn to use the poles, to allow them to charge and regenerate from each other. Thus he begins the essay with the passage I cited above, arguing that the reconciliation of opposites is impossible and that we can only "obey our polarity." Hegel, perhaps like Goethe, only sees the double consciousness that Emerson outlines in "The Transcendentalist." He never arrives at the thought of the double consciousness that offers the alternating vision of life. The idea that there is one double consciousness that must be overcome, but also a second, positive form that is not found in reconciliation but in alternation, has been an important if hardly noticed current in those who wrote after Emerson, including Du Bois, Bergson, Senghor, and others. It is in learning to use the double consciousness, rather than in seeking to overcome it, that Emerson and those following him will develop a theory of relation not only between spirit and matter, but also between cultures.

This innovation in Emerson is thus related to his thoughts on culture. Cavell has argued that the difficulty of ending a practice as abominable as slavery marks both the moments of pessimism and the clarion calls that constitute "Fate."[100] Building on his work, Eduardo Cadava has noted that for Emerson, overcoming slavery requires a critique of the whole global system of imperial domination that makes slavery possible in the United States.[101] And Nikhil Bilwakesh has further noted that this critique in Emerson is generated not just by an insistence on the truth of freedom in European thinkers, but also through a serious engagement with the *Bhagavad Gita*.[102] By linking the critique of slavery to the question of America's global ambitions, these critics all underscore the ways in which unbearable identities are created by race prejudice. And Bilwakesh especially shows that overcoming these prejudices is not simply a matter of enacting a principle of freedom that otherwise remains an abstract theory, but also one of actual engagement with ways of life and thinking from around the world.

The difference between Hegel and Emerson here is thus not simply one of individual action and consciousness. It is also about the relationship between cultures because part of what is happening here is that part of Emerson's new idea of double consciousness relates to his rereading of the *Bhagavad Gita*.[103] We saw above how for Emerson the movement of alternation could happen by alternating within one's own culture, and that it might also require "some foreign force."[104] If we allow the possibility of cultural difference as a dynamic entity, and if we insist that difference is not determinate in the last instance, we can develop a theory of cultural contact within the frames of radical pluralism. We might call this the practice of alter-nations, in the double sense of engaging with an other (alter) nation and of altering our nation through this practice.

Emerson reread the *Bhagavad Gita* in 1854, prior to his first composition of "Fate."[105] The *Gita* is—among other things—the story of a man, Arjuna, who must learn to act in the world in ways that may destroy him because a deity, Krishna, has told him to do so ("take sides with the deity"). More than this, it is about a man who learns how to *alternate in this world* through his engagement with a deity. Thus the first words Arjuna speaks to Krishna (in the Wilkins translation that Emerson read) are: "I pray thee, Kreeshna, cause my chariot to be driven and placed between the two armies, that I may behold who are the men that stand ready, anxious to commence the bloody fight."[106] One reading of the phrase "take sides with the deity" is not that he will side with the deity against someone else, but that he will go with Krishna between the sides and take stock of them.

What Emerson learns here is another aspect of alternation itself. To alternate is not just to move between modes; it is to move into betweenness itself, with one foot on each horse, so to speak. Perhaps Emerson calls this a solution to fate, freedom, and foreknowledge because it shows that our human condition enables modes of betweenness—sometimes we are free in our private imagination, sometimes bound to public realities beyond our control, and sometimes, with the deity, we stand between the two. What Emerson will find in this space between is just what Arjuna does: that pure betweenness is only a temporary capacity for humans. We can learn from it, but we must return to choose a side.

Having seen both sides, Arjuna's famous realization is that he cannot renounce this world, but must act in it. That action will of course itself have many meanings. Emerson, a man of peace, must now support the Civil War, as Arjuna also had. Radical pluralism can no more bear the fact of contradiction than can any other edifice of thought. But it does not promise to: it overcomes unbearability through humility. Radical pluralists of course must make decisions, but they do so having seen the sides and knowing the partiality of their knowledge and the plurality that will again result from whatever action they take. They are radicals because they know they need to partialize, but they are pluralists because they never assume that their partialization outweighs the moral worth of all humans. There is no friend/enemy distinction in pluralism because everyone is at once friend and enemy. Pluralism undercuts unbearability again by reminding us that we cannot act alone, and the universe will do more than whatever choice we have made—thus it "benefits" by our "ruin." By alternating "between cultures," Emerson thus learns a new mode of alternation as such.

Without going further into the specifics of Emerson's reading of the *Gita*, the key point in relation to Hegel is the very fact that it was a resource for Emerson. Emerson wrote in his *Journal* in 1845: "It [the *Gita*] was the first of books; it was as if an empire spoke to us, nothing small or unworthy, but large, serene, consistent, the voice of an old intelligence which in another age and another climate had pondered and thus disposed of the same questions which exercise us . . . Let us cherish the venerable oracle."[107] This is a far cry from what Hegel had to say about the Indian epics. In his *Philosophy of History*, for example, he wrote, "Although the Chinese invented gunpowder, they did not know how to use it, while the Indians produced superb gems of poetry without any corresponding advances in art, freedom, and law."[108] Later in the lectures, Hegel will critique the "formalism" of looking at moral traits unhinged from their incarnation in cultural practices and the state.[109] In short, there is very little to be learned from India or China for Hegel, and whatever may be worthwhile has already been folded into the actual practices of the present day.[110] For Emerson, the truths of that time are still available to us. The persistence of truth in its original form is part of what differentiates Emerson from Hegel.[111]

Still, doubts may linger about Emerson's own break here. Eric Cheyfitz, for example, has fairly questioned whether Emerson managed to relate to the falsely named "Indian" closer to home in his failures to engage with indigenous forms of thought. Cheyfitz argues that such an engagement may have been especially fruitful in terms of Emerson's thinking about nature and hospitality by offering him the language of kinship, both across humanity and beyond it.[112] Ultimately, while appreciative of some moments of international engagement in Emerson, Cheyfitz concludes: "The limits of Emerson's progressive thought are in his inability to *sustain* the imagination of the value of other cultures *on their own terms* and to image this cultural difference as a crucial critique of Western power."[113] While I have suggested otherwise, I do not think my argument here rests on Emerson himself having achieved this. What I am arguing for is something slightly different: that Emerson strove to develop a framework of thought that would in principle enable such engagements through his radical pluralism. Whether or not he fully accomplished a practice of difference, he, like Marx, undoubtedly worked toward the breakup of the ethnocentric vision that would disallow such a revision. Moreover, like Senghor, he did so based on a cultural understanding of the radical plurality of others. This understanding suggests, first, that different cultures had worked through different ways of being, but, second, that those ways of being were complex and mutating in themselves, and, third, that their shared "essence" is not a static culture but was "what is essential," as Senghor put it: the fact of its availability to all in conditions of nondomination.

The importance of engagement without domination returns us to the essay "Fate." Emerson wrote in his journals from the time of its first composition (1850s): "The argument of the slaveholder is one & simple: he pleads Fate." Emerson continues that this notion of "fate" is linked to an idea of racial difference: "Here is an inferior race requiring wardship,—and it is sentimentality to deny it."[114] He responds that this is not in fact a matter of sentimentality, but one of law. What kind of law, he asks, permits you to steal a man but not his shoes? If there is something wrong with race here, Emerson seems to be suggesting, it is both the degradation of Africans and the false claims to superiority by whites.

This imagined superiority is part of what manifests as the "Atlas complex" and the idea that one's own thoughts about how to achieve freedom are so perfect that they should be imposed on the whole world. Emerson writes at the beginning of the essay a line that bears repeating: "We are incompetent to solve the times. Our geometry cannot span the huge orbits of the prevailing ideas, behold their return, and reconcile their opposition. We can only obey our own polarity."[115] While there is a certain pessimism about the capacity to overcome slavery here, we might also note that it is a critique of the very kind of thinking that instituted slavery in the first place. It was because people thought themselves competent to legislate for the world, and to span the orb of the globe and reconcile it under a single domain, that the terrors of the present are what they are. (This recalls the line from "Nominalist and Realist": Nature "will not remain *orbed in thought*, but rushes into persons.") Rather than such feigned competence about knowledge of others and their place in the world, Emerson suggests that we learn to respect the differences produced in ourselves and others by polarity.

Critics of Emerson might suggest that his other writing from the same time seems to affirm this very right of conquerors. In *English Traits* (1856), for example, he remarks: "It is race, is it not? that puts the hundred millions of India under the dominion of a remote island in the north of Europe." But to criticize these lines is to imagine that Emerson thinks domination is a good thing.[116] There is, however, nothing especially in his writing to imagine that he thinks dominion by a far-off power is good. Critics might, in response, point to an oft-maligned line that follows: "Race in the negro is of appalling importance."[117] These readers seem to imagine that this line about "appalling importance" means that Emerson thinks the fault lies with Africans and the diaspora, but it seems more likely that what is appalling is that *white* people treat the race of others with such appalling importance. Indeed, some pages later in *English Traits*, Emerson suggests something to this effect with regard to England: "The English uncultured are a brutal nation."[118] Emerson discusses the brutal practices that are rampant in England and notes how this plays out in race-hatred, specifically with "The Jews [who] have been the favorite victims of royal and popular persecution."[119] What is "appalling" in race is persecuting others because of it. This is the act of those "theoretic kidnappers" who refuse to see the infinitude of every human and instead see only their physiognomy. As such brutality could not find sufficient outlets on this small, remote island, the British "could not help becoming the sailors and factors of the globe."[120] That is not a good thing.[121]

It is fair to say, however, that it is not *clear* that Emerson is in fact critical here. As Cadava notes: "Emerson takes the risk of ventriloquizing the language of slavery propaganda—we can find in 'Fate' echoes of most of the important proslavery arguments . . .—[but] he seeks to recontextualize this language not only within antislavery argument but also within a more general reflection on the nature of race and the violence that takes place in its name."[122] This risk is worth taking, Cadava suggests, because the language itself must also be transformed.[123] Part of what the pro-slavery advocates have done, after all, is to suggest that the language of liberty is coextensive with enslavement, that the language of nation is coextensive with empire, and that the language of race is coextensive with hierarchy. Cadava cites Emerson's talk on the Kansas-Nebraska Act, where Emerson notes that the Act equates "enlarging the area of Freedom" with the expansion of slavery. The result: "Language has lost its meaning in the universal cant . . . *Manifest Destiny, Democracy, Freedom*, fine names for an ugly thing."[124] Emerson is working to turn that language against itself and to recover the meaning of these words, even if—we should concede to his critics—he does not always succeed.

The remarks about race in *English Traits* have corollaries in "Fate." Emerson remarks, for example:

> The population of the world is a conditional population; not the best, but the best that could live now; and the scale of tribes, and the steadiness with which victory adheres to one tribe and defeat to another, is as uniform as the superposition of strata. We know in history what weight belongs to race. We see the

English, French, and Germans planting themselves on every shore and market of America and Australia, and monopolizing the commerce of these countries.[125]

Cadava's essay is largely dedicated to explicating this passage and the rest of the paragraph from which it comes. Building on the work of Patricia Seed, he shows how the idea of someone "planting themselves" is etymologically related to the idea of plantations. If this is indeed an essay against slavery, it is clear that Emerson is not congratulating these European nations, whose act of planting has reaped nothing but slavery and extermination. When Emerson later speaks of the "mysteries of human condition," he is perhaps referring back to this "conditional population," whose ability to plant the flag of freedom in the name of barbarity is indeed a mystery—not in the sense that it is difficult to explain, but in that it mystifies the truth with linguistic magic. If this is the "best that could live now," we had better hurry up and overcome our fate!

When Emerson speaks, in the paragraph on "double consciousness," about those who are "ground to powder by the vice of [their] race," or the need to "offset the drag and temperament of race," it is—at least in part—to these conquering populations that he is speaking. This vice is not the curse of Canaan (or Ham); it is the curse of having placed that burden on others.[126] The troubled temperament is not that of "lazy native," but that of the people whose irascibility and greed leads them to beat those who do not work to their liking. Emerson is not calling on "inferior races" to overcome their inferiority because of course no inferiority could exist in the first place for anyone who believes in the "singular equality of all ages." He is calling on racists to remember that no race is fated to dominate while another suffers perpetually. Those who do not see this will one day find themselves on the other side of that "steadiness with which victory adheres to one tribe and defeat to another, [which] is as uniform as the superposition of strata." That is, this cycle of domination will continue unless we can find a way to break this constant layering of mutilated fates, and enable some other world to emerge.[127]

Thus Emerson is not only using language against itself here. He is also trying to develop a new language—of alternation, unhanding, double consciousness, among others—that might enable a different mode of global relation. In this way, the incompetence to "solve" the times might enable a "solution to the mysteries of human condition." "Solution," we should remember, has a number of meanings. The OED lists, among others: "The termination or crisis of a disease. The action of releasing or setting free; deliverance, release. The action of paying; a payment. The action of discharging or fulfilling. The action of dissolving. The action of fusing."[128] Solution, in other words, is not the single thing that "solves" the problem, but rather a complex and layered word that invokes ideas of ending, freedom, and compensation, at the same time that it simultaneously conjoins the actions of separating and fusing—the action of the double consciousness. If it is also the case, as Cavell argues, that Emerson purposefully leaves the article off "*the* human condition,"[129] then we see yet again that no possible solution to life's conundrums can be singular, and any viable solution must take account of the evolving historical and social contexts in which we find ourselves. And yet, because Emerson's pluralism remains radical and critical, this does not devolve into relativism. There must be some *solution*, some "setting free," that will enable the freedom of alternation for all people and peoples.

My pluralist vision of Emerson is very close to, but importantly different from, a recent engaged reading of his work by Jeffrey Stout. Stout's reading, which is focused on the essay "Experience" (1844), argues that Emerson's work is very much aligned with Hegel's. He writes: "While he had not yet read Hegel by 1844, Emerson's response to skepticism closely resembles Hegel's . . . [The essay] seeks to overcome a rift in modern life between subjective ideals and material reality." The process through which the essay does this is akin to the *Phenomenology of Spirit*: "by critically examining various outlooks that have appeared historically and have tended to reinforce the rift."[130]

For Stout, "idealism" is one side of a problematic modern dichotomy with "materialism" that Emerson aims to overcome. Stout argues that Emerson's strategy is not to look toward a future reconciliation, but to show that "the rift has *already* been overcome, *more than once*."[131] In fact, the rift is overcome every time we "*stand for* something . . . *before others*."[132] In those moments, we are revealing the "truth of idealism," which is that, in Stout's clever phrasing, "ideals matter." In other words, the rift here is between a materialism bent on "explaining all idealized motivations away" and an idealism that is "too rarified to be actualized."[133] That rift is overcome not when the ideal becomes permanently real, but when we realize the need to stand for something and become exemplars of virtuous lives. This virtue, of course, cannot remain personal, but must be concretized (if not absolutized) in our institutions. "Abolitionism must be incorporated into a larger and deeper process of personal and societal change that *actually embodies* the highest ideals of the age."[134] The point is not that this desire guarantees success, but that all we can do is attempt to enact our values to the best of our abilities.[135]

I am very appreciative of this general reading of Emerson, but I think the dialectical casing may overlook Emerson's pluralist insights and the accompanying idea of alternation. Stout's argument is based on a reading of the closing line of "Experience": Emerson writes, "the true romance which the world exists to realize, will be the transformation of genius into practical power." In focusing his attention here, Stout cuts out the preceding half of the sentence, "Never mind the ridicule, never mind the defeat; up again, old heart!—*it* seems to say,—there is victory yet for all justice . . ."[136] But what is the "it" that is speaking? The previous sentence indicates that this is "the solitude to which every man is always returning." It is in our solitude that we have this vision of genius being transformed into practical power. Stout does not consider this. I don't think that makes his reading wrong so much as partial. It is certainly true that at moments we will wish, in our solitude, to transform genius into actualized structures in the world. But it is equally true, in day-to-day affairs, that this will be thwarted by the difficulties of experience. The message here thus seems to me to be the same as what we have seen throughout Emerson—not the hopeful reconciliation of ideal and real, but the ongoing understanding that we need this energy of solitude in order to continue in our necessary tasks of transforming the world. But, at the same time, we cannot get stuck in this reverie of solitude and neglect the difficulty of action. Thus the "true romance" is one that recognizes the equality of the opposing poles and learns to move between them. As I cited above from "Society and Solitude" (1857), "Here again, as so often, Nature delights to put us between extreme antagonisms, and our safety is in the skill with which we keep the diagonal line."[137] *As we move between them*, we should find changes in both spheres. Again from "Society and Solitude": "The remedy is to reinforce each of these moods from the other."[138] On this point of transformation I agree with Stout. But my concern is that a focus on realization may obscure the necessity of continuing to alternate.

I am not saying that there are no vestiges of such idealist thinking in Emerson; there certainly are. But what appears to me more exciting about his work—and more apposite for thinking through the global self—is his vision of an alternating world teeming with diversity. Thus where Stout looks to overcome rifts, I argue that Emerson wants to *move between the sides of the rift*. The aim is not only to reconcile subject and object (though we may do that sometimes), nor is it only (as Voelz might have it) to generate new energy and ideas and provocations from our failure to do so (though we may do that sometimes as well). Both this dialectical and this deconstructive move can be contained as part of a radical pluralism that sees that subject and object, ideal and material, are opposites whose "polarity" we have to learn to obey. *Unhanding our hope to grasp them in an instant, we instead alternate between their powers through our learning the movement of the double consciousness.* When the real threatens to tyrannize us, we pull back into ideals, and when the ideal has no traction in the world, we move more into material concerns. Sometimes we will find that this movement creates newly constituted entities (ideals matter), and sometimes we will find that it breaks up entities that have gone stale (ideals fracture). At no time is there a pure rift or a pure overcoming.

This plurality is not, however, necessarily a good thing. This is why radical pluralism must remain critical. It is true that all sides of a rift have something to "contribute," but that contribution may be detrimental, such as the claims of racism or a right to slavery. Radical pluralism is thus both descriptive and normative, and its norm is against those moments in plurality that seek to bind others to singular determinations. This is why "standing before," as Stout calls it, or "partialization," as I have named it, or "taking sides with the deity," as Emerson puts it, are necessary acts.[139] To take sides with the deity *against* something is to say that there is no available dialectic between justice and injustice, or between slavery and freedom. These are "real opposites," as Marx had it, and must be understood beyond the dialectical frame. They also have no relation to alternation, except as something to alternate out of. This is where we need the Emersonian practice of "aversion." And this is part of the logic of this complex Emersonian writing, which guides us in the movements of alternating through diversities.[140]

Emerson enjoins us to think of different modes of life that we can utilize as we negotiate the world. Sometimes this will require alternating into the construction of ideals; sometimes this will require tarrying with factious realities; sometimes this will require emptying ourselves of any thought entirely and seeing what we find beyond our inherited concepts and language games. This is why Emerson's practices, which may appear to be matters of the private self, are always bound up with the globe, how we share it, and how we view others on it.

6

Radical Pluralism II
Du Bois

Few intellectuals have understood the globality of the modern condition so well as W. E. B. Du Bois. In Du Bois's self-explanation of this understanding, his "early interest in the color problems in the United States and Africa led to the habit of travel"—a habit that would take him across the known world over the span of the near-century which he lived.[1] This habit of travel in turn led him to see that the race issues of the United States were not confined there, but were part of longer histories of anti-Semitism and colonial oppression.[2] Du Bois's increasing understanding of the global reach of modern problems is part of what he would call the "gift of second-sight," a bilingual pun in which the *gift* (German for poison) of oppression had been converted into a gift for seeing the world, its connections, and what needed to be done to remove the poison with unflinching clarity. As a scholar, novelist, essayist, and institutional activist, Du Bois wrote volumes of articles, tracts, pamphlets, speeches, fictions, and editorials about this global condition and his place in it. His constant rethinking of his own path, from an early liberal elitism to an increasing investment in the values of the communal to be found in Pan-Africanism, socialism, communism, and the global peace movement; and his unsettling praise of Stalin's Russia and Mao's China in his late years, have left a complex mass of ideas for scholars to untangle. I discuss some of these complexities below, but my primary aim in this chapter is to understand how Du Bois built on—and moved beyond—the preceding history told here, especially Emerson's legacy.

As he developed his global self, he pluralized radical pluralism. That is to say, he showed that different versions of pluralism would be necessary for subjects who found themselves subjected in the global order of things. To this end, Du Bois reinvented double consciousness, advocated specific ethical modalities for intercultural contact, engaged in an explicit and extended *practice* of making such contacts, innovated the humanistic understanding of the self with new methods from the social sciences, and experimented with genre to imagine alternative presents and futures for all peoples. These were his practices of the global self. I explore them as the intertwined themes that they are over the rest of this chapter.

The idea of double consciousness that I have discussed at such length in Emerson is, today, a phrase more generally associated with W. E. B. Du Bois and his famous analysis of the phenomenon in African Americans. In his oft quoted lines:

> After the Egyptian and Indian, the Greek and Roman, the Teuton and Mongolian, the Negro is a sort of seventh son, born with a veil, and gifted with second-sight in this American world—a world which yields him no true self-consciousness, but only lets him see himself through the revelation of the other world. It is a peculiar sensation, this double-consciousness, this sense of always looking at one's self through the eyes of others, of measuring one's soul by the tape of a world that looks on in amused contempt and pity.[3]

The phrasing here is remarkable, and much of what I have to say about Du Bois in this section amounts to an interpretation of these few lines. I argue that they are an extension of Emerson's ideas that help move beyond a reserved radical pluralism to a more globally available understanding of the notion. By this I mean that Emerson's radical pluralism, while not fully determined by his subject position, was still limited by it. Emerson's advice is thus certainly available to all and will have relevance for many, but he is simply and necessarily partial, as he himself admits and insists that everybody admit. There is nothing specific in his analysis of double consciousness, for example, that helps us to understand the phenomenon being described here by Du Bois. As a result, practices of the global self need to be developed for subjects who are produced in unbearable impositions of identity in ways that Emerson did not explore.[4] Du Bois offered a major revision of what radical pluralism could be that extends Emerson at the same time that Du Bois also—and necessarily—had his own limitations of vision.

My argument here is not, however, that Du Bois should be considered a "reader" of Emerson or that his conceptual innovation is a mere extension of the latter's work. Instead, my aim is to show how they are both part of an ongoing struggle to understand how relations of global interdependence (and forced dependence) shaped the possibilities for modern subjects. Du Bois is no more an Emersonian than Emerson is a Montaignian. They are all, rather, working to essay a bearable place in this violent world and arriving at different means for doing so. Du Bois explored what global practices would be for those who were told they could not perform Emersonian alternations because they had already been *forced* to "alter nations" through slavery and exile. He thus opened an inquiry into an element largely missing from Emerson's thought; namely, he asked what practices of the global self would look like from the position of those who did not have the "health and a day" to overcome empire and perform the tasks of alternation.

Central to my argument in this chapter is the claim (which goes against some elements of contemporary scholarship) that there are *two* forms of double consciousness in Du Bois—one critiqued and one affirmed.[5] To arrive at this claim requires a close reading of his literary language in this dense paragraph. His writing, here as elsewhere, is filled with polysemy. We see it even with the first word, "after." The American "Negro" is "after" in the sense of being the product of New World slavery, and so more recent as a race concept than the others.[6] More directly, in America, the Negro is "after" in the sense of being looked down on and degraded as stuck in an earlier time of historical evolution from which black men and women are told that they, at once, cannot transcend and must transcend. But "after" here also registers a third sense: to be going after, or working to achieve, something. Black people are "after" these other races in the sense that they are complex cultural beings who inhabit many spaces and seek the plural knowledges of the world. They are chasing after the meaning of human plurality and seeking to find their emancipated place in it.

There are also multiple meanings to the "gift" of "second-sight." The gift, though a product of terror, results in the ability to see the multiplicity of being. It is also the ability to see that one *has* two sights—the vision of the world as it appears and the vision of the world as it is forced by the "revelation of the other world." And it is also the gift that black people bring to the world—the gift of the knowledge of duality, of the fact that we are never simply a single identity, but always part of the complex interactions of the world. Finally, it is the gift of *seeing through* whiteness. As one of Du Bois's fictional characters will state, "We black folk of America are the only ones . . . who see white folk and their civilization with level eyes and unquickened pulse."[7] At the same time, Du Bois also had a sinister sense of what this gift meant, registered in his bilingual pun on gift as "poison." And it is in part because of the poison of being forced to alter nations that African Americans have the power of second-sight. And this poison has not yet fully become a proper gift in the English sense, because African Americans are not yet fully enabled to be these kind of multiple subjects and are constantly forced into a prescribed identity of ignorance and toil.[8]

There is further polysemy in the phrase "revelation of the other world." In Emerson, again, double consciousness was the product of just such a revelation in the positive sense of another, more peaceful world. He argued that such a "revelation" in fact obscured the perpetual doubling of what is already in this world. Du Bois's phrase adds a great many meanings. If "the other world" is a religious revelation for him, as it was for Emerson, it is in several competing senses: the possibility of a perfected humanity, the damnation in which most of the world now lives, and the imposition of Christianity through colonial missionary work and slavery. Du Bois's thinking constantly strives toward the first revelation—the realization of another, better world that is, as in Emerson, meant to occur in *this world*. Du Bois, following the spiritual tradition, thus links emancipation to the biblical account of Exodus and the founding of a new land. Writing nearly forty years after emancipation, Du Bois invokes the Hebraic sensibility of struggling to arrive at the promised other world of freedom: "Canaan was always dim and far away . . . but . . . the journey at least gave leisure for reflection and self-examination . . . [T]he child of Emancipation . . . saw in himself some faint *revelation* of his power . . . He began to have a dim feeling that, to attain his place *in the world*, he must be himself, and not another."[9] Achieving revelation in this world will thus mean not viewing oneself through the revelation of the other world, but through one's own eyes—eyes that themselves, of course, have their perception shaped by pluralities.

This does not mean that Du Bois has an unambiguous sense of the religious themes of the "revelation of the other world." The troubling fact is that the dueling possibilities for revelation overlap with each other. This reversal within the very language of biblical redemption is best expressed in *The World and Africa* (1947). Du Bois writes: "With this new world came fatally the African slave trade and Negro slavery in the Americas."[10] This new world brought with it a new "scientific" revelation: the doctrine of racial inferiority. "In line with this conviction the Christian Church . . . at first damned the heathen blacks with the 'curse of Canaan,' then held out hope of freedom through 'conversion,' and finally acquiesced in a permanent status of human slavery."[11] Canaan (now signifying a person) here shifts from promised land to a new form of damnation. The "curse of Canaan," also known as the "curse of Ham," comes from the story in Genesis where Ham sees a drunk Noah passed out naked. He tells Shem and Japteth, who clothe Noah. When Noah awakens he says, " 'Cursed be Canaan [Ham's son]; lowest of slaves shall he be to his brothers.' He also said, 'Blessed by the Lord my God be Shem [and Japheth]; and let Canaan be his slave.' "[12] According to David Goldenberg, while there is no mention of race in the biblical story, Near Eastern writers as early as the seventh century CE began to link "dark skin" to a permanent condition of slavery based on an imputed racialization of the original story.[13] So Canaan, the new world, the land that was meant to signify freedom, instead became the name of a curse justified by an impossible reading of the meaning of the "revelation of the other world."[14] Those justifying slavery, of course, did not bother themselves with the facts.

"The other world" in *Souls* also has a more directly secular meaning derived from this same structure of justification: it is the white world and its claim of supremacy. An African American is forced to see herself through the ideas and measurements of the white world. The white world claims to reveal the black soul to itself as something worthy of "amused contempt and pity," rather than respect and dignity. In his later essay "The Souls of White Folk" (1920), Du Bois will show that this revelation by white folk amounts to a single claim: "whiteness is the ownership of the earth forever and ever, Amen!"[15] Here again we see the co-optation of religious language by white supremacy. While *The Souls of Black Folk* explores what that revelation means for African Americans, this later essay asks, "what is the effect on a man or a nation when it comes passionately to believe such an extraordinary dictum as this?"[16] The answer, in short, is jealousy, hatred, and violence. Du Bois traces Euro-America's "practices of the global self" from its civilizing missions, its imperial adventures, and its claims to universality to its implosion in World War I. It was the terror of the war that revealed the other world to itself: "This is not Europe gone mad; this is no aberration nor insanity; this *is* Europe; this seeming Terrible is the real soul of white culture."[17] Here is Du Bois turning the revelation back against itself: where the world of whiteness attempts to show its grandeur, it in fact reveals the terror at its heart.

Finally, this revelation of the other world is also a revelation of the ties that bind oppressed peoples. At the end of *Souls*, Du Bois will write to white

America, "Your country? How came it yours? Before the Pilgrims landed we were here."[18] All the glosses I have consulted (in the Norton, Barnes & Noble, and Oxford editions) state that Du Bois is alluding to the fact that the Pilgrims arrived in 1620, and the first slaves arrived at Jamestown in 1619. But while this is certainly the most direct referent, the phrase ("Your country? How came it yours?") implies *both* that it became yours by slave labor *and* that it became so by conquest. This link of oppressed peoples will of course become a dominant theme throughout Du Bois's career as he increasingly thinks in terms of how those in the "other world" of the color line (and, increasingly, class line) can unite to abolish discrimination and instill some forms of global justice.

(There is perhaps one irony here, which is the possibility that Du Bois himself should be asked how this line of argument itself became his. In her 1892 essay "Has America a Race Problem? If So, How Can It Best Be Solved?" Anna Julia Cooper makes a very similar set of remarks. She notes first that "the red men used to be owners of this soil" and appear to have the best claim to it, and then writes: "the Mayflower . . . landed in the year of Grace 1620, and the first delegation from Africa just one year ahead of that." Thus: "Exclusive possession [of the land] belongs to none."[19] Cooper also argues that African Americans have enriched American culture in various ways, and Du Bois similarly concludes his discussion with talk of the contributions of black folk.[20] Whether or not Du Bois had read Cooper at this point is debatable. Chike Jeffers concludes that it is "eminently plausible" when discussing the similarities of their notions of the "black gift thesis."[21] Joy James—bringing out the problematic nature of what David Levering Lewis describes more factually in his biography—has noted that Du Bois in general failed to acknowledge the voice and agency of women writers.[22] I simply mark this here and return to it below.)

The revelation of the other world is to see oneself as part of a country that began with genocide and grew with slave labor, and to realize the horror that you are born and conditioned, but also emancipated, within the "folds" of *that* world. As Du Bois put it at the beginning of *Dusk of Dawn* (1940): "In the folds of this European civilization I was born and shall die, imprisoned, conditioned, depressed, exalted and inspired."[23] These are the troubling overlaps of the "revelation of the other world," of the promise of Canaan that is also the curse of Canaan. This is why a radical pluralism must remain critical: it must always critique those elements of a culture (an enfolding of people) that deny the true liberation of others. But it also remains radically plural in the sense that it always finds the "gift" within even those layers of oppression. Du Bois notes this by speaking of the inspirations of Western culture and then continuing with his language of folding (here as enveloping): "Had it not been for the race problem early thrust upon me and enveloping me, I should have probably been an unquestioning worshipper at the shrine of the social order and economic development into which I was born."[24] Du Bois thus locates his own criticality within his oppression, within the fact that even oppression is a plural form whose results always and necessarily escape the oppressor, who, try though they might, cannot be victorious in the last. Du Bois concludes the book in the same language: "there is infinite joy in seeing the Word, the most interesting of continued stories, unfold, even though one misses THE END."[25] These are again rich and polysemic lines, ones that suggest another "revelation"—not as the dominion of one, but as the power of language to instill new meanings and *develop* what has been too tightly *enveloped*, allowing its layers to again emerge. And one "misses" the end herein the sense that this is a process never to be fulfilled, but also in the sense that there is a certain melancholy (famously discerned in Buddhism) in the fact that no satisfaction can ever be ultimately achieved in so shifting a world. But, Du Bois reminds us, there is also the possibility of "infinite joy" if we can but learn to take pleasure in this very fact of pluralities unfolding.

Du Bois speaks of how unbearable identities are produced when cultures remain too tightly folded by the revelation of the supremacist world. Right after the sentence cited above about the African American beginning to find "his place in the world," Du Bois continues: "For the first time he sought to *analyze the burden* he bore upon his back, that dead-weight of social degradation partially masked behind a half-named Negro problem."[26] The burden that bears analysis—the burden of being a modern self on the underside of global modernity—is the unbearable identity produced by those global encounters. When Du Bois speaks of the "half-named Negro problem," he may be implicitly evoking an understanding of reality furthered by Richard Wright: "There is not a black problem in the United States, but a white problem."[27] Du Bois's claim may be more truthful, if less rhetorically powerful. It suggests that the problem of what it means to be in this violent, interconnected world is best understood as a problem for all peoples. It is unbearable to be a master (as Hegel knew), of course, for incommensurably different reasons than why it is unbearable to be a slave. Recognizing this dual unbearability may help some overcome their desire to be masters of the world, but, Du Bois asks, what is there for those whom Emancipation is failing?

Of course a revolution in the social order must come, and part of that path is a particular way of navigating the double consciousness produced by these revelations. Here at last we can understand the duality of this doubling:

> One ever feels his two-ness,—an American, a Negro; two souls, two thoughts, two unreconciled strivings; two warring ideals in one dark body, whose dogged strength alone keeps it from being torn asunder. The history of the American Negro is the history of this strife,—this longing to attain self-conscious manhood, to merge his double self into a better and truer self. In this merging he wishes neither of the older selves to be lost. He would not Africanize America, for America has too much to teach the world and Africa. He would not bleach his negro soul in a flood of white Americanism, for he knows that Negro blood has a message for the world. He simply wishes to make it possible for a man to be both a Negro and an American, without being cursed and spit upon by his fellows, without having the doors of Opportunity closed roughly in his face.

Double consciousness is unbearable for Du Bois less because it bifurcates the subject than because after doing so it traps him in two fixed, unbearable identities. The situation can be reversed, he says, if one is allowed to freely move between the multiplicities of being. This is obviously quite a task, because it requires overcoming the entire "revelation of the other world"—that is, the histories of racism, oppression, and violence—that created the condition in the first place. Although we can see the beginnings of this kind of thinking in Emerson and Marx, it is really in Du Bois that we see a full argument that overcoming the unbearable identities of modernity requires nothing less than a continual push for conceptual *and* institutional practices of racial justice the world over.

In "The Transcendentalist," Emerson saw his contemporaries lament the fact that the two sides of consciousness do not eventually "reconcile themselves." He continued, "When we pass [beyond this condition] . . . it will please us to reflect that, though we had few virtues or consolations, we bore with our indigence, nor once *strove* to repair it with hypocrisy or false heat of any kind."[28] Part of what Du Bois rejects in Emerson is this. While his works are concerned with dignity and avoiding false solutions (such as the terrorism attempted in *Dark Princess*), there is no pleasure in reflection on this fact. There is no reason to bear our indigence now. It is in fact unbearable to be told to wait for problems to be solved with time, and thus not act for change in the present. And there is no happy day off in the future when we can look back at the struggle and feel proud. Du Bois believes that happy day may just come—the "far-off Divine event" he frequently invokes—but nothing can redeem having lived through such brutal oppression.[29]

Nevertheless, Du Bois seems to appreciate Emerson's rejection of "striving" to reconcile what cannot be reconciled. Du Bois, as I read him, is not trying to reconcile the "unreconciled strivings." He wants "to be both." Like Emerson, he doubles double consciousness. In one form, we are trapped in an unlivable distinction; in the other, we learn to use the very thing that has divided us to generate new powers for action. Du Bois here is trying to make it possible for a subject to strive in multiple ways; to be a writer, a politician, an aloof intellectual, and a sentimentalist; or to cherish the ideals of liberty and the pursuit of happiness as much as simple living at home in the natural world. These themes and multiple desires constitute both his life and his writing. Du Bois explicitly does not want to reconcile his double consciousness into a single mode of being. He wants to live in a culture that promotes the multiplicities of his soul.

Like Emerson, and unlike Hegel, he strives to live with double consciousness and to learn from it the powers and gifts of alternation. Freedom in Du Bois, as in Emerson, is not just about the self's capacity for expression, or about the reconciliation of the subject with its world. Rather, it is the bold claim that freedom is the freedom to alternate. Slavery, its opposite, functions by at once refusing alternation (being reduced to a single trait, say, a body that labors or reproduces) and forcing alter-nation (in the slave trade, which refuses plural, global becoming, and insists that slaves take on a singular, unbearable identity in a new land).

The claim that "double consciousness" in Du Bois is more closely aligned with Emerson than with Hegel is not the major critical position today.[30] Evidence for the Hegelian reading appears in lines like "merge his double self into a better and truer self. In this merging he wishes neither of the older selves to be lost." Indeed, this sounds like sublation: canceling, preserving, and lifting up into a third term. But it is important that this citation continues, "He would not Africanize America, for America has too much to teach the world and Africa. He would not bleach his Negro soul in a flood of white Americanism, for he knows that Negro blood has a message for the world." Although these lines are often read as Hegelian, it should be clear by now why they are not: Hegel is not interested in the "gifts" of non-European cultures. Du Bois is. Hence, he does not say that Africa must become part of American history. Nor, for that matter, does he say that America must become part of African history. Rather, he maintains the same polycentrism of souls that he will speak of at a geopolitical level in his advice given to Kwame Nkrumah in 1957: "The consequent Pan-Africa, working together through its independent units, should seek to develop a new African economy and cultural center standing between Europe and Asia, taking from and contributing to both."[31] Du Bois is as insistent in 1903 as in 1957 that global connectivity is about plural alliances, not singular frameworks. Through these alliances both within the self and across nations, the poison of second-sight can be turned into a true gift, and the meaning of that gift will be the ability of a woman to be plural within herself.[32] She will not be forced to become something she is not or be reduced to a single aspect of her identity. She will be free to alternate between the sides of herself and her culture that make the most sense. Only then will we move past the stasis in which "the freedman has not yet found freedom in his promised land."[33]

This is related to the critique of the revelation of the other world and is part of Du Bois's ongoing critical engagement with Hegel. He absolutely appreciated Hegel's logic and his understanding of the processes of history. But, like Fanon, he knew that accessing Hegel's philosophy meant first counteracting the historical and geographic basis of that philosophy. It cannot be mere coincidence, after all, that Du Bois ends *Souls* saying that black folk brought three gifts to America: "story and song . . . sweat and brawn . . . [and] Spirit."[34] If for Hegel the European character carried the universal Spirit, for Du Bois, it is but one Spirit among many—one with the terrible desire to eviscerate other Spirits in its path to domination.[35] By refracting Hegel's solely European Spirit into multiple meaningful Spirits with plural contributions, Du Bois breaks with this philosophical version of the "revelation of the other world" and attempts to reveal another world of his own making, one wherein he can embody the true double consciousness of an alternating subject.

Because double consciousness here, as in Emerson, signifies the constancy of division, of always making new spaces to alternate into, it is central to Du Bois's version of radical pluralism. Du Bois's importance in the development of cultural pluralism is well-known.[36] His writings on racial difference and the possibility that each race offers "gifts" during global contact is also well-known and fiercely debated, and I return to these positions below.[37] Part of what I want to suggest here is that the language of radical pluralism can help explain why Du Bois was, at once, a critic of essentialism, a fountain of race-talk, and a committed universalist.[38] Rather than viewing these positions as contradictory, I see them as part of his unfolding radical pluralist commitment to understand that the facts of group formation do not overwhelm the facts of difference within groups or individuals. Nor does that ceaseless difference overwrite our general shared sympathies as humans—perhaps, most significantly, a leaning toward a plurality that we at once embrace and fear. Du Bois's version of radical pluralism, like Emerson's, is thus based not on an exclusion of the universal, but on an insistence that universals be themselves understood as conflicting goals whose possibility for just implementation rests on their capacity to remain humble and allow for multiple institutional forms.

Du Bois offered a version of this global pluralism in a 1948 essay on the history of race relations in the United States, which, he insisted, had to be understood as "part of a world situation."[39] And the "problem which faces the world today," according to Du Bois, is that "one single white European standard" is simply not sufficient for how to organize humanity.[40] But Du Bois believed that, in spite of it all, the experience of the United States should lead us to believe "that it is possible to have in this world a variety of cultural patterns . . . [and that] out of those different cultures may arise in the future a more and more unified culture, but never completely unified, which would express and carry out the cultural possibilities of the mass of men."[41] We can clearly see his striving to relate the universal drive against violence and exploitation to the fact that there are many ways of redressing these issues.

Du Bois's radical pluralism finds its basis in the multiplicity of the individual soul, as radical pluralism does in Emerson. Where these thinkers most greatly differ is in their understanding of the historical specificities that produce some of these multiplicities. It is here that double consciousness plays a key role in Du Bois's rethinking of the global origins of the modern self. I noted in the previous chapter that there is a relation between Emerson's and Feuerbach's critiques of "the other world." But Emerson's critique is liable to the same criticism Marx leveled at Feuerbach: that it has no actual social basis. In a certain sense, Du Bois does to Emerson's critique of double consciousness with regard to race what Marx does to Feuerbach's critique of religious consciousness with regard to class. For Feuerbach, the critique of religion aimed to restore to humanity the question of how to overcome its alienation in general terms. Feuerbach banished the idea that suffering could be overcome in the other world, but, according to Marx, he did not explain the suffering of this one: "It is therefore the *task of history*, once the *other-world of truth* has vanished, to establish the *truth of this world*."[42] Marx's philosophy is aimed at understanding how the issue of class relations explains the truth of suffering in this world, and that only by overcoming exploitation can suffering also be overcome. Du Bois shares (or will come to share) this understanding with Marx. But his intervention at this point is slightly different, if analogous, with regard to race. Emerson, like Feuerbach, had said "there is no other world."[43] For him that fact resolved an abstract issue about how his contemporaries had misunderstood that double consciousness was *of* this world and not formed in opposition to it. Even if, as I have argued, Emerson developed these ideas through his global engagement, he still did not see the possibility that double consciousness could be *produced* historically by identity formations like race. What he had said with regard to race was that a proper understanding of the double consciousness could help us overcome the racist ascriptions we place on others. As Marx takes up the overturning of the other world problem by analyzing class, so Du Bois extends Emerson's ideas by recognizing a bifurcation *caused* by race.[44] Whereas Emerson was first prompted to his reflection by a Goethean vision of the split between matter and spirit, Du Bois begins in response to an oppressive gaze. Du Bois sides with Emerson's goal but shows the need for practices of the self that begin with the situation of oppression.

Although the scholarship about double consciousness has tended to negatively assess Emerson in relation to Du Bois, Du Bois himself seems to have understood his relation to Emerson along the lines of what I have suggested.[45] Part of the current critical vision has to do with a focus on Emerson's first evocation of "double consciousness" in "The Transcendentalist." Indeed, most critics entirely ignore the second mention, with all its reformations. Another reason is that Du Bois's other references to Emerson have gone, for the most part, unanalyzed.[46] One has recently been unearthed by Robert Williams from a 1905 speech by Du Bois at the Third Annual Convention of the Religious Education Association. In this speech, Du Bois criticizes the kind of assumptions about other cultures that we have seen since Rousseau, ones based on abstract conceptions rather than actual knowledge. Du Bois sums up: "To induce, then, in men a consciousness of the humanity of all men, of the sacred unity in all the diversity, is not merely to lay down a pious postulate, but it is the active and animate heart-to-heart knowledge of your neighbors, high and low, black and white, employer and employed."[47]

Du Bois here stresses the need for a race contact based not just on the idea of equality, but also on actual knowledge and engagement. And, curiously enough, he suggests that part of how one can become the kind of being who achieves this engagement with diversity is through a "reverent listening . . . not simply to the first line but to the last line of Emerson's quatrain: 'There is no great, no small, / To the Soul that maketh all; / Where it cometh, all things are— /And it cometh everywhere.' "[48] These are the first lines in Emerson's first book of *Essays*, and they function as the epigraph to the essay "History." That Du Bois invokes the practice of "reverent listening" suggests that he learned something significant from these lines in terms of how he thought about practices of the global self. Emerson, he is suggesting, can teach one how to move past vague invocations of universalism and toward the actual engagements that allow one to understand the values of human life everywhere; as I quoted above, "As Nature has put fruits apart in latitudes, a new fruit in every degree, so knowledge and fine moral quality she lodges in distant men."[49]

Du Bois invokes another Emerson poem nearly four decades later in *The World and Africa*. At this moment, a perhaps less hopeful Du Bois registers Emerson's understanding of what happens when we attempt to dominate the values of the world. The citation appears at the end of the second chapter, "The White Masters of the World." Du Bois imagines a young woman in a "lovely British home," playing the "ivory keys of a grand piano" as she imagines her possible summer vacations.[50] Du Bois breaks his description of this quaint scene with the abrupt question: "How far is such a person responsible for the crimes of colonialism?" He notes that we cannot say for this particular individual without an actual accounting, but the likelihood of her connection to human destruction is high. The verdict: "The frightful paradox that is the indictment of modern civilization and the cause of its moral collapse is that a blameless, cultured, beautiful young woman in a London suburb may be the foundation on which is built the poverty and degradation of the world."[51]

What Du Bois essays to pierce through here is the concealment of the relation between these facts. And he gives credit to one other person who could make the connection: "Only an Emerson could see the paradox." He then cites from Emerson's poem "Mithridates": "O all you virtues, methods, mights; / Means, appliances, delights; / Reputed wrongs, and braggart rights; / Smug routine, and things allowed; / Minorities, things under cloud, / Hither take me, use me, fill me, / Vein and artery, though ye kill me."[52] The quote is not as obvious to me as it appears to have been to Du Bois, who does not explain it, but one can deduce a certain reading of Emerson here. The beginning of the poem, which speaks of collecting goods "from the earth-poles to the [equator] line," might help secure how this is a poem about an imperial excess. If so, this is a quote about the willingness of the European mind to seek to encompass so much—both beautiful and terrifying—that it eventually wills its own destruction via excess. If the poem from "History" signaled the possibility of human connection when we registered that meaningful humanity came from everywhere, the citation from "Mithridates" suggests the horror that results when a part of humanity seeks to take from everywhere. This is the difference between handing and unhanding the globe. It results in "the illogic in modern thought," such that, in Du Bois's example, Jan Smuts can at once suppress the black population of South Africa and go before the United Nations and call for "human rights."[53]

In the gap between these two citations of Emerson poems resides one key to Du Bois's practices of the global self. It is the possibility that we might live in such a way as neither to take from everywhere nor to give to everywhere without recompense, but rather to begin a worldwide practice of conscientious exchange. If this seems simple in theory, it is perhaps because it is so difficult in practice. This is the problem Du Bois had signaled in his 1905 address. This possibility is sketched later in *The World and Africa* when Du Bois conjectures the history of race in ancient Egypt. Using conjectural history to dislodge the present, Du Bois suggests that the Egyptians' "attitude toward people, white or black, was based on cultural contact." He then describes different groups of people, defined by skin color, but with no determinate relation between color and status. "Black people and yellow people were often depicted as conquered and yielding obeisance to their brown conquerors. Sometimes they appeared as equals, exchanged gifts and courtesies." Sometimes there were slaves, too, but "slavery was never attributed solely to black folk."[54]

I return to this idea of gifts and exchange below. For now I simply want to mark how Du Bois thinks across time and space to find the resources for moving past the "revelation of the other world" that had bound some to oppression. For Du Bois (as it should be for all us), it was imperative to find other means of relating between cultures to overcome this situation. To do so, the questions of race and cultural contact were "more significant for the meaning of the world today" than anything else.[55] Like Fanon, Du Bois articulated the question of meaning as being inextricable from the question of race. And, from his earliest work, he also understood this *as* a question: "How does it feel to be a problem?"⁵⁶ This is the question, silent or spoken, that was addressed to every African American. Its point of pressure, Du Bois tells us, occurs "between me and the other world."⁵⁷ Again like Fanon, he finds that his quest to understand his place in the world is abutted by the imposition of race. Thus his is a critique of Heidegger *avant la lettre*: to pose the question of being in the world without posing the questions of race and culture is to begin in the wrong place. The problem of the twentieth century is not "Being" in the abstract; it is "the problem of the color-line—the relation of the darker to the lighter races of men in Asia and Africa, in America and the islands of the sea."⁵⁸

As Brent Hayes Edwards has reminded us, these lines of Du Bois were first articulated not in *Souls of Black Folk*, but at the first Pan-African Congress in London in 1900 in his speech "To the Nations of the World."⁵⁹ In that speech, Du Bois spoke, as Kant had, of a world where contacts were accelerating and where learning to share a finite planet was imperative. But unlike Kant, who thought of how to handle this situation from the angle of European dominance, Du Bois insisted on a vision engaged with the entirety of humanity: "The modern world must . . . remember that in this age, when the ends of the world are being brought so near together, the millions of black men in Africa, America and the islands of the sea, not to speak of the brown and yellow myriads elsewhere, are bound to have great influence upon the world in the future."⁶⁰ Du Bois went on to argue that such a situation calls for a cooperative effort to create the "broadest opportunity for education and self-development."⁶¹ Otherwise, he warned, the situation would eventually prove fatal not only for the oppressed, but also for the shared, global values of freedom and justice and culture.

About a decade later, in his book on John Brown (1909), Du Bois linked this insight to Darwin's writing on evolution. He saw two possible ways of understanding Darwin. The first, white supremacist version saw Darwin's ideas as justifying the view that there was an "essential and inevitable inequality among men and races of men." Accompanying this is the idea that "civilization is a struggle for existence" to be at the top of that inequality. The white supremacist idea is that those of "white European stock" are the ones destined to be at the top of that heap of humanity.⁶²

Seeing that such social Darwinist arguments needed to be countered, Du Bois returned to his vision of shared improvement from 1900. He couples the idea of geographic interconnectedness across space with biological interconnectedness through the process of evolution. The logical result of Darwinian science is not hierarchy, but the shared destiny of the species. In a remarkable move to which I return in the coda of this book, Du Bois suggests that this changes our very ideas of self, freedom, and equality: "Freedom has come to mean not individual caprice or aberration,[63] but social self-realization in an endless chain of selves." Similarly, equality becomes the "equality of opportunity, for unbounded future attainment is the rightful demand of mankind." Thus the racial and geographic vision of shared improvement is redoubled after passing "through the fire of scientific inquiry."[64] This is what I later call "being-toward-bequeathment," or the idea that what makes us who we are is not our individual end (as in Heidegger's "being-toward-death"), but what we leave to the future in this "endless chain of selves." It is a remarkable insight of Du Bois's into how to connect Darwin to his pursuit of freedom and equality, and it logically builds on his exploration of a global self trying to reveal another world.

This need to keep transforming one's own understanding is part of why the racism that Du Bois dissects is not only a struggle for the black soul. The belief in whiteness also infects and perverts the practices of the global self for those called white. As Du Bois wrote in "The Souls of White Folk," the idea of the supremacy of whiteness led some to "desire to spread the gift abroad."[65] (Gift, here, again, is both poison and beneficence.) Like Chakrabarty after him, Du Bois saw that universalization gave both the power of critique and the damage of imposition.[66] Du Bois thus underlies the fact that race has always been a factor in global practices, and that by misconceiving it, many practices of the self constructed in modernity have gone awry. What the world requires is not the abolition of difference, but the ability to move between differences. This is what Emerson began to see with the increasing concern he showed with the problem of "whiteness" and the need to unhand the globe and learn to alternate. Du Bois furthers this by articulating the paradox of the racialized conditions of the "gift of second-sight," and so he begins to construct practices of the global self that are both open to radical pluralism and able to confront the penuries of the past.[67]

Although Du Bois wrote his original lines about global engagement in 1900, he would narrate his own life as a slow and continual awakening to the differences and similarities between cultures. Like Emerson and Marx, he needed to overcome the prejudices that formed from the culture into which he was born. Central to arriving at the second kind of double consciousness was just such an act of learning. Once he began to understand the values of African civilizations, he could think of them as a resource for alternation.

Du Bois's reflections on how and when he arrived at this understanding are somewhat uneven. In *Black Folk Then and Now* (1939), he credits Franz Boas's 1906 commencement address at Atlanta University with disabusing him of the idea—learned in high school, Harvard, and the University of Berlin—that "the Negro has no history." Boas told the graduating class: "'You need not be ashamed of your African past;' and then he recounted the history of the black kingdoms south of the Sahara for a thousand years." Du Bois recalls: "I was too astonished to speak."[68] In two later biographical accounts, Du Bois—consciously or not—did not mention Boas and instead referred to his own seeing through the ideology of ahistoricity by a "logical deduction" that the humanity and history of Africa simply must exist.[69] In his final *Autobiography*, he relates: "I am not sure when I began to feel an interest in Africa."[70]

The exclusion of Boas may be less forgetful or unfair and more a matter of registering that though Boas taught him specifics about African *history*, Du Bois's reading about Africa did predate this moment. As Richard Rath has shown, Du Bois's research into African cultures began in at least the 1890s, although he frequently found himself frustrated by the accounts of colonial missionaries.[71] Nevertheless, even if Du Bois knew little of African history then, he had already begun to understand some of the "philosophies of life" of people like the Tshi in present-day Ghana. Rath even makes the significant claim that what little he managed to understand of Tshi "animism" helped him conceive of the idea of "souls" in *Souls of Black Folk*. Like Emerson with the *Bhagavad Gita*, Du Bois alternated to another geography to find the idea of alternation itself in another ontological understanding. In the Tshi ontology, Rath relates, a "person could have more than one soul. Souls could come and go from the person at will, occasionally even fighting each other, usually to the detriment of their host's health."[72] One could, in other words, be radically plural not just as a self, but in fact as but a temporary host for the ceaseless multiplicity of the world itself. Part of the problem of the color line here was that it made it impossible to see such other ways of seeing the world. This is where Du Bois had to essay a global relation by crossing over the line of prejudice that keeps us from understanding other ontologies. Rath continues, in a similar vein to Viveiros de Castro, that such practices overcome "narcissism, the phenomenon of recognizing only one's own knowledge in the articulations of others."[73]

This connection to the Tshi, it seems to me, is central to understanding the complexity of Du Bois's own primitivism. In his early writings, he offered somewhat banal reflections. He wrote in *Souls*, for example, "Like all primitive folk, the slave stood near to Nature's heart."[74] Later, in "Criteria of Negro Art," Du Bois used such imagery to establish the ideals of simple, creative life as the necessary contribution of contemporary black arts.[75] Such an ideal appears in the character of the mother Du Bois himself used in his novel *Dark Princess*.[76] And he did partake, as many have noted, of certain basic Romantic tropes about the primitive other.[77] But Du Bois learned from his engagements, and he came to write against the very idea that primitive peoples are primitive in a pejorative sense.

In *Dusk of Dawn*, he tells us that he did not fully learn this lesson until his travels to Africa in 1923:

> Primitive men are not following us afar, frantically waving and seeking our goals; primitive men are not behind us in some swift foot-race. Primitive men have already arrived. They are abreast, and in places ahead of us; in others behind. But all their curving advance line is contemporary, not prehistoric. They have used other paths and these paths have led them by scenes sometimes fairer, sometimes uglier than ours, but always toward the Pools of Happiness.[78]

Part of what it means to essay the globe, of course, is always to be essaying it again, remaining open to its lessons. Du Bois breaks from a kind of primitivism, like Emerson realizing the "singular equality" of all ages, but he does not thereby succumb to the belief that only modern civilization is the best way to live. On the other side of primitivism is the understanding that all cultures have their advantages and disadvantages and that no final culture can bring all of those together. It is simply a matter of striving, of learning to be multiple, and learning to let others be multiple, too.

Of great importance here is the very fact of Du Bois's traveling. Unlike Rousseau, who simply called for philosophers to travel, or Kant, who thought travel a waste of time because there was so much of the world in books, Du Bois *actually went places*. As he noted in what reads like a rebuke of the post-Rousseau tradition of global thought: "It is impossible for the individual to reach the larger social conscience by sheer expansion, by a benevolent endeavor to be interested in all men . . . We can only be interested in men by knowing them."[79] Of course, there is nothing inherently good in travel. Cecil Rhodes traveled widely as well. What is crucial is to combine travel with conscientiousness, radical pluralism, and a refusal to impose unbearable identities. This forms a significant practice of the global self.

Conscientious traveling is perhaps also part of the scholar in Du Bois and his training in historical and sociological methodology. Indeed, one of the most significant ways in which he differs from many of the figures considered here is that he combined his humanistic reflections on global selves with new methods for understanding the embeddedness of those selves within social networks and institutions. As early as *Souls*, Du Bois had championed a multidisciplinary methodology across all his works, studying "physical proximity . . . economic relations . . . political relations . . . forms of intellectual contact and commerce . . . [and] the varying forms of religious enterprise."[80] This five-pronged method of analysis allowed him to explore comparative cultural inquiry as something that is both spatially and temporally embodied in social practices, as well as something that touches on the "less tangible" forms of existence.

But there does sometimes appear a gap between Du Bois's ideals and the realities he experienced. Scholars have begun to debate with increasing interest in the past few years, for example, his embrace of Maoism and Stalinism.[81] As recent scholars have shown, Du Bois's capacity for pluralist analysis tends to disappear here. Although he was aware of the race problems *within* both of their countries, he almost never wrote about them and instead focused on their attempts to make egalitarian social relations and fight the colonial racism of Europe and America. Du Bois did not arrive at this conclusion lightly, but only after his lifelong effort to analyze the failures of the United States to achieve anything like full enfranchisement and a fair distribution of goods to those in need. In response, he granted to communism what Vaughn Rasberry calls the "right to fail."[82] As Du Bois puts it in his *Autobiography*: "I know well that the triumph of communism will be a slow and difficult task, involving mistakes of every sort."[83] But Du Bois did not seem to foresee what history has revealed: that "mistakes of every sort" would destroy the project he believed in so deeply, that the revolutionary project can become so unbearable that it can no longer bear its own ideals. Du Bois almost seems to go in the opposite path of Emerson and Marx, as his ideas about other cultures lose their plurality over time in this single-sighted focus on overcoming racial capitalism at any cost.

Scholars like Rasberry, Robeson Taj Frazier, and Etsuko Taketani have done their best to articulate the logic of Du Bois's position. First, his argument began by refusing to interpret historical mistakes in a vacuum. Taketani and Rasberry both, for example, argue that Du Bois saw the excesses of the Soviet Union, China, and also Japan as *responses* to the violent world made by colonialism. Second, Du Bois showed at least minimal self-reflexive awareness that his writings were playing the role of a partisan.

Du Bois himself had spoken of this role earlier, in *Black Folk Then and Now* (1939), when he admitted that he might overemphasize the qualities of black history and ignore the faults. But such, he claimed, was necessary to right the wrongs of the propaganda on the other side. He sought out a dialogic "truth" in the absence of his claims to "science": "I realize that the truth of history lies not in the mouths of partisans but rather in the calm Science that sits between. Her cause I seek to serve, and wherever I fail, I am at least paying truth the respect of earnest effort."[84] This idea of "failure," and a right to fail on the way to truth (perhaps part of the Hegelian side of Du Bois), is central to Rasberry's explanation of Du Bois's position. A truly radical pluralist analysis, in my opinion, would move past Du Bois's partisan dichotomy and allow one to simply praise what is good in a place while still openly expressing criticisms of its failings. Because this would have increased his trustworthiness, it may have proved better propaganda anyway.

Nevertheless, as Frazier has pointed out, where Du Bois's social science was hampered, his fictions explored the very problems he would himself enact. In the *Worlds of Color* trilogy, Frazier argues, Du Bois demonstrates the "ineluctable challenges of foreign travel and articulating transnational and transracial connection."[85] Frazier points to a moment when his main character realizes that he is not in fact seeing China and its complexity, but only seeing China through the eyes of America's problems. This fictional realization is precisely what Du Bois fails to articulate in his travel writings. In his own limitations, then, Du Bois reminds us of the complex relation between experience and reflection. It is this ever present need to embody and reflect on our global relations—to alternate not just between spaces but between how we process them—that the multiple genres and multiple disciplines of his writings work though. If Du Bois erred—and perhaps less so than many of us—he still set forward paths of practice and theory for contemporary global selves to follow.

This future-oriented aspect of Du Bois's writing has also drawn increasing interest of late, especially in the wake of Afrofuturism. As Juliet Hooker defines it in her reading of Du Bois's fiction, "Afro-futurism is an aesthetic and literary movement that aims to counter the overwhelming absence of people of color and concomitant assumptions of racelessness in dominant conceptions of futurity."[86] Du Bois, Hooker argues, offered an Afrofuturist vision in his novel *Dark Princess*, in which he sought out a future "beyond racism." The question Hooker poses is if the narrative—with its triumphant arc of a worldwide uprising of peoples of color through the marriage of an African American man and an Indian princess—is also beyond races: "it is important to consider whether Du Bois posited interracial intimacy itself as a kind of racial utopia, or, if his vision of the racial politics of mixture was more complex."[87] If Du Bois is the radical pluralist I have made him out to be, then it will be the case that his future visions are about neither racelessness nor the continuance of the present, but the continuous creation of newly constituted social forms *through* mixture (as Senghor argued as well). As the novel ends with the birth of a child said to be a "messenger and messiah to *all* the dark world*s*," there is at least some evidence for new multiplicities being projected into the future in Du Bois's fictions.[88]

This is not just because diversity is a value in itself to Du Bois, but because diversity *produces* values, or gifts. Du Bois had said since at least 1903 that "we are compelled daily to turn more and more to a conscientious study of the phenomena of race-contact."[89] Such conscientious interactions would allow for the exchange of what Du Bois had even earlier called "race ideals" in his "Conservation of the Races" (1897).[90] And still by *Dusk of Dawn* the language is almost unchanged: "here in subtle but real ways the communalism of the African clan can be transferred to the Negro American group, implemented by higher *ideals* [that arise] through the contact of black folk with the modern world."[91] (The language here is also similar to Marx's late writings on the perseverance of the commune in Russia.) In speaking of race ideals, Du Bois, as I understand him, and as the passages from *The World and Africa* above make clear, held no essentialized vision of race, but rather a conception of human culture and race similar to Senghor's.[92] While human groups that bind or are bound together have no permanent differences, they do produce within themselves competing visions of the good. They may, in turn, come to uphold one or several of these visions as an offering to other cultural groups. In so doing, they project internal ideals, and individuals may find that these ideals either match or fail to align with their own ways of being. The trick, here as ever, is to avoid imposition and allow for multiplicity while remaining critical of just any claim to aversion. When Du Bois speaks of a "conscientious" understanding of cultural contacts, I take him to mean the seemingly obvious but in fact very difficult practice of being able to offer ways of being without constraining others to adopt them. Part of the difficulty is to remain humble while still following the accompanying demand to criticize those elements in others that may have pernicious effects—such as a culture of patriarchy. The difficulty, now as ever, is how to engage as a plurality with another plurality in ways that are both respectful and critical. Like Cooper before him and Césaire and Senghor after him, Du Bois suggested the possibility of thinking of contact as exchange and gift giving, but he certainly was always aware of the pun of *gift*—the possibility that an offering may be (or become) poison.

Some have suggested that Du Bois's own conception of racial gift giving is itself such a poison. Critics from Anthony Appiah in the 1990s to more recent work by Kenneth Warren have questioned the very idea of race on which Du Bois's "ideals" are based.[93] Although they have between them different politics, Appiah and Warren share a sense that "race" is a fictive entity whose continued purported existence only masks other forms of oppression—be they questions of identity in Appiah's case or economy in Warren's. There is a sense in both of their thinking that once the problem of race is eliminated as a way of *naming* injustice, the proper name can emerge and thus better be dealt with. This strikes me as a bit of political fantasy, both in the sense that one could simply annul a problem by demonstrating its falsity and in the sense that once we knew what our problem "really" was we would necessarily deal with it more effectively.

In response to Appiah and to Warren's collaborator Walter Benn Michaels, Paul Taylor has demonstrated a certain fallacy here in how people understand social construction. Following Ian Hacking, Taylor suggests that these other thinkers conflate two different meanings of social construction. In some instances it is a "debunking device, revealing to us that the allegedly natural fact is not any kind of fact at all." This is how Appiah, Michaels, and Warren seem to intend their discussions of race. In other cases, however, it should signal to us "that we are dealing with institutional facts, facts that depend for their existence on constitutive networks of social conventions."[94] Taylor argues that here, in fact, is where race exists: at a nexus of histories, memories, legal conventions, social and cultural assumptions, and nondetermining biological and physiognomic differences.[95] All of these categories, under this analysis, are not meant to imply some essential characteristic pertaining to a race, but rather a set of experiences and circumstances that are "likely to apply" or be experienced.[96]

What is perhaps most interesting, and where I think Du Bois's contribution may have especial relevance today, is that *all* of these authors share a basic concern with the politics of racial classification. Taylor's concern with these arguments, after all, is that "an appeal to racial eliminativism can not only obscure existing inequities but also preclude the most efficient means of addressing them."[97] For Michaels, it is the reverse: "What we owe the victims of injustice is justice, not a causal account of how they came to be victimized."[98] Curiously, Milton Friedman would probably agree with Michaels, in theory if not in practice: "There is every reason to help the poor man who happens to be a farmer, not because he is a farmer but because he is poor."[99] I note this similarity not to say that Michaels is secretly neoliberal, but rather the opposite: that no determinate politics follows from either racialist or eliminativist thinking. One may very well become a communist or a free-market capitalist in seeking to eliminate race, and a white supremacist or a multiculturalist in seeking to preserve race as a category of analysis.

This, I think, is what Du Bois, and Taylor following him, understood. I cited above Du Bois's late essay on race relations and its call for dynamic cultural pluralism. This is not about difference for the sake of difference. Rather, Du Bois's concern is that without the maintenance of cultural difference, we will in fact all slide into capitalist or other relations of dominance. Du Bois writes: "The populations of the world will tend to solve all of their problems of living according to one standard and, if that standard is wrong or inadequate, it means the dissolution of modern civilization or its revolutionary change."[100] As Emerson had said, even a truth becomes noxious when it is held fast for too long.[101] Some notion of race, Du Bois hypothesizes, may hold off this closure. He does note, importantly, that racial difference will become increasingly defined by culture and less and less by biology, and he does, as I noted above, hope for some possible unity within all this diversity.[102]

The overall, radical pluralist point, then, is that Appiah, Michaels, and Warren are perfectly correct to say that no feature of human understanding is eternal, and there is no reason to presume that race will not continue to evolve and may in fact someday disappear. But this does not mean that such a disappearance will happen by the stroke of a pen, or that it has already happened because *certain* biological notions have been debunked. As Étienne Balibar noted some decades ago, there has for a long time been a "racism without races . . . a racism whose dominant theme is not biological heredity but the insurmountability of cultural differences," and whose recent acceleration in debates about immigration has a long-standing historical precedent in anti-Semitism.[103] Thus, the critique of scientific racism means only that certain layers of racial thinking should be and, in some parts of our global culture, have been removed. If, when the last pernicious layers of racial thinking are gone, race, in toto, has disappeared, then so be it, so long as some other grist for the critique of domination, perpetual change, and openness to human evolution remains.

To show that Du Bois expands the range of practices of the self certainly does not make him the final word on the topic. The ceaseless plurality of existence means not only that new dimensions of oppression will always have to be factored in, but also that each of us, as we necessarily focus on partial aspects, will miss significant issues. I have noted consistently in this book that the authors chosen are largely limited by a focus on male subjectivity. While I have also claimed that male subjectivity is radically plural and involves dimensions that extend beyond gender, it is certainly not the case that the explorations of global subjectivity and practices I explore here cover all the bases of what modern selfhood means.

The limits of Du Bois's analyses and practices have been the subject of feminist critique for some time. Critics like Hazel Carby and Debra Clark Hine have questioned how applicable Du Bois's ideas are for black women.[104] For example, in an oft-cited phrase, Hine argued that had Du Bois factored in the questions of gender and class, "instead of writing, 'One ever feels his twoness,' he would have mused about how one ever feels her 'fiveness': Negro, American, woman, poor, black woman."[105] This is a critique that could apply to practically any of the thinkers I have discussed so far in this book, as well as to the book itself. (Again, by confessing this partiality and offering a radical pluralist framework attuned to feminist critiques since the introduction, I have hoped to show how this book may function in relation to these kinds of readings, even if the readings themselves focus elsewhere.) And Joy James and others have shown that, already in Du Bois's time, there were struggles between him and feminist leaders such as Anna Julia Cooper and Ida B. Wells Barnett. James notes that Du Bois, while remarkably progressive on public issues of women's rights, frequently failed to recognize these fellow activists as agents.[106] The point is not that Du Bois did not have illuminating things to say about gender; only that he, like others, is limited here in ways that will force us to keep thinking about how the modern self is shaped in a variety of competing and intersecting contexts.[107]

One illuminating point brought out in this context relates directly to the "gift thesis," as Chike Jeffers has called it.[108] I noted parenthetically above that Du Bois's thinking about the claims of the oppressed in ownership of America may have been influenced by Cooper. Jeffers has also suggested that Cooper is a potential influence on the idea of cultures as gift givers, and her essays on race-contact and what Jeffers calls the "female gift" are worth reading both on their own and in conversation with Du Bois. There is some debate as to whether Du Bois and Cooper share the same idea of the gift thesis. Jeffers affirms their similarity against the reading of Kathryn Gines, who suggests that Cooper envisions conflict and interaction against

Du Bois's separatism.[109] On my reading, there are clear differences, though not for the reason Gines gives. Cooper's vision is much more traditionally Hegelian than Du Bois's multiple spirit thesis. She writes, almost quoting *The Philosophy of History* (or *Subjective Spirit*): "As the European was the higher and grander than the Asiatic, so will American civilization be broader and deeper and closer to the purposes of the Eternal than any the world has yet seen."[110] While Cooper thus shares a certain vision of the need for cultural exchange with Du Bois, her teleological vision, at least at this point in her writings, is significantly different. It would, however, be unfair to read Cooper as an apologist for bland Americanism through cultural struggle. Eschewing the valorization of woman against "the primitive" that can be traced from Wollstonecraft to de Beauvoir, Cooper clearly registers an alliance: "Why should woman become plaintiff in a suit versus the Indian, or the Negro or any other race or class who have been crushed under the iron heel of Anglo-Saxon power and selfishness?"[111]

A more detailed reading of Cooper's ideas about cultural contact would take us beyond the scope of this chapter. What interests me here ultimately is, in fact, her most famous contribution to Africana philosophy when she writes:

> Not by pointing to sun-bathed mountain tops do we prove that Phoebus warms the valleys. We must point to homes, average homes of the rank and file of horny handed toiling men and women of the south (where the masses are) lighted and cheered by the good, and the true,—then and not until then will the whole plateau be lifted into the sunlight. Only the BLACK WOMAN can say when and where I enter, in the quiet, undisputed dignity of my womanhood, without violence and without suing or special patronage, then and there the whole *Negro race enters with me.*[112]

It is in these lines where Cooper makes her significant challenge for the theorization of the practices of the global self. The context here is important: she is responding to Martin Delaney's claim that he was representative of the race in certain contexts "when and where he entered." Cooper responds that this is effectively like saying that certain mountain-tops are representative of the valley. The focus on an exalted status misses the fact that the global problems we face will not be overcome when we have some good ideas, or some lofty theorists of pluralism, but only when all humans transcend any degraded status and are recognized for the meaningful beings that they are.

Throughout his career, Du Bois became more and more aware of the difficulties that making just global selves would require. It demanded not only change at the level of knowledge, but also adaptations of "folkways, habits, customs and subconscious deeds."[113] Part of this for him meant engagements with the aesthetic in novels like the *Worlds of Color* trilogy and *Dark Princess*. In *Dark Princess*, for example, Du Bois suggests that love, heartbreak, deception, and redemption are as important to becoming a global subject as theories of universalism, pluralism, or dialectics. It is hard to find a critic of his novels who does not remark on their aesthetic mediocrity, but some of what hampers Du Bois is that his fictions are more "essay-novels" than anything else. He is trying to essay a transformed relation between self and world not just intellectually, but also at the level of our habits, customs, and unconscious prejudices. Into the novel thus flood bits of his philosophy, psychology, and a sense of politics—the multidisciplinary methodology he recommended in *Souls*.

I want to highlight Du Bois's mode of analysis because—in spite of the limits noted above—it exceeds much of the work any of us does. He insisted throughout his career that "Negroes must live and eat and strive, and still hold unfaltering commerce with the stars."[114] *The Souls of Black Folk*, which avoids overemphasis on either of these goals, is an exemplary work of material and spiritual comparison. In an oft-cited critique of those who focus on Du Bois's notion of double consciousness, Adolph Reed suggested—correctly—that this multiple mode of engagement has been lost in the analysis. "Double consciousness" has become the primary concern, and the questions of economic struggle, such as those found in the chapter "Of Mr. Booker T. Washington and Others," have been lost under analyses of an idea about psychic strife. This "reduces to ephemera strategic arguments concerning mobilization for willful, collective action in public life."[115] Reed's argument was largely directed at currents in African American studies at the time, but it was also for him and for us a larger question about the importance of thinking about psychic-social relations.

This kind of critique of the focus on humanistic questions has recently been launched in an essay very closely related to my own project—Pheng Cheah's "The Material World of Comparison." There Cheah argues that we in the humanities have long operated with a model of comparison inherited from Rousseau, Kant, and Hegel. In this model, we extend our sympathy and imagination to construct a "common humanity" that can effectively inhabit the world together.[116] Even its most Eurocentric version in Hegel proves to have had a revolutionizing impact, as peoples once excluded from this vision come to fight for recognition within it. Cheah locates classical postcolonial fiction and theory (focusing on the work of Edward Said) in this "ethical dialectic of self and other."[117]

The problem, he suggests, is that this kind of consciousness-raising criticism deals with an epiphenomenon of the real, "material world of comparison." Following Foucault's work on biopolitics, Cheah suggests that we need to understand a more primary modality of comparison operative today, one that derives from Adam Smith's *The Wealth of Nations*. The mode of comparison there is between national resources, and it outlines the material conditions in which nations compete: not at the level of individual consciousness, but at the level of individual productivity. This mode of comparison "conditions, influences, and shapes any intellectual consciousness that is engaged in ethical comparison and, thus, also exceeds and circumscribes such endeavors."[118] Furthermore, he writes, our age "does not operate by directly impacting on the consciousness or even the psyche of its targets . . . [but] acts instead on . . . the physical-material milieu or environment for the biological existence of the population."[119] It is here, Cheah suggests, that the true ethical ground of comparison lies today: in the "aesthetic-cognitive mapping" of these uneven material relations.[120] To turn, rather, to something like "lamenting the degradation of the human" would be but "sentimental and nostalgic."[121]

In lectures given at Dartmouth in 2007, likely around when Cheah was writing his essay, Anthony Bogues turned to the *same thoughts* about biopolitics in Foucault but arrived at the opposite conclusion.[122] Bogues argued that Foucault's question about the shaping of human subjectivity "is the central political question of our time."[123] Bogues continued:

> [Normally] the political is nested within questions of how we are ruled, and as a consequence we study the various technologies of power centering on forms of what is called democracy. My argument is simply that this question of rule is no longer structured around questions of political obligation but rather around creating subjectivities.[124]

It was on this basis that Bogues shifted his center of focus from standard political analysis to the question of how subjectivity is being shaped and what kinds of other subjectivities we might try to shape in the present.

One of the thinkers Bogues turns to in this moment is Du Bois: "What Du Bois is pointing to is this. All historically catastrophic events, while wounding, produce cries. In hearing and listening to these cries we begin to glimpse alternative possibilities in relation to the historically catastrophic present."[125]

My own reading above has clearly more closely followed Bogues's concern. But I want to close by suggesting that the power of the *Souls of Black Folk* and Du Bois's other works is that they are radically pluralist essays that understand that different methods are needed at different moments within a variegated and complex present. Cheah and Bogues, I assume, are mostly arguing about emphasis, but even this seems to me to miss Du Bois's point that we need both. In our own work we will often fall on one side or the other, but an openness to the partialness of our analyses—we cannot all be Du Bois—seems necessary for a productive scholarly community. And interestingly enough, this is closer to Foucault's own position as well. He thought of his work on biopolitics and governmentality not as a break with questions of subjectivity, but as a locating of the struggle over subjectivity: "Quite simply, this means that in the type of analysis I have been trying to advance for some time you can see that power relations, governmentality, the government of the self and of others, and the relationship of self to self constitute a chain, a thread, and I think it is around these notions that we should be able to connect together the question of politics and the question of ethics."[126]

Emerson had said that the times put to him one question: "How shall I live?"[127] The question means three things: what conditions make your life possible; what do you do in the face of so much suffering; and what is the best way to live in such a world? Du Bois is unrepentant in his answers: the conditions of your life are the history of death and enslavement; in the face of such massacres you are to refuse any narrative of redemption; and your tasks in this place are to struggle for justice without hope, study without belief that you will have complete knowledge, and translate so that you never forget that your world is part of many worlds, and they are all connected. It is through struggle, study, and connection that the unbearable identity is overcome. It is by insisting that through your struggle, study, and connection you are more than what has been said of you. The lesson of pluralism is precisely this: people must find their own path beyond the unbearable identity, and they must struggle to ensure that in doing so they do not bind others—those to whom they are connected—into a new form of unbearability. In the final chapter, I turn at last to how D. T. Suzuki took up this challenge.

7

Emptying the Global Self
Suzuki

Throughout D. T. Suzuki's intellectual career, he argued that a very specific experience was necessary for the perception of truth.[1] He called this experience "satori," a Japanese word meaning, roughly, "awakening."[2] This awakening, Suzuki told his readers in *An Introduction to Zen Buddhism* (1934), is the only path to Zen: "At all events," he wrote, "there is no Zen without satori."[3] Unfortunately, the eager student looking to master the term will quickly be frustrated, because satori cannot be described in words, but only experienced in existence: "To understand Zen, it is essential to have an experience known as *satori*, for without this one can have no insight into the truth of Zen."[4] When Suzuki lectured at Columbia in 1952, he told his audience that though it was difficult to "give expression to the experience that is enlightenment . . . it is necessary . . . to make the experience possible."[5] He hoped his writings and lectures could help his readers and listeners find their way to satori. As he attempted to convince them to embark on this difficult quest for Zen, he did give hints of what the word meant. One of the ways Suzuki expressed this, as cited by his disciples Alan Watts and John Cage, was that Zen was like everyday experience, but about two feet off the ground.[6] This was Suzuki's essential promise to his readers and followers: if you pursue Zen and if you achieve satori, you will live in this world with a kind of miraculous "super-consciousness."[7]

As I show in this final part of the book, that super-consciousness bears a remarkable resemblance to what I have called "instinctual reason."[8] By "instinctual reason," again, I do not mean an essential human instinct for reason. Rather, I refer to the achievement of making reason a kind of instinct. To be "Zen," according to Suzuki, means that you are in the flow of the world, unburdened by the anxieties of reflection. Unlike Hamlet or

Descartes, you are not trapped in your private subjectivity, unsure of what is true, incapable of concrete action. You simply know and enact what is right. This idea evokes certain doubts. How, after all, can someone just "in the flow" know what is right? Is not that kind of knowledge something achieved by rational reflection? But satori promises something greater: after the experience, you will know what to do, and you will know how to do it as habit or instinct. This is your "original nature," what Suzuki will call "primal man." If the story of the Fall from Rousseau on is the story of falling into knowledge and needing to reconnect it to instinct, for Suzuki we have fallen into instinct (habits, karma) and need to reconnect to this other kind of knowledge: "Ignorance is conquered only when the state of things prior to Ignorance is realized, which is satori, seeing into one's own nature as it is by itself."[9] This is absolutely central to Suzuki's place in this story: whereas Rousseau and his followers, especially Hegel, sought the synthesis of global being in the development of the concept, Suzuki insisted that this way of being was only possible by renouncing concepts as such. "Intellect," he told his Columbia audience, "holds in itself the contradiction it is unable in itself to solve."[10] Only by finding a path to the moment *before* intellect began could we overcome the burdens of being.

Suzuki illustrated this overcoming with a Christina Rosetti poem in which she asks God to help her bear the burden of herself. But it was this very feeling of self-alienation, this double consciousness, he argued, that caused the self to feel like a burden in the first place.[11] His solution to the problem was not the Emersonian and Du Boisian move of alternation or the Hegelian attempt at reconciliation through the concept, although he learned, as we shall see, from each. His proposed solution demanded another path: neither to flee into your private ego nor try to grasp the world nor try to share being pluralistically. Instead you must go through the arduous process of abandoning everything you have inherited to arrive at satori. This is when you experience the "isness" of the universe. You neither conceive nor perceive the world; you simply *are* it. There is neither separation of subject and object nor an achievement of identity between them. It is identity itself that is vanquished. Satori is beyond (or, perhaps better put, before) language and intellection. Thus Zen is not about "a kind of meditation or contemplation directed toward some fixed thought," but rather about a "general mental upheaval which destroys the old accumulations of intellection and lays down the foundation for a new life."[12] That new life, Suzuki claimed, could overcome the otherwise unbearable demands of being a global self: not because it solved the problems, but because it ceased to view the self as separate from the world. The world is no more a burden for us than the weight of the earth is for the earth itself.[13]

I try to show across this chapter how the self is global for Suzuki in multiple ways. On an intellectual level, it is because he understood the problem of the burden of being through the philosophies he encountered in his global travels. Also at this level, it is because the way in which he articulated the answer—the achievement of instinctual reason—was explicitly grounded in the history we have seen so far. Suzuki kept the aim; but he changed the method: not the concept, but the overcoming of conceptual thought. At another level, which emerged more and more in his post–World War II writings, it was because Suzuki understood the interdependence of subjects as a global problem. "You cannot have enlightenment all by yourself," he said in 1952, "for your existence is conditioned by the existence of others."[14] This does not necessarily make enlightenment impossible until some moment when the whole world becomes enlightened at once. But it does mean that enlightenment is partial—and may always remain partial. "You can never be free without helping others to freedom, so there is no absolute freedom. Everything is bound together, there is no real freedom."[15] The closest we can get, then, is to achieve our moment of satori and, in that moment, to experience our connection to the world in a way that is beyond the limits of both intellect and affect: "This very moment of enlightenment experience takes in the whole world and is totality."[16]

But while the moment of connection may be liberating, there are unanswered questions within Suzuki's work about how the subject can reconnect to the fractured present. This is the moment when, as Melville predicted, identity comes flooding back. Suddenly the subject who has pierced into the true nature of reality and lost all sense of self must return to this phenomenal world *as* that very self. As some critics of Suzuki such as Ichikawa Hakugen suggested after World War II, emptying the mind of concepts and entering into the flow of things is a dangerous modality in fascist times. Instinctual reason may not help when revolutionary reason is called for.

More recently, Slavoj Žižek has suggested that Suzuki's nonthinking subject is the perfect complement to global capitalism's laissez-faire ideology. There are, as I suggest below, ways of defending Suzuki from these claims. It is especially hard to see how Zen, which Suzuki always stressed was an ascetic and antimaterialist practice, relates to the excesses of capital. But these critiques do hit at the heart of what remained unbearable within Suzuki's work itself. His aconceptual globality does not suffer from the Atlas complex of German idealism—he does not seek to prescribe institutional laws for all the world. Rather, it suffers from the opposite problem: it gives few or only vague suggestions for how to relate the experience of satori to ethical life.[17] As Ichikawa put it, "The problem is that of what, once the ego is emptied, it should do."[18]

My suggestion here is that Suzuki's Zen, like Hegel's dialectics or Senghor's rhythm, needs to be partialized. Seen as one "mood" (as Emerson would put it) of an expanding pluralism, it offers rich possibilities for subject formation such as we will see in two essayists who worked in Suzuki's wake: John Cage and bell hooks. To see what Suzuki makes possible, I trace the development of satori in his thought, showing its relation to Buddhist history (both philosophical and institutional), transcendentalism, and idealism. Suzuki was truly a global theorist in the sense that he engaged theories from around the world and also because his ideas of Zen are deeply related to how to be a global subject.

Suzuki's voice, however, has been lost in contemporary debates about global subjectivity. In part, this is because he is looked on as a naive philosopher who peddled a vague mysticism. His renown is explained away as a kind of Orientalism: it was only his Eastern guise that made him so popular; there was no true philosophical wizard behind the curtain. He is taken seriously only by New Age hippies, not by the world's leading philosophical and artistic minds. (Never mind that in his lifetime he went to some lengths to distance his work from what he himself viewed as the nonsense of his followers.) Further still, in spite of the fact that he was consistently if quietly critical of Japanese imperialism, it is common today to view his version of Zen as being designed to create a passive subject, pliable by authoritarian and corporatist influences.[19]

How are we to explain this discrepancy? Is it merely that we are savvier than our 1950s forerunners? Were they all really just under the thrall of Orientalism? It seems to me rather the reverse: under our own thrall of having revealed the structure of Orientalism, we can no longer take seriously the productions of a thinker like Suzuki. Even if some of his popularity was created by an "Asian craze," and even if some of his ideas demand critique and scrutiny, it simply does not follow that all of his work and its influence can be explained away or dismissed. Suzuki was indeed a profound thinker whose work demands a reevaluation. He was also a profoundly interesting writer, and his complex and suggestive style is indebted to the figures already encountered in this book—especially Emerson, on whose *Essays* Suzuki based his own major work, *Essays in Zen Buddhism* (1927).[20]

Furthermore, his formal innovations chart new territory by linking the essay to the concept of satori, or enlightenment. Reciprocally, he updates the very meaning of enlightenment, transforming it into a way of life aimed at essaying the globe.[21]

Satori after Globalism

One way to enter Suzuki's vast corpus of writings is through the seemingly simple question from his *Essays in Zen Buddhism, First Series*: "How can this [satori] be effected?"[22] In other words, he wanted to explore not just what satori was or how it related to the historicity of thought, but how it could come into being in our modern world. And he perhaps feared, as Cavell speaks of Thoreau fearing, that "his readers will take the project of self-emancipation to be merely literary."[23] In other words, it will sound nice on paper, and they will dream of it, but they will not take the steps to make it real. Some of his appropriations of Orientalism—of an idea of the Orient as a place where enlightenment had been actualized for centuries—were aimed precisely at inducing an otherwise distracted audience to take his proposals to heart.

After all, Suzuki's answer to the question of effect reveals it to be an arduous task: one achieves satori by "meditating on those utterances or actions that are directly poured out from the inner region undimmed by the intellect or the imagination, and that are calculated successfully to exterminate all the turmoils arising from ignorance and confusion."[24] The answer one might presume, that one achieves satori simply by emptying one's mind, is nowhere apparent here. Suzuki wants us to understand that the event of satori occurs through a rigorous process of meditation on both thoughts and actions.

In the historical Zen tradition, various modes of writing have been used to help practitioners achieve satori.[25] Perhaps most famous is the kōan.[26] As Victor Hori has argued, the kōan is not simply a paradox that provokes a nonconceptual insight, but an actual activity of coming to understand something about the paradoxical nature of reality. He discusses the activity of thinking through the kōan in a particularly helpful way when dealing with the classic: "Two hands clap and there is a sound. What is the sound of one hand?" Hori explains that this is not simply an unanswerable question that should liberate the mind, but that as one thinks about the kōan to such an extent that one becomes one with it, one realizes that the answer is in fact this oneness: the sound of the one is the meditator's being one with the world.²⁷

Suzuki relates his own experiences with the kōan in his autobiographical essays "Early Memories" (1961) and "An Autobiographical Account" (1969, published posthumously). In these autobiographical sketches, Suzuki describes the first time he went to a Zen temple as an experience of frustration and alienation. The head monk yelled at him for his stupidity, and no one was there to offer him any advice besides to just keep meditating.²⁸ A few years later he came across the Zen modernizer Imakita Kosen, who was a key figure in attempts to make Zen into a "practical pursuit" during the Meiji Restoration. As Janine Sawada has shown, Imakita was particularly important because he abandoned his contemporaries' interest in scholastic study in favor of an intensive practice for achieving enlightenment.²⁹ As part of the general trend of modern religions, Imakita set out to remake Buddhism in the face of Western scientific critique and imperial power.³⁰ Like many other modernists, he did this through a renewed focus on meditative practice, something that has been, perhaps surprisingly, largely absent from the actual history of Buddhism.³¹ The point, again, is not to deride this turn as part of the Europeanization of Buddhism; it is rather to understand the turn to transformative practice within a larger, transnational history of attempts to essay the globe.

Imakita insisted that students at his temple focus on a single kōan given to them by their master. For Suzuki, this was "the sound of one hand" kōan.³² However, Imakita's method was not successful for Suzuki: "I was not at all prepared to receive a koan at that time."³³ He pursued his Zen studies nevertheless and eventually received a different kōan from his new teacher, Shaku Sōen, after Imakita passed. Sōen was, like Imakita, a central figure in the transformations of Zen in the twentieth century. He was deeply committed to the preservation and dissemination of Buddhism, and his most important act in this regard may have been sending Suzuki to the United States.³⁴

Sōen's first move in helping Suzuki was to give him the "*mu*" kōan. (Q: Does a dog have Buddha nature, or not? A: *Mu* [no].³⁵) At first this switch made little difference. Suzuki struggled with the new kōan for four years without much progress. "Life in the monastery," he writes, "was exceedingly miserable."³⁶ It seems even to have driven him to suicidal thoughts: "It often happens that just as one reaches the depths of despair and decides to take one's life then and there that satori comes. I imagine that with many people satori may have come when it was just too late. They were already on their way to death."[37] Suzuki's crisis in the end, however, seems milder: he was about to leave for the United States to work with Paul Carus, a German émigré in the States who became interested in Buddhism after Sōen's speech (translated by Suzuki and the novelist Natsume Sōseki[38]) at the 1893 Parliament of World Religions in Chicago.[39]

Desperately seeking satori before his departure, Suzuki rededicated himself to the task. One night he had his experience while "seeing the trees in the moonlight. They looked transparent and I was transparent too."[40] Whatever one makes of this account (some critics deny the meaningfulness of satori; others have said that if Suzuki really had satori he would have more bravely spoken out against the war[41]), it is clear that his experience is mediated by the transnational world he lives in. First, because his lay training is a specifically modern form introduced by Imakita and Sōen; second, because his interest in Zen is spurred by its promotion in the West at the Parliament and by Carus. Moreover, it is this latter context of his imminent departure for the States that finally drives Suzuki to his realization. These elements of the story can help us to understand the intertwining of the kōan and the essay form in Suzuki's work to "effect satori": the essay extends the kōan out into the modern, global world and makes it available for Suzuki's readers.

But what it is that Suzuki claims to have experienced here is not so obvious. It is not simply about overcoming dualism. The key word to understand is "transparent," and doing so will take some philosophical labor across Suzuki's vast readings in both Mahayana Buddhism and German idealism. Suzuki frequently used the word transparency when describing satori. The word (alongside "luminosity") is a possible translation for a kind of inherent purity of the mind available through certain meditative techniques.[42] But Suzuki is not just talking about the mind—he is also talking about the world; here, the trees. There is something about the transparency of satori that is about the relation between self and world.

Suzuki was concerned to forestall the assumption that satori was about a kind of blissful calm or general mental blankness: "To tell the truth, there is here not the remotest hint of tranquility or serenity, nor of the identity of Nature and man. If anything is suggested here, it is the idea of utmost transparency."[43] There is no conceptual identity here, but rather the "identity" of both Nature and humans has been undone in order to produce transparency. By transparency, Suzuki meant that we experience the world as it is, without assumptions. And yet, at the same time, we experience the world as the kind of place in which there are things called "nature" and "man."

In other words, Suzuki is claiming that satori is not simply the breaking down of all categories, but the breaking down of all categories in such a way as to see the foundation of category making itself. This is what the word "transparency" means: *both* that one has broken with categories and the world has become transparent as what it is *and* that, in this experience, one sees that the world as it is has categories.

When Suzuki says that he experienced transparency, then, what he means is that he has broken with his standard intellection that told him that trees were trees and he was a man observing them. In a moment of mental upheaval, he realized the *foundation* of why this was both the case and not the case. In other words, he saw that, indeed, as he experienced the world every day, there were trees, and he was a man, and that was real. But he also saw, viscerally, experientially, that these trees, and he himself, were made of infinite and infinitesimal interdependence. Every part of him and every part of the tree are themselves broken down into infinite parts. But when those infinite parts connect in the right way, they form everyday realities like trees and consciousness. The famous Zen saying for this is "Before Zen practice, there are mountains and rivers. When Zen begins, there are neither mountains nor rivers. After enlightenment, mountains are mountains and rivers are rivers again."[44] Suzuki uses the word "transparency," I believe, to signal this double movement of the truth.

Here a question arises: if in satori everything is interpenetrating and transparent, does that mean that our average everyday world is false? Is a tree just a mental projection, for example? And wouldn't that contradict Suzuki's promise that the world after achieving satori is basically the same, only that one feels a few feet off the ground? Suzuki attempted to answer this question by innovating concepts from both German idealism and Mahayana Buddhism.

In one of several essays Suzuki wrote on satori (1949), he put the problem in very philosophical terms: "a genuine satori is at once transcendental and immanental."[45] This is explicitly Kantian language. Kant (whom Suzuki had studied[46]) had made an important distinction between the transcendent, as in that which passed beyond the possibilities *of* human experience, and transcendental, as in that which created the conditions of possibility *for* human experience.[47] Suzuki's neologism, "immanental," suggests a similar distinction. Immanence is simply the daily world that we live in and experience before satori. It is the opposite of transcendent and implies a full, unconscious immersion in everyday life. "Immanental" means that we have shattered our ordinary perception of the world and come into direct contact with reality. Just as the transcendental shows the conceptual conditions for the possibility of experience, so immanental marks the non-conceptual possibility of our being in the world.

It is thus equally important here that Suzuki is not denying the transcendental: he is not claiming that the categories of the mind are meaningless, and only the immanental experience is the truth. To the contrary, he is suggesting that in our very experience of the world is the *potential for* categories of thought. The very immanental shattering of the categories of perception is what eventually allows us to see those categories in a new light. These categories, however, are not permanent, as Kant had thought, but open to constant transformation. This is so because they only have "conventional" and not "ultimate" truth. (There may come a time, after all, when mountains and rivers simply no longer exist, and this is equally true for the more abstract categories of thought.) This standard distinction in Buddhist philosophy needs some explication.

The doctrines of emptiness and the two truths are some of the most widely discussed and debated in Buddhist studies, and no simple overview can do justice to these concerns that cut to the heart of Buddhism and its quest to end suffering. What I offer here is simply an overview of these positions so that Suzuki's unique take on them can be understood.[48] The canonical account of these doctrines is in Nagarjuna's *Fundamental Wisdom of the Middle Way*, chapter XXIV. Nagarjuna claims, "The Buddha's teaching of the Dharma / Is based on two truths: / A truth of worldly convention / And an ultimate truth."[49] These are the two truths, then: a conventional one and an ultimate one. It is tempting to assume that "ultimate" signifies in some way a higher truth, and conventional a lower one. But Nagarjuna is explicit: "Without a foundation in the conventional truth, / The significance of the ultimate cannot be taught."[50] So what are these two truths, and how do they relate? Conventional truth is more or less what it sounds like: the agreed upon truth formed by a community of thinkers and actors about the world they live in. Ultimate truth is the truth of things from their own side, that is, not as we impute reality to them but as they are in themselves.[51]

How are things in themselves? They arise by dependent origination and are empty in themselves.[52] This means that there is no intrinsic essence to anything; everything comes into being through dependence on other things, all of which are dependent on other things. The very condition of a thing being conventionally true for a community of thinkers and actors is that that thing has no essence. For, Nagarjuna argues, if a thing had an essence, then it could neither come into being nor go out of being: "If something comes from its own essence, / How could it ever be arisen?"[53] The logic here is not dissimilar from that of deconstruction: a thing can only come into being because of the passage of time, but it is the passage of time that also means that that thing must cease.[54] It is only because of this passage that anything can come to be or go out of being. This is the ultimate truth. But it is not too hard to see how this ultimate truth is entirely dependent on conventional truth, for without the conventional world of existing entities that dependently co-arise, *there would be nothing to be the ultimate truth of.* This is how I understand Nagarjuna's comment: "Whatever is dependently co-arisen / That is explained to be emptiness. / That [statement], being a dependent designation, / Is itself the middle way." In other words, emptiness itself is only a conventional name for this process, and the doctrine of emptiness itself is bound to dissolution.[55]

(I want to mark here that this thinking has been central in my formulation of radical pluralism. The two truths help us understand the relationship between an object's actual, existent constitution and its ongoing reconstitution across global networks; how interdependence—local and global—produces real entities; and the fact that, like the doctrine of emptiness itself, it is a way of viewing the world that may someday lose its purpose.)

Suzuki was a close reader of this tradition of thought, and what he means by transparency is bound up with the idea of understanding the two truths simultaneously. But there is a key difference here between Nagarjuna and Suzuki. According to Suzuki, "Emptiness is the result of an intuition and not the outcome of reasoning . . . When one tries to unravel it without the experience, the system becomes all the more a mass of confusion or an unintelligible jargon."[56] For Nagarjuna, one arrived at emptiness through a process of ratiocination. *The Fundamental Wisdom of the Middle Way* is a philosophical treatise, not a guide to meditation. Of course, its aim is to transform the subject, but it does so at the level of rational thought.[57] For Suzuki, one can only understand the transparency of the two truths once one has had the experience of satori.

This focus on experience is both what made Suzuki's work attractive and what has left it subject to extensive critique over the past several decades. David McMahan well summarizes the duality of his reception:

> Suzuki claims that Zen supersedes [the] personal perspective . . . by directly accessing reality per se . . . However philosophically problematic it maybe be in light of post-Kantian, analytic, phenomenological, and postmodern epistemological critiques,

this influential picture gives Buddhism, and particularly Zen, a special place in the western imagination.[58]

Suzuki is said to be popular because he promises something that "we" in the West have banished: the idea of direct, unmediated access to reality. This does explain some of Suzuki's appeal, but there are problems with this kind of analysis. Why is it, after all, that these "epistemological critiques" are given pride of place, as if they had proven something that Suzuki was entirely unaware of? McMahan is not suggesting that there is no tradition of questioning the access to reality in the history of Buddhist thought—that is simply not the case.[59] Rather, he is analyzing the cultural configuration in which Suzuki promises something that "we" now know better than, and, because he is outside "our" tradition, "we" are inclined to believe in his promise in spite of this fact. The hope once placed in "the primitive" is now transferred to Zen.

And, to a real extent, this does describe how Zen has been received. For Foucault, Watts, Cage, and others (my young self included), Suzuki promised a kind of feeling about the world that we no longer believed possible within the confines of our immediate culture. What I disagree with in McMahan's claims, then, is not the cultural analysis, but the lack of acknowledgment that Suzuki was in fact directly responding to these very sorts of critiques. It is true, as McMahan notes, that Kant did not believe in the possibility of this kind of experience, famously arguing that we could not experience the world in itself, but only apprehend it through our transcendental categories. Furthermore, he claimed that even if we could experience the world as is, it would mean nothing because we could not cognize it. He thus specifically denied the coherence of an "immanental and transcendental" experience of the world, writing:

> Assume that nature were completely exposed to you; that nothing were hidden from your senses and to the consciousness of everything laid before your intuition: even then you still could not, through any experience, cognize *in concreto* the object of your ideas (for besides this complete intuition, a completed synthesis and the consciousness of its absolute totality would be required, but that is not possible through any empirical cognition).[60]

Kant's basic point is that such an intuitive grasp of reality is not in any way meaningful because it necessarily remains divorced from the ability to cognize it. Intuitions without concepts, as he famously put it, are blind.[61]

Suzuki, as we have seen, does not exactly disagree. He is not saying that this moment of absolute exposure solves the whole problem of experience and cognition. But he *is* saying that this experience is necessary in order to make any claims about the world. Suzuki is not naive about Kant; he is directly criticizing him. And what he is saying is that if Kant thinks he can understand the nature of reality without the experience of satori, he is sadly mistaken.[62] The problem is that one comes to believe in something like transcendental categories and never learns the truth of emptiness. Kant is thus stuck with an idea about the immutability of the mind—something that, as Foucault points out, is in deep tension with his historical writings.[63] Suzuki's response, *avant* Foucault's, is to say that what is required is not a series of rational claims about knowledge, but the actual experience of transforming the mind:

> Theorists may say this [experience of satori] is impossible, for we put our subjectivity into every act of perception, and what we call an objective world is really a construction of our innate ideas. Epistemologically this may be so, but *spiritually* a state of perfect freedom is obtained *only* when all our egoistic thoughts are not read into life and the world is accepted . . . When therefore I say Buddhism is radical empiricism,[64] this is not to be understood epistemologically but spiritually.[65]

This is a key moment in which Suzuki grapples with the idealist tradition. He takes Kant's point about the subjectivity of perception seriously, but he then claims it only applies to perception prior to satori. When he says that there is a spiritual possibility beyond this epistemology, we should not understand this as mystical or religious in an unprovable sense. Rather, Suzuki is using the word spiritual in much the same way that Foucault does. He is concerned, as Foucault is, that "a philosopher may think out a deep system of thought, without necessarily living that thought himself."[66] Through practices of the self, indeed, through the breakdown of the very entity called the self in the achievement of satori, we can arrive at an experience of the world in its transparency and thus actually begin to live out philosophy.

It should be no surprise, then, that as Foucault prepared his lectures on the *Hermeneutics of the Subject*, he was, according to his partner, Daniel Defert, a "great reader" of Eugen Herrigel's *Zen and the Art of Archery*.[67] Herrigel's book, in both French and English, had a preface by Suzuki and many references to him throughout. A principle thread that runs through these chapters starts with this very fact: that as Foucault theorized the split between spirituality and truth in modern Western thought, his own *actual practice* was oriented toward thinking with other cultures in order to create a more global set of practices of the self. The wonderful irony is that while Foucault looked to Japan as a way of thinking outside the West, Suzuki articulated his Zen as a new interpretation of the Japanese religion based on contact with the West: "Until now we have seen Zen solely through the medium of Chinese and Japanese texts . . . Allow me to conclude by stating that we must now begin to consider how to interpret Zen in the context of Western thinking and feeling."[68] Rather than degrading Suzuki's thought because of its contact with the West, I think we are better to appreciate him within this broader context of "practices of the global self." Then some of Suzuki's more provocative claims in this regard can really be appreciated and debated.

One of the most attractive components of Suzuki's idea of satori is the kind of subject that it claims to produce after the "immanental and transcendental" experience. It is, as I suggested above, a version of Rousseau's "savage made to inhabit cities."[69] And although Suzuki borrowed the goal, he did not keep its geographic presumptions. So far as I know, he never wrote about "primitive cultures," but he certainly did keep the generic idea of a sublated "primitive."[70] Indeed, Suzuki spoke of his "Copernican Revolution" (in another explicit response to Kant) as giving us access to the "primal man," that is, the transparent being that exists before the Fall.[71] He also spoke of the fact that "we all seem to have an innate longing for primitive simplicity, close to the natural state of living."[72] What he argued was that current attempts to arrive at that state did not understand that we *can* return to the "primal man," but only if we abandon our hope at dialectical integration. In other words, Suzuki's Copernican Revolution is that this progress happens not by grasping our mental categories, as Kant's followers had claimed, but—quite the opposite—by overcoming those very mental categories through the immanental experience of aconceptuality.

After satori, Suzuki promised his readers, one would be both in the moment and aware. One would act instinctually, but one's instincts would have the utmost perspicacity. Moreover, one would be freed from the alienating burdens of rationality and returned to an immersive life, but with the same promise of gain from the experience of alienation that we have seen in idealism and Romanticism: "the restoration is more than a mere going back, the original content is enriched by the division, struggle, and resettlement . . . Zen proposes to do this for us and assures us of the acquirement of a new point of view in which life assumes a fresher, deeper, and more satisfying aspect."[73] For Hegel, one had a concept of the world after such a movement. For Suzuki, the struggle has been to lose concepts altogether. He flips Hegel on his head yet again.

Suzuki's claims about this aconceptual moment have been heavily criticized in recent years. Even those like Victor Hori who defend Suzuki's basic insights think that the aconceptual interpretation is a mistake: "there is no Zen enlightenment beyond thought and language in a realm of pure consciousness" any more than humans would be "free as birds" without gravity.[74] Gravity is the condition of our physical existence, and any physical freedom we might have cannot be thought outside it. Similarly, thought and language are the conditions of our mental existence, and any freedom we might have is *through* them. The use of gravity is not incidental here—it recalls Suzuki's claim that Zen enlightenment was like everyday experience "except about two feet off the ground." But Suzuki was not naive here. He affirmed, "As . . . human beings we cannot help thinking and talking."[75] And he insisted on the continuity of "particular experiences" with "pure experience," suggesting that pure experience—the moment before conceptualization—was the ground of all these other experiences, whether we actually *arrived* at that original experience or not.[76]

But even with these qualifications factored in, the problem, Hori and others claim, is that Suzuki had been blinded by the primitivism of Rousseau and his followers.[77] Hori argues that Suzuki's idea of an enlightenment experience outside language and consciousness is as fallacious as the idea of a pure, idyllic state of nature: "Just as the state of nature is said to exist prior to the development of society and state, so also the state of pure consciousness is said to exist prior to the development of thought and language."[78] He continues, "To the extent that this is so, the breakthrough to pure consciousness labeled *kenshō* [seeing reality] is the psychological version of a return to the innocence of the state of nature before dehumanizing society got started."[79] Any notion of "pure consciousness" is thus a "political concept" naming a critique of society.[80] It has nothing to do with what can actually be attained in consciousness.

In this critique, I believe that Hori senses a real proximity of concepts that he does not properly contextualize. Indeed, the idea that pure consciousness names a return to some primordial, unblemished state is exactly the argument that I want to make about Suzuki. However, whereas Hori views this as a debilitating historical thought that should be abandoned, I am arguing here that it shows how perfectly Suzuki both engaged and critiqued modern attempts to essay the globe. Since at least Rousseau, there has been a concern to develop subjects who could integrate reflective rationality with instinctual capacity in order to handle their new, global situation. And whereas such ideas of integration can certainly be found in earlier subject positions, such as what Aristotle called *phronēsis*, or Ikkyū called *fūryū*, it is only in the modern era that this achievement is thought to require global engagement with the problematic concept of "primitive life."

Suzuki is seeking a state very similar to what Rousseau, Schiller, and Hegel imagined: a way of being that would unite our conscious intellect with the sensual world. And like them, he believes that this is neither impossible nor immediately given, but rather an achievement. He stated this more or less explicitly: satori "is a kind of super-consciousness in which there is no opposition of subject and object, and yet there is a full awareness of things . . . In a sense 'the originally pure' is emptiness but an emptiness charged with vitality."[81] When Suzuki speaks of pure consciousness, then, he is speaking at the same time of this "super-consciousness," and this super-consciousness is nothing other than a new method for reaching Rousseau's proposed solution for global subjectivity, that is, a mode of being in the world that unites both the immersion and the reflection; both the transcendence and the immanence, which are required to think and act effectively in an interconnected world. Again, whether or not Rousseau and his followers were right about this need, the key point for the history of modern thought is to recognize that their conception of how to be global subjects formed within this troubled anthropological and colonial context. And while we might criticize Suzuki's solution on similar grounds, we should not criticize it simply because it is a Westernization. Rather, we should see him as critically participating in this tradition of modern global thought.

It is thus no coincidence, then, that when Suzuki sets up this movement toward instinctual rationality, he does so with explicit reference to the process of Hegelian dialectics. First, he summarizes the dialectical method as follows:

> The rationalistic way of dissolving contradictory concepts is to create a third concept in which they can be harmoniously set up. To find out such a new concept is the work taken up by the philosopher. While it is a great question whether he can finally succeed in discovering an all-embracing . . . concept, [they] cannot stop short . . . Endless and fruitless may be [their] efforts, but [they] shall have to go on this way.[82]

Suzuki leaves open the question of whether or not such a concept can be found, but he is not actually concerned with it, because this mode of thought is mistaken from the start. Therefore, "[t]he Zen way has taken an altogether different course."[83] It appreciates the intellect, but it does not think that this dialectical method is the path to what we are looking for. Rather, Zen "steps backwards."[84] It breaks out of the stream of history, of habits and ego formation, and enters into the moment of the immanental and transcendental. Neither the concept of the ego nor the categories of thought is the goal; the pure negation of the ego is. After this negation, we return to our original state of freedom and instinct, but at a higher level.[85]

Heidegger, too, spoke of this non-Hegelian movement in remarkably similar words[86]: "For us, the character of the conversation with the history of thinking is no longer *Aufhebung* . . . but the step back [*der Schritt zurück*]."[87] But again, the difference is that Heidegger conceptualizes this movement within a particular history—"Western thinking"—and not within the broader frameworks that such an analysis would require.[88] I cite again from his last interview:

> It is my conviction that any reversal of the modern technological world can only occur from out of the same location in which it originated. It cannot take place through the adoption of Zen Buddhism or other Eastern experiences of the world. In order to achieve a shift in thinking, one needs the European tradition as well as a new appropriation of it. Thinking will only be transformed through thought that has the same origin and determination.[89]

If I think Suzuki needs to be ranked with Heidegger as a thinker of modernity, it is because he understood the global condition to which Heidegger was utterly oblivious. Indeed, as I have argued throughout this book, if we look seriously at the history of modern thought, we find not an unbroken line of abstract "European thought," but a continual, unequal, fraught, and oftentimes violent attempt to think the globe carried out by writers the world over. To state that what we need is a "new appropriation" of the European tradition as something that excludes "other . . . experiences of the world" is precisely to misunderstand that tradition itself. Heidegger, like many theorists today, was blinded by the idea of Europe and so misunderstood the actual context in which he operated. This was not the case for Suzuki. He developed his concepts not based on a false historical geography, but on the needs of the present global condition. And again, this does not simply mean that he "Westernized" Zen, for "Western thinking and feeling" is itself a plural category that in the modern era is indissociably bound up with the need to think globally. Thus what is interpreted by Hori and others as Suzuki's greatest weakness may in fact be his greatest strength as a theorist of his present.

Suzuki and Emerson's Provocation

Suzuki's engagement with Emerson is equally if not more complex. Suzuki was widely appreciative of Emerson.[90] He even published an essay before coming to the States, which has not been translated, titled "Emaason no Zengakuron" or "Emerson's Zen Treatise." Suzuki quotes extensively from the Divinity School Address as well as "Circles" and "The Over-Soul" in the essay.[91] He seems, at this early point, to believe that Emerson and Zen are aiming at the same thought. At some point, however, he began to discern a difference: Emerson stopped at a point beyond which Suzuki insisted we go. In *Zen and Japanese Culture* (1938/1959), he looks back on his younger self and writes, "I am now beginning to understand the meaning of the deep impressions made upon me while reading Emerson in my college days. I was not then studying the American philosopher but digging down into the recesses of my own thought . . . I was, indeed, making acquaintance with myself then."[92] This is a warmly Emersonian response to Emerson. As Emerson himself had written: "Truly speaking, it is not instruction, but provocation, that I can receive from another soul. What he announces, I must find true in me, or wholly reject." Or again: "whosoever propounds to you a philosophy of the mind, is only a more or less awkward translator of things in your consciousness."[93] And if Suzuki will claim, as he does in the following paragraph, to have surpassed Emerson, then this, too, is Emersonian: "great men exist that there may be greater men."[94] So we should read the following passage with some sense of this indebtedness:

> It was raining one day, and Kyōshō (d. 937) the master said to a monk, "What is the sound outside the door?" The monk answered, "The pattering of rain drops, master." This was an honest answer, and the master knew it from the first. His verdict, however, was: "All beings are confused in mind, they are pursuing outside objects always, not knowing where to find

the real self." This is a hard hit. If the outside pattering is not to be called rain, what is it? What does it mean to pursue the outside objects, and to be confused in the notion of the ego? Sechō comments:

An empty hall, and the sound of pattering rain!
Indeed, an unanswerable question even for an accomplished master!

The American Transcendentalist's attitude toward Nature has no doubt a great mystical note, but the Zen masters go far beyond it and are really incomprehensible.[95]

Suzuki's claim, then, is that Emerson opened up for him the thought that Emerson did not himself pursue. But it is not very clear what exactly this greater thought is. Suzuki tells us at best that it is "incomprehensible." What that would seem to mean, based on his other work, is that it cannot be "comprehended," that is, put into rational or logical language. And yet it is unclear why this would function as a criticism of Emerson, who was himself often criticized for his openness to what was beyond the given order of thought and expression. There appears to be something else on Suzuki's mind here.

Stanley Cavell seems to have intuitively grasped the nature of the relation between Suzuki's thought and Emerson's. His brief remarks on the seventeenth-century Zen popularizer Bankei (whom Suzuki not only first brought to an American audience, but also recovered for Japanese Buddhist history[96]) cut to the heart of matters. Cavell writes:

This fantasy of a noumenal self as one's true self seems to me rather to be a certain expression or interpretation of the fantasy of selflessness (Kant's holy will; Bankei's Unborn . . .); the idea would be that the end of all attainable selves is the absence of self, of partiality. Emerson variously denies this possibility ("Around every circle another can be drawn," from "Circles"), but it seems that all he is entitled (philosophically) to deny is that such a state can be *attained* (by a self, whose next attainment is always a self). Presumably, a religious perfectionism may find that things can happen otherwise.[97]

Cavell's suggestion is that in Bankei, as in Suzuki, there is the belief in a moment beyond any partiality. Suzuki calls this the "immanental" and "transparency." And indeed, if we recall the moment of Emerson's "transparent eyeball" we can quickly see the difference. For Suzuki, there is no eyeball, there is nothing left, there is just transparency (even if it is a transparency pregnant with the mutable categories of reality). For Emerson, something always remains, even if just the eye/I—the circle of partiality and perception.

The question here, as Cavell puts it, is one of attainability: can one attain a position beyond the last circle, the fragment of perception? Emerson had said no: "When we discern justice, when we discern truth, we do nothing of ourselves, but allow a passage to its beams. If we ask whence this comes, if we seek to pry into the soul that causes, all philosophy is at fault."[98] The task of the self then, as Cavell interprets it, is not arriving at something attainable, but always maintaining a relationship to one's "next self." This is what Emerson had called our "unattained but attainable self."[99] It is the task of essayists, whether "Stoic, or oriental or modern," to describe such a self to us.[100] Cavell comments: "I do not read Emerson as saying . . . that there is one unattained/attainable self we repetitively never arrive at, but rather that 'having' 'a' self is a process of moving to, and from, nexts."[101] I have called this the perpetual movement of alternation in the context of Emerson's radical pluralism. Emerson, as I argued, banishes the anxiety of presuming that there is a singular truth out there that we must come into contact with in order to grasp our self, or the world. As Cavell puts it, Emerson's task in writing then becomes "to present nextness, a city of words to participate in."[102]

Suzuki is not presenting us with a city of words in his writing. Indeed, he is offering us an experience that promises to be both beyond language and the very ground of language itself—both immanental and transcendental. This is what Suzuki refers to when he speaks of what is "incomprehensible" in Zen. This moment unites both what is and what is not. Suzuki claims that we can go beyond what we think we can know, which is to say that we can know more than we can think. Whether this is a progress of thought through Emerson's provocation or a regression to some vague mysticism is precisely Suzuki's burden of proof.

The place where he takes on this burden most directly is an essay whose title is an implicit response to Emerson (and anticipatorily a response to Cavell), "Self the Unattainable" (1960/1970). There he writes:

> Relatively or dualistically, it is true, the self is "the unattainable" (*anupalabdha*), but this "unattainable" is not to be understood at the level of our ordinary dichotomous thinking. The

> Unattainable, so termed, subsists in its absolute right which we must now take hold of in the way hitherto unsuspected in our intellectual pursuit of reality. The intellect is to be set aside for a while in spite of "a certain sense of intellectual discomfort" one may have, and we must plunge into the nothingness which is beyond the intellect, threateningly opening its maw in the form of an abysmal pit. The Unattainable is attained as such in its just-so-ness . . . The Unattainable is attained as unattainable—this is the experience not of the psychological or logical self, but of the Unattainable self.[103]

That Emerson is on Suzuki's mind is clear from how he translates *anupalabdhi*, which is a Sanskrit term generally meaning "nonperception." It is part of the classical Indian system of epistemology and is a debated term, concerned with what it means to perceive an absence.[104] Suzuki, as he often does, sees within this scholastic debate a potential to address a more existential issue.[105] The epistemological category of "nonperception" opens up for Suzuki a way to discuss the possibility of having real knowledge of something that cannot be cognitively verified.

This is further underscored by the fact that he capitalizes "Unattainable," just as Emerson had in the essay "Circles" where he speaks of "the Unattainable, the flying perfect, around which the hands of man can never meet."[106] It is because there is this Unattainable, this beyond human perception, that we must accept the fact of our perception and learn to alternate, rather than "pry into the soul that causes." But it is exactly this prying that Suzuki recommends: not only can we, but we must experience the transparency of the universe. Without this experience, our knowledge falters at the very instant before it could have understood the world. For Suzuki, the Unattainable is in fact available to the self, but not as the self classically conceived, which is to say, that self that Suzuki interchangeably calls ego or atman, and that Buddhism from its start has sought to show the nonexistence of. This is not exactly "selflessness," and so Cavell's interpretation is limited here. What it is, rather, is that experience in one instant of both having and not-having a self that Suzuki called transparency. It is that thin instant in which we are between the ultimate and the conventional. It is the experience of what is, of "just-so-ness," the point at which the attained, the attainable, and the so-called Unattainable meet. This moment is not self-less, because, as Suzuki insists, the self is still there—mountains will once again be mountains, and rivers will be rivers, and Emerson Emerson.

What he claims we can experience then is not this moment as a finality, but as the moment *from which all other selves spring*. Thus, if Emerson and Cavell are right to say that to have a self is to always be moving on to new selves, what Suzuki suggests is the possibility of a liberatory moment in which we could *experience the condition* of this movement. This would not refute Emerson, philosophically or religiously; it would simply suggest the human capacity to reach beyond, to seek to pry, to plunge into the vitality of nothingness.

For Cavell, nextness is Emerson's (post-Kantian) insight that the thing is barred to me and that I must receive it and acknowledge it rather than asking for the security of experiencing it. But the point of something called enlightenment—achieved suddenly as in a flash, or through gradual means of purification of the mind, or in a combination of the two—is that this is not given in experience, but achieved by an experience. Emersonian experience, then, is a perpetual movement, a perfectionism of nextness, of what we can do given that to be human is to live in two worlds, one from which we are always already barred or, as Emerson had put it in "Experience," always "too late" to enter.[107] Suzukian experience, to the contrary, is a single movement in which the whole is felt, known to be, and then the rest of one's life is lived out as the deepening of this moment, its extension into other domains of life. One mistake we can make reading Suzuki is to think that this is a kind of perfection, attained and absolute and after which we will make no mistakes or have any problems. All that Suzuki promises us is that this experience frees us—not *from* the world, but *to the world*.

In claiming the possibility of such an experience, Suzuki places the phrase "a certain sense of intellectual discomfort" in quotation marks, which suggests that he is citing Bertrand Russell's introduction to Wittgenstein's *Tractatus Logico-Philosophicus* (a text we know that he had read and underlined.)[108] The full context of the phrase is this: "[Wittgenstein's] defense would be that what he calls the mystical can be shown, although it cannot be said. It may be that this defence is adequate, but, for my part, I confess that it leaves me with a certain sense of intellectual discomfort."[109] In saying that we must pass through this discomfort, Suzuki seems to both be affirming Wittgenstein's (early) work and availing himself of the latter's attempt to prove the limits of what can be done in language and what must be left to "showing" or to experience: "There are, indeed, things that cannot be put into words. They *make themselves manifest*. They are what is mystical."[110] A fuller discussion of Suzuki and Wittgenstein would take us beyond the scope of this chapter. Suffice it to say that, at this moment, Suzuki thinks that he has found in Wittgenstein a helpful attempt to articulate the limits of philosophy and the needs of manifest experience.

In response to Emerson's double consciousness, then, Suzuki posits a kind of nonconsciousness. For Emerson, to be a global self was to learn of the plurality embedded in the world's dualities and to learn to move between them. For Suzuki, the task is to overcome all concept of number, all concepts really, and, at last, be. To be global is to be transparent with the world, not to have a concept of it, not to have a manner of handling its multiplicity. Suzuki, as we will see below, thus left himself open to the charge of quietism and empty abstraction because this experience of the world's isness has no necessarily positive outcome. And while I believe that radical pluralism is a stronger solution to the challenge of essaying the globe without winding up in an unbearable identity, I also believe that the experience described by Suzuki is real and attainable and that it can be one of the moods of truth that helps to positively construct a pluralistic world. The challenge of its relation to politics is what we now must address.

The Limits of Satori

> "What about what happens when someone turns from divine study to the evils of human life?"
>
> —Plato, *The Republic*

Whether one agrees that we can simultaneously experience the ultimate and the conventional or not, this account of satori leaves a thorny question about conventional truth: if a community of thinkers and actors accepts something as true (say, that some human beings are inherently slaves), must this conventional truth be accepted as conventionally true even if ultimately false? Claims like this can in fact be easily refuted because no one could *inherently* be a slave. That would not be a conventional truth at all because it would force the conventional truth to contradict the ultimate truth, whereas we have seen them to be inextricably related. But the following situation is harder to dismantle on these grounds: for contingent historical reasons (war, for example), certain people have become slaves and are accepted as such in a society. Nothing in the ultimate truth would seem to contradict this conventional reality. "Interdependence" is often invoked, with the idea being that because we are all connected, we need to do what is best for each other.¹¹¹ In theory, an enlightened humanity would act for collective interest. But while this sounds nice, it does not necessarily hold, because the fact of interdependence does not necessarily lead to beneficence. Indeed, interconnectedness may equally lead one to aggression, as in Hegel's dialectic. Connection therefore must be *interpreted*, and this brings us back into the conventional world with its norms and disputes. Indeed, although there is a robust field of Buddhist social ethics, there is no normatively agreed-on relation between the epistemology of the two truths and those ethics.¹¹²

One of the most probing questions in recent studies of Suzuki has been about the relationship between his work and Japanese fascism during World War II. On all sides, there is agreement that Suzuki never became swept up in war fever, and, by comparison with many Japanese intellectuals at the time, he remained largely resistant to nationalistic tendencies.¹¹³ Nevertheless, Suzuki's work has been criticized for a lack of serious engagement with these problems. Although he did not encourage the war effort, he did little, publicly, to oppose it.¹¹⁴ After the war, he did begin to make public criticisms of imperialism and fascism and even criticized his own culpability for not having taken a stronger public stance.¹¹⁵ Suzuki also made strong political claims throughout his life, and these appear increasingly in his postwar writings in both Japanese and English. This can be seen especially in his Columbia lectures and dialogue with Thomas Merton. And in his Japanese-language writings, Suzuki tended to be more critical of the Japanese state and people, whereas externally he was often chauvinistic.¹¹⁶ Critics like Žižek might be surprised to discover remarks in these works such as "Lately I have had a desire to study socialism, for I am sympathetic to its views on social justice and equality of opportunity. Present-day society (including Japan, of course) must be reformed from the ground up."¹¹⁷

But there is a deeper logic to the critiques than mere ignorance of such statements by Suzuki. The question that has driven much of these concerns is: How could Zen Buddhists, with their claims to enlightenment and their Mahayana precepts of compassion and nonviolence, have aligned themselves with the war effort? The thinker most closely associated with pursuing this question is Hakugen Ichikawa, a priest, professor, and activist who has written extensively on issues relating to Zen and social justice. There is unfortunately very little of Ichikawa's work available in English, but his critique was popularized by Brian Daizen Victoria in his work *Zen at War*, which, as we will see shortly, has (mis)informed Žižek's critique of Zen.¹¹⁸

As a young man, Ichikawa was influenced by Suzuki's work and admired his modernizing tendencies.¹¹⁹ He distanced himself from Suzuki after the war because he did not feel that Suzuki's criticisms of Zen offered a sufficient explanation for the failure of Zen Buddhists during the war. Suzuki's own response, in short, was to insert a wedge between satori and politics. Satori could ease anxiety, open one's mind, change one's sense of the world, but it could not tell one how to act in such terrible times. This would require a difficult return from the sun to the cave, an adjustment of one's intellect from clear vision to radically problematic conditions. As Suzuki wrote after the war:

> With *satori* alone, it is impossible [for Zen priests] to shoulder their responsibilities as leaders of society. Not only is it impossible, but it is conceited of them to imagine they could do so . . . In *satori* there is a world of *satori*. However, by itself *satori* is unable to judge the right and wrong of war. With regard to disputes in the ordinary world, it is necessary to employ intellectual discrimination.[120]

Suzuki admits the unbearability: satori cannot "shoulder" the responsibilities of this world. But it still can help free one of egotism, make one more spontaneous, and reduce one's anxiety. The basic concepts of no-mind, original nature, and spontaneity are all still correct; they simply need to be more firmly wedded to a rigorous adherence to basic Buddhist precepts of compassion and antiviolence.

The difference between Suzuki and Ichikawa was about this question of the meaning of satori. For Ichikawa, it is precisely such concepts as no-mind and aconceptuality that have to be discarded. Zen is not about a carefree satori; it is about a satori that gives one a discriminating and powerful intellectual vision.[121] This is perhaps most clearly articulated in Ichikawa's idea of the "origin," which he turns from Suzuki's primitivist revision into a mathematical point. Thus in his essay "A Preliminary Conception of Zen Social Ethics" he links Suzuki's basic notions to Rousseau, Goethe, and Schiller, similarly to how I have above.[122] Such notions, he says, were meaningfully uprooted by Hegel and Marx because they were not adequate to the difficult social problems of a global world.[123] Suzuki's brilliance, which I have touted above, indeed solves a problem of global thought, but for Ichikawa it fails to solve *the* problem of contemporary social existence. Rather than finding a new path to the primacy of the primitive via a deconceptualized origin, a path to a revived "original naïveté," Ichikawa suggests that an origin *must* be found at the point of two axes between "seeing into the non-duality of Nature and . . . researching into the laws and constructions of the world."[124] Enlightenment in his conception, then, should not be directed first toward a nondual insight and then toward a hopeful worldly praxis, but rather should be concerned with finding this crossing point: "To die a 'Great Death' [such as in the satori experience] signifies, in my view, not merely to eradicate our dichotomy of reasoning, but also to awaken our humble and open minds of inquiry, aiming at the establishment of a peaceful and blissful world for all mankind."[125]

The main difference between Suzuki and Ichikawa, then, is that Suzuki, like Plato, insists on a possible errancy within the process of satori during the subject's return to the world, while Ichikawa wants to remove or at least reduce this possible errancy by finding a juncture between enlightenment and the world. The fact of the matter is that neither of these positions is perfect, for the simple fact that life, which unfolds in *time*, offers no perfect *position*. I think that Suzuki understood this very well when he wrote a now infamous remark in *Zen and Japanese Culture* that Zen "may be found wedded to anarchism or fascism, communism or democracy, atheism or idealism, or any political or economic dogmatism."[126] His point was not that Zen had no ethics, but that one could not have a satori process separated from the ethics of one's time (that the ultimate truth could not be separated from the conventional; it could only deny its inherency). At the same time, from Sato's archival research, we know from Suzuki's letters and early essays that he was indeed a very political thinker who praised socialism and excoriated nationalism.[127] In his later writings, Suzuki was simply trying to understand how it was that the beauty of satori could go awry, and what he saw was that it could not be separated from social conditions. Rather than denying the power of satori, he chose to hold onto its potential, insisting that we combine our pure experience with our intellectual discrimination to guide us during the unbearability of war. War, in effect, made Suzuki a pluralist in spite of himself. Suddenly intellectual discrimination was no longer subordinated to satori, but rather on par with it.

As a useful comparison, consider how Slavoj Žižek took up Ichikawa's critique of Suzuki in his *For They Know Not What They Do: Enjoyment as a Political Factor*.[128] For Žižek, like Ichikawa and indeed like Suzuki, we should be concerned with the ways in which Zen is being used as form of thought to mollify subjects in the face of capitalist excess. Žižek thus writes against "this pop-cultural phenomenon preaching inner distance and indifference towards the frantic pace of free-market competition."[129] But he then adds that this is not merely a pop-cultural concern for those without satori; rather, it cuts to the very heart of Zen itself. He argues that what satori gives us is only the thought that "even the most horrifying crimes eventually *do not matter*."[130] He calls this the "horrible thought!" that "Zen is ambiguous" and is simply "a spiritual *technique*, an ethically neutral *instrument* which can be put to different sociopolitical uses."[131] He then approves of the accuracy of Suzuki's remark that Zen can be part of any political system. But whereas Suzuki says this *so that* he can argue for making this neutral event into a positive politics, Žižek comes to the frighteningly absurd conclusion that "this means . . . that all-encompassing Buddhist Compassion has to be opposed to intolerant, violent Christian Love."[132] To be sure, he means that this Love can be used for revolutionary aims, but it is somewhat inconceivable that he would claim that this intolerance that has been so horrifyingly used through the past two millennia is somehow unscathed.

Rather than opposing one ideology with another, then, it would be better to think of politics as precisely the kind of negotiation Suzuki envisions. Whether we should spend our time reducing ourselves so that we can become better political subjects, as Thoreau, Gandhi, and Suzuki suggest, or whether we should directly seek a kind of worldly wisdom that aims less at absolute enlightenment and more at its point of intersection with social good, as Ichikawa, Marx, and Žižek suggest, is more of a personal choice than a metaphysical absolute. Indeed, Žižek is right: the "horrible thought" is that the universe simply is, and we do not ultimately know what is right and true, but can only feel our way toward justice within our conventional worlds. But, ironically, it is Suzuki who is willing to confront this horrible thought and go into the "abysmal pit," whereas Žižek flees away from it and runs to Christian Love.

The relation of thought and politics, the move to praxis, and the possible intersection of political and spiritual liberation: these are eternal themes. The task is not to answer them once and for all, but to see what connections between them we can enable. Suzuki does not offer us perfection, then, but he does offer a way of thinking that might help open us to create better conditions for our global times. Freed from materialism, we are free to inhabit the world in a way that might make the more equitable distribution of wealth (which Žižek himself claims to champion) possible:

> Are we not constantly engaged in warlike preparations everywhere in order to raise or maintain our precious standard of living? . . . Instead of raising the so-called standard of living,

will it not be far, far better to elevate the equality of living? This is a truism, but in no time of history has such a truism been more in need of being loudly declared than in these days of greed, jealousy, and iniquity. We followers of Zen ought to stand strongly for the asceticism it teaches.[133]

Or again, "To be poor, that is, not to be dependent on things worldly—wealth, power, and reputation"—that is what Suzuki thinks of as the potential politics of Zen.[134] And finally: "The individual gains meaning when we share in existence; one individual has no meaning. When we speak of one, this one brings others along—not just humans, but all the universe, or cosmos."[135] To open oneself to the world, to lose one's ego in the world, and then to return to the world not with demands but with gifts of clarity and insight—this is Suzuki's practice of the global self.

My argument here is not quite Suzuki's, however. While I have no doubt that the mystical experience of unity is real and meaningful, I do not believe that satori is necessary for everyone any more than I believe calculative analysis is necessary for everyone. These are all moods available to the radically pluralist self. As soon as one becomes necessary, it becomes unbearable. Moreover, satori itself is unbearable in the sense that it cannot tell us what to do without the other tools of the intellect, as Suzuki himself was forced to admit. It is wonderful to experience the world as transparency, and that transparency can teach us to let go of pernicious aspects of human life, but it cannot prevent us from letting go of those other elements that make our global existence livable. To overcome the unbearable identity is not to lose oneself in the world; it is to combine that experience with other ways of being in the world and learning how to alternate between them without imposing singularity on others in the process. It is, in short, still the lesson of Emerson and Du Bois.

What Suzuki offers us is something else. A phrase of Cavell's names it succinctly: "suppose the issue is not to win an argument . . . but to manifest for the other another way."[136] Rather than arguing for or against a particular experience, what Suzuki did at his best was to manifest the possibility of a kind of experience that had been banished from many forms of modern thought. Suzuki recovered mysticism as a practice of the global self. His Zen would not have been possible without the history of attempts to essay the globe that preceded him. In turn, he made possible a new path for the modern global subject.

Extensions of Suzuki: Cage and hooks

The number of thinkers whom Suzuki influenced is, as I noted in the preface, bewildering—not just because it is so impressive, but also because there exists very little critical literature that assesses his global impact. In these brief extensions of the discussion of his work, I have chosen to focus on two of his followers: John Cage, who studied directly with him, and bell hooks, who was led into much broader studies of Buddhism through the range of his influence. I discuss Cage here for a few reasons: he was an excellent interpreter of Suzuki's thought; his own work is often misunderstood because Suzuki has been misunderstood; he not only directly returns to the themes of practices of the global self and global aesthetics, but he also extends the scope of these practices to questions of sexuality. I discuss hooks because she shows the surprising places where an engagement with Suzuki may lead; because she adds to this account a complexity of vision around class, gender, and race that might otherwise go missing; and because she brings recent popularizations of Buddhism around mindfulness and presence into the discussion of what practices of the global self might look like today. Overall, both thinkers extend Suzuki by connecting his thoughts to the revolutionary essay tradition, suggesting why practices of the global self today will be unbearably partial unless they connect up to transformations in the social world.

The Global Politics of Cage's Zen

Cage is not often read as espousing such a social vision. Perhaps not surprisingly, his critics have raised critiques of his work that parallel those of Suzuki's. Edward Said (in his role as a music critic), for example, said of Cage that "a kind of joyous freedom, *jouissance*, underlies every one of his efforts in either prose, music, or silence."[137] For Said, this positions Cage on the side of those who withdraw "into self and solitude" and refuse the difficult political work that requires us to "speak truth to power . . . to exist through irony and skepticism, mixed in with the languages of the media, government, and dissent, trying to articulate the silent testimony of lived suffering and stifled experience."[138] Similarly, Theodor Adorno argued that Cage had reacted to the troubles of the present like other composers by merely "renouncing any control of their music by their ego. They prefer to drift and to refrain from intervening, in the hope that, as in Cage's *bon mot*, it will be not Webern speaking, but the music itself. Their aim is to transform psychological ego weakness into aesthetic strength."¹³⁹ And perhaps most vociferous is Fredric Jameson in *Postmodernism, or the Cultural Logic of Late Capitalism*:

> Think, for example, of the experience of John Cage's music, in which a cluster of material sounds . . . is followed by a silence so intolerable that you cannot imagine another sonorous chord coming into existence, and cannot imagine remembering the previous one well enough to make any connection with it if it does.¹⁴⁰

Cage, in short, retreats (Said), embraces weakness (Adorno), and undoes our temporal capacities to comprehend the present (Jameson). All of these critiques do speak some aspect of Cage's work. But there is more to Cage's opaque and difficult music and writing than these critiques would have us believe, and to understand what his work offers we will need to situate it within the context of Suzuki's global enlightenment.

In a series of remarks on Marcel Duchamp collected in the book *A Year from Monday*, Cage made this commentary:

> There are two versions of ox-herding pictures. One concludes with the image of nothingness, the other with the image of a fat man, smiling, returning to the village bearing gifts. Nowadays we have only the second version. They call it neo-Dada. When I talked with M. D. [Marcel Duchamp] two years ago he said he had been fifty years ahead of his time.¹⁴¹

There is a lot happening in these few sentences, and unpacking them can help us understand quite a bit about Cage's practice of essaying the globe.

To begin with, we need to know what the "two versions of the ox-herding pictures" are. An alternative translation, "The Ten Cow-Herding Pictures," is the final essay of Suzuki's first series of *Essays in Zen Buddhism* (1927). It is about a series of pictures by the twelfth-century Rinzai Zen monk Kakuan. The pictures depict the spiritual progress of a young man. It is often argued that the ox represents our untutored mind before we have embarked on the Buddhist path. We must find the ox, tame it, and then transcend it, because it is only a nominal (or pictorial) designation for what is in fact beyond words. Suzuki notes that Kakuan's paintings are an innovation on an earlier version. In the earlier version, the paintings end with an empty circle representing the transcendence of the karmic cycle. The second version, as Cage notes, ends with an image of a man returning to the world and bearing gifts. The lesson of the second version is that the point of spiritual practice is not transcendence but the Bodhisattva path of returning to express one's understanding and help others on their way.

We now know the context of the first few lines of Cage's quote: the two versions of the tale mentioned by Suzuki. But why does Cage go on to say, "Nowadays we have only the second version," that is, what is it about his moment that means that there is no longer the possibility of ending with an empty circle? To understand this, we have to go to Cage's foreword to the book. He describes there a question he has been pondering: whether or not his work has changed from a kind of inner meditation to a concern with changing the world. Building on Suzuki's teaching about the interdependence of subjects (implicitly) and Marshall McLuhan's idea that changes in technology have created a situation in which our minds extend into the world (explicitly), Cage collapsed the distinction:

> To me that means that the disciplines, gradual and sudden (principally Oriental), formerly practiced by individuals to pacify their minds, bringing them into accord with ultimate reality, must now be practiced socially—that is, not just inside our heads, but outside of them, in the world, where our central nervous system effectively now is.[142]

This quote by Cage has been central to my formulation of "practices of the global self" and "essaying the globe." It extends Suzuki's focus on how work on the self can help one engage social concerns by showing that engaging social concerns is part of our work on the self. I do not agree with Cage's timeline or his technological determinism, but I do believe that he is describing here precisely what happens with the modern essayist: that her self-transformative writing activity is directed toward a new relationship to the world as a whole. In the afterword, Cage gives this goal a name: "World-enlightenment."[143] By saying that only the second version of the ox-herding pictures is operative these days, he is repeating his stance that the once solitary practices of mind are now, of necessity, social and global.

To further understand Cage's practice, we need to ask about his relationship with Duchamp in the above citation. Cage obliquely refers here to a conversation he once had with Duchamp in which Cage told Duchamp that he had discovered chance operations fifty years before Cage did.¹⁴⁴ It is to this remark that Duchamp responds that he was ahead of his time. For example, in *Three Standard Stoppages*, Duchamp threw a piece of tape measuring one meter three times. He then made sculptures of the resulting falls that, because they do not fall straight, demonstrate their varying "lengths." This stressed not just the relativity of measurement, but its randomness as well. In another piece called *Erratum Musical*, Duchamp had a trio of musicians play random notes drawn from a bag. Such operations would become central to Cage's own mode of using chance in the making of his music and writings. Originally derived from his reading of the *I Ching*, Cage would use different methods throughout his career to determine how his work would be structured.

Cage theorized this practice in various places. One of the most important versions is in his preface to "Lecture on the Weather," a piece composed of quotes from the works of Henry David Thoreau. Cage notes that some might think this a contradiction because Thoreau warns us in *Walden* against "blind obedience to a blundering oracle." But, Cage says, this misunderstands what chance operations are:

> [They] are not mysterious sources of "the right answers." They are a means of locating a single one among a multiplicity of answers, and, at the same time, of freeing the ego from its taste and memory, its concern for profit and power, of silencing the ego so that the rest of the world has a chance to enter into the ego's own experience whether that be outside or inside.¹⁴⁵

Cage here takes what was often implicit in Suzuki and puts it into a concrete plan for global selves. This is perhaps the most straightforward example of what such a practice would look like from the vantage of modern Zen.

On the same page, Cage opposes chance operations to empires, which are planned and willed constructions. Chance operations are about opening to the world and its multiplicity of practices while still knowing that one has to act and cannot do everything. They are meant to free us of our determination but not of our necessity to act: we must return after this moment of freedom in order to bring gifts to the village.¹⁴⁶ If Duchamp's practice was Dada, then what Cage is doing here is connecting such practices in his own work—neo-Dada—to the legacy of the ox-herding tales. The practice of neo-Dada, then, is nothing other than the practice of opening the self into a field of global possibilities so that the meaning of its enlightenment can only be to become a bearer of gifts.

This is an important context for understanding all of Cage's work. It is often thought that randomness in his work is just that—a kind of pure, pointless chaos concerned only with the freedom of the subject. We saw this above in Edward Said's suggestion that Cage seeks to avoid confronting power and so fails to "articulate the silent testimony of lived suffering and stifled experience." But another way to understand Cage's work is as a scrambling of those very discourses of power *so that* those silent testimonies can be brought to light. Cage's most famous piece, *4'33"*, can productively be seen in this way. In *4'33"*, a pianist comes out on stage and, for the duration of the piece, plays no music.[147] It is easy to understand why this would make it seem that Cage was interested in some kind of vague freedom. But the question is, what can happen when the concert scene is framed by this action? For, as Cage repeatedly stated, he was not interested in expressing something, but rather making an open "field of possibilities."[148] The challenge for the global self is to choose within this field. But Cage, like Emerson, always insisted that there was no single answer. The point was to develop practices that could allow different answers to come forth. If one practice works, you partialize around it for a time until, like a stream of air on the body, it goes from refreshing to rancid, and you must open up again.

Cage's hope was that his work—his music, performances, lectures, and essays—would lead people to listen to things other than what had already been determined for them. Thus, when he reflected on *4'33"* some years later, he noted that it had for him a political legacy and memory in a speech that he had given in high school: "It was called 'Other People Think,' and it was about our relation to the Latin American countries. What I proposed was silence on the part of the United States, in order that we could hear what other people think, and that they don't think the way we do, particularly about us."[149] And it is not a coincidence that when Cage writes about this same moment in *Empty Words*, it is in the middle of the discussion about Thoreau, which concludes with the following quote: "The best communion men have is in silence."[150]

Cage, as I noted just now, was opposed to an idea, which he most often associated with Beethoven, that music was the expression of an artist's emotion.[151] He was particularly opposed, it would seem, to the idea of art as the representation of an infinite and unfulfilled longing. He wanted to think of music not as the expression of an emotional state that an audience member might also experience, but rather as a process of undoing those very emotional energies. His essay writing operated in the same way:

> When Art comes from within, which is what it was for so long doing, it be-came a thing which seemed to elevate the man who made it a-bove those who ob-served it or heard it . . . But since everything's changing, art's now going in and it is of the utmost importance not to make a thing but rather to make nothing. And how is this done? Done by making something which then goes in and reminds us of nothing.[152]

In other words, art is to become something that creates a space of enlightenment for the subject. This enlightenment is not anxious; it is the calm opening to the sounds of the world that a listener of *4'33"* would experience. There is nothing onstage for the listener to try to re-create in herself. Rather, the stage is there only as an opening for the transformation of all involved. Visually on the page, these openings are transcribed right into Cage's writings.

In spite of his reputation, Cage was neither naive nor whimsical. He did not think that this openness was de facto good, only that it offered the possibility for various transformations toward justice and equality. He was fond, for example, of quoting Buckminster Fuller's remark that so long as one person in the world is hungry, we are all hungry, but the problem was that we did not all *feel* this hunger. (We are not, in Suzuki's terms, "transparent" to it.) In creating interactive spaces of interpenetrating selves in a general field, Cage hoped that aesthetic experience could open us to this interdependency. But it could only do so, he believed, if it abandoned the dictatorial position of proscribed experience. This was for him the very definition of the inhuman—the creation of a "Frankenstein monster," of parts stitched together by an imposing conductor figure. This practice "when concerned with humane communication only move[s] over from Frankenstein monster to dictator."[153] Within the field of communication, then, the idea was for everyone to be open to everyone and build together some other possibility for living. Merely abandoning the conductor "is not a sign of identification with no matter what eventuality but simply of carelessness with regard to the outcome."[154] Like Suzuki, Cage was unfailingly precise. And he understood that any process of nonduality was not the end in itself, but part of an ongoing movement. *Unlike* Suzuki, and this is crucial, he did not view this as a process of a single enlightenment that then expressed itself for social good, but rather of enlightenment itself as a social process. This is one of his key innovations in this story.

It is in general important to note that while Cage learned an incredible amount from Suzuki, he did not follow his teacher to the letter. Suzuki's aesthetics were, in fact, of the precise Romantic variety that Cage wanted to get past. In a 1950 lecture on "Zen Buddhism and the Arts," for example, Suzuki stated, "Here is the origin of poetry and of all other arts. When there is a perfect identification of subject and object . . . something moves in the depths of what we might call the cosmic spirit, and it is from this movement that the utterance flows out."[155] What interested Cage in Suzuki was the *philosophy* of this relation of subject and world. But Cage's signal contribution was to level the difference between philosophy, experience, and art: it was not, for him, that we experienced something and then communicated it in art, but, rather, that art itself was this possible communion of subject and object. As he put it with regard to Suzuki's teaching about subjectivity, an individual ego "either closes itself off from its experience . . . or suppresses itself as ego and becomes open to all possibilities . . . What Suzuki said about this seemed, and still seems, to me directly applicable to music."[156] For Cage, Suzuki's thoughts were *applicable* to music, but not about music itself. His essays, like his art, were less about provoking a particular experience and more simply about opening the subject to new forms of global relation.

Cage scholarship has constantly failed to understand how he continued the task of essaying the globe through his work with Suzuki. This is missed even by Cage's defenders, including Branden Joseph, who has been, in other respects, perhaps his most sophisticated reader. Joseph's work has been instrumental in showing both the rigor and complexity of Cage's thought as well as in redressing the critical silence on his role in the artistic avant-garde from the 1960s on.[157] Unfortunately, however, Joseph believes that the reading of Cage's fundamental concepts as signs of "irrationality or mystical oneness" were, when "combined with Zen," "almost unavoidable."[158] Whereas Joseph excuses this confusion about Zen and tries to make Cage more sophisticated by bringing him into conversation with Foucault and Deleuze, I think this fundamentally misunderstands both Cage's work and modernity in general. The problem with Joseph's treatment of Cage is his assumption that these French thinkers provide the most important framework for understanding the modern condition to which Cage was responding. It then becomes easy to write out his Zen as unimportant to his actual claims within that context. But if the groundwork I have laid in this book has any purchase, then Cage's importance as a thinker is, like Suzuki's, *due to* his global engagement.

We can also return in this context to Jameson's critique of Cage. Jameson's concern is that the situation of contemporary capitalism has led to the breakdown of our active capacities to connect experience across time and space.[159] This is largely the case because of globalization—because the "experience" of politics is no longer subjectively available in daily life, but is rather spread out across global networks of capital. Postmodernism, rather than seeking to subvert or at least actively engage this situation, has come to celebrate it. This, in essence, is Jameson's reading of Cage, which is not significantly different from Adorno's: it makes an aesthetic value out of a political failure. But consider Jameson's own response to this situation:

> For neither Marx nor Lenin was socialism a matter of returning to small (and thereby less repressive and comprehensive) systems of social organization; rather, the dimensions attained by capital in their own times were grasped as the promise, the framework, and the precondition for the achievement of some new and more comprehensive socialism. How much the more is this now the case with the even more global and totalizing space of the new world system, which demands the invention and elaboration of an internationalism of a radically new type?[160]

This is precisely what Cage is doing: attempting to use new technological means to increase the capacities of the subject to understand and listen to the world around her. Given what we have seen about the actual plurality of Marx's own vision (in chapter 4), and given the notorious difficulties of Jameson's proposed solutions to this problem, one wonders if he too might have produced more integrated approaches had he learned to *listen* better to others—whether to Cage's music or the voices of "Third World literature."[161] Cage himself was often appropriative and not always as actively engaged with global alternatives as he might have been. Nevertheless, as Jameson's own notion of "cognitive mapping" provided us with techniques of spatializing the present, so Cage's music opened up new kinds of global listening.

One site in which we can see these new modes at work is Cage's own queer politics. In an essay on the relationship between Cage's silence and the closeted homosexuality of Cold War America, Jonathan Katz offers an exemplary model of reading Zen as part of Cage's practice of the global self. Katz suggests that we often read Cage's practice of silence as part of his own being silenced as a gay man. But he offers readings that allow us to see Zen as both personally and socially liberating. For example:

> In essence, Zen repositioned the closet not as an accomplice to repression nor a source of anxiety but as a partner in healing; it was in not talking about—and hence reifying—one's troubles that healing began. Hence, perhaps what made Zen so attractive to Cage was its unhinging of the connection between problems and passions. Zen provided a way to negotiate traumas by acknowledging the pain and then moving beyond or through it. This is not to say that problems are to be ignored nor passions smothered, but rather that they are not to become obsessively rehearsed.[162]

Zen thus offers a rigorous practice beyond a standard psychoanalytic model of repression. It allows us to see silence—not talking about it—as a globally available mode of handling the burdens of psychic life imposed by social structures.

And, Katz further argues, it offers a model of social change: "My point is that if silence was, paradoxically, in part an expression of Cage's identity as a closeted homosexual during the Cold War, it was also much more than that. Silence was not only a symptom of oppression, it was also, I want to argue, a chosen mode of resistance."[163] Also noting the speech about Latin America that I referenced above, Katz shows how silence opens up a kind of dialogic politics of humility and openness. It is, in effect, through his practices of the global self (his engagement with Zen's globalism) that Cage opened up new ways of understanding his own local practice. Through silence, his unbearable closeted identity became what bell hooks might have called an "identity in resistance."[164]

Katz rightly hedges his claim by noting that this mode of politics may be limited to the culturally specific moment of Cold War America.[165] And indeed, the history of queer politics is largely a history of public organizing. As Yannik Thiem has noted, we are in a historical moment when expanding bourgeois rights for queer subjects may result in an all-too-comfortable position of silence.[166] But here again I am a pluralist. The point is not to pick a position and say that politics today requires us to be either silent or public and organized. The point is to learn when to rely on which modality. As James Scott has argued, for instance, when we assume that only one kind of politics is "correct" and effective, we ignore the complex forms of "everyday resistance" and their remarkable power.[167] And Jeffrey Stout, who has perhaps argued more for broad-based organizing than any other contemporary theorist, notes not only that there are plural modes of politics, but also that humility and listening are fundamental to organizing.[168] These ideas of humility and listening are also fundamental to another essayist who wrote in Suzuki's wake: bell hooks. But hooks is not just a reader of Suzuki; her work presents a significant challenge to modern Buddhism as a practice of the global self from the vantage of race, class, and gender.

bell hooks's Global Presence

Globalization is not the only thing that disappears from Foucault's account of what has happened to practices of the self in the modern age. He also neglects the fundamental contributions of two things at the heart of bell hooks's writing career: feminism and pedagogy. The link between these two modes of practice goes all the way back to Mary Wollstonecraft. For Wollstonecraft, the problem was not that practices of the self had been lost, but that they had been denied to women.[169] This was especially the case with education.

Modern feminism has further specified that feminist pedagogy implies not just an education in ideas, but a revolution in ideas. As Adrienne Rich argues:

> Perhaps this is the core of the revolutionary process, whether it calls itself Marxist or Third World or feminist or all three . . . [It is] a rebellion against the idolatry of pure ideas, the belief that ideas have a life of their own and float along above the heads of ordinary people—women, the poor, the uninitiated.[170]

For Rich, revolution is not just about access; it is about a general transformation. Feminism is not, as it was for Wollstonecraft, an extension of men's rights to women. It is a calling into question the very abstraction of rights that has so often bristled against lived experience. It is a demand that thought not be extracted from life and then roughly reapplied (as in certain forms of the dialectic), but that thought become continuous with our becoming materially equal.

Similar ideas can be found in the kinds of radical pedagogy with which I began this book: the type hinted at by Montaigne, developed by Rousseau (for men to learn the social contract), and systematized and democratized by Paolo Freire and others, including bell hooks. Freire, who could have been a chapter of this book by himself, insisted on education as the site that mediated the coming-to-consciousness of theoretical reflection and the praxis of revolutionary transformation. This was because he did not aim to teach people about their situation. Rather, he acted as a guide to the situation, posing questions and spurring critical reflection through everyday understanding.[171] hooks, whose respect for Freire was enormous, remained concerned that he had imported too many ideas from the patriarchal order into his vision of the result of this pedagogic process. Freire, she writes, "constructs a phallocentric paradigm of liberation—wherein freedom and the experience of patriarchal manhood are always linked as though they are one and the same."[172] hooks offers instead visions of freedom grounded in a loving community of equals, not a single liberated subject.[173]

hooks is known for her critiques from the angle of race and gender that are focused on the transformation of individuals and communities. As the editors of a critical volume on her work make clear, hooks's work is structured on a series of "practices" that enable "spiritual and existential enrichment" within the context of what hooks refers to as "white supremacist capitalist patriarchy."[174] These practices include, but are not limited to, talking back, constructing "creative spaces," narrating and naming one's own life, theoretical claims that allow us to take distance on the pain of experience so as to reshape it, and a writing style that essays an engagement beyond academic confines.[175] Like Du Bois, Senghor, and Fanon, she thickens the account of this book through her reminder that practices of the global self will necessarily change depending on where one finds oneself in the global order. Beyond them, she enlarges this perspective through her reflections on her position as black woman in the United States of the late twentieth and early twenty-first centuries. More specifically here, she brings this position and this set of methods into her engagement with American Buddhism.

hooks's interest in Buddhism began through Suzuki's influence, especially as embodied in the poet and essayist Gary Snyder, whom she met at a poetry event in college. hooks does not seem to have followed too deeply into Suzuki's Zen, however, as she mainly references the Vietnamese monk and peace activist Thich Nhat Hanh and the notorious wild man of Tibetan-American Buddhism, Chögyam Trungpa, as her Buddhist teachers. Nevertheless, the very fact of her interest in Buddhism begins with Suzuki's influence. Her work is yet another testament to the double globality of Suzuki's practices, which took in the world in their formation and also had an extensive worldly influence.

While hooks's later works have tended to present Buddhism more or less in line with mainstream mindfulness approaches, her early 1990s essays and interviews in *Tricycle* magazine represent an important critical voice on both the limits and potentials of Buddhist practice.[176] In "Waking Up to Racism," for example, hooks takes on the fallacy that becoming enlightened, or "waking up," means that one becomes free of racism. Enlightenment, she suggests, would be more a matter of waking up to the *fact* of racism, that is, to the fact that if one lives with the conventional truths of a white supremacist culture, shades of racism will inflect one's attitude, regardless of one's race. What this necessitates, then, is the ongoing double movement of critiquing both institutional and personal racism. This, too, is a practice of the global self. It is about acknowledging that who we are, as we are, is racist, and that overcoming racism requires both a work on ourselves and a work on our cultures and institutions. To think that a moment of satori can end one's inner racism is as foolish as thinking that it could have ended Japan's imperial war.

This waking up also has specific effects on one's practices. hooks's essay represents a brief but sincere engagement with the question of the ego. For both Suzuki and Cage, a practice of the global self required the dismantling of the ego so as to open up the individual and the world to their shared transparency. hooks notes the problematic relation to race this inspires in some of her liberal, white Buddhist friends: "They are so attached to the image of themselves as nonracists that they refuse to see their own racism or the ways in which Buddhist communities may reflect racial hierarchies. This is made more problematic where the emphasis in predominately white communities is on letting go of the self."[177] The problem with simply letting go of the ego as a mantra is that it does not recognize the fact of difference in subjectivity. How could it be the same for Emerson, who feels secure in his potential for self-reliance, as it is for Du Bois, who feels his self already split by the racism of his culture? Overcoming the ego is simply not the same for someone who has been told they do not have a meaningful ego to begin with.

What hooks suggests, instead, is that one think through the precise locations in which a Buddhist practice might take place for a black woman from rural Kentucky, such as herself. And that begins to look like the difficult tarrying with two truths: to assert at once that there is a world beyond egos and racism and that nevertheless, that is not the case with our conventional world. And what hooks finds in this process is not so different from what Du Bois had polysemically called "the gift [German for poison] of second-sight." hooks writes: "It is often racism that allows white comrades to feel comfortable with their 'control' and 'ownership' of Buddhist thought and practice in the United States. They have much to learn, then, from those people of color who embrace humility in practice and relinquish the ego's need to be recognized." This capacity for humility, hooks avers, is part of an entrenched "practice of humility" that has roots in the African American experience and Afro-Christianity.[178] To tie these complex threads together, then, hooks accepts the values of reducing the ego, of humility, of mindfulness, and of compassion, but she denies the claim that the path to these is—or ought to be—the same for every subject. Black people in the United States have been told that they are not subjects with egos, but pliable bodies. If Buddhism is to be a meaningful practice within that historical context, it must be attentive to the resistant subjectivities formed in this process.

This analysis for hooks is also intersectional with the question of gender:

> Ten years ago if you talked about humility, people would say, I feel as a woman I've been humble enough, I don't want to try to erase the ego—I'm trying to get an ego. But now, the achievements that women have made in all areas of life have brought home the reality that we are as corruptible as anybody else. That shared possibility of corruptibility makes us confront the realm of ego in a new way. We've gone past the period when the rhetoric of victimization within feminist thinking was so complete that the idea that women had agency, which could be asserted in destructive ways, could not be acknowledged.[179]

Part of what makes hooks such an engaging essayist is that her critiques range in all directions. On the one hand, she critiques Buddhism for its unwillingness to meet subjects where they are. In this interview, she is especially suspicious of American Buddhism's willingness to countenance sexual misconduct between teachers and students. On the other, she critiques feminism's unwillingness to see the value of Buddhism's critique of the ego. Her work is radically pluralist at such moments, as it refuses to hypostasize a culture and looks both for what is positive and negative in a constituted concept.

But hooks is not always so pluralist in her writing style. There is also at least one concept that seems wholly good in her imagination: love. In her interview with *Tricycle*, hooks goes so far as to declare that beyond any particular critical affiliation she views as herself as being "steadfastly on a path about love." She explains: "To commit to love is fundamentally to commit to a life beyond dualism. That's why love is so sacred in a culture of domination because it simply begins to erode your dualisms: dualisms of black and white, male and female, right and wrong."[180] As we have seen, however, going beyond dualism has no necessary relation to justice. This is apparent even in hooks's own claims about the problems of assuming that enlightenment means being beyond racism. Love is thus called on to do an incredible amount of work in hooks's thinking. Not only must it push us beyond dualism, but it must also lead us to "commitment and involvement with the world."[181] Love, which is of course itself an endlessly changing and mutating concept (capable of bringing out the most tortured parts of our nature, capable of creating dualisms between couples and others, and capable of extending beyond any possible scope of engagement, as in Augustinian Christianity), is forced by hooks to simply be the catchword for the thing that heals the world. But love, of course, is but one word with many meanings, some of whose logics aid us to bear the burden of global living, and others that rend our frames of global competence.

There is also the lingering issue here, in both Cage and hooks, about what we might call their "unreconstituted Buddhism." Like many in the West, they have confused Buddhist scripture with Buddhist practice and effectively ignored the complex lived realities of Buddhism.[182] This has often meant relying on specific Buddhist notions such as nonduality and assuming that they represent the universal claims of Buddhist philosophers. This is far from the case. Indeed, much of Buddhism relies precisely on a distinction between conditioned existence and the nonconditioned achievement of nirvana. The idea that "samsara is nirvana" and other recurring clichés do certainly exist in Buddhist history, but they are heavily debated.[183] The argument I have made in this part of the book is that we need not insist on some more authentic Buddhism elsewhere so much as begin to understand modern Buddhism as part of an ongoing, dynamic series of attempts to essay the globe.

By reconstituting some of this history of Buddhism, we can see what is innovative and engaging in Suzuki, Cage, and hooks at the same time that we appreciate the historical limits of their vision. This second step is crucial lest we fall prey to continued exoticizations and Oriental imaginings of some pure Buddhist culture, which will produce unbearable identities for Buddhists and others. Such a vision of Buddhism has allowed many in the West to ignore the ongoing Buddhist massacres of Muslims in Myanmar, while also imprisoning Tibetan Buddhists in a peaceful identity that many argue has hindered their ability to effectively respond to Chinese imperialism there.[184] This does not mean, however, that a reconstituted global Buddhism lacks effective messages for today's world. So long as we bear in mind that this is an evolving tradition that should be critiqued as any other, we can also extract some of its lessons to extend the domain of practices of the global self, such as Suzuki, Cage, and hooks offer.

One final practice that hooks's work has increasingly focused on is presence. At first glance, presence may seem like the opposite of a global practice. How can focusing on one's immediate surroundings connect one to the rest of the world? But this is precisely what we have seen since Montaigne: that the rest of the world is deeply part of one's immediate surroundings—whether that is in books, clothing, spices, commodities, ideas, or people themselves. The general response to this condition has been to develop practices that allow one to extend thought into new spaces—whether by skepticism, teleology, revolution, pluralism, or emptiness. hooks, now following more Thich Nhat Hanh than Suzuki, suggests mindful presence as a means of finding the global through immediacy, but without abandoning conceptual thought.

In a recent collection of essays largely centered around her decision to return home to rural Kentucky, hooks writes, "Walking, I will establish my presence, as one who is claiming the earth, creating a sense of belonging, a culture of place."[185] hooks's point is not to ignore the global as she returns, but rather to use the local as a site through which she can come to terms with how she has been produced as a subject. It is essaying the local that allows her to understand her place in the world: "I had to return to those Kentucky hills to reclaim my sense of belonging on the earth."[186] In some ways, hooks's claim here is a kind of weak ecology of the land. But it is also about reconstituting the ways in which the globe produced her local. In returning, she found that her identity is bound up with "the power of geographical location, of ancestral imprints, of racialized identity." This situation calls for a "psychological practice that specifically focuses on recovery from racist victimization."[187] To overcome the unbearable identities that global modernities have produced requires such specific practices attuned to the present realities that one finds in Appalachia as much as in Rakhine, London, or Kinshasa.

Coda

Being-Toward-Bequeathment

There will always be new practices for the global self to develop, both as revisions of tradition and as inventions of the moment. And each individual will have to find their own way of coping with the fact that the world floods into their experience in ways that both buoy and drown. The point is not that we all need to be fully global. Indeed, as we have seen, this tends to cause as many problems as it solves. Rather, it is that we all need to give over some part of both our subjective and institutional lives to an understanding of how the world constitutes us and how we, in turn, can caringly constitute it. Much of what we see today under the guise of globalism—global markets, global spectacle culture, the global university—threatens to write over the lessons of the past few hundred years by insisting that one way of life is best for all.

An attentive listening to the intellectual history of these times urges us in a different direction—that of radical and critical pluralism. Not the facile pluralism that merely "tolerates" others, but the engaged and self-critical pluralism that remains open to transformation, dynamism, and preservation as related parts of what makes an individual or a culture what it is. This radical pluralism refuses to impose an identity on others at the same time that it critically denies self-presentations of absolutism. Yet it does not deny the right of any culture or individual to engage a strategic partialization by working steadfastly on a part of their plurality that is threatened. This combination of moves helps overcome what is unbearable in being global by simply learning to share the burden of being. It does not find the truth of life in a single thought—whether that be skepticism, dialectics, or mysticism. All of these can be brought together, can be alternated to, can be made available to all. And it does not presume that these options are themselves singular. Each individual, understanding as much as they can of their place in the world through acts of reconstitution, can fashion their own practices of the global self. In so doing, they can leave for future generations a testament to what made life on this planet bearable or even flourishing.

Of course, the continuity of such practices requires that the planet itself survive.

The possibility of planetary destruction is not new to our current moment. Communities that have survived attempted genocides know all too well that the end of the world has already come many times. That this possibility is felt today on a planetary scale is an extension of the actual and imagined ends of humanity. Just as thought has always extended as far into the world as it could, it has also imagined the possibility of the end of the world. Visions of floods, fires, and man-made catastrophes are ever present in the human mind. Climate change, in this sense, is not so different from the threat of nuclear annihilation faced in the mid-twentieth century. The difference is that rather than a two-nation struggle for dominance, it is a worldwide and unequally distributed mode of energy extraction and consumption that now threatens us. If practices of the global self are to have any real-world relevance, certainly it is here.

But, as Emerson warns, it is not "as if a child's hand could pull down the sun."[1] We work on all fronts, changing our organizations, our political structures, our research agendas, our frames of mind, our cultural habits, our sense of humility, and our willingness to obey or disobey. Practices of the global self are not perfect and complete solutions to the world's problems. To presume that they could be is to create a new, unbearable identity of responsibility, imagining that we may pull down the sun with our overstretched arm. The task of practices is to keep that unbearability at bay. They remind us to bear our burden, but not to take on more than is ours or impose on others more than is theirs. One of the most important things that the humanities can do now, I believe, is to continue to make the case for the alternating balance of pluralisms and partialisms: pluralisms that allow for new ideas to flourish and partialisms that allow us to rally around a single cause.

In *Learning to Die in the Anthropocene* (2015), Roy Scranton has made a very interesting claim about the role of the humanities and what practices of the global self should look like today. He argues, like many scientists, that catastrophic climate change is unavoidable. Our task is not only to mitigate its effects, but also, more importantly, to learn to live after the death of our current civilization. Like Hamlet, Descartes, and Heidegger, he thus returns to an ancient practice of the self: Socrates's "learning how to die."

He is insistent on the importance of this: "The greatest challenge we face is a philosophical one: understanding that this civilization is already dead." "If we want to learn to live in the Anthropocene, we must first learn how to die. . . . The rub now is that we have to learn to die not as individuals, but as a civilization."[2]

What I would say in response is that learning to die is but one practice among many, and certainly not the most important. I would not go so far as Spinoza, but I would register his complaint: "A free man thinks of nothing less than of death, and his wisdom is a meditation on life, not on death."[3] This book has been a meditation on one aspect of human life over the past four hundred or so years: how that life has been global. If we take *this* vision of the self, rather than the singular individual who dies, we can see that we do not need to perform the bizarre act of transferring the individual's death onto the civilization's, for the individual and the civilization have not been sundered in the first place. Scranton refers back to ancient practices, but "we" have been global for a very long time. The thing to figure out now is how to better be so, and falling back on ancient ways is the mistake of Hamlet, Descartes, and Heidegger. It is not time to be an antique Roman or a Dane. It is time to welcome others from the "Polack Wars," climate wars, or wars on terror and drugs, and to begin to tell the shared stories of our mistakes. Private, individual practices of course continue to have a place here. But what matters for both self and world is not only how we die, but how we give, what we bequeath. We certainly are beings-toward-death, in Heidegger's phrase, but also, and more importantly, we are beings-toward-bequeathment.

I excavate this notion from Stanley Cavell's beautiful book on Henry David Thoreau's *Walden*.[4] Cavell ends his book: "The boon of Walden is *Walden* . . . He is bequeathing it to us in his will, the place of the book and the book of the place. He leaves us in one another's keeping."[5] Thoreau says in *Walden* that he left the pond because he had "more lives to live."[6] *Walden* was not about the practice of dying so much as the practice of renewal, rebirth, and bequeathment. Dying, of course, is a part of that, but only a part. There is, I think, an implicit rebuke of Heidegger's notion of being-toward-death in Cavell's interpretation.[7] For Heidegger, our authenticity comes in the shattering of our projects that the fact of our own death brings home to us. This is what Scranton wants us to learn anew. Thoreau, Cavell suggests at the end of *Walden*, has "bequeathed" something to us. He has "left us in each other's keeping." He is a thinker of being-toward-bequeathment: he is not interested in the authenticity of the individual or the civilization in the face of their death; he is interested in what it is that the universe gives and keeps giving and how we can bring it into our world and show it to each other. It is not our death that matters, in other words, but what we leave to the next generation. We have seen Du Bois call this "social self-realization in an endless chain of selves," and it is, of course, at the heart of the idea of the Bodhisattva in some forms of Buddhism, such as those that appear in Suzuki's postwar writings.[8] In short, it is the question of how to avoid the unbearable: for ourselves, by not reducing our lives to our death, and for the future, by not taking away from them the very planet that can sustain their existence. The reciprocal structure for the next generation is what Cavell elsewhere speaks of as "bearing the responsibility of the inheritance."[9]

Our global identities are in time as much as in space. In an era of rapid technological transformation, rising nationalism, economic insecurity, ongoing wars, and the catastrophic threat of climate change, we are called on to have an ever deepening responsibility to both the past and the future. Being-toward-bequeathment is a style of living dedicated to the responsibility to inherit and pass on the multiple forms of existence. It is equally to remain open to new forms of life that may yet appear. While this way of understanding a global self in time cannot guarantee the continuation of the planet, it at least allows us a vision of self-reference as beings whose subjectivity is responsible not just to ourselves, but also to the histories of life and death that constitute the globe we share.

Notes

Introduction

1. A note on the word "globe." Some critiques of this term have been advanced, and alternatives have been offered, most notably "world" (*monde*) by Jean-Luc Nancy and "planet" by Gayatri Spivak. For each of them, the other term opens up a possibility for thinking that the totalizing force of globalization is said to close off. I respect and appreciate both of these claims. But some of what I am examining here is precisely "globe" in the worst sense, as something that certain thinkers did want to be constrainable and totalizable. I also want to invoke the geographic space of the globe and the fact that its finitude forces us to interconnectivity, as shown in the epigraphs. At the same time, I am examining counterpractices that sought to undo totalizing visions, to remake the globe as much as Spivak and Nancy do with their linguistic interventions. Because it is this contested space that interests me, "globe" seems the most apposite term for this study. Jean-Luc Nancy, *The Creation of the World or Globalization*, trans. Francois Raffoul and David Pettigrew (Albany: State University of New York Press, 2007); Gayatri Chakravorty Spivak, *An Aesthetic Education in the Era of Globalization* (Cambridge: Harvard University Press, 2012), 335–50. On the utility of the globe as a figure for a shared planet, see Ngũgĩ wa Thiong'o, *Globalectics: Theory and the Politics of Knowing* (New York: Columbia University Press, 2012), 8. For a reflection on how to think the globe and the planet together, see Eric Hayot, *On Literary Worlds* (New York: Oxford University Press, 2012), 91–117. For a helpful historical overview of the difference between "universal" and "global" history, see Sanjay Subrahmanyam, "On World Historians in the Sixteenth Century," *Representations* 91, no. 1 (2005): 26–57.

2. I cannot here do as Foucault and Taylor have done and show the millennia-long histories of self-making. There is ongoing work about the deep roots of today's globalism, and I do not intend at all to suggest here that the modern period is the only time when cultures have interacted. Like Glissant, I believe that thought always extends out into the world. I do suspect, however, that since the end of the fifteenth century CE, the increase in the accuracy of geographical knowledge

and the pace of contact across the totality of the earth's surface accelerated and significantly transformed thinking about global selves. Subrahmanyam points to this as the transition from an ordered universal history to an essayistic and fragmented global history. From a European perspective, one might think here of John Mandeville's fourteenth-century *Book of Marvels and Travels*, where he writes that Jesus of Nazareth died in "the middle of the world" (Jerusalem) so that his sacrifice would be "known to everybody in all parts of the world" just as "one shouts out in the middle of a city or town, so that all parts of the city know what is happening." While it is clear that there is a type of worldly thinking happening here, this particular spatial configuration for thinking a self-world relation would be practically impossible just over a century later. Other historical documents would, of course, produce different angles of comparison, and a fuller investigation of the long histories of global self-making from around the world would uncover different global origins of the modern self. Subrahmanyam, "On World Historians in the Sixteenth Century"; John Mandeville, *The Book of Marvels and Travels*, trans. Anthony Bale (Oxford: Oxford University Press, 2012), 5. For a brief overview of the ongoing work in the "global Middle Ages," see Geraldine Heng and Lynn Ramey, "Early Globalities, Global Literatures: Introducing a Special Issue on the Global Middle Ages," *Literature Compass* 11, no. 7 (July 2014): 389–94.

3. I understand, of course, the debates around the word "postcolonial," with its implication of the end of a colonial situation that in fact continues, and that there is a difference between postcolonial theorists and the history of "anticolonial" struggle and recent work in "decolonial" scholarship. These issues are central to some of the twentieth-century writers I discuss, and all of these different strands of scholarship have been influential for me and are discussed in the chapters to follow. At this point in the book, I am simply using "postcolonial" as the name of a field of general scholarship, that is, as the commonly accepted term for work that views colonialism as central to the marking of modern life.

4. Edward W. Said, *Orientalism* (New York: Vintage Books, 2004), 3.

5. See, for example, Edward W. Said, *Culture and Imperialism* (New York: Random House, 1993), 66. Said notes that the word "constitutive" comes from a quote from Williams on the previous page (65).

6. The details of this history are beyond my scope here, but suffice it to say that postcolonial theory of the self has moved in multiple directions. Among them, it has aimed to dislodge the claims of self-mastery in Europe; to understand how European domination was part of the making of colonial subjects; and, more recently, to move past too narrow a focus on colonialism to think about internal histories and South-South relations in self-formation. While learning from all of this work, this book is more concerned with how the globe as a delimited sphere produced relations between subjects across spaces. I discuss this further below. Lisa Lowe has recently given a powerful overview of such a project, writing: "Intimacy as interiority is elaborated in the philosophical tradition in which the liberal subject

observes, examines, and comes to possess knowledge of self and others. Philosophy elaborates this subject with interiority, who apprehends and judges the field of people, land, and things, as the definition of human being. Ultimately, I would wish to frame this sense of intimacy as a particular fiction that depends on the 'intimacies of four continents,' in other words, the circuits, connections, associations, and mixings of differentially laboring peoples, eclipsed by the operations that universalize the Anglo-American liberal individual." My project here takes up from hers, but focuses more on philosophical circuits than material ones, and more on the varieties of self than just those of liberalism. Lisa Lowe, *The Intimacies of Four Continents* (Durham: Duke University Press, 2015), 21. See also the explicit responses to Taylor in Malcolm Bull, "Slavery and the Multiple Self," *New Left Review; London*, no. 231 (September 1, 1998): 94–131; Peter van der Veer, *Imperial Encounters: Religion and Modernity in India and Britain* (Princeton: Princeton University Press, 2001), 160.

7. I wholeheartedly agree with Wilder's and Shih's remarks on this topic, which are worth citing at length. Wilder: "My argument pushes against a recent tendency in comparative history and colonial studies to insist upon multiple, alternative, or countermodernities, thus granting to Europe possession of a modernity which was always already translocal. What is the analytic and political cost of assigning to Europe such categories or experiences as self-determination, emancipation, equality, justice, and freedom, let alone abstraction, humanity, or universality? Why confirm the story that Europe has long told about itself? Modern, concrete universalizing processes (like capitalism) were not confined to Europe. Nor were concepts of universality (or concepts that became universal) simply imposed by Europeans or imitated by non-Europeans. They were elaborated relationally and assumed a range of meanings that crystallized concretely through use." And Shih: "No theory emerges in a historical vacuum or geographical isolation, and place, understood here as a nodal point of connection, produces and embodies relations on the world scale, however small or marginal it may be. The given place is part of, partakes of, and is constitutive of the world, and it is thus not merely a recipient but a coproducer of global processes, and hence a coproducer of the world as we know it." Gary Wilder, *Freedom Time: Negritude, Decolonization, and the Future of the World* (Durham: Duke University Press, 2015), 11; Shu-mei Shih, "Theory in a Relational World," *Comparative Literature Studies* 53, no. 4 (2016): 723.

8. In speaking of "reaction," I have in mind what Freud describes as the relation of a "*reactive thought*" and its repressed "contrary." In a sense, what I am arguing is that "the West" is a reactive thought and "the globe" is its repressed contrary. The Freudian notion hems me in a bit too much, and I am convinced by Foucault's claim in the *History of Sexuality* that production is a more operative mode of power than repression (we will see in general that globality produces thoughts more than being a repressed thought), but I think there is something to the idea that the strength and tenacity by which we have held to the concept of the West have to do with a deep yearning for a kind of community that the fact of the globe

constantly throws into question. The "treatment," as it were, of such a condition would be to think through how collectivities and globality are not a contradiction. This is part of what I am calling "radical pluralism." Sigmund Freud, *The Freud Reader* (New York: W. W. Norton, 1989), 200; emphasis in original.

9. The criticism of disciplinary divisions has been at the heart of much of the work I follow here. See, for example, Lewis R. Gordon, *Disciplinary Decadence: Living Thought in Trying Times* (Boulder: Paradigm Publishers, 2006); Susan Buck-Morss, *Hegel, Haiti and Universal History* (Pittsburgh: University of Pittsburgh Press, 2009), 22–23; Lowe, *The Intimacies of Four Continents*, 1–2.

10. Cornelius Castoriadis, *The Castoriadis Reader*, ed. David Ames Curtis (Oxford: Wiley-Blackwell, 1997), 149.

11. I am very appreciative, for example, of Adorno's thoughts on the essay. In his reflections on the form, nevertheless, he always seems to believe there is something powerful called "the essay," which stands outside its appropriations. See for example Theodor Adorno, *Notes to Literature, Volume 1*, ed. Rolf Tiedemann, trans. Sherry Weber Nicholsen (New York: Columbia University Press, 1991), 22–23.

12. Sanjay Subrahmanyam, "Global Intellectual History beyond Hegel and Marx," *History and Theory* 54, no. 1 (February 2015): 132.

13. This is perhaps a contentious claim about revolutionary history, and I unfortunately cannot pursue it in any great depth in this study. My point is not to criticize revolution so much as to suggest a different basis for its enactment. Fortunately, Gary Wilder's recent work offers a magnificently sketched vision of what a pluralist revolution (if not deep organizing) would look like; see Wilder, *Freedom Time*. For a rethinking of revolution as something that must happen *within* the plurality of historical conditions, see David Scott, *Conscripts of Modernity: The Tragedy of Colonial Enlightenment* (Durham: Duke University Press, 2004). On the importance of deep organizing for politics, see Jeffrey Stout, *Blessed Are the Organized: Grassroots Democracy in America* (Princeton: Princeton University Press, 2010).

14. I have especially learned from the analyses in Raymond Williams, *Culture and Materialism* (New York: Verso, 2006); Janet Jakobsen, *Working Alliances and the Politics of Difference: Diversity and Feminist Ethics* (Bloomington: Indiana University Press, 1998); William Connolly, *Pluralism* (Durham: Duke University Press Books, 2005); Susan Hegeman, *The Cultural Return* (Berkeley: University of California Press, 2012).

15. I owe my use of the word "radical" to my engagements with Gabriel Rockhill's work over the past few years. In speaking of his own work on "radical history," he writes, "The adjective *radical* refers both to the dissolution of the supposedly natural objects of history and to the dynamic role of different forms of agency in history." In other words, radical history goes down to the roots (the radicals) of things, and shows their dissolution in their constituent parts. At the same time, it shows how roots grow into things—agents of history. Gabriel Rockhill, *Radical History and the Politics of Art* (New York: Columbia University Press, 2014), 3.

The phrase "radical pluralism" also appears elsewhere, for example, in both William James and Dipesh Chakrabarty (as "radically plural"), but they mean the phrase slightly differently. See William James, *Writings 1902–1910* (New York: The Library of America, 1988), 650; Dipesh Chakrabarty, *Provincializing Europe: Postcolonial Thought and Historical Difference* (Princeton: Princeton University Press, 2008), 88.

16. Ralph Waldo Emerson, *Essays & Poems* (New York: Library of America, 1996), 844.

17. See the account in Nelson Mandela, *Long Walk to Freedom: The Autobiography of Nelson Mandela* (Boston: Back Bay Books, 1995), 167–70. Such acts are what underwrite Mahmood Mamdani's important critique of legal pluralism: "The language of pluralism and difference is born in and of the colonial experience." I would amend this slightly to say that the language of *traditional* pluralism is born here. Radical pluralism would not have fallen into this universal versus cultural schism. Mahmood Mamdani, *Define and Rule: Native as Political Identity* (Cambridge: Harvard University Press, 2012), 44. See also Tomoko Masuzawa, *The Invention of World Religions, or, How European Universalism Was Preserved in the Language of Pluralism* (Chicago: University of Chicago Press, 2005).

18. William James, *Essays in Radical Empiricism and a Pluralistic Universe*, ed. Ralph Barton Perry (New York: E. P. Dutton & Co., 1971); Hannah Arendt, *The Human Condition* (Chicago: University of Chicago Press, 1958); María Lugones, "Playfulness, 'World'-Travelling, and Loving Perception," *Hypatia* 2, no. 2 (1987): 3–19; Mariana Ortega, *In-between: Latina Feminist Phenomenology, Multiplicity, and the Self*, SUNY Series, Philosophy and Race (Albany: State University of New York Press, 2016); James Tully, *Strange Multiplicity: Constitutionalism in an Age of Diversity* (New York: Cambridge University Press, 1995); Connolly, *Pluralism*; Richard J. Bernstein, "Cultural Pluralism," *Philosophy & Social Criticism* 41, no. 4–5 (May 2015): 347–56. A similar idea of culture is in Williams, *Culture and Materialism*, 37–42. Connolly's idea of a "deep, multi-dimensional pluralism" was particularly formative (Connolly, *Pluralism*, 10). Arendt, I should say, is unrepentantly Eurocentric, in large part because she seems to believe pluralism is an invention of the Greeks. Probably the theory closest to my own can be found in Jakobsen's work, although, ironically, Jakobsen calls her project an alignment of diversity with complexity as against pluralism. But the kind of liberal pluralism she critiques is also critiqued by radical pluralism. Radical pluralism further extends Jakobsen's argument by showing how diversity occurs in the historical emergence of *concepts*. Because my concern is also more with individuals than political networks, I focus more on "alternation" across plurality, whereas Jakobsen focuses on "alliances." That said, the general set of theoretical claims here is very similar. Jakobsen, *Working Alliances and the Politics of Difference*, 4–15.

19. There are of course disagreements here: Ortega, for example, writes both appreciatively and critically of aspects of Lugones's own theory of pluralism. Ortega, further, distinguishes "multiplicity" from "plurality" in order to suggest a greater

sense of coherence within a given entity. In speaking of a "radical pluralism" that cuts across all of existence, my position is closer to Lugones's, but I appreciate and try to continue Ortega's call for a language that allows us to understand the coherence of selves. I speak of this, however, not in the phenomenological language she mobilizes, but rather from a language developed out of pluralism itself: the idea of partialities. Ortega, *In-Between*, 87–102.

20. One of the troubling claims we will see constituting the critical theory tradition is the idea that non-European cultures were singular and static. While any number of scholars in indigenous studies, history, anthropology, and other fields have contested this idea, it remains strong enough to this day for Jodi Byrd to note that in poststructual theories, "Indianness can be felt and intuited as a presence, and yet apprehending it as a process is difficult, if not impossible, precisely because Indianness has served as the field through which structures have always already been produced." As we will see, this false thinking about humanity affects the entire critical theory tradition. Byrd offers as a corrective a number of innovative concepts from "indigenous critical theory." Her work stands as a reminder to the limits of the Euro-American tradition I analyze here, and, I think, can be read profitably with some of the authors considered later in this book. It is also important to note in this context that these misperceptions of the past have effects on our present and future. In addition to Byrd's work on the critique of empire, one can consider Kyle White, for example, who has spoken of the importance of understanding indigenous plurality for thinking through the futures of climate change. And Emilio Kourí's ongoing research into the limits of agrarian reform in Mexico has suggested the problems that occur when we presume singular formations in the past in plans for revisions in the present. Jodi A. Byrd, *Transit of Empire: Indigenous Critiques of Colonialism* (Minneapolis: University of Minnesota Press, 2011), xviii; Kyle White, "Indigenous Philosophizing in Our Ancestors Dystopia" (Philosophy and Coloniality Symposium, New School for Social Research, April 16, 2018); Emilio Kourí, "Sobre La Propiedad Comunal de Los Pueblos, de La Reforma a La Revolucion," *Historia Mexicana* 66, no. 4 (264) (2017): 1923–60.

21. Eduardo Viveiros de Castro, "Cosmological Deixis and Amerindian Perspectivism," *Journal of the Royal Anthropological Institute* 4, no. 3 (1998): 469–88.

22. Dipesh Chakrabarty (whom I discuss at greater length in the chapter on Marx) raises an important possible objection here, namely, that globalizing the history of European thought can lead us to lose the specificity of how claims about "the West" were made in the colonies. Thus Chakrabarty writes, "I am aware that an entity called 'the European intellectual tradition' stretching back to the ancient Greeks is a fabrication of relatively recent European history . . . The point, however, is that . . . this is the genealogy of thought in which social scientists finds themselves inserted." In other words, no amount of deconstructing the idea of Europe is going to change the fact that Chakrabarty, coming of age in India, was confronted with Europe as a monolithic and universalizable entity. I want to hold onto Chakrabarty's

insight while also partializing it. That is to say, I want to show throughout this book that part of the West that was received by figures like Gandhi and Senghor and Fanon was not a monolith to which they had to respond, but rather a set of thoughts concerning global relations about which they also had claims to make. To accept the ideology of the West and to play it out yields tremendous insights, but so does denying that ideology. Throughout this book, and especially when dealing with modern Zen, I am going to suggest that it is only by globalizing the idea of the West that we can understand what modern thought is. By making this move, I am not wanting to erase the tremendous reality effects of the discourses of rationalism or secularism or law or modernity. Rather, I am trying to show that there was also a discourse of globality that was both an unbearable imposition (in the form of certain legal structures, for example, or an idea about what "art" is) and a shared and contested arena. Chakrabarty, *Provincializing Europe*, 5. He echoes these points at 27–29. See also Talal Asad, *Formations of the Secular: Christianity, Islam, Modernity* (Palo Alto: Stanford University Press, 2003), 13, 212–15.

23. For a statement to this effect (albeit one that does not acknowledge the global constitution of Europe), see Akeel Bilgrami, "Occidentalism, the Very Idea: An Essay on Enlightenment and Enchantment," *Critical Inquiry* 32, no. 3 (2006): 381–411.

24. For a provocative set of questions and reflections on how to think through the long histories of domination around the world in relation to Euro-America's more recent colonialism, see Bruce Robbins, "Prolegomena to a Cosmopolitanism in Deep Time," *Interventions* 18, no. 2 (March 3, 2016): 172–86. Gayatri Spivak has also made some recent remarks on how the shift in postcolonial studies to South-South relations will also lead to a necessary engagement with South-South domination. Gayatri Chakravorty Spivak, "Vicissitudes of the Postcolonial" (Postcolonial Humanities Working Group, Princeton University, 2018).

25. Erich Auerbach, *Mimesis: The Representation of Reality in Western Literature*, trans. Willard Trask (Princeton: Princeton University Press, 1953), 3–24.

26. Jane Anna Gordon, *Creolizing Political Theory: Reading Rousseau through Fanon* (New York: Fordham University Press, 2014); Jane Anna Gordon and Neil Roberts, eds., *Creolizing Rousseau* (London: Rowman & Littlefield International, 2014); Michael Monahan, "Introduction: What Is Rational Is Creolizing," in *Creolizing Hegel*, ed. Michael Monahan (Lanham: Rowman & Littlefield International, 2017), 1–22; Shu-mei Shih, "Comparison as Relation," in *Comparison: Theories, Approaches, Uses*, ed. Rita Felski and Susan Stanford Friedman (Baltimore: Johns Hopkins University Press, 2013), 79–98; Shih, "Theory in a Relational World."

27. Martin Bernal, *Black Athena: The Afroasiatic Roots of Classical Civilization* (New Brunswick: Rutgers University Press, 1987); Paul Gilroy, *The Black Atlantic: Modernity and Double Consciousness* (Cambridge: Harvard University Press, 1993); Gayatri Chakravorty Spivak, *A Critique of Postcolonial Reason: Toward a History of the Vanishing Present* (Cambridge: Harvard University Press, 1999); van der Veer,

Imperial Encounters; Buck-Morss, *Hegel, Haiti and Universal History*; Sankar Muthu, *Enlightenment against Empire* (Princeton: Princeton University Press, 2003); Antony Anghie, *Imperialism, Sovereignty, and the Making of International Law* (Cambridge: Cambridge University Press, 2005); Kevin Anderson, *Marx at the Margins: On Nationalism, Ethnicity, and Non-Western Societies* (Chicago: University of Chicago Press, 2010); Lowe, *The Intimacies of Four Continents*; Wilder, *Freedom Time*. Other works in this field that have been influential to me include George Makdisi, *The Rise of Humanism in Classical Islam and the Christian West: With Special Reference to Scholasticism* (Edinburgh: Edinburgh University Press, 1990); Terry Eagleton, Edward W. Said, and Seamus Deane, *Nationalism, Colonialism, and Literature* (Minneapolis: University of Minnesota Press, 1990); Mary Louise Pratt, *Imperial Eyes: Travel Writing and Transculturation* (London: Routledge, 1992); Ann Stoler, *Race and the Education of Desire: Foucault's History of Sexuality and the Colonial Order of Things* (Durham: Duke University Press Books, 1995); Naoki Sakai, *Translation and Subjectivity: On Japan and Cultural Nationalism* (Minneapolis: University of Minnesota Press, 1997); Robert Bernasconi, "With What Must the Philosophy of World History Begin? On the Racial Basis of Hegel's Eurocentrism," *Nineteenth Century Contexts* 22 (2000): 171–202; George Saliba, *Islamic Science and the Making of the European Renaissance* (Cambridge: MIT Press, 2007); Gordon, *Creolizing Political Theory*; Timothy Brennan, *Borrowed Light: Vico, Hegel, and the Colonies* (Palo Alto: Stanford University Press, 2014); Samuel Moyn and Andrew Sartori, eds., *Global Intellectual History* (New York: Columbia University Press, 2015). There are of course many disagreements across these texts, and I return to some of them throughout this book. But what they all share is an understanding that the history of ideas is, in part, a history of their travels across political borders. I note especially the influence of Anghie and Van der Veer because they constituted the formative moments of this project many years ago when David Scott introduced me to the former book at the end of my undergraduate education and Kenneth Dean to the latter just after I graduated.

  28. David Scott, "Antinomies of Slavery, Enlightenment, and Universal History," *Small Axe: A Caribbean Journal of Criticism* 14, no. 3 33 (October 26, 2010): 154; emphasis added.

  29. Buck-Morss, *Hegel, Haiti and Universal History*; Brennan, *Borrowed Light*; George Ciccariello-Maher, *Decolonizing Dialectics* (Durham: Duke University Press Books, 2017).

  30. Such diffusionist thinking about conceptual history can be seen across the otherwise very exciting essays collected in Moyn and Sartori, *Global Intellectual History*.

  31. Ciccariello-Maher is also interested in the global spread of dialectical thought. The main difference is that what I am tracking in the movements of the dialectic are how these geographical origins are contested—something that is simply not his focus.

  32. Important works that show the power of deconstruction for postcolonial critique that I engage with here include Spivak, *A Critique of Postcolonial Reason*; Pheng

Cheah, *Spectral Nationality: Passages of Freedom from Kant to Postcolonial Literatures of Liberation* (New York: Columbia University Press, 2003). On the other side, several recent works have criticized deconstruction in the name of a renewed dialectics: Brennan, *Borrowed Light*; Ciccariello-Maher, *Decolonizing Dialectics*. One can see this debate play out in the context mentioned here in David Kazanjian's review of Buck-Morss's book: David Kazanjian, "Hegel, Liberia," *Diacritics* 40, no. 1 (2010): 6–28.

33. Linda Martín Alcoff, "Philosophy, the Conquest, and the Meaning of Modernity: A Commentary on 'Anti-Cartesian Meditations: On the Origin of the Philosophical Anti-Discourse of Modernity' by Enrique Dussel," *Human Architecture* 11, no. 1 (Fall 2013): 61–65.

34. This is something that I think escapes even many postcolonial critics. Spivak's most recent work, for example, ignores the global aspect of Schiller's thought. Dipesh Chakrabarty's important work on Marx, Heidegger, and the postcolonial sidesteps an engagement with these thinkers' own global thought. Pheng Cheah's philosophically rich studies of postcolonial literature tend to present philosophy as a purely abstract enterprise, unrelated to these moments of representation. And though Akeel Bilgrami calls on us to consult the ontologies of non-European thinkers, he still presumes that these engagements would be sudden and unique future engagements of thought. Spivak, *An Aesthetic Education in the Era of Globalization*; Chakrabarty, *Provincializing Europe*; Cheah, *Spectral Nationality*; Akeel Bilgrami, *Secularism, Identity, and Enchantment* (Cambridge: Harvard University Press, 2014). For an exception in Cheah, see Pheng Cheah, "The Material World of Comparison," *New Literary History* 40, no. 3 (2009): 523–45.

35. Said, *Orientalism*. As I noted above, a line of constitutive criticism can also be traced from Said, especially his later *Culture and Imperialism* (New York: Knopf, 1993). This lineage is claimed by Anghie, *Imperialism, Sovereignty, and the Making of International Law*; van der Veer, *Imperial Encounters*.

36. Spivak, *A Critique of Postcolonial Reason*.

37. Judith Butler, *Parting Ways: Jewishness and the Critique of Zionism* (New York: Columbia University Press, 2013); Brennan, *Borrowed Light*; Amy Allen, *The End of Progress: Decolonizing the Normative Foundations of Critical Theory* (New York: Columbia University Press, 2016). Allen's work is somewhere between reconstitution and resources. She writes, for example, "Adorno and Foucault, for all their faults and their own tendencies toward Eurocentrism and their blindness to issues of colonialism and imperialism, nevertheless offer important resources within the tradition of critical theory for the crucially important project of decolonizing critical theory" (201). But she also joins the constitutive school with an important acknowledgement that the idea of "progress" that she criticizes was formed in colonial encounters (18–23). On the concept of resources, see also the work of François Jullien, which I discuss further in chapter 2: François Jullien, *On the Universal: The Uniform, the Common and Dialogue between Cultures*, trans. Michael Richardson and Fijalkowski Krzysztof (Cambridge: Polity, 2014).

38. I take the phrase "rummaging" in intellectual history from Stanley Cavell. The implied idea is that we are not adding something to the texts, but recovering what has always been there but has been discarded by the criticism. Stanley Cavell, *The Claim of Reason: Wittgenstein, Skepticism, Morality, and Tragedy* (New York: Oxford University Press, 1979), 467.

39. Agamben writes at the end of *The State of Exception*, for example: "The only [*soltanto*] truly political action, however, is that which severs the nexus between violence and law. And only [*soltanto*] beginning from the space thus opened will it be possible to pose the question of a possible use of law after the deactivation of the device that, in the state of exception, tied it to life." He derives this claim from a reading of modern Europe's inheritance of Roman law. But to speak of the "only truly political action" as one based on this genealogy is to fail to understand that the modern world was made by more than this inheritance. Giorgio Agamben, *State of Exception*, trans. Kevin Attell (Chicago: University of Chicago Press, 2005), 88; Giorgio Agamben, *Stato Di Eccezione* (Torino: Bollati Boringhieri, 2003), 112–13.

40. Van der Veer is referencing Taylor's work here, albeit quite briefly. van der Veer, *Imperial Encounters*, 160.

41. Michel Foucault, *The Hermeneutics of the Subject: Lectures at the Collège de France, 1981–1982*, trans. Graham Burchell (New York: Palgrave-Macmillan, 2005), 14; Michel Foucault, *L'herméneutique du sujet: Cours au Collège de France, 1981–1982* (Seuil/Gallimard, 2001), 15.

42. Foucault, *The Hermeneutics of the Subject*, 15; Foucault, *L'herméneutique du sujet: Cours au Collège de France, 1981–1982*, 16.

43. Foucault, *The Hermeneutics of the Subject*, 14–17; Foucault, *L'herméneutique du sujet: Cours au Collège de France, 1981–1982*, 15–19.

44. Foucault, *The Hermeneutics of the Subject*, 251–52; Foucault, *L'herméneutique du sujet: Cours au Collège de France, 1981–1982*, 241.

45. Foucault, *The History of Sexuality, Volume 1: An Introduction*, 82; Foucault, *L'histoire de la sexualité*, 1:109.

46. Foucault, *The History of Sexuality, Volume 1: An Introduction*, 89; Foucault, *L'histoire de La Sexualité*, 1:118.

47. Foucault, *The Hermeneutics of the Subject*, 252; For Foucault's reflections on the continuity of his work, see Foucault, *The Government of Self and Others*, 3–5; Foucault, *L'herméneutique du sujet: Cours au Collège de France, 1981–1982*, 241–42; Foucault, *Le Gouvernement de Soi et Des Autres: Cours Au Collège de France, 1982–1983*, 3–5.

48. Foucault, *The Hermeneutics of the Subject*, 253; Foucault, *L'herméneutique du sujet: Cours au Collège de France, 1981–1982*, 243.

49. "The question . . . would be: how can the indivisibility of knowledge and power in the context of interaction and multiple strategies induce both singularities, fixed according to their conditions of acceptability, and a field of possibles, of

openings, indecisions, reversals, and possible dislocations which make them fragile, temporary . . . ?" Michel Foucault, "What Is Critique?," in *The Politics of Truth*, ed. Sylvere Lotringer (Los Angeles: Semiotext, 2007), 66; Michel Foucault, "Qu'est-Ce Que La Critique? (Critique et Aufklärung)," *Bulletin de La Société Française de Philosophie* 84, no. 2 (1990): 52–53.

50. Foucault, *The Order of Things*, xv; Foucault, *Les Mots et Les Choses: Une Archéologie Des Sciences Humaines*, 7.

51. Stoler, *Race and the Education of Desire*, 5.

52. See, for example: Bernal, *Black Athena*; Bernasconi, "With What Must the Philosophy of World History Begin?"; Peter K. J. Park, *Africa, Asia, and the History of Philosophy: Racism in the Formation of the Philosophical Canon, 1780–1830* (Albany: State University of New York Press, 2014).

53. Foucault, *The Birth of Biopolitics*, 56; Foucault, *Naissance de La Biopolitique: Cours Au Collège de France, 1978–1979*, 57–58.

54. For some of the debates around these moments, see Michel Foucault, "Michel Foucault and Zen," in *Religion and Culture*, ed. Jeremy Carrette (New York: Taylor & Francis, 1999), 110–14; Naoki Sakai and Jon Solomon, "Introduction: Addressing the Multitude of Foreigners, Echoing Foucault," in *Translation, Biopolitics, Colonial Difference* (Hong Kong: Hong Kong University Press, 2006), 1–36; Behrooz Ghamari-Tabrizi, *Foucault in Iran: Islamic Revolution after the Enlightenment* (Minneapolis: University of Minnesota Press, 2016); Janet Afary and Kevin Anderson, *Foucault and the Iranian Revolution: Gender and the Seductions of Islamism* (Chicago: University of Chicago Press, 2005).

55. Cited in Afary and Anderson, *Foucault and the Iranian Revolution*, 203; my emphasis.

56. Foucault, "Foucault and Zen," 113; Foucault, "Michel Foucault and Zen," 113; Michel Foucault, *Dits et Écrits, 1954–1988*, vol. 3 (Paris: Gallimard, 1994), 622–23.

57. It is of course fair to point out that while I am focusing on the question of the globe, I am myself ignoring some of the other issues that Foucault's work brings up, especially the importance of his late work for feminist politics. I would ultimately hope to stress the connectivity of these issues and the fact that there can be no practices of the global self that are not attuned to issues of race, class, gender, and other historically constituted differences. I do address these concerns at various points in the book, especially when considering the essays of bell hooks. For a strong reading of Foucault's use for feminism, see Amy Allen, *The Politics of Our Selves: Power, Autonomy, and Gender in Contemporary Critical Theory* (New York: Columbia University Press, 2007).

58. Judith Butler, *Precarious Life: The Powers of Mourning and Violence* (New York: Verso, 2004), xii–xiii.

59. Butler, *Precarious Life*, xiii.

60. Judith Butler, *Giving an Account of Oneself* (New York: Fordham University Press, 2005), 22–26, 111–136.

61. Butler, *Giving an Account of Oneself*, 131.

62. Foucault, *The Hermeneutics of the Subject*, 252.

63. Wendy Brown's recent work on neoliberalism challenges the idea that the development of practices of the self are even possible to develop in our contemporary world. "No longer is there an open question of how to craft the self or what paths to travel in life," Brown writes in light of her claim that a neoliberal rationality has "vanquished" all other forms of the modern self. But while it is certainly true that our self-transformations must now *contend* with economic rationality, it is simply untenable to claim that it has defeated all other modes of self-making. Indeed, if that were the case, Brown's book itself would have been impossible to write. The framework of radical pluralism developed here is intended to refute such totalizing analyses. Wendy Brown, *Undoing the Demos: Neoliberalism's Stealth Revolution* (New York: Zone Books, 2015), 41. The argument is repeated and extended at 107–111.

64. See, for example, the overview in Jorge Cañizares-Esguerra, *How to Write the History of the New World: Histories, Epistemologies, and Identities in the Eighteenth-Century Atlantic World* (Palo Alto: Stanford University Press, 2002), chapter 2.

65. There are of course a great many debates about liberalism and empire. See, for example, Uday Mehta, *Liberalism and Empire: A Study in Nineteenth-Century British Liberal Thought* (Chicago: University of Chicago Press, 1999); Jennifer Pitts, *A Turn to Empire: The Rise of Imperial Liberalism in Britain and France* (Princeton: Princeton University Press, 2006); Andrew Sartori, *Liberalism in Empire: An Alternative History* (Berkeley: University of California Press, 2014); Lowe, *The Intimacies of Four Continents*; Jeremy Adelman, *Earth Hunger: Markets, Resources and the Need for Strangers* (Princeton: Princeton University Press, forthcoming).

66. Peter Linebaugh and Marcus Rediker, *The Many-Headed Hydra: Sailors, Slaves, Commoners, and the Hidden History of the Revolutionary Atlantic* (Boston: Beacon Press, 2013), 135.

67. I want to acknowledge again the tremendous diligence of Anna Leader in tracking down and checking all of these citations. For an ambivalent take on how global English has become the lingua franca of global history, see Jeremy Adelman, "Is Global History Still Possible, or Has It Had Its Moment?," Aeon, March 2017, https://aeon.co/essays/is-global-history-still-possible-or-has-it-had-its-moment.

68. Hazel Carby, "The Souls of Black Men," in *Next to the Color Line: Gender, Sexuality, and W. E. B. Du Bois*, ed. Susan Gillman and Alys Weinbaum (Minneapolis: University of Minnesota Press, 2007), 236.

69. I have been helped in articulating this point by the "self-fashioning" via a "feminist reading" of Henry David Thoreau (in spite of Thoreau's supposed ultra-masculine pretensions) in Laura Dassow Walls, "'Walden' as Feminist Manifesto," *Interdisciplinary Studies in Literature and Environment* 1, no. 1 (1993): 137–44.

70. I am especially interested here in "practices of the global self" that appear in writings beyond my focus here. There are many examples of these writings, such as Chakrabarty, *Provincializing Europe*, 117–148 (the phrase "practices of the self" can be found at 148); the analysis of the zombi in Joan Dayan, *Haiti, History, and the Gods* (Berkeley: University of California Press, 1998), 34–38; the idea of "world enlargement" in Epeli Hau'ofa, "Our Sea of Islands," *The Contemporary Pacific* 6, no. 1 (Spring 1994): 147–61; the double bind of subjecthood explored in Saidiya Hartman, *Scenes of Subjection: Terror, Slavery, and Self-Making in Nineteenth-Century America* (New York: Oxford University Press, 1997); and the brief suggestion in Veena Das, *Life and Words: Violence and the Descent into the Ordinary* (Berkeley: University of California Press, 2007), 221.

71. Wilson Harris, "The Frontier on Which 'Heart of Darkness' Stands," *Research in African Literatures* 12, no. 1 (1981): 86.

72. Emerson, *Essays & Poems*, 581.

73. Stanley Cavell, *Pursuits of Happiness: The Hollywood Comedy of Remarriage* (Cambridge: Harvard University Press, 1981), 28.

Chapter 1

1. Freire puts justice at the heart of critical consciousness in a way that remains only implicit in Montaigne. Paolo Freire, *Pedagogy of the Oppressed*, trans. Myra Bergman Ramos (New York: Seabury, 1970), 58.

2. Michel de Montaigne, *The Complete Essays of Montaigne*, trans. Donald Frame (Palo Alto: Stanford University Press, 1958), 110; Michel de Montaigne, *Les essais de Michel de Montaigne*, ed. Pierre Villey and V.-L. Saulnier (Paris: Presses Universitaires de France, 1965), 150.

3. On Montaigne's relation to the idea of the "practice of the self," see R. Lanier Anderson and Joshua Landy, "Philosophy as Self-Fashioning: Alexander Nehamas's Art of Living," *Diacritics* 31, no. 1 (April 1, 2001): 25–54; Pierre Force, "Montaigne and the Coherence of Eclecticism," *Journal of the History of Ideas* 70, no. 4 (2009): 523–44; Alexander Nehamas, *The Art of Living: Socratic Reflections from Plato to Foucault* (Berkeley: University of California Press, 1998). The term, as noted above, comes from the late lectures of Michel Foucault. Foucault argues that though Montaigne's work should be read within the Hellenic tradition of self-transformation, he does not believe a single author like Montaigne can overcome the force of the loss of these practices in modernity. My reply throughout this book is that Montaigne is in fact part of a new modern tradition that transforms the practices of the individual self into practices of the global self. Foucault, *The Hermeneutics of the Subject*, 251–52. For two masterly works on Montaigne's ideas about self-transformation in a more local sense, see Lawrence D. Kritzman, *The*

Fabulous Imagination: On Montaigne's Essays (New York: Columbia University Press, 2012); Jean Starobinski, *Montaigne in Motion*, trans. Arthur Goldhammer (Chicago: University of Chicago Press, 2009).

    4. Montaigne, *The Complete Essays of Montaigne*, 850–51; Montaigne, *Les essais de Michel de Montaigne*, 1108.

    5. Montaigne, *The Complete Essays of Montaigne*, 177–78; Montaigne, *Les essais de Michel de Montaigne*, 241.

    6. Montaigne, *The Complete Essays of Montaigne*, 112; Montaigne, *Les essais de Michel de Montaigne*, 153.

    7. The essay has had many, many readers. Some recent influential accounts include Michel de Certeau, *Heterologies: Discourse on the Other*, trans. Brian Massumi (Minneapolis: University of Minnesota Press, 1986), 67–79; Eric Cheyfitz, *The Poetics of Imperialism: Translation and Colonization from the Tempest to Tarzan* (Philadelphia: University of Pennsylvania Press, 1997), 142–72; Stephen Greenblatt, *Marvelous Possessions: The Wonder of the New World* (Chicago: University of Chicago Press, 1991), 146–50; George Hoffmann, "Anatomy of the Mass: Montaigne's 'Cannibals,' " *PMLA* 117 (2002): 207–21; Muthu, *Enlightenment against Empire*, 14–23; Tzvetan Todorov, *On Human Diversity: Nationalism, Racism, and Exoticism in French Thought*, trans. Catherine Porter (Cambridge: Harvard University Press, 1993), 39–43. There is also a helpful recent collection of essays edited by Philippe Desan, *Montaigne Studies* 22, no. 1–2 (2010). De Certeau's reading is the one that most focuses on Montaigne's self-transformation as fundamental to his writing practice. A critical and I think mistaken reading, Muthu's, receives some attention below. Hoffmann is unique in attempting to downplay the international question and viewing Montaigne's essay as in fact a reflection on contemporary religious politics in France.

    8. Montaigne, *The Complete Essays of Montaigne*, 852; Montaigne, *Les essais de Michel de Montaigne*, 1110.

    9. Emerson, *Essays & Poems*, 403.

    10. Montaigne, *The Complete Essays of Montaigne*, 150, 390; Montaigne, *Les essais de Michel de Montaigne*, 202, 525.

    11. Emerson, *Essays & Poems*, 414.

    12. Cited in Pierluigi Donini, "The History of the Concept of Eclecticism," in *The Question of "Eclecticism": Studies in Later Greek Philosophy*, ed. John M. Dillon and Anthony A. Long (Berkeley: University of California Press, 1996). On the relation to Montaigne, see Force, "Montaigne and the Coherence of Eclecticism."

    13. Emerson, *Essays & Poems*, 694–96.

    14. As Philippe Desan expresses it: "The New World becomes a space where everything is possible, a space of fantasies that authorize the boldest and most improbable comparisons. This liberation of the spirit enables a questioning of the Old World." Philippe Desan, " 'Il est des peuples où . . .': Montaigne et le Nouveau Monde," *Montaigne Studies* 22, no. 1–2 (2010): 4.

    15. Montaigne, *The Complete Essays of Montaigne*, 215; Montaigne, *Les essais de Michel de Montaigne*, 296.

16. Montaigne, *The Complete Essays of Montaigne*, 824; Montaigne, *Les essais de Michel de Montaigne*, 1076.

17. Montaigne, *The Complete Essays of Montaigne*, 150; Montaigne, *Les essais de Michel de Montaigne*, 202.

18. For a beautiful reading of the process of coming to truth (and its limits) in Montaigne, see Starobinski, *Montaigne in Motion*, 67–88.

19. Reason is mixed up with chance as well: "But if you take it rightly, it seems that our counsels and deliberations depend just as much on Fortune, and that she involves our reason also in her confusion and uncertainty. 'We reason rashly and inconsiderately,' says Timaeus in Plato, 'because, like ourselves, our reason has in it a large element of chance.'" Montaigne, *The Complete Essays of Montaigne*, 209; Montaigne, *Les essais de Michel de Montaigne*, 286.

20. Montaigne, *The Complete Essays of Montaigne*, 151; Montaigne, *Les essais de Michel de Montaigne*, 203.

21. Montaigne, *The Complete Essays of Montaigne*, 153; Montaigne, *Les essais de Michel de Montaigne*, 206.

22. Montaigne, *The Complete Essays of Montaigne*, 695; Montaigne, *Les essais de Michel de Montaigne*, 910.

23. Montaigne, *The Complete Essays of Montaigne*, 849; Montaigne, *Les essais de Michel de Montaigne*, 1107.

24. Montaigne, *The Complete Essays of Montaigne*, 150, 151; Montaigne, *Les essais de Michel de Montaigne*, 203, 204.

25. For an account of the importance of the Flood story in relation to Montaigne's religious context, see Hoffmann, "Anatomy of the Mass."

26. Peter Linebaugh and Marcus Rediker have also pointed out the brutal extent to which nascent capitalists, like the lords of Carthage, quashed the hopes for "alternatives" that the global commons offered. Linebaugh and Rediker, *The Many-Headed Hydra*, 20–26.

27. In "Of Coaches," Montaigne will also come to wish that antiquity *had* known about these lands, for they perhaps might have realized the hopes rather than destruction. Montaigne, *The Complete Essays of Montaigne*, 684–85.

28. On Léry's influence, see Lison Baselis-Bitoun, "Jean de Léry, Précurseur de Montaigne," *Montaigne Studies* 22, no. 1–2 (2010).

29. Montaigne, *The Complete Essays of Montaigne*, 152; Montaigne, *Les essais de Michel de Montaigne*, 205.

30. Montaigne, *The Complete Essays of Montaigne*, 152; Montaigne, *Les essais de Michel de Montaigne*, 205.

31. Greenblatt, *Marvelous Possessions*, 148.

32. Ibid., 150.

33. Montaigne, *The Complete Essays of Montaigne*, 80; Montaigne, *Les essais de Michel de Montaigne*, 112.

34. Montaigne, *The Complete Essays of Montaigne*, 829; Montaigne, *Les essais de Michel de Montaigne*, 1082.

35. Montaigne, *The Complete Essays of Montaigne*, 828; Montaigne, *Les essais de Michel de Montaigne*, 1081.

36. Montaigne, *The Complete Essays of Montaigne*, 829; Montaigne, *Les essais de Michel de Montaigne*, 1081.

37. Montaigne, *The Complete Essays of Montaigne*, 152; Montaigne, *Les essais de Michel de Montaigne*, 205.

38. Montaigne, *The Complete Essays of Montaigne*, 152; Montaigne, *Les essais de Michel de Montaigne*, 205.

39. *Oxford English Dictionary*, s.v. "barbarous (*adj.*)," December 2014, http://www.oed.com.proxy.libraries.rutgers.edu/view/Entry/15397.

40. Anthony Pagden, *The Fall of Natural Man: The American Indian and the Origins of Comparative Ethnology* (New York: Cambridge University Press, 1982), 15. Pagden goes on to argue that not speaking Greek specifically meant being excluded from the Greek polis, which was defined as the only space in which rational thought was said to occur (15–26).

41. Joachim du Bellay, *Joachim Du Bellay: "The Regrets," with "The Antiquities of Rome," Three Latin Elegies, and "The Defense and Enrichment of the French Language." A Bilingual Edition* (Philadelphia: University of Pennsylvania Press, 2006), 324.

42. Stanley Cavell, *The Senses of Walden* (Chicago: University of Chicago Press, 1992), 66.

43. Ibid., 67.

44. Montaigne, *The Complete Essays of Montaigne*, 152; Montaigne, *Les essais de Michel de Montaigne*, 205.

45. Erich Auerbach underscores this point as well: "nothing is further from his method than isolating his subject in any manner, than detaching it from the accidental conditions and circumstances in which it is found at a particular moment, in order to arrive at its real, permanent, and absolute essence." Auerbach, *Mimesis*, 299. Sankar Muthu does not: "Indeed . . . it only 'seems' as if we have no other standard of truth than our own customs." Muthu's argument that Montaigne believes in some eternal standard of truth is simply incorrect. *Enlightenment against Empire*, 21.

46. Montaigne, *The Complete Essays of Montaigne*, 152; Montaigne, *Les essais de Michel de Montaigne*, 205.

47. Montaigne, *The Complete Essays of Montaigne*, 153; Montaigne, *Les essais de Michel de Montaigne*, 206.

48. Montaigne, *The Complete Essays of Montaigne*, 158; Montaigne, *Les essais de Michel de Montaigne*, 213.

49. Margaret T. Hodgen, "Montaigne and Shakespeare Again," *Huntington Library Quarterly* 16, no. 1 (November 1, 1952): 29.

50. For a history of other European attempts to understand the practice and the various peoples it was associated with, see Frank Lestringant, *Cannibals: The Discovery and Representation of the Cannibal from Columbus to Jules Verne*, trans. Rosemary Morris (Berkeley: University of California Press, 1997). For a sophisti-

cated and nonromanticized contemporary account of the ontological foundations of cannibalism in the Arawaté (a Tupi-Guarani people), which is somewhat critical of Montaigne, see the works of Eduardo Viveiros de Castro, *The Inconstancy of the Indian soul: The Encounter of Catholics and Cannibals in 16th-Century Brazil* (Chicago: Prickly Paradigm Press, 2011), and *From the Enemy's Point of View: Humanity and Divinity in an Amazonian Society* (Chicago: University of Chicago Press, 1992), 273–308.

51. Montaigne, *The Complete Essays of Montaigne*, 155; Montaigne, *Les essais de Michel de Montaigne*, 209.

52. Montaigne, *The Complete Essays of Montaigne*, 159; Montaigne, *Les essais de Michel de Montaigne*, 213.

53. Hoffmann, "Anatomy of the Mass," 208–10.

54. Montaigne, *The Complete Essays of Montaigne*, 159; Montaigne, *Les essais de Michel de Montaigne*, 214.

55. Montaigne, *The Complete Essays of Montaigne*, 159; Montaigne, *Les essais de Michel de Montaigne*, 214.

56. Montaigne, *The Complete Essays of Montaigne*, 115; Montaigne, *Les essais de Michel de Montaigne*, 156–57.

57. Montaigne, *The Complete Essays of Montaigne*, 131; Montaigne, *Les essais de Michel de Montaigne*, 177.

58. Muthu, *Enlightenment against Empire*, 257.

59. Ibid., 23.

60. Ibid., 19.

61. Montaigne, *The Complete Essays of Montaigne*, 332; Montaigne, *Les essais de Michel de Montaigne*, 454–55.

62. Jean-Jacques Rousseau, *Basic Political Writings*, trans. Donald Cress (Indianapolis: Hackett Publishing, 1987), 54; Jean-Jacques Rousseau, *Œuvres complètes*, ed. Bernard Gagnebin and Marcel Raymond, vol. 3 (Paris: Gallimard, 1964), 156.

63. Eduardo Viveiros de Castro, "Cannibal Metaphysics," trans. Peter Skafish, *Radical Philosophy* 182 (December 2013): 18.

64. See, for example, Viveiros de Castro, "Cosmological Deixis and Amerindian Perspectivism."

65. Muthu, *Enlightenment against Empire*, 232.

66. Castro, *The Inconstancy of the Indian Soul*, 60.

67. Philippe Descola, "Beyond Nature and Culture," *Proceedings of the British Academy* 139 (2006): 137–55; Saba Mahmood, *Politics of Piety: The Islamic Revival and the Feminist Subject* (Princeton: Princeton University Press, 2005), 153; Ichikawa Hakugen, "A Preliminary Conception of Zen Social Ethics," *Journal of Indian and Buddhist Studies* 11, no. 1 (1963): 359–48 (page numbers go in reverse direction, perhaps because this is an English-language article in a Japanese journal); Mohandas Gandhi, *Mahatma Gandhi: The Essential Writings*, ed. Judith Brown (Oxford; New York: Oxford University Press, 2008), 56.

68. James C. Scott, *Weapons of the Weak: Everyday Forms of Peasant Resistance* (New Haven: Yale University Press, 1985), 180, 310; Partha Chatterjee, *Our Modernity* (Rotterdam and Dakar: SEPHIS and CODESRIA, 1997); Frantz Fanon, *Black Skin, White Masks*, trans. Richard Philcox (New York: Grove Press, 2008), 100–19.

69. Eduardo Gudynas, "Buen Vivir: Today's Tomorrow," *Development* 54, no. 4 (December 2011): 441–47.

70. James C. Scott, *The Art of Not Being Governed: An Anarchist History of Upland Southeast Asia* (New Haven: Yale University Press, 2009), 8, 172–74, 237.

71. Richard Bernstein, "Pragmatism, Pluralism, and the Healing of Wounds," in *Pragmatism: A Reader*, ed. Louis Menand (New York: Vintage, 1997), 397.

72. Montaigne, *The Complete Essays of Montaigne*, 158; Montaigne, *Les essais de Michel de Montaigne*, 212–13.

73. Auerbach, *Mimesis*, 311.

74. Charles Taylor, *Sources of the Self: The Making of the Modern Identity* (Cambridge: Cambridge University Press, 1989), x.

75. Ibid., 111.

76. Ibid., 185.

77. Cornel West, *The American Evasion of Philosophy: A Genealogy of Pragmatism* (Madison: University of Wisconsin Press, 1989), 36.

78. Ibid., 10.

79. The mood is well described by Hannah Arendt as an effect of the rise of the private realm: "The presence of others who see what we see and hear what we hear assures us of the reality of the world and ourselves, and while the intimacy of a fully developed private life, such as had never been known before the rise of the modern age and the concomitant decline of the public realm, will always greatly intensify and enrich the whole scale of subjective emotions and private feelings, this intensification will always come to pass at the expense of the assurance of the reality of the world and men." What I am suggesting here is that it is not only the rise of the private that is to blame, but also the choice to privatize one's life as a way of avoiding the burden of global engagement. Arendt, *The Human Condition*, 50.

80. Critical ideas of evasion appear, for example, in Emmanuel Levinas, *On Escape/De l'évasion*, trans. Bettina Bergo (Stanford: Stanford University Press, 2003); Stefano Harney and Fred Moten, *The Undercommons: Fugitive Planning & Black Study* (Minor Compositions, 2013).

81. René Descartes, *Discourse on Method; and, Meditations on First Philosophy*, trans. Donald Cress (Indianapolis: Hackett Publishing, 1998), 2–3; translation modified; René Descartes, *Discours de la méthode*, ed. Étienne Gilson (Paris: Librairie philosophique J. Vrin, 1925), 4.

82. Descartes, *Discourse on Method*, 17.

83. Benjamin Franklin, *The Autobiography of Benjamin Franklin* (Mineola: Dover, 1996), 65.

84. Descartes, *Discourse on Method*, 5; Descartes, *Discours de la méthode*, 9.

85. Descartes, *Discourse on Method*, 6; Descartes, *Discours de la méthode*, 10.

86. Descartes, *Discourse on Method*, 7; Descartes, *Discours de la méthode*, 12.

87. I have amended the translation and capitalized Cannibals here because it is in the original. This more closely resembles the parallel structure: "des Français ou des Allemands . . . des Chinois ou des Cannibales." "Cannibals," it should be remembered, were originally named after the Carib peoples whom Columbus recorded in his diary and were originally written about as a group of people and only later as a modality. On this history see Lestringant, *Cannibals*, 13–51.

88. Descartes, *Discourse on Method*, 9–10; Descartes, *Discours de la méthode*, 16.

89. A more developed account of this path in Descartes (with different but not unrelated aims) can be found in Ernest Gellner, *Reason and Culture: The Historic Role of Rationality and Rationalism* (Cambridge, MA: Basil Blackwell, 1992), 1–13.

90. Descartes, *Discourse on Method*, 13; Descartes, *Discours de la méthode*, 22–23.

91. Descartes, *Discourse on Method*, 15; Descartes, *Discours de la méthode*, 26.

92. Foucault, *The Hermeneutics of the Subject*, 190, 294.

93. Michel Foucault, *History of Madness*, trans. Jonathan Murphy and Jean Khalfa (New York: Routledge, 2006), 47.

94. Ibid., 47.

95. Whether or not Descartes himself believed in such a dualism is not the current scholarly position. For a critique of Dussel on these grounds, see Diego Soto Morera, "Crítica de La Razón Corporal: Dussel y Las Meditaciones Anti-Cartesianas," *Tabula Rasa*, no. 26 (June 2017): 141–69.

96. Enrique Dussel, *The Invention of the Americas: Eclipse of "the Other" and the Myth of Modernity*, trans. Michael D. Barber (New York: Continuum, 1995), 43.

97. Nelson Maldonado-Torres, "On the Coloniality of Being: Contributions to the Development of a Concept," *Cultural Studies* 21, no. 2–3 (2007): 244–45.

98. Enrique Dussel, "Anti-Cartesian Meditations: On the Origins of the Philosophical Anti-Discourse of Modernity," trans. George Ciccariello-Maher, *Journal of Cultural and Religious Theory* 13, no. 1 (2014): 35.

99. Alcoff, "Philosophy, the Conquest, and the Meaning of Modernity," 61.

100. Sanjay Subrahmanyam, "On World Historians in the Sixteenth Century," *Representations* 91, no. 1 (August 2005): 26–57.

101. Alcoff, "Philosophy, the Conquest, and the Meaning of Modernity," 65.

102. Dussel's later essay does consider the historical context of Descartes's reading, focusing especially on his engagement with Iberian Jesuit philosophers. He does not yet, however, engage the specific remarks on other cultures in Descartes's own text.

103. It is also entirely possible that Descartes makes explicit claims about this in other works with which I am unfamiliar.

104. William Shakespeare, "Hamlet," in *The Norton Shakespeare*, ed. Stephen Greenblatt (New York: W. W. Norton, 1997), II.II.243–50.

105. Ibid., V.I.155–56.

106. Ibid., V.I.250–1.

107. Ibid., V.II.346.
108. Ibid., V.II.353–4.
109. Ibid., V.II.381.
110. Sophocles, *Sophocles I: Oedipus the King, Oedipus at Colonus, Antigone*, trans. David Grene (Chicago: University of Chicago Press, 1991), 79.
111. For an exception, see Margreta De Grazia, *Hamlet without Hamlet* (New York: Cambridge University Press, 2007), chapter 3.
112. Oswald de Andrade, "Cannibalist Manifesto," trans. Leslie Bary, *Latin American Literary Review* 19, no. 38 (July 1, 1991): 38; in English in original.
113. The only qualification is that "'primitive phenomena' are often less hidden and complicated by extensive self-interpretation." In other words, the point of engaging other cultures is not to think about the diversity of human thinking and feeling; it is to use their lives to develop a theory that is then handed back to them as a universal truth. Martin Heidegger, *Being and Time: A Translation of Sein Und Zeit*, trans. Joan Stambaugh (Albany: State University of New York Press, 1996), 47; Martin Heidegger, *Gesamtausgabe*, vol. 2 (Frankfurt am Main: Vittorio Klostermann, 1977), 68.
114. Heidegger, *Being and Time*, 48; Heidegger, *Gesamtausgabe*, 2:69.
115. Heidegger, *Being and Time*, 164; Heidegger, *Gesamtausgabe*, 2:233.
116. Heidegger, *Being and Time*, 166; Heidegger, *Gesamtausgabe*, 2:236.
117. Heidegger, *Being and Time*, 341–45; Heidegger, *Gesamtausgabe*, 2:492–98.
118. Heidegger, *Being and Time*, 20; Heidegger, *Gesamtausgabe*, 2:31.
119. See Peter Warnek, "The History of Being," in *Martin Heidegger: Key Concepts*, ed. Bret W. Davis (Durham: Acumen Publishing, 2010), 166.
120. Martin Heidegger, "Der Spiegel Interview with Martin Heidegger," in *The Heidegger Reader*, ed. Gunter Figal, trans. Jerome Veith (Bloomington: Indiana University Press, 2009), 331.
121. Contemporary critics who think overcoming "Cartesian dualism" will somehow automatically lead to better ways of being in the world ought to remember Heidegger's example—both in the academic sense that Descartes is more complex than this allows and in the political sense that there is no necessary relation between dualistic thinking and bad politics any more than there is between nondualist thinking and good politics. I have discussed some of these concerns with Dussel and others above. For an intriguing book that is insufficiently attuned to these problems, see Jason Moore, *Capitalism in the Web of Life* (New York: Verso, 2015).
122. Taylor, *Sources of the Self*, 143.

Chapter 2

1. Rousseau, *Basic Political Writings*, 34; emphasis in original; Rousseau, *Œuvres complètes*, 3:123–24.
2. Rousseau, *Basic Political Writings*, 38; Rousseau, *Œuvres complètes*, 3:132.

3. Rousseau, *Basic Political Writings*, 70; Rousseau, *Œuvres complètes*, 3:178.

4. This point is explored at great length with regard to the economy in David Graeber, *Debt: The First 5,000 Years* (Brooklyn: Melville House, 2012).

5. For some context on Rousseau's work in conjectural history, see Cañizares-Esguerra, *How to Write the History of the New World*, 44–51.

6. Rousseau, *Basic Political Writings*, 35, 38; Rousseau, *Œuvres complètes*, 3:125, 132.

7. Rousseau, *Basic Political Writings*, 39; Rousseau, *Œuvres complètes*, 3:133. Rousseau is in some sense here working toward an evolutionary biology. His point, however, is not that science will someday clarify what philosophy can only conjecture. Rather, it is that empirical observation and theoretical conjecture must go hand in hand. For a reading of Rousseau in relation to historical biology, see Robert Wokler, *Rousseau, the Age of Enlightenment, and Their Legacies*, ed. Bryan Garsten (Princeton: Princeton University Press, 2012), chapter 1.

8. Rousseau, *Basic Political Writings*, 45; Rousseau, *Œuvres complètes*, 3:142.

9. Rousseau, *Basic Political Writings*, 59; Rousseau, *Œuvres complètes*, 3:162.

10. David Graeber and David Wengrow have recently written a very interesting essay that questions how Rousseau is used to this day to justify the present order of society. They suggest that most people misread Rousseau by ignoring that his method was entirely conjectural. But this *also* misreads Rousseau and ignores his use of the ethnographic data. This continues to write the ways in which colonized peoples shaped modern thought out of our sense of intellectual history. I appreciate that they correct the record to show that human history was fraught and complex, and not so teleological as Rousseau and his followers imagined. But Rousseau's basic method—to combine research with conjecture and ethical argument—is more their own than they realize. David Graeber and David Wengrow, "How to Change the Course of Human History," *Eurozine* (blog), March 2, 2018, https://www.eurozine.com/change-course-human-history/.

11. Jean-Jacques Rousseau, *Rousseau: "The Discourses" and Other Early Political Writings*, ed. Victor Gourevitch (Cambridge: Cambridge University Press, 1997), 355e6–56e6; Frederick Neuhouser, *Rousseau's Critique of Inequality: Reconstructing the Second Discourse* (Cambridge: Cambridge University Press, 2014), 35.

12. Rousseau, *Basic Political Writings*, 38–39; Rousseau, *Œuvres complètes*, 3:133.

13. Descartes, *Discourse on Method; and, Meditations on First Philosophy*, 24.

14. Ibid., 24–31.

15. Ibid., 33.

16. Rousseau, *Basic Political Writings*, 65; Rousseau, *Œuvres complètes*, 3:171.

17. Rousseau, *Basic Political Writings*, 65; Rousseau, *Œuvres complètes*, 3:171.

18. For Muthu's critique of Rousseau, see Muthu, *Enlightenment against Empire*, 32–47.

19. That Rousseau's method required a transformation of self in relation to other, and that it required a repudiation of Cartesian philosophy, was a point underscored by Claude Lévi-Strauss: "To attain acceptance of oneself in others . . . one must

first deny the self in oneself. To Rousseau we owe the discovery of this principle, the only one on which to base the sciences of man. Yet it was to remain inaccessible and incomprehensible as long as there reigned a philosophy which, taking the Cogito as its point of departure, was imprisoned by the hypothetical evidences of the self . . . Descartes believes that he proceeds directly from a man's interiority to the exteriority of the world, without seeing that societies, civilizations—in other words, worlds of men—place themselves between these two extremes." Claude Lévi-Strauss, *Structural Anthropology, Volume 2*, trans. Monique Layton (Chicago: University of Chicago Press, 1983), 36. While appreciative of the general claims, I don't think Rousseau begins with a denial of self so much as an expansion of it, and Descartes, as I have argued, knows full well he is attempting to evade exteriority.

20. Rousseau, *Basic Political Writings*, 9; Rousseau, *Œuvres complètes*, 3:14.

21. Rousseau, *Basic Political Writings*, 21; Rousseau, *Œuvres complètes*, 3:30.

22. Montaigne, *The Complete Essays of Montaigne*, 105; Montaigne, *Les essais de Michel de Montaigne*, 143.

23. Rousseau, *Basic Political Writings*, 81; Rousseau, *Œuvres complètes*, 3:194.

24. Lévi-Strauss, *Structural Anthropology, Volume 2*, 34–35.

25. Rousseau, *Basic Political Writings*, 100n10; Rousseau, *Œuvres complètes*, 3:214n10.

26. Rousseau, *Basic Political Writings*, 99n10; Rousseau, *Œuvres complètes*, 3:212n10.

27. Rousseau, *Basic Political Writings*, 65; Rousseau, *Œuvres complètes*, 3:171.

28. Rousseau, *Basic Political Writings*, 107n16; Rousseau, *Œuvres complètes*, 3:220n16.

29. Rousseau, *Basic Political Writings*, 72; translation revised; Rousseau, *Œuvres complètes*, 3:181.

30. Rousseau, *Basic Political Writings*, 73; translation revised.; Rousseau, *Œuvres complètes*, 3:182.

31. Rousseau, *Basic Political Writings*, 60; Rousseau, *Œuvres complètes*, 3:164.

32. On the persistence of Locke's colonial fantasies into present understanding, see William M. Denevan, "The Pristine Myth: The Landscape of the Americas in 1492," *Annals of the Association of American Geographers* 82, no. 3 (1992): 369–85.

33. John Locke, *Political Writings* (New York: Mentor, 1993), V. 28, 37.

34. Jean-Jacques Rousseau, *Emile: Or, On Education*, trans. Allan Bloom (New York: Basic Books, 1979), 99; Jean-Jacques Rousseau, *Œuvres complètes*, Bernard Gagnebin and Marcel Raymond, vol. 4 (Paris: Gallimard, 1964), 332–33.

35. Rousseau, *Emile*, 98; Rousseau, *Œuvres complètes*, 4:330–31.

36. Rousseau, *Basic Political Writings*, 152; Rousseau, *Œuvres complètes*, 3:366.

37. Rousseau, *Basic Political Writings*, 153; Rousseau, *Œuvres complètes*, 3:367.

38. Rousseau, *Basic Political Writings*, 153; Rousseau, *Œuvres complètes*, 3:367.

39. Rousseau, *Basic Political Writings*, 171; Rousseau, *Œuvres complètes*, 3:393.

40. Rousseau, *Basic Political Writings*, 171; Rousseau, *Œuvres complètes*, 3:392.

41. Nelson Maldonado-Torres, "Rousseau and Fanon on Inequality and the Human Sciences," in *Creolizing Rousseau*, ed. Jane Anna Gordon and Neil Roberts (London: Rowman & Littlefield International, 2014), 133.

42. See Philip P. Boucher, *Cannibal Encounters: Europeans and Island Caribs, 1492–1763* (Baltimore: Johns Hopkins University Press, 1992); Stephan Lenik, "Carib as a Colonial Category: Comparing Ethnohistoric and Archaeological Evidence from Dominica, West Indies," *Ethnohistory* 59, no. 1 (January 1, 2012): 79–107.

43. Jean-Baptiste Du Tertre, "Concerning the Natives of the Antilles," trans. Marshall McKusick and Pierre Verin (New Haven: HRAF, 1958), 21, HTML file.

44. Ibid., 21.

45. Ibid., 21.

46. E. P. Thompson, *Customs in Common: Studies in Traditional Popular Culture* (New York: The New Press, 1993), 164. See pages 159–75 for Thompson's overview of this global process.

47. Rousseau, *Basic Political Writings*, 46. Rousseau repeats this point about foresight at 62 and 66. Rousseau, *Œuvres complètes*, 3:144, 167, 173.

48. Maldonado-Torres, "Rousseau and Fanon on Inequality and the Human Sciences," 133.

49. Robert Pippin, *Idealism as Modernism: Hegelian Variations* (Cambridge: Cambridge University Press, 1997), 93–94.

50. For an exception to this trend, see Mary Nyquist, *Arbitrary Rule: Slavery, Tyranny, and the Power of Life and Death* (Chicago: University of Chicago Press, 2013), esp. 257–92.

51. Taylor, *Sources of the Self*, 297.

52. Ibid., 359.

53. Ibid., 363.

54. Buck-Morss, *Hegel, Haiti and Universal History*; Brennan, *Borrowed Light*, especially 89–132; Andrew Cole, *The Birth of Theory* (Chicago: University of Chicago Press, 2014), 42–57; Ciccariello-Maher, *Decolonizing Dialectics*.

55. Buck-Morss, *Hegel, Haiti and Universal History*, 59–60.

56. Jean-Jacques Rousseau, *Reveries of the Solitary Walker* (New York: Penguin Books, 1979), 88; Jean-Jacques Rousseau, *Œuvres complètes*, ed. Bernard Gagnebin and Marcel Raymond, vol. 1 (Paris: Gallimard, 1964), 1046.

57. Rousseau, *Basic Political Writings*, 150; Rousseau, *Œuvres complètes*, 3:364.

58. Rousseau, *Basic Political Writings*, 151; Rousseau, *Œuvres complètes*, 3:364.

59. Rousseau, *Emile*, 205; Rousseau, *Œuvres complètes*, 4:484.

60. Michael Forster, "Hegel's Dialectical Method," in *The Cambridge Companion to Hegel*, ed. Frederick C. Beiser (New York: Cambridge University Press, 1993), 132.

61. Ernst Cassirer, *The Philosophy of the Enlightenment*, trans. Fritz C. A. Koelin and James Pettegrove (Boston: Beacon Press, 1955), 263; Jean Starobinski, *Jean-Jacques Rousseau, Transparency and Obstruction*, trans. Arthur Goldhammer (Chicago: University of Chicago Press, 1988), 206.

62. For general reflections on Rousseau's influence, see Ernst Cassirer, *Rousseau, Kant, Goethe: Two Essays* (New York: Harper & Row, 1963); Richard L. Velkley, *Being after Rousseau: Philosophy and Culture in Question* (Chicago: University of Chicago Press, 2002); Frederick Neuhouser, *Foundations of Hegel's Social Theory: Actualizing Freedom* (Cambridge: Harvard University Press, 2003).

63. Rousseau, *Emile*, 82–83; Rousseau, *Œuvres complètes*, 4:307–8.

64. Rousseau, *Reveries of the Solitary Walker*, 88–91; Rousseau, *Œuvres complètes*, 1:1046–49.

65. Rousseau, *Emile*, 411; Rousseau, *Œuvres complètes*, 4:771.

66. Lucius Annaeus Seneca, *Letters from a Stoic. Epistulae Morales Ad Lucilium*, trans. Robin Campbell (Harmondsworth: Penguin, 1969), 38; my emphasis.

67. Plato, *Ion, Hippias Minor, Laches, Protagoras: The Dialogues of Plato, Volume 3*, trans. Reginald E. Allen (New Haven: Yale University Press, 1996), 97.

68. Rousseau, *Basic Political Writings*, 40; Rousseau, *Œuvres complètes*, 3:135.

69. On this point, see the magisterial introduction: Allan Bloom, "Introduction," in *Emile: Or, On Education*, by Jean-Jacques Rousseau (New York: Basic Books, 1979). Bloom, however, ignores the global elements at play here.

70. It is not surprising that Bernard Stiegler, whose account of philosophy begins with the problem of this myth, should spend some time thinking about Rousseau's relationship to it. While critical of Rousseau's appropriation of the Carib, Stiegler's choice to maintain a singular ontology of human time does not account for the historical geography that we can see here. Bernard Stiegler, *Technics and Time, 1: The Fault of Epimetheus*, trans. Richard Beardsworth and George Collins (Stanford: Stanford University Press, 1998), 100–33.

71. "He was also an eager reader of all sorts of travel reports, and he—who never left Königsberg—. . . said he had no time to travel precisely because he wanted to know so much about so many countries." Hannah Arendt, *Lectures on Kant's Political Philosophy*, ed. Ronald Beiner (Chicago: University of Chicago Press, 1989), 44. Eze has questioned this claim more rigorously than Arendt: Emmanuel Chukwudi Eze, "The Color of Reason: The Idea of 'Race' in Kant's Anthropology," in *Postcolonial African Philosophy: A Critical Reader* (Cambridge: Blackwell, 1997), 127–30.

72. See James Tully, *Public Philosophy in a New Key: Volume 2, Imperialism and Civic Freedom* (Cambridge: Cambridge University Press, 2009), 15–18.

73. Actually, these are the notes recorded by one of the students in his anthropology lectures, but they accord clearly with Kant's general philosophy. Immanuel Kant, *Lectures on Anthropology*, trans. Robert B. Louden et al. (Cambridge: Cambridge University Press, 2013), 224. Kant citations will all be to the Cambridge editions, which include the pagination for the original German.

74. Emmanuel Eze's provocative account reignited research in this field. Eze, "The Color of Reason: The Idea of 'Race' in Kant's Anthropology." For a recent overview of the scholarship since, see Jon M. Mikkelsen, ed., *Kant and the Concept*

of Race: Late Eighteenth-Century Writings (Albany: State University of New York Press, 2014).

75. A powerful, detailed account of the racism of the Idealist tradition can be found in Peter Park, *Africa, Asia, and the History of Philosophy*. See also Jon M. Mikkelsen, "Translator's Introduction," in *Kant and the Concept of Race: Late Eighteenth-Century Writings*, ed. Jon M. Mikkelsen (Albany: State University of New York Press, 2014), 1–20.

76. Claude Lévi-Strauss, *Tristes Tropiques*, trans. John Weightman and Doreen Weightman (New York: Penguin Books, 1992), 392.

77. Cited in Cassirer, *Rousseau, Kant, Goethe*, 1–2.

78. Kant, *Practical Philosophy*, 51.

79. Ibid., 51.

80. Ibid., 51.

81. Immanuel Kant, *Anthropology, History, and Education*, ed. Robert B. Louden and Günter Zöller, trans. Mary Gregor et al. (Cambridge: Cambridge University Press, 2011), 171. For a synthetic reading of Kant in a broader context of this kind of teleological thinking, see the overview in M. H. Abrams, *Natural Supernaturalism: Tradition and Revolution in Romantic Literature* (New York: Norton, 1971), 204–6.

82. For a rich intellectual history of Kant and Herder's relationship, albeit one that mostly avoids some of the thornier political issues relating to race and global governance, see John H. Zammito, *Kant, Herder, and the Birth of Anthropology* (Chicago: University of Chicago Press, 2002).

83. Kant, *Anthropology, History, and Education*, 166.

84. Ibid., 166.

85. Kant, *Lectures on Anthropology*, 407.

86. Kant, *Anthropology, History, and Education*, 169; emphases in original.

87. Ibid., 170n. The governmental specifics of this form of global governance are nicely and quickly summarized in Tully, *Public Philosophy in a New Key*, 15–17.

88. Eze, "The Color of Reason: The Idea of 'Race' in Kant's Anthropology," 114.

89. Kant, *Anthropology, History, and Education*, 109. One might wonder if Kant would have come up with the same schema had the scientific models of his day been less mechanistic and determined. But Kant did have such a thought available in the Epicurean *clinamen*, and he explicitly rejects it in this essay. Ibid., 115.

90. Ibid., 118.

91. Adorno, *Notes to Literature, Volume 1*, 16.

92. Kant, *Anthropology, History, and Education*, 115.

93. Ibid., 111.

94. Ibid., 111–12.

95. Ibid., 112.

96. Immanuel Kant, *Religion within the Boundaries of Mere Reason and Other Writings*, ed. and trans. George Di Giovanni and Allen Wood (Cambridge: Cambridge University Press, 1998), 56.

97. One wonders if this duality might be a point at which to unravel, in a deconstructive fashion, Kant's presumptions about instinct. Kant himself, however, never takes this step and seems to believe that instinct in whatever direction is simply what is at the origins of humanity.

98. Kant, *Religion within the Boundaries of Mere Reason and Other Writings*, 108n. Whether or not this is an accurate reading of Hobbes—it does not appear to be—is not immediately my concern here.

99. See Reinhard Brandt, "The Guiding Idea of Kant's Anthropology and the Vocation of the Human Being," in *Essays on Kant's Anthropology*, by Brian Jacobs (Cambridge: Cambridge University Press, 2003), 96–97.

100. Kant, *Anthropology, History, and Education*, 112; emphasis in original.

101. Ibid., 113; emphasis in original. Herder responds: "Reverse the proposition: a man who needs a master is an animal; as soon as he becomes a human being, he no longer needs any actual master." Johann Gottfried Herder, *Another Philosophy of History and Selected Political Writings*, trans. Ioannis D. Evrigenis and Daniel Pellerin (Indianapolis: Hackett Publishing, 2004), 127.

102. Emerson, *Essays & Poems*, 488.

103. Kant, *Anthropology, History, and Education*, 114.

104. Ibid., 114.

105. Ibid., 115; my emphasis.

106. Ibid., 116; my emphasis, 116–18.

107. Pierre Clastres, *Society against the State: Essays in Political Anthropology*, trans. Robert Hurley and Abe Stein (Cambridge: Zone Books, 1989), 30.

108. Muthu, *Enlightenment against Empire*, 207.

109. Kant, *Practical Philosophy*, 451.

110. Muthu, *Enlightenment against Empire*, 208.

111. Kant, *Practical Philosophy*, 329; my emphasis.

112. Muthu has responded to a similar argument advanced by Thomas McCarthy by arguing that whatever Kant says is actually about hope for progress in spite of injustice. The aspect about hope is no doubt true, but the question is, *where* does Kant's hope come from? It comes, unequivocally, from a teleological vision of the federation of states. Sankar Muthu, "Commerce, Conquest, and Cosmopolitanism in Enlightenment Political Thought," in *Empire and Modern Political Thought*, ed. Sankar Muthu (Cambridge: Cambridge University Press, 2014), 226n28. For McCarthy's argument, see Thomas McCarthy, *Race, Empire, and the Idea of Human Development* (Cambridge: Cambridge University Press, 2009), 42–68.

113. Kant, *Practical Philosophy*, 418; Kant, *Religion within the Boundaries of Mere Reason and Other Writings*, 180n.

114. Pauline Kleingold, "Kant's Second Thoughts on Colonialism," in *Kant and Colonialism: Historical and Critical Perspectives*, ed. Katrin Flikschuh and Lea Ypi (Oxford: Oxford University Press, 2015), 43–67. For a recent and very interesting argument about how Kant's anticolonialism originated in his concern for how it was

creating war *in Europe*, see Inés Valdez, "It's Not about Race: Good Wars, Bad Wars, and the Origins of Kant's Anti-Colonialism," *The American Political Science Review* 111, no. 4 (November 1, 2017): 819–34. Valdez also gives a helpful overview and citations to the current literature in English on the topic.

115. Kant, *Anthropology, History, and Education*, 145.

116. Ibid., 294–95.

117. Ibid., 294.

118. Ibid., 427, 429; emphases in original.

119. I thus agree with Valdez's conclusion, although I have taken a different path through Kant's writings: "Condemning violence against non-European groups and the violent means of conquest does not in and of itself require an acceptance of those groups as racially equal or their civilization as comparable to Europe's." Valdez, "It's Not about Race," 832.

120. Henry Ford and Samuel Crowther, *My Life and Work* (Garden City: Garden City Publishing, 1922), 72.

121. Kant, *Anthropology, History, and Education*, 117.

122. Kant, *Practical Philosophy*, 20.

123. Michel Foucault, "What Is Enlightenment?," in *The Foucault Reader*, ed. Paul Rabinow (New York: Pantheon Books, 1984), 38.

124. Ibid., 43.

125. Ibid., 43.

126. Ibid., 46.

127. Ibid., 46.

128. Ibid., 45.

129. Ibid., 43.

130. François Jullien, *A Treatise on Efficacy: Between Western and Chinese Thinking*, trans. Janet Lloyd (Honolulu: University of Hawai'i Press, 2004), vii.

131. Ibid., 15.

132. For a critique of Jullien's work along these lines, see Sakai and Solomon, "Introduction: Addressing the Multitude of Foreigners, Echoing Foucault."

133. Jullien, *On the Universal*, 140–56.

134. Spivak, *A Critique of Postcolonial Reason*, 9.

135. Ibid., 17.

136. For a brief overview of how just how much—both materially and intellectually—the United States owes to indigenous infrastructure and ways of life, see the synoptic account in Roxanne Dunbar-Ortiz, *An Indigenous Peoples' History of the United States* (Boston: Beacon Press, 2015), 15–31.

137. Spivak, *A Critique of Postcolonial Reason*, 4–6.

138. Ibid., 13n20.

139. Ibid., 13n20.

140. On the need to revise the canon of canonical thinkers by factoring in their geographic writings, see Anderson, *Marx on the Margins*.

141. Adorno, *Notes to Literature, Volume 1*, 10.
142. Brian Jacobs and Patricia Kain, eds., *Essays on Kant's Anthropology* (Cambridge: Cambridge University Press, 2003).
143. Immanuel Kant, *Critique of Pure Reason*, trans. Paul Guyer (Cambridge: Cambridge University Press, 1998), 100–1.
144. Ibid., 99–100.

Chapter 3

1. As M. H. Abrams argues, these are Schiller's two key contributions to much of the art and philosophy that followed in his wake: "Schiller . . . inaugurates the concept of the cardinal role of art . . . [and] introduces the use of *aufheben* in the multiple dialectical sense (which Hegel later annexed)." Abrams, *Natural Supernaturalism: Tradition and Revolution in Romantic Literature*, 212.
2. Frederick C. Beiser, *Schiller as Philosopher: A Re-Examination* (Oxford: Oxford University Press, 2005), 156. See also the brief discussions in Walter Hinderer, "Schiller's Philosophical Aesthetics in Anthropological Perspective," in *A Companion to the Works of Friedrich Schiller*, ed. Steven D. Martinson (Rochester: Camden Press, 2005), 27–46; Maurice Boucher, "Le 'Sauvage' et Le 'Barbare' Dans Les Lettres Sur l'education Esthétique," *Études Germaniques* 14 (1959): 333–37. These are very preliminary discussions, however, that focus on Schiller's use of anthropological ideas and ignore the actual people he claims to be writing about. In general, of the many texts that discuss Schiller's "anthropologie," most do so within the context of his abstract "philosophical anthropology of Man," not with specific reference to what this means for and about geographic others.
3. Rousseau, *Emile*, 205.
4. Kant, *Anthropology, History, and Education*, 171.
5. Friedrich Schiller, *On the Naive and Sentimental in Literature*, trans. Helen Watanabe O'Kelly (Manchester: Carcanet New Press, 1981), 22; Friedrich Schiller, "Über Naive Und Sentimentalische Dichtung," in *Schillers Werke*, ed. Arthur Kutscher, vol. 8 (Berlin: Deutsches Verlagshaus Bong & Co, 1910), 116. I should note that "they" here refers to all those Schiller considered "more natural," including also children and "country folk."
6. E. M. Wilkinson and L. A. Willoughby, "Introduction," in *On the Aesthetic Education of Man in a Series of Letters*, by Friedrich Schiller (Oxford: Oxford University Press, 1967), lvii; Friedrich Schiller, *On the Aesthetic Education of Man in a Series of Letters*, trans. E. M. Wilkinson and L. A. Willoughby (Oxford: Oxford University Press, 1967), 219. This is a bilingual edition with German on the left-hand page.
7. Schiller, *On the Aesthetic Education of Man in a Series of Letters*, 163, 147; translation modified.
8. Ibid., 79.

9. Ibid., 11, 173. For similar claims in Rousseau and Kant, see Rousseau, *Basic Political Writings*, 38; Kant, *Practical Philosophy*, 296–97.
10. Schiller, *On the Aesthetic Education of Man in a Series of Letters*, 191–93.
11. Ibid., 81.
12. Ibid., 119–21.
13. Ibid., 15.
14. Ibid., 97.
15. Ibid., 103–5.
16. Ibid., 105.
17. Ibid., 124–25; translation modified.
18. Ibid., 127.
19. Ibid., 161.
20. Schiller, *On the Naive and Sentimental in Literature*, 22.
21. Schiller, 28–29; my emphasis; Schiller, "Über Naive Und Sentimentalische Dichtung," 124; my emphasis.
22. T. J. Demos, "Moving Images of Globalization," *Grey Room*, no. 37 (Fall 2009): 6–29; Sven Lütticken, "Neither Autocracy nor Automatism: Notes on Autonomy and the Aesthetic," *E-Flux* 69 (January 2016), http://www.e-flux.com/journal/neither-autocracy-nor-automatism-notes-on-autonomy-and-the-aesthetic/; Peter Bürger, *Theory of the Avant-Garde*, trans. Michael Shaw (Minneapolis: University of Minnesota Press, 1984); Jacques Rancière, "The Aesthetic Revolution and Its Outcomes," *New Left Review*, no. 14 (2002): 133–51; Spivak, *An Aesthetic Education in the Era of Globalization*.
23. Beiser, *Schiller as Philosopher*, 156.
24. Peter Bürger, *Theory of the Avant-Garde*, trans. Michael Shaw (Minneapolis: University of Minnesota Press, 1984), 46.
25. Ibid., 46.
26. As when Aubrey Williams met Pablo Picasso, and the latter greeted the former not as a fellow painter, but as a potential object for a sketch. See Simon Gikandi, "Picasso, Africa, and the Schemata of Difference," *Modernism/Modernity* 10, no. 3 (September 5, 2003): 455–80.
27. As when André Breton and Aimé and Suzanne Césaire met and expressed mutual admiration and influence. See Gregson Davis, *Aimé Césaire* (Cambridge: Cambridge University Press, 1997), 67–73.
28. Abrams, *Natural Supernaturalism: Tradition and Revolution in Romantic Literature*, 210–11; Schiller, *On the Aesthetic Education of Man in a Series of Letters*, 35–43.
29. Schiller, *On the Aesthetic Education of Man in a Series of Letters*, 107–9; my emphasis; as cited in Jacques Rancière, *Dissensus: On Politics and Aesthetics*, trans. Steven Corcoran (New York: Bloomsbury Academic, 2010), 115.
30. Rancière, *Dissensus*, 132.

31. For a helpful overview of Rancière's work on aesthetics and politics, see Jacques Rancière, *The Politics of Aesthetics*, trans. Gabriel Rockhill (London: Bloomsbury Academic, 2013).

32. Rockhill, *Radical History and the Politics of Art*, 144.

33. Schiller, *On the Naive and Sentimental in Literature*, 21; my emphasis; Schiller, "Über Naive Und Sentimentalische Dichtung," 116; my emphasis. "Urwelt" means "primitive world" more generally, but in context, and in most translations, it refers to the people who lived there as well.

34. Jacques Rancière, *The Ignorant Schoolmaster: Five Lessons in Intellectual Emancipation*, trans. Kristin Ross (Palo Alto: Stanford University Press, 1991); Jacques Rancière, *Proletarian Nights: The Workers' Dream in Nineteenth-Century France* (New York: Verso, 2012).

35. Antenor Firmin, *The Equality of Human Races*, trans. Asselin Charles (Urbana: University of Illinois Press, 2002).

36. Claude Lévi-Strauss, *Structural Anthropology*, trans. Claire Jacobson and Brooke Grundfest Schoepf (New York: Anchor, 1967); Mahmood, *Politics of Piety*; Viveiros de Castro, "Cosmological Deixis and Amerindian Perspectivism."

37. Bilgrami, *Secularism, Identity, and Enchantment*, 291–306.

38. Linebaugh and Rediker, *The Many-Headed Hydra*, 141.

39. Spivak, *An Aesthetic Education in the Era of Globalization*, 3.

40. Ibid., 319.

41. Ibid., 8–9.

42. Ibid., 333.

43. Ibid., 4.

44. Ibid., 1.

45. Ibid.

46. The clearest exposition of Derrida's relation to Kant that I know is Martin Hägglund, *Radical Atheism: Derrida and the Time of Life* (Palo Alto: Stanford University Press, 2008), 13–49.

47. Jacques Rancière, *The Emancipated Spectator* (London: Verso, 2011), 49.

48. Rancière, *Dissensus*, 218.

49. Spivak, *An Aesthetic Education in the Era of Globalization*, 24.

50. Spivak mostly sides with Paul de Man's reading of Schiller. I am not alone in thinking that Schiller's writing is more persuasive than de Man allows. See, for example, Beiser, *Schiller as Philosopher*.

51. Spivak, *An Aesthetic Education in the Era of Globalization*, 1.

52. Ibid., 141.

53. Ibid., 6.

54. Jacques Derrida, *Of Grammatology*, trans. Gayatri Chakravorty Spivak, corrected edition (Baltimore: Johns Hopkins University Press, 1998), 120.

55. Ibid., 114.

56. Ibid., 158.

57. Gayatri Chakravorty Spivak, "Translator's Preface," in Derrida, *Of Grammatology*, lxxxiii–lxxxiv. See, for example, her remarks on the occasion of the fortieth anniversary of the translation. ICLS Columbia, *Of Grammatology Re-Translated: 40th Anniversary Edition: A Tribute*, https://www.youtube.com/watch?v=lLCOOld 3fto&feature=youtu.be.

58. Spivak, "Translator's Preface," lxxxii.

59. Spivak, *An Aesthetic Education in the Era of Globalization*, 324–25.

60. Emmanuel Levinas, *Emmanuel Levinas: Basic Philosophical Writings*, ed. Adriaan T. Peperzak, Simon Critchley, and Robert Bernasconi (Bloomington: Indiana University Press, 1996), 148.

61. For a balanced overview of the historical criticism, see F. Abiola Irele, *The Negritude Moment: Explorations in Francophone African and Caribbean Literature and Thought* (Trenton, NJ: Africa World Press, 2010), especially 95–122. For examples of recent work that are at once appreciative and critical, see, for example, Donna V. Jones, *The Racial Discourses of Life Philosophy: Négritude, Vitalism, and Modernity* (New York: Columbia University Press, 2010), 132–50; Elizabeth Harney, *In Senghor's Shadow: Art, Politics, and the Avant-Garde in Senegal, 1960–1995* (Durham: Duke University Press, 2004), 38–48; Emmanuel Chukwudi Eze, *Achieving Our Humanity: The Idea of the Postracial Future* (New York: Routledge, 2001), 115–76. Harney's book as a whole offers an illuminating and complex portrait of the effects of Senghor's cultural policy choices on the postindependence history of Senegalese art. Jones has noted, meanwhile, that she continues to evaluate her own work in light of other recent criticism. Donna V. Jones, review of *African Art as Philosophy: Senghor, Bergson and the Idea of Negritude*, by Souleymane Bachir Diagne, *Journal of Anthropological Research* 69, no. 1 (2013): 132–34. Finally, for a helpful review essay on recent work on Négritude in general, see Chike Jeffers, "Recent Work on Negritude," *Journal of French and Francophone Philosophy* 24, no. 2 (December 21, 2016): 304–18.

62. One of the limits of Senghor scholarship in English has been a lack of translations. While much of his poetry is translated, very few of his essays are. I have translated from the French when an English-language copy was not available. I was greatly aided in my selection of sources to read by Diagne's and especially Wilder's bibliographies.

63. Souleymane Bachir Diagne, *African Art as Philosophy: Senghor, Bergson and the Idea of Negritude* (London: Seagull Books, 2011); Wilder, *Freedom Time*. The claims of these books are not, of course, undebated. Reiland Rabaka, though not responding directly, has generally questioned the tendency to read what Négritude offers under the sign of Western philosophy, and Diagne has been queried on this account by Cheik Thiam. My position, as I explore below, follows Wilder's suggestion to see Senghor as pluralizing the very distinctions between geographies of thought on which these criticisms rely. This is not to say, for myself or for Wilder as I understand him, that Senghor is *merely* global. Indeed, he is insistent throughout

his life that *to be global* is to offer a particular vision of human arrangements. See Reiland Rabaka, *The Negritude Movement: W.E.B. Du Bois, Leon Damas, Aime Cesaire, Leopold Senghor, Frantz Fanon, and the Evolution of an Insurgent Idea* (Lanham: Lexington Books, 2015), 197–246; Cheikh Thiam, *Return to the Kingdom of Childhood: Re-Envisioning the Legacy and Philosophical Relevance of Negritude* (Columbus: Ohio State University Press, 2014). For a helpful overview of the debates, see Jeffers, "Recent Work on Negritude."

64. Léopold Sédar Senghor, *Liberté 5: Le dialogue des cultures* (Paris: Seuil, 1993), 96.

65. Given that I read Senghor as a radical pluralist in a line from Emerson and Du Bois, it might make sense to discuss him chronologically after the chapters on their work. But my point about radical pluralism is not that it is "invented" by Emerson and available only after him. Rather, it is that it is a way of thinking that comes and goes throughout human history, and different thinkers offer different variations on its possibility. In this section I explore how Senghor's version of radical pluralism offers a direct response to Schiller's dialectics.

66. The two are often distinguished from each other. As James Clifford wrote: "It is becoming common to describe two negritudes. Senghor's looks back to tradition and eloquently gathers up an African essence. Césaire's is more syncretic, modernist, and parodic." Without taking a strong position here, I have generally followed Wilder and Diagne in seeing strong similarities between the two. Clifford is cited in Harney, *In Senghor's Shadow*, 38. For Diagne's reading of Césaire, see Souleymane Bachir Diagne, "Rereading Aimé Césaire: Negritude as Creolization," *Small Axe* 19, no. 3 (December 2, 2015): 121–28.

67. Wilder, *Freedom Time*, 9.

68. Ibid., 98–101.

69. Jones, *The Racial Discourses of Life Philosophy*, 5.

70. In the context of relations between India and Britain, Peter van der Veer has similarly noted that both nations equally invented their own pasts in the nineteenth century. But whereas Britain's work is understood as part of the ongoing logic of the invention of tradition, India's is viewed as a "sign of an inferiority complex." He suggests that we are better to understand them on a level playing field: "Both British and Indian thoughts on origins belong to a history of colonial interactions and might be understood in the context of a shared colonial imaginaire." van der Veer, *Imperial Encounters*, 158–59.

71. Senghor uses these terms repeatedly throughout his work to contrast to the "discursive" or "eye" reason of post-Cartesian European thought.

72. I thus read Senghor, as I later do Suzuki, as a version of what Stanley Cavell has called a "democratic perfectionist." Such perfectionism without elitism requires, he suggests, that we transform perfectionism from a path toward the one good person (Socrates is his example), "to the idea of each of us being representative for each of us." He finds in Emerson an example of someone who "elects himself"

to be representative: to show to others the possibility for a kind of living that is potential in us but not yet brought out in our realities. In this sense, Senghor, *as an essayist*, is less making empirical claims about how every African *is* (which would, he clearly knows, be rather absurd) so much as perfectionist claims about an ideal form of being. Cavell cites Emerson to this effect: "So all that is said of the wise man by Stoic, or oriental or modern essayist, describes to each reader his own idea, describes his unattained but attainable self." This is of course a risky strategy, as essentialisms and denials may abound. Cavell notes two tendencies: "[1] the form of moralism that fixates on the presence of ideals in one's culture and promotes them to distract one from the presence of otherwise intolerable injustice . . . [And (2)] the enforcement of morality, or a moral code, by immoral means, represented in the theocratic state, but still present in reforming states . . ." Cavell says that he keeps the name perfectionism, in spite of these two associations, as a means to "struggle against [such] false or debased perfectionisms." Senghor's critics, one might say, suggest that he falls into both of these moves at various moments. I do think, nevertheless, that there are positive elements of his perfectionist essaying worth engaging. Stanley Cavell, *Conditions Handsome and Unhandsome: The Constitution of Emersonian Perfectionism* (Chicago: Open Court, 1990), 9–13.

73. I believe that Césaire himself, in a revealing moment, improperly makes a dialectician out of Senghor. He argues that Senghor must "transcend . . . the contradiction that you feel between lived existence and the marvelous dimension of life, a glimpsed instant." As I hope to show extensively in my discussion of "double consciousness" in Emerson and Du Bois, it is *learning to learn from this gap* that enables radical pluralism and a higher form of double consciousness; one that "alternates" between these moments of life to draw power from each. In this chapter, I allude to this resolution through the discussion of "rooting and uprooting" below. Césaire cited in Wilder, *Freedom Time*, 49.

74. Wilder, *Freedom Time*, 2. Wilder gives increasing depth and context to this idea throughout his book. He is not alone in returning to this moment in time to suggest that our understanding of national liberation as a de facto good is ahistorical. See, for example, Frederick Cooper, *Africa in the World: Capitalism, Empire, Nation-State* (Cambridge: Harvard University Press, 2014), 66–89.

75. Léopold Sédar Senghor, *Prose and Poetry*, trans. John Reed and Clive Wake (London: Heinemann, 1965), 99.

76. Senghor, *Prose and Poetry*, 99; Jean-Paul Sartre, "Black Orpheus," trans. John MacCombie, *The Massachusetts Review* 6, no. 1 (1964): 47–52. Senghor frequently returned to Sartre's introduction to his own edited volume of poetry, and I discuss this below. As an aside, I note that Sartre's position is perhaps more nuanced than he is usually given credit for. His claim should be contextualized by noting, first, that he is trying not to impose his understanding on Négritude so much as suggest that the authors of the movement are themselves moving in the direction of universal class consciousness (47). Second, he concludes the essay by suggesting

that these issues are ultimately less important than a general historical vision that comprehends the perpetual production of classes, groups, races, and nations who speak for the oppressed. He ends the essay citing a line from Césaire: "Let us greet today the historic chance that will permit black men to 'shout out the great negro cry so hard that the world's foundations will be shaken'" (52).

77. Senghor, *Liberté 5: Le dialogue des cultures*, 96.
78. Diagne, *African Art as Philosophy*, 15.
79. Senghor, *Liberté 5: Le dialogue des cultures*, 97.
80. Diagne, *African Art as Philosophy*, 196.
81. Léopold Sédar Senghor, *Liberté 1: Négritude et humanisme* (Paris: Seuil, 1964), 70.
82. Cited in Diagne, *African Art as Philosophy*, 84.
83. Senghor, *Liberté 5: Le dialogue des cultures*, 18–19. For more on these elements of Senghor's ontology, see Diagne, *African Art as Philosophy*, 45–96.
84. Senghor, *Liberté 1: Négritude et humanisme*, 216.
85. I'm not sure if this is what Diagne has in mind, but, according to the *OED*, "ratio" is a possible etymological root for "race." *Oxford English Dictionary*, s.v. "race (*n.6*)," accessed January 4, 2018, http://www.oed.com.ezproxy.princeton.edu/view/Entry/157031.
86. Diagne, *African Art as Philosophy*, 95.
87. Senghor, *Liberté 1: Négritude et humanisme*, 310.
88. Ibid., 216.
89. Kant, *Practical Philosophy*, 333–34.
90. Senghor, *Liberté 1: Négritude et humanisme*, 42.
91. Senghor, *Liberté 5: Le dialogue des cultures*, 86.
92. Ibid., 113, 180.
93. Léopold Sédar Senghor, *La poésie de l'action: conversations avec Mohamed Aziza* (Les Grands leaders) (Paris: Stock, 1980), 84–85. I profited greatly from the discussion of this time in Senghor's life in Wilder, *Freedom Time*, 52–59.
94. Senghor, *Liberté 5: Le dialogue des cultures*, 51. I have translated from Senghor's French: "Chacun doit être grec à sa façon, mais doit l'être." The original line is: "Jeder sei auf Seine Art ein Grieche! Aber er sei's." The standard English translation runs: "Let everyone be a Greek in his own way, but let him be a Greek!" Johann Wolfgang von Goethe, *Essays on Art and Literature*, ed. John Gearey, trans. Ellen von Nardroff and Ernest H. von Nardroff, vol. 3 of *The Collected Works of Goethe* (Princeton: Princeton University Press, 1994), 93. Johann Wolfgang von Goethe, *Goethes Werke / textkritisch durchgesehen und kommentiert von Erich Trunz*, vol. 12 (Munich: C.H. Beck, 1981), 176.
95. Léopold Sédar Senghor, "Goethe m'a Dit," *La Nouvelle Revue Des Deux Mondes* (May 1981), 326.
96. Senghor, *Liberté 1: Négritude et humanisme*, 86.

97. Joel Porte, ed., *Consciousness and Culture: Emerson and Thoreau Reviewed* (New Haven: Yale University Press, 2004), 3; Werner Sollors, "Of Mules and Mares in a Land of Difference; or, Quadrupeds All?," *American Quarterly* 42, no. 2 (1990): 182; Johann Wolfgang von Goethe, *Faust I & II*, trans. Stuart Atkins, vol. 2 of *The Collected Works of Goethe* (Princeton: Princeton University Press, 1994), I.1110–15.

98. Senghor, *Liberté 5: Le dialogue des cultures*, 25. The language here may come in part from Césaire, who had used half of the same phrasing in an essay on African art a few years earlier: "If Négritude involves taking root in a particular soil [*un enracinement particulier*], Négritude is also transcendence and expansion into the universal." Aimé Césaire, "Discours sur l'art africain (1966)," *Études littéraires* 6, no. 1 (1973): 103. The translation of Césaire here is from Davis, *Aimé Césaire*, 53.

99. Simon Critchley, "Black Socrates? Questioning the Philosophical Tradition," *Theoria: A Journal of Social and Political Theory*, no. 86 (1995): 79–98.

100. Ibid., 89.
101. Ibid., 90.
102. Ibid., 93.
103. Ibid., 94.
104. Ibid., 94.
105. Ibid., 96–98.
106. Ibid., 98.

107. The deconstructive practitioner who seems most free from doubt, and most comfortable with deconstruction as an all-encompassing mode of thought, is Hägglund, *Radical Atheism*.

108. Senghor says this in various places. Although Césaire is frequently cited in the criticism as the source, I could not trace a citation to where he says it. For Senghor's use, see, for example, Senghor, *Liberté 5: Le dialogue des cultures*, 23.

109. Senghor, *La poésie de l'action*, 87.

110. Senghor, *Liberté 1: Négritude et humanisme*, 318.

111. Wilder offers an economic version of this thinking in Senghor based on his archival research into Senghor's arguments about a postimperial federation. "Senghor's argument [for federalism] was based on four propositions. First the world is composed of many distinct civilizations, 'each of which places the accent on a singular aspect of the human condition.' Second, every great civilization is a 'cultural crucible' and 'devouring factory' that requires a 'constant influx of human raw materials and foreign contributions.' Third, imperialism created a situation of intense cultural interaction through which metropolitan and African peoples had a historic opportunity to 'fertilize' themselves. Finally, Senghor announced, 'together we will create a new civilization, whose center will be Paris, a new humanism . . . on the scale of the universe and of humanity.'" This was not just a matter of combination, but also of removal. This meant here, particularly, to kill off any vestiges of colonial or Nazi thinking—which were, for him, of the same root. Wilder, *Freedom Time*, 142.

112. Senghor often leaves the phrase without this qualification, perhaps to invoke the ambiguity of what exactly this new universal might look like. However, he does specify it at some points. For example: "We will construct the *civilization of the universal*, wherein each different civilization will contribute [*apportera*] its most creative—because most complementary—values." Léopold Sédar Senghor, *Liberté 3: Négritude et civilisation de l'universel* (Paris: Seuil, 1977), 241.

113. Senghor, *Liberté 5: Le dialogue des cultures*, 52.

114. Senghor, *Liberté 1: Négritude et humanisme*, 309.

115. Ibid., 43.

116. Senghor, *Prose and Poetry*, 49.

117. Aimé Césaire, "Culture and Colonization," trans. Brent Hayes Edwards, *Social Text* 28, no. 2 103 (June 1, 2010): 141–42.

118. Ibid., 136.

119. Ibid., 132. It is somewhat indicative of the early—if necessary—criticisms of Négritude that its critics would often chastise its authors for not offering claims that they themselves foreground in opposition. For example, just after stridently criticizing Césaire's essentialism, Paulin Hountondji would write lines that could have followed these in Césaire's talk: "Pluralism in the true sense did not stem from the intrusion of Western civilization into our continent . . . It is an internal pluralism, born of perpetual confrontations and occasional conflicts between African themselves . . . Far from having come to Africa with colonization, it is highly probably that cultural pluralism was checked and impoverished by its advent." I agree with Hountondji, but so did Césaire, who is further explicit in this lecture about the same fact of colonization: that it tends to ossify in the name of domination. I understand Hountondji's polemical concern with elements of Négritude, but I follow today's critics in wanting to see what else the philosophy offered. Paulin J. Hountondji, *African Philosophy, Second Edition: Myth and Reality*, 2nd ed. (Bloomington: Indiana University Press, 1996), 165; Césaire, "Culture and Colonization," 131–32.

120. Senghor, *Liberté 5: Le dialogue des cultures*, 108.

121. Aimé Césaire, "Letter to Maurice Thorez," trans. Chike Jeffers, *Social Text* 28, no. 2 103 (June 1, 2010): 150.

122. Thus among the various gifts that Césaire and Senghor believe African cultures can give to the world is what Nelson Maldonado-Torres calls the "decolonial gift": "an epistemic perspective that would help them [oppressors] to understand themselves better and address their crisis in a way that leads to the formation of a more human world." Nelson Maldonado-Torres, "Césaire's Gift and the Decolonial Turn," in *Critical Ethnic Studies: A Reader*, ed. Critical Ethnic Studies Editorial Collective (Durham: Duke University Press, 2016), 455.

123. Senghor, *Liberté 5: Le dialogue des cultures*, 23.

124. Leopold Senghor, "What the Black Man Contributes," in *Race and Racism in Continental Philosophy*, ed. Robert Bernasconi and Sybol Cook, trans. Mary Beth Mader (Bloomington: Indiana University Press, 2003), 287–301.

125. Ibid., 288. For Fanon's critique of Senghor, see Fanon, *Black Skin, White Masks*, 101–9; Frantz Fanon, *Œuvres*, vol. 1 (Paris: La Découverte, 2011), 163–68.
126. Senghor, "What the Black Man Contributes," 287.
127. Ibid., 288.
128. Diagne, *African Art as Philosophy*, 103.
129. Cited in ibid., 117–18.
130. In spite of the many critiques of Senghor as an essentialist of a primitive African identity, he was clear from very early in his writing that what was "essential" was simply that "under our differences" there are "more essential similarities." Furthermore, he is clear that "reason" is "*identical* in all men" and that he did not "believe in a 'prelogical mentality.'" Senghor, *Liberté 1: Négritude et humanisme*, 43.
131. I emphasize this because while I readily accept Thiam's claim that we can derive Senghor's thinking from African sources, it seems to me that part of why Senghor emphasized Bergson was that it helped him build the strength of his argument from within the geography of European thought. See especially Thiam, *Return to the Kingdom of Childhood*, 61–68.
132. Senghor states at one point that art itself is not the means, but the transformation of self required to see art is, though this claim does not always appear in his writing. "I acknowledge that it is no small task to achieve, without sacrilege, the state of grace required to be in communion with Negro art. One does not easily traverse this immeasurable gap that spiritually separates the contemporary civilized individual, fed on logic and reason, from his distant ancestor, who did not create his art but lived it, integrating it into his cave, hut, or sacred wood, and into the rituals of the family, clan, or tribe." Léopold Sédar Senghor, "Critical Standards of African Art," trans. Brian Quinn, *African Arts* 50, no. 1 (February 3, 2017): 10–15.
133. Diagne notes that Senghor thus makes an "ethnologization" of the "Bergsonian theses." Donna Jones has expressed concern that this act carries within it the problematic "racial discourses" already embedded in Bergson's philosophy. There is simply no place in this already crowded book for a discussion of Bergson, and I won't attempt one here. What does seem to me important in his work is its essentially pluralistic impulse to understand the human mind as one universally capable potential that has resulted in various dispositions. I take it that this was what Senghor found inspiring in his work. Diagne, *African Art as Philosophy*, 127; Jones, *The Racial Discourses of Life Philosophy*. As I trace this understanding of the plurality of the "one mind" resulting in a double consciousness (one analytic/finite and one intuitive/infinite) back to Emerson, it is perhaps not surprising that Bergson was a fervent reader of Emerson. Bergson said that as a young man growing up bilingual, he "loved Emerson." See also Bergson's invocation of Emerson in his lectures on the will (1906–7). Henri Bergson, *Mélanges: l'idée de lieu chez Aristote, Durée et simultanéité, correspondance, pièces diverses, documents* (Paris: Presses universitaires de France, 1972), 1244; 717.
134. Senghor, *Liberté 5: Le dialogue des cultures*, 18.

135. Senghor, *Liberté 1: Négritude et humanisme*, 71.

136. Jones makes a suggestion to this effect, although she qualifies it through other thinkers (Dilthey and Merleau-Ponty) who have questioned the one-sidedness of analytic knowledge. I disagree with Jones, however, that Senghor's approach to knowledge, unless "freed from Bergsonian absolutism," leads one to "devalue the importance of scientific and technological framing as less true than participant reason." On my reading, both Bergson and Senghor are quite clear that the aim is to recover *both* of these forms of human thinking in a world in which the technical is overly predominant. Indeed, Senghor made frequent remarks on the necessity of science and technology for development. His only insistence, and I think it quite reasonable, was that that development not occur separated from humanistic values. For example, quite explicitly: "We will reconcile modern technique and African humanism." Senghor will also admit, after the Second World War, that while early forms of Négritude had perhaps been myopically cultural, they now knew that it was necessary for their philosophy to also "reflect our economic and social evolution by integrating, through an active assimilation, the scientific progress of Europe." Jones, *The Racial Discourses of Life Philosophy*, 142–44, 146. Léopold Sédar Senghor, "Les Négro-Africains et La Union Française," *Revue Politique et Parlementaire*, June 1947, 208. Senghor, *Liberté 1: Négritude et humanisme*, 85.

137. Wilder, *Freedom Time*, 214.

138. Léopold Sédar Senghor, "Marxisme et Humanisme," *La Revue Socialiste* 19 (1948): 216.

139. See the summary in Wilder, *Freedom Time*, 206–40.

140. Senghor, "Les Négro-Africains et La Union Française," 208. I have used here the translation by Frederick Cooper, although I augmented and revised it slightly. (It seems Cooper found the same article reprinted in a different source, with slight changes.) Cooper also gives some helpful context in the pages around this quote. Cooper, *Africa in the World*, 75. I learned of this speech from Wilder, who discusses it in a broader discussion of Senghor's writings on federalism. Wilder, *Freedom Time*, 149; chapter 6.

141. Senghor, *Liberté 5: Le dialogue des cultures*, 22.

142. I unfortunately am in no position to evaluate Senghor's specific claims about the languages of Senegal and how they construct meaning. On the importance of thinking through the plurality of philosophy via the plurality of languages, see Chike Jeffers, ed., *Listening to Ourselves: A Multilingual Anthology of African Philosophy* (Albany: State University of New York Press, 2013); Souleymane Bachir Diagne, "Pour une histoire postcoloniale de la philosophie," *Cités*, no. 72 (December 21, 2017): 88–93.

143. My reading here was deeply influenced—indeed only made possible—by Diagne's book. He discusses at length the philosophical, anthropological, and art historical contexts that underline Senghor's phrase and shows how it refers most explicitly to African art. I have developed my reading of Senghor's philosophy and

politics through Diagne and Wilder. On the specifics of this famous sentence, see Diagne, *African Art as Philosophy*, 69–96.

144. On Levinas's Greco-Hebraic philosophy in opposition to global thought, see Avram Alpert, "Not to Be European Would Not Be 'to Be European Still': Undoing Eurocentrism in Levinas and Others," *Journal of French and Francophone Philosophy* 23, no. 1 (August 5, 2015): 21–41. I should note that I explicitly invoke Derrida in this text as a way of thinking through these problems and "opening" Levinas. Deconstruction, as I have said, needs to be partialized as a method of analysis, not in the least discarded. The essay ends, as Critchley's does, more with an invocation of future work than its practice. That is what I am trying to do more of in this book.

145. Fanon, *Black Skin, White Masks*, 202; Fanon, *Œuvres*, 1:248.

146. On Senghor's complex attempts to institutionalize Négritude and some of the reactions against it, see Harney, *In Senghor's Shadow*.

147. T. Denean Sharpley-Whiting, "Femme Negritude: Jane Nardal, La Depeche Africaine, and the Francophone New Negro," *Souls: A Critical Journal of Black Politics, Culture, and Society* 2, no. 4 (2000): 8–18.

148. Senghor, "What the Black Man Contributes," 288.

149. Gary Wilder, "Eurafrique as the Future Past of '"Black France"': Sarkozy's Temporal Confusion and Senghor's Postwar Vision," in *Black France / France Noire: The History and Politics of Blackness*, ed. Trica Danielle Keaton, T. Denean Sharpley-Whiting, and Tyler Stovall (Durham: Duke University Press Books, 2012), 57.

150. Ibid., 66.

151. Achille Mbembe, "France-Afrique: Ces Sottises Qui Divisent," *Africultures* (blog), August 8, 2007, http://africultures.com/france-afrique-ces-sottises-qui-divisent-6819/.

152. For examples: Achille Mbembe, "On the Postcolony: A Brief Response to Critics," *African Identities* 4, no. 2 (October 1, 2006): 153, 157; Achille Mbembe, *Critique of Black Reason*, trans. Laurent Dubois (Durham: Duke University Press Books, 2017), 90, 158.

153. Mbembe, *Critique of Black Reason*, 6.

154. This is a quote from Fanon, translated as "shake off the heavy darkness." Achille Mbembe, *Sortir de la grande nuit* (Paris: La Découverte, 2010), 17; Frantz Fanon, *The Wretched of the Earth*, trans. Constance Farrington (New York: Grove Press, 1968), 311.

155. Mbembe, *Sortir de la grande nuit*, 233.

156. See also his earlier statement: Achille Mbembe, "Afropolitanisme," *Africultures* (blog), December 25, 2005, http://africultures.com/afropolitanisme-4248/.

157. Achille Mbembe and Sarah Balakrishnan, "Pan-African Legacies, Afropolitan Futures," *Transition*, no. 120 (2016): 30.

158. Mbembe, *Critique of Black Reason*, 156–60.

159. Ibid., 157.

160. Ibid., 158.
161. Ibid., 173.
162. Ibid., 173.
163. Ibid., 180. Although my focus is more generally on colonial and other global contacts than the specific horrors of slavery, I share and hope to have echoed this general orientation in this book.
164. Ibid., 174. See also the reflections on the difficulties of this position via a reading "with and against Fanon" in Mbembe, "On the Postcolony," 153–57.
165. Mbembe, *Critique of Black Reason*, 176.
166. Ibid., 174.
167. In this sense, as deconstructions tend to do, Mbembe in turn invents a tradition of "classic Black art" that "has always been an art of sacrilege, sacrifice, and expenditure, multiplying new fetishes in pursuit of a generalized deconstruction of existence precisely through its use of play, leisure, spectacle, and the principle of metamorphosis. It is this utopian, metaphysical, and aesthetic supplement that the radical critique of race brings to democracy." Mbembe, 174.
168. Ibid., 173–74.
169. Diagne, *African Art as Philosophy*, 96.
170. The word "*sentir*" here may also mean smell or "breathe for oneself." Senghor noted in a text a few years later: "To greet, in Wolof, is *neyu*. A worthy elder told me that the word had the same etymology as *noyi*, to breathe. *Neyu* therefore means 'to breathe for oneself,' 'to smell' [*sentir*]. 'I think therefore I am,' wrote Descartes . . . The African might say, 'I smell, I dance the *Other*. I am.' . . . He does not need to think but live the *Other* in dancing him . . . Dancing is discovery and *re-creating* . . . It is the best mode of knowledge." Senghor, *Prose and Poetry*, 32; Léopold Sédar Senghor, "De la négritude. Psychologie du Négro-africain," *Diogène; Paris*, no. 37 (January 1, 1962): 7–8.
171. Senghor, *Liberté 1: Négritude et humanisme*, 216.
172. Ibid., 216.

Chapter 4

1. I am aware that some have questioned an excessive focus on this section—or the general isolation of passages in Hegel—as overshadowing the complexity and movements of his work and *The Phenomenology* as a whole. As my concern is with opening up dominant ways of conceiving the modern self, however, I find that reworking this paradigmatic part of Hegel is important for my study. On the problems with isolating the story for a reading of Hegel, see Rebecca Comay, "Resistance and Repetition: Freud and Hegel," *Research in Phenomenology* 45, no. 2 (September 2, 2015): 264; Michael Monahan, "Recognition Beyond Struggle: On a Liberatory Account of Hegelian Recognition," *Social Theory and Practice* 32,

no. 3 (2006): 390. Monahan, I note, also follows the strategy I have taken here of working back through this central passage in order to move it in another direction.

2. Works that have helped me in my ongoing understanding of the complexities of Hegel's thought include Julie E. Maybee, "Hegel's Dialectics," in *The Stanford Encyclopedia of Philosophy*, ed. Edward N. Zalta, Winter 2016 ed., https://plato.stanford.edu/archives/win2016/entries/hegel-dialectics/; Rebecca Comay, *Mourning Sickness: Hegel and the French Revolution* (Palo Alto: Stanford University Press, 2010); Stephen Houlgate, *The Opening of Hegel's Logic: From Being to Infinity* (West Lafayette, IN: Purdue University Press, 2005); Robert Stern, *The Routledge Guidebook to Hegel's Phenomenology of Spirit* (New York: Routledge, 2013); Robert Pippin, *Hegel on Self-Consciousness: Desire and Death in the Phenomenology of Spirit* (Princeton: Princeton University Press, 2011); Neuhouser, *Foundations of Hegel's Social Theory*; Michael Inwood, *A Hegel Dictionary* (Oxford: Wiley-Blackwell, 1992); Monahan, "Recognition Beyond Struggle: On a Liberatory Account of Hegelian Recognition." I have also greatly benefited from lecture courses on *The Phenomenology of Spirit* with Étienne Balibar, Jay Bernstein, and Kristin Gjesdal.

3. I have not, at least, found a passage in his works (or in the criticism) on these topics that seems to suggest otherwise.

4. I note that I differ from some of this scholarship, which often maintains a distinction between Hegel's philosophy "proper" and the unfortunate remarks he makes about other cultures. Some readers of Hegel are thus "resource" readers as opposed to "reconstitutive" readers, as I have laid out these terms in my introduction. I have, nevertheless, learned from all of them. Resource readers include Ciccariello-Maher, *Decolonizing Dialectics*; Michael Monahan, ed., *Creolizing Hegel* (Lanham: Rowman & Littlefield International, 2017); Nicholas Germana, "Revisiting 'Hegel and Haiti': Postcolonial Readings of the Lord/Bondsman Dialectic," in *Creolizing Hegel*, ed. Michael Monahan (Lanham: Rowman & Littlefield International, 2017); Brennan, *Borrowed Light*. Reconstitutive critics include Teshale Tibebu, *Hegel and the Third World: The Making of Eurocentrism in World History* (Syracuse: Syracuse University Press, 2011); Nelson Maldonado-Torres, *Against War: Views from the Underside of Modernity* (Durham: Duke University Press, 2008); Robert Bernasconi, "Hegel at the Court of Ashanti," in *Hegel after Derrida*, by Stuart Barnett (London: Routledge, 1998); Bernasconi, "With What Must the Philosophy of World History Begin?"; Park, *Africa, Asia, and the History of Philosophy*. For reasons I discuss below, I would place Buck-Morss somewhere in between. Buck-Morss, *Hegel, Haiti and Universal History*.

5. Rebecca Comay has argued that this reading of Hegel (one that he himself tends to confirm) overlooks the great many resistances to progress that overwhelm the seeming advances in his text. As history keeps churning, there is too much to process, and Spirit tends to misfire. She concludes, however, by finding meaning in these misfires: "it's only at moments of symbolic breakdown that history sheds its veneer as inexorable second nature." What interests me here is that this does

not happen in his writing about places outside Europe (with the possible exception of some interest in Asia). The Hegelian system functions without friction in his writing on the colonies. And this is my point here: if we are to get at the Hegel who is not the stereotype of himself, we have to find the *grounding* (pun intended) of where he enacts this triumphant vision. In other words, it is by going through and undoing his Eurocentrism that we can begin to read Hegel otherwise. I am not sure that the result of this reading is a lack of progress. In fact, I hope that it is not. The dream (the fantasy?) of this book is that a new mode of global relation based on a radical pluralism might actually enable a better shared future, albeit one more like what we find in Emerson and Du Bois and Senghor than in Hegel. There may be too many resistances to get there, but I still hope (wish?) to contribute to their overcoming. Comay, "Resistance and Repetition," 266.

6. Andrew Cole has argued with great erudition that the MSD is more properly about "lords and bondsmen" in the Medieval sense. Part of his evidence is that the particular terms used—*Herr and Knecht*—differ from Hegel's language about, for example, classical slavery (*Sklaverei*). Be that as it may, it does seem clear that Hegel also uses *Herrschaft*, at least in this context, to refer to colonial and imperial power as well. *Herrschaft* is also used somewhat generally in the *Phenomenology* to refer to "mastery" over material or concepts. See, for examples prior to the MSD in the *Phenomenology*, Georg Wilhelm Friedrich Hegel, *Phenomenology of Spirit*, trans. A. V. Miller (Oxford: Oxford University Press, 1977), 78, 84; Georg Wilhelm Friedrich Hegel, *Werke*, vol. 3 (Frankfurt am Main: Suhrkamp, 1969), 106, 112. Cole, *The Birth of Theory*, 68–70. For a counterinterpretation of the language here (noted but not discussed by Cole) in which a possible explanation is given through the translation of Aristotle into German, see Bull, "Slavery and the Multiple Self," 103–4.

7. Georg Wilhelm Friedrich Hegel, *Hegel's Philosophy of Subjective Spirit / Hegels Philosophie Des Subjektiven Geistes: Volume 2 Anthropology / Band 2 Anthropologie*, ed. and trans. Michael John Petry (Dordrecht: Springer, 1978), 61.

8. Jean Hyppolite points us to a useful quote from the *Jena Logic*: "The spirit of nature is a hidden spirit. 'It does not develop itself in the same form as spirit; it is only spirit for the spirit who is conscious of it, it is spirit in-itself, but not for-itself.'" Jean Hyppolite, *Studies on Marx and Hegel* (New York: Basic Books, 1969), 5.

9. Hegel, *Phenomenology of Spirit*, 3; Hegel, *Werke*, 3:13.

10. Cornelius Castoriadis, *Philosophy, Politics, Autonomy* (New York: Oxford University Press, 1991), 83.

11. In addition to Clastres, noted below, see, for example: Anthony Grafton, April Shelford, and Nancy G. Siraisi, *New Worlds, Ancient Texts: The Power of Tradition and the Shock of Discovery* (Cambridge: Belknap Press of Harvard University Press, 1992), 7–8.

12. As Clastres has ironically noted, ethnocentrism is what unites philosophers with "savages": "The savage belonging to some Indian or Australian tribe deems his

culture superior to all others without feeling obliged to deliver a scientific discourse about them. Ethnology, on the other hand, wants to situate itself directly within the realm of universality without realizing that in many respects it remains firmly entrenched in its particularity, and its pseudoscientific discourse quickly deteriorates into genuine ideology. (Some assertions to the effect that only Western civilization is able to produce ethnologists are thereby reduced to their true significance.)" Clastres, *Society Against the State*, 17.

13. Cole, *The Birth of Theory*, 67–68.

14. Ludwig Siep has offered just such a generalized account, looking at the relation between Hobbes and Hegel. I should note that he argues that though the earlier versions of the MSD relate to the transition out of the state of nature, this does not apply in the *Phenomenology*. This reading, so far as I understand it, seems to me to be based on a rather technical distinction in the evolution of Hegel's thinking as he advances on Hobbes. I hope to show here how the question of the transition very clearly applies in the *Phenomenology*. Ludwig Siep, "Der Kampf um Anerkennung. Zu Hegels Auseinandersetzung mit Hobbes in den Jenaer Schriften," *Hegel-Studien; Bonn* 9 (January 1, 1974): 198. Although I am ultimately less critical in the end of Hegel than Tishele Tibebu, I also learned a lot from his work on Hegel's references to the state of nature. Tibebu, Teshale, *Hegel and the Third World*.

15. Hegel, *Phenomenology of Spirit*, 1; Hegel, *Werke*, 3:11. This of course goes against Descartes's method of starting from scratch.

16. Hegel, *Phenomenology of Spirit*, 2; Hegel, *Werke*, 3:12.

17. Hegel, *Phenomenology of Spirit*, 11; Hegel, *Werke*, 3:24.

18. Hegel, *Phenomenology of Spirit*, 2; Hegel, *Werke*, 3:13.

19. Comay goes so far as to suggest that the book as a whole is an "anti-Bildungsroman," less about a process of learning than constant unlearning. This seems right at the level of the book as a whole, but Hegel himself, so far as I can tell, never unlearns his prejudices. Comay, "Resistance and Repetition," 262.

20. Hegel, *Phenomenology of Spirit*, 111; Hegel, *Werke*, 3:145.

21. Hegel, *Phenomenology of Spirit*, 113; Hegel, *Werke*, 3:148.

22. I had originally written here "*the* path" instead of one. Michael Monahan convinced me that this does not hold in a reading of Hegel as a whole. See Monahan, "Recognition Beyond Struggle: On a Liberatory Account of Hegelian Recognition."

23. Hegel, *Phenomenology of Spirit*, 113; Pinkard translation; Hegel, *Werke*, 3:148. (I have occasionally used Pinkard's unpublished translation to amend infelicities in the standard translation. Terry Pinkard, "Phenomenology of Spirit Page," Terry Pinkard, Georgetown University, accessed February 29, 2016, http://terrypinkard.weebly.com/phenomenology-of-spirit-page.html.)

24. Hegel, *Phenomenology of Spirit*, 113; Pinkard translation; Hegel, *Werke*, 3:148.

25. Hegel, *Phenomenology of Spirit*, 117. The "religious community" must also pass through this movement of overcoming "natural existence" toward the end of the *Phenomenology*. Ibid., 477.

26. Hegel, *Phenomenology of Spirit*, 119; Hegel, *Werke*, 3:155.

27. There are of course crucial differences between these two texts, but I have not found these differences to be important for my argument here, which is more concerned with Hegel's ongoing thinking about the state of nature than his entire system of thought. For some recent, more specific reflections on this part of the later work, see Marina F. Bykova, "The 'Struggle for Recognition' and the Thematization of Intersubjectivity," in *Essays on Hegel's Philosophy of Subjective Spirit*, ed. David Stern (Albany: State University of New York Press, 2013), 139–54.

28. Georg Wilhelm Friedrich Hegel, *Hegel's Philosophy of Subjective Spirit: Volume 3 Phenomenology and Psychology*, ed. and trans. Michael John Petry (Dordrecht: Reidel, 1978), 57.

29. "They must [*müssen*] engage in this struggle, for they must [*müssen*] raise their certainty of being for themselves to truth, both in the case of the other and in their own case. And it is only [*allein*] through staking one's life that freedom is won." Hegel, *Phenomenology of Spirit*, 114; Hegel, *Werke*, 3:149.

30. In the slightly later *Science of Logic* (1812–1816), Hegel follows Aristotle in suggesting that only after there had developed a social hierarchy could some be in a position to think. Again, it's important to note that Hegel believes *everyone* should be in this position. My concern is the path he seems to believe is necessary to get there. "As a matter of fact, the need to occupy oneself with pure thought presupposes that the human spirit must already have travelled a long road; it is, one may say, the need of the already satisfied need for the necessities to which it must have attained, the need of a condition free from needs, of abstraction from the material of intuition, imagination, and so on, of the concrete interests of desire, instinct, will, in which material the determinations of thought are veiled and hidden. In the silent regions of thought which has come to itself and communes only with itself, the interests which move the lives of races and individuals are hushed." Georg Wilhelm Friedrich Hegel, *Science of Logic*, trans. A. V. Miller (New York: Routledge, 2002), 43.

31. Hegel, *Phenomenology of Spirit*, 117; Hegel, *Werke*, 3:153.

32. Hegel, *Phenomenology of Spirit*, 117; Hegel, *Werke*, 3:153.

33. Hegel, *Phenomenology of Spirit*, 118; Hegel, *Werke*, 3:154–55.

34. Hegel, *Phenomenology of Spirit*, 43; Hegel, *Werke*, 3:65.

35. A more positive reading of Hegel might say that he does this because he is simply describing the world of ancient slavery, or medieval feudalism, or what he views as the submission to nature outside of Europe. But the risk, that Marx will later call Hegel's uncritical positivism, is that he naturalizes and justifies the very thing he is seeking to overcome.

36. Hegel, *Phenomenology of Spirit*, 118; Hegel, *Werke*, 3:155.

37. Rousseau, *Basic Political Writings*, 60–65.

38. Kant, *Anthropology, History, and Education*, 111.

39. Ibid., 114.

40. Schiller, *On the Aesthetic Education of Man in a Series of Letters*, 173.

41. For example: "*Negroes*, uninterested and lacking in interest, in a state of undisturbed naivety, are to be regarded as a nation of children. They are sold and allow themselves to be sold without any reflection as the rights or wrongs of it." Hegel, *Hegel's Philosophy of Subjective Spirit / Hegels Philosophie Des Subjektiven Geistes*, 55.

42. Monahan, "Recognition Beyond Struggle: On a Liberatory Account of Hegelian Recognition."

43. Monahan, *Creolizing Hegel*.

44. I return to this point below. For those who have taken some of these general problematics in Hegel more seriously, see, in addition to Tibebu and Bernasconi, Maldonado-Torres, *Against War*, 142–46.

45. Cole, *The Birth of Theory*, 65–82. Cole can only make his argument by explicitly avoiding discussion of the question of the state of nature, which he does twice (78, 80).

46. Gilroy of course had discussed Hegel in *relation* to slavery, but not with specific reference to Hegel's knowledge *of* slavery. Buck-Morss also notes the work of Pierre-Franklin Tavares, who had made this suggestion without the same archival research in an essay she only read after her original one was published. Buck-Morss, *Hegel, Haiti and Universal History*, 49.

47. Ibid., 52.

48. For an overview, see Teshale Tibebu, *Hegel and the Third World*, 34–41.

49. Siep, "Der Kampf um Anerkennung. Zu Hegels Auseinandersetzung mit Hobbes in den Jenaer Schriften."

50. Hegel, *Hegel's Philosophy of Subjective Spirit*, III:59; my emphasis.

51. Cole, whose reading focuses on the earlier version, does not engage this later moment. He does, however, note that of the text in the *Phenomenology*: "To be clear, the section . . . does not start out with feudal references, nor does it declare its medievalism from the first, until the episode itself passes from the struggle to the death to the struggle for recognition and for possession." My concern with Cole's reading is not that he is wrong about Hegel's interest in the critique of feudalism, but that he unnecessarily claims the critique of feudalism as the primary focus of the text, neglecting these other references and thus re-Europeanizing Hegel. Cole, *The Birth of Theory*, 80. Part of my concern is the very power of Cole's analysis, which has become authoritative and been used as evidence against readings like Buck-Morss's that extend Hegel into the colonies. See, for example, Germana, "Revisiting 'Hegel and Haiti': Postcolonial Readings of the Lord/Bondsman Dialectic," 100–1.

52. Hegel, *Hegel's Philosophy of Subjective Spirit*, 63; emphasis in original.

53. Hegel, *Phenomenology of Spirit*, 7; Hegel, *Werke*, 3:19.

54. Aimé Césaire, *Discourse on Colonialism*, ed. Robin D. G. Kelley (New York: Monthly Review Press, 2000), 45; my emphasis.

55. Hegel, *Phenomenology of Spirit*, 492; Hegel, *Werke*, 3:591.

56. On this latter point about prose, see the conclusion to Georg Wilhelm Friedrich Hegel, *Introductory Lectures on Aesthetics* (London: Penguin Books, 1993).

57. Buck-Morss, *Hegel, Haiti and Universal History*, 133.

58. Georg Wilhelm Friedrich Hegel, *Elements of the Philosophy of Right*, ed. Allen Wood, trans. H. B. Nisbet (New York: Cambridge University Press, 1991), 86; emphasis in original; Georg Wilhelm Friedrich Hegel, *Werke*, vol. 7 (Frankfurt am Main: Suhrkamp, 1969), 122.

59. Hegel, *Elements of the Philosophy of Right*, 86; emphasis in original; Hegel, *Werke*, 7:122.

60. Hegel, *Elements of the Philosophy of Right*, 87; emphases in original; Hegel, *Werke*, 7:123.

61. Hegel, *Elements of the Philosophy of Right*, 58; Hegel, *Werke*, 7:80–81.

62. Hegel, *Elements of the Philosophy of Right*, 230–31; Hegel, *Werke*, 7:350.

63. Hegel, *Elements of the Philosophy of Right*, 88; Hegel, *Werke*, 7:126.

64. "So even when Blacks revolt against slavery, as they did successfully in Haiti, this would seem, in Hegel's view, to be because they have come in contact with European views about freedom." Bernasconi also notes the research of Michael Hoffheimer, who has shown that Hegel's views were even used to justify slavery by a Mississippi congressman in 1860. Bernasconi, "Hegel at the Court of Ashanti," 61, 306n74. See also Bull, "Slavery and the Multiple Self," 109.

65. Hegel, *Elements of the Philosophy of Right*, 367; Hegel, *Werke*, 7:498–99.

66. Hegel, *Elements of the Philosophy of Right*, 376; emphasis in original; Hegel, *Werke*, 7:507.

67. Hegel, *Elements of the Philosophy of Right*, 120; emphasis in original; Hegel, *Werke*, 7:180.

68. Hegel, *Elements of the Philosophy of Right*, 376; Hegel, *Werke*, 7:508.

69. Hegel, *Elements of the Philosophy of Right*, 269; Hegel, *Werke*, 7:392–93.

70. Hegel, I should note, is pretty explicit about this himself: "In Haiti they ['the Negroes'] have even formed a state on Christian principles. They show no inner tendency to culture however. In their homeland the most shocking despotism prevails; there, they have no feeling for the personality of man, their spirit is quite dormant, remains sunk within itself, makes no progress, and so corresponds to the compact and *undifferentiated* mass of the African terrain." Hegel, *Hegel's Philosophy of Subjective Spirit / Hegels Philosophie Des Subjektiven Geistes*, 55.

71. Ibid., 63.

72. Judith Butler, Slavoj Žižek, and Ernesto Laclau, *Contingency, Hegemony, Universality: Contemporary Dialogues on the Left* (London: Verso, 2000), 20.

73. Hegel, *Phenomenology of Spirit*, 56; Hegel, *Werke*, 3:80.

74. George Ciccariello-Maher has recently taken a different tactic and suggested that we can "decolonize dialectics" by looking to how decolonial activists

enacted it. Like Butler, he looks what can be done *after* Hegel, and I am curious about what can be done *before*. Ciccariello-Maher, *Decolonizing Dialectics*.

75. As Bernasconi has shown with regard to Africa, Hegel purposefully misread his sources in order to construct his grand historical narrative. The point is not to "update" Hegel's readings so much as to insist on what happens if we take global cultural pluralities seriously. Bernasconi, "Hegel at the Court of Ashanti."

76. Philippe Descola, "Beyond Nature and Culture," in *The Handbook of Contemporary Animism*, ed. Graham Harvey (New York: Routledge, 2014), 79.

77. Ibid., 79.

78. Ibid., 79.

79. Stanley Cavell has also suggested a parallel to Hegel's "fight for recognition" in the idea of a "demand for acknowledgment." Cavell, *Pursuits of Happiness: The Hollywood Comedy of Remarriage*, 17.

80. As Spivak has argued, one part of Hegel's Eurocentrism is his claim that imperialism was invented by the West. Spivak, *A Critique of Postcolonial Reason*, 37.

81. Viveiros de Castro, *The Inconstancy of the Indian Soul*, 50–51.

82. Hegel makes this argument explicitly and famously in his *Lectures on the Philosophy of World History: Introduction*, trans. Hugh Barr Nisbet (Cambridge: Cambridge University Press, 1981).

83. Karl Marx, *Early Writings*, ed. Quintin Hoare, trans. Rodney Livingstone and Gregor Benton (New York: Vintage, 1975), 384–85; Karl Marx, *Gesamtausgabe (MEGA)*, vol. I, 2 (Berlin: Dietz, 1972), 403.

84. This is well explicated in Lucio Colletti, "Introduction," in *Early Writings*, by Karl Marx, trans. Tom Nairn (New York: Vintage, 1975), 20.

85. Marx, *Early Writings*, 155–56; Marx, *Gesamtausgabe (MEGA)*, I, 2:98.

86. Marx, *Early Writings*, 155; Marx, *Gesamtausgabe (MEGA)*, I, 2:97.

87. This of course does not mean that Hegel mechanistically applied the dialectic. Indeed, as his commentators have constantly confronted, the way in which Hegel describes the dialectical method shifts as he confronts different worldly contents. Given the relation between form and content central to his philosophy, this makes sense. My concern with Hegel, as noted above, is not with his general philosophy but with how, specifically, he applied the dialectic to questions of global contact. For a helpful overview of debates about Hegel's application of dialectics, see Maybee, "Hegel's Dialectics."

88. Marx, *Early Writings*, 174; Marx, *Gesamtausgabe (MEGA)*, I, 2:115.

89. Marx, *Early Writings*, 175; Marx, *Gesamtausgabe (MEGA)*, I, 2:115. For a more extensive treatment of these passages, see Bhikhu Parekh, *Marx's Theory of Ideology* (New York: Routledge, 2015), 86–95.

90. Louis Althusser and Étienne Balibar, *Reading Capital*, trans. Ben Brewster (London: NLB, 1970), 15.

91. Althusser and Balibar, 161–63.

92. Althusser and Balibar, 179.

93. Karl Marx, *Capital: A Critique of Political Economy, Volume 1*, trans. Ben Fowkes (New York: Vintage, 1977), 169; Karl Marx, *Gesamtausgabe (MEGA)*, vol. II, 8 (Berlin: Dietz, 1972), 104–5.

94. In an interesting reading of the late Marx that I discovered toward the end of my writing, Enrique Dussel similarly suggests that Marx's major "turn" [*viraje*] occurred not when he became more "scientific" but when he confronted the problem of how his theories related to the "people in Russia after the translation of *Capital* into Russian. For Dussel, this late "economic-anthropological" Marx, less concerned with the abstract theory of capital and more concerned with how to generate a national revolution through popular connections, is "pertinent to the extreme." A comparison of Anderson's and Dussel's thoughts on Marx's late writings would be worthwhile. Enrique Dussel, *El último Marx (1863–1882) y la liberación latinoamericana* (Mexico City: Siglo XXI, 1990), 268.

95. Anderson's work, which argues for a general shift in how we conceive of the canons of modern thought, helped me to better articulate my concerns throughout this book. The only slight difference I would mark from Anderson is that he tends to read Marx himself within the developmental framework of progress. For example, Anderson, in a response to critics, suggests that Marx's early writings "are simply too Hegelian in the bad sense, that of Hegel's rather conservative *Philosophy of History*, written long after the more revolutionary *Phenomenology of Spirit*." Marx's writings, as I try to show here, have incipient criticisms of historicism from the 1840s on. I suggest that Marx's early criticism of the *Phenomenology* was part of what set the stage for his later, more complex global engagements. Anderson, *Marx at the Margins*, 6–7. Kevin Anderson, "Marx at the Margins," *Dialectical Anthropology* 39, no. 2 (June 1, 2015): 229. While Anderson is far from the first to look at these elements of Marx—he himself credits his mentor, Raya Dunayevskaya—he offers an impressive and synthetic overview that has helped advance the conversation about Marx's writings on world cultures and how they might change our understanding of his work. For a helpful review, see Kohei Saito, "Learning from Late Marx," *Monthly Review* 68, no. 5 (2016), https://monthlyreview.org/2016/10/01/learning-from-late-marx/.

96. Marx did already show signs of understanding that the assumption of "primitivity" was flawed, at least according to Senghor. His early writings were influential for Senghor, especially when Marx wrote to Ruge in 1843: "Reason has always existed, but not always in form of rationality." Senghor often quoted this line, as he found generally in Marx's early writings a powerful critique of developmentalist models and a potential understanding of the plural forms of reason. I translate Marx from Senghor, "Marxisme et Humanisme," 206.

97. This aligns Marx with William Connolly's thoughts on the transformation of self as part of the "ethos of pluralization," an idea I explore at greater length when discussing Emerson in chapter 5. William Connolly, *The Ethos of Pluralization* (Minneapolis: University of Minnesota Press, 1995), 69–70.

98. For a clear version of the humanist critique of Althusser, see Colletti, "Introduction." Gareth Stedman Jones, whose monumental biography of Marx arrived too late for me to incorporate into this project, notes a similar continuity around the question of anthropology: "One of the most interesting features of Karl's new focus upon the durability and 'viability' of the archaic village community was the way in which it invited the restatement of the conception of human nature so eloquently spelled out by him in 1843 and 1844 during his time in Paris. This conception had not, as many commentaries assume, been discarded as the unwanted juvenilia of 'the young Marx.'" I would only nuance this statement by noting that this "restatement" required of Marx a "revision" of his understanding of non-European cultures. Gareth Stedman Jones, *Karl Marx: Greatness and Illusion* (Cambridge: Belknap Press of Harvard University Press, 2016), 584–85. Jeremy Adelman's review alerted me to the relevant passages in Stedman Jones's work. Jeremy Adelman, "The Mortal Marx," *Public Books*, December 1, 2016, http://www.publicbooks.org/the-mortal-marx/.

99. Marx, *Early Writings*, 348; emphases original except where noted; Marx, *Gesamtausgabe (MEGA)*, I, 2:389.

100. Marx, *Early Writings*, 366; Marx, *Gesamtausgabe (MEGA)*, I, 2:426.

101. It says something about how far critical theory still has to go that the most recent major work on alienation—Rahel Jaeggi's—has been acclaimed as a major advance on Marx because it articulates alienation without reference to essence. That's all well and good, but Jaeggi's work continues to ignore geographic histories or cultural differences. Rahel Jaeggi, *Alienation*, trans. Frederick Neuhouser and Alan E. Smith (New York: Columbia University Press, 2014).

102. Given Senghor's position and Dussel's writings on the late Marx (cited above), one might ask if Anderson's intervention in Marx studies is to show Western Marxists what other readers have known for a long time. Indeed, in a review of Anderson's book, Aijaz Ahmad noted that "the Marx Anderson presents is one that is rather familiar in India and among Asian Marxists more generally but much less so in the West." But there is a certain danger here of erasing local debates. Senghor was responding to those who used Marx's universalism against his ideas of Négritude, and Dussel is explicitly responding to similar problems in Latin American thought. Certainly there are universal Marxists in India, as well! The point is perhaps more that works like Anderson's are helping to restore important *debates* about Marx, which are insufficiently sketched in the current criticism in the West. Aijaz Ahmad, "Karl Marx, 'Global Theorist,'" *Dialectical Anthropology* 39, no. 2 (June 1, 2015): 201.

103. Cited in Anderson, *Marx at the Margins*, 2010, 234; my emphasis.

104. Karl Marx and Friedrich Engels, "The Communist Manifesto," in *The Marx-Engels Reader*, ed. Robert C. Tucker (New York: Norton, 1978), 476.

105. Ibid., 467–77.

106. Ibid., 477; my emphasis.

107. Ibid., 477.

108. Ibid., 500.

109. Karl Marx and Friedrich Engels, *The Marx-Engels Reader*, ed. Robert C. Tucker (New York: Norton, 1978), 658.

110. Ibid., 658.

111. The classic positions are in Said, *Orientalism*, 153–56; and the critique of Said's position in Aijaz Ahmad, *In Theory: Classes, Nations, Literatures* (London; New York: Verso, 1992), 221–42. Ahmad himself was less interested in the debate (he calls it merely a "formal" occasion) and more invested in thinking past the way in which Said's brief critique had begun to circulate as a shorthand for dismissing Marx out of hand. Ahmad, 14.

112. In addition to Ahmad's essay, see Anderson, *Marx at the Margins*, 9–28; 37–41; 185–87; 208–18.

113. Marx and Engels, *The Marx-Engels Reader*, 471–72.

114. This is true in Buck-Morss, for example, who ironically blames Marxism for writing over the place of geography in Hegel's thought. And even those who do notice these moments, such as Fredric Jameson, may come to dismiss them. Jameson argues that the reflections on the value of the Russian commune are the most "conservative" and "opportunist" elements of Marx, and that they do not bear on our political present. Jameson instead claims that Marx wanted to "demonstrate that socialism was more modern than capitalism and more productive." He continues: "To recover that futurism and that excitement is surely the fundamental task of any left 'discursive struggle' today." My fear is that such muscular statements produce the unbearable identities that relegated all of those outside modern productivity to be grist for its Satanic mills. Moreover, Jameson here is dismissive of entire ways of life, not only those that resist capitalist development, but also the interstices of difference within capitalist cultures that Marx himself was pointing to. And the statement is particularly troubling—if not unique—today, when ecological crises should make us doubt this logic of productivity as well as its political utility. I am not, to be sure, opposed to some elements of Jameson's thinking here and appreciate his call for imagining better futures (which can surely incorporate elements of the past). It is simply his dismissal tout court of anything not modern and productive that is troubling both for a reading of Marx and for the politics of the present. In a different spirit, Harry Harootunian has also noted not only the effective political alliances made possible by "residualism," but also how this has been central to capitalism's own success. He enjoins us to negotiate this dueling possibility. His work, as a whole, is a rich addition to Anderson's in that it looks at the variegated global history of Marx's reception. Buck-Morss, *Hegel, Haiti and Universal History*, 56–57; Fredric Jameson, *Representing Capital: A Commentary on Volume One* (London; New York: Verso, 2011), 89–90; Harry Harootunian, *Marx After Marx: History and Time in the Expansion of Capitalism* (New York: Columbia University Press, 2015). On the political needs of questioning such visions as Jameson's in the name of ecology, see Naomi Klein, *This Changes Everything: Capitalism vs. the Climate* (New York: Simon & Schuster, 2015); John Bellamy Foster, "The Long

Ecological Revolution," *Monthly Review* 69, no. 6 (November 1, 2017), https://monthlyreview.org/2017/11/01/the-long-ecological-revolution/. Klein's own veering into primitivist fantasies is troubling, but her insights can be preserved without them. A fuller discussion of these elements in her work is beyond my scope here.

115. Nelson Mandela engaged this practice himself with regard to Marx. He relates that after a patient reading of Marx's work, he came to see certain values of communism as indispensable for political development. Mandela, *Long Walk to Freedom*, 120–21.

116. Karl Marx, *The Ethnological Notebooks of Karl Marx*, ed. Lawrence Krader (Assen: Van Gorcum, 1972), 340; Anderson, *Marx at the Margins*, 204. The translation here is Anderson's from Marx's German notes. "Conventionalities" is in English in the original.

117. Anderson, *Marx at the Margins*, 212; the italicized line is Marx's addition to Kovalevsky.

118. Williams, *Culture and Materialism*, 37–42.

119. Marx and Engels, *The Marx-Engels Reader*, 472.

120. This point is well summarized in Ahmad, "Karl Marx, 'Global Theorist,'" 205.

121. Hobsbawm noted that Marx would have had very little accurate information about the cultures and histories of the Americas in the 1850s. This may overstate the case and more reflect the criticism of all-preceding ethnology in Hobsbawm's own moment. Eric Hobsbawm, "Introduction," 25.

122. Karl Marx, *Grundrisse: Foundations of the Critique of Political Economy*, trans. Martin Nicolaus (New York: Penguin, 1993), 83; my emphasis; Karl Marx, *Gesamtausgabe (MEGA)*, vol. II, 1 (Berlin: Dietz, 1972), 21.

123. Marx, *Grundrisse*, 485; emphases mine; Marx, *Gesamtausgabe (MEGA)*, II, 1:390.

124. Marx, *Grundrisse*, 473; emphasis mine; Marx, *Gesamtausgabe (MEGA)*, II, 1:381.

125. Marx, *Grundrisse*, 487; Marx, *Gesamtausgabe (MEGA)*, II, 1:391–92.

126. Friedrich Hayek, *The Road to Serfdom: Text and Documents—The Definitive Edition*, ed. Bruce Caldwell (Chicago: University of Chicago Press, 2007), 101.

127. Karl Polanyi, *The Great Transformation: The Political and Economic Origins of Our Time* (Boston: Beacon Press, 2001), 31.

128. These insights are scattered throughout their works, but see especially Thorstein Veblen, *The Theory of the Leisure Class* (Oxford: Oxford University Press, 2009), 10–15; Polanyi, *The Great Transformation*, 45–70. See also Raya Dunayevskaya, *Women's Liberation and the Dialectics of Revolution: Reaching for the Future* (Detroit: Wayne State University Press, 1996). For a recent invocation of anthropology to challenge economic orthodoxy, see Graeber, *Debt*.

129. This fact is at the heart of my disagreement with both Brennan and Muthu in the preceding chapters. Muthu focuses on an abstraction—cultural

agency—and so ignores the actual denigration of cultural agents. Brennan focuses on Hegel's historical vision but ignores what he actually says about those whom he incorporates in that vision. Cross-cultural value judgments matter more than either of these accounts allows.

130. Marx, *Capital: A Critique of Political Economy, Volume 1*, 171; Marx, *Gesamtausgabe (MEGA)*, II, 8:106–7.

131. Cited in Anderson, *Marx at the Margins*, 228.

132. Marx, *Early Writings*, 358; Marx, *Gesamtausgabe (MEGA)*, I, 2:398–99.

133. Senghor highlighted this line as well, using it in the post-WWII context to criticize totalitarian Marxisms as well as to call for general creative thinking on possible futures. Senghor, "Marxisme et Humanisme," 215–16. On Senghor's writings on Marx, see Wilder, *Freedom Time*, 206–40.

134. Chakrabarty, *Provincializing Europe*, 63.

135. Ibid., 254.

136. Ibid., xiii.

137. Ibid., 217.

138. Ibid., 254. Chakrabarty has continued to apply this model in his very interesting work on climate change. See, for example, Dipesh Chakrabarty, "Postcolonial Studies and the Challenge of Climate Change," *New Literary History* 43, no. 1 (2012): 1–18.

139. Chakrabarty, *Provincializing Europe*, 5.

140. In later work, Chakrabarty suggests that Indian thinkers did in fact have shifting positions on Europe, but he does not, so far as I know, revise his previous conclusions accordingly. Dipesh Chakrabarty, "From Civilization to Globalization: The 'West' as a Shifting Signifier in Indian Modernity," *Inter-Asia Cultural Studies* 13, no. 1 (March 2012): 138–52.

141. In addition to the works cited below, see the brief but incisive critique in Wilder, *Freedom Time*, 10–12.

142. Subrahmanyam, "On World Historians in the Sixteenth Century," 27.

143. Harootunian, *Marx After Marx*, 227.

144. Vivek Chibber, *Postcolonial Theory and the Specter of Capital* (New York: Verso, 2013), 291; emphasis in original.

145. In this way, Chakrabarty's critics misread him as primitivizing what he in fact complicates, just as Senghor's critics do. Perhaps this is part of why Chakrabarty has taken an interest in Senghor's works. See his "Legacies of Bandung: Decolonisation and the Politics of Culture," *Economic and Political Weekly* 40, no. 46 (2005): 4817.

146. These points are scattered throughout their books, but see, for example, Chibber, *Postcolonial Theory and the Specter of Capital*, 101–9; Harootunian, *Marx After Marx*, 225–34.

147. Bruce Robbins, "Subaltern Speak," *N+1*, Winter 2014, https://nplusonemag.com/issue-18/reviews/subaltern/.

148. Chakrabarty, *Provincializing Europe*, 6.
149. Ibid., 18, 68, 249–50.
150. Heidegger, *Being and Time*, 166.
151. Harootunian misses this point, focusing instead on a dubious reading of Heidegger and the history of being: "As for the claims of History II, it should be recognized that it is based on Being's historicality, which is actually prior to the production of history itself. Such historicality risked permanent and stationary immobility since it reflected Being in its primordial authenticity." We have seen, however, that this "primordial authenticity" has nothing to do with "stationary immobility" with respect to cultural transformations. Because Harootunian does not see Marx and Heidegger in conversation about global being (but rather about the nature of time), he concludes that they are merely "talking past each other." Harootunian, *Marx After Marx*, 230, 234.
152. Fanon, *Black Skin, White Masks*, xi; Fanon, *Œuvres*, 1:63.
153. Enrique Dussel, *The Underside of Modernity: Apel, Ricoeur, Rorty, Taylor, and the Philosophy of Liberation*, trans. Eduardo Mendieta (New York: Humanity Books, 1996).
154. See, for example, Robert Bernasconi, "The Assumption of Negritude: Aimé Césaire, Frantz Fanon, and the Vicious Circle of Racial Politics," *Parallax* 8, no. 2 (April 2002): 69–83; Gary Wilder, "Race, Reason, Impasse: Césaire, Fanon, and the Legacy of Emancipation," *Radical History Review* 90, no. 1 (2004): 31–61.
155. See, for example, Maldonado-Torres, *Against War*, 96–159; Ciccariello-Maher, *Decolonizing Dialectics*, 47–73; Nigel Gibson, "Dialectical Impasses: Turning the Table on Hegel and the Black," *Parallax* 8, no. 2 (April 1, 2002): 30–45; Lewis R. Gordon, *What Fanon Said: A Philosophical Introduction to His Life and Thought* (New York: Fordham University Press, 2015), 68–70, 130–34.
156. Fanon, *The Wretched of the Earth*, 41, 43; Fanon, *Œuvres*, 1:455, 457.
157. Fanon, *The Wretched of the Earth*, 44; Fanon, *Œuvres*, 1:458.
158. Fanon, *The Wretched of the Earth*, 312; Fanon, *Œuvres*, 1:673–74.
159. Robert Bernasconi, "The European Knows and Does Not Know: Fanon's Response to Sartre," in *Frantz Fanon's Black Skin, White Masks: New Interdisciplinary Essays*, ed. Max Silverman (Manchester: Manchester University Press, 2005), 101.
160. Fanon, *Black Skin, White Masks*, 161; Fanon, *Œuvres*, 1:211.
161. Fanon, *Black Skin, White Masks*, 14; Fanon, *Œuvres*, 1:81.
162. Fanon, *Black Skin, White Masks*, 15; Fanon, *Œuvres*, 1:82.
163. For a helpful recent collection on the book, see Max Silverman, ed., *Frantz Fanon's Black Skin, White Masks: New Interdisciplinary Essays* (Manchester: Manchester University Press, 2005).
164. Fanon, *Black Skin, White Masks*, 89; translation modified; Fanon, *Œuvres*, 1:153.
165. Fanon, *Black Skin, White Masks*, 89; Fanon, *Œuvres*, 1:153.

166. Fanon, *Black Skin, White Masks*, 27; Fanon, *Œuvres*, 1:94. "Blanc ou Noir, telle est la question." "Telle est . . ." is the standard translation of Shakespeare's line into French.

167. For a probing critique of Fanon's position on African philosophy, see Paget Henry, "Fanon, African and Afro-Caribbean Philosophy," in *Fanon: A Critical Reader*, ed. Lewis R. Gordon, T. Denean Sharpley-Whiting, and Renee T. White (Oxford: Wiley-Blackwell, 1996), 220–43. I agree with Henry that today we need to engage with more global philosophies but see this more as building on Fanon's work than departing from it. On the European side, Fanon is frequently taken to be following the work of Jean-Paul Sartre, but, as we will see, he in fact goes beyond Sartre in his activity of "destructuring" a history of philosophy that the former leaves intact.

168. Fanon, *Black Skin, White Masks*, xi; Fanon, *The Wretched of the Earth*, 316; Fanon, *Œuvres*, 1:63, 676.

169. I take this image of the dimension from Nancy Bentley's reading of a sketch of a short story by Du Bois: "the figure of a fourth dimension places emphasis not on color-line separation but on the coexistence of a distinct zone of experience with a three dimensional world that remains oblivious to it." Nancy Bentley, "The Fourth Dimension: Kinlessness and African American Narrative," *Critical Inquiry* 35, no. 2 (2009): 281.

170. Fanon, *Black Skin, White Masks*, 91; Fanon, *Œuvres*, 1:154.

171. I owe my focus on this passage, as well as much of my reading here, to conversations with Tal Corem and Cetin Gurer.

172. Fanon, *Black Skin, White Masks*, 91; Fanon, *Œuvres*, 1:154.

173. Fanon, *Black Skin, White Masks*, 92; Fanon, *Œuvres*, 1:155.

174. Fanon, *Black Skin, White Masks*, 205; translation modified; Fanon, *Œuvres*, 1:250.

175. Fanon, *Black Skin, White Masks*, 92; Fanon, *Œuvres*, 1:155. The idea may come from Sartre's *Anti-Semite and Jew*: "Authenticity, it is almost needless to say, consists in having a true and lucid consciousness of the situation, in assuming [*assumer*] the responsibilities and risks that it involves, in accepting [*revendiquer*] it in pride or humiliation, sometimes in horror and hate." "Accept," it should be noted, is a mistranslation here, too. *Revendiquer* means more to claim and thus aligns with this idea of assumption or taking up. Sartre does speak of acceptance later in the book, but this is with reference to the *situation*. One "accepts" only in the sense that one does not live in illusions about the grim reality of the present. Jean-Paul Sartre, *Anti-Semite and Jew* (New York: Schocken Books, 1965), 90, 136–37. Jean-Paul Sartre, *Réflexions sur la question juive* (Paris: P. Morihien, 1947), 116.

176. Fanon, *Black Skin, White Masks*, xv; Fanon, *Œuvres*, 1:66.

177. Fanon, *Black Skin, White Masks*, 201; Fanon, *Œuvres*, 1:247.

178. For a reading of Fanon along these lines, see Edward Said's "Travelling Theory Reconsidered," where he argues that Fanon's critique of reification is both about setting the world in motion and setting theory itself in motion by taking up

and rekindling a concept from Lukács. Edward W. Said, "Traveling Theory Reconsidered," in *Reflections on Exile and Other Essays* (Cambridge: Harvard University Press, 2000), 436–52. Gary Wilder has argued that Fanon learned this method from Césaire, who, in turn, likely learned it from Hegel and Homer—those other worldly thinkers. Wilder, "Race, Reason, Impasse." On Césaire's "exploration" of "racial selves," see also Davis, *Aimé Césaire*, 20–61.

179. Fanon, *Black Skin, White Masks*, 92–93; Fanon, *Œuvres*, 1:156.
180. Fanon, *Black Skin, White Masks*, 97; Fanon, *Œuvres*, 1:159.
181. Fanon, *Black Skin, White Masks*, 100; Fanon, *Œuvres*, 1:161. The necessity to surpass this moment is extreme. Fanon later relates a caption he saw in a children's book in which a black child says to a few white children, "Here is the pot where my ancestors cooked yours." Fanon, tongue in cheek, says that this is in fact "a service to the black man" because it represents him "not as eating the white man, but as having eaten him. Undeniably, this is progress." Fanon, *Black Skin, White Masks*, 180; Fanon, *Œuvres*, 1:225–26.
182. Fanon, *Black Skin, White Masks*, 101; Fanon, *Œuvres*, 1:163.
183. Fanon, *Black Skin, White Masks*, 102; Fanon's emphasis; Fanon, *Œuvres*, 1:163.
184. Fanon, *Black Skin, White Masks*, 106; Fanon's emphasis in a citation from Senghor; Fanon, *Œuvres*, 1:166.
185. Fanon, *Black Skin, White Masks*, 108; Fanon, *Œuvres*, 1:168.
186. Fanon, *Black Skin, White Masks*, 108; Fanon, *Œuvres*, 1:168.
187. Fanon, *Black Skin, White Masks*, 109; Fanon, *Œuvres*, 1:168.
188. Fanon, *Black Skin, White Masks*, 110; Fanon, *Œuvres*, 1:169.
189. Fanon, *Black Skin, White Masks*, 111; Fanon, *Œuvres*, 1:170. Of course, Négritude writers were not unaware of this mode of colonial relation. We find this explicitly, for example, in Césaire's *A Tempest*, when he rewrites Gonzalo's Montaignian paean to the Americas: "I meant that if the island is inhabited, as I believe it is, and if we colonise it, as is my wish, then we must shy away, as if from the plague, from importing here our defaults, yes, what we call civilization. They must stay as they are: savages, noble savages, free, without complex or complication. Something like a pool of eternal youth where we could come at intervals to revive our drooping urban spirits." Aimé Césaire, *A Tempest*, trans. Philip Crispin (London: Oberon, 2000), 30.
190. Fanon, *Black Skin, White Masks*, 111; Fanon, *Œuvres*, 1:170.
191. Fanon, *Black Skin, White Masks*, 111; Fanon, *Œuvres*, 1:170.
192. Fanon, *Black Skin, White Masks*, 112; Fanon, *Œuvres*, 1:171.
193. Fanon, *Black Skin, White Masks*, 24–25; Fanon, *Œuvres*, 1:91.
194. Fanon, *Black Skin, White Masks*, 88–89; Fanon, *Œuvres*, 1:153. I return to Hegel in the next chapter. For a critique of Hegel in Fanonian terms, see Nelson Maldonado-Torres, *Against War: Views from the Underside of Modernity* (Durham: Duke University Press, 2008), 143–50.

195. As Gibson puts it: "Rather than making generalizations about the human condition, Fanon's observations are grounded by the gravity of the historical specificity of racism and colonialism." Gibson, "Dialectical Impasses," 38.

196. Fanon, *Black Skin, White Masks*, 113; Fanon, *Œuvres*, 1:172.

197. Gordon, *What Fanon Said*, 24.

198. Ibid., 57.

199. As he notes later in the book, "Racist culture . . . erases itself as culture through forgetting its own flux." Gordon, 87.

200. Ralph Ellison, *Invisible Man*, 2nd ed. (New York: Vintage Books, 1995), 202.

201. I think this may be part of why Fanon's critique of Sartre is that he has forgotten his Hegelianism. What Fanon means, on my understanding, is that Sartre offers the racist Hegel who imposes his vision on others, rather than the radical Hegel, who posited self-sublation.

202. Fanon, *Black Skin, White Masks*, 114; translation modified; Fanon, *Œuvres*, 1:172.

203. This is why I disagree with Brennan's attempt to divide Fanon studies "down the middle" between those who read him through Hegel and those who consider him in light of poststructuralism. Such a division obscures Fanon's challenge to both and ignores his deep critical engagement with Hegel. Brennan, *Borrowed Light*, 84–85; 249n28.

204. This does not at all mean that Fanon denies the importance of Marxism. He only thinks that it, too, will need to be rethought through the specifics of colonial history. As we have seen, Marx himself agreed. Fanon, *The Wretched of the Earth*, 39–41; Fanon, *Œuvres*, 1:451–52.

205. Fanon, *The Wretched of the Earth*, 222–23; Fanon, *Œuvres*, 1:602.

206. Fanon, *Black Skin, White Masks*, 115; translation modified; Fanon, *Œuvres*, 1:173.

207. On Fanon's understanding of the multiplicity of Négritude, see Bernasconi, "The Assumption of Negritude."

208. Fanon, *Black Skin, White Masks*, 206; Fanon, *Œuvres*, 1:251.

209. Fanon, *Black Skin, White Masks*, 198; Fanon citing Marx; Fanon, *Œuvres*, 1:245.

210. See the overview in Azzedine Haddour, "Torture Unveiled: Rereading Fanon and Bourdieu in the Context of May 1958," *Theory, Culture & Society* 27, no. 7–8 (December 1, 2010): 66–74.

211. Frantz Fanon, *A Dying Colonialism*, trans. Haakon Chevalier (New York: Grove Press, 1994), 49; Fanon, *Œuvres*, 1:285–86.

212. My reading here follows Gordon, *Creolizing Political Theory*, 143–46.

213. Fanon, *A Dying Colonialism*, 50; Fanon, *Œuvres*, 1:287.

214. Fanon, *A Dying Colonialism*, 52; Fanon, *Œuvres*, 1:288–89.

215. Foucault, *The Hermeneutics of the Subject*, 304.

216. Ibid., 305.

217. "*Come un popolo si trasforma nel corso della sua emancipazione.*" A lecture by Neelam Srivastava brought this fact to my attention. See her article "Frantz Fanon in Italy," *Interventions* 17, no. 3 (May 4, 2015): 309–28.

218. Fanon, *A Dying Colonialism*, 96; Fanon, *Œuvres*, 1:328.

219. Fanon, *The Wretched of the Earth*, 36; Fanon, *Œuvres*, 1:452.

220. Fanon, *The Wretched of the Earth*, 46–71; Fanon, *Œuvres*, 1:455–78.

221. Fanon, *The Wretched of the Earth*, 75; Fanon, *Œuvres*, 1:481.

222. Fanon, *The Wretched of the Earth*, 98; Fanon, *Œuvres*, 1:500.

223. I have modified the translation, which here is "cleansing force." This problematic translation, kept in the new Philcox edition, is linguistically and conceptually inaccurate. It makes it seem as if violence purifies rather than removes a toxin. The idea is not that one is "clean" after anticolonial violence, but only that one has had the toxin of dependence removed.

224. Fanon, *The Wretched of the Earth*, 94; Fanon, *Œuvres*, 1:496.

225. William Shakespeare, "Henry V," in *The Norton Shakespeare*, ed. Stephen Greenblatt (New York: W. W. Norton, 1997), IV.III.60–65.

226. One could also say that in this context Fanon is attempting to use his essay to intervene in reality. He knows (and "The Conclusion" proves this) that violence produces a cycle of vengeance. We might see him here trying to cauterize the wound of violence by demonstrating its potential to secure and fashion a nation.

227. Fanon, *The Wretched of the Earth*, 95; Fanon, *Œuvres*, 1:496.

228. Jean-Paul Sartre, "Preface," in Fanon, *The Wretched of the Earth*, 13; Fanon, *Œuvres*, 1:433.

229. Fanon, *The Wretched of the Earth*, 106; Fanon, *Œuvres*, 1:506.

230. Fanon, *The Wretched of the Earth*, 193; Fanon, *Œuvres*, 1:576.

231. Fanon, 316; translation modified; Fanon, *Œuvres*, 1:676. On this translation, see Robert Bernasconi, "Casting the Slough: Fanon's New Humanism for a New Humanity," in *Fanon: A Critical Reader*, ed. Lewis R. Gordon, T. Denean Sharpley-Whiting, and Renee T. White (Cambridge: Wiley-Blackwell, 1996), 113–21.

232. Cheah, *Spectral Nationality*, 230.

233. Cheah has written against reducing philosophy to history, arguing that "[h]istorical analyses remain invaluable for reconstructing the concrete conditions under which contamination occurs in specific cases, but they do not acknowledge the irreducible character of contamination and its radical implications for the theory and practice of freedom." Sorting out our philosophy, he seems to suggest, should help us sort out our history and practice. My concern is how global histories inflect our philosophical judgments in ways that Cheah does not here recognize. Ibid., 10.

234. Nelson Maldonado-Torres has made this point explicitly: "Fanon is not satisfied with repeating the centuries-old slogan that philosophy is a 'way of life.' His critique of various European philosophers indicates that there are certain 'ways of life' that, when examined closely, rather appear as 'ways of death.' . . . For him

philosophy is, or should be, first and foremost an ethical and political activity that aims to promote the very possibility of life with others in community." In a footnote to this remark, Maldonado-Torres also makes a brief comparison between Fanon and a key interlocutor for Foucault: Pierre Hadot. Maldonado-Torres notes that Hadot fails to put justice at the center of his reflections. I agree, but have sought more generally here to think of *the globe* as the centerpiece of modern reckonings with philosophy as a way of life. Maldonado-Torres, *Against War*, 97; 278n7.

235. David Scott, *Refashioning Futures: Criticism after Postcoloniality* (Princeton: Princeton University Press, 1999), 194.

236. In addition to *Refashioning Futures*, see Scott, *Conscripts of Modernity*; David Scott, *Omens of Adversity: Tragedy, Time, Memory, Justice* (Durham: Duke University Press, 2014).

237. Scott, *Refashioning Futures: Criticism after Postcoloniality*, 203–8.

238. Ibid., 208–15.

239. Ibid., 218–20.

240. Ibid., 219–20.

241. There are, I think, deep problems with the critique of Foucault in the account by Afary and Anderson, but their work is a helpful resource at least. Afary and Anderson, *Foucault and the Iranian Revolution*. For a counter-reading, see Ghamari-Tabrizi, *Foucault in Iran: Islamic Revolution after the Enlightenment*.

242. Gilles Kepel, *Jihad: The Trail of Political Islam*, trans. Anthony Roberts (Cambridge: Belknap Press of Harvard University Press, 2003), 39. This is also cited by Homi K. Bhabha, "Foreword," in *The Wretched of the Earth*, by Frantz Fanon (New York: Grove Press, 2005), xxx.

243. Scott, *Refashioning Futures: Criticism after Postcoloniality*, 26.

244. Ibid., 34, 43.

245. Gordon notes that Fanon would likely reject the idea of being part of "theory from the Global South" because he is looking for "more *universalizing* practices. Although not *the* universal, because of the fundamental incompleteness at the heart of being human, the paradox of reaching beyond particularity is the simultaneous humility of understanding the expanse and possibility of reality and human potential." Gordon, *What Fanon Said*, 130.

Chapter 5

1. On Emerson as pluralist, see James M. Albrecht, *Reconstructing Individualism: A Pragmatic Tradition from Emerson to Ellison*, American Philosophy Series (New York: Fordham University Press, 2012), 25–126; Austin Bailey, "'The World Is Full': Emerson, Pluralism, and the 'Nominalist and Realist,'" *The Pluralist* 11, no. 2 (2016): 32–48. Generally positive reevaluations of Emerson that informed my thinking in this chapter include Stanley Cavell, *Emerson's Transcendental Etudes*

(Palo Alto: Stanford University Press, 2003); Branka Arsić, *On Leaving: A Reading in Emerson* (Cambridge: Harvard University Press, 2010); Russell Goodman, "Paths of Coherence through Emerson's Philosophy: The Case of 'Nominalist and Realist,'" in *The Other Emerson*, ed. Branka Arsic and Cary Wolfe (Minneapolis: University of Minnesota Press, 2010), 41–58; Jeffrey Stout, "The Transformation of Genius into Practical Power: A Reading of Emerson's 'Experience,'" *American Journal of Theology & Philosophy* 35, no. 1 (February 11, 2014): 3–24; Lawrence Buell, *Emerson* (Cambridge: Belknap Press of Harvard University Press, 2003); Wai-chee Dimock, *Through Other Continents: American Literature across Deep Time* (Princeton: Princeton University Press, 2006), 23–51; Len Gougeon, *Virtue's Hero: Emerson, Antislavery, and Reform* (Athens: University of Georgia Press, 1999); Laura Dassow Walls, *Emerson's Life in Science: The Culture of Truth* (Ithaca: Cornell University Press, 2003). For a few recent examples that fairly chart both Emerson's value and his ambivalence on political issues, especially race, see Anita Haya Patterson, *From Emerson to King: Democracy, Race, and the Politics of Protest* (New York: Oxford University Press, 1997); Peter S. Field, "The Strange Career of Emerson and Race," *American Nineteenth Century History* 2, no. 1 (March 2001): 1–32; Hugh Egan, "'On Freedom': Emerson, Douglass, and the Self-Reliant Slave," *ESQ: A Journal of the American Renaissance* 60, no. 2 (2014): 183–208; Donald Pease, "'Experience,' Antislavery, and the Crisis of Emersonianism," in *The Other Emerson*, by Branka Arsić and Cary Wolfe (Minneapolis: University of Minnesota Press, 2010); Johannes Voelz, *Transcendental Resistance: The New Americanists and Emerson's Challenge* (Hanover, NH: University Press of New England, 2010); Walls, *Emerson's Life in Science*, 166–87; Ian Finseth, "Evolution, Cosmopolitanism, and Emerson's Antislavery Politics," *American Literature* 77, no. 4 (December 1, 2005): 729–60.

2. Emerson, *Essays & Poems*, 806, 849.

3. Ibid., 990, 991.

4. Eduardo Cadava, "The Guano of History," in *The Other Emerson*, ed. Branka Arsic and Cary Wolfe (Minneapolis: University of Minnesota Press, 2010), 111.

5. Voelz, *Transcendental Resistance: The New Americanists and Emerson's Challenge*, 10.

6. Ibid., 246.

7. Ibid., 10 and passim.

8. Ibid., 10; F. O Matthiessen, *American Renaissance* (New York: Oxford University Press, 1941), 3; Philip Loveless Nicoloff, *Emerson on Race and History: An Examination of English Traits* (New York: Columbia University Press, 1961), 50. Only for Stout is Emerson successful. Stout, "The Transformation of Genius into Practical Power."

9. Deleuze's reading of Nietzsche (Nietzsche of course was an enthusiastic reader of Emerson) is similar here when he writes, "Pluralism sometimes appears to be dialectical—but it is its most ferocious enemy, its only profound enemy." For Deleuze this is so because "[t]he pluralist idea that a thing has many senses, the

idea that there are many things and one thing can be seen as 'this and then that' is philosophy's greatest achievement . . . its maturity and not its renunciation or infancy." This is part of what I want to say about Emerson: that he has been read as a failed dialectician where he has in fact been a profound thinker of pluralism via his concept of alternation. Gilles Deleuze, *Nietzsche and Philosophy*, trans. Hugh Tomlinson (New York: Columbia University Press, 1983), 8, 4.

10. Emerson, *Essays & Poems*, 979.

11. In addition to Voelz and Cadava, two magnificent readings of Emerson that make a similar claim and first opened my eyes to the power of Emerson's thinking are Arsić, *On Leaving*; Cavell, *Emerson's Transcendental Etudes*.

12. On the need to understand the lived experiences of slaves beyond "social death" and "dehumanization," see, for example, Vincent Brown, "Social Death and Political Life in the Study of Slavery," *The American Historical Review* 114, no. 5 (2009): 1231–49.

13. Emerson, *Essays & Poems*, 979.

14. It would be interesting to discuss Emerson's use of irony as a way of pulling us away from too great a dedication to an idea in order to enable our alternations. What Cadava calls Emerson's ventriloquism might be an aspect of this same alignment of racist rhetoric and critique of cultural norms. That Emerson uses rhetoric racist rhetoric against itself is a key claim of Cadava's essay.

15. Emerson, *Essays & Poems*, 980.

16. Ibid., 844.

17. Ibid., 780.

18. Ibid., 980.

19. Ralph Waldo Emerson, *The Early Lectures, Volume II*, ed. Robert E. Spiller (Cambridge: Harvard University Press, 1964), 175.

20. I discuss this idea at greater length below. On polarity in Emerson, see Walls, *Emerson's Life in Science*, 127–65.

21. Emerson, *Essays & Poems*, 769; emphasis added.

22. Ibid., 475.

23. See Cavell, *Emerson's Transcendental Etudes*, 8, 97, 113–14, 165–66, 181.

24. Emerson, *Essays & Poems*, 849.

25. Lévi-Strauss, *Tristes Tropiques*, 392.

26. Connolly, *The Ethos of Pluralization*, 69.

27. Cavell, *Emerson's Transcendental Etudes*.

28. Connolly, *The Ethos of Pluralization*, 69–70.

29. The argument here is effectively not so different from Chakrabarty's in *Provincializing Europe*. But my aim is not to provincialize the universal as opposed to the local so much as to show how the universal is one among many ways of developing global thought.

30. Emerson, *Essays & Poems*, 406.

31. Ibid., 310.

32. Ibid., 585.

33. Cited in George Kateb, *Emerson and Self-Reliance* (Thousand Oaks, CA: Sage, 1995), 19.

34. Emerson, *Essays & Poems*, 64.

35. Ralph Waldo Emerson, *The Journals and Miscellaneous Notebooks of Ralph Waldo Emerson* (Cambridge: Belknap Press of Harvard University Press, 1960), II:287.

36. Anthony Pagden notes, "America had been Europe's first 'new world,' its first encounter with a people of whose very existence it had hitherto been wholly unaware. Its second was with the peoples of the Pacific . . . in 1767." A more complex cartography of the relation of these different spaces and different modes of primitivism would be interesting to pursue but is not the focus of this study. Anthony Pagden, *Facing Each Other: The World's Perception of Europe and Europe's Perception of the World* (Burlington: Ashgate/Variorum, 2000), xxi.

37. Emerson, *The Journals and Miscellaneous Notebooks of Ralph Waldo Emerson*, 288.

38. Ibid., 288.

39. See for example the late essay "Civilization." Ralph Waldo Emerson, *Collected Works of Ralph Waldo Emerson, Volume VIII: Letters and Social Aims*, ed. Glen M. Johnson and Joel Myerson (Cambridge: Harvard University Press, 2010), 9–17.

40. Sheldon W. Liebman, "Emerson's Transformation in the 1820's," *American Literature* 40, no. 2 (1968): 147.

41. Alan Hodder, "Asia," in *Ralph Waldo Emerson in Context*, ed. Wesley T. Mott (New York: Cambridge University Press, 2013), 40–48.

42. Ian Finseth, "Evolution, Cosmopolitanism, and Emerson's Antislavery Politics"; Walls, *Emerson's Life in Science*, 166–98.

43. "Esquimaux" presents more problems than "Carib." Like Carib, it is a colonial category that generalizes groups that have different histories and languages. Unlike Carib, it is considered derogatory. Even though linguists no longer think the term was meant as such (meaning something like "those who make snowshoes"), it still carries negative connotations. I have decided to keep the word in quotation marks throughout my usage. For a quick, helpful overview, see Lawrence Kaplan, "Inuit or Eskimo? / Alaska Native Language Center," July 1, 2011, https://www.uaf.edu/anlc/resources/inuit-eskimo/.

44. Emerson, *The Early Lectures, Volume II*, 362.

45. I was not able to locate this anecdote in the sources Emerson mentions (John Franklin's *Narrative of a Journey to the Shores of the Polar Sea* or John Ross's *Narrative of a Second Voyage in Search of a Northwest Passage*), though it is possible I simply missed it. One imagines, however, that it is likely to have come from elsewhere because both authors make quite explicit that even in the morning sun, temperatures barely hover above freezing. The more likely source was William Robertson's *History of America*, which used the same anecdote from Du Tertre and which Emerson had read in his youth. That Robertson repeated the anecdote I

know from Jorge Cañizares-Esguerra, *How to Write the History of the New World: Histories, Epistemologies, and Identities in the Eighteenth-Century Atlantic World* (Palo Alto: Stanford University Press, 2002), 120. That Emerson read Robertson I know from Neal Dolan, *Emerson's Liberalism* (Madison: University of Wisconsin Press, 2009), 109.

46. Emerson, *The Early Lectures, Volume II*, 362.
47. Emerson, *Essays & Poems*, 690.
48. Ibid., 690.
49. Emerson, *The Early Lectures, Volume II*, 171.
50. Ibid., 171.
51. Ibid., 175, 186.
52. Emerson, *Essays & Poems*, 799.
53. A reading that helped me track Emerson's ambivalence here was Carolyn R. Maibor, *Labor Pains: Emerson, Hawthorne, and Alcott on Work and the Woman Question* (New York: Routledge, 2004), 34–52. At a political level, Maibor shows, Emerson was remarkably progressive. She further suggests that his general revision of values away from those generally associated with masculinity underscores a powerful normative critique of general cultural framing.
54. For an overview that is perhaps a little too kind to Emerson, see Len Gougeon, "Race," in *Ralph Waldo Emerson in Context*, ed. Wesley T. Mott (New York: Cambridge University Press, 2013), 196–203. Gougeon cites some of the more critical studies as well.
55. On the development of Emerson's thought in this regard, see Pease, " 'Experience,' Antislavery, and the Crisis of Emersonianism."
56. Ralph Waldo Emerson, *The Works of Ralph Waldo Emerson, in 12 vols. Fireside Edition* (Boston and New York, 1909), 54, http://oll.libertyfund.org/titles/1962.
57. Emerson, *Essays & Poems*, 641, 1049.
58. Ibid., 690.
59. In this universal mood, we might say that alternation itself is a generalizable human process, as I have suggested pluralism also is. Michael Jackson makes this claim, for example, in the context of thinking about philosophy in the lives of the Kuranko in Sierra Leone. Writing of our movements between abstraction and immersion, he states, "They are simply alternating forms of consciousness, either of which may provide a fleeting and consoling sense that we may comprehend our relationship to the world. They echo a distinction that precedes the development of modern science and is recognized in all human societies." The basic idea can also be found in the work of François Jullien. Speaking of the relationship between solitude and society, he writes, "Make no mistake, however: the precise middle way is not equidistant from withdrawal, on the one hand, and social life, on the other . . . The art of renewal instead lies in the alternation between tendencies." What I am suggesting is that Emerson offers a way of thinking about alternation to understand inter- and intracultural, as well as inter- and intrapersonal, engagements.

Michael Jackson, "Ajala's Heads: Reflections on Anthropology and Philosophy in a West African Setting," in *The Ground Between: Anthropologists Engage Philosophy*, ed. Veena Das et al. (Durham: Duke University Press, 2014), 28; François Jullien, *Vital Nourishment: Departing from Happiness*, trans. Arthur Goldhammer (Cambridge: Zone Books, 2007), 20.

60. Emerson wrote, for example: "I cannot myself use that systematic form which is reckoned essential in treating the science of the mind. But if one can say so without arrogance, I might suggest that he who contents himself with dotting a fragmentary curve, recording only what facts he has observed, without attempting to arrange them within one outline, follows a system also,—a system as grand as any other, though *he does not interfere with its vast curves by prematurely forcing them into a circle or ellipse*, but only draws that arc which he clearly sees, or perhaps at a later observation a remote curve of the same orbit, and waits for a new opportunity, well-assured that these observed arcs will consist with each other." I emphasize this part to show that Emerson's concern with the unbearable identity goes down to the level of geometry. Emerson, *The Works of Ralph Waldo Emerson, in 12 Vols.*, 11.

61. William Wordsworth, *William Wordsworth—The Major Works: Including The Prelude*, ed. Stephen Gill (New York: Oxford University Press, 2008), 199.

62. For example, Hegel argues that Socrates, who appears when "Athenian democracy had fallen into ruin," is an example of such a use of private conscience: "He evaporated the existing world and retreated into himself in search of the right and good." Hegel, *Elements of the Philosophy of Right*, 167.

63. Emerson, *Essays & Poems*, 1048. François Jullien has argued that there is a similar movement operative in certain forms of Taoism, as cited in note 59 above.

64. Walls, *Emerson's Life in Science*, 127.

65. Ibid., 136.

66. Ibid., 138.

67. Emerson, *Essays & Poems*, 575.

68. Ibid., 581.

69. Ibid., 577.

70. My reading here thus differs from Joseph Urbas, who claims that Emerson's "pluralism does not go all the way down" in his reading of "Nominalist and Realist." He bases his claim on the underlying unity Emerson posits, but, as I have argued, that "unity" is always already multiple. Urbas suggests that Russel Goodman, in his more pluralist reading, "stops just shy of the right conclusion." Urbas, on my reading, correctly sees Emerson's pluralism but then goes too far, finding a synthetic bottom rather than a ceaseless plurality. A proper discussion of Urbas and Goodman and their metaphysical commitments is beyond my scope here, but I want primarily to note that while I side here more with Goodman, I think the language of "radical pluralism" more completely captures Emerson's thought than Goodman's language of "aspects" and "process" (because these are part of the pluralist vocabulary), and, moreover, neither critic fully explores the place of global cultures

in the constitution of Emerson's thinking here. Joseph Urbas, "'Bi-Polar' Emerson: 'Nominalist and Realist,'" *The Pluralist* 8, no. 2 (2013): 82. Russell Goodman, "Paths of Coherence through Emerson's Philosophy: The Case of 'Nominalist and Realist,'" in *The Other Emerson*, ed. Branka Arsić and Cary Wolfe (Minneapolis: University of Minnesota Press, 2010), 41–58.

71. Emerson, *Essays & Poems*, 581; first emphasis in original, second emphasis added.

72. Ibid., 582.

73. Ibid., 583.

74. Goodman, "Paths of Coherence through Emerson's Philosophy: The Case of 'Nominalist and Realist,'" 48–52.

75. Emerson, *Essays & Poems*, 584.

76. Ibid., 585.

77. Ibid., 358.

78. Spivak, *A Critique of Postcolonial Reason*, 13.

79. Sara Danius, Stefan Jonsson, and Gayatri Chakravorty Spivak, "An Interview with Gayatri Chakravorty Spivak," *Boundary 2* 20, no. 2 (1993): 35.

80. Emerson, *Essays & Poems*, 414.

81. Ibid., 424.

82. Ibid., 480.

83. Ibid., 473.

84. Cavell, *Emerson's Transcendental Etudes*, 117; my emphasis.

85. Emerson, *Essays & Poems*, 485; my emphasis.

86. Cavell, *Emerson's Transcendental Etudes*, 133–34.

87. Emerson, *Essays & Poems*, 273.

88. Ibid., 62.

89. Ibid., 53.

90. Ibid., 15.

91. Emerson had used the phrase in a journal entry at least as early as 1838. Walls, *Emerson's Life in Science*, 144.

92. Emerson, *Essays & Poems*, 205.

93. Ibid., 205–6.

94. Cited in Albrecht, *Reconstructing Individualism*, 56.

95. Emerson, *Essays & Poems*, 793; my emphasis.

96. Anita Patterson, in her extensive reading of the race problem in Emerson, argues that the transition between the two essays has to do with how Emerson reconceives "double consciousness" through a racialized understanding of the American nation. I think it is correct that race becomes a key issue here, but, as I try to show later in the section, it is because double consciousness functions as a *critique* of certain forms of race-thinking, not as their hypostatization, as she suggests. Patterson, *From Emerson to King*, 153–55.

97. Hegel, *Phenomenology of Spirit*, 126.

98. Ibid., 127, 126.
99. Hegel, *Introductory Lectures on Aesthetics*, 60.
100. Cavell, *Emerson's Transcendental Etudes*, 192–214.
101. Cadava, "The Guano of History," 107–8. At the heart of the essay is a remarkable discussion about how Emerson enacts this critique by invoking "guano" (manure). Cadava details the complex history of this material and its importance in the 1850s and how Emerson relates the global dispossession of materials to the local murder and enslavement of labor (116–24).
102. Bilwakesh notes that most other critics only treat his engagements with Indian thought as metaphysics: "Prior criticism on Emerson and Sanskrit texts has almost completely overlooked how such reading may have affected his thinking and writing on questions of social action." Nikhil Bilwakesh, "Emerson, John Brown, and Arjuna: Translating the Bhagavad Gita in a Time of War," *ESQ: A Journal of the American Renaissance* 55, no. 1 (2009): 36.
103. Bilwakesh does not make this point, focusing more on how Emerson's ideas about action and war were influenced by his reading, but his research was very helpful in shaping my own reflections.
104. Emerson, *Essays & Poems*, 849.
105. Bilwakesh, "Emerson, John Brown, and Arjuna."
106. Charles Wilkins, *The Bhagvat-Geeta, or Dialogues of Kreeshna and Arjoon* (London: C. Nourse, 1785), 30. I have cited this passage in a similar reading of Thoreau in Alpert, "Sounding Conscience: *Walden*'s Global Bottoms."
107. Emerson, *The Journals and Miscellaneous Notebooks of Ralph Waldo Emerson*, X:356.
108. Hegel, *Lectures on the Philosophy of World History: Introduction*, 102.
109. While I am, like Fanon, very sympathetic to Hegel's critique of purely formal advances, his Eurocentric assumptions are simply absurd. How was he to speak of freedom, after all, in an era of slavery and colonization? Hegel, *Lectures on the Philosophy of World History: Introduction*, 140.
110. In light of such remarks, it is puzzling to me that Brennan argues that "[i]t is Hegel . . . who gives an explicit theoretical space to non-Western thought and provides an opening for scholars to explore such sources seriously." Some backing for Brennan's argument has, I should say, recently been given by Rathore and Mohapatra, who argue that the *extensiveness* of Hegel's grappling with Indian philosophy—something that surpasses what most scholars do today—is more meaningful than what he actually says, which, they add, can be explained away historically. I remain skeptical of these claims for the reasons given across this book. Moreover, there is reason to question whether Hegel wrote so much about India because he actually took an interest, or, what is more likely, because he sought to debunk the interest in India evident in those around him in his typically rigorous manner. This is the argument more convincingly advanced by Peter Park by setting Hegel in his historical context. Nevertheless, I do agree with their general claim that we

should engage with other historical philosophies as much as Hegel did, even though he himself did not consider them properly "philosophy," and what he says about them remains problematic. Brennan, *Borrowed Light*, 87. Aakash Singh Rathore and Rimina Mohapatra, *Hegel's India: A Reinterpretation with Texts* (New Delhi: Oxford University Press, 2017); Park, *Africa, Asia, and the History of Philosophy*, 113–31.

111. I agree here with Kateb: "He tends to see, I think, permanence, not eventual supersession, in the phenomena he interprets." Kateb, *Emerson and Self-Reliance*, 11. (Supersession is an alternative translation for *Aufhebung*.) That Emerson's dialectical movement of thought shares something with but ultimately departs from Hegel's has been registered regularly in recent secondary literature. See Cavell, *Emerson's Transcendental Etudes*, 81–82; Arsić, *On Leaving*, 38–39; Goodman, "Paths of Coherence through Emerson's Philosophy: The Case of 'Nominalist and Realist.' "

112. Eric Cheyfitz, "A Common Emerson: Ralph Waldo in an Ethnohistorical Context," *Nineteenth Century Prose* 30, no. 1–2 (2003): 260, 272.

113. Ibid., 275.

114. Ralph Waldo Emerson, *The Journals and Miscellaneous Notebooks of Ralph Waldo Emerson: 1852–1855* (Cambridge: Harvard University Press, 1977), 114. I was alerted to these passages by Cadava, "The Guano of History," 108.

115. Emerson, *Essays & Poems*, 769.

116. Cheyfitz, for example, writes that Emerson "admires" the "imperial power of the English . . . without equivocation." Cheyfitz, "A Common Emerson," 274.

117. Ralph Waldo Emerson, *English Traits*, ed. Howard Mumford Jones, John Harvard Library (Cambridge: Belknap Press of Harvard University Press, 1966), 30.

118. Ibid., 40.

119. Ibid., 40–41. Although he indicts all aspects of society, he makes this critique with some unfortunate and inexcusable classism.

120. Ibid., 41. There perhaps is a way of reading Emerson here as trying to answer a question later posed by Lucius Outlaw: "How might we work to conserve 'colored' populations and subgroupings (and white is a color as well), races and ethnies, without making it easier for racialism and ethnocentrism to 'go imperial' [in Appiah's phrase]?" How, in other words, might we have concepts of race that do not lead to domination? Emerson's answer, in part, is to criticize the very foundations of cultural imaginings that might spark such imperial fervor. This is coupled with an injunction: in whatever culture or racial formation where one finds oneself, one must simultaneously remain self- and group-critical and "oriented" (as Outlaw puts it) to the positive values of other lifeworlds. Lucius Outlaw, *On Race and Philosophy* (New York: Routledge, 1996), 21.

121. At least not for Emerson. Hegel believed that the lack of access to the sea was why Africans' spirit is "unexpressed, feels no impulse towards freedom, suffers universal slavery without resistance." Speaking of his ideas of the Indian caste system and its prohibition of sea navigation, he sums up the section: "This ossification [of caste] is fatal to freedom, and would not be tolerated by a nation given

to the free navigation of the sea." Such a nation, England, was itself fatal to the freedom of others. Hegel, *Hegel's Philosophy of Subjective Spirit / Hegels Philosophie Des Subjektiven Geistes*, 69.

122. Cadava, "The Guano of History," 121.

123. Ibid., 105.

124. Cited in ibid., 110.

125. Emerson, *Essays & Poems*, 775–76.

126. I understand that the ambiguity of the language here means that Emerson could be—and most likely is—speaking to multiple constituencies here, and I would not deny that. As some evidence for this position, however, I note that the phrase "ground to powder" surely echoes the gunpowder that would soon be used in a civil war. It is thus, again, about a race (whites) whose vices are driving them to self-destruction.

127. It should also be noted that Emerson did not have a static conception of race, as was common at the time. He writes, for example, "The fixity or inconvertibleness of races as we see them is a weak argument for the eternity of these frail boundaries." The fact that "we see" race as immutable is in no way proof of the fact. Emerson further notes that the English is a "composite character" with a "mixed origin," including the language. Susan Hegeman notes that one of Franz Boas's key contributions was to demonstrate "that there is no necessary relationship or spatial contiguity between nation-states, languages, races, and cultures." We should not give too much due to Emerson, but it is worth noting that he advanced at least some critique of this "necessary relationship" nearly a half-century before Boas. Emerson, *English Traits*, 31, 32; Hegeman, *The Cultural Return*, 14.

128. *Oxford English Dictionary*, s.v. "solution (*n.*)," http://www.oed.com.ezproxy.princeton.edu/view/Entry/184375.

129. Cavell, *Emerson's Transcendental Etudes*, 69–70.

130. Stout, "The Transformation of Genius into Practical Power," 7.

131. Ibid., 8.

132. Ibid., 9.

133. Ibid., 11.

134. Ibid., 19.

135. Ibid., 21.

136. Emerson, *Essays & Poems*, 492; my emphasis.

137. Ibid., 1049.

138. Ibid., 1048.

139. Stout, "The Transformation of Genius into Practical Power," 9.

140. Here I agree with Stout: "The essays aim to work a deep transformation in the reader. They do so by deliberately creating interpretive difficulties, through ellipses, allusions, aphorisms, paradoxical juxtapositions, and sublime examples." In my reading, however, these difficulties are meant as introductions into Emerson's alternating practices of the global self, not realizations of ideals. Ibid., 19.

Chapter 6

1. W. E. B. Du Bois, *In Battle for Peace: The Story of My 83rd Birthday* (Oxford: Oxford University Press, 2007), 11.

2. I will discuss the colonial relation at length below. The importance of witnessing anti-Semitism for Du Bois's early intellectual development in the 1890s was brought to my attention in Mitchell Duneier, *Ghetto: The Invention of a Place, the History of an Idea* (New York: Farrar, Straus and Giroux, 2016), 3–4.

3. W. E. B. Du Bois, *The Souls of Black Folk (Norton Critical Editions)*, ed. Henry Louis Gates Jr. and Terri Hume Oliver (New York: W. W. Norton & Company, 1999), 11.

4. Lawrie Balfour has read Du Bois on these grounds with reference to the texts of William Connolly that I cited above. She suggests that one limit to Connolly's argument is that it may ironically offer universal ideas about how to be pluralist that do not sufficiently take into account the specificity of racialized identities. Balfour calls Du Bois's works, especially his autobiographical relation to the race concept in *Dusk of Dawn*, "arts of the racialized self." I find that Du Bois's difference from Emerson is less a matter of critique and more a matter of expansion. Although I came across Balfour's book late in the writing of this chapter, I found it a useful resource in thinking about the complex links in Du Bois between practices of the self, racialization, feminism, and globalization, and it helped greatly in clarifications made during revision. Lawrie Balfour, *Democracy's Reconstruction: Thinking Politically with W. E. B. Du Bois* (Oxford: Oxford University Press, 2011), 87–95.

5. Although Robert Gooding-Williams and Shamoon Zamir, for example, disagree over the trajectory of Du Bois's thought, they appear to share the idea that "double consciousness" is a reified moment to be superseded in the path to a true self-consciousness. Adolph Reed offers a similar claim, from a different perspective. My hope is that the reading I provide here offers a compelling reason for why these interpretations are correct about a certain form of double consciousness, but there are *two* kinds of double consciousness in Du Bois, as in Emerson—one of which must be overcome and the other of which cannot be. Shamoon Zamir, *Dark Voices: W.E.B. Du Bois and American Thought, 1888–1903* (Chicago: University of Chicago Press, 1995), 116; Adolph L Reed, *W.E.B. Du Bois and American Political Thought: Fabianism and the Color Line* (New York: Oxford University Press, 1997), 130; Robert Gooding-Williams, *In the Shadow of Du Bois: Afro-Modern Political Thought in America* (Cambridge: Harvard University Press, 2009), 77–83. For a helpful overview of current writing about double consciousness, albeit one that strangely makes no mention of Zamir, see John P. Pittman, "Double Consciousness," in *The Stanford Encyclopedia of Philosophy*, ed. Edward N. Zalta, Summer 2016 (Metaphysics Research Lab, Stanford University, 2016), https://plato.stanford.edu/archives/sum2016/entries/double-consciousness/.

6. While it is true, as one reader pointed out to me, that all these "race concepts" are modern in their codification, this does not appear to me to be Du Bois's point in this passage. Rather, I see him as suggesting that even though African civilizations preexist these others, the diasporic "Negro" was born after the slave trade.

7. W. E. B. Du Bois, *Dark Princess: A Romance* (Jackson: Banner Books, 1995), 23.

8. Focusing on this passage as a description of alienation, Thomas Holt has also noted some of the potential positive results, including a better vision of the reality of the United States, endurance, discipline, knowledge of the need for struggle, and a capacity for refusal. Mitchell Aboulafia similarly notes the dual potential here: "Those who have a double-consciousness are in a unique position to achieve the impartiality of the spectator, because of a heightened awareness of otherness and multiplicity. This in fact can be a resource for marginalized peoples. Multiple standpoints can lead to a breadth of vision and insight not possessed by dominant groups. Yet this advantage can be undermined through the alienation inherent in dominate/subordinate relationships." Thomas C. Holt, "The Political Uses of Alienation: W. E. B. Du Bois on Politics, Race, and Culture, 1903–1940," *American Quarterly* 42, no. 2 (June 1990): 316; Mitchell Aboulafia, "W. E. B. Du Bois: Double-Consciousness, Jamesian Sympathy and the Critical Turn," in *The Oxford Handbook of American Philosophy*, by Cheryl Misak (Oxford: Oxford University Press, 2008), 182.

9. Du Bois, *The Souls of Black Folk (Norton Critical Editions)*, 14.

10. W. E. B. Du Bois, *The World and Africa: And, Color and Democracy*, ed. Henry Louis Gates Jr. (Oxford: Oxford University Press, 2014), 12.

11. Ibid., 13.

12. Coogan, Michael D., Marc Z. Brettler, and Carol Newsom, eds., *The Holy Bible: Containing the Old and New Testaments with the Apocryphal/Deuterocanonical Books: New Revised Standard Version* (New York: Oxford University Press, 1989), Genesis 9:25–26.

13. David M. Goldenberg, *The Curse of Ham: Race and Slavery in Early Judaism, Christianity, and Islam* (Princeton: Princeton University Press, 2003), 170.

14. It is also important to note that the Exodus narrative is one in which one people's liberation—the Hebrews—is premised on deliverance in another people's land—the Canaanites. For a critique of this vision of liberation from an indigenous perspective, resonant with Palestinian rights today, see Robert Allen Warrior, "Canaanites, Cowboys, and Indians: Deliverance, Conquest, and Liberation Theology Today," in *Voices Of The Religious Left*, ed. Rebecca Alpert (Philadelphia: Temple University Press, 2000), 51–58.

15. W. E. B. Du Bois, *Darkwater: Voices from Within the Veil* (Oxford: Oxford University Press, 2007), 16.

16. Ibid., 16.

17. Ibid., 19.

18. Du Bois, *The Souls of Black Folk (Norton Critical Editions)*, 162.

19. Anna Julia Cooper, *The Voice of Anna Julia Cooper: Including a Voice from the South and Other Important Essays, Papers, and Letters*, ed. Charles Lemert and Esme Bhan (Lanham: Rowman & Littlefield, 1998), 120, 121.

20. Cooper, *The Voice of Anna Julia Cooper*, 132–33; Du Bois, *The Souls of Black Folk (Norton Critical Editions)*, 162–63.

21. Chike Jeffers, "Anna Julia Cooper and the Black Gift Thesis," *History of Philosophy Quarterly* 33, no. 1 (January 1, 2016): 84.

22. Joy James, "The Profeminist Politics of W.E.B. Du Bois with Respects to Anna Julia Cooper and Ida B. Wells Barnett," in *W.E.B. Du Bois on Race and Culture: Philosophy, Politics, Poetics*, ed. Bernard W. Bell, Emily R. Grosholz, and James B. Stewart (New York: Routledge, 1996), 141–60.

23. W. E. B. Du Bois, *Dusk of Dawn: An Essay Toward an Autobiography of a Race Concept* (New York: Oxford University Press, 2014), 1; emphasis added.

24. Ibid., 14.

25. Ibid., 162.

26. Du Bois, *The Souls of Black Folk (Norton Critical Editions)*, 14; my emphasis.

27. Richard Wright, *Conversations with Richard Wright*, ed. Keneth Kinnamon and Michel Fabre (Jackson: University Press of Mississippi, 1993), 88. George Lipsitz notes about this phrasing, "I believe that it originated with Wright, or at least that is the earliest citation I have found so far." That seems accurate about the total claim, but Du Bois, if my interpretation is correct, should be seen as a partial origin. George Lipsitz, "The Possessive Investment in Whiteness: Racialized Social Democracy and the 'White' Problem in American Studies," *American Quarterly* 47, no. 3 (1995): 385n1.

28. Emerson, *Essays & Poems*, 206; my emphasis.

29. Ta Nehisi-Coates makes this point eloquently throughout his Du Bois–inspired essay *Between the World and Me*: "There is no uplifting way to say this. I have no praise anthems, nor old Negro spirituals. The spirit and soul are the body and brain, which are destructible—that is precisely why they are so precious." Ta-Nehisi Coates, *Between the World and Me* (New York: Spiegel & Grau, 2015), 103.

30. See especially Zamir, *Dark Voices*. For a reading of Du Bois that agrees with Zamir about Hegel's importance but differs on the details, see Aboulafia, "W. E. B. Du Bois: Double-Consciousness, Jamesian Sympathy and the Critical Turn." For a brief but trenchant critique of Zamir's Hegelian reading, see Gooding-Williams, *In the Shadow of Du Bois*, 284–85n37. For a recent defense of Zamir and further argument for Du Bois's Hegelianism, see Robert W. Williams and W. E. B. Du Bois, " 'The Sacred Unity in All the Diversity': The Text and a Thematic Analysis of W.E.B. Du Bois' 'The Individual and Social Conscience' (1905)," *Journal of African American Studies* 16, no. 3 (September 1, 2012): 456–97.

31. Du Bois cites his own advice in W. E. B. Du Bois, *The Autobiography of W. E. B. Du Bois: A Soliloquy on Viewing My Life from the Last Decade of Its First Century* (Oxford: Oxford University Press, 2007), 259.

32. Thomas Holt offers a different but still positive assessment of the paradox of second-sight: "Pressing the logic of Du Bois's formulation suggests a radical proposition: that African-Americans should celebrate their alienation, for it is the source of 'second-sight in this American world.'" Holt, "The Political Uses of Alienation," 306.

33. Du Bois, *The Souls of Black Folk (Norton Critical Editions)*, 12.

34. Ibid., 162.

35. Hegel in a sense agrees here: the power of the European Spirit is its ability to force the development of the universal spirit on the world. He is also explicit that Spirit divides into "Spirits," but he only finds that interesting national characteristics develop among the Europeans. In Africans, Spirit remains "dormant." See Hegel, *Hegel's Philosophy of Subjective Spirit / Hegels Philosophie Des Subjektiven Geistes*, 47–69.

36. See, for examples, Bernard Boxill, "Du Bois on Cultural Pluralism," in *W. E. B. Du Bois on Race and Culture: Philosophy, Politics, Poetics*, ed. Bernard W. Bell, Emily R. Grosholz, and James B. Stewart (New York: Routledge, 1997), 57–86; Bernstein, "Cultural Pluralism."

37. For some representative positions, which I discuss at greater length later in this chapter, see Kwame Anthony Appiah, *In My Father's House: Africa in the Philosophy of Culture* (New York: Oxford University Press, 1993); Lucius Outlaw, "If Not Races, Then What?: Toward a Revised Understanding of Bio-Social Groupings," *Graduate Faculty Philosophy Journal* 35, no. 1–2 (2014): 275–96; Paul C. Taylor, "Appiah's Uncompleted Argument: W.E.B. Du Bois and the Reality of Race," *Social Theory and Practice* 26, no. 1 (2000): 103–28. There is also an excellent volume on Du Bois on this and other issues in some ways spurred by Appiah's critique. Bernard W. Bell, Emily Grosholz, and James Benjamin Stewart, eds., *W.E.B. Du Bois on Race and Culture: Philosophy, Politics, and Poetics* (New York: Routledge, 1996).

38. Paul Gilroy suggests that the language of diaspora is better able to express Du Bois's commitments than pluralism: "As an alternative to these familiar positions, my aim here is to present and defend another more modest conception of connectedness which is governed by the concept of diaspora and its logic of unity and differentiation." Gilroy explains this logic a few pages down: "diaspora multiplicity is a chaotic, living, disorganic formation. If it can be called a tradition at all [as it is in Cedric Robinson's 'Black Radical Tradition'], it is a tradition in ceaseless motion—a changing same that strives continually towards a state of self-realisation that continually retreats beyond its grasp." Radical pluralism is meant to take seriously the ways in which Gilroy's notion of diaspora destabilizes traditional pluralist arguments. It also aims to give a more specified language of pluralization

and partialization as a means of understanding the "changing same." And by shifting from diaspora to a revised pluralism, it suggests a nonimpositional mode of universal thinking that is found in multiple histories, including the diasporic context. And yet, at the same time, by being *itself* a plural conception, it remains open to other modes of articulation, including those from diasporic thinkers like Du Bois. Part of the aim of this section is to show how Du Bois performs this pluralization of radical pluralism. Gilroy, *The Black Atlantic*, 120, 122.

39. W. E. B. Du Bois, "Race Relations in the United States 1917–1947," *Phylon (1940–1956)* 9, no. 3 (1948): 245.

40. Ibid., 246, 245.

41. Ibid., 247.

42. Marx, *Early Writings*, 244.

43. I do not know if Du Bois would have been aware of this remark by Emerson. It is worth noting that William James, Du Bois's influential teacher at Harvard, cites the remark in his lecture on Emerson's centenary in 1903 (six years after Du Bois published the original form of the essay but some years after he had studied with James). It is also in this lecture where James remarked of Emerson that he had a "drastic perception of differences" and "could perceive the full squalor of the individual fact." James, *Writings 1902–1910*, 1124, 1125. James cites the version from Emerson's late lecture "Essential Principles of Religion." Ralph Waldo Emerson, *The Later Lectures of Ralph Waldo Emerson, 1843–1871*, ed. Ronald A. Bosco and Joel Myerson, vol. 2 (Athens: University of Georgia Press, 2010), 269.

44. I have argued that Emerson viewed "double consciousness" as a method for overcoming race prejudice, but not as itself produced by race.

45. Many of the negative takes rely on somewhat hasty readings of Emerson. Adolph Reed, after citing Emerson's passage on "riding alternately," states, "Where Du Bois's notion pointed to a specific product of black American experience, Emerson's indicated a generic human condition, prior to and outside history." And Brian Bremen claims that Emerson's ideas have "genocidal implications" and thus, "[n]ot surprisingly . . . the compensation afforded Black folk by Emerson's 'propounding . . . of the double consciousness' is precious little." And finally, Shamoon Zamir is equally dismissive, though he considers Emerson more insipid than genocidal: "Emerson fails to reconcile thought and action in his critical perceptions and so also does not grasp the relationship of self and society in material and historical terms." And further, "Emerson not only abolishes society and history, but the self itself." Reed, *W.E.B. Du Bois and American Political Thought*, 100; Brian A. Bremen, "DuBois, Emerson, and the 'Fate' of Black Folk," *American Literary Realism, 1870–1910* 24, no. 3 (April 1, 1992): 84, 85; Zamir, *Dark Voices*, 165, 166. More appreciative readings of their relation can be found in the (still critical) writings of West, *The American Evasion of Philosophy*; Patterson, *From Emerson to King*. West, too, criticizes Emerson's racist remarks at some length, and not unfairly. Rampersad and Levering Lewis note that Emerson was a stylistic influence on Du Bois's essays.

Lewis goes so far as to say that Emerson was a "favorite" writer of Du Bois. Arnold Rampersad, *The Art and Imagination of W.E.B. DuBois* (New York: Schocken, 1990), 72; David Levering Lewis, *W. E. B. Du Bois, 1868–1919: Biography of a Race* (New York: Holt Paperbacks, 1994), 282.

46. Although I disagree with her interpretation, Anita Patterson is an important exception here, as she reads deeply into Emerson's work. Her argument is that Emerson's critique of liberal contracturalism and simultaneous belief in community led him to the notion of race as a way to bind the nation. She argues that this in turn binds him to a contradictory logic caught between "rights and race." Double consciousness, somewhat confusingly on my reading, comes to represent this contradiction between rights and race. I have tried to show in the previous chapter why I do not find this reading convincing. Patterson also very helpfully catalogues most of Du Bois's references to Emerson, though she does not note the important one in *The World and Africa* that I discuss here. Patterson, *From Emerson to King*, 1–5, 153–55, 162–64.

47. Williams and Du Bois, "The Sacred Unity in All the Diversity," 459.

48. Williams and Du Bois, 459.

49. Emerson, *Essays & Poems*, 806, 849.

50. The materiality of the ivory is of course important here for understanding the situation. As Du Bois puts it elsewhere in the book: "All these things and a hundred others became necessary to modern life, and modern life thus was built around colonial ownership and exploitation." Later in the book, speaking specifically of the keys, Du Bois writes of the murder of elephants: "Far away over miles and years, on lovely keys chipped from her curving tusks, men played the *Moonlight Sonata*. Neither for the keys nor the music was the death of the elephant actually necessary." Du Bois, *The World and Africa*, 26, 22, 47.

51. Ibid., 26.

52. Ibid., 27; Emerson, *Essays & Poems*, 1073.

53. Du Bois, *The World and Africa*, 27.

54. Ibid., 67.

55. Du Bois, *Dusk of Dawn: An Essay Toward an Autobiography of a Race Concept*, 1.

56. Du Bois, *The Souls of Black Folk (Norton Critical Editions)*, 9.

57. Ibid., 9.

58. Ibid., 17.

59. Brent Hayes Edwards, *The Practice of Diaspora: Literature, Translation, and the Rise of Black Internationalism* (Cambridge: Harvard University Press, 2003), 1.

60. W. E. B. Du Bois, *W. E. B. Du Bois: A Reader*, ed. David L. Lewis (New York: H. Holt and Co., 1995), 639. For a more extensive comparison between Du Bois and Kant, see Inés Valdez, *Transnational Cosmopolitanism*, forthcoming.

61. Du Bois, *W.E.B. Du Bois*, 639.

62. W. E. B. Du Bois, *John Brown* (Oxford: Oxford University Press, 2007), 162.

63. As this was Rousseau's problem as well, Du Bois can be seen as suggesting that evolutionary science is another—if equally unlikely—path to the achievement of the general will.

64. Du Bois, *John Brown*, 164.

65. Du Bois, *Darkwater (The Oxford W. E. B. Du Bois)*, 16.

66. Chakrabarty, "From Civilization to Globalization." Chakrabarty also explicitly uses the language of gift at the end of *Provincializing Europe*: "At the end of European imperialism, European thought is a gift to us all. We can talk of provincializing it only in an anticolonial spirit of gratitude." Chakrabarty, *Provincializing Europe*, 255.

67. On Du Bois's practical efforts here, see, for example, Balfour, *Democracy's Reconstruction*, 22–45. Jack Turner has elsewhere suggested that other African American reformers of Emerson (especially Frederick Douglass, James Baldwin, and Ralph Ellison) reformulated and expanded his practices beyond their original limits. Jack Turner, *Awakening to Race: Individualism and Social Consciousness in America* (Chicago: University of Chicago Press, 2012), 112–17.

68. W. E. B. Du Bois, *Black Folk Then and Now: An Essay in the History and Sociology of the Negro Race* (New York: Oxford University Press, 2007), xxxi. I thank Inés Valdez for pointing out this citation to me. A text of Boas's speech is available at Franz Boas, "Boas' Atlanta Commencement Address (1906)," http://www.webdubois.org/BoasAtlantaCommencement.html.

69. Du Bois, *In Battle for Peace (The Oxford W. E. B. Du Bois)*, 7; Du Bois, *The Autobiography of W. E. B. Du Bois (The Oxford W. E. B. Du Bois)*, 221.

70. Du Bois, *The Autobiography of W. E. B. Du Bois (The Oxford W. E. B. Du Bois)*, 221.

71. Richard Cullen Rath, "Echo and Narcissus: The Afrocentric Pragmatism of W. E. B. Du Bois," *The Journal of American History* 84, no. 2 (September 1, 1997): 474–76.

72. Ibid., 476.

73. Ibid., 492, 494.

74. Du Bois, *The Souls of Black Folk (Norton Critical Editions)*, 159.

75. W. E. B. Du Bois, "Criteria of Negro Art," *The Crisis*, October 1926.

76. For example, the description found at Du Bois, *Dark Princess*, 221.

77. Reed, *W.E.B. Du Bois and American Political Thought*, 122; Dickson D. Bruce Jr., "W. E. B. Du Bois and the Idea of Double Consciousness," in *The Souls of Black Folk (Norton Critical Editions)*, by W. E. B. Du Bois, ed. Henry Louis Gates Jr. and Terri Hume Oliver (New York: W. W. Norton & Company, 1999), 238–40.

78. Du Bois, *Dusk of Dawn: An Essay Toward an Autobiography of a Race Concept*, 64.

79. Williams and Du Bois, "The Sacred Unity in All the Diversity," 458.

80. Du Bois, *The Souls of Black Folk (Norton Critical Editions)*, 106.

81. There is a growing body of scholarship on this once overlooked contentious time in Du Bois's life. I engage here only with the recent works by Taketani, Frazier, and Rasberry, but a general overview would also include Gerald Horne, *Black and Red: W.E.B. Du Bois and the Afro-American Response to the Cold War, 1944–1963*, SUNY Series in Afro-American Society (Albany: State University of New York Press, 1986); Katherine Anne Baldwin, *Beyond the Color Line and the Iron Curtain: Reading Encounters between Black and Red, 1922–1963*, New Americanists (Durham: Duke University Press, 2002); Eric Porter, *The Problem of the Future World: W.E.B. Du Bois and the Race Concept at Midcentury* (Durham: Duke University Press, 2010); Etsuko Taketani, *The Black Pacific Narrative: Geographic Imaginings of Race and Empire between the World Wars* (Hanover, NH: Dartmouth, 2014); Robeson Taj Frazier, *The East Is Black: Cold War China in the Black Radical Imagination* (Durham: Duke University Press Books, 2014); Vaughn Rasberry, *Race and the Totalitarian Century: Geopolitics in the Black Literary Imagination* (Cambridge: Harvard University Press, 2016).

82. Rasberry, *Race and the Totalitarian Century*, 206.

83. Du Bois, *The Autobiography of W. E. B. Du Bois (The Oxford W. E. B. Du Bois)*, 35.

84. Du Bois, *Black Folk Then and Now (The Oxford W.E.B. Du Bois)*, xxxii.

85. Frazier, *The East Is Black*, 68.

86. Juliet Hooker, *Theorizing Race in the Americas: Douglass, Sarmiento, Du Bois, and Vasconcelos* (Oxford: Oxford University Press, 2017), 119.

87. Ibid., 117, 120.

88. Du Bois, *Dark Princess*, 311; my emphasis.

89. Du Bois, *The Souls of Black Folk (Norton Critical Editions)*, 106; my emphasis.

90. W. E. B. Du Bois, "The Conservation of Races," in *The Souls of Black Folk (Norton Critical Editions)*, ed. Henry Louis Gates Jr. and Terri Hume Oliver (New York: W. W. Norton & Company, 1999), 181.

91. Du Bois, *Dusk of Dawn: An Essay Toward an Autobiography of a Race Concept*, 110.

92. Janet Vaillant notes that according to Senghor, he came to Du Bois's writings later in life, after his ideas had largely developed (even if he had absorbed some of Du Bois's basic lessons through the Harlem Renaissance). Senghor, in retrospect, "called Du Bois one of the fathers of Négritude," and saw many of his own themes echoed there. This may also be because they both shared roots in Emerson (which Senghor would have arrived at, perhaps unknowingly, through Bergson). However, these latter two share an important difference from Emerson: Emerson had to work to deny the claimed values of (white) supremacist culture, while Du Bois and Senghor had to refound the values of their cultures precisely because of supremacist cultures. This is another part of the plurality of radical pluralism. Janet

Vaillant, *Black, French, and African: A Life of Léopold Sédar Senghor* (Cambridge: Harvard University Press, 1990), 135.

93. Appiah, *In My Father's House*; Kenneth W. Warren, *What Was African American Literature?*, The W.E.B. Du Bois Lectures (Cambridge: Harvard University Press, 2011).

94. Paul C. Taylor, "Race, Rehabilitated—Redux," *Critical Sociology* 36, no. 1 (January 1, 2010): 185.

95. On this last factor, see also the work of Lucius Outlaw. Outlaw argues that "biology" has itself become essentialized as a negative category, whereas it in fact has interesting and dynamic contributions to make to our ongoing understanding of race in the modern world. Outlaw, "If Not Races, Then What?: Toward a Revised Understanding of Bio-Social Groupings," 283–90.

96. Taylor, "Race, Rehabilitated—Redux," 185–86. One place to see the potential disagreement between Taylor and Warren is in how they read Du Bois's famous claim in *Dusk of Dawn* that blackness can be defined as anyone who is forced to ride Jim Crow in the South. For Warren, this means that race is ultimately defined either as a legal category or, once that category is removed, as a *memory* of a legal category. For Taylor, this is not specific to legal categories but to general social experiences that may or may not be inscribed in law. Du Bois, *Dusk of Dawn: An Essay Toward an Autobiography of a Race Concept*, 77; Warren, *What Was African American Literature?*, 94–97; Taylor, "Appiah's Uncompleted Argument," 108–10.

97. Taylor, "Appiah's Uncompleted Argument," 127.

98. Walter Benn Michaels, *The Shape of the Signifier: 1967 to the End of History* (Princeton: Princeton University Press, 2004), 167.

99. Milton Friedman, *Capitalism and Freedom: Fortieth Anniversary Edition* (Chicago: University of Chicago Press, 2002), 191.

100. Du Bois, "Race Relations in the United States 1917–1947," 246.

101. As Nicholas Bromell has shown in a trenchant synopsis of Du Bois's thinking, this concern for plurality against dominance manifested as early as his 1890 Harvard commencement address and continued to deepen and transform into his later writings on what Bromell calls his "democratic epistemology." Nicholas Knowles Bromell, *The Time Is Always Now: Black Thought and the Transformation of US Democracy* (New York: Oxford University Press, 2013), 113–22.

102. Du Bois, "Race Relations in the United States 1917–1947," 246–47.

103. Étienne Balibar, "Is There a Neo-Racism?," in *Race, Nation, Class: Ambiguous Identities*, by Immanuel Maurice Wallerstein and Étienne Balibar (New York: Verso, 1991), 21, 23.

104. Carby, "The Souls of Black Men"; Darlene C. Hine, "'In the Kingdom of Culture': Black Women and the Intersection of Race, Gender, and Class," in *Lure and Loathing: Essays on Race, Identity, and the Ambivalence of Assimilation* (New York: Penguin, 1993), 337–51.

105. Hine, "In the Kingdom of Culture," 338.

106. James, "The Profeminist Politics of W.E.B. Du Bois with Respects to Anna Julia Cooper and Ida B. Wells Barnett."

107. For an enlarged discussion of these themes, see Susan Gillman and Alys Weinbaum, eds., *Next to the Color Line: Gender, Sexuality, and W. E. B. Du Bois* (Minneapolis: University of Minnesota Press, 2007).

108. Jeffers, "Anna Julia Cooper and the Black Gift Thesis."

109. Ibid., 84–86; Kathryn T. Gines, "From Color-Blind to Post-Racial: Blacks and Social Justice in the Twenty-First Century," *Journal of Social Philosophy* 41, no. 3 (2010): 377–78.

110. Cooper, *The Voice of Anna Julia Cooper*, 129.

111. Ibid., 108.

112. Ibid., 63.

113. Du Bois, *Dusk of Dawn: An Essay Toward an Autobiography of a Race Concept*, 111.

114. Ibid., 3.

115. Reed, *W.E.B. Du Bois and American Political Thought*, 130.

116. Cheah, "The Material World of Comparison," 525.

117. Ibid., 536.

118. Ibid., 536.

119. Ibid., 538–9.

120. Ibid., 543.

121. Ibid., 342.

122. Published as Anthony Bogues, *Empire of Liberty: Power, Desire, and Freedom* (Hanover: Dartmouth College Press: University Press of New England, 2010).

123. Ibid., 16.

124. Ibid., 17.

125. Ibid., 58.

126. Foucault, *The Hermeneutics of the Subject*, 251.

127. Emerson, *Essays & Poems*, 769.

Chapter 7

1. Richard Jaffe noted to me in correspondence that Suzuki's ideas, while consistent, did of course change over time, especially as he found new elements of both the Buddhist tradition and contemporary philosophy in Europe and the United States. After all, Suzuki, like Du Bois (who was born just two years before him), lived for nearly a century. To give a general overview of his thought in this chapter, I decided to look less at Suzuki's development and more at his later writings, focusing largely on his writings from the late 1920s on. I do look a bit more explicitly at the chronology of his thinking about politics at the end of this chapter. Richard M. Jaffe, "E-Mail," December 27, 2017.

2. Suzuki sometimes italicized satori and sometimes did not. I have not used italics unless it appears as such in the cited material. For a criticism of Suzuki's use of this term, see Hakamaya Noriaki, "Critical Philosophy versus Topical Philosophy," in *Pruning the Bodhi Tree: The Storm over Critical Buddhism*, ed. Jamie Hubbard and Paul Swanson (Honolulu: University of Hawai`i Press, 1997), 56–80.

3. Daisetz Teitaro Suzuki, *An Introduction to Zen Buddhism* (New York: Grove Press, 1964), 98.

4. Daisetz Teitaro Suzuki, "An Autobiographical Account," in *A Zen Life: D. T. Suzuki Remembered*, ed. Masao Abe (New York: Weatherhill, 1986), 27.

5. Daisetz Teitaro Suzuki, *Columbia University Seminar Lectures (1952 & 1953)*, ed. Shigematsu Sōiku and Gishin Tokiwa (Kamakura, Japan: Matsugaoka Bunko, 2016), 11.

6. Alan W. Watts, *The Way of Zen* (New York: Vintage, 1999), 20; John Cage, *A Year from Monday: New Lectures and Writings* (Middletown: Wesleyan University Press, 1967), 96.

7. Daisetz Teitaro Suzuki, "Satori," in *A Zen Life: D. T. Suzuki Remembered*, ed. Masao Abe (New York: Weatherhill, 1986), 49.

8. I have in the preceding chapters traced the desire for this capacity back to Rousseau's anthropology, in which a global subject had to be made who would break with "primitive instinct," arise into rationality, and then return to an instinctual way of being with the lessons gained from rational discourse intact and with the negative aspects of both pure instinct and alienated reason discarded. The phrase that encapsulates this for me is when Rousseau says that Emile must be a "savage made to inhabit cities."

9. Suzuki, "Satori," 48.

10. Suzuki, *Columbia University Seminar Lectures (1952 & 1953)*, 35.

11. Ibid., 34–35.

12. Suzuki, *An Introduction to Zen Buddhism.*, 96.

13. Suzuki, *Columbia University Seminar Lectures (1952 & 1953)*, 35.

14. Ibid., 22.

15. Ibid., 22–23.

16. Ibid., 79.

17. Suzuki did attempt to do this, especially, as I discuss below, later in his life. See, for example, his 1959 dialogue with Thomas Merton: Daisetz Teitaro Suzuki and Thomas Merton, "Wisdom in Emptiness: A Dialogue by Daisetz T. Suzuki and Thomas Merton," in *Zen and the Birds of Appetite*, by Thomas Merton (New York: New Directions Publishing, 1968), 99–138. I thank Richard Jaffe for pointing out this reference to me.

18. Cited in Christopher Ives, *Imperial-Way Zen: Ichikawa Hakugen's Critique and Lingering Questions for Buddhist Ethics* (Honolulu: University of Hawai'i Press, 2009), 79.

19. For critiques of Suzuki's thought, see Robert H. Sharf, "Buddhist Modernism and the Rhetoric of Meditative Experience," *Numen* 42, no. 3 (1995): 228–83; Robert H. Sharf, "The Zen of Japanese Nationalism," *History of Religions* 33, no. 1 (1993): 1–43; Bernard Faure, *Chan Insights and Oversights: An Epistemological Critique of the Chan Tradition* (Princeton: Princeton University Press, 1993). A slightly less critical though still skeptical account appears in David L. McMahan, *The Making of Buddhist Modernism* (Oxford: Oxford University Press, 2008). On Orientalism as cause of Suzuki's success, see Jane Iwamura, *Virtual Orientalism: Asian Religions and American Popular Culture* (New York: Oxford University Press, 2010). On Suzuki's own distancing from his followers, see Daisetz Teitaro Suzuki, "Self the Unattainable," in *Selected Works of D.T. Suzuki*, ed. Richard M. Jaffe, vol. 1 (University of California Press, 2015), 90–95. On the question of war and passivity, see Brian Daizen Victoria, *Zen at War* (Lanham: Rowman & Littlefield Publishers, 2006). For a response, see Kemmyō Taira Sato, "D. T. Suzuki and the Question of War," trans. Thomas Kirchner, *Eastern Buddhist* 39, no. 1 (2008): 61–120. For more balanced works, both critical and appreciative of Suzuki's place in the history of Buddhist studies, if not global culture, see Luis O. Gomez, "D. T. Suzuki's Contribution to Modern Buddhist Scholarship," in *A Zen Life: D. T. Suzuki Remembered*, ed. Francis Haar and Masao Abe (New York: Weatherhill, 1986); Thomas Kasulis, "Reading D. T. Suzuki Today," *Eastern Buddhist* 38, no. 1/2 (2007): 41–57. The best available overview of Suzuki, his reception history, and the possibility of a new interpretation of his thought that I know of is now in Richard Jaffe's extensive introduction to his selected writings. Jaffe's work came out long after I began my research, and I was pleased to see the essential agreement between his project and my own. The difference is that I am emplotting Suzuki within these broader theoretical questions. Richard M. Jaffe, "Introduction," in *Selected Works of D. T. Suzuki, Volume I: Zen*, by Daisetsu Teitaro Suzuki (Berkeley: University of California Press, 2014), xi–lvi. On this general trend toward reevaluation, see Michael Mohr, "Plowing the Zen Field: Trends Since 1989 and Emerging Perspectives," *Religion Compass* 6, no. 2 (2012): 113–24.

20. In some respects, Suzuki's fate in reception history mirrors Emerson's own. As Stanley Cavell has argued, a reappreciation of Emerson requires a renewed focus on the hybridity of literature and philosophy in his essays. My hope in this chapter is to offer a groundwork for returning to Suzuki. Stanley Cavell, "Thinking of Emerson," in *The Senses of Walden* (Chicago: University of Chicago Press, 1992). Cavell, *Emerson's Transcendental Etudes.*

21. Some interesting reflections have been written on whether or not the term "enlightenment" is appropriate, given its cultural meaning in the North Atlantic and elsewhere today. My general sense is that once we understand "enlightenment" to be one among many concepts aimed at global understanding, there is not much of an issue here. For differing positions, see Dale Stuart Wright, *Philosophical Medita-*

tions on Zen Buddhism (New York: Cambridge University Press, 1998), 182–206; Sakai and Solomon, "Introduction: Addressing the Multitude of Foreigners, Echoing Foucault," 14.

22. Daisetz Teitaro Suzuki, *Essays in Zen Buddhism, First Series* (New York: Grove Press, 1961), 32.

23. Cavell, *The Senses of Walden*, 81.

24. Suzuki, *Essays in Zen Buddhism, First Series*, 32.

25. It should be noted that there is an extensive debate on whether or not "satori" is in fact something that Zen monks would have ever sought after. For a negative assessment, see Faure, *Chan Insights and Oversights*, 54–60. For a positive take, see Steven Heine, "What Is on the Other Side? Delusion and Realization in Dōgen's 'Genjōkōan,'" in *Dogen: Textual and Historical Studies*, ed. Steven Heine (New York: Oxford University Press, 2012).

26. On the difficulties of kōan interpretation, see Steven Heine, *Like Cats and Dogs: Contesting the Mu Koan in Zen Buddhism* (New York: Oxford University Press, 2014). For a dark literary investigation of ambiguous interpretation, see Yukio Mishima, *The Temple of the Golden Pavilion.*, trans. Ivan Morris (New York: Knopf, 1959).

27. Victor Hori, "Kōan and Kenshō in the Rinzai Zen Curriculum," in *The Koan: Texts and Contexts in Zen Buddhism*, ed. Steven Heine and Dale Wright (New York: Oxford University Press, 2000), 288–89.

28. Daisetz Teitaro Suzuki, "Early Memories," in *A Zen Life: D. T. Suzuki Remembered*, ed. Masao Abe (New York: Weatherhill, 1986), 5.

29. Janine Anderson Sawada, *Practical Pursuits: Religion, Politics, and Personal Cultivation in Nineteenth-Century Japan* (Honolulu: University of Hawai`i Press, 2004), 132.

30. This is a name for the general process of how Buddhist communities the world over reformulated themselves in the late nineteenth and early twentieth centuries, especially in relation to colonialism and scientific advances in Europe. For helpful overviews, see Donald S. Lopez, "Introduction," in *A Modern Buddhist Bible: Essential Readings from East and West.*, ed. Donald S. Lopez (Boston: Beacon Press, 2004), vii–xli; McMahan, *The Making of Buddhist Modernism.*

31. For an extensive history of this turn, albeit focused on Burma, see Erik Braun, *The Birth of Insight: Meditation, Modern Buddhism, and the Burmese Monk Ledi Sayadaw* (Chicago: University of Chicago Press, 2013). For a critique of this turn, see Sharf, "Buddhist Modernism and the Rhetoric of Meditative Experience."

32. Suzuki, "An Autobiographical Account," 6.

33. Ibid., 6–7.

34. For more on Sōen, see Michael Mohr, "The Use of Traps and Snares: Shaku Sōen Revisited," in *Zen Masters*, by Steven Heine and Dale Wright (Oxford: Oxford University Press, 2010); Richard M. Jaffe, "Seeking Sakyamuni: Travel and the Reconstruction of Japanese Buddhism," *The Journal of Japanese Studies* 30, no. 1 (2004): 65–96.

35. On the general instability of the meaning of this kōan, see Heine, *Like Cats and Dogs*. The kōan makes a famous appearance in American literature in Robert Pirsig's *Zen and the Art of Motorcycle Maintenance*, where Pirsig argues that it means something like "unask the question." Pirsig's reading is not entirely implausible. Robert M. Pirsig, *Zen and the Art of Motorcycle Maintenance* (San Francisco: HarperCollins, 2009), 327.

36. Suzuki, "An Autobiographical Account," 19.

37. Suzuki, "Early Memories," 10–11.

38. Sōseki's novel *The Gate* presents his own experiences with modern Zen meditation at Sōen's temple in a much less favorable light. Sōseki Natsume, *The Gate*, trans. William F. Sibley, New York Review Books Classics (New York: New York Review Books, 2013).

39. On Carus's importance for the American reception of Buddhism, as well as Buddhism's international modernization, see Judith Snodgrass, *Presenting Japanese Buddhism to the West: Orientalism, Occidentalism, and the Columbian Exposition* (Chapel Hill: The University of North Carolina Press, 2003).

40. Suzuki, "Early Memories," 11.

41. See Hakamaya, "Critical Philosophy versus Topical Philosophy"; Robert H Sharf, "Suzuki, D. T.," in *The Encyclopedia of Religion*, 2nd ed., vol. 13 (New York: Macmillan, 2005), 8884–87.

42. Robert H Sharf, "Is Mindfulness Buddhist? (And Why It Matters)," *Transcultural Psychiatry* 52, no. 4 (2015): 475.

43. Daisetz Teitaro Suzuki, *Zen and Japanese Culture* (Princeton: Princeton University Press, 2010), 356.

44. Daisetz Teitaro Suzuki, *Eight Lectures on Chan* (Kamakura-shi: Matsugaoka Bunko, 2011), 25.

45. Suzuki, "Satori," 28.

46. This was not only through his engagement with Paul Carus but also in his own reading. Suzuki's library in Kamakura retains to this day some dozen volumes on or by Kant.

47. Kant, *Critique of Pure Reason*, 385–86; 219–34.

48. My overview is deeply indebted to Jay L. Garfield, "Commentary," in *The Fundamental Wisdom of the Middle Way: Nagarjuna's Mulamadhyamakakarika*, by Nagarjuna (New York: Oxford University Press, 1995); The Cowherds, *Moonshadows: Conventional Truth in Buddhist Philosophy* (Oxford: Oxford University Press, 2011). Of course, the meanings of the two truths are widely debated across Buddhist history, as with any philosophical tradition. For a sense of the complexity and evolving ideas, see Richard Hayes, "Madhyamaka," ed. Edward N. Zalta, *The Stanford Encyclopedia of Philosophy* (Metaphysics Research Lab, Stanford University, 2017), https://plato.stanford.edu/archives/spr2017/entries/madhyamaka/.

49. Nagarjuna, *The Fundamental Wisdom of the Middle Way: Nagarjuna's Mulamadhyamakakarika*, trans. Jay L. Garfield (New York: Oxford University Press, 1995), 68.

50. Ibid., 68.
51. Garfield, "Commentary," 297–98.
52. Nagarjuna, *The Fundamental Wisdom of the Middle Way*, 69.
53. Ibid., 70.
54. There is a significant difference here, which is that the logic of Nagarjuna is in fact a soteriology and thus is directed not toward knowledge for its own sake, but toward the end of suffering. For a clear elucidation of this topic, see Georges B. J. Dreyfus, *The Sound of Two Hands Clapping the Education of a Tibetan Buddhist Monk* (Berkeley: University of California Press, 2003), 186–91; 238–46.
55. I believe this to be consistent with Garfield's commentary. He states: "[E]verything, including this very thesis, has only nominal truth, and nothing is either inherently existent or true in virtue of designating an inherently existent fact." I take this further to be the meaning of the difficult idea of the "emptiness of emptiness." Garfield, "Commentary," 305–7.
56. Daisetz Teitaro Suzuki, *Essays in Zen Buddhism, Third Series* (London: Rider, 1970), 263, 269–70.
57. Jan Westerhoff, *Nagarjuna's Madhyamaka: A Philosophical Introduction* (New York: Oxford University Press, 2009), 13.
58. McMahan, *The Making of Buddhist Modernism*, 134.
59. For just one example from within a strand of the Tibetan tradition, see Georges Dreyfus, *Recognizing Reality: Dharmakirti's Philosophy and Its Tibetan Interpretations* (Albany: State University of New York Press, 1997).
60. Kant, *Critique of Pure Reason*, 506–7. This passage, and the discussion of the "unconditioned" that follows, were also of central concern for the early German Romantics, with whom Suzuki would seem to share a lot. However, for thinkers like Novalis and Hölderlin, the point was not to merge with the absolute (something they agreed with Kant was impossible), but to approach the absolute through "infinite approximation." For recent research on the philosophical complexity of German Romanticism, see Manfred Frank, *The Philosophical Foundations of Early German Romanticism*, trans. Elizabeth Millan-Zaibert (Albany: State University of New York Press, 2004).
61. Kant, *Critique of Pure Reason*, 352.
62. "Philosophers and logicians are not experiencing enlightenment itself, yet at the back of their minds something makes them assume this experience and they have to talk as if they have it." Suzuki, *Columbia University Seminar Lectures (1952 & 1953)*, 75.
63. Foucault, "What Is Enlightenment?"
64. In speaking of "radical empiricism," Suzuki is alluding to the later work of William James, from which he also takes the term of "pure experience." But he is doing so with a significant difference. For James, there was no transcending the "field of consciousness." Mystical experience, he believed, could push us past the claims of rationality, but only because it offered a "tremendous *muchness*" in the

field of thought. James, ever the pluralist and ever open to revision, admitted that this was only a "suggestion" and that those with mystical experience might suggest otherwise. Suzuki attempted to do exactly this, and stated that what Zen offered was not a tremendous *m*uchness, but a rather ordinary *s*uchness. James, *Essays in Radical Empiricism and a Pluralistic Universe*; James, *Writings 1902–1910*, 1274.

65. Suzuki, *Essays in Zen Buddhism, First Series*, 140; my emphasis.

66. Suzuki, *Columbia University Seminar Lectures (1952 & 1953)*, 59.

67. Defert is cited as the reference for this point in Frédéric Gros's notes to the *Hermeneutics of the Subject*. Foucault, *The Hermeneutics of the Subject*, 227n58.

68. Suzuki, "An Autobiographical Account," 26.

69. Rousseau, *Emile*, 205.

70. More like classical writers than moderns fascinated by colonial anthropology, he will occasionally refer to Zen as close to animal life, avoiding the invidious distinctions between humans, though running the risk of creating them between species. Suzuki, *Columbia University Seminar Lectures (1952 & 1953)*, 20, 42.

71. Suzuki, *Zen hakko*, 67.

72. Suzuki, *Zen and Japanese Culture*, 23 cited above as well.

73. Suzuki, *Essays in Zen Buddhism, First Series*, 131, 229.

74. Hori, "Kōan and Kenshō in the Rinzai Zen Curriculum," 309.

75. Suzuki, *Columbia University Seminar Lectures (1952 & 1953)*, 73.

76. Ibid., 20.

77. Hori also cites similar reflections by Dale Wright. McMahan suggests that Suzuki "reconfigures and radicalizes Rousseau's primitivism," as does Ichikawa Hakugen. Hori, "Kōan and Kenshō in the Rinzai Zen Curriculum," 312n28; McMahan, *The Making of Buddhist Modernism*, 133; Hakugen, "A Preliminary Conception of Zen Social Ethics," 356.

78. Hori, "Kōan and Kenshō in the Rinzai Zen Curriculum," 307.

79. Ibid., 308.

80. Ibid., 309.

81. Suzuki, "Satori," 49.

82. Ibid., 47.

83. Ibid., 47.

84. Ibid., 47.

85. Suzuki also discusses Hegel, via a citation to Simone de Beauvoir, in the Columbia lectures. De Beauvoir relates how she felt a "great calm" reading Hegel in the library, but could not sustain it once back on the street. Suzuki suggests that while Hegel, abstractly, makes one feel at home in the world, his concepts break down in reality: not because reality refuses calm, but because conceptual thought cannot provide the desired grounding. Suzuki, *Columbia University Seminar Lectures (1952 & 1953)*, 39–40.

86. Larson notes that Heidegger and Suzuki met in 1953 and were likely familiar with each other's work earlier. There is an apocryphal story, recorded by

William Barrett, that Heidegger, reading Suzuki's 1927 *Essays*, said, "If I understand this man correctly . . . this is what I have been trying to say in all my writings." The details of their engagement with each other's thought lie beyond the scope of my research. Kay Larson, *Where the Heart Beats: John Cage, Zen Buddhism, and the Inner Life of Artists* (New York: Penguin Press, 2012). William Barrett, "Zen for the West," in *Zen Buddhism: Selected Writings*, by Daisetz Teitaro Suzuki (Garden City, NY: Doubleday, 1956), xii.

87. Martin Heidegger, *Identity and Difference*, trans. Joan Stambaugh (Chicago: University of Chicago Press, 2002), 47.

88. Ibid., 50.

89. Heidegger, "Der Spiegel Interview with Martin Heidegger," 331.

90. The scholarship has overestimated this appreciation, at times even reducing Suzuki to Emerson. For George Leonard and David McMahan, Suzuki's Zen is a creative "misreading" of historical Zen through a Transcendentalist lens. Palmer Rampell, commenting on Suzuki's influence on Ginsberg, Cage, and Salinger, writes: "We may be forgiven if, for a moment, we are disappointed that Suzuki's philosophy was not entirely fresh, that some of our favorite artists thought they had been inspired by mystical visions of Japanese Zen when, all the while, some all-too-familiar New Englanders stood just behind the curtain." He even wonders why "Suzuki never distanced himself from Buddhism." George Leonard, *Into the Light of Things: The Art of the Commonplace from Wordsworth to John Cage* (Chicago: University of Chicago Press, 1994), 151; McMahan, *The Making of Buddhist Modernism*, 122; Palmer Rampell, "Laws That Refuse To Be Stated: The Post-Sectarian Spiritualities of Emerson, Thoreau, and D. T. Suzuki," *The New England Quarterly* 34, no. 4 (2011): 653, 638.

91. I owe this knowledge to Wayne Yokoyama in personal correspondence. The essay is mentioned also by Leonard, but he gives as its title "On Emerson." Rampell offers the most extensive discussion of the essay available in English. Leonard, *Into the Light of Things*, 151; Rampell, "Laws That Refuse To Be Stated: The Post-Sectarian Spiritualities of Emerson, Thoreau, and D. T. Suzuki," 629–33.

92. Suzuki, *Zen and Japanese Culture*, 343–44.

93. Emerson, *Essays & Poems*, 79, 427.

94. Ibid., 632.

95. Suzuki, *Zen and Japanese Culture*, 344.

96. Jaffe, "Introduction," xxxiii.

97. Cavell, *Conditions Handsome and Unhandsome*, xxxiv.

98. Emerson, *Essays & Poems*, 256.

99. Ibid., 239.

100. Ibid., 239.

101. Cavell, *Conditions Handsome and Unhandsome*, 12.

102. Ibid., 12. The phrase "city of words" is from Plato.

103. Suzuki, "Self the Unattainable," 92, 93.

104. J. N. Mohanty, *Classical Indian Philosophy* (Lanham: Rowman & Littlefield Publishers, 2000), 30.

105. On this tendency in Suzuki's translations, and on the amount of work he put into conceiving and reconceiving his word choice, see Mark Blum, "Introduction to the DT Suzuki Translation," in *Shinran's Kyogyoshinsho: The Collection of Passages Expounding the True Teaching, Living, Faith, and Realizing of the Pure Land*, by Shinran (New York: Oxford University Press, 2012), especially 7–8.

106. Emerson, *Essays & Poems*, 403.

107. Ibid., 487.

108. An annotated copy of this work is in Suzuki's library in Kamakura, and this passage from Russell is underlined.

109. Bertrand Russell, "Introduction," in *Tractatus Logico-Philosophicus*, by Ludwig Wittgenstein (London: Routledge, 2002), xxiv.

110. Ludwig Wittgenstein, *Tractatus Logico-Philosophicus* (London: Routledge, 2002), 6.522.

111. For an overview of this argument, see The Cowherds, *Moonpaths: Ethics and Emptiness* (Oxford: Oxford University Press, 2015), 203–20.

112. See, for example, Cowherds, *Moonshadows*, 111–13; 167–68; 221–31. For an overview of contemporary and historic approaches to Buddhist ethics, see "Part V: Ethics" in William Edelglass and Jay L. Garfield, eds., *Buddhist Philosophy: Essential Readings* (Oxford: Oxford University Press, 2009).

113. Victoria, *Zen at War*; Sato, "D. T. Suzuki and the Question of War."

114. Sato has shown the extent to which his private letters explicitly oppose the war, which, in a time of great censorship and persecution of even private thoughts, was no mere rhetoric.

115. Even Brian Victoria, who is ultimately an unnecessarily harsh critic of Suzuki, notes that Suzuki was the first to criticize Zen complicity, although he concludes that his response was insufficient (148–52).

116. For an overview of these writings, see Sato, "D. T. Suzuki and the Question of War."

117. Ibid., 80. See her essay for other similar remarks.

118. A very helpful summary of and engagement with Ichikawa's critique is available in Ives's book-length treatment, *Imperial-Way Zen*.

119. Ibid., *Imperial-Way Zen*, 192n65.

120. Cited in Sato, "D. T. Suzuki and the Question of War," 117.

121. Robert Sharf has shown that this dialogue between positions has historical precedents. Sharf, "Is Mindfulness Buddhist? (and Why It Matters)," 476–77.

122. Hakugen, "A Preliminary Conception of Zen Social Ethics," 356–55.

123. Ibid., 355.

124. Ibid., 358, 348. Ichikawa names these with the Sanskrit terms, tattvajñāna for the vertical axis of nonduality and upāyajñāna for the horizontal axis

of worldly laws. He states that these interpretations of the classical terms are his own modernization.

125. Ibid., 348.

126. Suzuki, *Zen and Japanese Culture*, 63. I note that Wendy Brown makes the same claim about democracy: "Democracy is an empty form that can be filled with a variety of bad content and instrumentalized by purposes ranging from nationalist xenophobia to racial colonialism, from heterosexist to capitalist hegemony; it can be mobilized within the same regimes to counter these purposes." Brown, *Undoing the Demos*, 209.

127. Sato, "D. T. Suzuki and the Question of War."

128. There have been several critiques of Žižek's position here. The most recent and in-depth one, to my knowledge, is offered by Timothy Morton in Marcus Boon, Eric Cazdyn, and Timothy Morton, *Nothing: Three Inquiries in Buddhism* (Chicago: University of Chicago Press, 2015). The volume offers three wide-ranging essays thinking through possible relations between Buddhist studies and the history of critical theory.

129. Slavoj Žižek, *For They Know Not What They Do: Enjoyment as a Political Factor* (London: Verso, 2002), xliii.

130. Žižek, xlviii. He actually says this after citing the *Bhagavad Gita* as if it were a Zen text, and I am simply following his mashed-up argument here.

131. Žižek, xlvii.

132. Ibid., xlviii.

133. Suzuki, *Zen and Japanese Culture*, 352.

134. Ibid., 23.

135. Suzuki, *Columbia University Seminar Lectures (1952 & 1953)*, 212.

136. Cavell, *Conditions Handsome and Unhandsome*, 31.

137. Edward W. Said, *Reflections on Exile and Other Essays* (Cambridge: Harvard University Press, 2000), 29.

138. Ibid., 526.

139. Theodor Adorno, *Quasi Una Fantasia: Essays on Modern Music* (London; New York: Verso, 1992), 283.

140. Fredric Jameson, *Postmodernism, or, The Cultural Logic of Late Capitalism* (Durham: Duke University Press, 1990), 28.

141. Cage, *A Year from Monday: New Lectures and Writings*, 71.

142. Ibid., ix.

143. Ibid., 167.

144. John Cage and Joan Retallack, *Musicage: Cage Muses on Words, Art, Music* (Middletown: Wesleyan University Press, 1995), 110.

145. John Cage, *Empty Words: Writings '73–'78* (Middletown: Wesleyan University Press, 1979), 5.

146. Although such a distancing from planning may rightly worry those like myself who think it necessary for progressive politics.

147. For more on the varieties and history of this piece, see Gann, *No Such Thing as Silence*, chapter 5.
148. John Cage, *Silence: Lectures and Writings* (Middletown: Wesleyan University Press, 1961), 11.
149. Richard Kostelanetz and John Cage, *Conversing with Cage* (New York: Limelight Editions, 1988), 222.
150. Cage, *Empty Words*, 5.
151. Cage, *Silence*, 75.
152. Ibid., 129; dashes in original.
153. Ibid., 36.
154. Ibid., 38.
155. Suzuki, *Zen hakko*, 71. The use of "identification" here contradicts Suzuki's earlier claims that it is transparency and not "identification" that is the goal. I presume this to be a careless error or a translation for a new audience and not a fundamental rethinking.
156. John Cage and Daniel Charles, *For the Birds* (Boston: M. Boyars, 1981), 106.
157. See Branden Wayne Joseph, "Chance, Indeterminacy, Multiplicity," in *The Anarchy of Silence: John Cage and Experimental Art*, by Julia Robinson (Barcelona: Museu d'Art Contemporani de Barcelona, 2009); Branden Wayne Joseph, *Beyond the Dream Syndicate: Tony Conrad and the Arts after Cage: (A "Minor" History)* (New York; London: Zone; MIT [distributor], 2011), 77–85.
158. Joseph, *Beyond the Dream Syndicate*, 80.
159. Jameson, *Postmodernism, or, The Cultural Logic of Late Capitalism*, 25.
160. Ibid., 50.
161. I am referring here to the infamous essay: Fredric Jameson, "Third-World Literature in the Era of Multinational Capitalism," *Social Text*, no. 15 (1986): 65–88. I have tremendous respect for Jameson and his work, but I do think that he falls too easily within a Hegelian line of appropriation of world cultures for his own historical purposes.
162. Jonathan Katz, "John Cage's Queer Silence; or, How to Avoid Making Matters Worse," *GLQ* 5, no. 2 (1999): 235.
163. Ibid., 238.
164. bell hooks, *Teaching to Transgress: Education as the Practice of Freedom* (New York: Routledge, 1994), 46.
165. Katz, "John Cage's Queer Silence; or, How to Avoid Making Matters Worse," 241.
166. Yannik Thiem, "Queer," in "Dictionary of the Possible," ed. Sreshta Rit Premnath and Avram Alpert, special issue, *Shifter* 22 (2016): 144–46.
167. James C. Scott, *Domination and the Arts of Resistance: Hidden Transcripts* (New Haven: Yale University Press, 1992).

168. Stout, *Blessed Are the Organized*.

169. Mary Wollstonecraft, *A Vindication of the Rights of Women*, ed. Candace Ward (New York: Dover, 1996), 25.

170. Adrienne Rich, *Arts of the Possible: Essays and Conversations* (New York: W. W. Norton & Company, 2002), 56.

171. Freire, *Pedagogy of the Oppressed*, especially chapter 2.

172. hooks, *Teaching to Transgress: Education as the Practice of Freedom*, 49.

173. See, for example, the essay "Love as the Practice of Freedom," in bell hooks, *Outlaw Culture: Resisting Representations* (New York: Routledge, 1994), 243–50.

174. Maria del Guadalupe Davidson and George Yancy, eds., *Critical Perspectives on bell hooks* (New York: Routledge, 2009), 1.

175. del Guadalupe Davidson and Yancy, 1–7.

176. For a balanced history of mindfulness meditation, see Jeff Wilson, *Mindful America: The Mutual Transformation of Buddhist Meditation and American Culture* (New York: Oxford University Press, 2014). For a characteristically critical take, see Sharf, "Is Mindfulness Buddhist? (And Why It Matters)."

177. bell hooks, "Waking Up to Racism," *Tricycle*, Fall 1994, https://tricycle.org/magazine/waking-racism/.

178. Ibid.

179. bell hooks and Helen Tworkov, "Agent of Change: Helen Tworkov Interviews Bell Hooks," in *Tricycle Conversations Volume 1* (e-book: Tricycle), http://www.tricycle.com/wisdom-collection/teachings/tricycle-conversations-volume-1.

180. Ibid.

181. Ibid.

182. Sharf, "Buddhist Modernism and the Rhetoric of Meditative Experience," 244. See also Donald S. Lopez, "Buddhism in Practice," in *Asian Religions in Practice: An Introduction*, ed. Donald S Lopez (Princeton: Princeton University Press, 1999), 56–87.

183. On the concept of nirvana, see Steven Collins, *Nirvana and Other Buddhist Felicities: Utopias of the Pali Imaginaire* (Cambridge: Cambridge University Press, 1998). For a complex discussion of nondualism and its discontents, see Jamie Hubbard and Paul Swanson, eds., *Pruning the Bodhi Tree: The Storm over Critical Buddhism* (Honolulu: University of Hawai`i Press, 1997).

184. On this latter point, see, for example, Robert Barnett, "Symbols and Protest: The Iconography of Demonstrations in Tibet, 1987–89," in *Resistance and Reform in Tibet: 40 Years On, Tibet 1950–90*, ed. Robert Barnett (Bloomington: University of Indiana Press, 1994), 238–58.

185. bell hooks, *Belonging: A Culture of Place* (New York: Routledge, 2009), 2.

186. Ibid., 58.

187. Ibid., 17, 71.

Coda

1. Emerson, *Essays & Poems*, 793.

2. Roy Scranton, *Learning to Die in the Anthropocene: Reflections on the End of a Civilization* (San Francisco: City Lights Publishers, 2015), 23, 27, 21.

3. Benedictus de Spinoza, *Ethics* (London; New York: Penguin Books, 1996), 151 (IV.67).

4. *Walden* is itself a masterpiece of global practices, which I have addressed elsewhere: Avram Alpert, "Sounding Conscience: Walden's Global Bottoms," *J19: The Journal of Nineteenth-Century Americanists* 4, no. 1 (2016): 41–63.

5. Cavell, *The Senses of Walden*, 119.

6. Henry David Thoreau, *Walden*, 150th Anniversary Edition (Princeton: Princeton University Press, 2004), 323.

7. For Cavell's thinking on the relation between the two, see Stanley Cavell, "Night and Day: Heidegger and Thoreau," in *Appropriating Heidegger*, by James E. Faulconer and Mark A. Wrathall (Cambridge: Cambridge University Press, 2000), 47.

8. Du Bois, *John Brown*, 64.

9. Cavell, *Pursuits of Happiness: The Hollywood Comedy of Remarriage*, 28.

Works Cited

Aboulafia, Mitchell. "W. E. B. Du Bois: Double-Consciousness, Jamesian Sympathy and the Critical Turn." In *The Oxford Handbook of American Philosophy*, by Cheryl Misak, 169–84. Oxford: Oxford University Press, 2008.

Abrams, M. H. *Natural Supernaturalism: Tradition and Revolution in Romantic Literature*. New York: Norton, 1971.

Adelman, Jeremy. *Earth Hunger: Markets, Resources and the Need for Strangers*. Princeton: Princeton University Press, forthcoming.

———. "Is Global History Still Possible, or Has It Had Its Moment?" Aeon, March 2017. https://aeon.co/essays/is-global-history-still-possible-or-has-it-had-its-moment.

———. "The Mortal Marx." *Public Books*, December 1, 2016. http://www.publicbooks.org/the-mortal-marx/.

Adorno, Theodor. *Notes to Literature, Volume 1*. Edited by Rolf Tiedemann. Translated by Sherry Weber Nicholsen. New York: Columbia University Press, 1991.

———. *Quasi Una Fantasia: Essays on Modern Music*. London: Verso, 1992.

Afary, Janet, and Kevin Anderson. *Foucault and the Iranian Revolution: Gender and the Seductions of Islamism*. Chicago: University of Chicago Press, 2005.

Agamben, Giorgio. *State of Exception*. Translated by Kevin Attell. Chicago: University of Chicago Press, 2005.

———. *Stato Di Eccezione*. Torino: Bollati Boringhieri, 2003.

Ahmad, Aijaz. *In Theory: Classes, Nations, Literatures*. London: Verso, 1992.

———. "Karl Marx, 'Global Theorist.'" *Dialectical Anthropology* 39, no. 2 (June 1, 2015): 199–209.

Albrecht, James M. *Reconstructing Individualism: A Pragmatic Tradition from Emerson to Ellison*. American Philosophy Series. New York: Fordham University Press, 2012.

Alcoff, Linda Martín. "Philosophy, the Conquest, and the Meaning of Modernity: A Commentary on 'Anti-Cartesian Meditations: On the Origin of the Philosophical Anti-Discourse of Modernity' by Enrique Dussel." *Human Architecture* 11, no. 1 (Fall 2013): 57–66.

Allen, Amy. *The End of Progress: Decolonizing the Normative Foundations of Critical Theory*. New York: Columbia University Press, 2016.

———. *The Politics of Our Selves: Power, Autonomy, and Gender in Contemporary Critical Theory.* New York: Columbia University Press, 2007.

Alpert, Avram. "Not to Be European Would Not Be 'To Be European Still': Undoing Eurocentrism in Levinas and Others." *Journal of French and Francophone Philosophy* 23, no. 1 (August 5, 2015): 21–41.

———. "Sounding Conscience: Walden's Global Bottoms." *J19: The Journal of Nineteenth-Century Americanists* 4, no. 1 (2016): 41–63.

Althusser, Louis, and Étienne Balibar. *Reading Capital.* Translated by Ben Brewster. London: NLB, 1970.

Anderson, Kevin. "Marx at the Margins." *Dialectical Anthropology* 39, no. 2 (June 1, 2015): 225–32.

———. *Marx at the Margins: On Nationalism, Ethnicity, and Non-Western Societies.* Chicago: University of Chicago Press, 2010.

Anderson, R. Lanier, and Joshua Landy. "Philosophy as Self-Fashioning: Alexander Nehamas's Art of Living." *Diacritics* 31, no. 1 (April 1, 2001): 25–54.

Andrade, Oswald de. "Cannibalist Manifesto." Translated by Leslie Bary. *Latin American Literary Review* 19, no. 38 (July 1, 1991): 38–47.

Anghie, Antony. *Imperialism, Sovereignty, and the Making of International Law.* Cambridge: Cambridge University Press, 2005.

Appiah, Kwame Anthony. *In My Father's House: Africa in the Philosophy of Culture.* New York: Oxford University Press, 1993.

Arendt, Hannah. *Lectures on Kant's Political Philosophy.* Edited by Ronald Beiner. Chicago: University of Chicago Press, 1989.

———. *The Human Condition.* Chicago: University of Chicago Press, 1958.

Arsić, Branka. *On Leaving: A Reading in Emerson.* Cambridge: Harvard University Press, 2010.

Asad, Talal. *Formations of the Secular: Christianity, Islam, Modernity.* Palo Alto: Stanford University Press, 2003.

Auerbach, Erich. *Mimesis: The Representation of Reality in Western Literature.* Translated by Willard Trask. Princeton: Princeton University Press, 1953.

Bailey, Austin. "'The World Is Full': Emerson, Pluralism, and the 'Nominalist and Realist.'" *The Pluralist* 11, no. 2 (2016): 32–48.

Baldwin, Katherine Anne. *Beyond the Color Line and the Iron Curtain: Reading Encounters between Black and Red, 1922–1963.* New Americanists. Durham: Duke University Press, 2002.

Balfour, Lawrie. *Democracy's Reconstruction: Thinking Politically with W. E. B. Du Bois.* Oxford: Oxford University Press, 2011.

Balibar, Étienne. "Is There a Neo-Racism?" In *Race, Nation, Class: Ambiguous Identities*, by Immanuel Maurice Wallerstein and Étienne Balibar, 17–28. New York: Verso, 1991.

Barnett, Robert. "Symbols and Protest: The Iconography of Demonstrations in Tibet, 1987–89." In *Resistance and Reform in Tibet: 40 Years On, Tibet 1950–90*, edited by Robert Barnett, 238–58. Bloomington: University of Indiana Press, 1994.

Barrett, William. "Zen for the West." In *Zen Buddhism: Selected Writings*, by Daisetz Teitaro Suzuki. Garden City, NY: Doubleday, 1956.
Baselis-Bitoun, Lison. "Jean de Léry, Précurseur de Montaigne." *Montaigne Studies* 22, no. 1–2 (2010).
Beiser, Frederick C. *Schiller as Philosopher: A Re-Examination*. Oxford: Oxford University Press, 2005.
Bell, Bernard W., Emily Grosholz, and James Benjamin Stewart, eds. *W.E.B. Du Bois on Race and Culture: Philosophy, Politics, and Poetics*. New York: Routledge, 1996.
Bellay, Joachim du. *Joachim Du Bellay: "The Regrets," with "The Antiquities of Rome," Three Latin Elegies, and "The Defense and Enrichment of the French Language." A Bilingual Edition*. Philadelphia: University of Pennsylvania Press, 2006.
Bentley, Nancy. "The Fourth Dimension: Kinlessness and African American Narrative." *Critical Inquiry* 35, no. 2 (2009): 270–92.
Bergson, Henri. *Mélanges: l'idée de lieu chez Aristote, Durée et simultanéité, correspondance, pièces diverses, documents*. Paris: Presses universitaires de France, 1972.
Bernal, Martin. *Black Athena: The Afroasiatic Roots of Classical Civilization*. New Brunswick: Rutgers University Press, 1987.
Bernasconi, Robert. "Casting the Slough: Fanon's New Humanism for a New Humanity." In *Fanon: A Critical Reader*, edited by Lewis R. Gordon, T. Denean Sharpley-Whiting, and Renee T. White, 113–21. Cambridge: Wiley-Blackwell, 1996.
———. "Hegel at the Court of Ashanti." In *Hegel after Derrida*, by Stuart Barnett. London: Routledge, 1998.
———. "The Assumption of Negritude: Aimé Césaire, Frantz Fanon, and the Vicious Circle of Racial Politics." *Parallax* 8, no. 2 (April 2002): 69–83.
———. "The European Knows and Does Not Know: Fanon's Reponse to Sartre." In *Frantz Fanon's Black Skin, White Masks: New Interdisciplinary Essays*, edited by Max Silverman, 100–11. Manchester: Manchester University Press, 2005.
———. "With What Must the Philosophy of World History Begin? On the Racial Basis of Hegel's Eurocentrism." *Nineteenth Century Contexts* 22 (2000): 171–202.
Bernstein, Richard J. "Cultural Pluralism." *Philosophy & Social Criticism* 41, no. 4–5 (May 2015): 347–56.
Bhabha, Homi K. "Foreword." In *The Wretched of the Earth*, by Frantz Fanon. New York: Grove Press, 2005.
Bilgrami, Akeel. "Occidentalism, the Very Idea: An Essay on Enlightenment and Enchantment." *Critical Inquiry* 32, no. 3 (2006): 381–411.
———. *Secularism, Identity, and Enchantment*. Cambridge: Harvard University Press, 2014.
Bilwakesh, Nikhil. "Emerson, John Brown, and Arjuna: Translating the Bhagavad Gita in a Time of War." *ESQ: A Journal of the American Renaissance* 55, no. 1 (2009): 27–58.

Bloom, Allan. "Introduction." In *Emile: Or, On Education*, by Jean-Jacques Rousseau. New York: Basic Books, 1979.
Blum, Mark. "Introduction to the D. T. Suzuki Translation." In *Shinran's Kyogyoshinsho: The Collection of Passages Expounding the True Teaching, Living, Faith, and Realizing of the Pure Land*, by Shinran. New York: Oxford University Press, 2012.
Boas, Franz. "Commencement Address at Atlanta University, May 31, 1906." *Atlanta University Leaflet*, no. 19 (S.l: s.n.).
Bogues, Anthony. *Empire of Liberty: Power, Desire, and Freedom*. Hanover: Dartmouth College Press: University Press of New England, 2010.
Boon, Marcus, Eric Cazdyn, and Timothy Morton. *Nothing: Three Inquiries in Buddhism*. Chicago: University Of Chicago Press, 2015.
Boucher, Maurice. "Le 'Sauvage' et Le 'Barbare' Dans Les Lettres Sur l'education Esthétique." *Études Germaniques* 14 (1959): 333–37.
Boucher, Philip P. *Cannibal Encounters: Europeans and Island Caribs, 1492–1763*. Baltimore: Johns Hopkins University Press, 1992.
Boxill, Bernard. "Du Bois on Cultural Pluralism." In *W. E. B. Du Bois on Race and Culture: Philosophy, Politics, Poetics*, edited by Bernard W. Bell, Emily R. Grosholz, and James B. Stewart, 57–86. New York: Routledge, 1997.
Brandt, Reinhard. "The Guiding Idea of Kant's Anthropology and the Vocation of the Human Being." In *Essays on Kant's Anthropology*, by Brian Jacobs. Cambridge: Cambridge University Press, 2003.
Braun, Erik. *The Birth of Insight: Meditation, Modern Buddhism, and the Burmese Monk Ledi Sayadaw*. Chicago: University of Chicago Press, 2013.
Bremen, Brian A. "DuBois, Emerson, and the 'Fate' of Black Folk." *American Literary Realism, 1870–1910* 24, no. 3 (April 1, 1992): 80–88.
Brennan, Timothy. *Borrowed Light: Vico, Hegel, and the Colonies*. Palo Alto: Stanford University Press, 2014.
Bromell, Nicholas Knowles. *The Time Is Always Now: Black Thought and the Transformation of US Democracy*. New York: Oxford University Press, 2013.
Brown, Vincent. "Social Death and Political Life in the Study of Slavery." *The American Historical Review* 114, no. 5 (2009): 1231–49.
Brown, Wendy. *Undoing the Demos: Neoliberalism's Stealth Revolution*. New York: Zone Books, 2015.
Bruce Jr., Dickson D. "W. E. B. Du Bois and the Idea of Double Consciousness." In *The Souls of Black Folk (Norton Critical Editions)*, by W. E. B. Du Bois, edited by Henry Louis Gates Jr. and Terri Hume Oliver. New York: W. W. Norton & Company, 1999.
Buck-Morss, Susan. *Hegel, Haiti and Universal History*. Pittsburgh: University of Pittsburgh Press, 2009.
Buell, Lawrence. *Emerson*. Cambridge: Belknap Press of Harvard University Press, 2003.

Bull, Malcolm. "Slavery and the Multiple Self." *New Left Review; London*, no. 231 (September 1, 1998): 94–131.
Bürger, Peter. *Theory of the Avant-garde*. Translated by Michael Shaw. Minneapolis: University of Minnesota Press, 1984.
Butler, Judith. *Giving an Account of Oneself*. New York: Fordham University Press, 2005.
———. *Parting Ways: Jewishness and the Critique of Zionism*. New York: Columbia University Press, 2013.
———. *Precarious Life: The Powers of Mourning and Violence*. New York: Verso, 2004.
Butler, Judith, Slavoj Žižek, and Ernesto Laclau. *Contingency, Hegemony, Universality: Contemporary Dialogues on the Left*. London: Verso, 2000.
Bykova, Marina F. "The 'Struggle for Recognition' and the Thematization of Intersubjectivity." In *Essays on Hegel's Philosophy of Subjective Spirit*, edited by David Stern, 139–54. Albany: State University of New York Press, 2013.
Byrd, Jodi A. *Transit of Empire: Indigenous Critiques of Colonialism*. Minneapolis: University of Minnesota Press, 2011.
Cadava, Eduardo. "The Guano of History." In *The Other Emerson*, edited by Branka Arsic and Cary Wolfe. Minneapolis: University of Minnesota Press, 2010.
Cage, John. *A Year from Monday: New Lectures and Writings*. Middletown: Wesleyan University Press, 1967.
———. *Empty Words: Writings '73–'78*. Middletown: Wesleyan University Press, 1979.
———. *Silence: Lectures and Writings*. Middletown: Wesleyan University Press, 1961.
Cage, John, and Daniel Charles. *For the Birds*. Boston: M. Boyars, 1981.
Cage, John, and Joan Retallack. *Musicage: Cage Muses on Words, Art, Music*. Middletown: Wesleyan University Press, 1995.
Cañizares-Esguerra, Jorge. *How to Write the History of the New World: Histories, Epistemologies, and Identities in the Eighteenth-Century Atlantic World*. Palo Alto: Stanford University Press, 2002.
Carby, Hazel. "The Souls of Black Men." In *Next to the Color Line: Gender, Sexuality, and W. E. B. Du Bois*, edited by Susan Gillman and Alys Weinbaum, 234–69. Minneapolis: University of Minnesota Press, 2007.
Cassirer, Ernst. *Rousseau, Kant, Goethe: Two Essays*. New York: Harper & Row, 1963.
———. *The Philosophy of the Enlightenment*. Translated by Fritz C. A. Koelin and James Pettegrove. Boston: Beacon Press, 1955.
Castoriadis, Cornelius. *Philosophy, Politics, Autonomy*. New York: Oxford University Press, 1991.
———. *The Castoriadis Reader*. Edited by David Ames Curtis. Oxford: Wiley-Blackwell, 1997.
Cavell, Stanley. *Conditions Handsome and Unhandsome: The Constitution of Emersonian Perfectionism*. Chicago: Open Court, 1990.
———. *Emerson's Transcendental Etudes*. Palo Alto: Stanford University Press, 2003.

———. "Night and Day: Heidegger and Thoreau." In *Appropriating Heidegger*, by James E. Faulconer and Mark A. Wrathall, 30–49. Cambridge: Cambridge University Press, 2000.

———. *Pursuits of Happiness: The Hollywood Comedy of Remarriage*. Cambridge: Harvard University Press, 1981.

———. *The Claim of Reason: Wittgenstein, Skepticism, Morality, and Tragedy*. New York: Oxford University Press, 1979.

———. *The Senses of Walden*. Chicago: University of Chicago Press, 1992.

———. "Thinking of Emerson." In *The Senses of Walden*. Chicago: University of Chicago Press, 1992.

Certeau, Michel de. *Heterologies: Discourse on the Other*. Translated by Brian Massumi. Minneapolis: University of Minnesota Press, 1986.

Césaire, Aimé. *A Tempest*. Translated by Philip Crispin. London: Oberon, 2000.

———. "Culture and Colonization." Translated by Brent Hayes Edwards. *Social Text* 28, no. 2 103 (June 1, 2010): 127–44.

———. "Discours sur l'art africain (1966)." *Études littéraires* 6, no. 1 (1973): 99–109.

———. *Discourse on Colonialism*. Edited by Robin D. G. Kelley. New York: Monthly Review Press, 2000.

———. "Letter to Maurice Thorez." Translated by Chike Jeffers. *Social Text* 28, no. 2 103 (June 1, 2010): 145–52.

Chakrabarty, Dipesh. "From Civilization to Globalization: The 'West' as a Shifting Signifier in Indian Modernity." *Inter-Asia Cultural Studies* 13, no. 1 (March 2012): 138–52.

———. "Legacies of Bandung: Decolonisation and the Politics of Culture." *Economic and Political Weekly* 40, no. 46 (2005): 4812–18.

———. "Postcolonial Studies and the Challenge of Climate Change." *New Literary History* 43, no. 1 (2012): 1–18.

———. *Provincializing Europe: Postcolonial Thought and Historical Difference*. Princeton: Princeton University Press, 2008.

Chatterjee, Partha. *Our Modernity*. Rotterdam and Dakar: SEPHIS and CODESRIA, 1997.

Cheah, Pheng. *Spectral Nationality: Passages of Freedom from Kant to Postcolonial Literatures of Liberation*. New York: Columbia University Press, 2003.

———. "The Material World of Comparison." *New Literary History* 40, no. 3 (2009): 523–45.

Cheyfitz, Eric. "A Common Emerson: Ralph Waldo in an Ethnohistorical Context." *Nineteenth Century Prose* 30, no. 1–2 (2003): 250–81.

———. *The Poetics of Imperialism: Translation and Colonization from The Tempest to Tarzan*. Philadelphia: University of Pennsylvania Press, 1997.

Chibber, Vivek. *Postcolonial Theory and the Specter of Capital*. New York: Verso, 2013.

Ciccariello-Maher, George. *Decolonizing Dialectics*. Durham: Duke University Press Books, 2017.

Clastres, Pierre. *Society Against the State: Essays in Political Anthropology.* Translated by Robert Hurley and Abe Stein. Cambridge: Zone Books, 1989.
Coates, Ta-Nehisi. *Between the World and Me.* New York: Spiegel & Grau, 2015.
Cole, Andrew. *The Birth of Theory.* Chicago: University of Chicago Press, 2014.
Colletti, Lucio. "Introduction." In *Early Writings*, by Karl Marx, translated by Tom Nairn. New York: Vintage, 1975.
Collins, Steven. *Nirvana and Other Buddhist Felicities: Utopias of the Pali Imaginaire.* Cambridge: Cambridge University Press, 1998.
Comay, Rebecca. *Mourning Sickness: Hegel and the French Revolution.* Palo Alto: Stanford University Press, 2010.
———. "Resistance and Repetition: Freud and Hegel." *Research in Phenomenology* 45, no. 2 (September 2, 2015): 237–66.
Connolly, William. *Pluralism.* Durham: Duke University Press Books, 2005.
———. *The Ethos of Pluralization.* Minneapolis: University of Minnesota Press, 1995.
Coogan, Michael D., Marc Z. Brettler, and Carol Newsom, eds. *The Holy Bible: Containing the Old and New Testaments with the Apocryphal/Deuterocanonical Books: New Revised Standard Version.* New York: Oxford University Press, 1989.
Cooper, Anna Julia. *The Voice of Anna Julia Cooper: Including a Voice from the South and Other Important Essays, Papers, and Letters.* Edited by Charles Lemert and Esme Bhan. Lanham: Rowman & Littlefield, 1998.
Cooper, Frederick. *Africa in the World: Capitalism, Empire, Nation-State.* Cambridge: Harvard University Press, 2014.
Cowherds, The. *Moonpaths: Ethics and Emptiness.* Oxford: Oxford University Press, 2015.
———. *Moonshadows: Conventional Truth in Buddhist Philosophy.* Oxford: Oxford University Press, 2011.
Critchley, Simon. "Black Socrates? Questioning the Philosophical Tradition." *Theoria: A Journal of Social and Political Theory*, no. 86 (1995): 79–98.
Danius, Sara, Stefan Jonsson, and Gayatri Chakravorty Spivak. "An Interview with Gayatri Chakravorty Spivak." *Boundary 2* 20, no. 2 (1993): 24–50.
Das, Veena. *Life and Words: Violence and the Descent into the Ordinary.* Berkeley: University of California Press, 2007.
Davis, Gregson. *Aimé Césaire.* Cambridge: Cambridge University Press, 1997.
Dayan, Joan. *Haiti, History, and the Gods.* Berkeley: University of California Press, 1998.
De Grazia, Margreta. *Hamlet without Hamlet.* New York: Cambridge University Press, 2007.
Deleuze, Gilles. *Nietzsche and Philosophy.* Translated by Hugh Tomlinson. New York: Columbia University Press, 1983.
Demos, T. J. "Moving Images of Globalization." *Grey Room*, no. 37 (Fall 2009): 6–29.
Denevan, William M. "The Pristine Myth: The Landscape of the Americas in 1492." *Annals of the Association of American Geographers* 82, no. 3 (1992): 369–85.

Derrida, Jacques. *Of Grammatology*. Translated by Gayatri Chakravorty Spivak. Corrected edition. Baltimore: Johns Hopkins University Press, 1998.
Desan, Philippe. " 'Il Est Des Peuples Où . . .': Montaigne et Le Nouveau Monde." *Montaigne Studies* 22, no. 1–2 (2010).
Descartes, René. *Discours de la méthode*. Edited by Étienne Gilson. Paris: Librairie philosophique J. Vrin, 1925.
———. *Discourse on Method; and, Meditations on First Philosophy*. Translated by Donald Cress. Indianapolis: Hackett Publishing, 1998.
Descola, Philippe. "Beyond Nature and Culture." *Proceedings of the British Academy* 139 (2006): 137–55.
———. "Beyond Nature and Culture." In *The Handbook of Contemporary Animism*, edited by Graham Harvey, 77–91. New York: Routledge, 2014.
Diagne, Souleymane Bachir. *African Art as Philosophy: Senghor, Bergson and the Idea of Negritude*. London: Seagull Books, 2011.
———. "Pour une histoire postcoloniale de la philosophie." *Cités*, no. 72 (December 21, 2017): 81–93.
———. "Rereading Aimé Césaire: Negritude as Creolization." *Small Axe* 19, no. 3 (December 2, 2015): 121–28.
Dimock, Wai-chee. *Through Other Continents: American Literature across Deep Time*. Princeton: Princeton University Press, 2006.
Dolan, Neal. *Emerson's Liberalism*. Madison: University of Wisconsin Press, 2009.
Donini, Pierluigi. "The History of the Concept of Eclecticism." In *The Question of "Eclecticism": Studies in Later Greek Philosophy*, edited by John M. Dillon and Anthony A. Long. Berkeley: University of California Press, 1996.
Dreyfus, Georges. *Recognizing Reality: Dharmakirti's Philosophy and Its Tibetan Interpretations*. Albany: State University of New York Press, 1997.
Dreyfus, Georges B. J. *The Sound of Two Hands Clapping: The Education of a Tibetan Buddhist Monk*. Berkeley: University of California Press, 2003.
Du Bois, W. E. B. *Black Folk Then and Now: An Essay in the History and Sociology of the Negro Race*. New York: Oxford University Press, 2007.
———. "Criteria of Negro Art." *The Crisis*. October 1926.
———. *Dark Princess: A Romance*. Jackson: Banner Books, 1995.
———. *Darkwater: Voices from Within the Veil*. Oxford: Oxford University Press, 2007.
———. *Dusk of Dawn: An Essay Toward an Autobiography of a Race Concept*. New York: Oxford University Press, 2014.
———. *In Battle for Peace: The Story of My 83rd Birthday*. Oxford: Oxford University Press, 2007.
———. *John Brown*. Oxford: Oxford University Press, 2007.
———. "Race Relations in the United States 1917–1947." *Phylon (1940–1956)* 9, no. 3 (1948): 234–47.
———. *The Autobiography of W. E. B. Du Bois: A Soliloquy on Viewing My Life from the Last Decade of Its First Century*. Oxford: Oxford University Press, 2007.

———. "The Conservation of Races." In *The Souls of Black Folk (Norton Critical Editions)*, edited by Henry Louis Gates Jr. and Terri Hume Oliver, 176–84. New York: W. W. Norton & Company, 1999.

———. *The Souls of Black Folk (Norton Critical Editions)*. Edited by Henry Louis Gates Jr. and Terri Hume Oliver. New York: W. W. Norton & Company, 1999.

———. *The World and Africa: And, Color and Democracy*. Edited by Henry Louis Gates Jr. Oxford: Oxford University Press, 2014.

———. *W. E. B. Du Bois: A Reader*. Edited by David L. Lewis. New York: H. Holt and Co., 1995.

Du Tertre, Jean-Baptiste. "Concerning the Natives of the Antilles." Translated by Marshall McKusick and Pierre Verin. New Haven: HRAF, 1958. HTML file.

Dunayevskaya, Raya. *Women's Liberation and the Dialectics of Revolution: Reaching for the Future*. Detroit: Wayne State University Press, 1996.

Dunbar-Ortiz, Roxanne. *An Indigenous Peoples' History of the United States*. Boston: Beacon Press, 2015.

Duneier, Mitchell. *Ghetto: The Invention of a Place, the History of an Idea*. New York: Farrar, Straus and Giroux, 2016.

Dussel, Enrique. "Anti-Cartesian Meditations: On the Origins of the Philosophical Anti-Discourse of Modernity." Translated by George Ciccariello-Maher. *Journal of Cultural and Religious Theory* 13, no. 1 (2014): 11–53.

———. *El último Marx (1863–1882) y la liberación latinoamericana*. Mexico City: Siglo XXI, 1990.

———. *The Invention of the Americas: Eclipse of "the Other" and the Myth of Modernity*. Translated by Michael D. Barber. New York: Continuum, 1995.

———. *The Underside of Modernity: Apel, Ricoeur, Rorty, Taylor, and the Philosophy of Liberation*. Translated by Eduardo Mendieta. New York: Humanity Books, 1996.

Eagleton, Terry, Edward W. Said, and Seamus Deane. *Nationalism, Colonialism, and Literature*. Minneapolis: University of Minnesota Press, 1990.

Edelglass, William, and Jay L. Garfield, eds. *Buddhist Philosophy: Essential Readings*. Oxford: Oxford University Press, 2009.

Edwards, Brent Hayes. *The Practice of Diaspora: Literature, Translation, and the Rise of Black Internationalism*. Cambridge: Harvard University Press, 2003.

Egan, Hugh. "'On Freedom': Emerson, Douglass, and the Self-Reliant Slave." *ESQ: A Journal of the American Renaissance* 60, no. 2 (2014): 183–208.

Ellison, Ralph. *Invisible Man*. 2nd ed. New York: Vintage Books, 1995.

Emerson, Ralph Waldo. *Collected Works of Ralph Waldo Emerson, Volume VIII: Letters and Social Aims*. Edited by Glen M. Johnson and Joel Myerson. Cambridge: Harvard University Press, 2010.

———. *English Traits*. Edited by Howard Mumford Jones. John Harvard Library. Cambridge: Belknap Press of Harvard University Press, 1966.

———. *Essays & Poems*. New York: Library of America, 1996.

———. *The Early Lectures, Volume II*. Edited by Robert E. Spiller. Cambridge: Harvard University Press, 1964.

———. *The Journals and Miscellaneous Notebooks of Ralph Waldo Emerson*. Cambridge: Belknap Press of Harvard University Press, 1960.

———. *The Journals and Miscellaneous Notebooks of Ralph Waldo Emerson: 1852–1855*. Cambridge: Harvard University Press, 1977.

———. *The Later Lectures of Ralph Waldo Emerson, 1843–1871*. Edited by Ronald A. Bosco and Joel Myerson. Vol. 2. Athens: University of Georgia Press, 2010.

———. *The Works of Ralph Waldo Emerson, in 12 vols. Fireside Edition*. Boston and New York, 1909. http://oll.libertyfund.org/titles/1962.

Eze, Emmanuel Chukwudi. *Achieving Our Humanity: The Idea of the Postracial Future*. New York: Routledge, 2001.

———. "The Color of Reason: The Idea of 'Race' in Kant's Anthropology." In *Postcolonial African Philosophy: A Critical Reader*, 103–40. Cambridge: Blackwell, 1997.

Fanon, Frantz. *A Dying Colonialism*. Translated by Haakon Chevalier. New York: Grove Press, 1994.

———. *Black Skin, White Masks*. Translated by Richard Philcox. New York: Grove Press, 2008.

———. *Œuvres*. Vol. 1. Paris: La Découverte, 2011.

———. *The Wretched of the Earth*. Translated by Constance Farrington. New York: Grove Press, 1968.

Faure, Bernard. *Chan Insights and Oversights: An Epistemological Critique of the Chan Tradition*. Princeton: Princeton University Press, 1993.

Field, Peter S. "The Strange Career of Emerson and Race." *American Nineteenth Century History* 2, no. 1 (March 2001): 1–32.

Finseth, Ian. "Evolution, Cosmopolitanism, and Emerson's Antislavery Politics." *American Literature* 77, no. 4 (December 1, 2005): 729–60.

Firmin, Antenor. *The Equality of Human Races*. Translated by Asselin Charles. Urbana: University of Illinois Press, 2002.

Force, Pierre. "Montaigne and the Coherence of Eclecticism." *Journal of the History of Ideas* 70, no. 4 (2009): 523–44.

Ford, Henry, and Samuel Crowther. *My Life and Work*. Garden City: Garden City Publishing, 1922.

Forster, Michael. "Hegel's Dialectical Method." In *The Cambridge Companion to Hegel*, edited by Frederick C Beiser, 130–70. New York: Cambridge University Press, 1993.

Foster, John Bellamy. "The Long Ecological Revolution." *Monthly Review* 69, no. 6 (November 1, 2017). https://monthlyreview.org/2017/11/01/the-long-ecological-revolution/.

Foucault, Michel. *Dits et Écrits, 1954–1988*. 1994th ed. Vol. 3. Paris: Gallimard, n.d.

———. *History of Madness*. Translated by Jonathan Murphy and Jean Khalfa. New York: Routledge, 2006.
———. *Le Gouvernement de Soi et Des Autres: Cours Au Collège de France, 1982–1983*. Hautes Études. Paris: Seuil/Gallimard, 2008.
———. *Les Mots et Les Choses: Une Archéologie Des Sciences Humaines*. Paris: Gallimard, 1966.
———. *L'herméneutique du sujet: Cours au Collège de France, 1981–1982*. Seuil/Gallimard, 2001.
———. *L'histoire de La Sexualité*. Vol. 1. Paris: Gallimard, 1976.
———. "Michel Foucault and Zen." In *Religion and Culture*, edited by Jeremy Carrette, 110–14. New York: Taylor & Francis, 1999.
———. *Naissance de La Biopolitique: Cours Au Collège de France, 1978–1979*. Hautes Études. Paris: Seuil/Gallimard, 2004.
———. "Qu'est-Ce Que La Critique ? (Critique et Aufklärung)." *Bulletin de La Société Française de Philosophie* 84, no. 2 (1990): 35–63.
———. *The Birth of Biopolitics: Lectures at the Collège de France, 1978–1979*. Translated by Graham Burchell. New York: Picador, 2010.
———. *The Government of Self and Others: Lectures at the College de France, 1982–1983*. Translated by Graham Burchell. New York: Picador, 2011.
———. *The Hermeneutics of the Subject: Lectures at the Collège de France, 1981–1982*. Translated by Graham Burchell. New York: Palgrave-Macmillan, 2005.
———. *The History of Sexuality, Volume 1: An Introduction*. Translated by Robert Hurley. New York: Vintage, 1990.
———. *The Order of Things: An Archaeology of the Human Sciences*. New York: Vintage Books, 1973.
———. "What Is Critique?" In *The Politics of Truth*, edited by Sylvere Lotringer, 23–82. Los Angeles: Semiotext, 2007.
———. "What Is Enlightenment?" In *The Foucault Reader*, edited by Paul Rabinow. New York: Pantheon Books, 1984.
Frank, Manfred. *The Philosophical Foundations of Early German Romanticism*. Translated by Elizabeth Millan-Zaibert. Albany: State University of New York Press, 2004.
Franklin, Benjamin. *The Autobiography of Benjamin Franklin*. Mineola: Dover, 1996.
Frazier, Robeson Taj. *The East Is Black: Cold War China in the Black Radical Imagination*. Durham: Duke University Press Books, 2014.
Freire, Paolo. *Pedagogy of the Oppressed*. Translated by Myra Bergman Ramos. New York: Seabury, 1970.
Freud, Sigmund. *The Freud Reader*. New York: W. W. Norton, 1989.
Friedman, Milton. *Capitalism and Freedom: Fortieth Anniversary Edition*. Chicago: University of Chicago Press, 2002.
Gandhi, Mohandas. *Mahatma Gandhi: The Essential Writings*. Edited by Judith Brown. Oxford: Oxford University Press, 2008.

Garfield, Jay L. "Commentary." In *The Fundamental Wisdom of the Middle Way: Nagarjuna's Mulamadhyamakakarika*, by Nagarjuna. New York: Oxford University Press, 1995.

Gellner, Ernest. *Reason and Culture: The Historic Role of Rationality and Rationalism*. Cambridge, MA: Basil Blackwell, 1992.

Germana, Nicholas. "Revisiting 'Hegel and Haiti': Postcolonial Readings of the Lord/Bondsman Dialectic." In *Creolizing Hegel*, edited by Michael Monahan. Lanham: Rowman & Littlefield International, 2017.

Ghamari-Tabrizi, Behrooz. *Foucault in Iran: Islamic Revolution after the Enlightenment*. Minneapolis: University of Minnesota Press, 2016.

Gibson, Nigel. "Dialectical Impasses: Turning the Table on Hegel and the Black." *Parallax* 8, no. 2 (April 1, 2002): 30–45.

Gikandi, Simon. "Picasso, Africa, and the Schemata of Difference." *Modernism/Modernity* 10, no. 3 (September 5, 2003): 455–80.

Gillman, Susan, and Alys Weinbaum, eds. *Next to the Color Line: Gender, Sexuality, and W. E. B. Du Bois*. Minneapolis: University of Minnesota Press, 2007.

Gilroy, Paul. *The Black Atlantic: Modernity and Double Consciousness*. Cambridge: Harvard University Press, 1993.

Gines, Kathryn T. "From Color-Blind to Post-Racial: Blacks and Social Justice in the Twenty-First Century." *Journal of Social Philosophy* 41, no. 3 (2010): 370–84.

Goethe, Johann Wolfgang von. *Essays on Art and Literature*. Edited by John Gearey. Translated by Ellen von Nardroff and Ernest H. von Nardroff. Vol. 3 of *The Collected Works of Goethe*. Princeton: Princeton University Press, 1994.

———. *Faust I & II*. Translated by Stuart Atkins. Vol. 2 of *The Collected Works of Goethe*. Princeton: Princeton University Press, 1994.

———. *Goethes Werke / textkritisch durchgesehen und kommentiert von Erich Trunz*. Vol. 12. Munich: C.H. Beck, 1981.

Goldenberg, David M. *The Curse of Ham: Race and Slavery in Early Judaism, Christianity, and Islam*. Princeton: Princeton University Press, 2003.

Gomez, Luis O. "D. T. Suzuki's Contribution to Modern Buddhist Scholarship." In *A Zen Life: D. T. Suzuki Remembered*, edited by Francis Haar and Masao Abe. New York: Weatherhill, 1986.

Gooding-Williams, Robert. *In the Shadow of Du Bois: Afro-Modern Political Thought in America*. Cambridge: Harvard University Press, 2009.

Goodman, Russell. "Paths of Coherence through Emerson's Philosophy: The Case of 'Nominalist and Realist.'" In *The Other Emerson*, edited by Branka Arsic and Cary Wolfe, 41–58. Minneapolis: University of Minnesota Press, 2010.

Gordon, Jane Anna. *Creolizing Political Theory: Reading Rousseau through Fanon*. New York: Fordham University Press, 2014.

Gordon, Jane Anna, and Neil Roberts, eds. *Creolizing Rousseau*. London: Rowman & Littlefield International, 2014.

Gordon, Lewis R. *Disciplinary Decadence: Living Thought in Trying Times.* Boulder: Paradigm Publishers, 2006.

———. *What Fanon Said: A Philosophical Introduction to His Life and Thought.* New York: Fordham University Press, 2015.

Gougeon, Len. "Race." In *Ralph Waldo Emerson in Context*, edited by Wesley T. Mott, 196–203. New York: Cambridge University Press, 2013.

———. *Virtue's Hero: Emerson, Antislavery, and Reform.* Athens: University of Georgia Press, 1999.

Graeber, David. *Debt: The First 5,000 Years.* Brooklyn: Melville House, 2012.

Graeber, David, and David Wengrow. "How to Change the Course of Human History." *Eurozine* (blog), March 2, 2018. https://www.eurozine.com/change-course-human-history/.

Grafton, Anthony, April Shelford, and Nancy G. Siraisi. *New Worlds, Ancient Texts: The Power of Tradition and the Shock of Discovery.* Cambridge: Belknap Press of Harvard University Press, 1992.

Greenblatt, Stephen. *Marvelous Possessions: The Wonder of the New World.* Chicago: University of Chicago Press, 1991.

Guadalupe Davidson, Maria del, and George Yancy, eds. *Critical Perspectives on bell hooks.* New York: Routledge, 2009.

Gudynas, Eduardo. "Buen Vivir: Today's Tomorrow." *Development* 54, no. 4 (December 2011): 441–47.

Haddour, Azzedine. "Torture Unveiled: Rereading Fanon and Bourdieu in the Context of May 1958." *Theory, Culture & Society* 27, no. 7–8 (December 1, 2010): 66–90.

Hägglund, Martin. *Radical Atheism: Derrida and the Time of Life.* Palo Alto: Stanford University Press, 2008.

Hakugen, Ichikawa. "A Preliminary Conception of Zen Social Ethics." *Journal of Indian and Buddhist Studies* 11, no. 1 (1963): 359–48.

Harney, Elizabeth. *In Senghor's Shadow: Art, Politics, and the Avant-Garde in Senegal, 1960–1995.* Durham: Duke University Press, 2004.

Harootunian, Harry. *Marx After Marx: History and Time in the Expansion of Capitalism.* New York: Columbia University Press, 2015.

Harris, Wilson. "The Frontier on Which 'Heart of Darkness' Stands." *Research in African Literatures* 12, no. 1 (1981): 86–93.

Hartman, Saidiya. *Scenes of Subjection: Terror, Slavery, and Self-Making in Nineteenth-Century America.* New York: Oxford University Press, 1997.

Hau'ofa, Epeli. "Our Sea of Islands." *The Contemporary Pacific* 6, no. 1 (Spring 1994): 147–61.

Hayek, Friedrich. *The Road to Serfdom: Text and Documents—The Definitive Edition.* Edited by Bruce Caldwell. Chicago: University of Chicago Press, 2007.

Hayes, Richard. "Madhyamaka." Edited by Edward N. Zalta. *The Stanford Encyclopedia of Philosophy.* Metaphysics Research Lab, Stanford University, 2017. https://plato.stanford.edu/archives/spr2017/entries/madhyamaka/.

Hayot, Eric. *On Literary Worlds*. New York: Oxford University Press, 2012.
Hegel, Georg Wilhelm Friedrich. *Elements of the Philosophy of Right*. Edited by Allen Wood. Translated by H. B. Nisbet. New York: Cambridge University Press, 1991.
———. *Hegel's Philosophy of Subjective Spirit / Hegels Philosophie Des Subjektiven Geistes: Volume 2 Anthropology / Band 2 Anthropologie*. Edited and translated by Michael John Petry. Dordrecht: Springer, 1978.
———. *Hegel's Philosophy of Subjective Spirit: Volume 3 Phenomenology and Psychology*. Edited and translated by Michael John Petry. Dordrecht: Reidel, 1978.
———. *Introductory Lectures on Aesthetics*. London: Penguin Books, 1993.
———. *Lectures on the Philosophy of World History: Introduction*. Translated by Hugh Barr Nisbet. Cambridge: Cambridge University Press, 1981.
———. *Phenomenology of Spirit*. Translated by A. V. Miller. Oxford: Oxford University Press, 1977.
———. *Science of Logic*. Translated by A. V. Miller. New York: Routledge, 2002.
———. *Werke*. Vol. 3. Frankfurt am Main: Suhrkamp, 1969.
———. *Werke*. Vol. 7. Frankfurt am Main: Suhrkamp, 1969.
Hegeman, Susan. *The Cultural Return*. Berkeley: University of California Press, 2012.
Heidegger, Martin. *Being and Time: A Translation of Sein Und Zeit*. Translated by Joan Stambaugh. Albany: State University of New York Press, 1996.
———. "Der Spiegel Interview with Martin Heidegger." In *The Heidegger reader*, edited by Gunter Figal, translated by Jerome Veith, 313–33. Bloomington: Indiana University Press, 2009.
———. *Gesamtausgabe*. Vol. 2. Frankfurt am Main: Vittorio Klostermann, 1977.
———. *Identity and Difference*. Translated by Joan Stambaugh. Chicago: University of Chicago Press, 2002.
Heine, Steven. *Like Cats and Dogs: Contesting the Mu Koan in Zen Buddhism*. New York: Oxford University Press, 2014.
———. "What Is on the Other Side? Delusion and Realization in Dōgen's 'Genjōkōan.'" In *Dogen: Textual and Historical Studies*, edited by Steven Heine. New York: Oxford University Press, 2012.
Heng, Geraldine, and Lynn Ramey. "Early Globalities, Global Literatures: Introducing a Special Issue on the Global Middle Ages." *Literature Compass* 11, no. 7 (July 2014): 389–94.
Henry, Paget. "Fanon, African and Afro-Caribbean Philosophy." In *Fanon: A Critical Reader*, edited by Lewis R. Gordon, T. Denean Sharpley-Whiting, and Renee T. White, 220–43. Oxford: Wiley-Blackwell, 1996.
Herder, Johann Gottfried. *Another Philosophy of History and Selected Political Writings*. Translated by Ioannis D. Evrigenis and Daniel Pellerin. Indianapolis: Hackett Publishing, 2004.
Hinderer, Walter. "Schiller's Philosophical Aesthetics in Anthropological Perspective." In *A Companion to the Works of Friedrich Schiller*, edited by Steven D. Martinson, 27–46. Rochester: Camden Press, 2005.

Hine, Darlene C. "'In the Kingdom of Culture': Black Women and the Intersection of Race, Gender, and Class." In *Lure and Loathing: Essays on Race, Identity, and the Ambivalence of Assimilation*, 337–51. New York: Penguin, 1993.
Hodder, Alan. "Asia." In *Ralph Waldo Emerson in Context*, edited by Wesley T. Mott, 40–48. New York: Cambridge University Press, 2013.
Hodgen, Margaret T. "Montaigne and Shakespeare Again." *Huntington Library Quarterly* 16, no. 1 (November 1, 1952): 23–42.
Hoffmann, George. "Anatomy of the Mass: Montaigne's 'Cannibals.'" *PMLA* 117 (2002): 207–21.
Holt, Thomas C. "The Political Uses of Alienation: W. E. B. Du Bois on Politics, Race, and Culture, 1903–1940." *American Quarterly* 42, no. 2 (June 1990): 301–23.
Hooker, Juliet. *Theorizing Race in the Americas: Douglass, Sarmiento, Du Bois, and Vasconcelos*. Oxford: Oxford University Press, 2017.
hooks, bell. *Belonging: A Culture of Place*. New York: Routledge, 2009.
———. *Outlaw Culture: Resisting Representations*. New York: Routledge, 1994.
———. *Teaching to Transgress: Education as the Practice of Freedom*. New York: Routledge, 1994.
———. "Waking Up to Racism." *Tricycle*, Fall 1994. https://tricycle.org/magazine/waking-racism/.
hooks, bell, and Helen Tworkov. "Agent of Change: Helen Tworkov Interviews bell hooks." *Tricycle*, Fall 1994. https://tricycle.org/magazine/agent-change-an-interview-with-bell-hooks/.
Hori, Victor. "Kōan and Kenshō in the Rinzai Zen Curriculum." In *The Koan: Texts and Contexts in Zen Buddhism*, edited by Steven Heine and Dale Wright. New York: Oxford University Press, 2000.
Horne, Gerald. *Black and Red: W.E.B. Du Bois and the Afro-American Response to the Cold War, 1944–1963*. SUNY Series in Afro-American Society. Albany: State University of New York Press, 1986.
Houlgate, Stephen. *The Opening of Hegel's Logic: From Being to Infinity*. West Lafayette, IN: Purdue University Press, 2005.
Hountondji, Paulin J. *African Philosophy, Second Edition: Myth and Reality*. 2nd ed. Bloomington: Indiana University Press, 1996.
Hubbard, Jamie, and Paul Swanson, eds. *Pruning the Bodhi Tree: The Storm over Critical Buddhism*. Honolulu: University of Hawai'i Press, 1997.
Hyppolite, Jean. *Studies on Marx and Hegel*. New York: Basic Books, 1969.
ICLS Columbia. *Of Grammatology Re-Translated: 40th Anniversary Edition: A Tribute*. https://www.youtube.com/watch?v=lLCOOld3fto&feature=youtu.be.
Inwood, Michael. *A Hegel Dictionary*. Oxford: Wiley-Blackwell, 1992.
Irele, F. Abiola. *The Negritude Moment: Explorations in Francophone African and Caribbean Literature and Thought*. Trenton, NJ: Africa World Press, 2010.
Ives, Christopher. *Imperial-Way Zen: Ichikawa Hakugen's Critique and Lingering Questions for Buddhist Ethics*. Honolulu: University of Hawai'i Press, 2009.

Iwamura, Jane. *Virtual Orientalism: Asian Religions and American Popular Culture.* New York: Oxford University Press, 2010.
Jackson, Michael. "Ajala's Heads: Reflections on Anthropology and Philosophy in a West African Setting." In *The Ground Between: Anthropologists Engage Philosophy*, edited by Veena Das, Michael D. Jackson, Arthur Kleinman, and Bhrigupati Singh, 27–49. Durham: Duke University Press, 2014.
Jacobs, Brian, and Patricia Kain, eds. *Essays on Kant's Anthropology.* Cambridge: Cambridge University Press, 2003.
Jaeggi, Rahel. *Alienation.* Translated by Frederick Neuhouser and Alan E. Smith. New York: Columbia University Press, 2014.
Jaffe, Richard M. "E-Mail," December 27, 2017.
———. "Introduction." In *Selected Works of D. T. Suzuki, Volume I: Zen*, by Daisetsu Teitaro Suzuki, xi–lvi. Berkeley: University of California Press, 2014.
———. "Seeking Sakyamuni: Travel and the Reconstruction of Japanese Buddhism." *The Journal of Japanese Studies* 30, no. 1 (2004): 65–96.
Jakobsen, Janet. *Working Alliances and the Politics of Difference: Diversity and Feminist Ethics.* Bloomington: Indiana University Press, 1998.
James, Joy. "The Profeminist Politics of W.E.B. Du Bois with Respects to Anna Julia Cooper and Ida B. Wells Barnett." In *W.E.B. Du Bois on Race and Culture: Philosophy, Politics, Poetics*, edited by Bernard W. Bell, Emily R. Grosholz, and James B. Stewart, 141–60. New York: Routledge, 1996.
James, William. *Essays in Radical Empiricism and a Pluralistic Universe.* Edited by Ralph Barton Perry. New York: E. P. Dutton & Co., 1971.
———. *Writings 1902–1910.* New York: The Library of America, 1988.
Jameson, Fredric. *Postmodernism, or, The Cultural Logic of Late Capitalism.* Durham: Duke University Press, 1990.
———. *Representing Capital: A Commentary on Volume One.* London: Verso, 2011.
———. "Third-World Literature in the Era of Multinational Capitalism." *Social Text*, no. 15 (1986): 65–88.
Jeffers, Chike. "Anna Julia Cooper and the Black Gift Thesis." *History of Philosophy Quarterly* 33, no. 1 (January 1, 2016): 79–97.
———, ed. *Listening to Ourselves: A Multilingual Anthology of African Philosophy.* Albany: State University of New York Press, 2013.
———. "Recent Work on Negritude." *Journal of French and Francophone Philosophy* 24, no. 2 (December 21, 2016): 304–18.
Jones, Donna V. Review of *African Art as Philosophy: Senghor, Bergson and the Idea of Negritude*, by Souleymane Bachir Diagne. *Journal of Anthropological Research* 69, no. 1 (2013): 132–34.
———. *The Racial Discourses of Life Philosophy: Négritude, Vitalism, and Modernity.* New York: Columbia University Press, 2010.
Jones, Gareth Stedman. *Karl Marx: Greatness and Illusion.* Cambridge: Belknap Press of Harvard University Press, 2016.

Joseph, Branden Wayne. *Beyond the Dream Syndicate: Tony Conrad and the Arts after Cage (a "Minor" History)*. New York: Zone, 2011.
———. "Chance, Indeterminacy, Multiplicity." In *The Anarchy of Silence: John Cage and Experimental Art*, by Julia Robinson. Barcelona: Museu d'Art Contemporani de Barcelona, 2009.
Jullien, François. *A Treatise on Efficacy: Between Western and Chinese Thinking*. Translated by Janet Lloyd. Honolulu: University of Hawai'i Press, 2004.
———. *On the Universal: The Uniform, the Common and Dialogue between Cultures*. Translated by Michael Richardson and Fijalkowski Krzysztof. Cambridge: Polity, 2014.
———. *Vital Nourishment: Departing from Happiness*. Translated by Arthur Goldhammer. Cambridge: Zone Books, 2007.
Kant, Immanuel. *Anthropology, History, and Education*. Edited by Robert B. Louden and Günter Zöller. Translated by Mary Gregor et al. Cambridge: Cambridge University Press, 2011.
———. *Critique of Pure Reason*. Translated by Paul Guyer. Cambridge: Cambridge University Press, 1998.
———. *Lectures on Anthropology*. Translated by Robert B. Louden, Allen W. Wood, Robert R. Clewis, and G. Felicitas Munzel. Cambridge: Cambridge University Press, 2013.
———. *Practical Philosophy*. Edited and translated by Mary Gregor. Cambridge: Cambridge University Press, 1996.
———. *Religion within the Boundaries of Mere Reason and Other Writings*. Edited and translated by George Di Giovanni and Allen Wood. Cambridge: Cambridge University Press, 1998.
Kaplan, Lawrence. "Inuit or Eskimo? | Alaska Native Language Center." July 1, 2011. https://www.uaf.edu/anlc/resources/inuit-eskimo/.
Kasulis, Thomas. "Reading D. T. Suzuki Today." *Eastern Buddhist* 38, no. 1/2 (2007): 41–57.
Kateb, George. *Emerson and Self-Reliance*. Thousand Oaks, CA: Sage, 1995.
Katz, Jonathan. "John Cage's Queer Silence; or, How to Avoid Making Matters Worse." *GLQ* 5, no. 2 (1999): 231–52.
Kazanjian, David. "Hegel, Liberia." *Diacritics* 40, no. 1 (2010): 6–28.
Kepel, Gilles. *Jihad: The Trail of Political Islam*. Translated by Anthony Roberts. Cambridge: Belknap Press of Harvard University Press, 2003.
Klein, Naomi. *This Changes Everything: Capitalism vs. the Climate*. New York: Simon & Schuster, 2015.
Kleingold, Pauline. "Kant's Second Thoughts on Colonialism." In *Kant and Colonialism: Historical and Critical Perspectives*, edited by Katrin Flikschuh and Lea Ypi, 43–67. Oxford: Oxford University Press, 2015.
Kostelanetz, Richard, and John Cage. *Conversing with Cage*. New York: Limelight Editions, 1988.

Kourí, Emilio. "Sobre La Propiedad Comunal de Los Pueblos, de La Reforma a La Revolucion." *Historia Mexicana* 66, no. 4 (264) (2017): 1923–60.
Kritzman, Lawrence D. *The Fabulous Imagination: On Montaigne's Essays*. New York: Columbia University Press, 2012.
Larson, Kay. *Where the Heart Beats: John Cage, Zen Buddhism, and the Inner Life of Artists*. New York: Penguin Press, 2012.
Lenik, Stephan. "Carib as a Colonial Category: Comparing Ethnohistoric and Archaeological Evidence from Dominica, West Indies." *Ethnohistory* 59, no. 1 (January 1, 2012): 79–107.
Leonard, George. *Into the Light of Things: The Art of the Commonplace from Wordsworth to John Cage*. Chicago: University of Chicago Press, 1994.
Lestringant, Frank. *Cannibals: The Discovery and Representation of the Cannibal from Columbus to Jules Verne*. Translated by Rosemary Morris. Berkeley: University of California Press, 1997.
Levinas, Emmanuel. *Emmanuel Levinas: Basic Philosophical Writings*. Edited by Adriaan T. Peperzak, Simon Critchley, and Robert Bernasconi. Bloomington: Indiana University Press, 1996.
Lévi-Strauss, Claude. *Structural Anthropology*. Translated by Claire Jacobson and Brooke Grundfest Schoepf. New York: Anchor, 1967.
———. *Structural Anthropology, Volume 2*. Translated by Monique Layton. Chicago: University of Chicago Press, 1983.
———. *Tristes Tropiques*. Translated by John Weightman and Doreen Weightman. New York: Penguin Books, 1992.
Lewis, David Levering. *W. E. B. Du Bois, 1868–1919: Biography of a Race*. New York: Holt Paperbacks, 1994.
Liebman, Sheldon W. "Emerson's Transformation in the 1820's." *American Literature* 40, no. 2 (1968): 133–54.
Linebaugh, Peter, and Marcus Rediker. *The Many-Headed Hydra: Sailors, Slaves, Commoners, and the Hidden History of the Revolutionary Atlantic*. Boston: Beacon Press, 2013.
Lipsitz, George. "The Possessive Investment in Whiteness: Racialized Social Democracy and the 'White' Problem in American Studies." *American Quarterly* 47, no. 3 (1995): 369–87.
Locke, John. *Political Writings*. New York: Mentor, 1993.
Lopez, Donald S. "Buddhism in Practice." In *Asian Religions in Practice: An Introduction*, edited by Donald S Lopez, 56–87. Princeton: Princeton University Press, 1999.
———. "Introduction." In *A Modern Buddhist Bible: Essential Readings from East and West.*, edited by Donald S Lopez, vii–xli. Boston: Beacon Press, 2004.
Lowe, Lisa. *The Intimacies of Four Continents*. Durham: Duke University Press, 2015.
Lugones, María. "Playfulness, 'World'-Travelling, and Loving Perception." *Hypatia* 2, no. 2 (1987): 3–19.

Lütticken, Sven. "Neither Autocracy nor Automatism: Notes on Autonomy and the Aesthetic." *E-Flux* 69 (January 2016). http://www.e-flux.com/journal/neither-autocracy-nor-automatism-notes-on-autonomy-and-the-aesthetic/.
Mahmood, Saba. *Politics of Piety: The Islamic Revival and the Feminist Subject*. Princeton: Princeton University Press, 2005.
Maibor, Carolyn R. *Labor Pains: Emerson, Hawthorne, and Alcott on Work and the Woman Question*. Literary Criticism and Cultural Theory. New York: Routledge, 2004.
Makdisi, George. *The Rise of Humanism in Classical Islam and the Christian West: With Special Reference to Scholasticism*. Edinburgh: Edinburgh University Press, 1990.
Maldonado-Torres, Nelson. *Against War: Views from the Underside of Modernity*. Durham: Duke University Press, 2008.
———. "Césaire's Gift and the Decolonial Turn." In *Critical Ethnic Studies: A Reader*, edited by Critical Ethnic Studies Editorial Collective, 435–62. Durham: Duke University Press, 2016.
———. "On the Coloniality of Being: Contributions to the Development of a Concept." *Cultural Studies* 21, no. 2–3 (2007): 240–70.
———. "Rousseau and Fanon on Inequality and the Human Sciences." In *Creolizing Rousseau*, edited by Jane Anna Gordon and Neil Roberts, 121–42. London: Rowman & Littlefield International, 2014.
Mamdani, Mahmood. *Define and Rule: Native as Political Identity*. Cambridge: Harvard University Press, 2012.
Mandela, Nelson. *Long Walk to Freedom: The Autobiography of Nelson Mandela*. Boston: Back Bay Books, 1995.
Mandeville, John. *The Book of Marvels and Travels*. Translated by Anthony Bale. Oxford: Oxford University Press, 2012.
Marx, Karl. *Capital: A Critique of Political Economy, Volume 1*. Translated by Ben Fowkes. New York: Vintage, 1977.
———. *Early Writings*. Edited by Quintin Hoare. Translated by Rodney Livingstone and Gregor Benton. New York: Vintage, 1975.
———. *Gesamtausgabe (MEGA)*. Vol. I, 2. Berlin: Dietz, 1972.
———. *Gesamtausgabe (MEGA)*. Vol. II, 8. Berlin: Dietz, 1972.
———. *Gesamtausgabe (MEGA)*. Vol. II, 1. Berlin: Dietz, 1972.
———. *Grundrisse: Foundations of the Critique of Political Economy*. Translated by Martin Nicolaus. New York: Penguin, 1993.
———. *The Ethnological Notebooks of Karl Marx*. Edited by Lawrence Krader. Assen: Van Gorcum, 1972.
Marx, Karl, and Friedrich Engels. "The Communist Manifesto." In *The Marx-Engels Reader*, edited by Robert C Tucker. New York: Norton, 1978.
———. *The Marx-Engels Reader*. Edited by Robert C. Tucker. New York: Norton, 1978.

Masuzawa, Tomoko. *The Invention of World Religions, or, How European Universalism Was Preserved in the Language of Pluralism*. Chicago: University of Chicago Press, 2005.

Matthiessen, F. O. *American Renaissance*. New York: Oxford University Press, 1941.

Maybee, Julie E. "Hegel's Dialectics." In *The Stanford Encyclopedia of Philosophy*, edited by Edward N. Zalta, Winter 2016. Metaphysics Research Lab, Stanford University, 2016. https://plato.stanford.edu/archives/win2016/entries/hegel-dialectics/.

———. "Hegel's Dialectics." In *The Stanford Encyclopedia of Philosophy*, edited by Edward N. Zalta, Winter 2016 edition. https://plato.stanford.edu/entries/hegel-dialectics/.

Mbembe, Achille. "Afropolitanisme." *Africultures* (blog), December 25, 2005. http://africultures.com/afropolitanisme-4248/.

———. *Critique of Black Reason*. Translated by Laurent Dubois. Durham: Duke University Press Books, 2017.

———. "France-Afrique: Ces Sottises Qui Divisent." *Africultures* (blog), August 8, 2007. http://africultures.com/france-afrique-ces-sottises-qui-divisent-6819/.

———. "On the Postcolony: A Brief Response to Critics." *African Identities* 4, no. 2 (October 1, 2006): 143–78.

———. *Sortir de la grande nuit*. Paris: La Découverte, 2010.

Mbembe, Achille, and Balakrishnan, Sarah. "Pan-African Legacies, Afropolitan Futures." *Transition*, no. 120 (2016): 28–37.

McCarthy, Thomas. *Race, Empire, and the Idea of Human Development*. Cambridge: Cambridge University Press, 2009.

McMahan, David L. *The Making of Buddhist Modernism*. Oxford: Oxford University Press, 2008.

Mehta, Uday. *Liberalism and Empire: A Study in Nineteenth-Century British Liberal Thought*. Chicago: University of Chicago Press, 1999.

Michaels, Walter Benn. *The Shape of the Signifier: 1967 to the End of History*. Princeton: Princeton University Press, 2004.

Mikkelsen, Jon M., ed. *Kant and the Concept of Race: Late Eighteenth-Century Writings*. Albany: State University of New York Press, 2014.

———. "Translator's Introduction." In *Kant and the Concept of Race: Late Eighteenth-Century Writings*, edited by Jon M. Mikkelsen, 1–20. Albany: State University of New York Press, 2014.

Mishima, Yukio. *The Temple of the Golden Pavilion*. Translated by Ivan Morris. New York: Knopf, 1959.

Mohanty, J. N. *Classical Indian Philosophy*. Lanham: Rowman & Littlefield Publishers, 2000.

Mohr, Michael. "Plowing the Zen Field: Trends Since 1989 and Emerging Perspectives." *Religion Compass* 6, no. 2 (2012): 113–24.

———. "The Use of Traps and Snares: Shaku Sōen Revisited." In *Zen Masters*, by Steven Heine and Dale Wright. Oxford: Oxford University Press, 2010.

Monahan, Michael, ed. *Creolizing Hegel*. Lanham: Rowman & Littlefield International, 2017.
———. "Introduction: What Is Rational Is Creolizing." In *Creolizing Hegel*, edited by Michael Monahan, 1–22. Lanham: Rowman & Littlefield International, 2017.
———. "Recognition Beyond Struggle: On a Liberatory Account of Hegelian Recognition." *Social Theory and Practice* 32, no. 3 (2006): 389–414.
Montaigne, Michel de. *Les essais de Michel de Montaigne*. Edited by Pierre Villey and V.-L. Saulnier. Paris: Presses Universitaires de France, 1965.
———. *The Complete Essays of Montaigne*. Translated by Donald Frame. Palo Alto: Stanford University Press, 1958.
Moyn, Samuel, and Andrew Sartori, eds. *Global Intellectual History*. New York: Columbia University Press, 2015.
Muthu, Sankar. "Commerce, Conquest, and Cosmopolitanism in Enlightenment Political Thought." In *Empire and Modern Political Thought*, edited by Sankar Muthu, 199–231. Cambridge: Cambridge University Press, 2014.
———. *Enlightenment against Empire*. Princeton: Princeton University Press, 2003.
Nagarjuna. *The Fundamental Wisdom of the Middle Way: Nagarjuna's Mulamadhyamakakarika*. Translated by Jay L. Garfield. New York: Oxford University Press, 1995.
Nancy, Jean-Luc. *The Creation of the World or Globalization*. Translated by Francois Raffoul and David Pettigrew. Albany: State University of New York Press, 2007.
Natsume, Sōseki. *The Gate*. Translated by William F. Sibley. New York Review Books Classics. New York: New York Review Books, 2013.
Nehamas, Alexander. *The Art of Living: Socratic Reflections from Plato to Foucault*. Berkeley: University of California Press, 1998.
Neuhouser, Frederick. *Foundations of Hegel's Social Theory: Actualizing Freedom*. Cambridge: Harvard University Press, 2003.
———. *Rousseau's Critique of Inequality: Reconstructing the Second Discourse*. Cambridge: Cambridge University Press, 2014.
Ngũgĩ wa Thiong'o. *Globalectics: Theory and the Politics of Knowing*. New York: Columbia University Press, 2012.
Nicoloff, Philip Loveless. *Emerson on Race and History: An Examination of English Traits*. New York: Columbia University Press, 1961.
Noriaki, Hakamaya. "Critical Philosophy versus Topical Philosophy." In *Pruning the Bodhi Tree: The Storm over Critical Buddhism*, edited by Jamie Hubbard and Paul Swanson, 56–80. Honolulu: University of Hawai`i Press, 1997.
Nyquist, Mary. *Arbitrary Rule: Slavery, Tyranny, and the Power of Life and Death*. Chicago: University of Chicago Press, 2013.
Ortega, Mariana. *In-between: Latina Feminist Phenomenology, Multiplicity, and the Self*. SUNY Series, Philosophy and Race. Albany: State University of New York Press, 2016.
Outlaw, Lucius. "If Not Races, Then What?: Toward a Revised Understanding of Bio-Social Groupings." *Graduate Faculty Philosophy Journal* 35, no. 1–2 (2014): 275–96.

———. *On Race and Philosophy*. New York: Routledge, 1996.
Pagden, Anthony. *Facing Each Other: The World's Perception of Europe and Europe's Perception of the World*. Burlington: Ashgate/Variorum, 2000.
———. *The Fall of Natural Man: The American Indian and the Origins of Comparative Ethnology*. New York: Cambridge University Press, 1982.
Parekh, Bhikhu. *Marx's Theory of Ideology*. New York: Routledge, 2015.
Park, Peter K. J. *Africa, Asia, and the History of Philosophy: Racism in the Formation of the Philosophical Canon, 1780–1830*. Albany: State University of New York Press, 2014.
Patterson, Anita Haya. *From Emerson to King: Democracy, Race, and the Politics of Protest*. New York: Oxford University Press, 1997.
Pease, Donald. "'Experience,' Antislavery, and the Crisis of Emersonianism." In *The Other Emerson*, by Branka Arsić and Cary Wolfe. Minneapolis: University of Minnesota Press, 2010.
Pinkard, Terry. "Phenomenology of Spirit Page." Terry Pinkard, Georgetown University. http://terrypinkard.weebly.com/phenomenology-of-spirit-page.html.
Pippin, Robert. *Hegel on Self-Consciousness: Desire and Death in the Phenomenology of Spirit*. Princeton: Princeton University Press, 2011.
———. *Idealism as Modernism: Hegelian Variations*. Cambridge: Cambridge University Press, 1997.
Pirsig, Robert M. *Zen and the Art of Motorcycle Maintenance*. San Francisco: Harper Collins, 2009.
Pittman, John P. "Double Consciousness." In *The Stanford Encyclopedia of Philosophy*, edited by Edward N. Zalta, Summer 2016 edition. https://plato.stanford.edu/archives/sum2016/entries/double-consciousness/.
Pitts, Jennifer. *A Turn to Empire: The Rise of Imperial Liberalism in Britain and France*. Princeton: Princeton University Press, 2006.
Plato. *Ion, Hippias Minor, Laches, Protagoras: The Dialogues of Plato Volume 3*. Translated by Reginald E. Allen. New Haven: Yale University Press, 1996.
Polanyi, Karl. *The Great Transformation: The Political and Economic Origins of Our Time*. Boston: Beacon Press, 2001.
Porte, Joel, ed. *Consciousness and Culture: Emerson and Thoreau Reviewed*. New Haven: Yale University Press, 2004.
Porter, Eric. *The Problem of the Future World: W.E.B. Du Bois and the Race Concept at Midcentury*. Durham: Duke University Press, 2010.
Pratt, Mary Louise. *Imperial Eyes: Travel Writing and Transculturation*. London: Routledge, 1992.
Rabaka, Reiland. *The Negritude Movement: W.E.B. Du Bois, Leon Damas, Aime Cesaire, Leopold Senghor, Frantz Fanon, and the Evolution of an Insurgent Idea*. Lanham: Lexington Books, 2015.
Rampell, Palmer. "Laws That Refuse To Be Stated: The Post-Sectarian Spiritualities of Emerson, Thoreau, and D. T. Suzuki." *The New England Quarterly* 34, no. 4 (2011): 621–54.

Rampersad, Arnold. *The Art and Imagination of W.E.B. DuBois*. New York: Schocken, 1990.

Rancière, Jacques. *Dissensus: On Politics and Aesthetics*. Translated by Steven Corcoran. New York: Bloomsbury Academic, 2010.

———. *Proletarian Nights: The Workers' Dream in Nineteenth-Century France*. New York: Verso, 2012.

———. "The Aesthetic Revolution and Its Outcomes." *New Left Review*, no. 14 (2002): 133–51.

———. *The Emancipated Spectator*. London: Verso, 2011.

———. *The Ignorant Schoolmaster: Five Lessons in Intellectual Emancipation*. Translated by Kristin Ross. Palo Alto: Stanford University Press, 1991.

———. *The Politics of Aesthetics*. Translated by Gabriel Rockhill. London: Bloomsbury Academic, 2013.

Rasberry, Vaughn. *Race and the Totalitarian Century: Geopolitics in the Black Literary Imagination*. Cambridge: Harvard University Press, 2016.

Rath, Richard Cullen. "Echo and Narcissus: The Afrocentric Pragmatism of W. E. B. Du Bois." *The Journal of American History* 84, no. 2 (September 1, 1997): 461–95.

Rathore, Aakash Singh, and Rimina Mohapatra. *Hegel's India: A Reinterpretation with Texts*. New Delhi: Oxford University Press, 2017.

Reed, Adolph L. *W.E.B. Du Bois and American Political Thought: Fabianism and the Color Line*. New York: Oxford University Press, 1997.

Rich, Adrienne. *Arts of the Possible: Essays and Conversations*. New York: W. W. Norton & Company, 2002.

Robbins, Bruce. "Prolegomena to a Cosmopolitanism in Deep Time." *Interventions* 18, no. 2 (March 3, 2016): 172–86.

———. "Subaltern Speak." *N+1*, Winter 2014. https://nplusonemag.com/issue-18/reviews/subaltern/.

Rockhill, Gabriel. *Radical History and the Politics of Art*. New York: Columbia University Press, 2014.

Rousseau, Jean-Jacques. *Basic Political Writings*. Translated by Donald Cress. Indianapolis: Hackett Publishing, 1987.

———. *Emile: Or, On Education*. Translated by Allan Bloom. New York: Basic Books, 1979.

———. *Œuvres complètes*. Bernard Gagnebin and Marcel Raymond. Vol. 3. 5 vols. Paris: Gallimard, 1964.

———. *Œuvres complètes*. Bernard Gagnebin and Marcel Raymond. Vol. 4. 5 vols. Paris: Gallimard, 1964.

———. *Œuvres complètes*. Bernard Gagnebin and Marcel Raymond. Vol. 1. 5 vols. Paris: Gallimard, 1964.

———. *Reveries of the Solitary Walker*. New York: Penguin Books, 1979.

———. *Rousseau: "The Discourses" and Other Early Political Writings*. Edited by Victor Gourevitch. Cambridge: Cambridge University Press, 1997.

Russell, Bertrand. "Introduction." In *Tractatus Logico-Philosophicus*, by Ludwig Wittgenstein. London: Routledge, 2002.
Said, Edward W. *Culture and Imperialism*. New York: Random House, 1993.
———. *Orientalism*. New York: Vintage Books, 2004.
———. *Reflections on Exile and Other Essays*. Cambridge: Harvard University Press, 2000.
———. "Traveling Theory Reconsidered." In *Reflections on Exile and Other Essays*, 436–52. Cambridge: Harvard University Press, 2000.
Saito, Kohei. "Learning from Late Marx." *Monthly Review* 68, no. 5 (2016). https://monthlyreview.org/2016/10/01/learning-from-late-marx/.
Sakai, Naoki. *Translation and Subjectivity: On Japan and Cultural Nationalism*. Minneapolis: University of Minnesota Press, 1997.
Sakai, Naoki, and Jon Solomon. "Introduction: Addressing the Multitude of Foreigners, Echoing Foucault." In *Translation, Biopolitics, Colonial Difference*, 1–36. Hong Kong: Hong Kong University Press, 2006.
Saliba, George. *Islamic Science and the Making of the European Renaissance*. Cambridge: MIT Press, 2007.
Sartori, Andrew. *Liberalism in Empire: An Alternative History*. Berkeley: University of California Press, 2014.
Sartre, Jean-Paul. *Anti-Semite and Jew*. New York: Schocken Books, 1965.
———. "Black Orpheus." Translated by John MacCombie. *The Massachusetts Review* 6, no. 1 (1964): 13–52.
———. *Réflexions sur la question juive*. Paris: P. Morihien, 1947.
Sato, Kemmyō Taira. "D. T. Suzuki and the Question of War." Translated by Thomas Kirchner. *Eastern Buddhist* 39, no. 1 (2008): 61–120.
Sawada, Janine Anderson. *Practical Pursuits: Religion, Politics, and Personal Cultivation in Nineteenth-Century Japan*. Honolulu: University of Hawai`i Press, 2004.
Schiller, Friedrich. *On the Aesthetic Education of Man in a Series of Letters*. Translated by E. M. Wilkinson and L. A. Willoughby. Oxford: Oxford University Press, 1967.
———. *On the Naive and Sentimental in Literature*. Translated by Helen Watanabe O'Kelly. Manchester: Carcanet New Press, 1981.
———. "Über Naive Und Sentimentalische Dichtung." In *Schillers Werke*, edited by Arthur Kutscher. Vol. 8. Berlin: Deutsches Verlagshaus Bong & Co., 1910.
Scott, David. "Antinomies of Slavery, Enlightenment, and Universal History." *Small Axe: A Caribbean Journal of Criticism* 14, no. 3 33 (October 26, 2010): 152–62.
———. *Conscripts of Modernity: The Tragedy of Colonial Enlightenment*. Durham: Duke University Press, 2004.
———. *Omens of Adversity: Tragedy, Time, Memory, Justice*. Durham: Duke University Press, 2014.
———. *Refashioning Futures: Criticism after Postcoloniality*. Princeton: Princeton University Press, 1999.

Scott, James C. *Domination and the Arts of Resistance: Hidden Transcripts.* New Haven: Yale University Press, 1992.

———. *The Art of Not Being Governed: An Anarchist History of Upland Southeast Asia.* New Haven: Yale University Press, 2009.

———. *Weapons of the Weak: Everyday Forms of Peasant Resistance.* New Haven: Yale University Press, 1985.

Scranton, Roy. *Learning to Die in the Anthropocene: Reflections on the End of a Civilization.* San Francisco: City Lights Publishers, 2015.

Seneca, Lucius Annaeus. *Letters from a Stoic. Epistulae Morales Ad Lucilium.* Translated by Robin Campbell. Harmondsworth: Penguin, 1969.

Senghor, Léopold Sédar. "Critical Standards of African Art." Translated by Brian Quinn. *African Arts* 50, no. 1 (February 3, 2017): 10–15.

———. "De la négritude. Psychologie du Négro-africain." *Diogène; Paris*, no. 37 (January 1, 1962): 3–16.

———. "Goethe m'a Dit." *La Nouvelle Revue Des Deux Mondes*, 1981, 322–26.

———. *La poésie de l'action: conversations avec Mohamed Aziza.* Les Grands leaders. Paris: Stock, 1980.

———. "Les Négro-Africains et La Union Française." *Revue Politique et Parlementaire*, June 1947, 205–8.

———. *Liberté 1: Négritude et humanisme.* Paris: Seuil, 1964.

———. *Liberté 3: Négritude et civilisation de l'universel.* Paris: Seuil, 1977.

———. *Liberté 5: Le dialogue des cultures.* Paris: Seuil, 1993.

———. "Marxisme et Humanisme." *La Revue Socialiste* 19 (1948): 201–16.

———. *Prose and Poetry.* Translated by John Reed and Clive Wake. London: Heinemann, 1965.

———. "What the Black Man Contributes." In *Race and Racism in Continental Philosophy*, edited by Robert Bernasconi and Sybol Cook, translated by Mary Beth Mader, 287–301. Bloomington: Indiana University Press, 2003.

Shakespeare, William. "Hamlet." In *The Norton Shakespeare*, edited by Stephen Greenblatt. New York: W. W. Norton, 1997.

———. "Henry V." In *The Norton Shakespeare*, edited by Stephen Greenblatt. New York: W. W. Norton, 1997.

Sharf, Robert H. "Buddhist Modernism and the Rhetoric of Meditative Experience." *Numen* 42, no. 3 (1995): 228–83.

———. "Is Mindfulness Buddhist? (And Why It Matters)." *Transcultural Psychiatry* 52, no. 4 (2015): 470–84.

———. "Suzuki, D. T." In *The Encyclopedia of Religion*. 2nd ed., 13:8884–87. New York: Macmillan, 2005.

———. "The Zen of Japanese Nationalism." *History of Religions* 33, no. 1 (1993): 1–43.

Sharpley-Whiting, T. Denean. "Femme Negritude: Jane Nardal, La Depeche Africaine, and the Francophone New Negro." *Souls: A Critical Journal of Black Politics, Culture, and Society* 2, no. 4 (2000): 8–18.

Shih, Shu-mei. "Comparison as Relation." In *Comparison: Theories, Approaches, Uses*, edited by Rita Felski and Susan Stanford Friedman, 79–98. Baltimore: Johns Hopkins University Press, 2013.
———. "Theory in a Relational World." *Comparative Literature Studies* 53, no. 4 (2016): 722–46.
Siep, Ludwig. "Der Kampf um Anerkennung. Zu Hegels Auseinandersetzung mit Hobbes in den Jenaer Schriften." *Hegel-Studien; Bonn* 9 (January 1, 1974): 155–207.
Silverman, Max, ed. *Frantz Fanon's Black Skin, White Masks: New Interdisciplinary Essays*. Manchester: Manchester University Press, 2005.
Snodgrass, Judith. *Presenting Japanese Buddhism to the West: Orientalism, Occidentalism, and the Columbian Exposition*. Chapel Hill: The University of North Carolina Press, 2003.
Sollors, Werner. "Of Mules and Mares in a Land of Difference; or, Quadrupeds All?" *American Quarterly* 42, no. 2 (1990): 167–90.
Sophocles. *Sophocles I: Oedipus the King, Oedipus at Colonus, Antigone*. Translated by David Grene. Chicago: University of Chicago Press, 1991.
Soto Morera, Diego. "Crítica de La Razón Corporal: Dussel y Las Meditaciones Anti-Cartesianas." *Tabula Rasa*, no. 26 (June 2017): 141–69.
Spinoza, Benedictus de. *Ethics*. London: Penguin Books, 1996.
Spivak, Gayatri Chakravorty. *A Critique of Postcolonial Reason: Toward a History of the Vanishing Present*. Cambridge: Harvard University Press, 1999.
———. *An Aesthetic Education in the Era of Globalization*. Cambridge: Harvard University Press, 2012.
———. "Translator's Preface." In *Of Grammatology*, by Jacques Derrida. Corrected edition. Baltimore: Johns Hopkins University Press, 1998.
———. "Vicissitudes of the Postcolonial." Postcolonial Humanities Working Group, Princeton University, 2018.
Srivastava, Neelam. "Frantz Fanon in Italy." *Interventions* 17, no. 3 (May 4, 2015): 309–28.
Starobinski, Jean. *Jean-Jacques Rousseau, Transparency and Obstruction*. Translated by Arthur Goldhammer. Chicago: University of Chicago Press, 1988.
———. *Montaigne in Motion*. Translated by Arthur Goldhammer. Chicago: University of Chicago Press, 2009.
Stern, Robert. *The Routledge Guidebook to Hegel and the* Phenomenology of Spirit. New York: Routledge, 2013.
Stiegler, Bernard. *Technics and Time, 1: The Fault of Epimetheus*. Translated by Richard Beardsworth and George Collins. Palo Alto: Stanford University Press, 1998.
Stoler, Ann. *Race and the Education of Desire: Foucault's History of Sexuality and the Colonial Order of Things*. Durham: Duke University Press Books, 1995.
Stout, Jeffrey. *Blessed Are the Organized: Grassroots Democracy in America*. Princeton: Princeton University Press, 2010.

———. "The Transformation of Genius into Practical Power: A Reading of Emerson's 'Experience.'" *American Journal of Theology & Philosophy* 35, no. 1 (February 11, 2014): 3–24.
Subrahmanyam, Sanjay. "Global Intellectual History beyond Hegel and Marx." *History and Theory* 54, no. 1 (February 2015): 126–37.
———. "On World Historians in the Sixteenth Century." *Representations* 91, no. 1 (2005): 26–57.
Suzuki, Daisetz Teitaro. "An Autobiographical Account." In *A Zen Life: D. T. Suzuki Remembered*, edited by Masao Abe, 13–26. New York: Weatherhill, 1986.
———. *An Introduction to Zen Buddhism*. New York: Grove Press, 1964.
———. *Columbia University Seminar Lectures (1952 & 1953)*. Edited by Shigematsu Sōiku and Gishin Tokiwa. Kamakura, Japan: Matsugaoka Bunko, 2016.
———. "Early Memories." In *A Zen Life: D. T. Suzuki Remembered*, edited by Masao Abe, 3–12. New York: Weatherhill, 1986.
———. *Eight Lectures on Chan*. Kamakura-shi: Matsugaoka Bunko, 2011.
———. *Essays in Zen Buddhism, First Series*. New York: Grove Press, 1961.
———. *Essays in Zen Buddhism, Third Series*. London: Rider, 1970.
———. "Satori." In *A Zen Life: D. T. Suzuki Remembered*, edited by Masao Abe, 27–62. New York: Weatherhill, 1986.
———. "Self the Unattainable." In *Selected Works of D.T. Suzuki*, edited by Richard M. Jaffe. Vol. 1. University of California Press, 2015.
———. *Zen and Japanese Culture*. Princeton: Princeton University Press, 2010.
Suzuki, Daisetz Teitaro, and Thomas Merton. "Wisdom in Emptiness: A Dialogue by Daisetz T. Suzuki and Thomas Merton." In *Zen and the Birds of Appetite*, by Thomas Merton, 99–138. New York: New Directions Publishing, 1968.
Taketani, Etsuko. *The Black Pacific Narrative: Geographic Imaginings of Race and Empire between the World Wars*. Hanover, NH: Dartmouth, 2014.
Taylor, Charles. *Sources of the Self: The Making of the Modern Identity*. Cambridge: Cambridge University Press, 1989.
Taylor, Paul C. "Appiah's Uncompleted Argument: W.E.B. Du Bois and the Reality of Race." *Social Theory and Practice* 26, no. 1 (2000): 103–28.
———. "Race, Rehabilitated—Redux." *Critical Sociology* 36, no. 1 (January 1, 2010): 175–90.
Thiam, Cheikh. *Return to the Kingdom of Childhood: Re-Envisioning the Legacy and Philosophical Relevance of Negritude*. Columbus: Ohio State University Press, 2014.
Thiem, Yannik. "Queer." In "Dictionary of the Possible," edited by Sreshta Rit Premnath and Avram Alpert. Special issue, *Shifter* 22 (2016): 144–46.
Thompson, E. P. *Customs in Common: Studies in Traditional Popular Culture*. New York: The New Press, 1993.
Thoreau, Henry David. *Walden*. 150th Anniversary Edition. Princeton: Princeton University Press, 2004.

Tibebu, Teshale. *Hegel and the Third World: The Making of Eurocentrism in World History*. Syracuse, NY: Syracuse University Press, 2011.
Todorov, Tzvetan. *On Human Diversity: Nationalism, Racism, and Exoticism in French Thought*. Translated by Catherine Porter. Cambridge: Harvard University Press, 1993.
Tully, James. *Public Philosophy in a New Key: Volume 2, Imperialism and Civic Freedom*. Cambridge: Cambridge University Press, 2009.
———. *Strange Multiplicity: Constitutionalism in an Age of Diversity*. New York: Cambridge University Press, 1995.
Turner, Jack. *Awakening to Race: Individualism and Social Consciousness in America*. Chicago: University of Chicago Press, 2012.
Urbas, Joseph. "'Bi-Polar' Emerson: 'Nominalist and Realist.'" *The Pluralist* 8, no. 2 (2013): 78–105.
Vaillant, Janet. *Black, French, and African: A Life of Léopold Sédar Senghor*. Cambridge: Harvard University Press, 1990.
Valdez, Inés. "It's Not about Race: Good Wars, Bad Wars, and the Origins of Kant's Anti-Colonialism." *The American Political Science Review* 111, no. 4 (November 1, 2017): 819–34.
———. *Transnational Cosmopolitanism*, forthcoming.
Veblen, Thorstein. *The Theory of the Leisure Class*. Oxford: Oxford University Press, 2009.
Veer, Peter van der. *Imperial Encounters: Religion and Modernity in India and Britain*. Princeton: Princeton University Press, 2001.
Velkley, Richard L. *Being after Rousseau: Philosophy and Culture in Question*. Chicago: University of Chicago Press, 2002.
Victoria, Brian Daizen. *Zen at War*. Lanham: Rowman & Littlefield Publishers, 2006.
Viveiros de Castro, Eduardo. "Cannibal Metaphysics." Translated by Peter Skafish. *Radical Philosophy* 182 (December 2013): 17–28.
———. "Cosmological Deixis and Amerindian Perspectivism." *Journal of the Royal Anthropological Institute* 4, no. 3 (1998): 469–88.
———. *The Inconstancy of the Indian Soul: The Encounter of Catholics and Cannibals in 16th-Century Brazil*. Chicago: Prickly Paradigm Press, 2011.
Voelz, Johannes. *Transcendental Resistance: The New Americanists and Emerson's Challenge*. Hanover, NH: University Press of New England, 2010.
Walls, Laura Dassow. *Emerson's Life in Science: The Culture of Truth*. Ithaca: Cornell University Press, 2003.
———. "'Walden' as Feminist Manifesto." *Interdisciplinary Studies in Literature and Environment* 1, no. 1 (1993): 137–44.
Warnek, Peter. "The History of Being." In *Martin Heidegger: Key Concepts*, edited by Bret W. Davis, 155–68. Durham: Acumen Publishing, 2010.

Warren, Kenneth W. *What Was African American Literature?* The W.E.B. Du Bois Lectures. Cambridge: Harvard University Press, 2011.
Warrior, Robert Allen. "Canaanites, Cowboys, and Indians: Deliverance, Conquest, and Liberation Theology Today." In *Voices Of The Religious Left*, edited by Rebecca Alpert, 51–58. Philadelphia: Temple University Press, 2000.
Watts, Alan W. *The Way of Zen*. New York: Vintage, 1999.
West, Cornel. *The American Evasion of Philosophy: A Genealogy of Pragmatism*. Madison: University of Wisconsin Press, 1989.
Westerhoff, Jan. *Nagarjuna's Madhyamaka: A Philosophical Introduction*. New York: Oxford University Press, 2009.
White, Kyle. "Indigenous Philosophizing in Our Ancestors' Dystopia." Presented at the Philosophy and Coloniality Symposium, New School for Social Research, April 16, 2018.
Wilder, Gary. "Eurafrique as the Future Past of '"Black France"': Sarkozy's Temporal Confusion and Senghor's Postwar Vision." In *Black France / France Noire: The History and Politics of Blackness*, edited by Trica Danielle Keaton, T. Denean Sharpley-Whiting, and Tyler Stovall, 57–87. Durham: Duke University Press Books, 2012.
———. *Freedom Time: Negritude, Decolonization, and the Future of the World*. Durham: Duke University Press, 2015.
———. "Race, Reason, Impasse: Césaire, Fanon, and the Legacy of Emancipation." *Radical History Review* 90, no. 1 (2004): 31–61.
Wilkinson, E. M., and L. A. Willoughby. "Introduction." In *On the Aesthetic Education of Man in a Series of Letters*, by Friedrich Schiller. Oxford: Oxford University Press, 1967.
Williams, Raymond. *Culture and Materialism*. New York: Verso, 2006.
Williams, Robert W., and W. E. B. Du Bois. "'The Sacred Unity in All the Diversity': The Text and a Thematic Analysis of W.E.B. Du Bois' 'The Individual and Social Conscience' (1905)." *Journal of African American Studies* 16, no. 3 (September 1, 2012): 456–97.
Wilson, Jeff. *Mindful America: The Mutual Transformation of Buddhist Meditation and American Culture*. New York: Oxford University Press, 2014.
Wittgenstein, Ludwig. *Tractatus Logico-Philosophicus*. London: Routledge, 2002.
Wokler, Robert. *Rousseau, the Age of Enlightenment, and Their Legacies*. Edited by Bryan Garsten. Princeton: Princeton University Press, 2012.
Wollstonecraft, Mary. *A Vindication of the Rights of Women*. Edited by Candace Ward. New York: Dover, 1996.
Wordsworth, William. *William Wordsworth—The Major Works: Including The Prelude*. Edited by Stephen Gill. New York: Oxford University Press, 2008.
Wright, Dale Stuart. *Philosophical Meditations on Zen Buddhism*. New York: Cambridge University Press, 1998.

Wright, Richard. *Conversations with Richard Wright.* Edited by Keneth Kinnamon and Michel Fabre. Jackson: University Press of Mississippi, 1993.
Zamir, Shamoon. *Dark Voices: W.E.B. Du Bois and American Thought, 1888–1903.* Chicago: University of Chicago Press, 1995.
Zammito, John H. *Kant, Herder, and the Birth of Anthropology.* Chicago: University of Chicago Press, 2002.
Žižek, Slavoj. *For They Know Not What They Do: Enjoyment as a Political Factor.* London; New York: Verso, 2002.

Index

Aboulafia, Mitchell, 363n8
Abrams, M. H., 107, 322n1
Adorno, Theodor, 76; on Cage, 276–77, 283; on the essay, 85, 298n11; eurocentrism of, 303n37; on Kant, 95
aesthetics, 103–10, 114; aesthetic geography, 106–8; of Mbembe, 132–33, 334n166; and Schiller, 24, 98, 103–10; of Suzuki, 282
aesthetics, global, 108, 127; of Cage, 276, 282; and history, 97; and intuition, 127; pluralization of, 115; of Schiller, 97, 106–7, 112, 115, 126, 128, 133–34, 137, 165; of Senghor, 97, 112, 113–14, 126, 129–30, 133–34
African American studies: and Du Bois, 246
Afrofuturity, 240–41
Agamben, Giorgio, 16, 304n38; Eurocentrism of, 17
Ahmad, Aijaz, 343n102, 344n111
Alcoff, Linda Martín, 14, 50–51
alienation, 158–59; in Emerson, 209–10; in Marx, 158–59, 343n101; Rousseau on, 158; and Suzuki, 261; and unbearability, 205–6
Allen, Amy, 15, 303n37
alternation, 356n59; and *Bhagavad Gita*, 212–13; and deconstruction, 120–21; and dialectics, 120; and double consciousness, 208–10; and Du Bois, 11, 229–30, 236–37, 240, 250, 363n8; and Emerson, 11, 24, 26, 122, 190–94, 197–98, 201–9, 212–13, 217–20, 223, 250, 267, 354n9, 356n59, 361n140; and freedom, 229; and liberation, 201; openness to, 11; and radical pluralism, 122; of self, 267; and slavery, 191, 229; universal plurality of, 201. *See also* Emerson, Ralph Waldo
Althusser, Louis: humanist critique of, 343n98; on Marx, 156–57
Anderson, Benedict, 168
Anderson, Kevin, 13, 159, 161, 342n95, 343n102
Andrade, Oswald de, 54–55
Anghie, Antony, 13, 302n27
anthropology, 138, 345n121; and critical theory, 76; and dialectics, 69–76; as European, 138; Heidegger on, 55; and Hegel, 152–55; and liberal economics, 163–63; and Marx, 156–58; and philosophy, 55, 89–90, 94; on Senghor, 331n132; and universality, 337n12. *See also* Du Tertre, Jean-Baptiste; Hegel, G. W. F.; Rousseau, Jean-Jacques; Schiller, Friedrich

415

Anthropology from a Pragmatic Point of View (Kant), 83, 88–90. *See also* Kant, Immanuel
Apostels, Leo, 117
Appiah, Anthony, 242, 243
Arendt, Hannah, 10; on evasive mood, 312n79; on pluralism, 299n18
Aristotle, 34, 263, 338n30
Auerbach, Erich, 12, 310n45; on Montaigne, 45, 46
Aurelius, Marcus, 180
Autobiography of W. E. B. Du Bois, The, 237, 239. *See also* Du Bois, W. E. B.
avant-garde, the, 104; and primitivism, 104

Balfour, Lawrie, 362n4
Balibar, Étienne, 243
Bankei, 266
Bantu Education Act (1953), 10
barbarism, 32, 36, 310n40
Barrett, William, 378n86
Bateson, Gregory, 108
Baudelaire, Charles, 91
Beethoven, Ludwig van, 280
being-toward-bequeathment, 27, 236, 293–94
Bentley, Nancy, 348n169
Bergson, Henri, 212, 332n135; Senghor, influence on, 113–14, 127, 134, 331nn131–32, 369n92
Bernal, Martin, 13, 119
Bernasconi, Robert, 18, 150, 154, 340n64
Bernstein, Richard, 10
Bhagavad Gita: and alienation, 212–13; and Emerson, 212–14; non-attachment in, 207
Bilgrami, Akeel, 107, 303n34
Bilwakesh, Nikhil, 212, 359n102
blackness: and Du Bois, 370n96; in Fanon, 174–75, 177–78

Black Skins, White Masks (Fanon), 170–79. *See also* Fanon, Frantz
Boas, Franz, 361n127
Bogues, Anthony, 247–48
Borges, Jorge Luis, ix, 18, 19
Bremen, Brian, 366n45
Brennan, Timothy, 13–14; on Fanon, 350n203; on Hegel, 14, 15, 25, 73–74, 150, 345n129, 359n110
Bromell, Nicholas, 370n101
Brown, John, 235
Brown, Wendy: Eurocentrism of, 17; on neoliberal tradition, 306n63
Buck-Morss, Susan, 344n114; on Haitian Revolution, 74, 144–46; on Hegelian dialectics, 13–14, 73–74; on Master Slave Dialectic, 25, 138, 144–46, 150, 339n46; on slavery, 138, 144, 150; on Spirit, 147; on state of nature, 144
Buddhism: and Cage, 289; emptiness in, 257, 260; as essaying the globe, 289–90; Mahayana, 255, 256, 271; and meditation, 254; and mindfulness, 276; and nonviolence, 271; and Orientalism, 289; presence in, 276; and the self, 268; two truths in, 257–59, 270–71. *See also* Suzuki, D. T.; Zen
Buddhism, American: and bell hooks, 286–89; and gender, 288; and racism, 287–88; and Zen, 266
Buddhist studies, ix
Butler, Judith: on Hegel, 151–52, 154; on interdependency, 19–20; on Levinas, 15
Byrd, Jodi, 300n20

Cadava, Eduardo, 189–90, 212, 216–17, 354n14, 359n101
Cage, John, ix, 249, 252; and Buddhism, 289; compositional methods of, 279; critiques of,

276–77, 82; essaying the globe, 277, 278, 282; essay writing of, 280–81; global aesthetics of, 276, 282; global self, practices of, 276, 278–84, 287, 299; and interdependence, 281; queer politics of, 283; randomness in, 279–80; and silence, 27; Thoreau in, 279, 280; and Zen, 259, 283–84

cannibalism, 39; Fanon on, 175–76; Hegel on, 153. *See also* Montaigne, Michel de

Capital: A Critique of Political Economy, Volume 1 (Marx), 156–57, 165, 342n94. *See also* Marx, Karl

capitalism, 108–9, 143, 159, 297n7; and cultural difference, 243; and empire, 129, 131; and Fanon, 182; and globalization, 109, 251; and Marx, 109–10, 143, 156–60, 164–66, 168, 196, 344n114; and neoliberalism, 26; racial, 121, 239; residual communal practices under, 162; and subjectivity, 251; and universalism, 147, 162; and Zen, 273

Carby, Hazel, 21–22, 244

Carus, Paul, 255

Cassirer, Ernst, 76

Castoriadis, Cornelius, 5, 32, 138

Cavell, Stanley, 27, 37, 275, 304n38, 326n72; on Emerson, 195, 206–7, 212, 218, 266–69, 373n20; on Hegel, 326n79; on Suzuki, 266–69; on Thoreau, 253, 293–94

Césaire, Aimé, 112, 115, 132, 170–71, 323n27; on colonialism, 124–25, 146, 161; and cultural pluralism, 330n119; dialectics of, 136; and essentialism, 330n119; in Fanon, 170–71, 176; gift, contact as, 242; and Harlem Renaissance, 130; and intersubjectivity, 125–26; on Négritude, 326n66, 329n98; racialism in, 123–24; on Sartre, 179; selective gift of, 124; on Senghor, 327n73; *A Tempest*, 349n189; and universal civilization, 123–24. *See also* Négritude; Senghor, Léopold Sédar

Césaire, Suzanne, 115, 323n27

Chakrabarty, Dipesh, 303n34, 346n140, 354n29, 368n66; Eurocentrism, critique of, 167; on European intellectual tradition, 300n22; and global interdependence, 169; on Heidegger, 169–70; on Marx, 168–70; on primitivism, 346n145; *Provincializing Europe*, 166–70, 354n29, 368n66; on universalism, 166–68, 236

chance operations, 279

Chatterjee, Partha, 44

Cheah, Pheng, 184, 246–47, 248, 303n34, 351n233

Cheyfitz, Eric, 214

Chibber, Vivek, 167–68

Ciccariello-Maher, George, 13, 73–74, 302n31, 340n74

Clastres, Pierre, 88, 336n12

Clifford, James, 326n66

climate change, 21, 292–94

Cole, Andrew, 25, 73, 76, 139; on Hegel, 144, 339n45, 339n51; on Master Slave Dialectic, 336n6; on slavery, 144

colonialism: anticolonialism, 80, 182; Césaire on, 124–25, 146, 161; and Descartes, 50–52; and dialectics, 74, 76, 135; Du Bois on, 233, 367n50; and ego, 171; and ethnography, 63; and Fanon, 76; and Hegel, 138–39, 146–47, 150–51, 161, 177; Marx on, 157; and Master Slave Dialectic, 138–39, 147, 150–51; and nationalist ego, 171; and philosophy, 52, 73, 94, 98; and reason, 185–87;

colonialism *(continued)*
  and representation, 15; and
  Rousseau, 50, 67, 69; and Senghor,
  76; and subjection, 70; and
  surrealism, 128; and universalism,
  166; violence of, 101, 171–72,
  181–82, 321n119
Columbus, Christopher, 102–3
Comay, Rebecca, 335n5, 337n14
communism, 166, 239, 243; Du
  Bois on, 239; and global struggles,
  162; and Marx, 25, 156–62, and
  pluralism, 157, 161–62, 166; and
  Rousseau, 24; Senghor on, 128; and
  universalism, 25, 158. *See also* Marx,
  Karl
Communist Manifesto, 159–62
Connolly, William, 10, 342n97,
  362n4; on plural practices of self,
  195–96
constitutive criticism, 14–15
Cooper, Anna Julia, 226, 242, 244–45
Critchley, Simon, 121
critical theory, 9, 15–16, 20,
  343n101; and anthropology, 76;
  deconstruction and dialectics
  polarity, 114; Eurocentrism of,
  300n20, 303n37; and Hegelian
  dialectic, 73–74, 76
Critique of Pure Reason (Kant), 96. *See
  also* Kant, Immanuel

Dark Princess (Du Bois), 228, 238,
  240–41, 246
Dassow Walls, Laura, 198, 201–2
de Beauvoir, Simone, 245, 377n85
de Certeau, Michel, 308n7
decolonial studies, 71, 296n3
decolonization, 128, 185; of critical
  theory, 303n37; of dialectics,
  171–72, 340n74; and Senghor, 128,
  330n122. *See also* colonialism

deconstruction, 110, 114, 258,
  333n143; of aesthetics, 114; and
  alternation, 120–21; and dialectics,
  14, 111, 113; and hybridity, 120–
  22; limits of, 111–12; and Mbembe,
  133–34; and radical pluralism,
  114–15, 122, 125. *See also* Derrida,
  Jacques
Defert, Daniel, 260
Delaney, Martin, 245
de las Casas, Bartalomé, 51, 52
de Léry, Jean, 34
Deleuze, Gilles, ix, 76, 282, 353n9
de Man, Paul, 324n50
Demos, T. J., 103–4
Derrida, Jacques, 16, 76, 80, 109,
  333n143; and deconstruction, 110;
  and hybridity, 121; on Lévi-Strauss,
  110; on logocentrism, 110; on
  Rousseau, 110
Desan, Philippe, 308n14
Descartes, René, 313n102; and
  anticolonialism, 52; and colonialism,
  50–52; conjectural history of, 63;
  and cultural relativity, 48; *Discourse
  on Method*, 46–47, 63–65, 67;
  evasion in, 46–47, 49–50, 58–59;
  Foucault on, 49–50; interiority of,
  58–59, 64, 250, 316n19; as modern
  thinker, 51; and the past, 293; self
  in, 2–3, 46–48; singular identity of,
  23, 140, 250
Descola, Philippe, 44, 152, 154
Diagne, Souleymane Bachir: on
  Césaire, 326n66; on Senghor, 112,
  116, 117, 126–27, 133, 325n63,
  326n66, 331n132, 332n142
dialectics, 13, 24, 25, 291; and
  alternation, 120; of Césaire, 136;
  and colonialism, 74, 76, 135;
  colonial origins of, 14, 69–76;
  decolonization of, 171–12, 340n74;

and deconstruction, 14, 111, 114; deracialization of, 172; and Emerson, 115, 191, 202, 354n9; and Fanon, 14, 25, 136, 171–72; Hegelian, 73–74, 76; of Kant, 98; and Marx, 14, 25, 155, 202; and pluralism, 353n9; and race, 178–79; and racism, 183–84; and radical pluralism, 114–15, 125; and Rousseau, 73–75, 97, 136–37, 164–65; and Schiller, 102, 130; of Senghor, 14, 136, 146, 327n73; and Suzuki, 14, 261, 263–64; as universal, 74; and Zen, 264
dialectics, Hegelian, 24, 73, 135, 137, 341n87; Buck-Morss on, 13–14, 25, 73–74, 138, 144–46, 150, 339n46; Cole on, 336n6; colonial logic of, 135; and critical theory, 73–74, 76; and Fanon, 146, 151–52, 178–79. *See also* Fanon, Frantz; Hegel, G. W. F.; Master Slave Dialectic (MSD)
diaspora, 216, 363n6; multiplicity of, 365n38
Diderot, Denis, 41; on the eclectic, 31
Diop, Cheikh Anta, 119
Discourse on Method (Descartes), 46–47, 63–65, 67. *See also* Descartes, René
Discourses (Rousseau), 64–65, 67. *See also* Rousseau, Jean-Jacques
dogmatism, 96
double consciousness: and alternation, 208–10; Du Bois on, 26, 119–20, 221, 228–29, 230–34, 236, 246, 287, 327n73, 362n4, 363n8; in Emerson, 119–20, 203–12, 217, 222, 224, 228, 230–34, 270, 327n73, 331n132, 358n96, 366n44–45, 367n46; and Hegel, 212, 229; and Marx, 228; and modern self, 231; and race, 232; and Suzuki, 250, 270; and transcendentalism, 208–9, 210; unbearability of, 228. *See also* Du Bois, W. E. B.; Emerson, Ralph Waldo
du Bellay, Joachim, 36–37
Du Bois, W. E. B., 2, 174, 348n169; on Africa, 237–38; and Afrofuturism, 240–41; and alternation, 11, 229–30, 236–37, 240, 250, 363n8; *The Autobiography of W. E. B. Du Bois*, 237, 239; and being-toward-bequeathment, 236; on colonialism, 233, 367n50; and communal values, 221; on communism, 239; *Dark Princess*, 228, 238, 240–41, 246; and Darwin, 235; on double consciousness, 26, 119–20, 221, 228–29, 230–34, 236, 246, 287, 327n73, 362n4, 363n8; *Dusk of Dawn: An Essay Toward an Autobiography of a Race Concept*, 226, 238, 241, 362n4, 370n96; and Emerson, 222–23, 229, 232–34, 362n4, 369n92; and essentialism, 8, 231; feminist critiques of, 244; on freedom, 229, 236; and futurity, 222, 229, 235–36, 240–41; gifts in, 221–26, 229–30, 234, 236, 242, 244–45; global self, practices of, 4, 222–23, 225–26, 234, 238, 244, 246, 286; global thinking of, 129, 221, 230, 235; on Greek hybridity, 119; and Hegel, 229, 230; on history, 237; methodology of, 239, 246; and ontology, 237; and philosophy, racial history of, 81–82; primitivism of, 237–38; on race, 221, 223–28, 231–32, 234–36, 241–43; radical pluralism of, 9, 187, 191, 221–22, 230–31, 236–42, 246,

Du Bois, W. E. B. *(continued)*
248, 326n65, 336n5; revelation of the other world, 224–28, 230, 236; and Romanticism, 238; on second-sight, 221–24, 236, 286, 365n32; and self-essentializing, 8; and Senghor, 369n92; on slavery, 224–25, 248; *The Souls of Black Folks,* 225–26, 230, 235–39, 246, 248; and sublation, 229–30; and travel, 221, 238–39, 240; and unbearable identity, 8, 227–30, 248, 294; and universalism, 81, 231, 236, 246; and whiteness, 225. See also double consciousness
Duchamp, Marcel, 277, 278–79
Dunayevskaya, Ray, 342n95
Dusk of Dawn: An Essay Toward an Autobiography of a Race Concept (Du Bois), 226, 238, 241, 362n4. *See also* Du Bois, W. E. B.
Dussel, Enrique, 50–52, 171; on Descartes, 313n102; on Marx, 342n94, 343n102
Du Tertre, Jean-Baptiste, 69–71, 74, 75, 78; colonial trade anecdote, 136, 165, 198–99. *See also* Emerson, Ralph Waldo; Kant, Immanuel; Rousseau, Jean-Jacques

Edwards, Brent Hayes, 235
Emerson, Ralph Waldo, ix, 1, 4, 326n72; alienation in, 209–10; alternation in, 11, 24, 26, 122, 190–94, 197–98, 201–9, 212–13, 217–20, 223, 250, 267, 354n9, 356n59, 361n140; and *Bhagavad Gita,* 212–14, 237; and circumscription, 30, 31; on culture, 192–93, 212; and dialectics, 115, 191, 202, 354n9; double consciousness in, 26, 119–20, 203–12, 217, 222, 224, 228, 230–34, 270, 327n73, 331n132, 358n96, 366n44–45, 367n46; Du Tertre anecdote, use of, 198–99, 355n45; epistemology of, 190, 204; and Eurocentrism, 189, 197–98; experience in, 269; freedom in, 229; gender in, 200; and global consciousness, 197; global self, practices of, 189–90, 195, 200–1, 220, 361n140; global subjectivity of, 193; as global thinker, x, 207; and Idealism, 193, 197, 206, 218–19; imposition, refusal of, 190, 211; "master tones" of, 10, 192, 206; on the other world, 231–32; partialized universalism of, 196–97; philosophy as social criticism, 46; on race, 197–201, 215–17, 358n96, 360n120, 361n127, 367n46; racial prejudice of, 189–90, 197, 200–1, 236; radical pluralism of, 9, 187, 190–95, 197, 203–4, 213–14, 218–20, 231, 267, 326n65, 336n5, 354n9, 357n70; on reason, 191; Romantic Orientalism of, 198; on slavery, 191–92, 198, 206, 212, 215, 216–17; and skepticism, 31, 218–19; and unbearability, 209, 357n60; unhanding in, 197, 206–7, 217, 220; and universalism, 202–3, 233; and whiteness, 236; and white supremacy, 189, 198, 215. *See also* double consciousness; Du Bois, W. E. B.
Emile: Or, On Education (Rousseau), 67, 75–79, 84, 98, 161, 194, 372n8. *See also* Rousseau, Jean-Jacques
empire, 34; and capitalism, 129, 131; and self-reliance, 49
Engels, Friedrich, 159–62
enlightenment: and art, 281; as experience, 269; and global understanding,

373n21; of Kant, 24, 165; and opening of self, 281; and operations of self, 279; and partialization, 251; and racism, 287, 289; and satori, 253; as social process, 281; in Suzuki, 251, 269; and the world, 273; and Zen, 262. *See also* satori

Enlightenment, The: as global phenomenon, 93; and imperialism, 41; and non-Europeans, 41

epistemology: of Emerson, 190, 204; Indian, 268; post-Kant, 80; and Suzuki, 260

essaying the globe, 5–7, 37; and Buddhism, 289–90; and Cage, 277, 278, 282; and contextual understanding, 39; and Du Bois, 238; and gender, 45; in Hegel, 140; Montaigne on, 40, 45, 200; and radical pluralism, 270; and unbearable identity, 28

essays, 85, 298n11; form of, 5–6, 45, 99, 255; and the kōan, 255; modes of, 6; and satori, 253; of Schiller, 99; and subjectivity, 45

Essays (Montaigne), 29–30, 42, 45. *See also* Montaigne, Michel de

Essays in Zen Buddhism (Suzuki), 252–53, 256, 277, 378n86. *See also* Suzuki, D. T.

essentialism: and Du Bois, 8, 231; and Césaire, 330n119; and Montaigne, 35; radical, 112; of Senghor, 112; strategic, 205; and strategic partialisms, 11, 167, 205

ethnocentrism: of Kant, 111; of Lévi-Strauss, 110; of liberalism, 164; Marx on, 214; and philosophy, 336n12; of Rousseau, 110–11; of Schiller, 111. *See also* Eurocentrism

ethnology. *See* anthropology

Eurocentrism: of Adorno, 303n37; of Agamben, 17; Chakrabarty on, 167; in critical theory, 15–20; and Emerson, 189, 197–98; of Foucault, 16, 17–20, 303n37; of Hegel, 137, 153, 247, 336n5, 341n80, 359n109; of Heidegger, 23, 170, 264; and history, 152; and Marx, 157–58, 161; and reason, 152; Senghor on, 119. *See also* ethnocentrism

evasion: in Descartes, 46–47, 49–50, 57–59; in *Hamlet*, 53–55, 59; and Heidegger, 56–57; of philosophy, 46; in Rousseau, 69

Fanon, Frantz, 24; *assumption* in, 174–75, 348n175; and authenticity, 185–86; blackness in, 174–75; *Black Skins, White Masks*, 170–79; on cannibalism, 175–76; and colonialism, 76; dialectical thought of, 14, 25, 136, 171–72; and dialectics, Hegelian, 146, 151–52, 178–79; freedom in, 178, 184; futurity of, 171; global self, practices of, 180, 181, 183–84, 286; and global self-making, 4, 171, 177; Heidegger, opposition to, 173; on Hegel, 135, 359n109; invention in, 179–81; and justice, 172; liberation in, 185; on Marx, 350n204; as naïve, 184; on Négritude, 171, 175–76; on nostalgia, 44; ontology in, 25, 173, 184; openness to alternation, 11; racialization in, 171, 173–74, 184; and racial history of philosophy, 81–82; on racial ontology, 178, 234–35; on rationality, 175–77, 180; reification, critique of, 348n178; on Sartre, 176–79; on Senghor, 126, 175–76; skepticism of, 171; on slavery, 175; unbearability in, 135, 171, 175; and universalism, 81, 171–72, 352n245; on the veil, 179–80; on violence,

Fanon, Frantz *(continued)*
  172, 181–84, 185, 351n226;
  Wretched of the Earth, The, 181–84
Feuerbach, Ludwig, 209, 231
Finseth, Ian, 198
Firmin, Anténor, 107
Forster, Michael, 75
Foucault, Michel, ix, 3; on Aurelius, 180; on biopolitics, 186, 247, 248; on biopower, 6; on Descartes, 49–50; Eurocentrism of, 16, 17–20, 303n37; and Fanon, 185–86; and feminist politics, 305n57; global engagement of, 18–20, 91; on governmentality, 186, 248; *The Hermeneutics of the Subject*, 3, 17; *The History of Sexuality*, 19, 297n8; and Iranian Revolution, 19, 186, 195; on Kant, 91, 95; on nationalism, 50; on production, 297n8; self, histories of, 18, 91–92, 295n2; self, practices of, 16–17, 20, 77, 185–86, 261, 307n3; on spirituality, 17, 19; and subjectivity, 247, 248; on violence, 185; and Zen, 19, 195, 259, 260–61
Frazier, Robeson Taj, 239, 240
freedom: and alternation, 229; Du Bois on, 229, 236; in Emerson, 229; in Fanon, 178, 184; in Hegel, 141–42, 144, 148–49, 340n64; Kant on, 80, 99, 148, 210; in Sartre, 178; and violent struggle, 150. *See also* liberty
Freire, Paolo, 29, 285–86
Freud, Sigmund, 80, 297n8; on *Hamlet*, 54; and primitivism, 126
Friedman, Milton, 242–43
Frobenius, Leo, 127
furyū, 263

Gandhi, Mohandas, 44, 107, 274

gender: and Buddhism, 288; in Emerson, 200; and essaying the globe, 45; and humility, 288; in Montaigne, 45; and Négritude, 130; in Senghor, 130–31; and subjectivity, 244
Gilroy, Paul, 13, 339n46; on Du Bois, 365n38
Gines, Kathryn, 244–45
Glissant, Édouard, 295n2
globalism, 291
globality, xi; in *Hamlet*, 53–55, 59; in Hegel, 108; in Kant, 108; in Marx, 108; and unbearability, 194
globalization, 123, 283, 295n1; and art, 104; and capitalism, 109, 251; and philosophy, 110; Spivak on, 109
global self. *See* self, global
globe, the, 295n1; as repressed contrary, 297n8
Goethe, 119, 132; and doubleness, 119–20, 212, 232; and Senghor, 119–20, 132
Goldenberg, David, 225
Goodman, Russel, 357n70
Gordon, Jane, 12
Gordon, Lewis, 177–78, 352n245
Greenblatt, Stephen, 35, 40, 68
Groundwork of the Metaphysics of Morals (Kant), 83, 88–89. *See also* Kant, Immanuel
Guatarri, Félix, 76
Guyot, Arnold, 203

Hacking, Ian, 242
Hägglund, Martin, 329n107
Haitian Revolution: and Hegel, 73–74, 144–46, 151; and MSD, 144–45, 340n70
Hamlet, 293; evasion of globality in, 53–55, 59; Freud on, 54; and modernity, 53; subjectivity in, 23, 46

Haraway, Donna, 16
Harootunian, Harry, 344n114, 347n151
Harris, Wilson, 22
Hayek, Friedrich, 163–64
Hegel, G. W. F., ix, 4, 13; and anthropology, 152, 341n75; and colonialism, 177; colonialism, justification for, 146–47, 150–51, 161; concepts, global origins of, 93, 137; conjectural history of, 145; on culture and nature, 137; dialectics of, 24, 73, 135, 137, 341n87; and double consciousness, 212, 229; Eurocentrism of, 137, 153, 247, 336n5, 341n80, 359n109; on freedom, 141–42, 144, 148–49, 340n64; geographic imagination of, 154; global history of, 136, 165; global subjectivity of, 138–39; global thinking of, 108, 139, 155; and Haitian Revolution, 73–74, 144–46, 151, 340n70; on history, 137, 341n75; and imperialism, 164; on India, 214, 359n110; on intuition and instinct, 143; Master Slave Dialectic of, 74, 75, 320n101, 338n30; ontology of, 177; on philosophy, 140, 211; and progress, 335n5; racism of, 25, 144; and recognition, 141–42, 151–54, 160, 247, 341n79; on Schiller, 211; self-other relation in, 100, 192, 335n4; self-world, relation of, 52; slavery, justification for, 141–44, 147–49, 161, 339n41, 340n64; state of nature in, 143–45, 147, 152; subjectivity in, 211; and sublation, 24, 73, 75, 135, 136, 229; totalizing vision of, 147, 155; uncritical positivism and idealism of, 155; on "unhappy consciousness,"
210–11; and universalism, 135, 137, 143, 151; and violence, 136, 141–43, 144, 147; on world cultures, 381n161. *See also* Marx, Karl; Master Slave Dialectic
Hegeman, Susan, 361n127
Heidegger, Martin, ix, 207; on being, 55, 56, 169–70, 235, 236, 347n151; being-toward-death, 27, 143, 236, 293; on Cartesian subject, 57–58; on ethnology, 55; Eurocentrism of, 23, 170, 264; evasive mood in, 58, 59; on forgetting of being, 16; global engagement, evasion of, 56–57; and modernity, 23; on the other, 55; and the past, 293; and race, 235; on the self, 56; and subject-object dualism, 52, 314n121; and Suzuki, 377n86; and universalism, 56, 57–58, 170, 173, 314n113; Zen Buddhism, engagement of, 58, 264
Herder, Johann Gottfried, x, 41, 43; on Kant, 320n101
Herrigel, Eugen, 260–61
Hine, Debra Clark, 244
History of Sexuality, The (Foucault), 19, 297n8. *See also* Foucault, Michel
Hobbes, Thomas, 62, 86–87; and slavery, 144; state of nature in, 135, 143; struggle in, 143
Hobsbawm, Eric, 345n121
Hodder, Alan, 198
Hoffmann, George, 39, 308n7
Hölderlin, Friedrich, 376n60
Holt, Thomas, 363n8, 365n32
Hooker, Juliet, 240–41
hooks, bell, ix, 252, 276; and American Buddhism, 286–89; and feminism, 285; on Freire, 286; global self, practices of, 286, 290; on "identity in resistance," 27, 284;

hooks, bell *(continued)*
  on love, 288–89; and mindfulness, 286, 290; openness to alternation, 11; pedagogy of, 285; as radical pluralist, 288
Hori, Victor, 253–54, 262, 265
Horkheimer, Max, 76
Hountondji, Paulin, 330n119
hybridity: and deconstruction, 120–22; in Emerson, 373n20; Greek, 119; and imperialism, 121; and racial capitalism, 121; in Senghor, 116

Ichikawa Hakugen, 44, 251–52, 271–73, 379n124; and social good, 274
I Ching, 279
idealism: and materialism, 218–19; and Suzuki, 26, 260; uncritical, 155–57, 161, 338n35; and Zen, 80
idealism, German, 80, 252; and Emerson, 193, 197, 206, 218–19; Marx, critique of, 154; and sublation, 201–2
identity, xi; and Descartes, 23, 140, 250; in resistance (hooks), 27, 284; and will to dominate, 7. *See also* unbearable identities
Ikkyū, 263
Imakita Kosen, 254, 255
immanence, 256–57
imperialism: and cultural agency, 42–43; and the Enlightenment, 141; Hegel on, 164; and hybridity, 121; and Kant, 89, 164; and Montaigne, 41–42, 164; and ontology, 42; and Rousseau, 164; and Schiller, 164
intellect, 127; and satori, 250–51, 253; Senghor on, 130; Suzuki on, 268
intelligence: of the marginalized, 109; as plural, 107

interdependence: and aggression, 271; and Cage, 281; global, 169, 194; and Marx, 169; Suzuki on, 278; and truth, 270–71
interiority, 296n6; of Descartes, 58–59, 64, 250, 316n19; as universal, 152
intuition, 127; and instinct, 143; Senghor on, 130, 259

Jackson, Michael, 356n59
Jaeggi, Rahel, 343n101
Jaffe, Richard, 371n1
Jakobsen, Janet, 10, 299n18
James, Joy, 226, 244
James, William, 10, 366n43, 376n64
Jameson, Fredric, 344n114, 381n161; on Cage, 277, 283
Jeffers, Chike, 226, 244
Jones, Donna, 113, 331n132, 332n135
Jones, Gareth Steadman, 343n98
Joseph, Branden, 282
Jullien, François, 92–93, 356n59
justice: and Fanon, 172; and reason, 152; Rousseau on, 61, 64, 74–75; and universalism, 94–95; and Zen, 274

Kakuan, 277
Kant, Immanuel, ix, 1; *Anthropology from a Pragmatic Point of View*, 83, 88–90; and anticolonialism, 80; anti-imperialism of, 89; categorical imperative of, 81; conjectural history of, 82, 150; cosmopolitanism of, 90–91, 113; *Critique of Pure Reason*, 96; dialectical method of, 98; enlightenment of, 24, 165; ethnocentrism of, 111; Eurocentrism of, 113; feminist readings of, 94; on freedom, 80, 99, 148, 210; geographic history of, 118; on global

cultures, 95, 192, 235; on global governance, 68, 137; global self, practices of, 82, 88–89, 91–93; as global thinker, x, 80–81, 108, 139; *Groundwork of the Metaphysics of Morals*, 83, 88–89; Hobbes, response to, 86–87; and imperialism, 164; on instinct, 103; parable of choice in, 198–99; on perfectibility, 85; as pluralist, 81; and primitivism, 126; and race, 81–82; on rationality, 83–84, 86, 103, 148–49; reality, experience of, 259; Rousseau, response to, 24, 84–85, 86, 89–90, 97; state of nature, 86–87, 99, 143, 320n97; and subjectivity, 125; as teleological, 82, 83–86, 88–89, 98, 320n112; on time, 92; on transcendental experience, 256–57, 259–60; transcendental writings of, 95; and travel, 80, 238; and unbearability, 81; universalism of, 7–8, 28, 81, 91, 96, 115
Katz, Jonathan, 283–84
King, Martin Luther, Jr., 111
Kleingold, Pauline, 89
kōan, 253–55
Kouri, Emilio, 300n20
Kovalevsky, Maxim, 161–62

La Boétie, Étienne de, 41, 65
Larson, Kay, 377n86
Leonard, George, 378n90
Levering Lewis, David, 226, 366n45
Levinas, Emmanuel, 15, 111–12, 130, 333n143
Lévi-Strauss, Claude, 65, 82, 107, 194, 315n19; ethnocentrism of, 110
liberalism: ethnocentrism of, 164; Fanonian, 185
liberal tradition, 21

liberation: and alternation, 201; and Exodus, 224–25, 363n14; in Fanon, 185; and radical pluralism, 226–27; and the self, 269
liberty: civil, 148–49; in global society, 154; in Hegel, 148–49; natural, 148–49; and possession, 68; and property, 163; Rousseau on, 66–67, 72, 148; and slavery, 216. *See also* freedom
Liebman, Sheldon, 198
Linebaugh, Peter, 21, 108, 309n26
Lipsitz, George, 364n27
Locke, John, 50, 67
Lowe, Lisa, 296n6
Lubbock, John, 161
Lugones, María, 10, 299n19
Lütticken, Sven, 103–4

Mahmood, Saba, 44, 107
Maibor, Carolyn R., 356n53
Maldonado-Torres, Nelson, 50–52; on decolonial gift, 330n122; on Fanon, 351n234; on Rousseau, 69, 71–72
Malinowski, Bronislaw, 124
Mandeville, John, 296n2
Marx, Karl, 13, 24, 342n94, 343n102; alienation in, 158–59, 343n101; on anthropology, 156–58; *Capital*, 156–57, 165, 342n94; on capitalism, 109–10, 143, 156–60, 164–66, 168, 196, 344n114; on colonialism, 157; on communism, 166; and cultural interdependence, 169; and dialectics of, 25, 155, 202; and double consciousness, 228; on ethnocentrism, 214; Eurocentrism of, 161; Eurocentrism, critique of, 157–58; German idealism, critique of, 154; and the global, 93; on global being, 347n151;

Marx, Karl *(continued)*
  and global cultures, 156; global thinking of, 156, 160–61, 164, 166; Hegel, critique of, 135, 154–57, 161, 338n35, 342n95; history in, 161, 163, 165; on India, 160; as Orientalist, 160, 344n111; pluralism of, 170, 283; and primitivism, 342n96; on property, 163; as radical pluralist, 154; on real opposites, 155–56, 196, 220; recognition, struggle for, 160; Rousseau, critique of, 163; social being of, 2–3; and social good, 274; and unbearable identities, 135; on uncritical idealism and positivism, 155–57, 161, 338n35; universalism of, 158, 166, 169–70
Master Slave Dialectic (MSD), 336n6, 337n30; and cannibalism, 153; colonialism, as defense of, 138–39, 147, 150–51; as conjectural history, 151; consciousness in, 140; and global history, 135, 137; global origins of, 138; and Haitian Revolution, 144–45, 340n70; and history of philosophy, 145; and recognition, 151; and relations among states, 150; slavery, as justification for, 138–39, 147–50; and state of nature, 145, 337n14; truth, capacity for, 141; and unbearability, 139; violent struggle in, 141–43, 150. *See also* Hegel, G. W. F.
Mbembe, Achille, 131; aesthetics of, 132–33, 334n166; Afropolitanism of, 131–33; on Aimé Césaire, 132; new deconstruction of, 133–34; on Senghor, 131–33
McCarthy, Thomas, 320n112
McLuhan, Marshall, 278

McMahan, David, 258–59, 378n90
Melville, Herman, v, 251
Merleau-Ponty, Maurice, 174
Merton, Thomas, 271
metaphysics, 96, 359n102; of presence, 16; Western, 4–5, 12, 110, 113
Michaels, Walter Benn, 242
mindfulness, 276, 286, 290
modernity: as global, x, 3, 51; and global self, 203; and *Hamlet*, 53; Heidegger, 23; history of, 4; and rationality, x; and self, 5, 7, 10, 12, 16–18, 46; and unbearable identity, 227
Mohapatra, Rimina, 359n110
Monahan, Michael, 12, 144, 334n1
Montaigne, Michel de, 1, 7, 190; ambivalence in, 38; and anti-imperialism, 41–42; and appropriation, 35; on Aristotle, 34; and circumscription, 30–31; difference in, 35–36, 39–40; eclecticism of, 23, 31, 36, 85; education, critique of, 29; on essaying the globe, 40, 45, 200; *Essays*, 29–30, 42, 45; and essentialism, 35; gender in, 45; global engagement of, 48–49; global self of, 50, 58, 171; global subjectivity in, 30–31; as global thinker, x; and imperialism, 164; on inequality, 63; on language, 32, 36–37, 39, 41; nature in, 42; on the New World, 34–35, 41, 309n26; and "noble savage" tradition, 41; "Of Cannibals," 30, 31–41, 45, 181, 197; on Plato, 34; practices of self in, 40–41, 44–45, 64, 307n3; on reason, 31–32, 33, 35, 37, 180, 309n19; skepticism of, 8, 23, 31–32; subjectivity in, 29–30, 172; and unbearable identity, 33

Morris, William, 107–8
Muthu, Sankar, 13, 308n7, 310n45; and cultural agency, 41–44, 345n129; on Kant, 88–89, 320n112; on reason, 42
mysticism: as practice of global self, 275; of Suzuki, 8, 26; and unbearability, 8

Nagarjuna, 257–58, 376n54
Nancy, Jean-Luc, 295n1
Nardal, Jane, 115, 130
Nardal, Paulette, 115, 130
native informants, 94
nature: in Hegel, 137; in Montaigne, 42; and practices of self, 128; in Rousseau, 98, 138; and subjectivity, 43–44
Négritude, 97, 107, 113, 115, 325n63; Césaire on, 326n66, 329n98; and class, 124–25, 327n76; criticisms of, 330n119; Fanon on, 171, 175–76; and gender, 130; and Harlem Renaissance, 130; and Marxism, 343n102; as practice of global self, 133; and race, 131–32; and reracialization, 171; Sartre on, 115, 124–25, 176–78, 327n76; Senghor on, 107, 112–13, 115–16, 129; and sublation, 136. *See also* Césaire, Aimé; Senghor, Léopold Sédar
Nehisi-Coates, Ta, 364n29
neoliberalism, 116, 306n63; and capitalism, 26; and rationality, 9
New World, 308n14; in Montaigne, 34–35, 41, 309n26
Nietzsche, Friedrich, 80, 207, 353n9; practices of self in, 195; and Zen, 195
nominalism, 203–4
Novalis, 376n60
Núñez de Balboa, Vasco, 67–68

Oedipus plays (Sophocles), 54
On the Social Contract, 67, 84. *See also* Rousseau, Jean-Jacques
ontology, 152; and Du Bois, 237; Fanon on, 25, 173, 189; Foucault on, 91; Heideggerian, 25, 55, 57–58, 173; of Hegel, 177; and imperialism, 42; racial history of, 127, 173, 186; and radical pluralism, 11, 44, 122; Senghor on, 117, 126–27
Orientalism, 3–4; and Buddhism, 289; and Emerson, 198; and Suzuki, 252–53
Ortega, Mariana, 10, 299n19
Outlaw, Lucius, 360n120, 370n95

Pagden, Anthony, 355n36
Paine, Thomas, 204
Park, Peter, 18, 359n110
partialization, 220, 292; in Emerson, 196–97; and enlightenment, 251; and radical pluralism, 213, 291, 365n38; and Zen, 252
Patterson, Anita, 358n96, 367n46
Paz, Octavio, ix
pedagogy, 285; of Rousseau, 25, 63
perfectibility: Kant on, 85; in Rousseau, 62–63, 80, 100, 136
Phenomenology of Spirit (Hegel), 138–47, 155, 210–11, 218; consciousness, history of, 140; essaying the globe in, 140; history in, 140; self-consciousness in, 140–42. *See also* Hegel, G. W. F.
philosophy: and anthropology, 55, 89–90, 94; and colonialism, 73, 94, 98; and the empirical, 109; and ethnocentrism, 336n12; of evasion, 46; and globalization, 110; Hegel on, 140, 211; and history, 351n233; and race, 173, 81–82; racial

philosophy *(continued)*
discourses in, 113; Spivak on, 109; and subjection, 94; transcendental, 108
Philosophy of Subjective Spirit (Hegel), 137, 138, 141, 145, 245. *See also* Hegel, G. W. F.
phronēsis, 263
physicality: as universal, 152
Picasso, Pablo, 323n26
Pippin, Robert, 72–73
Plato, 33, 78–79, 270, 273
pluralism, 299n18; and communism, 157, 161–62, 166; and dialectics, 353n9; of Marx, 170, 283; and tolerance, 291; traditional, 8, 10, 69, 192, 299n17; and unbearability, 194; as universal, 11. *See also* radical pluralism
Plutarch, 40–41, 65
Polanyi, Karl, 164
Poma de Ayala, Felipe Guamán, 51, 52
possession, 54, 67–68; communal, 68; Greenblatt on, 35, 40, 68; and liberty, 68
postcolonial: as term, 296n3
postcolonial theory, 3–5; and Eurocentrism, 167–68; and hybridity, 121; and reconstitutive reading, 21; of the self, 296n6
primitive, the: and civilization, 101
primitivism, 43, 55, 59; and the avant-garde, 104; Chakrabarty on, 346n145; discourse of, 127; of Du Bois, 237–38; and Eurocentrism, 43, 164–65; and Freud, 126; and Kant, 126; and Marx, 342n96; in Montaigne, 38–39; and Romanticism, 238; and Rousseau, 64, 127, 263–64, 377n77; in Schiller, 13–14, 126, 128; and Suzuki, 272–73; and Zen, 259

Provincializing Europe (Chakrabarty), 166–70, 354n29, 368n66

Rabaka, Reiland, 325n63
race: and anti-Semitism, 221, 243; and being, 234–35; and capitalism, 121, 239; and dialectics, 178–79; and double consciousness, 232; Du Bois on, 221, 223–28, 231–32, 234–36, 241–43; and Fanon, 178, 234–35; and global practices, 236; and Heidegger, 235; and injustice, 242; and Kant, 81–82; and Négritude, 131–32; and philosophy, 113, 173, 81–82; Senghor on, 117–18, 241; as social construction, 242
racialization: in Fanon, 171, 173–74, 184
racism: and dialectics, 183–84; and Emerson, 189–90, 197, 200–1, 236; and enlightenment, 287, 289; of Hegel, 25, 144; and satori, 187; scientific, 81–82; and unbearable identities, 212; and white supremacy, 287
radical pluralism, xi, 8–12, 22, 291–92, 299n18; and alternation, 122; and deconstruction, 114–15, 122, 125; and dialectics, 114–15, 125; and difference, 147; of Du Bois, 9, 187, 191, 221–22, 230–31, 236, 237–38, 240–42, 246, 248, 326n65, 336n5; of Emerson, 9, 187, 190–91, 193–95, 197, 203–4, 213–14, 218–20, 231, 267, 326n65, 336n5, 354n9, 357n70; and essaying the globe, 270; and global relations, 336n5; and global subjectivity, 28; of hooks, 238; and liberation, 226–27; of Marx, 154; and ontology, 11, 44, 122; and partialization, 213, 291, 365n38; and relativism, 194;

and revolution, 195; of Senghor, 24–25, 115, 117, 120, 129, 133, 214–25, 326n65, 336n5; and the two truths, 258; and unbearability, 213, 291; and unbearable identities, 9, 12, 194–95; and universalism, 122–23, 147; and universality, 231; and values, 124
Rampell, Palmer, 378n90
Rampersad, Arnold, 366n45
Rancière, Jean, 97, 101, 103–7; on aesthetics, 114; on philosophy, 109
Rasberry, Vaughn, 239
Rath, Richard, 237
Rathore, Aakash Singh, 359n110
rationality: Fanon on, 175–77, 180; Kant on, 83–84, 86, 103, 148–49; and modernity, x; and neoliberalism, 9; Rousseau on, 63–64, 83, 103, 111; and subjectivity, 91. *See also* reason
realism, 203–4
reason, 6; and colonialism, 185–87; Emerson on, 191; and Eurocentrism, 152; and instinct, 97, 251, 263; and justice, 152; Montaigne on, 31–33, 35, 37, 180, 309n19; and Muthu, 42; Schiller on, 102, 148–49; Senghor on, 114, 331n130; and Zen, 93. *See also* rationality
reason, instinctual: of Rousseau, 24, 103, 372n8; Schiller on, 102–3; and super-consciousness, 249–50; in Suzuki, 251
recognition: and freedom, 144; and global self, 154; Hegelian, 141–42, 151–54, 160, 247, 341n79; and intersubjectivity, 153; and MSD, 151; struggle for, 145, 150, 160; and violence, 151, 153
reconstitution, 12–15; and radical pluralism, 12; traditions of, 15–16

reconstitutive reading, 21
Rediker, Marcus, 21, 309n26
Reed Sampson, 209
Reed, Adolph, 246, 362n5, 366n45
Rich, Adrienne, 285
Rivet, Paul, 118
Robbins, Bruce, 168
Roberts, Neil, 12
Robertson, William, 355n45
Rockhill, Gabriel, 105, 298n11
Romanticism, 6; German, 376n60; and the ordinary, 36; and primitivism, 238
Rousseau, Jean-Jacques, 4, 15, 82; on alienation, 158; on colonialism, 50; colonization, critique of, 67, 69; and communism, 24; conjectural history of, 61–63, 65–66, 78–81, 85, 146, 165, 315n10; and dialectics, origin of, 74–75, 97, 136–37, 164–65; *Discourses*, 64–65, 67; Du Tertre anecdote in, 71–76, 84, 89–90, 97, 136, 165, 198–99; *Emile: Or, On Education*, 67, 75–79, 84, 98, 161, 194, 372n8; and essaying the globe, 200; ethnocentrism of, 110–11; evasion in, 69; on global self, 23–24, 59, 65–66, 72, 263; global self, practices of, 63, 71, 77–78, 80, 171; as global thinker, x, 139, 164–65; human perfectibility in, 62–63, 80, 100, 136; and imperialism, 164; on inequality, 61, 63, 65–66, 71; instinctual reason of, 24, 103, 372n8; on justice, 61, 64, 74–75; on land claims, 67–68; on liberty, 66–67, 72, 148; Locke, critique of, 50, 67; methodology of, 63–64, 315n19; Montaigne, citations of, 64–65; and myth, 61, 78–79, 318n705; nature in, 98, 138; on nature of man, 61–63;

Rousseau, Jean-Jacques *(continued)*
On the Social Contract, 67, 84;
on private property, 69–70; and
primitivism, 64, 127, 263–64,
377n77; on rationality, 63–64, 83,
103, 111; "savages," romanticizing
of, 65–66, 69, 72, 261; self, relation
to other, 64, 71–72, 315n19; and
slavery, 144; on state of nature, 99,
161; subjectivity, evolutionary theory
of, 23, 66, 71, 79; sublation of, 24;
and time, 71, 74–78; traditional
pluralism of, 69; unbearable identity
in, 71, 173; universalism of, 115.
See also Kant, Immanuel
Russell, Bertrand, 269

Said, Edward, 3–4, 12, 247, 303n35;
on Cage, 276; on Fanon, 348n178;
Marx, critique of, 344n111;
on mutual constitution, 13; on
representation, 14–15
Sarkozy, Nicolas, 131
Sartre, Jean-Paul, 348n175; "authentic
self" in, 186; dialectics of, 136; and
engagement, 128; freedom in, 178;
on Négritude, 115, 124–25, 176–
78, 327n76; and whiteness, 177
Sato, Kemmyō Taira, 274, 379n114
satori, 196, 249; and aconceptuality,
261–62; and enlightenment, 253;
and the essay, 253; and ethics, 252,
274; and global thought, 254–63;
and intellect, 250–51, 253; and
the kōan, 253–55; as original
nature, 250; and politics, 272,
276; and racism, 187; and super-
consciousness, 249–50, 263; and
unbearability, 272. *See also* Suzuki,
D. T.; Zen
Sawada, Janine, 254

Schiller, Friedrich, ix, 59, 303n34;
aesthetic education of, 24, 98,
102, 106; and aesthetic theory,
103–10; anthropological argument
in, 97, 104, 322n1; and class, 104;
conjectural history of, 98, 99–100,
104; and dialectics, 102, 130; essay
form of, 99; ethnocentrism of, 111;
evolutionary narrative of, 99–100;
on formal drive, 100; on freedom,
99, 102, 148; and the global, 93;
global aesthetics of, 97, 106–7,
112, 115, 126, 128, 133, 134, 137,
165; global thought of, 139; and
imperialism, 164; on instinct, 102;
instinctual reason in, 102–3; on
play drive, 101–2, 105; and politics,
128; primitive instinct in, 113–14,
126, 128; and radical pluralism,
326n65; on reason, 102, 148–49;
on sensuous drive, 99–100; on state
of nature, 99, 143; sublation in,
24, 98, 100, 101–2, 105, 322n1;
and unbearable identities, 97, 103;
universalizing vision of, 99, 100,
115, 128, 133
Schopenhauer, Arthur, 86
scientific racism, 81–82
Scott, David, 13, 185–86
Scott, James C., 44, 284
Scranton, Roy, 292
Seed, Patricia, 217
self: alternation of, 267; and
Buddhism, 268; Cartesian, 2–3,
46–48; in Foucault, 16–18, 20,
77, 91–92, 185–86, 261, 295n2,
307n3; and hooks, 286, 290; and
modernity, 5, 7, 10, 12, 16–18;
Montaigne, practices of, 40–41,
44–45, 64, 307n3; and other, 64,
71–72, 73, 134, 315n19; plurality

of, 5; and postcolonial theory, 296n6

self, global, 2–3, 16–18, 291–92; Cage, practices of, 276, 278–84, 287, 299; and class, 36; Du Bois, practices of, 4, 222–26, 234, 238, 244, 246, 286; Emerson, practices of, 189–90, 195, 200–1, 220, 361n140; Fanon, practices of, 170–71, 180, 181, 183–84, 286; Kant, practices of, 82, 88–89, 91–93; and language, 37; of Montaigne, 50, 58, 171; practices of, 37; and time, 77–78; white masculinist practices of, 22

self-making, 2–3, 4, 295n2; of Fanon, 4, 171, 177

Seneca, 78

Senghor, Léopold Sédar, 2, 10, 122, 242, 325n62; and alternation, 202; on analytic thinking, 127–28, 132n135; assimilation in, 123; on civilization of the universal, 123–24, 129, 147, 192, 329n111, 330n112; and colonialism, 76; on communism, 128; on culture, 241; and decolonization, 128, 330n122; as democratic perfectionist, 326n72; dialectics of, 14, 136, 146, 327n73; and Du Bois, 369n92; and Emerson, 369n92; on emotion, 126–28, 130; as essentialist, 116, 118–19, 121, 126–27, 331n130; on ethnology, 331n132; on Eurocentrism, 119; gender in, 130–31; global aesthetics of, 97, 112, 126, 133–34; global pluralism, vision of, 112, 325n63; global self, practices of, 114, 133–34, 286; Goethe, paraphrase of, 119–20, 132; and Harlem Renaissance, 130; hybridity in, 116; on intellect, 130; on intuition, 130; on Marx, 159, 342n96, 343n102, 346n133; on Négritude, 107, 112–13; Négritude, definition of, 115–16, 129; on ontology, 117, 126–27; as philosopher of mixture, 116–21, 123, 329n111; on race, 117–18, 241; and racial history of philosophy, 81–82; racialism in, 123–24; radical essentialism of, 112; radical pluralism of, 24–25, 115, 117, 120, 129, 133, 214–15, 326n65, 336n5; on reason, 114, 331n130; on Sartre, 125, 179; on Schiller, 112, 113; and self-essentializing, 8; strategic partialism in, 116; and unbearable identities, 114; and universalism, 123. *See also* Négritude

settler colonialism, 94

Sharpley-Whiting, T. Danean, 130

Shih, Shu-mei, 4, 12–13, 297n7

Siep, Ludwig, 337n14

skepticism, 96, 291; and Emerson, 31, 218–19; of Fanon, 271; of Montaigne, 8, 23, 31–32

slavery: and alternation, 191, 229; Du Bois on, 224–25, 248; Emerson on, 191–92, 198, 206, 212, 215, 216–17; Fanon on, 175; and Haitian Revolution, 74, 138, 144–45; and Hegel, 141–44, 147–49, 161, 339n41, 340n64; and Hobbes, 144; legacy of, 175; and liberty, 216; and Rousseau, 144; and Spirit, 139; as state of nature, 144. *See also* Master Slave Dialectic (MSD)

Smith, Adam, 142, 156, 247

Smuts, Jan, 234

Snowden, Frank M., 119

Snyder, Gary, 286

social Darwinism, 235
Socrates, 47, 292
Sōen, Shaku, 254, 375n38
Souls of Black Folks, The (Du Bois), 225–26, 230, 235–39, 246, 248. See also Du Bois, W. E. B.
South Africa, 10
Spinoza, Baruch, 293
Spirit, 146–47, 230, 365n35; and colonialism, 139; European, 137; and nature, 137; and the other, 137; and slavery, 139; and state of nature, 139. *See also* Hegel, G. W. F.
Spivak, Gayatri, 13, 15, 295n1, 301n24; aesthetics, deconstruction of, 114; on deconstruction, 110; on Derrida, 110–11; on globalization, 109; on Kant, 93–95, 109–10; on philosophy, 109; on Schiller, 97, 103–4, 108–9, 111, 303n34, 324n50; on strategic essentialism, 205
Starobinski, Jean, 76, 309n18
state of nature: in Hegel, 143–45, 147, 152; in Hobbes, 135, 143; and Kant, 86–87, 99, 143, 320n97; and *kenshō*, 262; and Master Slave Dialectic, 145, 337n14; and Rousseau, 99, 161; Schiller on, 99, 143; slavery as, 144; and Spirit, 139
Stiegler, Bernard, 318n70
Stoler, Ann, 18
Stout, Jeffrey, 218–20, 284–85, 361n140
strategic partialisms, 11, 167, 205, 216
subject, Cartesian, 7, 57–58; as evasion of the global, 57
subject, Hegelian: and European supremacy, 138; and nature, 138; and stages of culture, 138
subjectivity: and capitalism, 251; Cartesian, 7; and Foucault, 247, 248; and gender, 244; global, 20, 30–31, 97, 252; global practices of, 16, 98; in Hegel, 211; and Kant, 125; male, 244; in Montaigne, 29–30, 172; and nature, 43–44; and primitivism, 98; and rationality, 91; and Rousseau, 23, 66, 71, 79; and Suzuki, 8, 27, 252, 282; and universalism, 91; and violence, 182–83
sublation, 24, 73, 75; and Du Bois, 229–30; and Emerson, 193; and German idealism, 201–2; and Hegel, 24, 73, 75, 135, 136, 229; and Négritude, 136; of Rousseau, 24; in Schiller, 24, 98, 100, 101–2, 105, 322n1
Subrahmanyam, Sanjay, 7, 296n2; Chakrabarty, critique of, 167, 169; on global history, 7, 51
surrealism: colonialism, critique of, 128
Suzuki, D. T., 2; and aconceptuality, 261–62, 270, 272; aesthetics of, 282; and alienation, 261; class in, 36, 271, 275; conventional and ultimate reality in, 117; critiques of, ix, 258–59, 262–63, 265, 270, 378n90; and dialectics, 14, 261, 263–64; and double consciousness, 125, 270; and Emerson, 252, 265–70; and enlightenment, 251, 269; *Essays in Zen Buddhism*, 252–53, 256, 277, 378n86; and epistemology, 260; experience in, 269; and fascism, 271; *The Gate*, 375n38; and German Romanticism, 376n60; global self of, 36, 250–52; global self, practices of, 261, 270, 275, 287, 299; global thought of, 251–52, 263–66, 272–75; and Heidegger, 377n86; and Hegel, 377n86; idealism, relationship

to, 26, 260; and identification, 381n155; immanence in, 256–57; instinctual reason in, 251, 263; on intellect, 268; on interdependence of subjects, 278; on Kakuan paintings, 277–78; and Kant, 255–56, 260; on the kōan, 253; legacy of, ix, 286, 373n20; and Mahayana Buddhism, 255, 256; mysticism of, 8, 26; and Orientalism, 252–53; and primitivism, 272–73; on reason and instinct, 92–93; Rousseau, critique of, 24; self, breakdown of, xi, 260; social concerns in, 278; and socialism, 271, 273; and subjectivity, 8, 27, 252, 282; transcendentalism, relationship to, 26; transparency in, 255–56, 258, 266–68, 270, 281, 381n155; two truths in, 273; and unbearability, 272; and unbearable identity, 248, 250, 294; and war, 271–72, 273, 379nn114–15; and Wittgenstein, 269–70; and Zen, ix–x, 27, 195. *See also* satori; Zen

Taketani, Etsuko, 239
Tao Te Ching: grasping, critique of, 207
Taylor, Charles, 3, 6; on "inwardness," 46, 59; on Rousseau, 72–73; on the self, 7, 295n2
Taylor, Paul, 242–43, 370n96
Thiam, Cheik, 325n63, 331n131
Thich Nhat Hang, 286, 290
Thiem, Yannik, 284
Thoreau, Henry David, 107–8, 253, 274
transcendentalism, 13, 108; and double consciousness, 208–9, 210; and Kant, 95, 256–57, 259–60; and Suzuki, 26. *See also* Emerson, Ralph Waldo

transparency, 255–56; in Suzuki, 255–56, 258, 266–68, 270, 281, 381n155
Trungpa, Chögyam, 286
Tully, James, 10, 319n87
Turner, Jack, 368n67

unbearability, x–xi, 106; and alienation, 205–6; and alternation, 120, 197, 205; of colonial identity, 171; and double consciousness, 26, 197, 209, 212–24, 228–32, 250, 270; in Fanon, 135, 170–75; and globality, 131, 194, 289, 291; and Kant, 81, 89, 97, 103; and Master Slave Dialectic, 25, 139, 144, 227; of modernity, 190; and mysticism, 8; and necessity, 275; overcoming of, 6, 10, 114, 139, 213; and radical pluralism, 9, 115, 125, 213, 271, 291; and revolution, 8; and satori, 272–75; and Suzuki, 272; and traditional pluralism, 10; and universalism, 194; of war, 273
unbearable identities, 6–9; and Buddhism, 289; colonial, 171, 183; and Du Bois, 8, 222, 227–30, 239, 248, 294; and Emerson, 193–94, 205–6, 209, 248, 357n60; and essaying the globe, 28; and evasive mood, 47, 58; and Fanon, 25, 135, 170–75, 177; and global interdependence, 194; and Kant, 7, 28, 97, 103; and Marx, 135, 157–58, 163, 170; and modernity, 190, 227–28, 289; and Montaigne, 7, 33; overcoming of, 9, 12, 17, 58, 135, 194–95, 209, 248, 250–51, 275, 289; and racism, 212; and radical pluralism, 9, 12, 26, 169, 194–95; of responsibility, 292; and Rousseau, 71, 103, 194; and Schiller, 97, 103,

unbearable identities *(continued)*
106; and Senghor, 114, 130–31,
192; and Suzuki, 7, 26–27, 248,
250–51, 270, 272, 294
universalism: Chakrabarty on, 166–68,
236; and colonialism, 166; and
communism, 25, 158; and Du
Bois, 81, 231, 236, 246; and
Emerson, 196–97, 202–3, 233; and
Fanon, 81, 171–72, 352n245; and
feminism, 94; and global thought,
354n29; and Hegel, 135, 137, 143,
151; and Heidegger, 56, 57–58,
170, 173, 314n113; and justice,
274; of Kant, 7–8, 28, 81, 91, 96,
115; of Marx, 158, 166, 169–70;
and partialization, 196–97; and
radical pluralism, 122–23, 147; of
Rousseau, 115; and Schiller, 99,
100, 115, 128, 133; and Senghor,
123; and subjectivity, 91; and
unbearability, 194
universality, 22, 297n7; and capitalism,
162; and diversity, 167–69; and
ethnology, 337n12; and pluralism,
11
Urbas, Joseph, 357n70

Valdez, Inés, 321n119
van der Veer, Peter, 13, 16, 302n27,
326n70
Veblen, Thorstein, 80
Victoria, Brian Daizen, 271, 379n115
violence: anticolonial, 182; and
colonialism, 101, 171–72, 321n119;
and colonization, 181; Fanon
on, 172, 181–84, 185, 351n245;
Foucault on, 185; and freedom,
150; and Hegel, 136, 141–43,
144, 147, 150; and power, 88; and
recognition, 151–53; revolutionary,
181; and subjectivity, 182–83

Viveiros de Castro, Eduardo, 11, 43,
107, 237; on Hegel, 153–54
Voelz, Johannes, 190, 220

Walden, 293–94, 383n4
Warren, Kenneth, 242, 370n96
Watts, Alan, 249, 59
Weber, Max, 59
Wells Barnett, Ida B., 244
West, The: as constituted entity, 18; as
global, 301n22; plural effects of, 11;
as reactive thought, 297n8
West, Cornel, 46
White, Kyle, 300n20
whiteness: in Du Bois, 225; and
Emerson, 236; and practices of
global self, 236; and Sartre, 177;
and second-sight, 223–24
white supremacy: and the Bible, 225;
and Emerson, 189, 198, 215; and
racism, 287; and social Darwinism,
235
Wilder, Gary, 4, 13, 297n7, 327n73;
on Césaire, 326n66; on Marx, 128–
29; on Sarkozy, 131; on Senghor,
25, 112–13, 128–29, 133, 325n63,
326n66
Wilkinson, E. M., 99
Williams, Raymond, 4, 162, 164
Williams, Robert, 232
Willoughby, L. A., 99
Wittgenstein, Ludwig, 207, 269
Wollstonecraft, Mary, 80, 245, 285
Wretched of the Earth, The (Fanon),
181–84
Wright, Richard, ix, 227, 364n27

Zamir, Shamoon, 362n5, 366n45
Zasulich, Vera, 159
Zen: and Cage, 259, 283–84; and
capitalism, 273; and dialectics,
264; and enlightenment, 262; and

ethics, 274; and Foucault, 19, 195, 259, 260–61; and Heidegger, 58, 264; and idealism, 80; and justice, 274; modern, 13; and Nietzsche, 195; partialization of, 252; and passivity, 252; and political ideology, 273–74; and the primitive, 259; and queer politics, 283–84; and reason, 93; and satori, 249; and subject formation, 252; and World War II, 271; Žižek on, 271, 273–74. *See also* satori; Suzuki, D. T.

Žižek, Slavoj, 251; Zen, critique of, 271, 273–74

www.ingramcontent.com/pod-product-compliance
Lightning Source LLC
Chambersburg PA
CBHW032013230426
43671CB00005B/74